ECONOMICS FOR COMPETITI

ECONOMICS FOR COMPETITION LAWYERS

SECOND EDITION

GUNNAR NIELS
HELEN JENKINS
JAMES KAVANAGH

Oxera

OXFORD

UNIVERSITY PRESS

OXFORD
UNIVERSITY PRESS

Great Clarendon Street, Oxford, OX2 6DP,
United Kingdom

Oxford University Press is a department of the University of Oxford.
It furthers the University's objective of excellence in research, scholarship,
and education by publishing worldwide. Oxford is a registered trade mark of
Oxford University Press in the UK and in certain other countries

Published in the United States of America by Oxford University Press
198 Madison Avenue, New York, NY 10016, United States of America

British Library Cataloguing in Publication Data
Data available

ISBN 978–0–19–871765–2

FOREWORD

'There are no useful propositions in economics,' wrote the late J.K. Galbraith, 'that cannot be stated accurately in clear, unembellished and generally agreeable English.' Even allowing for some exaggeration in that observation, it may nonetheless invite scepticism from lawyers—and judges—faced with complex economic evidence in competition cases. However, for those dealing with such cases, an understanding of the economic questions and arguments is increasingly important. In the fifteen years since the European Commission ushered in a 'more economic' approach in its 2000 Guidelines on Vertical Restraints, an economic appreciation of the issues is now influencing all areas of competition law. Indeed, the issues themselves are sometimes framed primarily in economic terms.

This presents a significant challenge for those dealing with competition cases who lack an advanced education, and often any formal training at all, in economics. In meeting that challenge, this second edition of *Economics for Competition Lawyers*, like the first, will be of great assistance. The economic theories, concepts, and techniques relevant to different areas of competition law are explained in approachable language, and mathematical formulae that can cause the lawyer's eyes to glaze over are avoided. Here one can find an explanation of critical loss as applied to market definition; of the different metrics that may be used to measure economic profitability; of the various measures of cost that can be used for the consideration of exclusionary pricing; of the efficiencies that can justify vertical restraints; and of the different theories used to determine FRAND terms of supply. As I wrote in the foreword to the first edition, this is not to suggest that the text is always easy for the non-economist: the authors do not adopt a simplistic approach, and their sophisticated analysis and exposition inevitably make certain sections a demanding read. But the result is a rewarding explanation of the economic toolkit available to practitioners and decision-makers, and deployed by the economic experts now frequently involved in competition cases.

The structure of the book is based on the competition law of the European Union. A particular benefit of this work is the copious illustration from decided cases not only from the EU courts and Commission and the UK but also decisions and guidelines of national competition authorities and court judgments from other European countries, the United States, and beyond. Of some of those judgments the authors are critical, and some of their criticisms are controversial, but that makes this book more stimulating. The authors do not shrink from expressing their view as to how, from an economist's perspective, certain aspects of EU competition law should develop. The book concludes with a discussion of the role of the economist as expert, a valuable reminder for economists themselves of their duty to assist the court and avoid the temptation or inducement to partisan bias.

This work does not concentrate exclusively on the traditional focus for competition economists in industrial organization economics, but usefully extends to the techniques of financial analysis and includes a brief excursus into behavioural economics as a basis for considering consumer behaviour in the context of assessing market power and remedies. Perhaps the approach of behavioural economics might usefully also be applied to the conduct of enterprises, since companies and firms—or at least the individuals who direct them—do not necessarily behave like the rational profit-maximizers of economic models.

Competition law emphatically remains law not economics, as these authors with all their experience of competition litigation recognize. There may be sound policy reasons, whether of practicability or of principle, why the law may depart from a rigid application of economic theory, even when the theory commands general consensus. Courts and competition authorities will sometimes find that contemporary internal documents from the participants provide a more satisfactory basis for determination of the nature and operation of the market than more abstract economic analysis. In some cases, sufficient factual data on which to found a robust economic assessment will be lacking. But competition law continues to evolve. Whether for appropriate application of the developing legal principles or for critical assessment of the expert evidence, a clear understanding of the economic theories, concepts, and arguments remains essential. To that important task, this broad-ranging work makes a very significant and welcome contribution.

Mr Justice Roth
London
January 2016

ACKNOWLEDGEMENTS

We thank the readers of the first edition for making this second edition a worthwhile project. As before, this book reflects the collective wisdom and ideas developed in Oxera over the past fifteen years, and we are grateful to all those who have worked with us during this period. Special thanks go to Adriaan ten Kate and Kerry Hughes for their close involvement in reviewing the text. We have also received great support from Annabel Atkinson, Paul Breakwell, Avantika Chowdhury, Luis Correia da Silva, Pascale Déchamps, Cate Dominian, Enno Eilts, Michele, Granatstein, Christian Huveneers, Matthew Johnson, Anthony Julius, Michael Kraus, Leonardo Mautino, Andy Meaney, Robin Noble, Sahar Shamsi, Martina Thirtle, and Rein Wesseling, and indirectly from all our colleagues who took on a greater workload to allow us space to write. Last but certainly not least, we could not have completed the book without the support and patience of our families.

TABLE OF CONTENTS

LIST OF FIGURES

LIST OF TABLES

TABLE OF CASES

Note: Cases beginning with 'Re,' 'In Re,' 'In the matter of,' etc, are indexed under the first significant word which follows.

References are by paragraph number; chapter numbers appear in **bold,** paragraph numbers in plain.

UK CASES

US CASES

OTHER NATIONAL CASES

Australia

Austria

Belgium

Canada

Denmark

France

TABLE OF LEGISLATION

References are by paragraph (or footnote) number; chapter numbers appear in **bold**, paragraph numbers in plain. Footnote numbers are in *italic* and preceded by *n*.

INTERNATIONAL INSTRUMENTS

LIST OF ABBREVIATIONS

AAC	average avoidable cost
ABC	activity-based costing
ACM	Authority for Consumers and Markets (Netherlands)
ATC	average total cost
ATR	Attheraces
AVC	average variable cost
BA	British Airways
BHB	British Horseracing Board
CAPM	capital asset pricing model
CAT	Competition Appeal Tribunal (UK)
CB	Cartes Bancaires
CBA	cost–benefit analysis
CC	Competition Commission, now part of the Competition and Markets Authority (UK)
CFI	Court of First Instance, now General Court (EU)
CMA	Competition and Markets Authority (UK)
CPU	central processing unit
CRM	customer relationship management
DB	Deutsche Bahn AG
DCF	discounted cash flow
DEA	data envelopment analysis
DOJ	Department of Justice (USA)
EBIT	earnings before interest and tax
ECJ	European Court of Justice
EEA	European Economic Area
ETSI	European Telecommunications Standards Institute
FCA	Financial Conduct Authority (UK)
FCC	Federal Communications Commission (USA)
FRAND	fair, reasonable, and non-discriminatory
FTC	Federal Trade Commission (USA)
GSK	GlaxoSmithKline
GUPPI	gross upward price pressure index
HHI	Herfindahl–Hirschman Index
IO	industrial organization
IP	intellectual property
IRR	internal rate of return
JCRA	Jersey Competition Regulatory Authority
JV	joint venture
KVI	known-value item
LRAIC	long-run average incremental cost
LRIC	long-run incremental cost
MEA	modern equivalent asset
MFN	most-favoured-nation
MIF	multilateral interchange fee
MMC	Monopolies and Mergers Commission, succeeded by the Competition Commission and the Competition and Markets Authority (UK)

NBV	net book value
NMa	Nederlandse Mededingingsautoriteit, now part of the Authority for Consumers and Markets (Netherlands)
NPV	net present value
OEM	original equipment manufacturer
OFT	Office of Fair Trading, now part of the Competition and Markets Authority (UK)
Oftel	Office of Telecommunications, now part of Ofcom (UK)
OLS	ordinary least squares
OPTA	Onafhankelijke Post en Telecommunicatie Autoriteit, now part of the Authority for Consumers and Markets (Netherlands)
OTA	online travel agent
OTT	over-the-top
P&Ds	parity and differential agreements
PPI	payment protection insurance
ROCE	return on capital employed
ROE	return on equity
ROS	return on sales
RPM	resale price maintenance
SAA	South African Airways
SEP	standard-essential patent
SIEC	significant impediment to effective competition
SLC	substantial lessening of competition
SME	small- and medium-sized enterprise
SPLC	substantial prevention or lessening of competition
SSO	standard-setting organization
TFEU	Treaty on the Functioning of the European Union
TTBER	Technology Transfer Block Exemption Regulation
UPP	upward price pressure
WACC	weighted average cost of capital

1

INTRODUCTION:
STARTING FROM FIRST PRINCIPLES

1.1 Competition Economics and You

Does one of these descriptions apply to you? **1.01**

Reader 1—You studied law because you didn't like maths at school. After brief stints in commercial and European law you got involved in competition law, only to discover that the field is littered with economists who throw numbers and statistics at you—and competition authorities even seem to listen to them. Reluctantly, but bravely, you decide that to further your career in competition law you must overcome your aversion to equations and charts and learn some economics. This book will help you with that. **1.02**

Reader 2—You are a seasoned competition lawyer. Over the last ten–fifteen years you have noted a gradual but steady shift in the field: it is increasingly relying on economic theories and tools. You discover that having a good grasp of the economics gives you an important edge over your rivals. You decide that you want to gain more insight into the principles **1.03**

1

behind some of the economic tools that you have already been using to construct your winning legal cases. This book will help you with that.

1.04 Reader 3—You are an advocate, a barrister, or a judge. You encounter an economic expert who supports one side's case with rather complex quantitative analysis. Can you rely on this economist? Is the analysis robust? Or is it a smokescreen? You accept that economic models may always be something of a black box to you, but you decide that you want to be better equipped to peer inside that box, to shake and rattle it by asking critical questions, and see if it still holds together. This book will help you with that.

1.05 Whether you are a practising competition lawyer, a competition official, a member of the judiciary, or a legal scholar, economics matters to you because it matters to competition law. Legal provisions have economic concepts embedded in them. Competition authorities refer to economic principles and analysis in their decisions. Parties on either side of a competition dispute use economic arguments and evidence to support their case. The degree of influence of economics has differed historically across jurisdictions—US antitrust has relied on economic thinking for over a century, while in Europe this is a more recent phenomenon[1]—but nowadays economists are active in almost every competition regime around the world.

1.2 What Does Economics Contribute to Competition Law?

1.06 So what is it that economics has to offer? Why is it so influential in competition law? What do competition economists do? In answer to these questions, various roles of economics can be distinguished. Some of these roles are about shaping the legal principles of competition policy. Others are about developing tools and applying empirical techniques to competition cases in practice.

1.2.1 Economic origins of competition law

1.07 First, it is not an outlandish claim that economic thinking actually provides the main rationale for competition law. The very essence of this field of law is based on the economic notion that competition is 'good' and monopoly is 'bad'. This notion itself has existed since long before there were any economists (anti-monopoly laws go back to Roman times),[2] but economic theory has shown more formally that rivalry among suppliers in a market is something worth promoting and protecting. The founding father of the profession, Adam Smith, was the first to recognize, in 1776, that society is economically better off if business people can freely pursue their own self-interest (profit), as, in doing so, they will seek to serve the need of customers—the market mechanism known as the 'invisible hand'.[3] Under pressure from rivals, businesses are forced to make the best products and keep prices and costs low. A monopolist, in contrast, can artificially restrict output so as to extract higher prices from consumers, and has fewer incentives to be cost-efficient. Following this line of economic thinking, the objective of competition law is to keep markets competitive and to prevent monopoly situations from arising.

---

[1] See, for example, Kovacic and Shapiro (2000), Shenefield (2004), and Niels and ten Kate (2004).
[2] See Green (2010).
[3] Smith (1776), Book IV, Ch II.

2

In the same vein, economic logic explains why price-fixing cartels are generally regarded as the **1.08** 'supreme evil' in competition law, and are treated as a criminal offence in several jurisdictions.[4] Unfair on consumers it may be, but is price fixing really the equivalent of stealing or fraud? Philosophically and legally (though note that we are not lawyers), this argument seems far from clear—aren't firms in a cartel selling their own products? Rather, the explanation seems to be economic. It was again Adam Smith who recognized that 'people of the same trade' have an inherent tendency to get together and have conversations resulting 'in a conspiracy against the public, or in some contrivance to raise prices'.[5] The harsh treatment that cartels receive in competition law is meant to deter would-be price-fixers.

1.2.2 Understanding the effects of business practices

Second, beyond the basic insights into competition and monopoly, economic theory has **1.09** contributed to a greater understanding of the effects of certain common business practices that regularly become the subject of competition inquiries. When are these practices anti-competitive and when not? The answer is not always obvious. When you are on a flight, chances are that few other passengers in the cabin have paid exactly the same fare as you. Is such price discrimination between passengers anti-competitive? Or is there some economic efficiency rationale (e.g. fewer flights would be available overall if airlines were prevented from filling seats through yield management)? When you buy a car it often comes with a built-in multimedia player. Is such bundling anti-competitive, hindering the sale of portable DVD and music players? (If you are wondering why this is a relevant question, consider that until the late 1950s seatbelts were sold separately from cars, and that while the market for personal satellite navigation systems has been fast growing, the addressable market for independent producers of sat navs has begun to decline as built-in navigation systems become commonplace.) And what if Microsoft bundles its Media Player with the Windows operating system, or Google provides free maps with any online search results? Economics can help you in answering these questions.

It took competition law quite some time to realize that inherent trade-offs between restric- **1.10** tive effects and efficiency benefits must be made. In the 1960s, US antitrust law—then the most prominent competition regime in the world—was marked by substantial confusion about how best to achieve the goal of keeping markets competitive. Various decisions from that period were, with hindsight, more about protecting individual competitors than protecting competition. In *Brown Shoe* (1962), a merger between two shoe manufacturer–retailers in the United States, the Supreme Court held that competition would be best served by preserving 'fragmented industries and markets', even if this meant sacrificing efficiencies, with consequent 'occasional higher costs and prices'.[6] In *Federal Trade Commission v Procter & Gamble* (1967), a merger concerning the household liquid bleach market, the Supreme Court established the 'entrenchment doctrine', whereby mergers could be prohibited if they strengthened the position of the merging parties vis-à-vis rivals through efficiencies, broader product ranges, or greater financial resources.[7] Becoming too efficient was deemed bad. This period was also marked by per se prohibitions of various types of

---

[4] This label was given by the US Supreme Court, in *Verizon Communication Inc v Law Offices of Curtis V. Trinko, LLP* 540 US 398 (2004).
[5] Smith (1776), Book I, Ch X.
[6] *Brown Shoe Co v United States* 370 US 294 (1962).
[7] *Federal Trade Commission v Procter & Gamble* 386 US 568 (1967).

business practice that did not easily fit within the textbook model of perfect competition, such as tying and vertical restraints.

1.11 This was when the ideas of the 'Chicago School', led by proponents such as Harold Demsetz, Richard Posner, and Robert Bork, came to the fore (Demsetz, 1974; Posner, 1976; Bork, 1978). They showed that many practices and agreements that restrict the freedom or choice of some parties can be efficient and pro-competitive, and should therefore not be prohibited per se but assessed under a rule of reason. In addition, efficiencies should be welcomed because they benefit consumers, even if they harm individual competitors. These ideas revolutionized US antitrust law in the 1970s and 1980s, resulting in a less interventionist, and more economics-based, approach. Since the mid-1980s, competition law in the United States and elsewhere has increasingly been influenced by more modern economic theories of industrial organization (IO), sometimes grouped together under the heading 'post-Chicago'. These theories have provided further insights into the economic effects of the types of business practice that competition law often grapples with, including bundling, tying, predation, and leveraging of market power.[8]

1.12 Competition law in Europe and elsewhere has now caught up with these ideas. Since the late 1990s, the European Commission, at times spurred on and at times held back by the European courts, has sought to reform all the major pillars of the competition rules: restrictive agreements under Article 101 of the Treaty on the Functioning of the European Union (TFEU), mergers and acquisitions under the EU Merger Regulation, abuse of dominance under Article 102, and state subsidies and aid under Articles 106 and 107.[9] As discussed in this book, in each case these reforms allowed for greater consideration of economic effects and efficiencies. This 'effects-based' approach to competition policy contrasts with the more legalistic, or 'form-based', approach that had prevailed in European competition law since its inception in 1957.[10] Other jurisdictions are following suit—indeed, some, such as Mexico and South Africa, adopted more economic approaches before the European Commission did.[11]

1.2.3 Different strands of economics: Industrial organization, finance, and behavioural economics

1.13 The third role of economics is that it has helped develop practical tests and criteria that make the application of the law more workable, and provides a range of statistical and econometric techniques to produce empirical evidence to back up theories and arguments in competition cases. Here we should explain that in the economics discipline there isn't actually a strand called 'competition economics'. At university, economics students do not typically learn about concepts such as market definition and dominance (although increasingly there are specialized courses where they have this option). Instead, competition economics draws from different strands of economics.

1.14 The dominant strands are microeconomics and IO, which are concerned with how markets work, how demand and supply interact, and how rivals react strategically to each other's

---

[8] For a discussion, see Sullivan (1995), Hovenkamp (2001), and Kovacic (2007).
[9] Throughout the book we will mostly be using the article numbering in the TFEU, even where the original decisions or judgments were made under the numberings of previous treaties.
[10] See, for example, Vickers (2005), and Niels and Jenkins (2005).
[11] See ten Kate and Niels (2006), and Oxera (2005b).

actions. When you come across a competition economist nowadays, chances are they have an IO background. However, competition economics is not exclusively about IO. Two other important theoretical strands are financial economics and behavioural economics, and we will cover these in several places in this book. Finance tools are complementary to IO tools, even though in practice financial economists and IO economists often have different approaches to analysing concepts such as market power and cartel damages. Behavioural economics is a relatively new field in economics that builds on ideas from psychology and has been gaining traction in the last ten years—not surprising in a period of financial turmoil in which the rationality of markets is questioned.

While the economics that is relevant to competition law draws from different (and some-   **1.15**
times not well-integrated) strands of theory, you may be reassured by the fact that it is mainstream and accepted within those strands. As Areeda and Hovenkamp (2007, p. 112) put it:

> Antitrust economics employs what academic economists sometimes denigrate as 'applied
> economics'. The relation of applied economics to economics as an intellectual discipline is a
> little like the relationship of the tonsillectomy to the science of surgery or the oil change to
> the science of automotive engineering. Applied economics as a general matter is hardly at the
> frontier of economic science, but its very banality supplies the consensus needed to make it
> a successful antitrust tool.

Hence, in competition law you won't normally have to listen to academic economists tout-   **1.16**
ing their latest theories—indeed, one of the criteria for admissibility of expert evidence in
US courts is that it is based on accepted theories, not untested ones (see Chapter 10). Nor
should you expect to see too much disagreement among economists about which theory
is best. Rather, when competition economists disagree it is mostly about how a particular
theory has been applied to the particular facts of the case, and how case-specific data has
been analysed.

1.2.4 Different strands of economics: Econometrics

This leads us to another field of economics that has been highly influential in competition   **1.17**
law: econometrics. This can be described as the application of statistical techniques to economic problems. In the last twenty years or so, the toolkit of quantitative techniques available to economists has expanded significantly, and so has the body of theoretical models
that can be empirically tested using econometrics. At the same time, computing power
and real-world data availability have improved. Companies keep electronic records in data
warehouses, 'scanner data' is collected for many products sold over the counter or online,
and generally more and more 'big data' is available on consumer and business behaviour
online and offline. It is fairly standard for economists to seek to apply econometric analysis, testing for statistical patterns and relationships in the available data. Indeed, in some
US court cases there has been an expectation that economic experts use econometrics
when analysing data (see Chapter 9). Where used appropriately, this can lend greater rigour to competition decisions.

One of the first examples of a court case that was highly influenced by the relative merits   **1.18**
of the econometric analyses by both sides is the 1997 *Staples/Office Depot* merger case in
the United States.[12] This merger concerned two retail chains of large office supply stores.

---

[12] *Federal Trade Commission v Staples Inc* 970 F Supp 1066 (DDC 1997). See also Baker (1999).

The Federal Trade Commission (FTC) had found evidence in internal documents that the two chains saw each other as direct competitors and that they generally set lower prices in cities where both chains had a presence than in cities where only one of them had a store. The econometric analysis by the FTC confirmed this, showing a statistically significant price difference of more than 5 per cent between cities with just one of these stores and cities with both (taking account of any other factors that may have contributed to the price difference). The FTC concluded from this that the merger would lead to a price increase.[13] Econometrics is probably the area in economics that most closely resembles a black box in the eyes of the competition lawyer. In this book we set out the types of case in which econometrics can be helpful, and also seek to equip you with the means to ask some critical questions next time you are presented with an econometric analysis.

1.3 The Book's Approach to Explaining Competition Economics

1.19   Competition law is a complex field. As one specialized court put it, 'competition law is not an area of law in which there is much scope for absolute concepts or sharp edges'.[14] This is not the fault of economics. Determining whether a certain business practice or merger has on balance more negative or more positive effects on competition and consumers is difficult because markets are inherently complex. Yet economists can do a lot more to help lawyers navigate through the complexities of applying competition law to real-world problems. This begins with explaining economic principles and concepts clearly.

1.20   Later in this chapter we try to explain a number of important basic economic concepts in the way of the 'economic naturalist', an approach borrowed (loosely) from Robert Frank, one of a number of contemporary authors of 'popular' economics books (Frank, 2007). The idea is to make the reader think a bit like an economist and develop some economic intuition. We explain the concept of demand and supply curves without drawing any charts—not because some lawyers we know have an aversion to charts, but because we think that this will allow you to think through the drivers of demand and supply in a truly back-to-basics fashion. In the remaining chapters of the book we follow a more conventional approach to explaining economics (and do draw some charts), but throughout we try to keep the expositions relatively straightforward and to avoid the excessive use of jargon. There are hardly any equations in this book either.

1.21   Another feature of the style of this book is that we place emphasis on setting out the underlying economic principles of competition law, rather than on existing guidelines, decisions, or case law. We do not take an integrated or 'holistic' law-and-economics approach in this regard (as some other textbooks do). We do strongly believe that good competition law requires a blend of law and economics (and we like to think of ourselves as competition economists with a modest grasp of competition law). But we believe that you are best served by this book through reading and learning about economics (you already know about the law). This will allow you to exercise your own judgement and achieve that blend of the two

---

[13]   In 2015, eighteen years after their previous attempt, Staples and Office Depot agreed another merger. At the time of writing the deal was still under review by the FTC.

[14]   *Racecourse Association and British Horseracing Board v Office of Fair Trading* [2005] CAT 29, 2 August 2005 at [167].

fields. For example, on the topic of vertical restraints (Chapter 6), we focus on the basic economics behind such restraints. This helps you think through from first principles why businesses may adopt vertical restraints; what positive effects they may have on efficiency; and what negative effects they may have on competition. You can then judge for yourself how the relevant legal framework would apply in a specific case. The book does not start by setting out what, for example, the European Commission guidelines or European court judgments say on vertical restraints, followed by an explanation of the economics (if any) behind them. We do it the other way round. We start with the principles and then illustrate them with real-world case examples (and also show instances where existing guidelines or case law may not reflect 'good economics'). It follows that the economic principles explained in the book are not specific to any competition jurisdiction—most of them apply globally.

Economics is often about applying common sense, but sometimes it produces counter-intuitive results. The back-to-first-principles approach presented here also allows us to reveal some common misperceptions among competition practitioners (not just lawyers, also economists). For example, why is it relevant for market definition when, after a price increase for a product (e.g. online DVD rentals), consumers do not switch to a substitute product (such as bricks-and-mortar DVD rental), but simply consume less of that product? We address this in Chapter 2. And why might a network provider offer its services below cost without any anti-competitive intent (a relevant issue in abuse of dominance cases in high-tech industries, as discussed in Chapter 4)? **1.22**

1.4 Explaining Some Basic Principles the Economic Naturalist's Way

1.4.1 Demand curves, with no chart

Think of a two-dimensional field—it could be any sheet of paper, or this page of the book before you. Call this the 'price and quantity' field. Every point on it represents a particular price and quantity of a particular product (this could be any product: apples, foreign holidays, petrol, electricity, jumbo jets). The higher up we are in the field, the higher the price of the product; at the bottom of your sheet of paper the price is zero. Likewise, as we move from left to right, the quantity of the product increases; to the extreme left of your sheet of paper the quantity is zero. (If we had drawn a proper chart—which we do in Chapter 2—we would have said that the vertical axis represents price and the horizontal axis represents quantity.) **1.23**

Somewhere in this field, buyers and suppliers of the product are hoping to meet. Let's start with the buyers—the demand side. What happens to the quantity demanded as we move from bottom to top in the field? It seems logical that as the price of apples goes up, they will be less in demand (fewer consumers will buy apples, and those who still do may buy fewer of them). Some products, like foreign holidays, will lose a lot of demand immediately when moving upwards in the field (so we shoot rapidly from right to left in quantity as we go up in price). Demand for these products is said to be price-sensitive (or elastic; we explain the concept of elasticity in Chapter 2). For other products—such as petrol—we can go quite far up the field (raising price) without changing demand much—that is, we hardly move left in quantity (oil companies and tax authorities have found ways to exploit this price insensitivity). But even for those products there will come a point where demand drops—car use does eventually fall when petrol becomes prohibitively expensive, even if only for a small number **1.24** of 'marginal' consumers who can either switch to other modes of transport or who simply cannot afford the higher prices (the concept of marginal consumers is an important one in economics and we come back to it in Chapter 2).

1.25 So it is not unreasonable for economists to conclude that the demand curve in the price and quantity field is downward-sloping from top-left to bottom-right—to the left are those consumers with a higher willingness to pay; to the right are those with a lower willingness to pay.[15] We could draw a straight line, but economists prefer to use a more general shape like a curve (in fact, demand could take any irregular shape, as long as over a sufficiently large distance it slopes downwards as we move to the right). This demand curve is not merely some economist construct—businesses will know they can sell a bit more if they lower prices, and lose sales if they raise prices, and will try to find the right price and quantity where their profits are highest.

1.26 If you find this straightforward so far, that is a good sign because a lot of the time that economists spend working on competition cases actually involves trying to locate this demand curve. They need this, for example, to delineate the relevant market, to measure market power, or to simulate the price effect of a merger. Economists can normally observe only one price–quantity point in the field, which is the current price and quantity. If they are lucky, they can observe a few more points—for example, if the price has changed from last year, and a different quantity was sold at that price (even then, quantity changes may be due to factors other than price changes). But it is never possible to see the full relationship between price and quantity. Economists have to assess empirically the properties of demand in the vicinity of the price–quantity points they can observe. They will in particular want to know how sensitive demand is to price. The issues of market definition and market power critically turn on this, as shown further in Chapters 2 and 3.

1.4.2 The level of demand, and interaction with other products

1.27 There are additional relevant insights that we can obtain through this naturalist thought experiment. We have seen how demand is downward-sloping from top-left to bottom-right. But what determines where exactly we start in our field? In other words, ignoring its slope for the moment, what determines whether the demand curve is located somewhere very high up (or far to the right) in the field or somewhere very low (or far to the left)? The answer to this question is of greater relevance to competition law than many practitioners, including economists, realize. Remember that our price–quantity field represents one product only, and it shows how demand for that product interacts with its price. Take foreign holidays to the Greek Islands. One factor that determines the position of the demand curve to start with is income (usually thought of as household disposable income). As income rises—we all become richer—so does demand for Greek Island holidays, even at the same price. The demand curve as a whole shifts up and to the right.[16]

---

[15] There are products that sell more when the price is higher, because (perhaps somewhat irrationally) consumers' perception of them changes with price. Think of diamonds, designer handbags, and high-end French wines. Economists call these Veblen goods, after Thorstein Veblen who wrote about this in 1899 (Veblen, 1899). A later classic treatise on these effects was given in Leibenstein (1950).

[16] Again, there are exceptions. Some products sell less when income rises. Economists call these 'inferior goods' or Giffen goods, after Robert Giffen, as first recognized in Alfred Marshall's classic economics textbook of 1890 (Marshall, 1890). Examples of inferior goods are potatoes, other basic foodstuffs, and 'cheap' alcoholic beverages such as Mexican pulque and Japanese shochu, although empirical evidence for such Giffen effects is limited.

More interesting for competition law purposes, however, is the fact that the position of **1.28**
the demand curve is also determined by competition from other products—say, holidays
to the Maldives. Those products have their own price–quantity field and demand curve.
But there is a lively interaction between the demand curves of the different products—
something that is often overlooked by focusing on just one product. So imagine a whole
series of price–quantity fields, one for each sunny destination that holidaymakers might
conceivably go to. If holidays to the Maldives (or Madeira or Mallorca) become more
popular for some reason (they become cheaper, or the quality of tourist facilities improves),
this has the effect of shifting the demand curve for Greek holidays further down and to
the left. Higher demand for holidays to the Maldives means lower demand for holidays
to the Greek Islands. This interaction between demand curves of different products is the
essence of how products can be substituted for each other, and lies at the heart of market
definition and merger analysis.

1.4.3 Supply curves, still with no chart

Now let's turn to supply. Is the logic the same as for demand? Does the supply curve slope **1.29**
upwards from bottom-left to top-right, with higher price meaning more supply? Alas, not
necessarily. Some economic-naturalist thinking can explain this. Take the supply of apples.
Assume that entry is easy and cheap—many people can grow their own apple tree and
bring their produce to the apple market. This is a basic ingredient of the economic model
of perfect competition, to which we turn later. Where in our price–quantity field is this
supply located?

The answer depends on the level of cost per unit. This is intuitive: just as buyers make their **1.30**
buy/don't buy decisions by comparing price to their willingness to pay for the product, suppliers make their supply/don't supply decisions by comparing price to their cost of supplying
the product. Suppose it costs €1 to produce and market a kilo of apples. All producers are
perfectly happy to sell at that price as they cover all their costs.[17] So, we have then an unlimited supply of apples at €1 per kilo. The supply 'curve' is a horizontal line at that level. It
cannot be any lower or any higher. If the price falls below €1, no apples would be supplied to
the market as producers cannot recover their costs. Any price above €1 would immediately
attract more suppliers who are willing and able to sell at €1. Suppliers who can be lured into
the market only at a price above €1—or who are less efficient and cannot recover their costs
at €1—simply wouldn't stand a chance in this perfectly competitive market.

1.4.4 Where demand and supply meet

Where do demand and supply meet then? What is the market equilibrium? The downward- **1.31**
sloping demand curve will cross the horizontal supply curve at €1, and market quantity
in this 'market equilibrium' is whatever total quantity consumers demand at that price of €1.
At this point, we have a 'marginal consumer' who is willing to pay exactly €1 per kilo, and
gets apples at that price. Consumers to the left of that point get their apples at €1 per kilo
too, but are willing to pay more than that. They derive a 'consumer surplus' from their
purchase, a concept which we explore further below. The equivalent concept of 'marginal

---

[17] You are right to think at this point that this is perhaps rather odd: don't businesses want to make a profit
over and above the recovery of costs? Economists can live with this theoretical result by assuming that the
cost here also includes a 'normal' profit as reward for the producer's investment and risk.

producer' does not really apply here since all producers have the same cost of €1 and the supply curve is horizontal.

1.4.5 When supply curves are upward-sloping

1.32 From this basic premise that supply curves tend to be horizontal in competitive markets, we can explore the circumstances in which they are not. Supply curves can be upward-sloping (from bottom-left to top-right in our price–quantity field). This occurs when some producers have lower costs than others, but cannot serve the whole market due to capacity constraints (unlike in our apple example, in which all suppliers could produce at €1 per kilo without any constraint on capacity or on the number of suppliers with a tree in their garden). Electricity generation is an example. Say there is one nuclear plant that generates electricity at a price of €5 per MWh (megawatt hour), and has the capacity to produce 1,000 MW of electricity in every hour. However, total market demand is 5,000 MWh during peak hours, so the nuclear plant cannot serve the whole market. There is room for producers with higher costs—say, gas turbine plants producing at €30 per MWh. So our supply curve for electricity is horizontal at the level of €5 from where quantity is 0 MWh to where it is 1,000 MWh. The supply curve then makes a step-change up to the level of €30 and is horizontal again as we move further right in quantity. There may be a number of such steps as other generation technologies come into play, such as coal-fired power plants at €35 per MWh and oil-fired plants at €60 per MWh. In these situations, the market price in equilibrium will normally be determined by the level of cost of the higher-cost producers—the 'marginal producers'—who will make only a 'normal' profit (the market price just covers their costs). In peak hours the marginal producers may be oil-fired plants and the market price €60.[18] At the market price, the lower-cost suppliers will make a healthy margin above cost. This raises the interesting question for competition law of whether the low-cost producers can be said to have market power in these circumstances. There is another complication, however, to which we turn below. The nuclear plant in our example has by far the lowest cost of generating additional units of electricity (€5 per MWh versus €30 per MWh for the next cheapest technology), but this ignores the fact that the fixed cost of building the nuclear plant in the first place was substantially higher than for the other types of plant.

1.4.6 The level of demand, economies of scale, and the number of suppliers for which there is room in the market

1.33 The supply curves that we have pictured before us reflect the marginal cost of production—what it costs to produce the next unit of output: an apple or a megawatt of electricity. We discuss different cost concepts (such as marginal costs, incremental costs, and avoidable costs) in the context of pricing abuses in Chapter 4. In this section we consider the concept of average total cost (ATC), which is the cost per unit of output including fixed costs (i.e. those costs that do not vary with output, such as the cost of building a plant). This has an impact on how many suppliers can operate in the market. High fixed costs mean that there are economies of scale—average total production costs per unit decrease as output increases.

---

[18] Off-peak demand is lower (the demand curve is further to the left) and the gas turbine plants now become the marginal producers, resulting in a price of €30. The higher-cost coal- and oil-fired plants do not sell anything during off-peak hours, but they remain in the market as they can sell during peak hours. In other markets they might have been forced to exit.

Take the nuclear plant. It costs a lot to build, but then it costs relatively little to generate   **1.34**
electricity (€5 per MWh in our example). Say the fixed cost of building the nuclear plant is
€3 billion. If it is only ever used to generate 1 MWh, that unit of output has an average cost of
€3 billion (so the average-cost curve begins very high up to the far left of our price–quantity
field). The more electricity the plant generates, the lower the average cost. We saw earlier
that the plant in our example has a maximum capacity of 1,000 MW. Its average-cost curve
therefore slopes downwards from the far left of the field to where quantity is 1,000 MWh.
To generate more than 1,000 MW in one hour, another nuclear plant would have to be
built (or other generation technologies would have to be used, as in the above example). The
firm's average-cost curve goes up again as we move further right. The 1,000 MWh point is
therefore called the minimum efficient scale of production for the nuclear plant.

This basic logic of minimum efficient scale has significant implications for competition   **1.35**
law (again something that practitioners are not always aware of, and economists do not
always make explicit). It effectively determines how many suppliers can efficiently operate
in the market. Most real-world markets have economies of scale, and this is in fact the main
reason why they often have only a limited number of suppliers (think of car manufacturers, makers of washing powder, or supermarket chains). Even in apple production there are
economies of scale (planting and growing a tree is a fixed cost, so we slightly cheated with our
€1 per kilo example), but they are not so pronounced, and hence there is room for many
suppliers. However, in the case of electricity generation, if the total market demand size is
5,000 MWh during peak hours, there is room in the market for five nuclear plants. If the
electricity market size is 2,000 MWh, only two nuclear plants can operate at the minimum
efficient scale. A similar situation occurs in the production of large jumbo jets, where globally only two manufacturers remain (Boeing and Airbus), probably because demand is not
there to sustain a third. If the market size is below 2,000 MWh, only one nuclear plant can
produce efficiently (a second plant could still operate to meet the residual demand above
1,000 MWh, but the plants cannot both achieve the minimum efficient scale simultaneously). If the market size is 1,000 MWh or smaller, a situation of 'natural monopoly'
arises—there is room for only one firm in the market.

You can see how this interaction between market size (a demand-side feature) and econo-   **1.36**
mies of scale (a supply-side feature) often determines the 'natural' state of concentration
in markets. Sometimes having a greater number of suppliers in the market is simply not
possible, because it is not efficient. If there are too many suppliers, one or more of them are
bound to operate below the minimum efficient scale, and they are the ones compelled to
exit the market first if competitive forces are allowed to work freely. Consumers and competition authorities have to live with this economic reality. The same logic also explains
a main economic rationale for removing international trade barriers in the context of the
World Trade Organization or the European internal market—free trade enhances total
market size (as producers can sell beyond their national market), and hence allows more
companies to achieve minimum efficient scale, promoting competition and efficiency at
the same time.

1.4.7 Competition 'good'

In exploring demand and supply above, we already touched on the main features of per-   **1.37**
fectly competitive markets: free entry and exit, and no significant economies of scale in
production. The equilibrium price is determined by the interplay between demand and

11

supply. All suppliers are 'price-takers'. Economists have shown that such perfect competition produces desirable outcomes for the economy as a whole. First, production in a competitive market takes place at the lowest level of cost—in the apple example, no supplier with costs higher than €1 per kilo can survive. This is called productive efficiency. Second, all consumers who are willing to pay a price that covers this cost of production are indeed being served (only those with a willingness to pay less than €1 per kilo of apples do not buy any in the equilibrium situation). This means that the 'right' amount of resources in the economy is allocated to apple production; this is referred to as allocative efficiency. Another way of interpreting allocative efficiency is that the maximum number of efficient transactions takes place in the market.

1.38 For competition law purposes, it is useful to bear in mind the economic principle that any transaction between a willing buyer and a willing seller is inherently desirable. Think of that old bicycle that has been stored in your garden shed for years. You are perfectly willing to sell it to someone for €25. Equally there must be someone out there whose willingness to pay for your bike is equal to or greater than €25. If the two of you find each other and transact (sites like eBay are pretty useful for this), you both benefit compared with a situation in which the bike remains unused in the shed. Thus, when transactions take place, buyers benefit because the price is at or below their willingness to pay, and suppliers benefit because the price is at or above their cost of supply. As a rule of thumb, competition law should therefore generally look favourably upon business practices that enhance market output or create new markets (new buyer–supplier transactions) altogether, even if they also have some restrictive effect.

1.4.8 Monopoly 'bad'

1.39 Contrast that with monopoly. Suppose, hypothetically, that there is a single producer of apples (note that this is exactly what you are asked to suppose when applying the hypothetical monopolist test for market definition, discussed in Chapter 2). What happens to price and quantity? The monopolist clearly can do better than set the price at €1 and make only a 'normal' profit. It can restrict output, thus creating some artificial scarcity, and raise the price—remember that lower quantity and higher prices go hand in hand when the demand curve is downward-sloping. The monopolist is a price-setter, not a price-taker, and does not need to fear consumers switching to rival producers of apples (there is none). The monopolist reduces output and raises price up to the point where its profits are maximized (technically this occurs where the monopolist's marginal revenue equals its marginal cost; we return to this in Chapter 2).

1.40 Note here that the sky is not the limit for this monopoly price rise. It is unlikely that the price of apples will go up all the way to, say, €5 per kilo, even under monopoly. Any price increase has two offsetting effects: a higher price means a higher profit margin for each product sold (€5–€1=€4 in this case), but it also means fewer sales of apples (if the price rises to €5, we would probably move quite far to the left in our price–quantity field, leaving only those buyers who have a very high willingness to pay for apples). The consumers who no longer buy apples at this price will divert their money to other products, such as pears and kiwi fruit, thus pushing the demand curve for those products to the right in their respective price–quantity fields. This is demand substitution at work. Even a monopolist is therefore still constrained to some extent by competition from other products. At some price above

€1 but below €5—say, at €1.50 per kilo—the monopolist maximizes profit because the loss of customers from raising price any further becomes so large that it outweighs the gain in profit margin (this, in a nutshell, is the concept of 'critical loss' used in market definition, which we also cover in Chapter 2).

So what are the effects of monopoly on economic welfare? Why is monopoly 'bad'? The first effect that may be considered 'bad' is that the monopolist earns more profit than previously (€1.50−€1=€0.50 of profit on every kilo sold). This comes directly at the expense of those customers who still buy apples at the monopoly price. Economists say that there is a redistribution from consumer surplus to producer surplus. Producer surplus is simply the difference between price and costs (it's the same as profit). The concept of consumer surplus is less easy to grasp. Remember that our demand curve represents willingness to pay. At the competitive price, all customers with a willingness to pay of at least €1 buy those apples in equilibrium. These are all customers to the left in our price–quantity field, including those to the far left who are willing to pay as much as, say, €5 per kilo. But they have to pay only €1 (thanks to those 'good' competitive forces in the market). They therefore get a surplus of willingness to pay over price (the consumer equivalent of producers' profit). The consumer who was willing to pay €5 gets a surplus of €4 at the price of €1. In monopoly, price is increased to €1.50, so consumer surplus for all those who still buy apples is reduced by €0.50 per kilo. **1.41**

Economists do not have any particular reason to condemn such redistribution of surplus. No one among the remaining buyers is actually forced to purchase anything they are not willing to pay for. Most buyers still get a surplus, even those willing to pay €1.51. It is just a smaller surplus than previously. The new marginal consumers who are willing to pay exactly €1.50 no longer get any surplus; they used to get €0.50 surplus at the old price of €1, but they can at least still buy the product at a price they are willing to pay. Who is to say that €0.50 of surplus in the hands of consumers is better than €0.50 of surplus in the hands of producers? Yet most competition law regimes emphasize promoting consumer surplus among their objectives more than total surplus, as we discuss later on. **1.42**

Economists have more to say on the second 'bad' effect of monopoly, which is that output is artificially restricted. At the price of €1.50, several consumers who are perfectly willing to pay the cost of producing the apples are not being served by the monopolist—that is, those consumers who are willing to pay between €1 and €1.49. In the competitive situation they were served, but after the monopoly price rise they are no longer served. They are the previous marginal consumers who are now lost. This represents an allocative inefficiency. Too few of the economy's resources are allocated to the production of apples. No one gains from this, not even the monopolist (as it makes no profit on these sales that are no longer made). Economists describe this as a 'deadweight welfare loss'. **1.43**

The third 'bad' effect is that monopolists may have a 'quiet life'.[19] Free from pressure from any rivals, why would a monopolist do its best to produce efficiently, to bring down production costs, or to bring innovative new products to the market? The question is not as obviously rhetorical as it seems. An economist may point out that at a cost of, say, €0.80 per kilo, **1.44**

---

[19] The phrase 'The best of all monopoly profits is a quiet life' was coined by the economist John Hicks (Hicks, 1935).

the monopolist can make higher profits than at a cost of €1.00 per kilo, so it may still seek to reduce costs purely out of self-interest. Yet an apple monopolist may also pay its workers or (more likely) its managers a bit more than what a competitive supplier could afford—in money or in perks like first-class travel. The monopolist may face less pressure to invest in a new automated apple-picking technology that would reduce costs. And it may not have much incentive to make any bioengineering efforts to render its apples that little bit sweeter and juicier. This 'quiet life' effect is possibly the most damaging from the perspective of economic welfare. Monopolistic markets generally lack the rivalrous dynamism that leads to innovation and the introduction of new products.

1.4.9 Monopoly profit as a fundamental market signal

1.45 Unfortunately, the 'competition good, monopoly bad' story is not as black and white as you might think. Ending up with a monopoly may be a bad thing for economic welfare, but having a *process* in which suppliers want to become a monopolist is actually highly desirable. The lure of monopoly profit is what drives suppliers to be innovative. Companies in many markets, be they car manufacturers, soft-drink producers, or clothes shops, want to make their product a little bit different from competitors so as to be able to charge a premium. This is why in most markets products are 'differentiated', with each supplier having a degree of monopoly power over its own product (or brand). There is some debate in economics (and in other social sciences) about the merits of product differentiation, especially when it is achieved solely through advertising.[20] However, if you doubt whether product differentiation overall is a good thing, imagine a world in which we all had to wear the same clothes or drive the same car. In some markets the gains from successful innovation can be even larger. Ford achieved a decisive cost advantage over rivals in 1908 with its Model T, the first car to be mass-produced on assembly lines. Companies such as Hoover, Tetra Pak, 3M, Microsoft, and Apple created whole new markets for themselves (at least for a period) by launching innovative products: respectively, the vacuum cleaner in 1908, tetrahedron milk packaging in 1953, Post-it notes in 1977, MS-DOS in 1982, and the iPod digital music player in 2001.

1.46 This poses some fundamental problems for competition law (it is no coincidence that almost all the innovative companies listed above have come under scrutiny by competition authorities at some stage). First, competition law should tread carefully when tackling monopolies directly, since such action might affect the desirable incentives that other suppliers have to outperform their rivals in search of monopoly profits. As US Judge Learned Hand famously put it in 1945, 'The successful competitor, having been urged to compete, should not be turned upon when he wins.'[21] Instead, competition law should focus primarily on keeping markets sufficiently open and contestable, such that monopoly positions can be challenged over time by new entrants. Second, competition lawyers cannot really rely on evidence of intent in the same way as criminal lawyers can. In competitive markets, intentions to 'pound' a rival 'into the sand' or 'squish him like a bug' may actually be perfectly consistent with a healthy drive to compete.[22] Third, innovative activity is regarded as so desirable

---

[20] See the discussion in Comanor and Wilson (1979), and Becker and Murphy (1993).

[21] *US v Aluminum Co of America (ALCOA)* 148 F 2d 416 (2d Cir. 1945).

[22] Such intentions are cited in two US predation cases: *US Philips Corp v Windmere Corp* 861 F 2d 695 (Fed. Cir. 1988), cert denied, 490 US 1068 (1999) and *Kelco Disposal v Browning-Ferris Indus of Vermont* 845 F 2d 404 (2d Cir.) aff'd 492 US 257 (1989). We return to this in Chapter 4.

that there is a wholly separate area of law—intellectual property (IP) law—that creates monopolies by awarding patents for inventions and innovations. Copyright law has similar effects. Like competition law, IP law is built on a basic economic premise: that rewarding innovative effort by granting a temporary (often around twenty years) monopoly position to the innovator creates greater incentives to innovate in the first place. The tension with competition law is immediately obvious.

1.4.10 A recap of the concepts used so far

If you have followed the line of reasoning in our 'economic naturalist' thought experiment above, you have grappled with the following basic economic concepts: price, quantity, buyers, suppliers, price sensitivity, marginal consumers, willingness to pay, demand curve, substitutes, supply curve, market equilibrium, marginal producers, perfect competition, normal profit, entry, exit, capacity constraint, market power, marginal costs, average total costs, fixed costs, economies of scale, minimum efficient scale, natural monopoly, price-taker, productive efficiency, allocative efficiency, monopoly, hypothetical monopolist, price-setter, profit maximization, critical loss, consumer surplus, producer surplus, deadweight welfare loss, innovation, and product differentiation. You already know more about economics than you realize. Much of the material covered in the remainder of this book builds on these basic concepts.

1.47

1.5 Some Health Warnings on Competition, Competition Policy, and Competition Economists

1.5.1 Health warnings on competition

As we have seen, competition can achieve many benefits for society—lower prices, allocative efficiency, productive efficiency, innovation, and product variety. Not because producers are altruistic benefactors, but because their self-interested pursuit of profit, combined with pressure from rivals who are after the same, leads them to produce the kind of products that consumers want to buy, and to do so at the most efficient levels of cost. Adam Smith's invisible hand works, by and large. And the good thing is that markets do not need perfect competition to achieve all that (which is just as well, since hardly any real-world market is perfectly competitive). Sometimes a small number of suppliers, even two, may be sufficient to generate fierce rivalry (though in concentrated markets competition can also be highly ineffective). In some markets even a monopolist may be prevented from raising prices by the threat of immediate 'hit-and-run' entry—this concept of 'contestable markets' has been found to apply in competition cases involving helicopter services and local bus services, for example.[23]

1.48

However, there are some policy goals that competition *cannot* achieve, and it is important to be aware of these. Competitive markets may fail to serve certain customers where the costs of serving them exceed their willingness to pay. Think of a remote, small mountain village—no bus operator would consider it worthwhile running a service to it, and no postal

1.49

---

[23] Competition Commission (2000), 'CHC Helicopter Corporation and Helicopter Services Group ASA', January; and *Chester City Council and Chester City Transport Limited v Arriva PLC* [2007] EWHC 1373 (Ch).

operator would deliver letters there (the demand and supply curves in our price–quantity field never meet). That is why governments may choose to impose a universal service obligation or grant a subsidy to ensure that such 'essential' services are provided, sometimes in return for a degree of exclusivity (i.e. monopoly) for the service provider in question. Markets also fail in situations of natural monopoly, as described above. To achieve efficient production, a single supplier is warranted, but then specific constraints such as price caps may be imposed on that monopoly supplier, often by a sector regulator. The regulation of natural monopolies is not discussed specifically in this book; however, some of the most interesting and challenging competition cases arise in these industries since many natural monopolies—rail infrastructure, gas transportation networks, local telephony networks—interact with competitive layers in the supply chain. Competition law can also learn some useful lessons from regulation when it comes to designing remedies, a theme dealt with in Chapter 8.

1.50 Economic theory has identified several other common types of market failure where competition may not do the job. There may be externalities, where decisions by one market participant do not take into account the impact on other market participants. An example of a negative supply-side externality is a factory upstream that dumps its waste into the river, thus affecting a fish farm further downstream. An example of a positive demand-side externality is a social networking site whose attractiveness to any user depends on how many other users have joined (so no user would join individually if no one else joined—a chicken-and-egg externality). In the extreme, such network effects can give rise to a situation akin to natural monopoly, with the corresponding competition problems—witness the spate of competition actions against Microsoft and more recently Google. Furthermore, markets may not function properly if there is asymmetric information between buyers and suppliers (insurance and used cars are frequently cited examples)—there may be so little trust between them that no transactions take place at all. In a famous article published in 1970, the economist George Akerlof showed how owners of good second-hand cars have difficulty selling them because buyers cannot distinguish good cars from 'lemons' (Akerlof, 1970).

1.51 Finally, competition can do little to achieve distributive justice. Competition results in what economists have labelled Pareto efficiency, which means that in equilibrium there are no more transactions whereby one party can be made better off without making another party worse off.[24] All efficient transactions that make both parties better off have taken place (in terms of the earlier example, all used bicycles that people wanted to sell and buy have been sold and bought). But this says nothing about how welfare is distributed. One party may have everything and the other nothing, and this can still be Pareto-efficient. We saw above that, on the demand side, not all consumers may be served by competitive markets. On the producer side things are even harsher. Open markets may offer opportunities to many aspiring entrepreneurs, but the playing field is rarely level (e.g. large companies benefit from economies of scale and better access to capital) and not everyone succeeds in the marketplace. Competition inevitably produces winners and losers. The fate suffered by the losers can be unpleasant, and sometimes leads to calls for help or protection. This takes us to our health warnings on competition policy.

---

[24] This is after the economist Vilfredo Pareto (Pareto, 1906).

1.5.2 Health warnings on competition policy

The first health warning on competition policy is that it should not be equated with com- **1.52**
petition itself (as it sometimes is). Competition policy is normally aimed at promoting and
protecting competition. But it can also, unintentionally, stifle competition. Robert Bork
of the Chicago School wrote a book on this entitled *The Antitrust Paradox* (Bork, 1978).
Think of competition as a boxing match. The audience wants to see a fierce fight in which
the best boxer prevails; it doesn't care particularly about the fate of the loser, as long as a new
challenger takes his place rapidly. But in comes the referee. He tells the fighters to treat each
other in a gentlemanly fashion. No punches below the belt (prices below cost). No verbal
threats revealing an intention to massacre the opponent. The boxer who is slightly bigger
and more experienced is told he has a 'special responsibility' not to weaken his opponent any
further. And the winner is not allowed any excessive prize money. The result is clear. The
audience doesn't get the spectacle it wanted. Weaker fighters stay in the ring much longer
than they otherwise would. Stronger fighters feel hampered once they gain the upper hand,
so may try a little less hard. And new challengers are deterred because there is not much
prize money to be won. The referee's rules may ultimately induce the two boxers to stop
making much combative effort and instead agree tacitly to just pretend to be having a fierce
fight, and rake in fees paid by viewers. Competition policy can have the same dampening
effect on competition in the market. A feature of the EU regime that comes close to such
an antitrust paradox is the 'special responsibility' on any dominant firm 'not to allow its
conduct to impair genuine undistorted competition on the market'.[25] We return to this in
Chapter 4. The shoe and liquid bleach mergers in the United States that we referred to above
are also good examples; indeed, cases like these in the 1950s and 1960s were the inspiration
for Bork's book title.

1.5.3 Over- and under-enforcement

Competition authorities and courts have to distinguish between business practices that are on **1.53**
balance pro-competitive (they do more good than harm to competition and efficiency) and
those that are on balance anti-competitive. The only practices where the line can be drawn
reasonably clearly are hardcore price fixing and market sharing between competitors—these
practices almost invariably do more harm than good (as discussed in Chapter 5). For all
other business conduct, agreements, and mergers, competition policy must strike a balance
between minimizing the likelihood of prohibiting practices that are in reality pro-competitive
(false positives), and minimizing the likelihood of condoning practices that are in reality anti-
competitive (false negatives).[26] Economics can help by providing insight into the likely effects
of practices and by applying counterfactual and cost–benefit analysis, but economists cannot
accurately measure the effects of over-enforcement or under-enforcement. Where the line is
drawn is ultimately a matter of philosophy or policy judgement. In practice this will depend
on the degree to which decision-makers have confidence that markets can sort themselves
out (a confidence that seems to be weaker in Europe than in the United States), or the degree
to which they have confidence that government intervention can improve market outcomes
(a confidence that seems to be weaker in the United States than in Europe).

---

[25] Case 322/81 *Nederlandsche Banden-Industrie Michelin NV v Commission* [1983] ECR 3461 (*Michelin I*).
[26] False positives are known in statistics as type-I errors, and false negatives as type-II errors. (Type-III
errors are when you forget which is which.)

1.54 There is consensus (even in Europe now) that competition policy should protect the process of competition, not individual competitors. Competition can be very harsh on those companies that can't keep up with the more efficient ones, and competition law is not (or should not be) designed to help them (competition authorities should not over-enforce like the boxing referee above). From an economic perspective, competition policy is not about 'fairness'. Indeed, fairness can be a dangerous beacon when deciding on a course in a competition investigation. Markets are rarely 'fair' in the popular meaning of the word—is it fair that the likes of Walmart have displaced local, family-run shops all over the world, or that the major Hollywood studios have driven out many independents? Competition authorities that over-emphasize the importance of 'fair play' in markets may create unrealistic expectations among small businesses and consumers that competition policy will ensure a level playing field and a 'fair' market outcome.

1.5.4 Different objectives of competition law

1.55 The most frequently stated objectives of competition policy are efficiency, economic welfare, and consumer welfare. There has been some debate in certain jurisdictions about whether consumer welfare should have primacy over total welfare, and whether 'consumers' should be taken as end-consumers or also buyers in intermediate markets. Fortunately, efficiency and consumer welfare often go hand in hand and competition can enhance both simultaneously. There are some exceptions. One is price discrimination, which often enhances efficiency by allowing output to be increased, but which does not necessarily improve consumer welfare if it also allows the supplier to extract higher prices from each consumer (see Chapter 4). Another is a merger that results in significant cost efficiencies but also a small increase in price; total welfare may rise, but consumer welfare falls (see Chapter 7).

1.56 Historically, competition policy has been associated with several other goals, such as the dispersion of economic power (one of the original aims in the United States)[27] and economic integration (a major goal of the EU competition rules). However, we have already seen that competition is not necessarily good at achieving objectives other than efficiency. For example, by preventing mergers in concentrated markets and tackling abuses by dominant firms, competition law does contribute somewhat to the dispersion of economic power, but sometimes the forces of competition themselves result in, or even require, the emergence of powerful but efficient firms. Likewise, while the application of 'standard' competition principles to Articles 101 and 102 TFEU will often contribute to the internal-market objective as well (e.g. acting against exclusionary conduct by a dominant national company may result in entry from other Member States), sometimes EU competition law applies criteria that are specific to the aim of the internal market rather than to competition as such—an example is the negative stance towards exclusive car dealerships based on national boundaries, despite the fact that economic theory suggests that exclusive territories for distributors may have efficiency justifications (see Chapter 6).

---

[27] US antitrust started with the enactment of the Sherman Antitrust Act in 1890. While there has been much debate about the objectives of antitrust law ever since, early on it was established that at least one of the main goals was to protect competition and prevent monopolies in the interest of consumers. See *Standard Oil Co of New Jersey v United States* 221 US 1 (1911), a case also discussed in Chapter 8.

1.5.5 Health warnings on competition economists

Throughout the book we aim to give you a feel for what economics can contribute to competition law, and also for what its limitations are. An important theme is the role that economists play in competition cases. Just as competition and competition policy are not synonymous, there is a distinction between *economics* and *economists*. Knowledge of economics is important to any competition lawyer. But economists are not always essential. Competition lawyers are normally able to deal with bread-and-butter competition problems themselves, even when some economics is involved.[28] It is only in the more complex cases that they call in the help of economists (although we have seen that competition cases quite often fall into the complex category). This book aims to equip competition lawyers with the means to handle the bread-and-butter cases, and to understand and use an economist's analysis in the more complex cases.

The other side of the coin is that economists must carry out their analysis reliably and with integrity, and present their results with clarity. We believe that our profession can still improve on those fronts. Economists do not always recognize the limitations of their analysis (or do not make them explicit). They are sometimes, rightly or wrongly, perceived as hired guns—a perception that is reinforced every time two economic experts are seen to be slinging mud at each other's analysis. We would rather that economists be perceived as experts who can provide useful insight into the complex economics of a competition case. Various mechanisms can be, and have been, implemented to promote best practice in the use and conduct of economists, in order to make their contributions more helpful and credible. We address this topic in Chapter 10.

1.6 The Remainder of the Book, and What's New in this Second Edition

1.6.1 The chapters

This book covers all the major areas of competition law. It is organized such that you can either read it cover-to-cover, or use it as a reference when you want to find out about the economics behind specific topics or issues. We follow the structure of most legal textbooks in this field, starting with market definition (Chapter 2) and market power (Chapter 3), two 'building blocks' that are of relevance to most types of competition case. Chapter 4 deals with abuse of dominance; Chapter 5 with cartels and other types of horizontal agreement; Chapter 6 with vertical restraints; and Chapter 7 with mergers. We then have two chapters on topics that you may see less often in standard texts. Both deal with what happens after a competition law infringement has been found. Chapter 8 discusses the design of remedies for competition problems and infringements, an area that has attracted relatively little scholarly attention thus far compared with the identification of those problems. Chapter 9 deals with the quantification of damages arising from infringements, a topic of increasing interest as private damages claims against infringing parties are on the rise in many jurisdictions. Finally, in Chapter 10 we offer some thoughts on the use of economic evidence in competition cases in terms of best practice and future direction.

1.57

1.58

1.59

---

[28] In a recent High Court case the judge decided to apply the hypothetical monopolist test himself because neither of the parties had provided economic expert evidence. *Purple Parking Ltd, Meteor Parking Ltd v Heathrow Airport Ltd* [2011] EWHC 987 (Ch) (15 April 2011), at [111].

1.60 If this were a book on economics for competition economists we might have included separate chapters or annexes on specific methods that are applied across various types of case. Instead we decided to introduce these methods in specific chapters. Thus, profitability analysis is explained in Chapter 3 on market power, but is equally relevant to abuse of dominance and quantifying damages. In Chapter 3 we also explain the basics of behavioural economics, and come back to it under remedy design in Chapter 8. The use of survey analysis is explained in Chapter 7 on mergers, but is also relevant for market definition. Finally, the use of econometrics is explained in Chapters 2 and 9, but applies to mergers and other cases as well. We hope that you bear with us where we necessarily digress somewhat to explain the basics of these methodologies and cross-refer between chapters.

1.6.2 What's new?

1.61 The above structure is almost the same as in the first edition of this book, published in 2011. Economic principles and concepts do not change as rapidly as the case law; indeed some don't change at all. Yet there were good reasons for refreshing the book, and in this second edition we have made substantive changes in each chapter. We have included a number of recent high-profile investigations as useful examples to illustrate economic themes, such as the abuse of dominance cases against Intel and Google, the prohibitions of the Ryanair/Aer Lingus and UPS/TNT mergers, and the collusive actions by Apple and various publishers with respect to the sale of e-books.

1.62 In addition, we have expanded (or reduced) coverage of certain topics to reflect trends and developments in recent years, some of which we had predicted in the final chapter of the first edition (and some, as befits economists, we had not). For example, the trend to de-emphasize market definition in competition cases has continued, particularly in mergers. We have therefore shortened Chapter 2 (though it is still one of the longer chapters because market definition remains important in competition law), and some of the economic concepts that are relevant to both market definition and the assessment of unilateral merger effects—such as diversion ratios—are now explained in Chapter 7. Meanwhile, behavioural economics has continued to establish itself as a (modest) part of the economics toolkit for competition law. In addition to Chapter 8 on remedies we now also cover behavioural economics in Chapter 3, where we set out how, in markets characterized by consumer biases, suppliers may have a greater and more enduring degree of market power than would follow from traditional economics. Several restrictive agreements cases in recent years have raised complex economics questions, and we discuss these in Chapters 5 and 6. These include pay-for-delay agreements in pharmaceuticals and most-favoured-customer arrangements in online markets such as those for e-books and hotel bookings. How competition authorities should deal with acquisitions of minority shareholdings has become a hotly debated question in merger control, which we cover in Chapter 7. Economics has also made further inroads into the areas of private damages actions, and we have updated Chapter 9 accordingly.

1.63 The only major change in the structure of the book is that we no longer include a chapter on state aid. In the last five years the number of state aid cases in Europe has grown significantly, and state aid law and economics has become a discipline in its own right. Several of the economic principles and techniques discussed in this book are also of relevance to state aid cases—for example, the assessment of distortions to competition, profitability analysis, and remedies design. There are several books and journal articles on state aid setting out the economics used in such cases.[29]

To conclude the book, in Chapter 10 we venture again into exploring likely trends in com-   **1.64** petition law over the next five years. One is the enhanced use of 'big data'—competition authorities are keen to use this in cartel hunting, but are also concerned that companies can use 'big data' to create entry barriers in online and digital markets. Another trend is the growing emphasis placed by competition authorities on the consumer, bringing competition law closer to consumer protection. Finally, the debate on form-based versus effects-based approaches to abuse of dominance seems to be never-ending—the *Post Danmark I* and *Post Danmark II* rulings by the European Court of Justice (ECJ) in 2012 and 2015 provided some support for effects-based analysis, but the 2014 *Intel* judgment by the General Court swung the pendulum back towards form-based analysis.[30] Competition law will remain a thoroughly dynamic and exciting field in the years ahead. Economics, and economists, have a useful role to play in shaping it, as we hope you will agree.

---

[29] For example, Kavanagh et al. (2011) and Kavanagh (2013).
[30] Case C-209/10 *Post Danmark A/S v Konkurrencerådet*, judgment of 27 March 2012 (*Post Danmark I*); Case C-23/14 *Post Danmark A/S v Konkurrencerådet*, judgment of 6 October 2015 (*Post Danmark II*); and Case T-286/09 *Intel Corp v Commission*, Judgment of 12 June 2014.

2

MARKET DEFINITION

2.1 Why Market Definition?

2.1.1 An intermediate step

2.01 Two producers of high-quality chocolate want to merge. When notifying the deal, they argue that it should be cleared because there will be plenty of competition remaining post-merger. How should the competition authority go about assessing the merger? The basic approach is well established in competition law. First, you define the relevant market. Is it limited to high-quality chocolate or does it include mass-market chocolate as well? Second, you analyse the position of the merging parties in the relevant market. Do they have a high market share? Does the merger leave only a limited number of competitors in the market? If the answer to these last two questions is yes, the authority is more likely to find the merger to be anti-competitive.

2.02 You can see how market definition matters here. If the market is limited to high-quality chocolate, and the two merging parties have market shares of, say, 30 per cent and 20 per cent respectively, the merger is more likely to be blocked than if the market included all chocolate, and the parties have only 3 per cent and 2 per cent. Market definition plays a similar role as an intermediate step in cases of restrictive agreements and abuse of dominance: the relevant market is defined, and then an assessment is made of whether the parties concerned have market power or dominance in that market.

2.1.2 What market definition tries to do

Most products are to some extent substitutable, as we will see in this chapter. Market defini- **2.03**
tion tries to separate close substitutes from more distant substitutes. To test whether a group of products (say, apples) competes closely with another group (bananas), you can pretend that competition *within* the group does not exist and focus only on competition *between* the groups—that is, you hypothetically monopolize the supply of apples and test whether apples as a group face close competitive pressure from bananas. If not, bananas do not form part of the market for apples. Once the relevant market has been defined in this way to include all close substitutes, the analysis proceeds to the next stage, focusing on competition among the inside products, without worrying too much about outside products (more distant substitutes). This is why market definition can be a helpful intermediate step in the competition assessment.

2.1.3 Avoiding the submarket trap

Defining the market as a first step in the assessment of mergers and anti-competitive prac- **2.04**
tices wasn't always so common in the history of competition law (and nor may it remain so common, as we explain in this chapter and in Chapter 7). Courts, authorities, and scholars struggled for a long time to develop the notion of market definition.[1] A low point was reached in 1962 with the US Supreme Court ruling in *Brown Shoe*, a merger between two shoe manufacturer–retailers.[2] The Court endorsed the principle of submarkets within relevant markets. It first stated that 'The outer boundaries of a product market are determined by the reasonable interchangeability of use or the cross-elasticity of demand between the product itself and substitutes for it'. So far so good (we explain cross-elasticity in section 2.3 below). But the Court went on: 'However, within this broad market, well-defined submarkets may exist which, in themselves, constitute product markets for antitrust purposes.'[3] The lower court had defined separate relevant markets ('relevant lines of commerce') for men's shoes, women's shoes, and children's shoes, but according to the Supreme Court this did not rule out the possibility that narrower relevant markets could exist at the same time, such as by price, quality, age, or sex. In *Brown Shoe* itself such further submarkets were in fact rejected in the end, but several subsequent cases in the lower courts defined submarkets within markets. For example, in *US v Mrs Smith Pie Co* (1976), the market was defined as that for all desserts (based on consumer research), but a separate submarket was then found for frozen dessert pies, and it was in this submarket that the competition concerns were investigated.[4]

It is plain to see that defining a relevant market and then allowing for submarkets within **2.05**
that market is not a very helpful step in competition analysis. Commentators in the United States were quick to point this out. Some called the submarket principle 'an intellectual

---

[1] For a history, see Werden (1992). Some commentators advocated the term 'market delineation', which arguably reflects more accurately what the exercise is about than 'market definition'. However, the latter term has gained the upper hand in common usage.

[2] *Brown Shoe Co v United States* 370 US 294 (1962).

[3] Ibid., at 325.

[4] *US v Mrs Smith Pie Co* 440 F Supp 220 (ED Pa 1976).

monstrosity' (Hall and Phillips, 1964); others observed that 'either there is or there is not a market in which competition may be affected...If the line of commerce is men's shoes, it should not also be men's golf shoes: if one boundary is right, the other must be wrong' (Hale and Hale, 1966). The submarket concept was eventually abandoned. The 1982 US Merger Guidelines paved the way for the hypothetical monopolist test, which is now used by competition authorities around the world, and which we discuss at some length in this chapter.[5] Submarkets cannot exist under this test.

2.1.4 Avoiding the product characteristics trap

2.06   Market definition is about substitution and price pressure between products. It is not about the physical differences between products. Of course, physical features will often dictate whether products are substitutable—straw and twigs are not good substitutes for bricks. They need to be taken into account in any market definition exercise, if only as a sense-check. But a market definition that relies solely on product characteristics can be unsound. Products with different characteristics may still be substitutes in the eyes of the buyers—take sugar and high-fructose corn syrup, or plastic and glass bottles. One can have endless, and usually inconclusive, debates about market boundaries based on product features. Is chewing gum in a separate relevant market because people like to chew something?[6] Moreover, market definition based on product characteristics overlooks the fact that price pressure between products does not require all customers to consider them substitutes. Babies and elderly people with dentures may not switch from bananas to other fruits, but that in itself does not make bananas a relevant market. Many other people may well see different fruits as substitutes, and this could be sufficient for these other fruits to place a competitive constraint on bananas (see section 2.8 where we discuss the infamous *United Brands* case).[7]

2.1.5 Beware the product differentiation trap

2.07   Market definition works best when products are reasonably homogeneous, such that you can test whether one group of products competes with another (e.g. apples versus bananas, or cellophane versus other wrapping materials). Market definition works less well when product differentiation is an important feature of the market. Unfortunately from this point of view, many real-world products are differentiated—chocolate, cars, smartphones, and even apples come in different sizes, flavours, colours, and models, and under different brand names. Differentiation typically means that there is a spectrum of products that are close but imperfect substitutes. For example, there is a whole range of cars from superminis and small family cars to executive and luxury cars. Likewise, corner shops, shopping centres, and airports are differentiated geographically. Delineating a relevant market on such a spectrum can be difficult, artificial, and potentially misleading. Here is why:

- Difficult: There may be no clear cut-off points along the spectrum. You can buy a new car at virtually every price multiple of €1,000, from around €9,000–€10,000—you get a Kia Picanto or Skoda Citigo for that—to close to €100,000, where you're into variants of the BMW M6 and Mercedes SL-class (not to mention the Ferrari and Aston Martins that have prices an order of magnitude higher still).

---

[5] Department of Justice (1982), 'Merger Guidelines', 14 June.
[6] This was the question in the Mexican predatory pricing case *Chicles Canel's SA de CV v Chicle Adams SA de CV*, Mexican Federal Competition Commission, 15 February 1997. See ten Kate and Niels (2006).
[7] Case 27/76 *United Brands v Commission* [1978] ECR 207; [1978] 1 CMLR 429.

- Artificial: A very wide market for all cars would include not-so-close substitutes such as the Suzuki Alto and the Alfa Romeo Spider; but very narrow markets—for example, the market for Porsche 911 Carreras—may not be very informative for the competition analysis either.
- Potentially misleading: The reliance on market definition as an intermediate step in the competition analysis creates the impression that the question is all about products being 'in' or 'out'—products outside the relevant market are deemed not to be substitutes; products within the relevant market are treated as perfect substitutes. This is not the case in differentiated product markets. Product substitutability is a matter of degree, and market definition means that you have to draw the line somewhere, in the knowledge that a product that is just inside the line may not be so different from a product that is just outside.

For these reasons, the usefulness of market definition as an intermediate step has been questioned in recent years. (In fairness to the US Supreme Court, a recognition of the complications that arise in differentiated product markets was probably also one of the reasons why it endorsed the submarket principle in *Brown Shoe*.) Some commentators have gone so far as to proclaim that market definition should be abandoned entirely (e.g. Kaplow, 2010). Some competition authorities now often focus more directly on the competitive effects of mergers and place less emphasis on market definition. We come back to this later in this chapter and in Chapter 7.   **2.08**

However, we consider that market definition can still be appropriate in differentiated product markets. Several of the aspects of market definition that we discuss in this chapter—such as market aggregation and chains of substitution—can assist in dealing with the challenges of product differentiation. Moreover, concepts such as own-price and cross-price elasticity are relevant for other stages of the competition analysis beyond market definition.   **2.09**

2.1.6 The remainder of this chapter

Section 2.2 gives an overview of the various dimensions of a relevant market, in addition to the standard product and geographic dimensions. Section 2.3 explains the basic economic principles of demand that are of relevance to market definition (and competition analysis more generally), in particular demand systems, substitution, and elasticities. Section 2.4 deals with the hypothetical monopolist test for market definition, as defined in its most elaborate form in the 1992 US Horizontal Merger Guidelines.[8] Section 2.5 discusses critical loss analysis, the tool most frequently used to put the hypothetical monopolist test into practice. The subsequent sections address specific aspects of market definition, namely the cellophane fallacy (section 2.6), supply-side substitution, and market aggregation (section 2.7), price discrimination markets (section 2.8), chains of substitution (section 2.9), and other aspects of geographic market definition (section 2.10). Section 2.11 discusses market definition for complementary products (including aftermarkets and networks) and for bundles, while section 2.12 explains how market definition may depend on the relevant layer of the vertical supply chain. Section 2.13 addresses the question of product migration over time (e.g. from narrow-band internet access to broadband) and how this relates to product substitution. Section 2.14 discusses how relevant markets may be defined by reference to features other than price, such as quality and innovation. In section 2.15 we explain the main quantitative tools for market definition: regression analysis and price-correlation analysis. Finally, in section 2.16 we return to the question: 'Why market definition?'   **2.10**

---

[8] Department of Justice and Federal Trade Commission (1992), 'Horizontal Merger Guidelines'.

2.2 Dimensions of the Relevant Market

2.2.1 The product and geographic dimensions

2.11   When you read about relevant markets, you commonly see that they have both a product dimension and a geographic dimension. The relevant product market consists of the group of products that are considered close substitutes—for example, the market for broadband internet services (whether over cable, fibre, fixed-telephony, or mobile networks). The geographic dimension of the market is the area in which that group of products is sold or purchased—for example, the market for broadband internet services in the UK, or in the Greater London area. However, a relevant market may have several dimensions in addition to product and geography. Often these dimensions are implicitly or explicitly considered as part of the product dimension, but sometimes they are overlooked.

2.2.2 Time of purchase or consumption

2.12   A train journey from Oxford to London at 7.30 a.m. is not much different from a train journey from Oxford to London at 10.30 a.m.—it's the same rolling stock and journey time. And yet the two may be in separate relevant markets. Passengers on the 7.30 train are likely to be more time-sensitive than price-sensitive (they need to get to work on time), allowing operators to charge about twice as much for this service as for the 10.30 train. So not only are you more likely to find a free seat on the 10.30 train, you are also significantly better off financially. Such peak versus off-peak market distinctions can be made in many transport, communications, and leisure markets, where peak may refer to the time of day, day of the week, or the season. Time of purchase or consumption also matters for 'perishable' goods such as fresh fruits, newspapers, and sports broadcasting events. In the extreme this may give rise to different relevant markets by time dimension—for example, live broadcasting of sports events is generally seen as separate from deferred broadcasting of the same events (unless your team won, in which case you may want to see the whole match over and over again).

2.2.3 Period of investigation

2.13   This second additional market dimension is also related to time, but in a different way. It refers to the period of investigation, that is, whether it is forward- or backward-looking, and for how long. Merger assessments are forward-looking. They are generally concerned with how the merger will affect competition in the next one or two years. The analysis therefore focuses on competitive constraints in the next one or two years, and market definition should assist in identifying those constraints. Market analyses (including market definition) carried out by national telecoms regulators under the EU regulatory framework tend to focus on the next three years, as they must identify suitable regulatory measures for that period.[9] In contrast, investigations into abuse of dominance often relate to the current situation or to the recent past, when the alleged abuse took place. The question is then

---

[9] Council Directive (EC) 2009/140 of the European Parliament and of the Council of 25 November 2009 amending Council Directives (EC) 2002/21 on a common regulatory framework for electronic communications networks and services, 2002/19 on access to, and interconnection of, electronic communications networks and associated facilities, and 2002/20 on the authorization of electronic communications networks and services, Article 16(6) of the amended Framework Directive.

whether the company in question was dominant in that period. A forward-looking market definition in such a case may overlook the fact that a market has already been monopolized (and market power already exercised), and may erroneously conclude that there are close substitutes at the prevailing price (which is already a monopoly price). This is known as the cellophane fallacy, as explained further in section 2.6.

2.2.4 Different customer groups

There may be different markets for the same product corresponding to different custom- **2.14** ers (or groups of customers). This may occur where some customers have a greater choice of alternatives than others, and suppliers can exploit this difference by targeting the latter, 'captive', customers with higher prices. This gives rise to price discrimination markets, a topic that we discuss in section 2.8, where we also come back to the examples of the time-sensitive passengers and the babies and elderly people with dentures who can't switch from bananas to other fruits.

2.2.5 Different distribution channels

The same bottle of beer can be in a different relevant market depending on whether it is **2.15** sold in a supermarket or in a bar. The same holds for a pay-TV sports package that may be sold to residential customers and to owners of bars. This is not to say that different distribution channels always form separate markets. The main criteria are again the difference in demand patterns and the ability of suppliers to exploit this difference—when you are in a bar you are unlikely to switch to buying the same drink in the supermarket down the road, even if it is five times cheaper to do so. An increasingly important question related to this dimension is whether online and bricks-and-mortar sales of the same product (e.g. consumer electronics or package holidays) are close substitutes.

2.2.6 The vertical layer in the supply chain

The same product—a car, a washing machine, a bunch of fresh flowers—may pass through **2.16** a whole set of intermediaries on its way from producer to end-consumer. The relevant market can be different depending on which layer of the chain is considered (in Australia and New Zealand this is known as the functional dimension of the market). Which layer to look at will normally depend on where in the chain the competition problem in question arises in the first place—for example, is it a dispute between manufacturers, wholesalers, or retailers? Sometimes this poses difficult questions for market definition, and we discuss these further in section 2.12. One question concerns the relationship between demand by end-consumers and demand by intermediaries. If demand by the intermediary is derived from end-consumer demand, what does that mean for market definition higher up the chain? Other questions relate to the importance of intermediaries vis-à-vis end-consumers. Should competition law be mainly concerned with end-consumers as opposed to intermediaries? Does it matter if a whole layer of the chain is excluded from the market through the conduct in question if end-consumers are no worse off?

2.2.7 The seven dimensions

Above we have discussed seven different dimensions of the market: product, geographic, **2.17** time of purchase, period of investigation, customer group, distribution channel, and vertical. Not all of these will be relevant to all competition cases, and often the additional dimensions are considered implicitly as part of the definition of the product market. The dimensions also often overlap or interact with each other (e.g. different customer groups purchasing the product at different times or through different distribution channels). Nonetheless, we suggest that it is useful to check explicitly which of these dimensions may lead to further separate markets in any specific case at hand.

2.3 The Demand Side: Substitution and Elasticities

2.18 It is useful to draw a distinction between demand-side substitution, supply-side substitution, and new entry. Demand-side substitution refers to switching by customers. This is the most immediate competitive constraint that companies face. Supply-side substitution refers to suppliers in neighbouring markets using their existing production facilities to start producing the product in question (or supplying the geographic area in question). We explain supply-side substitution in section 2.7. It is a less immediate constraint on companies than demand-side substitution. Customers are generally quicker to vote with their feet if they are unhappy than wait for other suppliers to come to them. New entry by rivals takes even more time and investment than supply-side substitution, and is therefore not usually considered at the market definition stage (see further Chapter 3). In this section we focus on the demand side.

2.3.1 The demand curve, with chart

2.19 In Chapter 1 we saw how customers' responsiveness to price can be captured by the demand curve, how this demand curve is affected by the prices of substitute products, and how this forms the basis for market definition. We elaborate on that here. Figure 2.1 shows the demand curve that we didn't draw in Chapter 1. It represents a very simple demand schedule for, say, high-quality chocolate. As with your imaginary price–quantity space in Chapter 1, price is on the vertical axis and quantity on the horizontal axis. According to the demand schedule, no customer buys the chocolate if the price is 10, and for every price decrease of 1 monetary unit there is demand by one additional customer (we assume here that every customer buys one box of chocolates). So if the price is 9 there is one customer

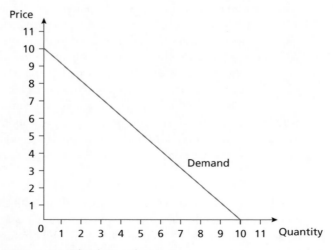

Figure 2.1 The demand curve

willing to pay for the chocolate; if the price is 8 there are two customers, and so on. If we write the formula for this demand schedule (something we generally try to avoid in this book), it would be $q = 10 - p$, where q stands for quantity and p for price. We could also write it as $p = 10 - q$, which is equivalent. The latter is called the inverse-demand relation, since it expresses price as a function of quantity, while the demand relation expresses quantity as a function of price. You may have noticed that Figure 2.1 is drawn as the inverse-demand relation (as price is on the y-axis and quantity on the x-axis) rather than the demand relation. For this counterintuitive way in which economists draw demand curves, blame Alfred Marshall, who laid the foundations for microeconomic analysis in the late nineteenth century (Marshall, 1890).

2.3.2 Shifts in the demand curve due to interaction with other products

The simple demand curve in Figure 2.1 allows us to explore some of the main principles that underlie market definition. As noted in Chapter 1, the exact position of the demand curve in the price–quantity space is influenced by two external factors: income and demand for substitute products. Let's say there is an increase in income in the economy as a whole such that at every price there is now one additional customer who is willing (and able) to pay for high-quality chocolate. The demand curve as a whole shifts 1 unit to the right (or 1 unit upwards, which is the same). We could write the new demand formula as $p = 11 - q$. This is shown in Figure 2.2. Now assume that a substitute product—say, mass-market chocolate bars—is reduced in price, such that some customers are lured away from the high-quality variety. At each price, there is now one customer less for high-quality chocolate. This can also be seen in Figure 2.2.

2.20

What this really says is that demand for high-quality chocolate is not just a function of the *own* price of high-quality chocolate, but also of income and of the price of substitute products. Such a general relationship holds for virtually any product in the real world. How much you buy of a product is influenced by its own price, by the price of other products, and by your income. Now picture a whole demand system in which demand for each good in the economy is expressed as a function of (i) the price of that good; (ii) total income; and

2.21

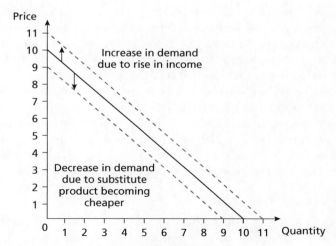

Figure 2.2 The demand curve shifts

31

(iii) the prices of all other goods in the economy (economists have developed several types of demand system, but the most common is the Marshallian demand system, after the same Alfred Marshall). For market definition it is obviously the closer substitutes that matter most, but it is useful to bear in mind that within this demand system (but also in the real world) all products are to some extent substitutes of each other. Any euro you don't spend on high-quality chocolate you can spend on designer clothes or MP3 downloads instead. This demand system forms the starting point for the hypothetical monopolist test, as we explain further in this chapter. Being aware of this demand system helps you understand the basics of market definition, and also avoid some of the mistakes that are sometimes made when defining relevant markets.

2.22   To help you picture the demand system, imagine a tablecloth. Each point on the cloth represents a product. Now lift the tablecloth at one specific point, and assume that this is like raising the price of that product. The neighbouring products on the cloth are lifted up as well—these are the closest substitutes. The next closest substitutes go up to a lesser extent, and more remote products show no noticeable change. For example, when you lift the tablecloth at the point where apples are, then you will drag up pears and other fruits to some extent as well. High-quality chocolate is in the demand system too, but probably so far away from the apples that there is no noticeable effect from you lifting the cloth a bit. The same would hold if you lifted the cloth at the point where the chocolate is—apples are unlikely to be noticeably affected by that. Market definition is in essence about identifying those products that are close substitutes in the demand system—that is, those products that move up in price when you lift the tablecloth.

2.3.3   Responsiveness of demand to price

2.23   What matters for market definition is how customers react to changes in price. Non-price features, such as quality, are generally taken as given for the purpose of market definition (although they may sometimes be considered explicitly, as discussed in section 2.13). The demand curve in Figure 2.1 shows prices and quantities for a given product quality. Changes in quality may have the effect of shifting the curve up or down, just like income and substitute products did in Figure 2.2.

2.24   The demand curve captures how customers react to price changes. There are two ways of looking at this: demand responsiveness and demand elasticity. Demand responsiveness can be inferred from the slope of the curve. In Figure 2.1 this slope has an angle of –1 (a 1-unit fall in price leads to a 1-unit rise in demand). If we draw a flatter curve, we would say that demand is more responsive to price (a small price change leads to a bigger change in quantity). The extreme would be a horizontal curve, where even a tiny increase or decrease in price leads to a loss or gain of all demand (this is the demand an individual supplier faces in perfect competition; recall from Chapter 1 that in this case the supplier is a price-taker and faces no choice but to supply at the market price). A steeper curve would represent less responsive demand. The extreme would be a vertical demand curve, where the same quantity is demanded regardless of what price is charged (this is unlikely to occur in reality).

2.3.4   Own-price elasticity of demand

2.25   A commonly used measure for price sensitivity is the price elasticity of demand. This represents the percentage change in quantity following a percentage increase in price. An elasticity of –2 means that a 1 per cent increase in price leads to a 2 per cent fall in demand. When demand is linear, price elasticity can also be described as the percentage change in quantity divided by the percentage change in price. So if a 10 per cent price increase results in a 20 per cent fall in demand, the elasticity is, again, −2.[10] If a 10 per cent price increase results in only a 3 per cent fall in demand, the elasticity is −0.3. This measure is more accurately known as the own-price elasticity of demand, as it relates the demand for a product to changes in its own price.

2.3.5 Cross-price elasticity of demand

Another measure that is relevant for market definition is the cross-price elasticity, which represents how demand for one product reacts to changes in the price of another product. If a 10 per cent increase in the price of flights between London and Paris results in a 15 per cent increase in demand for Eurostar train journeys, the cross-price elasticity of rail with respect to air travel between the two cities is 1.5 (15 per cent divided by 10 per cent). Note that while the own-price elasticity is usually negative (since price and demand move in opposite directions), the cross-price elasticity is positive when two products are substitutes. A price increase in one is associated with a demand increase for the other as a result of customers switching. The cross-price elasticity is negative for what economists call complementary goods—an increase in the price of gin not only reduces demand for gin itself but also demand for tonic water, as people will consume fewer gin-and-tonics. We return to the role of complements in market definition in section 2.11.

2.26

2.3.6 Own-price elasticities and market definition

Own-price elasticities play an important part in microeconomic theory and in competition analysis. As we explain in section 2.4 in the context of the hypothetical monopolist test, elasticities are directly linked to the price that monopolists set when maximizing their profits. The more elastic the demand to start with, the lower the price that the monopolist can set (intuitively, this is because elastic demand means that customers are responsive to price). If the own-price elasticity lies between 0 and −1, demand is said to be inelastic. Customers do not respond much to price changes—a 10 per cent price increase means customer demand falls by less than 10 per cent. Where demand is inelastic, there is clearly scope for increasing the price. Indeed, a profit-maximizing monopolist would always do so. In contrast, demand is said to be elastic if the own-price elasticity is greater than 1 in absolute terms—say, −2 or −3.[11] Elastic demand makes it less attractive to raise the price.

2.27

2.3.7 A health warning on elasticities: They change as you move along the demand curve

Own-price elasticities must be interpreted with care. Competition practitioners (be they lawyers or economists) do not always bear this in mind. The reason is that the elasticity value depends crucially on the price level at which it is measured. Demand for a product can be inelastic when the price is low, but elastic when the price is high.

2.28

---

[10] Below we explain that if you raise the price by 10 per cent, the elasticity itself may change, so this last interpretation of elasticity (10% divided by −20% equals −2), while intuitive and therefore often used, is not strictly correct. From a theoretical perspective, an elasticity value relates only to one specific point on the demand curve, and very small price changes from that point.

[11] Since the own-price elasticity is a negative number, more elastic means a more negative (so smaller) number, which makes it difficult to explain this intuitively as we keep having to add the qualifier 'in absolute terms'.

2.29 To see this, consider Figure 2.3, which shows the same demand curve as before. The (inverse) demand function for this curve was $p = 10 - q$. We defined the own-price elasticity as the percentage change in demand divided by the percentage change in price. We keep algebra to a minimum in this book, but it is useful to explain the steps in calculating elasticities here—see also Table 2.1. The elasticity can be expressed as $\Delta q/q$ divided by $\Delta p/p$ (where Δ is the symbol for a very small change, so the first expression shows the change in q divided by q, which gives the percentage change).[12] This can be rewritten as $\Delta q/\Delta p$ times p/q. Of these last two expressions, the one to explain our point here is p/q, that is, price divided by quantity.[13] The fact that the elasticity mathematically depends on the ratio between price and quantity implies that it matters where on the demand curve the elasticity is measured.

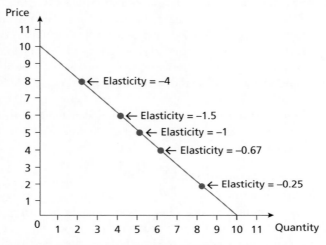

Figure 2.3 Elasticities vary along the demand curve

Table 2.1 An elasticity calculation step by step

Description of the step	Result
Demand curve function	$q = 10 - p$
Inverse demand curve function (shown in Figure 2.3)	$p = 10 - q$
Percentage change in demand (we omit multiplying by 100%)	$\Delta q/q$
Percentage change in price	$\Delta p/p$
Own-price elasticity	$(\Delta q/q) / (\Delta p/p) = (\Delta q/\Delta p) \times (p/q)$
Slope (first derivative) of the demand curve	$\Delta q/\Delta p = -1$
Own-price elasticity at $p = 2$ and $q = 8$	$-1 \times (2/8) = -0.25$
Own-price elasticity at $p = 4$ and $q = 6$	$-1 \times (4/6) = -0.67$
Own-price elasticity at $p = 8$ and $q = 2$	$-1 \times (8/2) = -4$

---

[12] In fact, it gives the per-unit change. Multiply this by 100% and you get the percentage change. Economists often do not make this distinction explicit as it is easier to speak of the percentage change, but leave out the 'multiply by 100%'.

[13] The other expression, $\Delta q/\Delta p$, represents the functional relationship between price and quantity and is the inverse of the slope of the curve in Figure 2.3 (the slope is $\Delta p/\Delta q$). Technically, $\Delta q/\Delta p$ is the first derivative of quantity with respect to price and equals −1 here (this is because the demand function is $q = 10 - p$; if the demand function had been $q = 10 - 2p$ then $\Delta q/\Delta p$ would have equalled −2).

It also implies that in most circumstances the elasticity increases as price increases, that is, as we move further up the demand curve. Take a point at the lower end of the curve, where price is 2 and quantity is 8. Our formula tells us that the elasticity at this point is −1 (see the last footnote) times 2/8, so −0.25. This implies highly inelastic demand. A bit higher up the curve, at a price of 4 and quantity of 6, demand is still inelastic, but less so—the elasticity is −1 times 4/6, so −0.67. At a price of 5 and quantity of 5 the elasticity equals −1. At any point above that, demand is elastic. So at a price of 6 and quantity of 4 the elasticity is −1.5, and at a price of 8 and quantity of 2 the elasticity is −4. All this is on the very same demand curve that has the same slope throughout.

You should therefore treat with some caution general statements such as 'the demand for **2.30** petrol is inelastic' or 'the demand for foreign holidays is elastic'. The demand for petrol may be relatively unresponsive to price changes—and this may be reflected in a steep slope of the demand curve—but whether demand for petrol is inelastic or elastic depends on the point of measurement, that is, whether petrol prices are already high or low.[14] Another implication of this is that the outcome of the hypothetical monopolist test also depends on the point of measurement—a theme to which we return below.

2.4 The Hypothetical Monopolist Test

2.4.1 Drawing the line: Hypothetical cartels and monopolists

You saw before that in the demand system, like on the tablecloth, all products are to some **2.31** extent substitutes. Market definition is about drawing the line somewhere such that the relevant market includes only the closest substitutes which impose the most significant price discipline. There are various methods to determine where the line is drawn, but you should be aware that the line itself will always have an element of arbitrariness.

One method is simply to raise the price of the product in question by, say, 5 per cent, and **2.32** include in the relevant market for that product those other products that move up in price as well up to a certain (arbitrary) point, say 4 per cent (assuming that the output of those other products stays constant). This approach would look purely at demand interactions between products within the demand system. It does not say anything about any supply-side factors that might cause such a price change in the first place.[15]

The debates leading up to the development of the hypothetical monopolist test in the United **2.33** States, however, focused on the supply side. They centred around the question: which products constrain suppliers in the market from imposing a price increase? An early idea was that of the hypothetical price-fixing cartel: which firms (and products) would need to be included in the cartel such that a price increase would not be undermined by outside competitors? This idea of the hypothetical cartel then made way for the hypothetical monopolist—after all, monopolizing a market outright is more likely to be effective than cartelizing it. In this approach to market definition it is the hypothetical monopolist who brings about the price rise in the demand system, and it is the impact on the profitability

---

[14] One exception to this is where the demand curve is 'iso-elastic', that is, it has the same elasticity along the whole of the curve. This is a demand curve specification that has some interesting theoretical properties but limited practical value.
[15] See ten Kate and Niels (2009).

of the monopolist that determines the likelihood and sustainability of the price rise, and hence the boundary of the relevant market. If it is not profitable (or profit-maximizing—see section 2.4.4 below) for a hypothetical monopolist to raise price by a small amount—usually 5 per cent or 10 per cent—that must be because too much demand is lost to other products. The nearest of those substitute products must be included in the market. In other words, a market is something worth monopolizing. In terms of the tablecloth analogy, the relevant market is formed by those products that constrain the hypothetical monopolist from lifting the cloth by more than 5–10 per cent.

2.4.2 The orthodox formulation of the hypothetical monopolist test

2.34 First introduced in the 1982 US Merger Guidelines, the wording of the hypothetical monopolist test was refined in the 1992 Horizontal Merger Guidelines, published jointly by the Department of Justice (DOJ) and FTC:

> A market is defined as a product or group of products and a geographic area in which it is produced or sold such that a hypothetical profit-maximizing firm, not subject to price regulation, that was the only present and future producer or seller of those products in that area likely would impose at least a 'small but significant and non-transitory increase in price', assuming the terms of sale of all other products are held constant. A relevant market is a group of products and a geographic area that is no bigger than necessary to satisfy this test.[16]

2.35 Each of these words in the definition has a specific meaning, and we will dissect it bit by bit. In the first sentence you will recognize the product and geographic dimensions of the market. Also in the first sentence you see the hypothetical monopolist, that is, the 'only present and future' supplier of those products in that area. Importantly, the monopolist is a profit-maximizing firm (just like any firm in a microeconomics textbook), and there is no regulation that would prevent it from raising prices. The hypothetical monopolist test draws the line for market definition by reference to a 'small but significant and non-transitory increase in price'—now commonly known as 'SSNIP'—that the monopolist 'likely would' impose (assuming no change in the price or 'terms of sale' for other products). We return to this below. Finally, the text implies that there is a distinction between 'a market' and 'a relevant market' as determined by the 'no bigger than necessary' criterion, a subtlety in the hypothetical monopolist test to which we also return later.

2.4.3 The hypothetical cartel once more

2.36 Before that, some further comments about the hypothetical cartel. Although market definition now focuses on the hypothetical monopolist, thinking in terms of cartel price increases can still be useful in certain cases. In a US damages action in 1989 against a concrete producer cartel, the question arose as to whether concrete in West Los Angeles was a relevant market. The plaintiff argued that the success of the cartel itself proved the existence of a relevant market. The court agreed:

> As a purely logical matter, French [the plaintiff] is unquestionably correct. A price-fixing conspiracy confined to manufacturers of concrete would not have been able to succeed if concrete were not a distinct product market: when the cartel attempted to raise prices,

---

[16] Department of Justice and Federal Trade Commission (1992), 'Horizontal Merger Guidelines', s 1.0, reprinted in 4 Trade Reg Rep 104. In the 2010 Horizontal Merger Guidelines you find a watered-down version of the hypothetical monopolist test. The 1992 version is more comprehensive.

customers would simply switch to sand, brick, gravel or some other construction material. Similarly, a price-fixing conspiracy confined to firms in West Los Angeles would not have succeeded if West Los Angeles were not a distinct geographic market: when the cartel attempted to raise prices, customers would simply take their business to East Los Angeles or San Diego or Phoenix. If a group of firms is able to fix prices, it is because their customers have nowhere else to turn. Every price-fixing conspiracy thus identifies directly, in a real world context, a group of firms which is insulated from outside competitive pressures. That is precisely what conventional market definition evidence attempts to identify artificially, by the collection and interpretation of economic data regarding the relationship between various demand curves, by common sense assumptions about the interchangeability of similar products, and the like.[17]

The notion of the hypothetical cartel made a reappearance in the 2010 Horizontal Merger Guidelines, which indicate that the concept of a hypothetical profit-maximizing cartel may be used instead of a hypothetical monopolist if the pricing incentives faced by the actual suppliers in the market differ substantially from those of the monopolist because they sell products outside the candidate market as well.[18] The example given is where the candidate market is one for durable equipment and the suppliers of that equipment derive substantial revenues from selling spare parts and maintenance and repair services for that equipment. We discuss such situations in section 2.11 on market definition for complements and bundles. **2.37**

2.4.4 What the hypothetical monopolist *would* do: Maximize profits

You start with the focal product, which is where the competition concern arises in the first place—let's say high-quality chocolate as in the merger at the start of this chapter. To define the boundaries of the market you then hypothetically monopolize the supply of high-quality chocolate. All of a sudden, instead of multiple suppliers (including your two merging parties) there is only one. Luckily, economic theory tells us what the monopolist is going to do in this candidate market. **2.38**

As explained in Chapter 1, the monopolist will set its price and quantity at the profit-maximizing level. Here we explain in a bit more detail (and with a chart) how the profit-maximizing point is found. In Figure 2.4, which is the standard monopoly representation that you will find in any microeconomics textbook, the monopolist faces the entire demand curve for high-quality chocolate (since by assumption there are no other suppliers). The demand function is the same as before, represented by the equation $p = 10 - q$. **2.39**

Profits for the monopolist equal revenue minus costs. Maximum profit is achieved when marginal profit is zero (profits can no longer be increased further), and this occurs at the point where marginal revenue equals marginal cost. We now set out the steps in calculating this optimal point. See also Table 2.2. Revenue equals price times quantity—so $p \times q$, which equals $(10 - q) \times q$. This means that marginal revenue is $10 - 2q$ (the first derivative of revenue with respect to quantity). The marginal revenue curve is shown in Figure 2.4. It starts at the same point as the demand curve (price equals 10 at zero quantity), but then slopes downward twice as steeply. Now suppose that marginal cost equals 2 per unit of output (so **2.40**

---

[17] *EW French & Sons v General Portland* 885 F 2d 1392, 1402 (9th Cir. 1989), at [65].
[18] Department of Justice and Federal Trade Commission (2010), 'Horizontal Merger Guidelines', 19 August, p. 9.

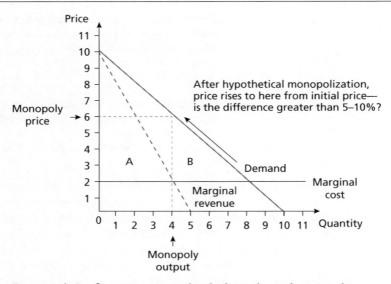

Figure 2.4 Profit-maximization by the hypothetical monopolist

Table 2.2 Calculating the profit-maximizing point step by step

Description of the step	Result
Inverse demand function	$p = 10 - q$
Monopoly revenue = price × quantity	$(10 - q) \times q$
Marginal cost per unit	2
Monopoly profit = revenue – total cost	$(10 - q) \times q - (2 \times q)$
Monopoly marginal revenue (first derivative of revenue with respect to quantity)	$10 - 2q$
Monopoly profits are maximized where marginal revenue equals marginal cost	$10 - 2q = 2$, so $q = 4$ and $p = 6$
Monopoly profit at $q = 4$ and $p = 6$ (optimum point)	$(6 \times 4) - (2 \times 4) = 16$
Monopoly profit at $q = 5$ and $p = 5$	$(5 \times 5) - (2 \times 5) = 15$
Monopoly profit at $q = 3$ and $p = 7$	$(7 \times 3) - (2 \times 3) = 15$

total cost is $2q$). This is also shown in the figure. Total profit is maximized at $q = 4$, since that is where marginal revenue equals marginal cost ($10 - 2 \times 4 = 2$). At this point, price equals 6 ($10 - 4$), and the profit margin on each unit equals 4 (price minus marginal cost), so total profit on the 4 units sold equals 16. Total profit is shown in the figure as area A. Another way of describing the profit-maximizing point is that it is where the surface of area A is the greatest. If you set price a bit lower, at 5, total profit falls to 15 (as quantity increases to 5 and the profit margin per unit is 3). If you raise price to 7 and the profit margin to 5, quantity falls to 3 and total profit is also 15. Hence, as a monopolist you cannot do better than set the price at 6 and quantity at 4, making a profit of 16.

2.41 Recall from section 2.3 that at this profit-maximizing point of $q = 4$ and $p = 6$ the own-price elasticity is –1.5. So the monopolist ends up on the elastic part of the demand curve. Contrast this with the perfect competition outcome, where price equals marginal cost, so $p = 2$, and quantity is 8, and the own-price elasticity equals –0.25. So here you are on the inelastic part of the demand curve when there is perfect competition on the supply side. You can see how a monopolist would rapidly move away from there, raising prices and not losing too much custom in the process. Area A in Figure 2.4 reflects a transfer of consumer surplus to producer profit when moving from perfect competition to monopoly. Area B reflects the consumer surplus that is lost because those units are no longer sold even though consumers were willing to pay more than the cost of producing them. It is known as the deadweight welfare loss to society resulting from monopoly (the lost consumer surplus accrues to no one; it's wasted).

2.4.5 Profit-maximization and the SSNIP

Back to what this means for market definition. You have seen now what price and quantity the profit-maximizing monopolist would choose. All you need to do next is compare that point with the position before the market was monopolized, and measure how much the price has changed—is this change 'small but significant'? If the starting point was perfect competition, monopolization of the market in our example would lead to an increase from $p = 2$ to $p = 6$, so by 200 per cent—clearly a large and significant increase in price. However, the starting point does not need to be perfect competition. The market pre-monopolization may have been characterized by some form of oligopolistic competition, such that price was already higher than marginal cost. If the market price pre-monopolization was, say, 5, the hypothetical monopolist would impose a price increase of 1 monetary unit to 6, so 20 per cent, which is more than the 5–10 per cent range for SSNIP. If the market price was 5.75, the change to 6 would represent a 4 per cent increase, so less than 5–10 per cent. If the market price was 6, monopolization would not result in any price increase. You can see that it therefore matters where exactly you start before applying the hypothetical monopolist test. If the product in question is already priced at the monopoly level, a hypothetical monopolist would not impose any further price increases. However, that does not imply that the market is not worth monopolizing, because it clearly is in this case. This result, and the erroneous conclusion that can be drawn from it, is known as the cellophane fallacy, which we discuss further in section 2.6.

2.42

2.4.6 Why the 'SS' in SSNIP?

The term 'SSNIP' has become widely known in competition law. Indeed, 'SSNIP test' and 'hypothetical monopolist test' are used interchangeably. You may have wondered why it has to be a 'small but significant' increase. Is this for some scientific reason? Would the test still work with a large price increase? The SSNIP is usually interpreted as 5 per cent or 10 per cent. You will recall from the earlier sections that substitution between products is a matter of degree. If you lift the tablecloth high enough, many remote products will move up as well. If you raise the price of high-quality chocolate far enough, there comes a point when even the more mundane types of chocolate become attractive alternatives. Any cut-off point for such a price increase is inherently arbitrary. You could in theory perform a market definition test that asks if a hypothetical monopolist would raise price by 20 per cent, 50 per cent, or 100 per cent. Why do most competition authorities use 5–10 per cent as the threshold? There are various reasons for this (although these are rarely made explicit).

2.43

First, competition law is generally concerned with mergers and anti-competitive prac- tices that reduce competition in the market and hence lead to higher prices. How high is too high? Some competition authorities consider that a 5 per cent increase is already

2.44

of significant detriment to consumers. The UK Competition Commission (CC, now part of the Competition and Markets Authority, CMA) stated in its previous (2003) Merger Guidelines:

> The Commission will normally use 5 per cent for the SSNIP test, rather than the more common 5–10 per cent, because in many instances an increase in the price of a product of around 5 per cent (with all other prices unchanged) might reasonably be judged to have a significant effect on customers' expenditure on the product and so provides an appropriate level at which to consider the test.[19]

2.45   Of course the hypothetical monopolist does not impose price increases for real. But the SSNIP threshold is related to the more general concern about price rises. An authority that applies a 5 per cent threshold can be said to be stricter than an authority that applies a 10 per cent or 20 per cent threshold. A higher threshold for the SSNIP means a greater chance of broader markets being defined and hence a lower likelihood of a finding of market power.

2.46   Second, how far the monopolist's profit-maximizing price lies above the initial price depends on the initial own-price elasticity. The more inelastic demand is (before hypothetically monopolizing the market), the more the monopolist will raise prices. As explained in section 2.3, elasticities vary depending on the price point at which they are measured. Economists usually have data to estimate elasticities only at current price levels, not at the (hypothetical) monopoly price level. The estimated elasticities can therefore be used to test only very small price increases above the current price level—hence 5 per cent or at most 10 per cent for the SSNIP threshold. Beyond that it is difficult to know how quickly demand becomes more elastic (so how quickly the profit-maximizing price is reached). A 20 per cent SSNIP threshold would lead to uncertain results because the elasticity value might differ too much between the starting price point (where we can measure the elasticity) and the hypothetical, profit-maximizing price (where the elasticity is unobserved). A 5–10 per cent threshold has greater scientific merit from this perspective.

2.4.7 Why the 'N' in SSNIP?

2.47   The other aspect of the SSNIP is the 'non-transitory' nature of the price increase. The 'N' in SSNIP is as arbitrary as the 'SS', and the cut-off point is usually chosen for policy and practical reasons. One rationale for considering a 'non-transitory' price increase is that competition authorities are not normally concerned with transitory market power. Positions of market power tend to be eroded over time (more on this in Chapter 3). If it suddenly starts to rain on a busy open-air market, vendors who sell umbrellas find themselves controlling a scarce good that is in strong demand, such that they can extract a hefty monopoly rent. The same is true for car hire and taxi companies when train drivers are on strike or air travel is disrupted.[20] Such a position of market power will not last, and does not usually merit a separate market definition by time of consumption (as discussed in section 2.2). Only persistent market power is of concern. The small but significant increase in price must therefore be 'non-transitory'. One exception to this is the electricity generation market, where authorities have been concerned about very short, thirty-minute, periods of market power and have

---

[19] Competition Commission (2003), 'Merger References: Competition Commission Guidelines', at [2.8].
[20] One of the authors paid €3,000 for a taxi ride from Rome to Paris when the European airspace was closed due to volcanic ash in April 2010. Economists do not learn about economics only from textbooks.

defined relevant markets accordingly.[21] These thirty-minute periods recur more frequently and predictably than the periods of rain or train strikes, so in reality in electricity generation the authorities are concerned about a series of regular short periods of market power over a longer time period.

How long is non-transitory? Competition authorities usually refer to a period of one to two years. In some markets, customers may sign contracts with providers for a minimum period—for example, a twelve-month mobile phone contract. By interpreting non-transitory as one or two years, you would still take into account the fact that customers may switch once the contract expires, even if they can't switch before then. Longer-term contracts, say, for three or five years, must be treated differently—customers on these contracts will be in the hypothetical monopolist's pocket for the duration of the non-transitory period. **2.48**

A practical reason for choosing a particular 'N' is that the analysis is likely to be more precise if you take one or two years than if you take longer periods. This is because future market dynamics are difficult to predict. Moreover, from a supply-side perspective, the profit-maximizing price over a one-year or two-year period would depend on which costs are marginal (variable with output) over the period. The longer the time period, the more costs become variable, so it becomes more difficult to predict where the monopolist would set the profit-maximizing price. **2.49**

Curiously, the 1997 European Commission Notice on market definition refers to a 'permanent' increase in price.[22] In line with the description above, this would imply that the Commission takes greater account of long-term market dynamics and tends to define wider markets as a result. However, another possible explanation for the European Commission text would be that the term 'permanent' is simply an alternative (and somewhat loosely worded) way of capturing the concept of 'non-transitory'. **2.50**

2.4.8 An iterative process: From the focal product to the smallest market

The test asks whether a hypothetical, profit-maximizing monopolist would impose a SSNIP. Here we discuss the importance of selecting the right start and end point for the test, that is, the right focal product and geographic area. **2.51**

Let's begin with the end point. The US Merger Guidelines make a subtle distinction between the definition of a market—which is where a hypothetical monopolist would impose a SSNIP—and the relevant market—which is 'no bigger than necessary to satisfy this test'. In other words, the relevant market is the smallest market in which the monopolist would impose a SSNIP.[23] A hypothetical commercial broadcast monopolist operating in the whole of Europe would be able to impose a SSNIP, so the whole of Europe would be a market. But a hypothetical broadcast monopolist in Germany would equally be able to **2.52**

---

[21] For example, Competition Commission (2001), 'AES and British Energy: A report on references made under section 12 of the Electricity Act 1989', 31 January; and Office of Fair Trading and Ofgem (2005), 'Application in the energy sector; competition law guideline', January.

[22] European Commission (1997), 'Notice on the Definition of Relevant Market for the Purposes of Community Competition Law', 97/C372/03, at [17].

[23] The 2010 Horizontal Merger Guidelines no longer refer to this smallest market principle. We think that this may cause confusion, as it is one of the fundamental principles of the hypothetical monopolist test.

impose a SSNIP. Which of these two candidate markets is the relevant market? Let's say it's the whole of Europe. We then find that there are quite a few commercial broadcasters in this European market and conclude that there is no competition concern. This would be erroneous. Within Europe there is at least one 'pocket' of market power—in this example, Germany—where a hypothetical monopolist can raise prices. Therefore, Germany should be the relevant market here. By taking the smallest market you avoid overlooking pockets of market power. It also means that you don't need to worry about submarkets within the relevant market.

2.4.9 Picking the right focal product and area

2.53 So the end point for market definition is to find the smallest market in which the hypothetical monopolist would impose a SSNIP. What is the starting point? Recall that market definition is not an end in itself, but only an intermediate step in the analysis of competitive constraints. For market definition to be informative, the starting point must always be the product in relation to which the competition concern arises. If the case relates to commercial broadcast services in Germany—two German broadcasters wish to merge, for example—the focal product and geographic area to hypothetically monopolize would be commercial broadcasting in Germany. If the concern arises from a proposed merger between two producers of frozen dessert pies in north-east United States, then that is the hypothetical monopolist's initial domain.

2.54 The focal product can be narrowly defined. After all, you are trying to find the smallest market in which a SSNIP can be imposed in order to identify pockets of market power. Thus, in the merger case at the beginning of this chapter you can start with high-quality chocolate, and hypothetically monopolize that market so as to test whether it faces competitive constraints from other types of chocolate—if the monopolist would impose a SSNIP, the relevant market is indeed confined to high-quality chocolate. However, in section 2.1 we also warned that in markets with differentiated products the whole market definition exercise may become uninformative. The focal products may become too broad (high-quality chocolate can be divided into various types and presentations which are not necessarily close substitutes), or too narrow (just Porsche 911 Carreras, or Godiva chocolate) to be informative. We recommend that in these situations you take a pragmatic view on whether the products concerned are so differentiated that market definition loses value as an intermediate step (because you potentially end up finding that each differentiated product is worth monopolizing and hence in theory constitutes a separate relevant market). If differentiation is that significant, it may be more appropriate to focus the analysis directly on the competitive constraints and closeness of competition between the differentiated products, skipping market definition altogether (we return to this in Chapter 7). However, we think that there is often no need for skipping market definition, because in many differentiated product markets you can still find meaningful groups of products that are reasonably similar and that you can hypothetically monopolize to test the constraints from other groups—for example, top-of-the-range sports cars, Belgian high-quality chocolates, or even all high-quality chocolates. An element of judgement will usually be required.

2.4.10 Multiple focal products

2.55 It is also important to bear in mind that in any competition case there can be more than one focal product (or area). Indeed, you should in principle define a relevant market for any product (or area) where you might have a competition concern. If a German and a UK commercial broadcaster wish to merge, you have to define a relevant market separately for broadcast services in Germany and for broadcast services in the UK. These are two different market definition exercises. Note that in this case you may well find that neither relevant market has the other product in it, and hence that there are no competitive overlaps between the merging parties. This is one of those rare situations in which a narrow market definition actually suits the merging parties; normally broader markets favour merging parties, and hence merging parties tend to favour broader markets.

Likewise, if a producer of frozen dessert pies merges with a producer of ice cream, you **2.56** have to apply the hypothetical monopolist test to each of these products separately. The two exercises may well lead to the same market definition that has both products in it, for example, a market for all desserts. However, you might also find that substitution is strong in one direction but not the other. Say that frozen dessert pies are not worth monopolizing because many consumers switch to ice cream and other desserts if the price is raised. At the same time, in the market with ice cream as the focal product, a hypothetical monopolist does find it profitable to impose a SSNIP because few consumers switch away to other desserts. So ice cream is in the market for frozen dessert pies, but frozen dessert pies are not in the market for ice cream.

2.4.11 Asymmetric markets

Markets can be asymmetric in this regard. One product may be in the market for another **2.57** product, even if that other product is not in its market (this is not the norm, but it can occur in practice). That is why it is important to identify clearly the focal product of a relevant market. It is also why a generally worded question such as 'Are frozen dessert pies and ice cream in the same relevant market?' is not meaningful as such—the answer depends on what the focal product is. The right questions are: 'Is ice cream in the relevant market for frozen dessert pies?', and 'Are frozen dessert pies in the relevant market for ice cream?' In our hypothetical example above, the answer to the first question was yes and to the second question no.

A case where asymmetric markets were considered is the *Bayer–Aventis Crop Science* merger **2.58** in 2002, involving agricultural crop-protection products.[24] The European Commission found evidence of substitution from foliar and soil applications of fungicides and insecticides to seed treatment, but not the other way round (from seed treatment to the other applications). The Commission also found another instance of 'one-way substitution'— between two specific types of cereal crop-protection products. Asymmetric markets have also been found in various supermarket inquiries in the UK—larger stores were considered to constrain smaller stores, but not the other way round.[25]

An example of where asking whether two products are in the same market, as opposed to **2.59** whether one is in the market for the other (focal) one, led to an erroneous analysis is the 2007 abuse of dominance case before the English High Court concerning local bus services. As pointed out in the judgment:

> [Counsel for the defendants] also made what I regard as a fair point of criticism of [the claimants' expert's] analysis. In any analysis of whether local buses form an exclusive

---

[24] *Bayer–Aventis Crop Science* (Case COMP/M.2547), Decision of 17 April 2002.
[25] For example, Competition Commission (2005), 'Somerfield plc/Wm Morrison Supermarkets plc', September.

product market, the usual approach is to hypothesize a small but significant non-transitory increase in price for bus services of 5 to 10% and determine what alternative modes of transport (if any) become a substitute. That is the right approach, whereas [the claimants' expert] appeared to regard it as equally relevant to consider whether buses were a substitute for cars. Buses may be competitively constrained by cars, but cars may not be competitively constrained by buses.[26]

2.4.12 Getting to the smallest market

2.60 You have now seen what the start and end points are for the hypothetical monopolist test. The way to get from the focal product and area to the smallest market in which a SSNIP would be imposed is through a process of iteration. You hypothetically monopolize the focal product—say high-quality chocolate. The hypothetical monopolist will set the price at the profit-maximizing level. Is this new profit-maximizing price more than 5–10 per cent higher than the existing price? If the answer is yes, you have found your relevant market. If the answer is no you must expand the market. Recall that if a SSNIP is not imposed, that must be because consumers switch to other products in the demand system—it does not matter whether this is switching to close substitutes, such as mass-market chocolate, or spending income on more remote substitutes, such as theatre tickets or expensive wine. In keeping with the aim of finding the smallest market, you take the closest substitute for the focal product and bring it within the realm of the hypothetical monopolist. You then apply the SSNIP question again. If the answer is now yes, you have found your relevant market. If the answer is still no, you proceed to the third iteration of the test by including the second closest substitute. And so on.

2.61 In reading this explanation of the iterative process, some questions may have occurred to you that we have not yet answered. First, how do you actually assess whether a SSNIP would be profitable? Second, if the test fails in the first iteration, how do you determine what the closest substitute is? Third, in the next iteration, do you consider a SSNIP only for the focal product, or for all products controlled by the hypothetical monopolist? The first question is addressed in section 2.5 on critical loss analysis. We answer the second and third questions next in this section. Before that, however, it is worth pointing out that while in theory the hypothetical monopolist test can have several iterations, in practice you'll quite often find that one iteration is sufficient. If you conclude that a hypothetical monopolist of high-quality chocolate would not find it profit-maximizing to impose a small price increase, in all likelihood any real producer of such chocolate—including the merged entity—would also not be able to raise the price. Hence you have the answer to your competition question, and there is no need to delineate exactly where the boundaries of the relevant market are beyond high-quality chocolate.

2.4.13 Ranking substitutes: Diversion ratios and cross-price elasticity

2.62 As you have now read several times, many products within the demand system are to some extent substitutes for each other. But clearly some are closer substitutes than others. For the purpose of the hypothetical monopolist test, you need to rank substitute products according to how close they are to the focal product. The closest substitute is normally the product

---

[26] *Chester City Council and Chester City Transport Limited v Arriva PLC* [2007] EWHC 1373 (Ch), at [157]. We acted for the defendants in this case.

that absorbs most of the sales that are lost by the hypothetical monopolist after imposing a price increase. That product poses the strongest competitive constraint on the focal product and is the one that the monopolist, if given the choice, would like to get its hands on most. Once that closest substitute product is grouped with the focal product, the hypothetical monopolist no longer cares about losing sales from the latter to the former because it controls both products. The most significant obstacle to raising the price of the focal product has thus been removed (internalized, as economists would say), and the price of the focal products will increase by more than in the first iteration.

Exactly the same logic applies when you are trying to assess the effects of a merger directly, without market definition. In that case the central question is whether the merging companies (or their products or brands) are each other's closest competitors, so the ranking of substitutes matters. We discuss unilateral effects analysis of mergers in Chapter 7, but it is useful to bear in mind that the economic principles that we explain here—demand systems, elasticities, ranking of substitutes—are of direct relevance to merger analysis as well. **2.63**

Substitutes can be ranked using the diversion ratio. The closest substitute is the one with the highest diversion ratio, that is, the product which benefits most from the loss of sales of the focal product after the price increase.[27] We explain this concept of diversion ratio in more detail in Chapter 7. You can see that it is closely related to the concept of cross-price elasticity: the higher the cross-price elasticity, the higher the diversion ratio. Note, however, that the product with the highest cross-price elasticity is not always the product with the highest diversion ratio; this also depends on the size of total demand for each product. To see this, recall that the cross-price elasticity is defined as the percentage change in the quantity of one product divided by the percentage change in the price of the other. Let's say that after a 10 per cent price increase by the hypothetical high-quality chocolate monopolist, most lost sales are captured by mass-market chocolate products—the diversion ratio is highest, and this is therefore the closest substitute for high-quality chocolate. Yet because demand for mass-market chocolate is vast, the percentage increase in that demand from capturing lost high-quality chocolate sales is relatively low, and so is the cross-price elasticity of demand for mass-market chocolate with respect to the price of high-quality chocolate. Conversely, pralines may capture fewer of the lost high-quality chocolate sales (the diversion ratio is lower, and hence pralines are not the closest substitute) but because pralines sales are smaller, the cross-price elasticity may well be higher than that for mass-market chocolate. **2.64**

There are two further points to make in relation to the ranking of substitutes and the use of cross-price elasticities. First, in the context of market definition, any sales loss matters to the hypothetical monopolist since it makes the price increase less profitable. It does not matter to the high-quality chocolate monopolist whether sales are lost to close substitutes (mass-market chocolate) or remote substitutes (expensive wine, or just basic groceries). Second, own-price elasticities are of greater interest in market definition than cross-price elasticities. This has not always been understood in competition law. Before the hypothetical monopolist test was developed, markets were frequently defined according to whether the cross-price elasticity between two products was high or low. The cross-price elasticity matters for the ranking of substitutes in the hypothetical monopolist test, which is a rather **2.65**

---

[27] A more accurate term would be the capture ratio. See ten Kate and Niels (2014).

secondary role. Nonetheless, a measurement of the cross-price elasticity may provide a use-ful sense-check on the own-price elasticity. This is because there is a theoretical relationship between the two (which we do not elaborate upon here): in the Marshallian demand system a general rule is that the higher the sum of all of a product's cross-price elasticities, the higher (more negative) that product's own-price elasticity will be. If you see an estimate of own-price elasticity that suggests very elastic demand for a product (a small price increase causes a large sales loss), you should also expect to see that product having some high cross-price elasticities with other products, since that sales loss will be mainly absorbed by other products in the demand system.

2.4.14 The second iteration onwards: Which of the monopolist's products does the SSNIP question apply to?

2.66 This is a frequently asked question, and has not been answered very well in competition authorities' guidance or other texts. And yet it is straightforward: even if the monopolist controls multiple products, the SSNIP question should apply only to the focal product as that is the product where the competition concern arises in the first place. Let's consider a merger between producers of apples. This is the focal product. In the first iteration of the test you find that the hypothetical monopolist would impose a 3 per cent price increase—insufficient to constitute a SSNIP. You find that pears are the closest substitute for apples. In the second iteration of the test the monopolist controls both apples and pears. As a result, it now no longer cares about losing sales to pears when raising the price of apples. The main constraint on raising apple prices has disappeared (in economic terms, it has been internalized by the monopolist). The monopolist can now raise prices for both products if required to maximize profits (remember that in the first iteration the assumption was that the terms of sale of all other products, including pears, are held constant). Say the hypo-thetical monopolist now imposes a price increase on apples of 13 per cent—a SSNIP. But pears increase in price by 4 per cent (the profit-maximizing price, obtained in the same way as in Figure 2.4). So in this example there is no SSNIP on pears, despite the monopolization of their supply, the reason being that pears face strong competition from other fruits that the monopolist does not control.

2.67 Must you therefore proceed to a third iteration of the test, where the group of products controlled by the monopolist includes bananas as well? Suppose you did, and you found that the price of apples now increases by 15 per cent and that of pears by 6 per cent (the monopolist no longer cares about switching to bananas, so can flex prices up a bit further), while bananas—monopolized for the first time in this third iteration—increase in price by only 2 per cent. Following the same logic that made you proceed to the third iteration—that is, you require *all* the hypothetical monopolist's prices to increase—you would eventually reach the conclusion that the market should include all fruits. Alas, the logic and the con-clusion are incorrect. Already in the second iteration you found a pocket of market power in apples. As soon as pears, their closest substitute, are added, the monopolist imposes a SSNIP on the apples. The relevant market for apples includes pears, but no more. It is a market worth monopolizing. The fact that you discover in the second iteration that pears in themselves are not a market worth monopolizing (even when taken together with apples) is irrelevant. You are focused on the scope for price increases in apples, because that is where the competition concerns from the merger arise. So in the second and any subsequent itera-tions of the hypothetical monopolist test, the SSNIP question is still applicable only to the focal product.

2.4.15 Purity of the SSNIP test, with some pragmatism

Thus far we have considered the hypothetical monopolist test in its purest form, which is **2.68** based on the definition of the test in the 1992 Horizontal Merger Guidelines. However, in practice, some flexibility will be required if the hypothetical monopolist test is to remain a useful concept for market definition. It is difficult enough to estimate elasticities and consumer responses to price changes. But once you have an estimate, identifying the profit-maximizing price that the monopolist would set gives rise to additional complications. It is easier—as we explain in the next section—to ask simply whether it would be profitable for the hypothetical monopolist to impose a SSNIP, rather than whether it would be profit-maximizing. This is the essence of critical loss analysis, a commonly used method to make the hypothetical monopolist test workable.

Another reason why some pragmatism is required is that, as we mentioned before, in **2.69** most markets there is a degree of product differentiation. The test works best when products are homogeneous. One pragmatic adjustment we have already discussed is that, for the purposes of the hypothetical monopolist test, you can to some extent ignore differentiation and group together products that may still be considered reasonably homogeneous (top-of-the-range sports cars or high-quality chocolate—no two products in these groups are exactly the same, but overall they constitute reasonably identifiable categories). There are markets, however, where the degree of differentiation is so high that the hypothetical monopolist test in its purest form becomes too uninformative. If that is the case, you should skip market definition altogether and focus directly on competitive constraints.

2.5 Critical Loss Analysis

2.5.1 Would or could: Two different hypothetical monopolists

In section 2.4 we quoted the definition of the hypothetical monopolist test from the 1992 **2.70** US Horizontal Merger Guidelines. Below are the definitions given in guidance from the Australian Competition & Consumer Commission and the European Commission. Can you spot the difference with the US guidelines?

> The process of applying the [hypothetical monopolist test] starts with one of the products and geographic areas supplied by one or both of the merger parties. If a hypothetical monopolist supplier of this product cannot *profitably* institute a SSNIP because of customers switching to alternative products, the next closest demand substitute is added. If a hypothetical monopolist supplier of this extended group of products cannot *profitably* institute such a price increase because of customers switching to alternative products, the next best substitute is added. The collection of products is expanded until a hypothetical monopoly supplier of all those products *could profitably* institute a SSNIP [emphasis added].[28]

> The question to be answered is whether the parties' customers would switch to readily available substitutes or to suppliers located elsewhere in response to a hypothetical small (in the range 5–10%) but permanent relative price increase in the products and areas being considered. If substitution were enough to make the price increase *unprofitable* because of the resulting loss of sales, additional substitutes and areas are included in the relevant market.

---

[28] Australian Competition & Consumer Commission (2008), 'Merger Guidelines', November, at [4.20].

This would be done until the set of products and geographical areas is such that small, permanent increases in relative prices would be *profitable* [emphasis added].[29]

2.71 Rather than ask what a monopolist *would* do to *maximize profits*—as in the US version—these other versions ask what a monopolist *could* do *profitably*. The US version is the theoretically purer one. Monopolists maximize profits. The other version is about breaking even: at what point does the monopolist make the same profits as before?

2.5.2 Would or could: Does it matter?

2.72 Having two different versions of the hypothetical monopolist test has caused confusion among practitioners (lawyers and economists). Some may not even have been aware that there was a difference. But does it really matter?

2.73 Theory tells us that it is not always the case that if a certain price increase is profitable, the hypothetical monopolist would actually impose it. A profit-maximizing monopolist would impose a smaller increase if that led to even higher profits. In fact it can be shown that the break-even price increase is twice as high as the profit-maximizing price increase (assuming linear demand and constant marginal cost, as we have in our examples). If you go back to Figure 2.4, the monopolist *would* go up to the profit-maximizing price, but *could* raise price even higher and still make a profit. As a consequence, markets defined using the break-even approach tend to be narrower than those defined using the profit-maximization approach (can you see why?).

2.74 In practice, however, the break-even approach in critical loss analysis has some advantages, even if it is theoretically less pure. One is that the critical loss threshold does not depend on the shape of the demand curve, and you therefore do not need to make any assumptions about demand. You need to know only the levels of demand before and after the price increase.

2.5.3 The concept of critical loss

2.75 If you raise the price of a product two things happen. You sell less of the product, as customers walk away or reduce their purchases. But you also make a higher profit margin than before on the units that you do sell. These two effects therefore work in opposite directions. The first decreases your profits; the second increases them. Any business in the real world faces this trade-off when considering a price increase. And so does a hypothetical monopolist. How do you know which of the two effects prevails? At what point do the two effects exactly cancel each other out, and leave you with the same amount of profits as before? This is what standard critical loss analysis is about. The critical sales loss is the percentage of sales at which the hypothetical monopolist makes the same profit before and after imposing a SSNIP. If the estimated actual sales loss following the SSNIP exceeds the critical loss threshold, the SSNIP is unprofitable (conclusion: the market is wider). If the estimated actual loss is below the critical loss, the SSNIP is profitable (conclusion: this is a relevant market).

2.76 You can already see from the description of the two effects which factors influence this threshold. The first effect is customers walking away or reducing purchases following the 5 per cent or 10 per cent price increase. So it matters whether you select 5 per cent or 10 per

---

[29] European Commission (1997), 'Notice on the Definition of Relevant Market for the Purposes of Community Competition Law', 97/C372/03, at [17].

cent as the SSNIP. With a 5 per cent SSNIP you expect a lower actual sales loss than with 10 per cent, but the critical loss will also be lower (see the discussion around Table 2.3 below). The reason why lost sales matter is that the monopolist made a profit on them before. So the initial profit margin (as before, defined as price minus marginal cost, divided by price) matters in determining the critical loss. The second effect of the price increase is the higher margin that is earned on the remaining sales. The higher margin equals the initial margin plus 5 per cent or 10 per cent, as that is by how much the price has increased (this assumes that marginal costs do not change over this range of output, which is a simplifying but often not unreasonable assumption). So, in sum, the critical loss depends on two factors: the percentage SSNIP on which you do the analysis, and the initial profit margin. Once you have estimated the actual sales loss after a SSNIP (a different challenge altogether), you compare this with the critical loss.

2.5.4 The critical loss formula

This is as far as we can take our verbal explanation of critical loss analysis. Some basic algebra **2.77** is required to explain the formula for working out the critical loss. A chart also helps. Consider the following. There is a starting situation in which q units of the product are sold at price p. This gives rise to a price–cost margin, m, equal to price minus marginal costs, divided by price—that is, $m = (p - c) / p$. Then there is a SSNIP of x, which is equal to the change in p divided by p ($x = \Delta p/p$)—note therefore that x can be any percentage, even though it is usually interpreted as 5 per cent or 10 per cent. Suppose that this SSNIP results in a fall in the quantity sold of Δq. The two effects of the SSNIP on profits can then be expressed as follows. The fall in quantity, Δq, gives rise to a loss of profits since on each of the units previously sold the profit was m times p—that is, the loss of profit is Δq times m times p.[30] The profit margin on the remaining sales is enhanced by x (the SSNIP)—this extra profit is $(q - \Delta q)$ times x times p. The critical loss question is: what is the maximum reduction in quantity that the hypothetical monopolist may suffer before the price increase becomes unprofitable? The answer is: the Δq for which the profit gain from the price increase offsets the profit loss from the decline in quantity. In other words, it is where the monopolist breaks even: $(q - \Delta q)$ times p times x (the loss in profit from reduced sales) equals Δq times m times p (the gain in profit on the remaining sales). A bit of rearranging leads us to the standard expression for the critical loss percentage: $\Delta q/q = x / (x + m)$.[31] Thus, in line with our verbal explanation earlier, the critical loss depends only on the SSNIP percentage used, x, and on the initial price–cost margin, m.

2.5.5 Critical loss illustrated

This situation is illustrated in Figure 2.5. F is the starting point, with a price p and a quantity **2.78** q. Total profits for the monopolist are equal to the area ACFD (points A and C are on the marginal cost curve and a profit margin of p minus A is earned on every unit of q). Then price is raised to ($p + \Delta p$) and output falls to ($q - \Delta q$). As above, it is assumed that marginal costs, c, are constant. The profits lost by the quantity reduction correspond to the shaded area BCFE. But there is also a profit gained by the price increase, as represented by the shaded area DEHG. Critical loss analysis is about comparing these two effects. If BCFE is larger than DEHG, the price increase is unprofitable (conclusion: the market is wider).

---

[30] You may have spotted that Δq is expressed as a positive number here, even though it represents a fall in quantity.
[31] The critical loss formula was first identified in Harris and Simons (1989).

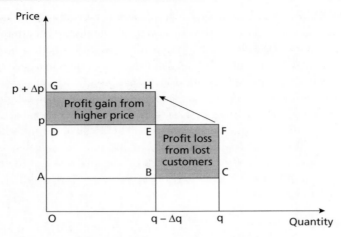

Figure 2.5 The profit effects of a price increase

If DEHG is larger, the price increase is profitable. You can see that this depends crucially on the level of Δq, the estimated fall in quantity of sales. Given the values of q, p, and Δp, the larger Δq is, the greater area BCFE becomes, and the more area DEHG gets squeezed. The Δq for which DEHG and BCFE have exactly the same surface area is the critical sales loss—this is where the monopolist breaks even.

2.79 You may have noted that Figure 2.5 does not have a demand curve. It just has two price–quantity points, F and H. This is because determining the critical sales loss—and the formula $x/(x+m)$—does not depend on the shape or nature of the actual demand curve at all (other than that it is downward-sloping). It simply follows from an arithmetic comparison between profits before and after a price increase. This is one of the practical advantages of critical loss analysis.

2.5.6 A numerical example of critical loss

2.80 Table 2.3 shows the critical loss percentages for 5 per cent and 10 per cent price increases and for different values for the initial price–cost margin. Various points are worth noting

Table 2.3 Critical loss values based on the formula $x / (x+m)$

Initial price–cost margin (m) (%)	Critical loss for 5% SSNIP— $0.05 / (0.05 + m)$ (%)	Critical loss for 10% SSNIP— $0.1 / (0.1 + m)$ (%)
0	100	100
10	33.3	50.0
20	20.0	33.3
30	14.3	25.0
40	11.1	20.0
50	9.1	16.7
60	7.7	14.3
70	6.7	12.5
80	5.9	11.1
90	5.3	10.0
100	4.8	9.1

in the table. If the initial margin is zero (price equals marginal cost, so no profits are made), the 5 per cent or 10 per cent price increase would be profitable for the monopolist regardless of the sales loss, as any remaining sales now generate a positive profit—hence the critical sales loss is 100 per cent, at which point profit is zero again. The general point is that the higher the profit margin you earn, the more every lost sale hurts you. Furthermore, you can see that the critical sales percentage for a 10 per cent SSNIP is higher than for a 5 per cent SSNIP, although not quite proportionately so—the choice between 5 per cent and 10 per cent matters somewhat here (with 5 per cent you tend to find slightly narrower markets than with 10 per cent). However, we recommend that your ultimate conclusions on market definition should not hinge on the exact choice of the SS in SSNIP.

2.5.7 The marginal customer matters

You can see from the critical loss percentages in the table that a price increase can be unprofitable even if only a relatively small proportion of customers switch. For a 5 per cent SSNIP, the critical loss is less than 20 per cent for any margins above 20 per cent. This means that you may have a result where more than 80 per cent of customers would continue to buy the product and yet the price increase is unprofitable.[32] Critical loss analysis is about what customers at the margin do, not what the average or typical customer does. A market is still not worth monopolizing if switching by the other 20 per cent makes the price increase unprofitable. In this case, those marginal customers with choice are in effect protecting the other customers who do not have, or do not exercise, a choice. Moreover, while from one perspective the percentages in the table may seem low, from another they may seem high. They almost all exceed the SSNIP percentage itself (except where the margin is very high). Going back to the elasticities in Figure 2.3, what this implies is that critical loss analysis is not really about testing whether the elasticity is higher or lower than –1 (which is often used as the cut-off point for calling demand elastic or inelastic).

2.5.8 Case study: Critical loss analysis in a holiday parks merger

The 2001 merger between Gran Dorado and Center Parcs, reviewed by the Dutch competition authority (NMa, now part of the ACM), illustrates how you can get stuck focusing on product characteristics, and how this can be overcome through critical loss analysis.[33] Gran Dorado and Center Parcs both operated self-catering accommodation in holiday parks with a range of facilities (indoor swimming pools, restaurants, playgrounds, etc.) in the Netherlands, Belgium, and Germany. These parks are typically used for short breaks. The NMa approved the merger, but only after the parties had agreed to divest a substantial number of parks.

Center Parcs and Gran Dorado were the two largest, and probably best-known, providers of holiday parks in the Netherlands and surrounding regions, popular with Dutch short-breakers. The NMa concluded that other types of holiday accommodation, such as family

2.81

2.82

2.83

---

[32] Technically we should say customers representing 80% of sales, rather than 80% of customers, as different customers may buy different quantities. But our main point here remains the same.

[33] Nederlandse Mededingingsautoriteit (2001), *Gran Dorado–Center Parcs*, Zaak 2209. See also Niels and van Dijk (2006). We advised the merging parties in this case.

hotels, hotels for city breaks, hotels close to theme parks, and luxurious camping sites, should not be included in the relevant market because of the distinct product characteristics. It also found that there were significant differences in quality and price between the various types of holiday park. Based on these considerations, the NMa narrowed the market down to four-season holiday villages, which included those operated by Center Parcs and Gran Dorado.

2.84 The differences in product characteristics that the NMa emphasized are no doubt of importance to holidaymakers. However, there are several product features that might make the holiday parks more interchangeable with other accommodation. For example, customer research carried out by the parties for their own commercial purposes (i.e. not specifically for the merger inquiry) showed that for many visitors walking and cycling through the surroundings outside the parks was one of the main activities during their short break (besides using the pool and other facilities inside the park). Indeed, these holiday parks are typically located in an attractive national park or coastal area, rather than, say, in the middle of an industrial estate. Seen from this perspective, other types of accommodation in such areas—including hotels, holiday homes, and holiday parks with fewer facilities—compete in the same market. An even broader perspective would be to include all accommodation for short breaks. The parties themselves regarded Eurodisney (now called Disneyland Paris) as a major competitor. Indeed, the short-break brochures in which Grand Dorado and Center Parcs advertised also typically included Eurodisney and other options for short breaks.

2.85 Hence, focusing on product characteristics is inconclusive. Does an indoor pool become a 'tropical' pool when it has a slide and some palm trees? Yet an even greater shortcoming of this approach is that it fails to address the crucial question for market definition: whether a sufficient proportion of consumers consider these products to be substitutes. As noted earlier, products do not need to be perfect substitutes to be in competition with each other. A small overlap of consumers who are willing to switch can be sufficient. With this in mind, the merging parties undertook a consumer survey to identify the level of sales that a hypothetical monopolist would lose as a result of a SSNIP. This type of survey is often the easiest (and fastest) way to obtain some relevant data on switching behaviour, even though it is not foolproof and the results should always be interpreted with care (see Chapter 7 for more discussion of surveys).

2.86 The survey was held among 250 short-breakers in the Netherlands, that is, those who had been on any short break in the past three years. In order to focus the minds of the respondents (and hence increase the chance of relevant answers), they were first asked about their current behaviour and preferences in relation to short breaks. Then, before turning to the SSNIP question, respondents were asked which type of short break they were considering for the next two years. Those who considered visiting a holiday park with facilities and indoor pool (i.e. of the Center Parcs or Gran Dorado type) were asked whether they would still do so after a 10 per cent price increase lasting for two years, or whether they would switch to an alternative type of short break, or not go on a short break at all (as noted earlier, the latter also represents a relevant sales loss to the monopolist). To help respondents interpret the question, they were not only informed of the 10 per cent increase but were also given a numerical example of what this, on average, would do to the price they would pay.

The results of the survey indicated that the relevant market was broader than only **2.87** holiday parks with a range of facilities and an indoor swimming pool. This is because 28 per cent of those who considered a short break in such a park said they would switch to another type of short break, or take no short break at all, after a 10 per cent price increase. This sales loss exceeded the estimated critical loss. A rough approximation indicated that the holiday parks had a margin in the range of 60–80 per cent (this is because a large part of their costs are fixed, that is, do not vary with sales). Applying the formula, this generates a critical loss of 11–14 per cent (10 per cent divided by 10 per cent plus 60 per cent equals 14 per cent, and 10 per cent divided by 10 per cent plus 80 per cent equals 11 per cent). You can see that in cases like these there is no need to identify the price–cost margin with great precision. The broad margin range of 60–80 per cent generates a narrow critical loss range of 11–14 per cent, and the estimated actual loss in this case (28 per cent) was sufficiently in excess of the critical level to conclude that the market was wider.

2.5.9 Critical loss in markets with differentiated products

In markets with differentiated products you may end up having to perform a very large **2.88** number of SSNIP tests, as each variety of the product is potentially a focal product for market definition. Earlier we explained two paths you could take to avoid this. First, you could to some extent ignore differentiation and group together products that may still be considered reasonably homogeneous (top-of-the-range sports cars, high-quality chocolate, holiday parks with self-catering accommodation), and take that group as a focal product for the SSNIP test. In line with the smallest-market principle, you could do this conservatively and take relatively narrow groups to start with. The hypothetical monopolist test would then be applied to each of the groups as if they consisted of homogeneous goods. Second, you could skip the market definition stage altogether and focus directly on the competitive constraints and closeness of competition between the differentiated products. In the holiday park example, you would assess whether Center Parcs and Gran Dorado are each other's closest competitor.

Economists have recently developed some tools that provide a third alternative.[34] You **2.89** can still define the relevant market through the hypothetical monopolist test by applying critical loss analysis to a group of differentiated products. In essence this is the same as applying the SSNIP question in the second and subsequent iterations of the hypothetical monopolist test, but here you can potentially take any product in the group as the focal product. You effectively take a shortcut by starting with a monopolist who already controls all the products where competition concerns may arise. You can then apply the break-even SSNIP question to any one of the products in the group, or to all the products. The focus in this new critical loss test for differentiated products is on the diversion ratio between these products—the critical loss formula depends not just on the SSNIP (x) and the initial margin (m), but also on the percentage of total sales loss after the SSNIP that is diverted to other products within the monopolist group as opposed to outside the group. This percentage can be called the intra-group diversion ratio (some economists call it the aggregate diversion ratio, but we believe that this term has more than one meaning). The higher

---

[34] See Farrell and Shapiro (2008), Daljord, Sørgard, and Thomassen (2008), and ten Kate and Niels (2010).

the intra-group diversion ratio, the less the monopolist cares about losing sales of one of its products (as more of these lost sales are captured by its other products), and the more profitable the SSNIP.

2.90 We can show this in a formula. Recall that the critical loss formula for the standard case (homogeneous products) was x divided by $x + m$. With differentiated products the critical loss can be expressed as x divided by $x + m (1 - d)$, where d is the intra-group diversion ratio. The factor $(1 - d)$ has crept into the formula as the percentage of sales that is lost to outside products. To see how it makes a difference, take the critical loss for a 10 per cent SSNIP and 40 per cent margin from Table 2.3—equal to 20 per cent in the standard formula. In the new formula, if d equals zero (i.e. 100 per cent of sales is lost to outside products), the formula becomes the same as before, and the critical loss is still 20 per cent. But with a positive intra-group diversion ratio this changes. Say d equals 0.2 (20 per cent). The new formula then gives a critical loss of 24 per cent—this is higher than the 20 per cent you had before, since it takes a greater sales loss before the monopolist starts to care. Thus, the more the products under the control of the hypothetical monopolist are each other's closest substitutes, the more the monopolist can profitably increase price.

2.6 The Cellophane Fallacy

2.6.1 Back to the 1950s

2.91 The 'cellophane fallacy' is a widely known concept in competition law. Less well-known are the finer details of the original case, which is 60 years old. In 1956, the US Supreme Court ruled on a monopolization case brought by the government against Du Pont.[35] Du Pont had a 75 per cent share of US sales of cellophane. The producer of the other 25 per cent had a licence from Du Pont and paid it royalties. Cellophane constituted only 20 per cent of all flexible packaging materials. The decision therefore turned on the definition of the relevant product market. The Supreme Court, unlike the government, considered that there was sufficient evidence of interchangeability between cellophane and other materials (such as paper, film, and foils). There were similarities in functionality, and large-user industries such as meat production switched regularly between different types of packaging material. While cellophane was two to three times as expensive as its nearest competitors (glassine and grease-proof papers), the court found that further price increases were prevented by those other materials. Can you see the fallacy in this reasoning?

2.92 Cellophane production was already a (near-) monopoly at the time. Du Pont owned the technology, and competition from the other cellophane producer was restricted through a licence agreement and apparent tacit co-ordination between the two. If the prevailing price was already the monopoly price, a hypothetical cellophane monopolist (Du Pont nearly was one for real) would not raise prices any further, since at the monopoly price other competing products start to bite. But that does not mean that cellophane is not a market worth monopolizing—it could still be a relevant market of its own. Many commentators

---

[35] *US v EI du Pont de Nemours & Co* 351 US 377 (1956).

have pointed this out since. Indeed, three dissenting Supreme Court judges said it in the judgment itself:

> We cannot believe that buyers, practical businessmen, would have bought cellophane if close substitutes were available at from one-seventh to one-half cellophane's price. That they did so is testimony to cellophane's distinctiveness.[36]

The cellophane fallacy can be explained through Figures 2.3 and 2.4. We explained how own-price elasticities depend on where you start on the demand curve. The hypothetical monopolist test assesses the price at which the monopolist maximizes profits, and asks whether this price is at least 5–10 per cent higher than the initial (pre-monopolization) price. You can see that if the price is already at (or very near to) the monopoly price, the monopolist would not impose a further SSNIP. The logic of the test would then dictate that the market is broader than the product in question, but this could lead to the erroneous conclusion that cellophane producers have no market power. **2.93**

2.6.2 Is the fallacy a problem?

The cellophane fallacy is not normally a concern in merger cases. Competition authorities review whether mergers reduce competition compared with the present situation. It is therefore valid to take the prevailing price level as the starting point for the hypothetical monopolist test where the market is reasonably competitive before a merger. The exception is where markets, pre-merger, are already characterized by a form of (tacit) price co-ordination between competitors, such that hypothetical monopolization would not lead to significant further price increases, hence giving rise to the cellophane fallacy again. The fallacy is most likely to arise in cases where there is already a dominant company, or more generally where it is suspected that the party or parties under investigation have already exercised some degree of market power. In any such case, competition authorities or claimants can invoke the cellophane fallacy to refute attempts by the defendants to demonstrate a wider market based on a SSNIP question applied to prevailing prices. Are they right? **2.94**

In theory, the cellophane fallacy arises only when prevailing prices are at, or very close to, the monopoly level. If prices are more than 5–10 per cent below the monopoly level, you would find a hypothetical monopolist imposing a SSNIP—your analysis would not suffer from the cellophane fallacy. The question is: how do you know where prevailing prices lie relative to the monopoly price level? We suggest that the answer to this question cannot be inferred just from the existing market structure (except where you have an unregulated real profit-maximizing monopolist). You cannot say that there is a cellophane fallacy just because the market structure does not look perfectly competitive. Prices in oligopolistic markets may lie anywhere between the competitive and monopoly levels. Even companies with very high market shares may still be constrained from raising price all the way up to the monopoly level. In these cases, asking the SSNIP question based on prevailing prices can still provide useful insight into substitution and competitive constraints. You just have to bear in mind that some degree of market power (short of monopoly power) may already have been exercised at those prices. At the very least you can apply a one-way test. If at the prevailing price level a monopolist can profitably impose a SSNIP, you can be confident that the market is no wider. If, in contrast, you find that the monopolist cannot profitably **2.95**

---

[36] Ibid., at [417].

increase price, you have to consider that there may be a cellophane fallacy and that the market may be defined too broadly. Ultimately, if there is a high probability that your analysis will suffer from a cellophane fallacy, you may have to conclude that market definition is not a useful intermediate step and instead focus directly on indicators of market power and competitive constraints (see Chapter 3).

2.6.3 Start from the competitive price level?

2.96 A frequently cited solution to the cellophane fallacy is to start the hypothetical monopolist test from the competitive price level rather than the prevailing price level. Because the test has its foundations in microeconomic theory, it is tempting to take marginal cost as the competitive price level (since in perfect competition, prices equal marginal cost). However, as we discuss in greater detail in Chapter 3, there are many real-world markets in which prices are set above marginal costs, but which can still be considered competitive—prices above marginal costs may be required to cover fixed costs, or may reflect a temporary position of pricing power that is eroded over time. Therefore, to get a better approximation of the competitive price level you would need to carry out an analysis of profitability over a longer time period. The problem is, however, that such an analysis makes the market definition stage redundant. After all, profitability sheds light directly on whether companies can persistently earn high returns without attracting entry or inducing consumer switching. This is precisely how competition law defines market power. Indeed, the US Supreme Court itself cited profitability in the 1956 cellophane case as a reason to reject the monopolization claim and, implicitly, reject the presence of a cellophane fallacy (the court referred to arguably less sophisticated techniques of measuring profits than have been developed since—see Chapter 3):

> Nor can we say that du Pont's profits, while liberal (according to the Government 15.9 per cent net after taxes on the 1937–1947 average), demonstrate the existence of a monopoly without proof of lack of comparable profits during those years in other prosperous industries. Cellophane was a leader, over 17 per cent, in the flexible packaging materials market. There is no showing that du Pont's rate of return was greater or less than that of other producers of flexible packaging materials.[37]

2.7 Supply-side Substitution and Market Aggregation

2.7.1 What if the hypothetical monopolist is not 'the only future supplier'?

2.97 In section 2.3 we explained the distinction between demand-side substitution, supply-side substitution, and new entry. Thus far in this chapter we have dealt with demand-side substitution, that is, switching by customers. The only supply-side aspect of market definition that has come up at this stage is our hypothetical monopolist, that is, the supplier who imposes the price changes to which customers react. Supply-side substitution is about the reactions of suppliers of other products to the monopolist's price changes. It is usually a less immediate constraint on companies than demand-side substitution (we said before that customers are generally quicker to vote with their feet if they are unhappy than wait for other suppliers to come to them). Nonetheless, supply-side substitution may also render price increases by the monopolist unprofitable.

---

[37] Ibid., at [404].

In the formal definition of the hypothetical monopolist test in the 1992 US Horizontal **2.98** Merger Guidelines—cited in section 2.4—supply-side substitution is expressly ruled out because the monopolist is the 'only present and future producer or seller of those products in that area'. This version of the test considers only demand-side substitution. However, other jurisdictions regard supply-side substitution as part of the market definition stage. Ultimately, it should not matter too much when in the analysis you consider supply-side substitution since all competitive constraints must be taken into account in the assessment (recall that market definition is only an intermediate stage). Under the US approach, those suppliers that are not in the market but could easily supply-side substitute into it are taken into account at the point of calculating market shares. This should give the same result as calculating shares in a wider market based on supply-side substitution. Nevertheless, there are some traps that you might inadvertently walk into when relying on supply-side substitution at the market definition stage. We discuss these below.

2.7.2 Classic examples: Paper and bus services

Paper production is a frequently cited example of supply-side substitution. Paper comes in **2.99** a range of qualities, from standard printer paper (uncoated) to high-quality paper (often coated) used, for instance, in fine art books. From a demand point of view, different qualities of paper are not substitutes—a pricey art book cannot be printed on low-quality paper. However, paper plants may be able to manufacture different qualities of paper, switching their existing production facilities at little cost within a short timeframe, if the commercial opportunity arises—for example, if the price of a paper variety that they are currently not producing increases by 5–10 per cent. In such circumstances, the various qualities of paper may be included in the relevant market. The European Commission uses the paper example in its 1997 Notice on the Definition of Relevant Market, and first dealt with the issue in a 1992 merger decision:

> Demand-side substitutability
>
> There is limited substitutability between uncoated and coated papers because of their different characteristics (such as discolouring and printing quality). In addition uncoated paper is much cheaper than coated paper. The above table shows that the price of the cheapest coated paper is even higher than the price of the most expensive uncoated paper and that coated paper is on average 15% more expensive than uncoated paper.
>
> Supply-side substitutability
>
> From the supply side, there is a rather high substitutability. Indeed, since the difference between coated and uncoated paper results from extra processing, the coating processing can be included whenever required. Since the different grades of paper result mainly from the blend used, the coating materials used and some other extra processing, it is relatively easy for a producer to switch from production of one paper type to another.[38]

Bus services are another classic example of supply-side substitution. From a demand-side **2.100** perspective, point-to-point bus routes would form separate markets. People who need to travel from A to B normally won't switch to another route. However, from a supply perspective, a bus operator can expand into new routes and compete with existing operators

---

[38] *Torras/Sarrio* (Case No IV/M.166), Decision of 24 February 1992, at [17–8]. See also European Commission (1997), 'Notice on the Definition of Relevant Market for the Purposes of Community Competition Law', 97/C372/03, at [22].

with relative ease, provided that it has an existing bus depot nearby (where buses can park overnight and be maintained). This means that geographic markets for bus services are often defined more widely, covering the whole area that can economically be served from an existing depot.

2.7.3 Three criteria for supply-side substitution: No sunk costs, swiftness, and scale

2.101　From both the paper and the bus examples you can see what kind of criteria matter for supply-side substitution. First, there must be no significant additional 'sunk' investments or costs of switching. Second, supply-side substitution must be swift. Third, it must be of a sufficient scale to constrain the hypothetical monopolist.

2.102　The first of these criteria refers to a commonly used concept in economics: sunk investments. These are different from other investments in that they cannot be recovered upon exit from the market. A typical example is an investment in a new brand by a market entrant, which will lose its value once the company exits the market again (and the brand cannot be sold). In contrast, investments that are not sunk still have value at the point of exit (e.g. machinery or vehicles). This matters for entry decisions. If you know you can get rid of your assets for a decent price in the event of your new business venture failing, you are more likely to go ahead than in the situation where you would have to scrap the assets.

2.103　The second criterion relates to timeliness of the supply switch. As with the 'N' in SSNIP there are no hard and fast rules for what is timely, but often the reference is to a one-year period, or simply to existing production facilities being used (existing paper plants or bus depots). Use of existing facilities implies swift entry, and also tightens the first criterion somewhat from no sunk investment to no major investment in new facilities (sunk or not). The 1992 US Horizontal Merger Guidelines call supply-side substitution 'uncommitted entry', which is contrasted with 'committed entry'. The 2010 Guidelines simply refer to 'rapid entrants'. In economic theory, industries without sunk costs and where entry is rapid are called 'contestable markets'. In such markets, the possibility of 'hit and run' entry would prevent even a monopolist from raising prices (and hence, according to the hypothetical monopolist test, they may actually not be relevant markets in themselves in the first place).

2.104　To continue with the bus example, the provision of local bus services has some features of a contestable market. If the operator has a bus depot nearby, adding services to an existing route or opening new routes can be done swiftly (in the UK a new route can be opened fifty-six days after registration). Any investment in additional buses is not sunk, since there is often a liquid market for second-hand buses should the operator decide to exit the route (buses can also be leased or rented).

2.105　With regard to the third criterion mentioned above—scale—in the provision of bus services even entry on a small scale can have a strong competitive impact on a particular bus route—for example, if the entrant runs its service only on the busiest part of a route or during the busiest times of the day.

2.7.4 The risk of overstating competitive pressure from supply-side substitution

2.106　There is something inherently odd about supply-side substitution. Demand-side substitution is about whether consumers see products as substitutes. If they do to a sufficient degree, you put the two products together in the relevant market. Supply-side substitution, however, is not so much about the products as about the *suppliers* of those products. The high-quality paper monopolist is constrained by the producers of low-quality paper because they can also produce high-quality paper, not by the low-quality paper itself. This oddity is one of the reasons why the US Guidelines prefer to focus on demand-side substitution, and then treat suppliers that can supply-side substitute as participants in the market by including them in the market share calculation. As noted earlier, this should ultimately lead to the same conclusion as in the approach where you include supply-side substitution in the market definition itself. But there is a risk that you will overstate the competitive pressure from supply-side substitution as a result of this oddity.

Consider the following example. You have six producers of high-quality paper. The two largest ones (A and B) have 25 per cent of production each, the other four 12.5 per cent, as shown in Table 2.4. Considering demand-side substitution only, you find that a hypothetical monopolist for high-quality paper would impose a SSNIP—customers would not switch to low-quality paper. If the two largest producers were to merge, they would have a combined market share of 50 per cent, sufficient to raise some competition concerns. But you haven't considered supply-side substitution yet. Suppose low-quality paper is produced by completely different companies, but you find that their existing plants and equipment can easily be switched to produce high-quality paper. So on a supply-side basis the relevant market for the merger should include low-quality paper. As you can see from the table, the total market is now two-and-a-half times as large, and the merging parties have a combined market share of only 20 per cent—not enough to warrant competition concerns. This may well be the correct conclusion. But there is a risk that you have overstated the importance of supply-side substitution as a competitive constraint, and hence understated the merged entity's market power. You have effectively assumed that all production of low-quality paper can be readily switched to high-quality paper (you have added all 600 tonnes to the relevant market). This may not reflect reality. There may be various reasons why some of the capacity cannot readily be switched. Producers of low-quality paper may not want to upset relationships with their existing customers, they may have long-term supply

2.107

Table 2.4 **Stylized example of supply-side substitution**

	High-quality paper production (tonnes)	Market share in high-quality paper	Market share in all paper	Market share in high-quality paper plus available low-quality capacity
Producer A	100	25%	10%	21.7%
Producer B	100	25%	10%	21.7%
Producer C	50	12.5%	5%	10.9%
Producer D	50	12.5%	5%	10.9%
Producer E	50	12.5%	5%	10.9%
Producer F	50	12.5%	5%	10.9%
Market size (tonnes)	400	400	1,000	460
Low-quality paper production (tonnes)	600			
Low-quality capacity available for substitution (tonnes)	60 (10% of all low-quality capacity)			

contracts with them, or they may still consider the low-quality market more lucrative despite the price increase in high-quality paper. In essence, this comes down to the scale of the supply-side substitution, the third criterion mentioned above. Suppose producers of low-quality paper would switch only 10 per cent of their capacity to high-quality paper. Then you should count only that available capacity when you calculate market shares. You would find that according to this calculation the merged entity has a 43.5 per cent market share (200 tonnes out of 460).

2.7.5 The risk of getting supply-side substitution in the wrong direction

2.108 Another potential pitfall with using supply-side substitution is getting the direction of the substitution wrong. This happens when you include all products or geographic areas which suppliers can substitute into, regardless of whether this substitution is towards, or away from, the focal product or area. This leads to overly broad markets, since only supply-side substitution *towards* the focal product or area in question is relevant in capturing the competitive constraints on that product or area.

2.109 An example of where such an error was made is the abuse of dominance case before the English High Court involving bus services, as referred to previously. The dispute concerned alleged predation on several local routes in Chester in the north-west of England—this was the focal area. Both sides' experts had agreed that the geographic market should be defined according to supply-side substitution, including all existing bus depots that could economically serve routes in Chester (a drive time of thirty minutes was considered the maximum distance between the depot and the route). However, the claimants' expert subsequently expanded the geographic market by including all areas that could be served from the depots, including areas in the other direction from Chester. This led to an overly broad market (in this case, the defendant had a higher market share in the wider market because it had substantial operations in areas adjacent to Chester). The court agreed with the defendants' expert that this was incorrect:

> [The claimants' expert's] starting point was to identify which depots can economically provide bus services to Chester...He then defined the market as comprising the areas that those depots serve or can serve, and he concluded that for practical purposes that meant it comprises the eight local authority districts in which the depots are situated; and with that approach [the defendants' expert] disagreed. Thus, for example, Arriva's Winsford depot (to the east of Chester...) is said to be capable of economically operating into Chester, and the Crewe and Nantwich administrative district lying to its south-east (and increasingly remote from Chester) into which services from Winsford are also possible is therefore also said to fall within the geographic market...
>
> The effect of [the claimants' expert's] approach...is thus to include in his market depots from which he accepts it would *not* be possible for any operator economically to provide local bus services in Chester...
>
> I accept [the defendants' expert's] opinion...that when identifying a geographic market by reference to supply-side considerations it is a mistake to include all geographic areas into which suppliers can substitute regardless of whether this is towards or away from the focal market; and that only supply-side substitution towards the focal market is relevant to capture competitive constraints on that market.[39] [Emphasis in original]

---

[39] *Chester City Council and Chester City Transport Limited v Arriva PLC* [2007] EWHC 1373 (Ch), at [163–4] and [190]. We acted for the defendants in this case.

2.7.6 Keeping an eye on the focal product

If you have defined the product market based on supply-side substitution, you should still **2.110** bear in mind the focal product for the rest of your analysis, for example, when assessing the geographic market. Take the following example, based on an abuse of dominance investigation by the water regulator in England and Wales.[40] The investigation concerned the treatment of leachate. An arguably less appealing product than high-quality chocolate, leachate is the liquid that originates from rain percolating through the different layers of waste on a landfill site. It can be toxic and therefore needs to be treated appropriately before being discharged in the sewer. This occurs mainly at waste-water treatment works. The leachate is normally transported by tanker—'tankered'—from the landfill site to these treatment works. The complaint concerned access for companies tankering leachate to the waste-water treatment works which were owned by the incumbent regional water and sewerage company. There was discussion about the possibility of supply-side substitution by other treatment works that could treat any liquid waste but that did not currently treat leachate. Such supply-side substitution was deemed feasible overall, although there were some limitations on the available capacity of these other treatment works, and other types of liquid waste were more profitable to treat (recall the paper example above). Let's ignore these limitations and assume that the product market is extended to the treatment of all liquid waste, on the basis that any treatment works can treat any type of liquid waste, including leachate. This brings us to the geographic market. Tankering leachate is expensive—it ceases to be economical if the distance between the landfill site and treatment works is greater than 30 miles. But most other types of liquid waste are more economical to ship over longer distances—say, up to 60 miles. Given that the product market has been defined as all liquid waste (in this stylized example), should you consider this longer distance when delineating the geographic market?

The answer is no. To see why, consider the (again slightly stylized) situation in which all **2.111** waste-water treatment works that currently treat leachate and lie within 30 miles of the major landfill sites in the region are owned by the incumbent. Beyond the 30 miles are several other treatment works that could switch (supply-side substitute) to treating leachate, and therefore have been included in your relevant product market. But you can clearly see that leachate cannot be economically tankered to those supply-side substitutes because the distance is too great. If you had taken your product market—treatment of all liquid waste—as the starting point for your geographic market, you would have overlooked the pocket of market power in leachate treatment itself. Your geographic market definition should therefore always refer back to the focal product, that is, the product where the competition concern arose in the first place (in this case treatment of leachate only).

2.7.7 Market aggregation

Market aggregation is a phenomenon closely related to supply-side substitution. It is one **2.112** of those pragmatic adjustments to the theoretically pure hypothetical monopolist test that make it more usable. Consider a merger between two shoe manufacturers. How wide is the market? From a demand-side perspective, size 38 shoes and size 39 shoes are not

---

[40] Ofwat (2005), 'Investigation into charges for the treatment of tankered landfill leachate by United Utilities Plc following a complaint made by Quantum Waste Management Ltd', Case CA98/01/32, Decision, 20 May. We advised the investigated party.

substitutable. Thus, on this basis you should define a separate relevant market for each shoe size. Clearly that would be somewhat absurd. Your conclusions on competitive constraints would be exactly the same for each of these size-based markets, since each producer makes and sells all the sizes (except where producers specialize in very large or small shoe sizes). The competitive conditions are the same. So you might as well aggregate all shoe sizes into one market. The same logic applies to various transport and communications markets, where demand-side considerations would lead to many different point-to-point markets, but where competitive conditions are often similar for all of these markets, and hence for practical reasons you can aggregate them. An express delivery service from Oxford to Brussels is not a substitute for a service from Oxford to Berlin, and yet it makes sense to aggregate them if most operators can offer services to both these and other places. In its decision in 2013 to prohibit the acquisition by UPS of TNT the European Commission defined national markets for both domestic and international delivery services rather than numerous point-to-point markets.[41]

2.8 Price Discrimination Markets

2.8.1 Comparing apples with bananas

2.113 In the 1978 *United Brands* judgment, the ECJ considered whether bananas are a separate market.[42] The case concerned banana distribution arrangements in the north-west of Europe. There was some statistical evidence that banana demand and prices are under pressure in the summer months when domestic fruits are in ample supply, and during the 'orange season' at the end of the year. The ECJ agreed with the European Commission that these periods of substitution were too limited—bananas are available the whole year round, so candidate substitute fruits would have to be too, it held. Oranges were regarded as too distinct, and apples were seen as interchangeable only to a small degree. The ECJ (and the Commission) reasoned as follows:

> This small degree of substitutability is accounted for by the specific features of the banana and all the factors which influence consumer choice.
>
> The banana has certain characteristics, appearance, taste, softness, seedlessness, easy handling, a constant level of production which enable it to satisfy the constant needs of an important section of the population consisting of the very young, the old and the sick.[43]

2.114 This reasoning may remind you of the holiday park merger discussed before, which also sought to define markets primarily based on product characteristics. You can debate at length whether babies, elderly people, and the sick really can't replace bananas with other fruits (our own experience would suggest otherwise, but then supermarkets nowadays offer a much greater variety of fruits year round than in the 1970s). More importantly, the ECJ's reasoning misses the point about critical loss. Even if one particular 'section of the population' cannot switch away from bananas, there are other sections that can. If too many of those other customers would switch to apples, oranges, and the like after a banana price increase, a hypothetical banana monopolist would not impose such an increase. The

---

[41] *UPS/TNT Express* (Case COMP/M.6570), Decision of 30 January 2013.
[42] Case 27/76 *United Brands v Commission* [1978] ECR 207; [1978] 1 CMLR 429.
[43] Ibid., at [30–1].

very young, the old, and the sick would thus be protected by the less captive customers. Crucially, this is because banana suppliers and retailers are unable to target their captive customers (for a start, babies, the elderly, and the sick may not be doing their own shopping). If the monopolist raises price, it has to do so across the board to all customers. It cannot price-discriminate, that is, charge a different price to different groups of customers for the same product.

2.8.2 Captive customers and price discrimination

Price discrimination can give rise to separate markets by (groups of) customers. This may **2.115** occur when some customers have a greater choice of alternatives than others, and suppliers can exploit this difference by targeting the latter, 'captive', customers with higher prices, without this being undermined by arbitrage (where the non-captive customers can resell the product to the captive ones, or purchase it on their behalf). Banana suppliers are unable to achieve such price discrimination. But other suppliers can. A common example is the travel industry. A flight from London Heathrow to Milan Linate at 7.40 a.m. will have a mix of time-sensitive and non-time-sensitive passengers on board. The former have no choice but to be on that particular flight—they may have a meeting in Milan at lunch time. The latter passengers could have chosen a different time to fly, or perhaps even a different destination (e.g. a city break in Madrid instead of Milan). Airlines are able to exploit this difference since time-sensitive passengers tend to book their tickets less far in advance of flying (airlines usually raise fares closer to the flight date), and are more likely to demand flexible tickets in case their meeting times change (airlines target this by offering more expensive flexible economy and business tickets). Competition cases involving airlines therefore frequently define separate markets for time-sensitive and non-time-sensitive passengers.[44] Returning to the bananas case, there was perhaps some economic merit in the ECJ's argument that competition from seasonal fruits is not quite sufficient to prevent a banana price rise—it is just that this banana price rise would occur outside those seasons. Rather than applying the criterion that substitute fruits for bananas must be available all year round, the ECJ could have followed the price discrimination logic and argued that bananas still form a separate relevant market during those times of the year in which other fresh fruits are in less ample supply. It would then probably still have found United Brands to be dominant in those periods.

Where suppliers cannot specifically target the captive customers, there are no separate price **2.116** discrimination markets. If you live two minutes' walking distance from a major supermarket, you are probably a captive customer—you wouldn't drive ten minutes to the other major supermarket in town. Fortunately for you, the supermarket has no way of distinguishing between you and the next customer in the queue who lives exactly halfway between the two supermarkets and hence has more choice (though beware that these days supermarkets know a lot about you through your loyalty cards and online shopping behaviour). The supermarket cannot discriminate against you. You are 'protected' by other customers who live further away and therefore do have a choice between supermarkets. This protection of

---

[44] The European Commission made this distinction in a large number of airline mergers, including *Lufthansa/Swiss* (Case COMP/M.3770), Decision of 4 July 2005. More recently, the Commission has refined this distinction to 'premium passengers' versus 'non-premium passengers'. See, for example, *US Airways/American Airlines* (Case COMP/M.6607), Decision of 5 August 2013.

customers who don't have a choice by those who do is a feature of demand that arises in many markets.

2.117 Clearly, price discrimination is a common business practice. It would not make sense to define separate price discrimination markets wherever different prices are charged. You might discover that almost every passenger on your London–Milan flight has paid a different fare, but you would not want to define a separate market for each passenger. Again, some pragmatism is required. The most consistent approach is to consider instances of price discrimination where the captive group of customers is significant (a group of customers worth having a monopoly over, such as time-sensitive passengers), and where the price difference is significant and sustainable for a non-transitory period.

2.8.3 Are absolute price differences relevant?

2.118 You have seen that the hypothetical monopolist test is about reactions to relative price changes between products. It is not about absolute price differences. Branded soft drinks may provide a competitive constraint on own-label soft drinks, and hence be included in the market, despite being more expensive. Customers make a price–quality trade-off, so if the price difference between the two products becomes too narrow they may switch from own-label to branded (just like customers of branded soft drinks may switch to own-label if the price difference becomes too large). However, just as differences in product characteristics sometimes provide a useful sense-check on market definition, so do differences in price. For example, if you can buy a business ticket for a flight from London Heathrow to Milan Linate Airport at 7.40 a.m. next Wednesday for £519, while an economy ticket from London Stansted to Milan Bergamo Airport at 8.00 a.m. that day costs £58, chances are that these two flight tickets do not provide much competitive pressure on each other. You would expect them to be in separate relevant markets. How can you establish this? It may be that there is a break somewhere in the chain of substitution from cheap to expensive flights between London and Milan (see the next section on chains of substitution). Or it may be that you have to define separate markets along various dimensions, such as by geography (the question being which airports you should include around London and which around Milan) or by type of customer (time-sensitive versus non-time-sensitive passengers).

2.9 Chains of Substitution

2.9.1 Examples of chains: Holiday parks and broadband internet

2.119 The relevant market for a focal product or area may be extended to include several indirect substitute products or areas through a chain of substitution. Consider the example of the holiday park merger in the Netherlands presented in section 2.5. The survey that was used to assist the product market definition also shed some light on the geographic scope of the market. Respondents were asked how far they would be willing to travel for a weekend break. The maximum travel time cited was four hours and the median answer was three and a half hours (the median is the middle one if you rank all observations in a sample from lowest to highest). This confirmed the view of the merging parties that people are willing to travel for around three to four hours to their weekend break destination. This travel time determines the catchment area of each park. The Netherlands being a small country (in three to four hours you will reach a border regardless of where you start), the geographic market for short breaks thus covers at least the Netherlands, Belgium, some nearby parts of Germany (in particular the Eifel region), and the north of France. This is the first link in the chain of substitution. Holiday parks in this broader area do not only compete for Dutch custom but also for visitors from neighbouring countries (the Dutch represented only around 45 per cent of customers of Center Parcs at the time, while 30 per cent were German, 15 per cent French, and 10 per cent Belgian). German customers within a three- to four-hour drive would come from places like Düsseldorf or Hamburg. For them, there are other popular short-break destinations within a three- to four-hour drive in the other direction, including the Ostsee region, Thüringer Wald, or the Schwarzwald. This means that Center Parcs in the Netherlands competes directly with holiday accommodation in those other destinations to attract German custom, despite the fact that Dutch holidaymakers are less likely to travel to those destinations. This is the second link in the chain of substitution. This chain could be further extended since, for example, the Schwarzwald competes in turn with nearby destinations in France, Switzerland, and Austria. Following this logic, there could well be a geographic market for short-break destinations spanning large parts of western and central Europe.

Chains of substitution may also arise in product market definition. In a 2010 market review, Ofcom, the UK communications industry regulator, defined a broadband internet access market that includes all available download speeds:

> In 2008 we concluded that the [broadband access market] definition did not have an upper speed limit, i.e. there is a 'chain of substitution' through the available broadband internet access speeds . . .

> Current broadband packages available in the market tend to be at specific clusters of speed, such as 2Mbit/s, 8Mbit/s, and 20Mbit/s. One of the key characteristics of broadband packages is the download (and to some extent upload) speeds, with higher speed services commanding higher prices. Therefore for a given speed service, a 5–10% SSNIP would decrease the price differential between the speed of the service in question and the next service up. If there are sufficient consumers who switch up, it would render the SSNIP unprofitable and suggest a single product market between the two speeds . . .

> In addition, end users are almost as likely to switch up to a higher quality service as they would switch down to a lower quality service . . . This further suggests that consumers see the range of price/speed options as potential substitutes should the price of their package increase. As a result there is unlikely to be an identifiable break across the range of speeds available to warrant separate markets for low and high speed services within the current generation broadband access services available in the market.[45]

2.120

Ofcom thus found a continuous chain of substitution among internet speeds available in 2010. It then addressed the question of whether the chain might break following the introduction of 'super-fast broadband services' over fibre, which were becoming more common and offered speeds of 40–50Mbit/s or higher. The regulator considered that over time some breaks in the speed chain may occur because of the continued development and growth of internet applications that require very high speeds (such as online games and internet TV). We explore this phenomenon of breaks in the chain next.

2.121

---

[45] Ofcom (2010), 'Review of the wholesale broadband access markets', March, at [3.88–91].

2.9.2 Breaking the chain

2.122 You should perhaps be somewhat sceptical of chains of substitution that are too long. Remember that in every further iteration of the hypothetical monopolist test, the monopolist gets to control another substitute product (or area), and so has a little bit more pricing power than previously. Before long, pricing power would be such that a SSNIP would be imposed for the focal product (or area)—remember that the SSNIP question still applies only to the focal product or area in these further iterations, so once the price increases there you have a relevant market. For a link in the chain to be strong, the next substitute must place substantial competitive pressure on the product or area that you have just added to the group controlled by the monopolist.

2.123 One particular situation in which the chain of substitution may be long is where you have one supplier that competes nationally with several regional suppliers and follows a national pricing strategy. In a number of European countries, a national telephony incumbent competes with a number of regional cable companies in the provision of telephony and internet services. The cable operators do not compete directly with each other (often this is for legacy reasons; many of these operations used to be run as monopolies owned by local authorities). But each of them competes with the national operator. Now take the hypothetical situation where one of the bigger regional cable operators reduces the price of a bundled telephony/internet/TV package (see section 2.10 on market definition for bundles). The national operator decides that it needs to match this decrease because it does not want to lose customers in that region. But that means reducing prices in the whole country, because it always charges the same everywhere (it advertises its packages at the national level, which is one of its competitive advantages over the regional operators). Hence, the other regional cable operators are also forced to lower their prices, so as to keep in line with the national operator. In effect, the first regional operator, through a chain of substitution via the national operator, has placed an indirect competitive constraint on all other regional operators. Clearly, if the national operator decides to abandon its policy of uniform pricing and to flex prices regionally instead, the chain breaks down and different regional markets may be defined.

2.10 Other Aspects of Geographic Market Definition

2.10.1 Transport costs as a basis for geographic market definition

2.124 Geographic patterns of supply and demand are often driven by transport costs. It is therefore relevant to consider these costs when delineating geographic markets. Concrete is a classic example of an industry where geographic markets are highly localized because of transport costs. In-transit mixers generally have to reach the construction site within ninety minutes from loading at the plant to prevent the concrete from becoming hard and unusable. Other products may be more easily shipped—fresh flowers grown in the Netherlands make it in large quantities to homes in the United States and Japan. But even for those products, transport costs matter—air freight charges on Dutch flowers will add to the cost faced by the US purchaser, more so than on flowers grown in nearby Mexico, and this may ultimately affect market definition.

2.125 At its simplest, you can incorporate transport costs directly in the hypothetical monopolist test. If transport costs between two regions represent more than 5–10 per cent of the prevailing prices, a monopolist in one region could increase the price by 5–10 per cent without attracting supply from the other region. The NMa applied this test when reviewing (and ultimately approving) a merger in 2007 between the only two major sugar producers in the Netherlands.[46] Transport costs for industrial sugar were found to be around €0.08 per tonne/kilometre. With a prevailing price of around €650 per tonne, a 5 per cent price increase might invite imports from a distance of 400 km (5 per cent of €650 equals €32.50; transporting a tonne of sugar over a distance of 400 km at €0.08 per kilometre costs €32, so becomes attractive with the new price). The NMa also took into account the fact that the then new EU internal market regime for sugar—promoting greater market integration—was expected to lead to a fall in market prices to around €500 per tonne in the coming years. Assuming the same transport costs, the corresponding distance over which imports would be profitable after a 5 per cent price increase is 300 km, and the NMa took this as the basis to expand the relevant market beyond the Netherlands.

When applying the hypothetical monopolist test with transport costs, the usual caution **2.126** is required. For example, prevailing prices may already encapsulate the transport cost differential (this is akin to the cellophane fallacy discussed in section 2.6). Likewise, transport costs may change over time, as new technologies or modes of transport are developed (mix-at-site trucks can now deliver smaller amounts of concrete with less time pressure than in-transit mixers, so some concrete customers have greater choice than previously).

Sometimes it may be more relevant to consider transport costs from the perspective of **2.127** the buyer rather than the supplier. In our holiday park example, the customers travel to the supplier rather than the other way round (this is a purer form of demand-side substitution; where it is the supplier that moves, this is more closely related to supply-side substitution). When it is the customers that move, instead of focusing on transport costs as such, you would measure what in transport economics is commonly known as the generalized cost of travel. This is the sum of the monetary costs of a journey (the cost of the ticket if using public transport or the fuel if using the car) and its non-monetary costs. The latter consists mainly of the value of the total time spent on the journey. Calculating this value can take into account many different factors, such as opportunity costs (what else you could have done during that time), or the fact that some of the time spent has a greater 'cost' (waiting at a railway station is more 'costly' than sitting in a comfortable leather seat while on the move).[47]

2.10.2 Trade and travel patterns as a basis for geographic market definition

Another way of assessing geographic markets is to consider actual trade or travel patterns. If **2.128** there is a lot of movement of goods between two regions—by either suppliers or buyers—it is likely that they form part of the same geographic market. A formal approach to this is the Elzinga–Hogarty test, named after two economists who proposed that a region is a separate geographic market if there are few imports—'little in from outside' (LIFO)—and few exports—'little out from inside' (LOFI) (Elzinga and Hogarty, 1973). The test has been widely applied, including in several hospital mergers in the United States, where it was assessed whether hospitals attract patients from far afield.[48] As with the SSNIP, exactly

---

[46] Nederlandse Mededingingsautoriteit (2007), *Cosun–CSM*, Zaak 5703/304, 20 April.
[47] More background on generalized cost can be found in Button (1993).
[48] One example is *Federal Trade Commission v Tenet Healthcare Corp* 17 F Supp 2d 937 (ED Mo 1998), rev'd 186 F 3d 1045 (8th Cir. 1999).

how you set the threshold for LIFO and LOFI is inherently arbitrary. Elzinga and Hogarty proposed two thresholds at 75 per cent and 90 per cent of supply. According to this logic, if imports and exports as a proportion of total supply are above the threshold, the geographic market is likely to be wider. The French competition authority defines local markets in the retail industry based on the area around each store where customers representing 80 per cent of sales are located.[49]

2.129   Using current trade and travel patterns to define geographic markets can lead to erroneous conclusions. In particular, it misses the basic logic of the hypothetical monopolist test, which is about demand and supply responses to small changes in price. Even if you observe few imports or exports at present, what matters is whether trade would start to take place after the hypothetical monopolist imposes a SSNIP. Despite these potential shortcomings of the Elzinga–Hogarty test, examining current trade and travel patterns can still provide a useful starting point or sense-check for your geographic market definition.

2.10.3 Attack of the isochrones

2.130   In the past, geographic markets were often delineated by drawing circles of various sizes around production facilities or population centres to determine catchment areas. In the Dutch sugar merger that we saw earlier, the authority drew circles of a 300 km radius around each merging party's production facilities. The geographic market was thus extended to include producers in Belgium, France, and Germany—the so-called European 'sugar belt'. In this broader market the two Dutch producers had a share of around 20 per cent (compared with nearly 100 per cent in the Netherlands only). You can see that circles are rather unsophisticated—they may accurately reflect distances as the crow flies, but not how far you can travel in a truck filled with leachate or sugar. Modern technology has allowed for some refinement of this type of analysis. Mapping software is now regularly used to delineate more coherent geographic markets that take into account the characteristics of the underlying road network and travel speeds. Instead of circles you get isochrones. An isochrone is a line that joins together all of the points that can be reached within a constant journey time from a given starting location. To draw the isochrones, the relevant drive time threshold first needs to be determined—you can use evidence from surveys, analyse transport costs, or observe existing travel patterns. There is an inevitable element of judgement in this, but you can always test the sensitivity of your results by drawing slightly broader and narrower isochrones to see whether the competitive landscape within the isochrones changes.

2.131   What do you take as the central point of the isochrone? In line with the logic of the hypothetical monopolist test, this should reflect the focal product as closely as possible. In the bus example discussed earlier, the competition concern arose with respect to certain routes in the centre of Chester. Based on supply-side considerations, the geographic market was found to include all existing bus depots within thirty minutes' drive time of the routes. In theory, you could draw an isochrone around every point on the route from which the bus can begin service in the early morning. Pragmatically, however, an isochrone around one particular main stop on the route (e.g. the central bus station in Chester) will often provide

---

[49] Autorité de la concurrence (2013), 'Lignes directrices de l'Autorité de la concurrence relatives au contrôle des concentrations', July, at [366].

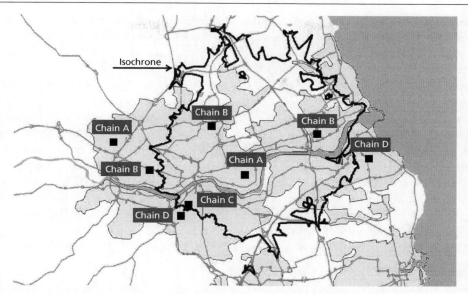

Figure 2.6 Twenty-minute isochrone for the cinema owned by chain A

sufficient insight. The next step is to analyse market shares and other indicators of competitive strength of the various operators in this geographic market.

In other cases you would draw the isochrones around the relevant outlets in question—each **2.132** supermarket or holiday park. This gives the catchment area of each outlet, which provides useful information on the competitive constraints they face. For example, in a cinema merger in the UK—*Odeon/UCI* (2005)—the Office of Fair Trading (OFT, now part of the CMA) and the parties drew isochrones for a twenty-minute drive time around each cinema, a distance considered to reflect the cinema's core catchment area.[50] A thirty-minute isochrone was used as a sensitivity check. Figure 2.6 shows the boundaries of the twenty-minute isochrone for a cinema owned by one of the merging parties (chain A) in one of the cities considered.[51] The irregular shapes and peaks of the isochrone reflect the configuration and speed of the underlying road network. The other merging party (chain B) has two cinemas in the area, while only one competing cinema is present (chain C). The other competing operator in the city, chain D, has no presence in this isochrone.

Strictly speaking, such isochrones do not accurately reflect the relevant geographic market, **2.133** since they are supply-centred rather than demand-centred. Two cinemas do not compete because they are within twenty minutes' drive time of each other, but because they are both within reach (i.e. within twenty minutes' drive time) of the same customers. One simple adjustment to the supply-centred isochrones is therefore to perform a 'population re-centring', which comes down to drawing the isochrones around major population centres and then assessing which outlets are within their reach. For pragmatic reasons, you do this

---

[50] Office of Fair Trading (2005), 'Acquisition by Terra Firma Investments (GP) 2 Ltd of United Cinemas International (UK) Limited and Cinema International Corporation (UK) Limited', 7 January. We acted for the merging parties.

[51] The authors offer a bottle of wine to the first reader who guesses which city this is.

only for the major population centres, rather than for every single customer as pure theory would dictate, since a focus on the major centres will usually give a sufficiently clear picture.

2.10.4 The curious case of the geographic dimension of transport markets

2.134   In transport markets there is the curious feature that the product itself has a geographic aspect to it. Transport services take a person or object from one place to another. So what is the product dimension of the transport market in question, and what is the geographic dimension? In most cases, this would be a matter of semantics, and make no difference to the competition assessment. One case where it did matter was the 2011 air cargo cartel case before the High Court of New Zealand, in which the Commerce Commission prosecuted several airlines.[52] The first stage of the case focused on whether there was a market 'in New Zealand' for inbound air cargo services—the Commerce Act 1986 requires there to be a market in New Zealand for the Commission to have jurisdiction. This boiled down to a question of geographic market definition. The second stage of the process—involving the actual cartel prosecution—would proceed only if the Commission prevailed in the first stage.

2.135   Most air cargo is transported in the belly-hold of passenger planes. The airlines agreed with the Commission that there is a market in New Zealand for cargo services from an origin (O) airport in New Zealand to an overseas destination (D) airport. However, the cartel investigation focused mainly on services *to* New Zealand. For these the airlines argued that the market is not located in New Zealand, but rather at the O airport outside New Zealand (e.g. London Heathrow, Hong Kong, or Sydney). Most air cargo services are arranged through freight forwarders at the airport of origin, and negotiated between these freight forwarders and the airlines at that airport. The airline experts argued that the market is located at the O airport because that is where supply and demand meet, or where prices are formed.

2.136   A principled approach to market definition would start with the product being offered: air cargo services from, for example, Sydney (the O airport) to Auckland (the D airport). This represents the product dimension of the market. Each OD service that is relevant to the investigation forms a focal point for a market definition exercise. There are therefore multiple relevant markets in this case (in principle, one for every inbound OD route serviced by the defendant airlines). Within the product dimension, one market definition question is whether air cargo services from Sydney to Auckland face a competitive constraint from, for example, sea cargo services from Sydney to Auckland. The answer will be no for many products, but the point here is that within the product dimension of the market you can explore whether air cargo services from O to D are constrained by other modes of transport.

2.137   Having determined the product dimension of the market, the approach turns to the geographic dimension. This concerns the geographic extent of the O end of the service and that of the D end. If the focal product for which the market is being delineated is air cargo services from London Heathrow to Auckland, the geographic market analysis asks which other airports compete with London Heathrow and Auckland as O or D airports (you could assess this using catchment area or isochrone analysis). At the O end, the question

---

[52] *Commerce Commission v Air New Zealand and others*, CIV-2008-404-008352, 24 August 2011. We acted as experts for the Commerce Commission.

is whether London Heathrow faces a competitive constraint from, say, London Gatwick, London Stansted, or Birmingham International. At the D end, the question is about the constraints on Auckland. The answer may well be that Auckland does not face a significant competitive constraint from other airports, but the point is that market definition requires an assessment of the geographic dimension at both ends of the service. Figure 2.7 illustrates. The product that forms the starting point for the analysis is the air cargo service from O to D. The geographic market around airport O contains airport P (a close substitute) but not airport Q (a more remote airport). The geographic market around airport D contains no other airports (airport E is too remote to provide a significant competitive constraint). Services between airports P and D are included in the market for the focal OD service. In this way, the relevant market (with its product and geographic dimensions) has been identified—the analysis is complete. All the inbound OD flights represent relevant markets that are, in part, in New Zealand, given that the D airport of this product is in New Zealand.

Limiting the market to the O end of the service—as the airlines' economic experts did in the **2.138** New Zealand case—is not in line with the hypothetical monopolist test. If a SSNIP were imposed on the London Heathrow–Auckland service, shippers would consider the London Gatwick–Auckland service as an alternative option at the O end. Faced with a SSNIP on the Heathrow–Auckland route, shippers would equally consider alternative airports at the D end of the service as a substitute for Auckland. Any such substitution would also make the SSNIP less profitable for the hypothetical Heathrow–Auckland monopolist. The airline experts agreed that the SSNIP test applies as described above, but they considered it to be a test for the product dimension of the market, not the geographic dimension. Yet having defined what the airline experts refer to as the product market, the SSNIP analysis that they then applied to identify the geographic market is exactly the same as that for the product market, except that they applied it to only the O end of the market. This is an artificial way of excluding the destination points of air cargo services from any consideration of whether there is a market in New Zealand.

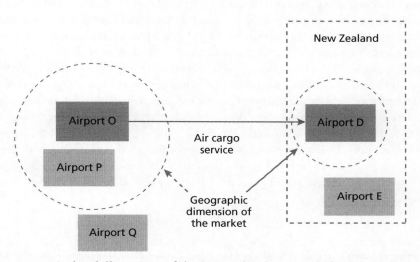

Figure 2.7 Stylized illustration of the geographic dimension of air cargo markets

71

2.11 Market Definition for Complements and Bundles

2.11.1 Substitutes, complements, and bundles

2.139 Recall from section 2.3 that substitute products have a positive cross-price elasticity while complements have a negative one. This has important implications for the assessment of mergers. If you merge two substitute products, you can expect them both to increase in price—this is commonly understood and lies at the heart of merger control in competition law. Merging two complementary products has the opposite effect: there is downward pressure on prices.[53] What are the implications of complements for market definition? If you expand the hypothetical monopolist's influence by adding a substitute product, prices will go up. The monopolist now no longer cares about losing sales to those substitutes. Following the same logic as above, if you add a complementary product instead, a profit-maximizing monopolist will set a lower price than before. A hypothetical monopolist in the supply of gin would selfishly raise the price to extract maximum profits, without caring about the negative effect that this has on tonic water sales. If the monopolist controlled tonic water as well, it would care about lost tonic water sales, and hence would not raise the price of gin by as much when maximizing the profits of both products. This is exactly the opposite effect of adding a substitute product—a complementary product acts as a pricing constraint when it is inside the monopoly group, whereas a substitute product acts as a constraint when it is outside. How do you apply the hypothetical monopolist test here?

2.11.2 Selecting the right starting point

2.140 The test itself can readily be applied in cases where there are complementary products. The main difficulty lies in choosing the right starting point: in the first iteration of the test, does the monopolist control just one product, or does it control the two (or more) complements? The outcome of the test may differ substantially. A gin monopolist might impose a SSNIP while a gin-and-tonic monopolist might not. The choice will have to be determined by the specific market and the specific competition problem that you are considering. If the real companies in the market supply just one product, your hypothetical monopolist should do so as well. The production and sale of gin by spirits companies are usually separate from those of tonic water, so it is not unreasonable to take gin as the focal product if that is where the competition concern arises, and ignore the complementarities with tonic water at the market definition stage. In contrast, if the real companies normally control two complementary products already, or consumers in the market usually buy the complementary products together (in a bundle), it may be more appropriate to start the test from a hypothetical monopolist that controls both of those products. An obvious, if somewhat absurd, example is that of left shoes and right shoes. They are different products, and they are complements, not substitutes. Shoe producers supply and sell them together, and consumers buy them together. You can therefore safely start your market definition exercise with a hypothetical monopolist who produces both left and right shoes, and ask if it could impose a SSNIP on pairs of shoes.

---

[53] That a monopolist with two complementary goods sets a lower price than in a situation where each good is controlled separately is called the 'Cournot effect', after the French mathematician/economist Antoine Augustin Cournot—he of the famous oligopoly model, discussed in Chapter 7 (Cournot, 1838).

2.11.3 Markets for bundles

The same logic holds for bundled products more generally. Bundling occurs when two or   **2.141**
more products are sold more cheaply together than individually (this is known as mixed
bundling), or when they are sold only together (pure bundling). Bundling is a very common business practice—with a left shoe comes a right shoe, with a car come four wheels
and a multimedia system, with your mobile phone contract comes a smartphone. Bundling
has many economic justifications, but it may also raise competition concerns—we address
this in Chapter 4. Here we explore how bundling may affect market definition. There is an
economic case for defining relevant markets for bundles, as opposed to individual products,
where: (i) bundling is pure rather than mixed—the two products are available only as a
package, not separately (you can't buy just a right shoe); (ii) the complements are consumed
in fixed proportions (one left and one right shoe, one car and four wheels); and (iii) all suppliers in the market sell bundles. However, there are also markets where the picture is more
mixed—only some suppliers sell bundles, or bundling is a relatively new phenomenon. An
example is the various 'triple-play' and 'quadruple-play' packages that you can get from
telecoms providers (fixed telephony, broadband internet, TV, and mobile telephony). These
packages have been on offer for several years and are steadily gaining ground among consumers, but still there are operators in the market with different combinations of services in
the bundles (some are traditionally stronger in TV services, others in telephony services),
and some customers still obtain individual services from different providers. Here there is
no clear-cut case for defining relevant markets either at the level of the individual products
or at the level of the bundles. It is good practice to do both. This allows you to explore the
relative strengths of the different operators in each product separately, and at the same time
to assess whether some operators are particularly strong in the offering of the bundles (not
all providers of the individual services may be able to offer all services in the bundle), and
identify any scope for market power in that way.

2.11.4 Market definition for aftermarkets

In most circumstances, you buy a product, you consume it, and that's the end of the story.   **2.142**
In some markets, however, buying the product is just the beginning. In order to make full
use of it, you subsequently have to buy associated products or services that are complements
to the original product. Examples of this include razors and razor blades, printers and
cartridges, game consoles and video games, and proprietary software and further upgrades
to that software. The same holds for durable equipment (such as photocopiers, machinery,
cars, and cash registers), and subsequent maintenance services and spare parts for that
equipment. The market in which you buy the associated product or service is commonly
referred to as the secondary market or aftermarket. Many competition cases have arisen
in aftermarkets. Often they involve complaints that the supplier of the primary product
is using its control over that product to exclude independent suppliers from selling the
secondary product. A classic example is the *Kodak* litigation in the United States, which
lasted from 1987 to 1998.[54] Kodak was found guilty of monopolizing the market for the
servicing of its high-volume copier and micrographics equipment. It had a strong position

---

[54] The two main rulings in this case are *Eastman Kodak Co v Image Technical Services, Inc et al.* 504 US 451
(1992), and *Image Technical Services, Inc et al. v Eastman Kodak Co* 125 F 3d 1195 (9th Cir. 1997). A discussion of the economics of the case can be found in MacKie-Mason and Metzler (2009).

in the supply of this equipment (the primary product), which required extensive, ongoing maintenance (the secondary product). Many independent organizations serviced Kodak equipment at the time, in direct competition with Kodak's own national network of service technicians, but then Kodak stopped selling spare parts to these organizations, such that they could no longer provide maintenance services. In Chapter 4 we discuss abuse of dominance. The issue addressed here is whether market definition can be a helpful intermediate step in assessing such practices.

2.143 Two main questions arise: Does the primary producer have the ability to foreclose the secondary market from competition? And if competition in the secondary market is foreclosed, does the primary producer have the ability to exploit its customers there (in other words, are customers worse off if Kodak keeps the aftermarket to itself)? In essence you want to know what the competitive constraints are on the primary producer. Market definition normally helps in identifying these competitive constraints. In this case, the main market definition question is whether the secondary market is a separate relevant market from the primary market, or whether there is a 'systems market' that includes both the primary and secondary product. However, regardless of how you delineate the market exactly, the source of any market power of the primary producer is its control over the primary product. So even if you conclude that the aftermarket is a separate market, you would still need to take into account the link between the primary market and the aftermarket.

2.11.5 A systems market or separate markets?

2.144 Defining a systems market would be appropriate if customers are fully aware at the time of purchase that what they buy is a system. They know that they need to purchase the secondary product or service as well, and take this into account when making the primary purchase decision. One example would be game consoles and video games. When choosing between a Nintendo Wii U, a Sony PlayStation 4, and a Microsoft Xbox One, you (or, more likely, your children) will normally consider which games are available for that console. If the market is a systems one, you could test whether a hypothetical monopolist controlling one system faces competition from other systems—does the Nintendo Wii U face a pricing constraint from the PlayStation and Xbox? Does Kodak face strong competition from other producers of high-volume copiers and micrographics equipment? You would also take into account the general logic of complements that we discussed earlier. If there were a genuine systems market, and companies priced on a systems basis, Kodak would be constrained from raising the price of the secondary product if that negatively affected sales (and hence profits) of the primary product, and vice versa. This market definition therefore helps you identify cases where any negative effects on customers are limited, that is, cases where system competition is so strong that it constrains any exploitation of market power in the secondary market.

2.145 There are other circumstances, however, in which system competition is not sufficiently strong to constrain market power in the secondary market, and where a systems market definition would therefore be less appropriate. This can occur where customers do not fully take the need for the secondary product into account when choosing the primary product, or have insufficient information at the time of the primary purchase (see Chapter 3 on the effect of consumer biases in such situations). It can also arise when the primary product already has a large installed base of customers who are locked in for the foreseeable future (they would face high switching costs if they were to move to another primary product).

You can also be more doubtful about a systems market if there is evidence (as there was in *Kodak*) that the supplier of the primary product does not engage in system pricing. Finally, there may be a separate market for the secondary product if the competitive dynamics of the primary and secondary markets are very different, or where many secondary products are compatible with multiple primary products—for example, spare car parts such as tyres that fit on any make of car, or garages that service any make of car.

2.11.6 Market definition in two-sided platform markets

Two-sided markets caught the attention of economists following the interchange fee investigations into Visa and MasterCard beginning in the 1990s.[55] We return to these when discussing horizontal agreements in Chapter 5. Here we explore the two-sided nature of credit card schemes and the implications for market definition. Credit card schemes are among the many examples of networks or platforms that face demand from two groups of customers, with positive demand externalities between them. In credit card schemes, these externalities arise between issuers—the participating banks that issue cards to their accountholders—and acquirers—the banks that sign up retailers (traditionally referred to as 'merchants' in this context). A card becomes more valuable to retailers the more consumers hold and use it. Likewise, it becomes more valuable to have in your wallet the more retailers accept it in their shops. Other examples of two-sided platforms include video game consoles (externalities between users and game developers), PC operating systems (PC users and applications developers), newspapers (readers and advertisers), and speed-dating events (men and women).

2.146

In setting their pricing structure, platforms must get both sides on board. In order to get participants on one side they need to have sufficient participants on the other side. This is not dissimilar to a situation where you have two complementary products—if demand for one goes up, then so does demand for the other. It makes commercial sense to set a pricing structure that optimizes the size of the network. This usually means setting relatively low prices for the more price-sensitive customer side, and relatively high prices for the less price-sensitive side. Likewise, it may imply setting lower prices to the side that is more important in terms of attracting the other side, that is, the side that generates larger network effects. For this reason, 'free' newspapers are free to users and recover costs from advertisers, and some speed-dating events are free to women and thus recover more of their costs from men. There is nothing inherently anti-competitive about these pricing practices. Indeed, to the extent that they have the effect of expanding the platform or network size, they may increase overall welfare compared with the situation where all sides are charged the same price.

2.147

A first step in the competition analysis is to define the relevant market—does the platform face competitive constraints from other platforms? The hypothetical monopolist test can be used here. We illustrate this below with a stylized application to a credit card scheme. The question that arises is what you take as the starting point—a hypothetical monopolist on one side, on the other side, or on both sides? It may not make much sense to consider a hypothetical monopolist on one side in isolation. In the context of a credit card scheme, if the question is whether the scheme competes with other payment systems, you want to test

2.148

---

[55] Early decisions in these investigations include Reserve Bank of Australia (2001), 'Reform of credit card schemes in Australia', December; and *Visa International—Multilateral Interchange Fee* (Case COMP/ 29.373), Decision of 24 July 2002.

competition on both sides. The complementary and network effects between the two sides mean that no real card scheme would set prices on one side without considering the effects on demand from the other side. A reduction in the number of card transactions on one side would by definition mean a reduction in transactions on the other side—one retailer transaction necessarily involves one cardholder transaction (the two sides are like complements in this respect). Furthermore, because of the network effects between the two sides, when setting prices, the monopolist would take into account the fact that a reduction in demand on one side also makes the product less attractive for the other side. Applying the hypothetical monopolist test to a credit card scheme is therefore similar to a second-round iteration of the test, where the monopolist controls two products. The main difference with the standard situation is that the two products are complements, not substitutes.

2.11.7 A numerical example of critical loss analysis in two-sided markets

2.149 How do you apply critical loss analysis? You follow the same logic as in standard critical loss analysis, but now take into account two sides of the market. So you test whether the hypothetical monopolist can profitably impose a 5–10 per cent increase in charges to retailers (known as merchant service charges), a 5–10 per cent increase in cardholder charges, or a combination of the two that results in an overall increase in the 'system price' of 5–10 per cent. To determine the critical loss, you need an estimate of the actual sales loss on either side that would result from the price increase, and an estimate of the profit margin.

2.150 Let's start with the margin. Suppose that the issuing banks that participate in the scheme (those banks that have relationships with cardholders) incur a cost per transaction of €1.20, and the acquiring banks (those that deal with retailers) a cost of €0.30. Such a cost imbalance between issuing and acquiring banks is not uncommon in payment systems, since the former incur costs such as fraud prevention, bad-debt write-offs, and cardholder loyalty awards. The total 'system cost' is €1.50 per transaction. As to revenues, suppose that issuing banks receive €1.00 per transaction from cardholder charges, while acquiring banks receive €1.50 per transaction from merchant service charges. This revenue imbalance is also not uncommon since retailers tend to have greater willingness to pay than cardholders—indeed, the combination of the cost and revenue imbalances provides the economic rationale for the interchange fees paid from acquirers to issuers, as discussed in Chapter 5. The total 'system price' per transaction is €2.50, so the initial price–cost margin equals €1.00, or 40 per cent.[56]

2.151 Now suppose you have evidence on retailers' and cardholders' responses to price increases. A survey among retailers suggests that a 10 per cent increase in merchant service charges would lead to a loss of 15 per cent of total card transactions, as the retailers where those transactions take place would cease to accept the card or discourage card payments by imposing a surcharge or minimum purchase value. Econometric evidence on cardholder elasticity of demand suggests that a 10 per cent increase in cardholder charges would lead to a 30 per cent drop in transactions—cardholders are apparently quite prone to switching

---

[56] You may work out that if both acquirers and issuers are to earn a 40% margin, the scheme requires an interchange fee paid by acquirers to issuers equal to €1.00 per transaction so as to make up for the cost–revenue imbalance in the scheme (the acquiring banks then receive €0.50 net per transaction while incurring a cost of €0.30, and the issuing banks receive €2.00 net with a cost of €1.20).

to other payment methods. The last step in this hypothetical example is for you to compare the estimated actual loss with the critical loss. You have to do this according to the system price and system cost. The merchant service charge (€1.50) represents 60 per cent of the system price (€2.50). A 10 per cent increase in that charge is therefore equivalent to a 6 per cent increase in the system price. This 6 per cent increase leads to a 15 per cent loss in transactions. Applying the critical loss formula of section 2.6 gives you 6 per cent divided by 6 per cent + 40 per cent, which equals 13 per cent, so the estimated actual loss exceeds the critical loss. The cardholder charges (€1.00) represent 40 per cent of the system price. A 10 per cent increase in those charges is therefore equivalent to a 4 per cent increase in the system price. The critical loss for this is 4 per cent divided by 4 per cent + 40 per cent, or 9 per cent, so is again exceeded (transactions fall by 30 per cent). Hence a 10 per cent price increase is unprofitable both on the retailer side and on the cardholder side. In this stylized example the market is broader than just credit cards.

2.12 Markets Along the Vertical Supply Chain

2.12.1 The vertical dimension of the market

As noted in section 2.2, an additional market dimension is the vertical layer in the supply chain. The same product—a car, a washing machine, a bunch of fresh flowers—may pass through a series of intermediaries on its way from producer to end-consumer. The relevant market may be different depending on which layer of the chain is considered. This in turn will depend on where the competition problem in question arises. If the concern relates to an exclusive distribution arrangement between a washing machine manufacturer and a large retail chain, the product market should be defined with reference to that upstream level of the supply chain. Washing machines are the focal product, and the first question to ask is whether the manufacturer has market power in the supply of washing machines. However, it will still be relevant to consider the final layer of the supply chain (the down-stream market) as well, which is the layer where you purchase a washing machine from a retail outlet. This is for several reasons, as discussed below. **2.152**

2.12.2 Markets in different vertical layers and their interaction

First, even if the upstream market between manufacturer and retail chain is the focal product where the exclusive arrangement arises, this arrangement is likely to have an effect on the final consumer market as well—you as a consumer may face less choice of where to buy your washing machine. The downstream market can therefore be an additional relevant market. In this market you want to analyse the competitive position of the retailer, and the effects of the arrangement on prices and other terms offered to consumers. **2.153**

Second, even if the focus is on the upstream market, the demand in this market—in this case the demand for washing machines—is often largely driven by the demand of final consumers. Whether different types of washing machine—high-capacity versus low-capacity; those with and without a tumble dryer—are close substitutes depends on the preferences of final consumers. The demand of retailers for washing machines is a 'derived' demand—that is, derived from that of consumers. Retailers will buy and stock the products that consumers want. Indeed, the main evidence on substitution will often relate to consumer behaviour rather than retailer behaviour. If that is the case, you have to exercise some care when applying the hypothetical monopolist test to the upstream market. Suppose that you find that **2.154** consumer demand falls by 10 per cent if the retail price of washing machines increases by 5 per cent, from €500 to €525. The own-price elasticity of demand for washing machines is –2. Is this price increase profitable? That depends on whether you look at it from the perspective of the retailer or the manufacturer. Recall Table 2.3, which shows the critical loss threshold depending on the initial price–cost margin and the percentage price increase. Suppose that the retailer obtains washing machines from the manufacturer at a wholesale price of €250. The retailer margin is therefore 50 per cent (half of the retail price of €500). From Table 2.3 you can see that the critical loss threshold for a 5 per cent price increase and 50 per cent margin equals 9.1 per cent. The 10 per cent fall in demand (just) exceeds this critical level, which would lead you to conclude that the price increase is unprofitable. However, what you have just determined is that a hypothetical monopoly retailer of washing machines could not impose a SSNIP. The focal question here, in contrast, is whether a hypothetical monopoly manufacturer could profitably increase price. How can you use the consumer evidence from the downstream market to infer any conclusions on this last question in relation to the upstream market? You can use the principle that retailer demand is derived from consumer demand and apply critical loss analysis. The manufacturer might achieve the increase in the retail price from €500 to €525 by increasing the wholesale price from €250 to €275 (assuming that the retailer fully passes on this price increase of €25 to its customers). The wholesale price increase is 10 per cent. The sales loss is still 10 per cent—retailer demand is simply derived demand. Now suppose that the cost of production of the washing machine is €125, which means that the manufacturer has an initial margin of 50 per cent as well. As you can see from Table 2.3, for a 10 per cent price increase the critical loss threshold is 16.7 per cent, so for the hypothetical monopoly manufacturer this price increase is profitable and the market is no wider than washing machines.

2.155 Note that in this example we assumed that the retailer passes on 100 per cent of the wholesale price increase. However, even if the pass-on rate is lower, your conclusion that the manufacturing layer is worth monopolizing remains unchanged, since a lower pass-on rate means that even fewer sales are lost, so the wholesale price increase is even more profitable. We discuss the economic principles of pass-on in more detail in Chapter 9 on the quantification of damages.

2.12.3 Derived demand and market definition: The air cargo example

2.156 Derived demand across different layers of the supply chain played a crucial role in market definition in the New Zealand air cargo cartel case discussed in section 2.10. Recall that the airlines argued that the relevant markets for inbound flights were located at the origin (O) airports outside New Zealand, as that is where freight forwarders negotiate with the airlines. The New Zealand High Court considered this view to be too narrow because the demand of freight forwarders at the O airport is a derived demand from importers in New Zealand:

> To limit the market to the geographic market available to freight forwarders at origin is unduly restrictive and ignores certain practical realities. It ignores the reality that those who ultimately dictate the terms of the transaction, who are often importers in New Zealand, ultimately pay for the services, and have their own options should they be subjected to unacceptable competitive practices by the airlines, which they can exercise to the detriment of the airlines.[57]

---

[57] *Commerce Commission v Air New Zealand and others*, CIV-2008-404-008352, 24 August 2011, at [183].

Freight forwarders at the O airports do not purchase air cargo services for their own use. **2.157** Their demand is derived from that of the importers and exporters. This has consequences for the hypothetical monopolist test. Say there is a hypothetical monopolist on flights between Sydney and Auckland. When setting prices, the monopolist will be guided not only by the reactions of the freight forwarders in Sydney. Other commercial considerations come into play, not least the possible reaction of importers in New Zealand. If these importers reduce their total demand in response to the air cargo price increase (e.g. some importers decide to make fewer shipments, while others switch to sea transport), this will also have an impact on the profitability of that price increase. Air cargo rates constituted a significant proportion of the price charged by freight forwarders to the importers—around 60–90 per cent. This would mean that a 10 per cent price increase by the hypothetical air cargo monopolist on an OD route would translate into a noticeable 6–9 per cent price increase to importers in New Zealand (assuming that the freight forwarders pass the increase on in full). If the importers in New Zealand then reduce their total demand in response to that increase, this will have an impact on the hypothetical monopolist's profits. The court accepted this reasoning:

> Therefore, we prefer the evidence of the Commission's experts. We are satisfied that a hypothetical monopolist in considering the consequences of a SSNIP would look beyond the port of origin to where the price impact will affect the demand for its air cargo service. That place is where the ultimate person who pays for the goods resides, either the place of the exporter or the place of the importer.[58]

The importance of derived demand in the court's conclusion on market definition raises an **2.158** interesting question about the orthodox formulation of the hypothetical monopolist test set out in section 2.4. Recall that the test states that when the monopolist imposes a SSNIP, the prices of all other goods remain unchanged. The main reason for this is to identify the direct effects of the price increase on the focal product and keep the analysis tractable (the prices of other products outside the control of the monopolist could be adjusted in response to the SSNIP, but this would be complex to analyse). The court asked the pertinent question of whether the hypothetical monopolist framework allows for the SSNIP in air cargo to be passed on to downstream prices (i.e. the freight-forwarder charges), or whether those prices should remain constant. We noted that the hypothetical monopolist framework allows for sufficient flexibility to ask the right question. Testing the effects of an air cargo SSNIP without changing freight-forwarder charges downstream does not shed much light on the substitution behaviour that occurs in reality, which also depends on the importers to whom the SSNIP is passed on. The court agreed:

> In a case alleging price fixing, then, it is important that market definition should be conducted with an eye to capturing the point at which quantities of goods and services transacted will be affected by a price increase. In particular, if a price fix occurs in a market for a good that is purchased by middlemen who simply turn around and sell it on to consumers, then the anti-competitive effect of the price fix really occurs in the next market downstream, to the extent that the price increase faced by the middlemen is simply passed through to their customers.[59]

This is not to say that derived demand should influence market definition in all competi **2.159** tion cases. In this particular case, the factual evidence showed that the original demand by

---

[58] Ibid., at [180].
[59] Ibid., at [161].

the importers in New Zealand has a sufficiently close and significant impact on the derived demand by freight forwarders at the O airports, such that the airlines take this original demand into account (among other factors) when making business decisions and setting terms and conditions of supply. The court thus set a useful relevant standard for market definition across vertical layers of the supply chain, which can be applied to other cases as well:

> The point at which a SSNIP ceases to have significant impact will as a matter of practice be discernible. That point will be the boundary of the market.[60]

2.12.4 Turning the supply chain upside down for market definition

2.160 Another issue related to defining markets in the context of a vertical supply chain arose in the European Commission's investigation into loyalty rebates offered by British Airways (BA) to travel agents.[61] The concern was about the effects of such rebates on competition between airlines, and therefore ultimately on passengers. A sensible first stage in the analysis would therefore be to define the relevant market with airline services as the focal product. You can then assess whether the airline has a dominant position in the provision of flights. The European Commission took a different approach. It defined the relevant market the other way round, as that for the provision of air travel agency services, which are purchased from travel agents by airlines. It found that BA had a dominant position as a buyer in that market, with a (declining) market share as a buyer of over 40 per cent of all relevant flights. Perhaps in this case the outcome might have been the same if the Commission had defined the market for the supply of airline services (where the 40 per cent market share would also have been used as an indicator of dominance). But defining the market in the way the Commission did carries the risk of focusing the attention of the competition analysis on the wrong market, that is, it leads you to focus on the effects of the rebates in the travel agent market, while the real concern is with distortions to the supply of airline services to final customers. To capture this concern, defining a market for the supply of airline services is more informative.

2.12.5 Self-supply by vertically integrated companies

2.161 The issue of self-supply comes up in market definition where a vertically integrated company sells inputs both to its own downstream business and to competitors. Should the former, captive, sales be included in the market? Take the example of fixed telephony networks (where this issue has often arisen). The incumbent network operator supplies two-thirds of its wholesale connections to its own retail business, and one-third to rival retailers. Two competitors have built their own networks, both a third of the size of that of the incumbent. Suppose that they open their networks to independent retailers. So at the network level the incumbent has a 60 per cent share of wholesale connections and the two competitor networks have 20 per cent each. However, two-thirds of the incumbent's sales (40 per cent of total connections) are captive. Should the relevant market include these or should it be limited to the 'open market'? You can see that excluding captive sales gives the incumbent a share of 33.3 per cent—not enough to label it dominant. But would that underestimate the strength of the incumbent's network, which is three times larger than each of its rivals? Now suppose that the two competitor networks supply only their own respective retail arms. Here the incumbent is the only network that grants third-party access, and its share of the

---

[60] Ibid., at [181].
[61] *Virgin/British Airways* (Case IV/D-2/34.780), Decision of 14 July 1999.

open market is 100 per cent. Does that now overestimate its market power, given that there are two rival networks with 40 per cent of connections between them?

The question of whether self-supply should be included in the market can be answered **2.162** by reference to the criteria for supply-side substitution. There is a good case for inclusion if the capacity used for self-supply can easily be switched to service third parties and if this is sufficiently lucrative for the vertically integrated company. In the above example, if the incumbent fixed-telephony network can readily supply more wholesale connections to independent retailers it makes sense to include self-supply in the market.

2.12.6 Do end-consumers always matter most?

Retailer or wholesaler demand is not always fully derived from consumer demand. It may **2.163** be the case that even where final consumers are willing and able to switch between different products, retailers cannot because some products are 'must-stock' items. For your flight from London to Paris you can choose from several airlines. When you book the ticket through an online travel agent, you expect that agent to offer tickets for all the major airlines. So travel agents have less choice than final consumers—each major airline may be a 'must-have' for each travel agent. What do you do in situations where consumers have choice (so you don't have to worry about them) but retailers or other intermediaries in the chain do not?

Competition policy is often, implicitly or explicitly, more concerned with effects on final **2.164** consumers than effects on intermediaries. This is why the analysis of mergers and business practices upstream in a supply chain will frequently consider effects further downstream as well (as in the washing machine example above). Sometimes you can go a step further and place the main weight of the analysis on the downstream market—you may not care what effect a practice or agreement has on certain intermediaries in the chain, as long as final consumers are not negatively affected. This may occur where the main effect of the practice or agreement is to redistribute profits from one layer in the chain to another—for example, from manufacturer to retailer, or vice versa. Such arrangements are very common and can lead to fierce commercial disputes in which competition law arguments are often invoked, but the final consumer may be unaffected. Some policy judgement may be required in such cases. Is a particular intermediary layer in the value chain really worth preserving? Consider the example of the leachate abuse of dominance case discussed in section 2.7.[62] The complaint was made by an intermediary acting as a broker between landfill sites and the providers of leachate tanker and treatment services. The incumbent water and sewerage company, which owned the treatment works and also had its own tanker operations, began to contract with some of the landfill sites directly, thereby 'squeezing' the intermediary broker out of the market. If you take a narrow view on market definition at the layer of intermediary brokerage services, you might find that the broker—given the nature of its activities—had no choice but to deal with the landfill sites and treatment works in that area. If you take a broader view, you might conclude that what matters is whether the landfill sites, as the customers in this market, have sufficient choice (the authority found that they did have some choice, including building their own treatment facilities). The position of the

---

[62] Ofwat (2005), 'Investigation into charges for the treatment of tankered landfill leachate by United Utilities Plc following a complaint made by Quantum Waste Management Ltd', Case CA98/01/32, Decision, 20 May.

broker as intermediary matters less if you take that view—customers are unharmed, so why care if the broker goes out of business?

2.13 Product Substitution Versus Product Migration

2.165 There are markets where consumers migrate from one product to another over time. Many modern examples come from the digital world: consumers have migrated from dial-up (narrowband) internet access to broadband internet, from analogue TV to digital TV, from VHS to DVD to Blu-ray, and from letters and faxes to email and social media. Product migration occurs in other industries as well—for example, from wooden and then metal tennis rackets to those made of graphite and other high-tech materials, and from bricks-and-mortar retailing to online sales. Sometimes the shift from one product to the next may happen overnight, but often the old and new products are sold alongside each other for some time. In competition investigations, the question then regularly arises as to whether the two products form part of the same relevant market—are the old and new products regarded as close substitutes? As you have seen in this chapter, the hypothetical monopolist test is defined in terms of relative price changes. Product migration is not driven by small price changes. Yet this is not to say that it should be ignored when defining relevant markets. Product migration can still have implications for whether a product is worth monopolizing.

2.166 Product migration is normally in one direction—from the old product to the new. The question of whether one is in the other's relevant market can take two forms, depending on which is the focal product. The first is whether the old product places a competitive constraint on the new product. At some point in time this becomes a less interesting question. Once you have switched to broadband internet or digital TV, you are unlikely to ever switch back to narrowband or analogue TV. Nonetheless, in the early stages of the new product, the old one may still be very attractive to consumers, such that suppliers of the new product have to compete not only with each other but also with the suppliers of the old product. The other question is whether the new product imposes a pricing constraint on the old product. An example is the analysis of the leased-lines market by OPTA, the Dutch telecoms regulator, in 2005. A leased line is a permanently connected communications link between two premises, dedicated to a customer's exclusive use. At the time, business users had begun to switch from leased lines to other data services, such as those based on internet protocol technology. While these newer data services had more variable capacity and required more outsourcing of network management functions, customers considered them a lower-cost alternative to leased lines. Having noted a high degree of migration from leased lines to the newer data services between 2002 and 2004, OPTA nonetheless concluded that the movement between the products was not relevant for market definition:

> Switching and migration from service A to B does not automatically constitute demand substitution. Demand substitution requires that switching from A to B is caused by changes in the price difference between A and B. In this case, there is price pressure. Migration, however, can result from other factors, such as the emergence of a completely new service (B) or changes in user preferences. Consumers migrate as a result, where this migration no longer depends on further small (5 per cent to 10 per cent) changes in the price difference between A and B.[63]

---

[63] OPTA (2005), 'Ontwerpbesluit huurlijnen' (draft decision leased lines), 1 July, at [280] (translated from Dutch).

Is this an overly restrictive interpretation of the hypothetical monopolist test? What ulti-   **2.167**
mately matters is whether the old product is a product worth monopolizing. Here, product
migration does have relevance. Recall the charts earlier in this chapter. In Figure 2.2 you
saw how the demand curve of a product can shift downwards if a close substitute product
gains in popularity (or becomes cheaper). Product migration has precisely this effect. The
rise of graphite tennis rackets meant that, over time, the demand for wooden and other
rackets declined. The same happened to the demand for dial-up internet access and VHS
players (DVD players may follow suit). Going back to Figures 2.2 to 2.4 you can see the
consequences of the demand curve shifting downwards. The intersect between demand
and marginal costs moves ever further towards the left-hand side of the demand curve.
Remember from Figure 2.3 that this left-hand side is the elastic part of the curve. There
comes a point when demand for the old product has fallen so far that it is no longer a product
worth monopolizing and therefore does not constitute a separate market.

2.14 Market Definition for Features Other than Price

2.14.1 It's not just the price that matters

The traditional hypothetical monopolist test focuses on the ability to raise price, and this   **2.168**
is what we have discussed so far in this chapter. Raising prices is the most direct, and often
most visible, way of exploiting a position of market power. However, products also compete on non-price aspects such as quality, design, and brand. A hypothetical monopolist
can exploit customers by downgrading those aspects of the product offering and thereby
saving costs—for example, it could cut corners on quality or not improve the design of
the product. This could equally be of concern to competition authorities. In principle,
therefore, the logic of the hypothetical monopolist test can be applied to non-price aspects
as well. You could ask: would the hypothetical monopolist put into effect a 5–10 per cent
reduction in quality? The difficulty often lies in establishing a clear metric for those non-
price aspects (how do you measure quality?), and in identifying how a small change in a
particular product feature affects the monopolist's profits (does lower quality mean lower
costs?). But these difficulties have not prevented economists and competition authorities
from using the hypothetical monopolist framework to define relevant markets with reference to product features other than price.

2.14.2 The example of football pools

The 2007 *Sportech/Vernons* merger in the UK provides an example.[64] The merging par-   **2.169**
ties operated the major weekly football pools, which consisted of the stakes received from
people playing in the pools. Football pools had been very popular, but had shrunk by a
factor of 10 since 1994 when the National Lottery was introduced (you could say that
this is a form of product migration as discussed in the previous section). The stakes in the
pool are influenced by the entry prices set by the pool operators. Only a portion of the
pool money goes into the prize fund—the payout ratio is in the range of 20–25 per cent.
Most of the prize fund is paid out to the winning player as a jackpot. Thus, there are three
important features of the product—the entry price, the payout ratio, and the size of the

---

[64] Competition Commission (2007), 'A Report on the Anticipated Acquisition by Sportech plc of the
Vernons Football Pools Business from Ladbrokes plc', 11 October.

jackpot. The hypothetical monopolist test in its purest form would apply to the entry price only. However, the CC considered evidence on the effect of a small but significant deterioration in the merging parties' product offering more generally—that is, a small increase in the entry price, a small reduction in the jackpot, and a small reduction in the payout ratio. Note that for each of these features there is a clear metric (they are all expressed as a monetary value) and a directly observable link with the profitability of the operators (the greater the payout, the smaller the profit left for the operator). This makes the test more straightforward to apply than for some other non-price features. The evidence indicated that not many customers actually switched between the two major pools in response to changes in the product offering. This suggested that the two were not close competitors, and this was the main reason why the CC concluded that the merger did not substantially lessen competition. As to competition with other gambling products, there was evidence that many customers would simply play the pools less if the product offerings worsened, but not switch to the National Lottery or other gambling products. The CC drew a somewhat confusing conclusion from this:

> Survey evidence shows that customers who stop playing the pools either save the money or spend it in a wide range of other ways. However, we considered that expanding the market definition to include all alternative uses of disposable income would not be appropriate. We therefore conclude, at this stage, that the market is no wider than the football pools . . .
>
> In our view, given the wide range of alternative spending or saving products to which football pools customers might switch in response to a price rise, a market definition which took account of all these alternatives would not be workable, even if we thought they were a constraint on pools prices.[65]

2.170 In line with the market definition principles set out in this chapter, you would instead conclude that the market *is* wider than football pools—customers who stop playing the pools are a relevant sales loss to the hypothetical monopolist. You cannot determine where exactly the market boundaries lie because there is no clear closest substitute for the football pools, but nor is there any need to do so, because the fact that a hypothetical monopolist in football pools could not profitably worsen the product offering implies that the merging parties could not either.

2.14.3 Time elasticities in geographic market definition

2.171 In section 2.10 we discussed transport costs as a factor in geographic market definition, and how in the case of individual consumers you can analyse the generalized cost of travel, which incorporates monetary and non-monetary costs (mainly the value of the time spent). Transport costs can determine the extent of the geographic market. Economists have taken this a step further and introduced the concept of time elasticity as a substitute for price elasticity in defining relevant markets, specifically in the context of hospital mergers (Capps et al., 2001). In many countries the government regulates the prices charged by hospitals and other healthcare providers, so the main concern when implementing the hypothetical monopolist test is not a price rise but a reduction in the quality of service. However, measuring the quality of healthcare delivery is notoriously difficult and patients generally have little information with which to judge the quality, which can complicate the market definition analysis. As an alternative to measuring changes in price and quality, the time

---

[65] Ibid., at [6] and [5.81].

elasticity approach measures how many consumers would switch to competing healthcare providers in response to a hypothetical 5–10 per cent increase in travel time. The increase in travel time does not reflect what the hypothetical monopolist is really going to do—it is not actually going to relocate the hospital (though it may close down certain departments in one of the hospitals)—but rather is an approximation for other reductions in quality of service. The willingness to switch gives an indication of the responsiveness in demand to changes in other aspects of the service. The analysis then makes certain assumptions about how the time elasticity relates to the price elasticity, which in turn allows the identification of a critical loss level above which the increase in travel time (and reduction in quality) becomes unprofitable because too many patients switch elsewhere.

You may get the impression that this is a rather roundabout way of applying the hypothetical monopolist test to non-price aspects of a product. Yet time elasticities have been used in several healthcare merger cases in the United States and Europe, as responsiveness to travel time to hospitals can be measured more easily than reactions to other non-price features of the service. In other markets, customer responses to changes in quality may be assessed more directly. Would our hypothetical monopolist for high-quality chocolate exploit its market power by compromising on its ingredients? The principles would be the same as for the time elasticity, and based on the same logic as critical loss analysis. The main challenge is, again, identifying how a small change in quality affects the hypothetical monopolist's profits—if quality worsens, how much extra profit does the monopolist make through saved costs, and how much profit is lost due to customers switching? These questions are generally easier to answer for price changes than for quality changes.

2.172

2.14.4 Market definition in innovation markets

In industries such as high-tech, IT, and pharmaceuticals, companies compete not only, or even mainly, on price, but also on who brings the most innovative products to market. Market power can be reflected in the control over innovative capabilities as much as in the control over prices. How can you capture this scope for market power during the market definition stage of your competition analysis? The DOJ and FTC came up with an 'innovative' solution, treating innovation capability as a market in its own right:

2.173

> An innovation market consists of the research and development directed to particular new or improved goods or processes, and the close substitutes for that research and development. The close substitutes are research and development efforts, technologies, and goods that significantly constrain the exercise of market power with respect to the relevant research and development, for example by limiting the ability and incentive of a hypothetical monopolist to retard the pace of research and development. The Agencies will delineate an innovation market only when the capabilities to engage in the relevant research and development can be associated with specialized assets or characteristics of specific firms.[66]

This principle had been applied in the DOJ's review of the proposed merger of General Motor's Allison Division and ZF Friedrichshafen, a German company.[67] GM Allison and ZF were the world's largest producers of medium and heavy automatic transmissions (used in buses, heavy trucks, and similar types of vehicle). ZF was dominant in Europe,

2.174

---

[66] Department of Justice and Federal Trade Commission (1995), 'Antitrust Guidelines for the Licensing of Intellectual Property', p. 11.
[67] *United States v General Motors Corp* Civ No 93-530, filed 16 November 1993.

whereas GM was dominant in the United States. For the purposes of assessing the merger, the DOJ defined both product markets and innovation markets. The production and sale of transmissions for buses and heavy trucks constituted the relevant product markets. Geographically they were confined to the United States (this was because it was a review by the DOJ; applying the same logic to Europe would probably have resulted in a separate European geographic market as well). In contrast, the innovation market was defined as the worldwide market for technical innovation in the design, development, and production of transmissions. This influenced the outcome of the case. While GM and ZF did not compete in many of the defined product markets in the United States—and hence the merger caused little concern in those markets—together they controlled most of the relevant worldwide innovation market. The DOJ was concerned that the merger would significantly lessen the competition in innovation. The proposed merger was ultimately abandoned.

2.15 Quantitative Tools for Market Definition

2.175 The economic principles set out in this chapter help you to ask the right questions about market definition in any specific case. You would usually seek to support this with empirical evidence: is a small price increase profitable for the hypothetical monopolist? This is where economists usually come in with their toolbox of empirical methods to measure customers' responsiveness to price. In this section we aim to provide a flavour of two of the main empirical tools used in market definition: regression analysis and price-correlation analysis. We also indicate how you can ask some critical questions when you are presented with the results of such empirical analyses. Chapter 9 further discusses regression analysis in the context of quantifying damages. Another empirical tool for market definition is survey analysis. We explain the basics of this in Chapter 7 on mergers.

2.15.1 Using regression analysis to estimate demand elasticities

2.176 If you want to know how customers respond to price changes, one option is to observe actual prices and quantities for the product. How much of the product customers have actually purchased at different price levels tells you something about their 'revealed preferences' (as opposed to 'stated preferences', which is what you get from surveys). If you have a sufficient number of observations, you may be able to identify the demand curve and price elasticities. Imagine that you observe prices and quantities of the product—say, high-quality chocolate—at regular intervals (monthly) over an extended period of time (two years). All observations are plotted in the price–quantity space in Figure 2.8. This is a stylized example—in reality you would not get such wide variation in the observed prices (economists like variation in the data, as that generally allows for more robust measurement). While eyeballing the figure already gives you some idea of the relationship between price and quantity (again, you would rarely see this in practice), you need to identify a demand curve that is accurate and statistically meaningful. This is where regression analysis comes in. Regression is a generic term for statistical methods that can be used to explain the variation in data using other factors.[68]

---

[68] Econometrics is the application of regression analysis and other statistical and mathematical principles to economic data. You will often hear the terms regression analysis and econometrics being used interchangeably in competition cases, which is not strictly correct but acceptable for practical purposes.

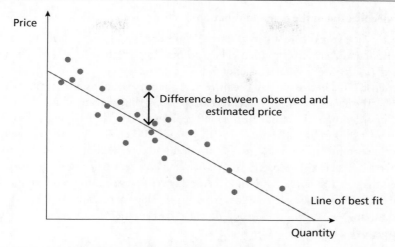

Figure 2.8 The demand curve as the 'line of best fit'

Recall that the theoretical demand function in Figure 2.1 was expressed as $p = 10 - q$. Using   **2.177** regression analysis, you can estimate a demand function of this form that best matches the dots in Figure 2.8. You start by writing the equation for this line as $p = a - b \times q$ + error term. In this equation, p is the dependent variable, q is an explanatory variable, and a and b are the coefficients to be estimated—a is where the demand curve intersects with the y-axis, usually referred to as the 'constant term' ($a = 10$ in Figure 2.1), while b is the coefficient that represents the slope of the curve ($b = 1$ in Figure 2.1). The error term represents the distance from the estimated line of best fit to each of the dots. In Figure 2.8 this difference is illustrated for one of the observations. In other words, it reflects how far off the line you are at each given quantity. Some observations are closer to the line than others. 'Line of best fit' means that you want to minimize the differences overall. Statistically, the trick to this involves several steps. First, you draw a line that you think fits reasonably well. Second, at each quantity you take the difference between the line and the actual observation (this can be positive or negative, depending on whether the observation is above or below the line you drew). Third, you take the square of each difference. Squaring has two rationales: you are treating points below and above the line the same (squaring a negative number gives a positive number), and you are giving more weight to the larger differences (as squares get bigger for higher numbers). Fourth, you take the sum of all the squares. Fifth, you follow the above four steps again for other possible lines, until you have found your line of best fit, which is where the sum of the squared differences is the smallest. This is why this approach is called 'ordinary least squares' (OLS) estimation. It is the most commonly used technique in econometrics and you will often see it when empirical studies are presented in competition cases. More sophisticated techniques can be used where this suits the nature of the data, but the basic logic remains that the objective of the analysis is to find the line of best fit. When OLS was first developed in the 1930s, econometricians used to calculate the minimum sum of the squares themselves. Fortunately, these days you can use statistical packages such as Stata to do it for you.[69]

---

[69] OLS and other techniques are explained in basic econometrics textbooks, such as Wooldridge (2013) and the aptly named *Mostly Harmless Econometrics* by Angrist and Pischke (2009). For technical expositions

2.15.2 Specification of the demand function

2.178 In practice, when you are presented with the results of a regression analysis, you will often see that the demand curve is specified in logarithms ('logs') rather than 'levels'. Instead of a function '$p = a - b \times q +$ error term', economists often estimate the function '$\log p = a - b \times \log q +$ error term'. This means that all the price and quantity data has been transformed into logarithms. The logarithm of a number to a given base is the power to which that base must be raised in order to produce that number (10 is often used as the base; $10^3 = 1,000$, so the logarithm of 1,000 to base 10 equals 3). The regression then simply tests the relationship between these transformed series instead of the original series. One reason for using this statistical trick is that the log specification is better at capturing the price–quantity interaction when the demand curve is not linear. Another reason is that the coefficient b directly represents the own-price elasticity, rather than just the slope of the curve—that is, it directly gives you the answer you are after (this is due to a mathematical relationship to do with the first derivative of a logarithmic function).

2.179 There is a potential problem with the interpretation of the observations plotted in Figure 2.8. Each observation reflects the quantity that was actually purchased at the particular price. These actual outcomes are not just reflective of the demand curve, they are the result of the interaction between demand and supply. Economists refer to this as the endogeneity of prices. When you look at the position of any two dots in the price–quantity field, you cannot tell whether the difference between the two is attributable to a shift *along* the demand curve, or to a shift *of* the demand curve *itself* to the left or to the right. Only shifts along the demand curve are relevant for the estimation of the slope of the demand curve. To isolate the shifts along the curve, economists look for instances where a difference between two observations has resulted from a shift of the *supply* curve rather than of the demand curve. A typical cause of a shift in the supply curve is production cost changes. Hence, cost data is often included in the estimation to identify supply changes. In economics jargon, the cost data is used as a control variable or as an 'instrument' in the regression analysis to address the endogeneity problem. Sometimes other variables can be suitable as instruments—for example, the weather conditions at particular times can be used as an instrument to explain supply shocks in agricultural products or ice cream.

2.15.3 A fishy example of regression analysis

2.180 To illustrate how regression analysis is used to estimate elasticities for market definition, consider the merger between Pan Fish and Marine Harvest, two farmers of Atlantic salmon, which was examined by the CC and a number of other national competition authorities in 2006.[70] An important question was whether salmon farmed in Scotland constituted a product market that was distinct from salmon farmed in Norway. The CC used regression analysis to estimate own- and cross-price elasticities for Scottish salmon. The equation specified by the CC was of the form: 'log of quantity of Scottish salmon = $a - b \times$ log of price of Scottish salmon + $c \times$ log of price of Norwegian salmon + $d \times$ log of income + error term'. Note that this is the demand function where quantity is a function of price,

---

of how econometrics techniques can be applied to market definition we refer you to Davis and Garcés (2009), Bishop and Walker (2010), and Motta (2004).

[70] Competition Commission (2006), 'Pan Fish ASA and Marine Harvest NV merger inquiry', 18 December.

rather than the inverse demand function that is shown in Figures 2.1 and 2.8, where price is a function of quantity. The CC had data on quantities, prices, and income, and could estimate the coefficients *a* (the constant term), *b* (the own-price elasticity of demand for Scottish salmon), *c* (the cross-price elasticity of Scottish salmon with respect to the price of Norwegian salmon), and *d* (the income elasticity). The CC recognized that prices might be endogenous, so it used exchange rate data as an instrument for Scottish and Norwegian salmon prices. The regression results showed an own-price elasticity for Scottish salmon of −3.5, and a cross-price elasticity with respect to the price of Norwegian salmon of 3. These estimates suggest that the demand for Scottish salmon is highly sensitive to price, and also that it responds strongly to Norwegian salmon price changes. While the CC did not perform a formal critical loss analysis based on the own-price elasticity estimate, it considered that the own- and cross-price elasticities were high, and concluded that this evidence was consistent with Norwegian salmon being in the same product market as Scottish salmon.

2.15.4 Questions you can ask when presented with regression analysis

Estimating elasticities through regression analysis is conceptually straightforward, but there are often pitfalls and complexities (endogeneity of prices, discussed above, is one). High standards need to be met before a regression analysis can be considered robust. Economists have developed a reasonably clear idea of what constitutes 'good economic practice', and econometrics has developed a range of diagnostics tests that you would normally expect to have been met. The econometrics toolbox may always be something of a black box to you, and debates on which particular econometric method is most appropriate in the case at hand can be rather esoteric, but there are some critical questions you can ask. These fall into three categories. **2.181**

First, you can ask questions about the data. What is the data coverage in terms of time period and products or market participants? How frequent is the data (monthly, yearly)? How large is the dataset? Are there enough observations to estimate elasticities robustly using econometric methods? Is the data of good quality (are there many missing observations or measurement errors)? The more observations there are, and the greater the variance between them, the higher the likelihood of finding statistically significant results. In the extreme, if you have only two observations, chances are that the line drawn from one to the other will not accurately reflect the demand curve. Even twenty-four observations, as in Figure 2.8, is on the low side. **2.182**

Second, you can ask questions about the econometric approach. Is the method appropriate for the market concerned and in light of the available data (does OLS work, or is a more sophisticated technique needed)? What assumptions underlie the econometric approach? Is the equation specified correctly, and is it in line with economic theory and market reality? Does it solve the price endogeneity problem, for example, through the use of instruments or a structural model?[71] Does the model explain most of the variation in price or quantity? R-squared (or an adjusted version of it) is the main statistic used to indicate how well a model fits the data. An R-squared of 1 means the model fits the data perfectly (but is rare, **2.183**

---

[71] Rather than estimate the simple demand equation discussed here, modern practice in econometrics would be to try to estimate a structural model with a number of equations recognizing that price and quantity simultaneously determine each other. Such models are a more sophisticated way of dealing with the problem of endogeneity than using instruments.

and suspicious if you see it). An R-squared of 0.6 means the model explains 60 per cent of the variance in the dependent variable. There are no clear thresholds for what constitutes an acceptable R-squared; indeed, one can always increase R-squared by adding more explanatory variables, without necessarily improving the regression analysis.

2.184 The third category consists of questions about the elasticity estimate. Are the estimated elasticity values plausible (is the own-price elasticity negative as theory would predict)? Are the estimated coefficients statistically significant? Statistical significance means you can be confident that the true parameter value lies within a particular interval from the estimated parameter value (often a 95 per cent confidence interval is used, applying the t-test or p-test).

2.185 You should expect any econometric results to be accompanied by a range of statistical diagnostic tests, ideally with some explanation for non-economists. Apart from the tests for the goodness of fit of the model (adjusted R-squared) and statistical significance for each parameter (t-test or p-test), there should be diagnostics for other potential statistical problems such as endogeneity, heteroscedasticity (a favourite word among non-economists), and multicollinearity. Heteroscedasticity ('unequal spread' in plain English) with respect to a particular explanatory variable arises where the variation in the dependent variable is not uniform across the values for that explanatory variable. For example, when you estimate the demand for different types of cars, age of the buyer could be one explanatory variable. However, variation in demand among the younger age bands (late teens and early twenties) will be lower than for the thirty- to fifty-year-olds, as in the latter group there is much more variation in personal income—and hence expenditure on cars—than for the former group (most students and young workers will buy cheap cars). Multicollinearity arises where two explanatory variables are closely related to each other and therefore capture the same effect on the dependent variable. An example is personal income and postcode area in which the person lives; you should avoid including both of them as explanatory variables for the demand of cars.

2.15.5 Price-correlation analysis

2.186 Before the concept of the relevant market was developed for the purpose of competition law, economists used to regard a market as something where the 'law of one price' holds. The logic is that products that constitute a market should be priced very similarly. Any price differences within such a market would be removed through a combination of entry (by suppliers who can undercut higher prices), exit (by suppliers who can't compete at lower prices), and arbitrage (intermediaries buying low and selling high). Relevant markets in competition law are more practical and acknowledge that products can place competitive pressure on each other even if prices are not the same. Yet the idea of the law of one price still has its use for market definition, and lies behind price-correlation analysis. If products are close substitutes, and even if they have different prices, you would still expect those prices to move together over time. If some event causes the price of one of the products to change with respect to the other, this will trigger demand and supply substitution (customers switching, intermediaries engaging in arbitrage), and eventually prices will come back into line. The statistical term for such moving in parallel is correlation. This is usually measured by the correlation index, which can take any value between +1 (when there is perfect positive correlation) and −1 (perfect negative correlation, i.e. if one goes up the other goes

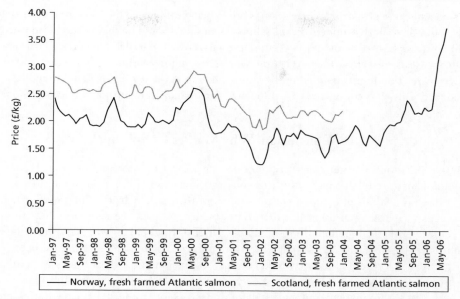

Figure 2.9 Price correlation to support market definition: monthly farm gate prices of Scottish and Norwegian salmon

Source: Competition Commission (2006), 'Pan Fish ASA and Marine Harvest NV Merger Inquiry', 18 December, Figure 7.

down), with a correlation of zero meaning no correlation at all. The closer the correlation between the price series of two markets is to +1, the more likely it is that the two are in the same relevant market.

The *Pan Fish/Marine Harvest* merger, discussed earlier, provides a good illustration of how price-correlation analysis can assist with market definition.[72] To answer the question of whether salmon farmed in Scotland constitutes a distinct product market from salmon farmed in Norway, the CC not only carried out a regression analysis but also considered the correlation between the prices of Scottish salmon and Norwegian salmon over time. This is shown in Figure 2.9. You can see that prices of Scottish and Norwegian salmon tend to move in parallel, that is, they are highly correlated (the correlation coefficient is 0.91). Scottish salmon is consistently priced at a premium, but this does not alter the observation that the prices move in parallel, which suggests that Scottish and Norwegian salmon belong to the same relevant market.   **2.187**

Just like other empirical methods, price-correlation analysis comes with a number of health warnings. The CC was well aware of this: '[W]hile informative, neither the correlation test, nor the extent of co-movement in prices (stationarity) test, can be viewed as definitive evidence of the existence of a relevant market.'[73] The main potential problem with the price-correlation test is that prices of two products can be correlated over time for reasons other than these products being in the same relevant market—you can have spurious correlation.   **2.188**

---

[72] Competition Commission (2006), 'Pan Fish ASA and Marine Harvest NV merger inquiry', 18 December.
[73] Ibid., at [5.36].

A frequent cause of spurious correlation is prices being influenced by changes in costs that are common to both products. In the salmon example, it could be that salmon feed prices cause prices of Scottish and Norwegian salmon to move in parallel. However, in this particular case, there were no obvious reasons why prices might have moved in parallel, and the price-correlation results pointed in the same direction as the regression analysis and other evidence. This gives confidence that the conclusion on market definition is the correct one.

2.16 Conclusion: Why Market Definition?

2.189 Market definition is about whether a product (or geographic area) is in or out. Is mass-market chocolate in the market for high-quality chocolate? If it is in, you consider it as part of your analysis of competitive constraints in the market. If it is out, you don't. In this regard, market definition is a useful intermediate step in the competition analysis, and the hypothetical monopolist test provides a useful threshold for whether something is in or out—based on the question of which products constrain each other in raising price. Without such a threshold, there would be much confusion and lack of clarity on market definition, just like there was before the hypothetical monopolist test was introduced—submarkets within markets and market definitions based on product characteristics might well begin to creep in again. Furthermore, having market definition as a standard intermediate step in the analysis contributes to a degree of legal certainty. Competition lawyers and courts understand the concept and it is embedded in case law. It assists companies and their legal advisers in carrying out self-assessments of risks (or opportunities) under competition law. By trying to identify relevant markets, a company can calculate its own market share and that of rivals, and thus assess the likelihood of competition law intervention. Market shares are still a useful initial guide to the existence of market power (see Chapter 3).

2.190 In this chapter we have explained the basic logic and some of the advanced features of the hypothetical monopolist test for market definition. We have also explained how exercising some judgement is crucial when setting the threshold of whether something is in or out, and a measure of pragmatism is required when trying to apply the threshold in practice. Sometimes the required degree of judgement and pragmatism will be so high that market definition becomes less useful as an intermediate step. As explained in this chapter, a particular situation in which this may arise is when markets are characterized by a high degree of product differentiation. Asking whether something is in or out can be difficult, artificial, and potentially misleading in those cases. The question becomes more about which products are each other's closest substitutes, than about which products are in or out. In these situations you can focus on the analysis of competitive constraints directly, and skip the market definition stage altogether. Rather than asking whether the relevant market contains high-quality chocolate or all chocolate, you ask whether Godiva and Neuhaus, prior to a merger, provide a strong competitive constraint on each other. We return to this in Chapter 7. Nonetheless, you should bear in mind that many of the economic concepts underlying market definition that we discussed in this chapter—such as demand elasticities, diversion ratios, and supply-side substitution—are also at the heart of the economic questions arising at subsequent stages of competition analysis. The principles of market definition are not past their sell-by date yet.

3

MARKET POWER

3.1 A Central Concern in Competition Law

3.1.1 A long-standing concern

3.01 Market power means you can exploit your customers. You can restrict output and raise price for a sustained period, without being undermined by competitors. Concerns about market power pre-date competition law. In the late sixteenth century, Edward Darcy, a member of Queen Elizabeth's court, received an exclusive licence for twenty-one years to sell playing cards in England. This arrangement was driven by the Queen's concern that card playing was becoming a problem among her subjects, and the hope that having one person controlling the trade would regulate the activity. No one else was allowed to make cards 'upon pain of the Queen's gracious displeasure, and of such fine and punishment as offenders in the case of voluntary contempt deserve'.[1] When a London-based haberdasher, T. Allein, sold his own playing cards, Darcy sued him. The court ruled against Darcy in 1602 and determined that the granting of a monopoly was invalid.[2] It argued that while the Queen had intended to permit this monopoly for the public good, she must have been 'deceived' because such a monopoly can be used only for the private gain of the monopolist. The court considered monopoly to be bad for others who exercise the same trade (condemning them to 'live in idleness and beggary'), and for the wider public. It also held that while provisions might be added to moderate the monopoly's behaviour, 'it is meer folly to think that there is any measure in mischief or wickedness'.

3.02 Four centuries on we have competition law, based on the very same notion that competition is 'good' and monopoly is 'bad'.[3] In this chapter we explore the concept of market power. What are its main economic characteristics? How can it be measured? What is its role in competition law? We will see that market power is a matter of degree: Darcy had monopoly power, which lies at one end of the spectrum, but a small corner shop has some market power too if there are no other shops nearby. Competition law is concerned only with higher degrees of market power.

---

[1] This quote is from a contemporaneous report entitled 'The Case of Monopolies' by Sir Edward Coke, a prominent lawyer and judge of that era, as reproduced in Sheppard (2003).

[2] *Darcy v Allein* 77 Eng Rep 1260 (QB, 1602).

[3] Yet the thinking behind the playing card monopoly still rears its head. In 2014 Greece's Council of State (its highest administrative court) ruled in favour of the country's monopoly betting company, OPAP. In 2013 the ECJ had found the OPAP monopoly to be incompatible with EU law, but left open the possibility for the state to allow a monopoly in the interest of 'consumer protection and the preservation of order in society'. The Greek authorities and court considered that OPAP helps in fighting illegal gambling and controlling expansion of the sector (never mind that it also makes healthy monopoly profits). Greek Council of State, Judgments 3167/2014 and 3168/2014, 30 September 2014; and Joined Cases C-186/11 and C-209/11, *Stanleybet International Ltd and Others v Ypourgos Oikonomias kai Oikonomikon*, Ypourgos Politismou, Judgment of 24 January 2013.

3.1.2 A central concern, but not tackled directly

Central as the concern may be, competition law does not actually tackle market power   **3.03**
directly. Companies are not normally fined merely because they have market power. Nor
have there been many instances where competition authorities ordered the break-up of
companies with market power (see Chapter 8 for some rare examples). Instead, competition law addresses the *abuse* of market power. It prevents companies with market power
from excluding competitors and (though infrequently, as we discuss in Chapter 4) from
exploiting customers. In this regard market power often functions as a threshold for
intervention—a practice that is harmless when undertaken by a company that faces competitive constraints may be considered heinous when conducted by a company with market power. Competition law also addresses the *creation* and *enhancement* of market power
through merger and acquisition. The idea is that companies are allowed to 'earn' their
market power through organic growth and superior performance, but not simply to 'buy'
it by merging with a competitor.

So why does competition law not tackle market power directly? The main reason is that   **3.04**
the quest for market power is an integral feature of well-functioning markets. It provides
a strong spur to achieve cost efficiencies, to invest, and to innovate. It is therefore not normally illegal to establish a position of market power through organic growth, investment,
or serving customers well. Recall the referee of the boxing match in Chapter 1. The audience wishes to see a good fight. A boxer should therefore not be prevented from getting better and stronger than his rivals. The referee intervenes only when there is punching below
the belt or fixing of matches among opponents. As US Judge Learned Hand famously put
it: 'The successful competitor, having been urged to compete, must not be turned upon
when he wins.'[4]

3.1.3 Market power is a matter of degree

Market power comes in degrees, as we noted earlier. Small degrees of market power exist in   **3.05**
many markets simply because products are differentiated in some way. We mentioned the
corner shop that has no rival shops nearby (or is the only shop open during evening hours).[5]
A corner shop charges more for a litre of milk than a major supermarket. In a model of
perfect competition this should not be sustainable. In reality, however, the characteristics
of the litre of milk include the time cost of purchasing (the time to get to the shop and buy
the milk) and the urgency with which it is required (running out of such essential household items leads to what are known as 'distress' purchases). The customer is willing to pay a
premium for the opportunity to buy the milk quickly and immediately. Such market power
is arguably of no real concern to competition authorities. When considered over a longer
(non-transitory) period, the small corner shop probably faces significant competition from
the larger supermarkets on the outskirts of town.[6]

---

[4] *United States v Aluminum Co. of America*, 148 F.2d 416, 430 (2d Cir. 1945).
[5] Another example of geographic differentiation is that of ice-cream vendors who spread out along a
beach. This comes from the classic article by Hotelling (1929), who identified the importance of product differentiation at a time when economists were still mainly using models of perfect competition and monopoly
in homogeneous goods markets.
[6] The story may be different in a small village where the shop is truly the only option, as some of our colleagues who live in rural Oxfordshire can attest.

3.06 Similarly, a degree of market power commonly arises from branding and product differentiation. Chocolatiers, soft drink manufacturers, banks, and law firms all seek to make their products distinct from the competition so as to gain a little bit of pricing power. At Tesco you can buy a 2-litre bottle of Tesco Cola for £0.55, while a bottle of Pepsi Regular costs £1.98.[7] There may be some quality and hence cost differences between the two bottles (though have you ever tried the Pepsi test?), but these are unlikely to account for the 3.5 times price difference in full. Instead, the higher margins earned by Pepsi indicate a degree of market power, driven by brand preference and loyalty. As long as consumers have the option to choose freely from a wide range of colas (or other soft drinks), this brand-based market power as such is not really of concern under competition law.

3.1.4 Monopolistic competition

3.07 A market structure in which there is competition between many brands of similar products is often described as 'monopolistic competition'. This is not an oxymoron. Each supplier can be seen as having a monopoly over its own brand. Prices will be higher than the marginal cost of production as each supplier has some market power due to customers' brand preferences. However, profit margins are competed away as suppliers need to keep investing in advertising and quality for their brand to preserve its differentiating character (or, in the case of corner shops, they need to pay for the fixed costs of running the shop). In this market environment, prices are in line with average costs and no company makes profits above the 'normal' economic level for its industry. Where successful differentiation results in very high profits, new brands come in and fill the space until profits return to normal again. Many real-world markets fit this description. There is no problematic degree of market power.

3.08 So when does product differentiation raise concerns? One situation is where there are only a few brands in the market, and one brand has a high degree of market power that cannot easily be challenged. Many cases of abuse of dominance and vertical restraints arise from such situations (see Chapters 4 and 6). Another is where two brands that compete closely with each other are combined through a merger—as discussed further in Chapter 7. A model similar to monopolistic competition is that of Bertrand oligopoly with differentiated products. Each supplier is again a monopolist over its own products and faces varying degrees of competition from other products depending on the degree of differentiation. However, there is no free entry, so the degree of market power can be high. You will often see economists referring to differentiated Bertrand oligopoly as it forms the basis for the analysis of unilateral effects of mergers (see further Chapter 7).

3.1.5 Market power: A stockpile that can be exhausted

3.09 There is another sense in which market power is a matter of degree: you can use it, but typically only once. A company with market power can hike up the price. But as the price gets higher, so does the resistance to further increases—recall from Chapter 2 that demand tends to become more elastic at higher prices. There comes a point when the company has exhausted all its market power and cannot raise price any further. At that point, would you say it has market power? This question is akin to the notion of the cellophane fallacy that we discussed in Chapter 2.[8] At prevailing price levels, cellophane was subject to competitive

---

[7] Prices correct as of January 2015.
[8] *US v El du Pont de Nemours & Co* 351 US 377 (1956).

constraint from other wrapping materials. But those prevailing price levels had resulted from Du Pont exploiting its near-monopoly in cellophane. Du Pont faced strong competition at those high prices, but for competition policy purposes you may still want to take into account the fact that the company clearly had market power to start with and had effectively used it up by raising prices.

By the same token, monopolizing a market tends to be costly. A company that seeks to foreclose the market often has to spend a lot of its market power—for example, signing up customers or distributors to exclusive contracts requires offering them attractive terms or discounts. In this sense market power is like a stockpile that you gradually use up, and cannot easily make bigger without some profit sacrifice (we return to this in Chapter 4). This notion of market power as a finite and changing stockpile is not commonly used in competition law—market power tends to be regarded as a fixed state. However, it is useful to bear in mind that market power has its limits. **3.10**

3.1.6 Degrees of market power that worry competition authorities

The first threshold for market power that features in competition law is where there is sufficient influence from a practice or a company for there to be an appreciable effect on competition. The concept of appreciable effect is often applied under Article 101(1) TFEU in the assessment of non-hardcore horizontal and vertical agreements (i.e. agreements other than those relating to price fixing, market sharing or bid rigging). Appreciability can be determined by reference to the degree of market power of the companies concerned, or the proportion of the market covered by the agreement in question. No clear thresholds exist. European Commission guidance refers to certain market share thresholds below which an agreement may be regarded as not problematic—these range from 10 per cent to 30 per cent depending on the type of agreement (in particular whether it is horizontal or vertical). We discuss this in Chapters 5 and 6.[9] **3.11**

3.1.7 Dominance

Dominance is the core market power threshold in competition law in the European Union and many other jurisdictions. It can be interpreted as a significant degree of market power—a dominant company is large and powerful enough to have a substantial effect on the market. This notion is captured in the *United Brands* and *Hoffmann-La Roche* judgments, where the ECJ referred to the ability to behave independently and to hinder or exclude competitors: **3.12**

> UBC is an undertaking in a dominant position enjoying a degree of general independence in its behaviour on the relevant market which enables it to hinder to a large extent any effective competition from competitors.[10]

> The dominant position thus referred to relates to a position of economic strength enjoyed by an undertaking which enables it to prevent effective competition being maintained on the relevant market by affording it the power to behave to an appreciable extent independently of its competitors, its customers and ultimately of the consumers.[11]

---

[9] Under the Block Exemption Regulation 330/2010, most vertical agreements benefit from a safe harbour if both the supplier and the buyer have a market share below 30 per cent. The De Minimis Notice (2014/C 291/01) provides a safe harbour for horizontal agreements where the parties have a combined market share below 10 per cent.

[10] Case 27/76 *United Brands v Commission* [1978] ECR 207, at [65].

[11] Case 85/76 *Hoffmann-La Roche & Co AG v Commission* [1979] ECR 461, at [38].

3.13   These legal definitions do not accord strictly with the underlying economics of market power. No company can really behave independently of its competitors and customers. The very nature of a downward-sloping demand curve means that even a monopolist will lose customers as it raises price. However, the caveat 'to an appreciable extent' suggests that the independence is not absolute but a matter of degree, which makes economic sense. In a competitive market, all firms are 'price-takers'—that is, they have little or no ability to set the selling price. Behaving independently means that a dominant company is not too concerned about whether its customers will find alternative suppliers, or that its competitors are able to assail its position.

3.1.8 Super-dominance and monopoly

3.14   Monopoly is the strongest form of market power. Literally it means sole seller. Competition law takes a slightly broader view. US antitrust law uses the term 'monopoly power' to mean a significant degree of market power, or more specifically as 'the power to control prices or exclude competition'.[12] Monopoly power does not necessarily require an actual monopoly position, and in practice will often coincide with the concept of dominance in other jurisdictions. EU case law has at times referred to a level of market power between dominance and monopoly, namely 'super-dominance'. This was first defined as 'a position of overwhelming dominance verging on monopoly' in the case of a shipping conference that controlled 90 per cent of the market.[13]

3.15   As regards actual monopolies, the best-known types are the natural and statutory ones. A natural monopoly (as explained in Chapter 1) is an industry where the underlying cost of production means that it is most efficient to have a single producer. Common examples include water, electricity, and gas transportation networks that have high fixed costs, but once built can serve each additional customer at low cost. Monopolies can also arise from demand-side economies of scale, known as network effects, for products such as social networking sites or technology standards (as discussed further in section 3.3). Statutory or legal monopolies are those established by the state or a court.

3.16   Historically, for utility services (transport, energy, water) that are considered essential to society, public ownership was a solution to the need for subsidy to provide these services. For other services, such monopolies have been a popular form of revenue raising, either through state ownership or through the licence fees extracted from private operators in return for the right to exploit that monopoly. The licences for the first Independent Television (ITV) franchises for UK commercial broadcasts in the 1950s were dubbed the original 'licence to print money'.[14] The scarcity of analogue broadcast spectrum meant that there was initially only one (monopoly) channel on which advertising would be carried in each region. Postal services were another statutory monopoly in countries across the world, built on the desire to ensure a universal service. Recognition of the difficulty of enforcing a single, affordable price for a delivery service to any point in a country when faced with competition has led governments to preserve national postal monopolies. Historically they have retained state ownership to ensure that no private entity can exploit monopoly power. In recent years several postal incumbents have been privatized (in search of funding and cost efficiency) and

---

[12] *US v El du Pont de Nemours & Co* 351 US 377 (1956).
[13] Opinion of Advocate General Fennelly of 19 October 1998, in Case C-395/96 P *Compagnie Maritime Belge and Dafra-Lines v Commission* [2000] ECR I-1365.
[14] See Johnson and Turnock (2005).

subjected to price regulation. We do not discuss the economics of regulation of monopolies in utility and network industries here. Nevertheless, there are some lessons that competition law and regulation can learn from each other, as we discuss in Chapter 8 on remedies. Moreover, as we shall see in Chapter 4, many examples of abuse of dominance arise in these industries. IP rights and the patent system are a further source of monopoly. While the ownership of these rights does not infringe competition law as such, we will see several examples of IP owners being challenged for anti-competitive practices.

3.1.9 The remainder of this chapter

So far we have discussed the concept of market power and its different degrees. We now turn   **3.17**
to its use in practice. Market power is often assessed with reference to market shares and concentration measures—the subject of section 3.2—and to entry and exit barriers—dealt with in section 3.3. In section 3.4 we explore the role of profitability as an indicator of market power. High profits sustained over a long period of time capture the essence of market power, and yet profitability analysis is not frequently used by competition authorities. This section contains a brief explanation of the basics of profitability analysis. Section 3.5 discusses buyer power and bidding markets. Buyer power may be so strong that it offsets the seller's market power. A specific type of buyer power exists in bidding markets, where sellers periodically have to bid for a major customer's business rather than compete on an ongoing basis—competition *for* the market rather than competition *in* the market. Section 3.6 explores the insights from behavioural economics into the interaction between consumers and suppliers. Consumer biases and bounded rationality mean that in a range of consumer markets companies have a greater and more persistent degree of market power than would follow from traditional models of competition. This section also contains a brief explanation of the basics of behavioural economics. Finally, section 3.7 considers another area where assessing market power is far from straightforward: dynamic, innovative markets. In such markets it is pertinent to return to the notion that we discussed at the start of this section: the prospect of obtaining market power provides a compelling incentive for companies to innovate and outperform rivals. It lies at the heart of efficient market functioning and is therefore not a bad thing as such.

3.2 Market Shares and Concentration Measures

3.2.1 Market shares and market power

Once you have defined the relevant market you can measure market shares. These are cen-   **3.18**
tral to understanding the degree of market power and existing competition in the market. Market shares can be a means to determine 'safe harbours'—that is, where a company is so small in a properly defined market that it is highly unlikely to have substantial market power. Conversely, is a large market share synonymous with market power? In the European Union there is a strong presumption that it is:

> The existence of a dominant position may derive from several factors which, taken separately, are not necessarily determinative but among these factors a highly important one is the existence of very large market shares . . .

> very large market shares are in themselves, and save in exceptional circumstances, evidence of the existence of a dominant position.[15]

---

[15] Case 85/76 *Hoffmann-La Roche & Co AG v Commission* [1979] ECR 461, at [39] and [41].

3.19 In *AKZO* (1991), the ECJ ruled that a company with a stable market share of more than 50 per cent in a relevant market would be deemed dominant unless there were exceptional circumstances.[16] A 40 per cent dominance threshold was used, for example, in the 2004 Coca-Cola undertakings with respect to exclusivity, rebates, and tying, in those countries where Coca-Cola's soft drinks represent more than 40 per cent of national sales (and more than double the share of the nearest competitor).[17] In the German Act against Restraints of Competition—last amended in July 2014—a company is presumed dominant if it has a market share of at least 40 per cent. In South Africa's Competition Act of 1998 this is 45 per cent.

3.20 Economics tells us that market shares should, in any case, not be seen as the sole answer. They are a useful summary indicator of the relative strength of a company, but do not capture other important market characteristics, such as the position of potential competitors and of buyers. Before we turn to those other factors we consider the measurement of market shares in some more detail.

3.2.2 Measuring market shares: Not as easy as it might seem

3.21 Market shares seem straightforward to calculate. You take the output of the relevant supplier and divide it by the total market output. But in practice it can be surprisingly difficult. This starts with the question of market shares in terms of what: turnover, volume of sales, number of suppliers, number of customers, capacity? Each of these metrics has its merits and limitations, and which is the most appropriate will depend on the specific case at hand. As set out in the 2010 US Horizontal Merger Guidelines:

> In most contexts, the Agencies measure each firm's market share based on its actual or projected revenues in the relevant market. Revenues in the relevant market tend to be the best measure of attractiveness to customers, since they reflect the real-world ability of firms to surmount all of the obstacles necessary to offer products on terms and conditions that are attractive to customers. In cases where one unit of a low-priced product can substitute for one unit of a higher-priced product, unit sales may measure competitive significance better than revenues . . .

> In markets for homogeneous products, a firm's competitive significance may derive principally from its ability and incentive to rapidly expand production in the relevant market in response to a price increase or output reduction by others in that market. As a result, a firm's competitive significance may depend upon its level of readily available capacity to serve the relevant market if that capacity is efficient enough to make such expansion profitable. In such markets, capacities or reserves may better reflect the future competitive significance of suppliers than revenues, and the Agencies may calculate market shares using those measures.[18]

3.2.3 Market shares by value and volume

3.22 The most common measure of market share is turnover or sales value. Especially in markets where products are differentiated this allows them to be aggregated, with more weight placed on the suppliers of more expensive products. Consider the merger between Nestlé

---

[16] Case C-62/86 *AKZO Chemie BV v Commission*, [1991] ECR I-3359; [1993] 5 CMLR 215.

[17] *Coca-Cola* (Case COMP/A39.116/B2), Decision of 22 June 2005.

[18] Department of Justice and Federal Trade Commission (2010), 'Horizontal Merger Guidelines', 19 August, p. 17.

and Perrier, two companies involved in bottling water from natural sources. The European Commission set out why it preferred market shares in value terms:

> The market shares in value terms better reflect the real market strength in this market than the market shares in volume because the French water market is composed of two categories of products which are very different in terms of price, ie the nationally distributed mineral waters and the local waters, which are mainly spring waters. There exists a wide and constantly increasing price gap between these two categories of waters... Given this considerable price difference between these two categories of waters and the importance of financial resources in the water market for investment in publicity and marketing, the Commission considers that it is more appropriate to take account of the market shares expressed in value than in volume.[19]

Yet using value market shares may sometimes underestimate the competitive significance of lower-price suppliers. Volume (in terms of units supplied) is a common alternative measure of market shares, especially when the products in question are sufficiently homogeneous. An example is the 2014 *Holcim/Cemex West* merger in the German cement industry, where the Commission defined a relevant product market for all grey cement (as distinct from white cement) and presented market shares on the basis of tonnes sold in the various geographic markets.[20] The number of customers can be a useful volume-based metric for market share calculations where customers buy the same quantities and broadly pay the same price. In the airline industry, market shares for a given route are often calculated in terms of the number of passengers flown, as seen, for example, in the 2013 *Ryanair/AerLingus* merger case.[21] Each passenger occupies one seat on the plane, and through yield management airlines tend to set fares with the aim of filling all seats. A pragmatic reason for using this metric is that data on passenger numbers is often readily available. Turnover is much less observable, especially as few passengers on the same flight pay exactly the same fare (which can render the passenger numbers metric less informative if the fare differences become too large—e.g. between business and leisure passengers). **3.23**

3.2.4 Capacity market shares

Value- and volume-based measures of market share give information about the constraints from other companies based on the choices made by customers. As we know from Chapter 2, supply-side substitution can also broaden the market. A market share measure that captures the capacity of potential suppliers is relevant in such cases since capacity is a better indicator of supply-side substitution, and hence of competitive significance. This principle is reflected in the US Horizontal Merger Guidelines as quoted above, and in the New Zealand Commerce Commission guidelines: **3.24**

> where a capacity-based measure of market share produces a significantly lower share of the market for the combined entity than one based on sales volumes, the implied unemployed capacity available to competitors, or to possible market entrants, might be taken into account as a potential constraint on the combined entity from actual or near competitors.[22]

---

[19] *Nestlé/Perrier* (Case IV/M.190), Decision of 22 July 1992, at [40].
[20] *Holcim/Cemex West* (Case COMP/M.7009), Decision of 5 June 2014.
[21] *Ryanair/Aer Lingus III* (Case COMP/M.6663), Decision of 27 February 2013. We advised the acquiring party in this inquiry.
[22] New Zealand Commerce Commission (2003), 'Mergers and Acquisitions Guidelines', at [5.2].

3.25 Consider a hypothetical example from the bus sector. There are two operators in a given local market: operator A with a depot with sixty buses, and operator B with forty buses. If operator B runs mainly inter-urban services (with high passenger mileage) and operator A runs mainly local services (with low passenger mileage), a market share based on passenger miles would give the impression that B was the stronger competitor. A capacity-based measure would reveal that operator A has a greater ability to substitute to new routes as it has more buses and is therefore a stronger supply-side competitor than operator B. In Chapter 2 we discussed the *Chester City Council and Chester City Transport v Arriva* predatory pricing case involving local bus services, where it was accepted that the geographic market should be defined in terms of supply-side substitution. The case then turned on the relevant market share metric, with the candidates being bus hours (i.e. the hours a bus spends on the road—proposed as a proxy measure for turnover) and capacity (by number of buses and depot capacity). The High Court concluded as follows:

> As regards [the claimants' expert's] 'bus hours' metric, I also regard this as wrong in principle... I regard the metric as at least an unreliable proxy for turnover. But even if it is to be regarded as a proper such proxy, I also accept [the defendants' expert's] opinion that such a metric is not an appropriate one for measuring market power in a case where the market is being determined on a supply-side basis, even though it may be where it is being determined on a demand-side basis. Turnover measures what operators are *actually* doing, not what they are capable of doing, whereas in a supply-side case the inquiry is what they are *capable* of doing. [The defendants' expert's] opinion... is that in such a case *capacity* is the best metric for measuring market power. I accept that opinion and agree that a vehicle count is one way of measuring it. I understood [the defendants' expert] also to agree that an alternative way is to measure the bus capacity of particular depots. I find that [the claimants' expert] used the wrong metric in order to ascertain market shares in a wrongly identified market.[23] [Emphasis in original.]

3.26 Another example of the use of capacity as the basis for market share calculations is the *Cott/ Macaw* (2006) merger in the United Kingdom, where the relevant market for own-label carbonated soft drinks (CSDs) was defined on the basis of supply-side substitution. The CC concluded that:

> For that reason, capacity-based market shares potentially better represent the potential for competition by taking into account each supplier's total capacity to provide own-label PET-bottled CSDs.[24]

3.27 However, it acknowledged that market shares based on capacity might overstate some companies' share of capacity available for producing soft drinks since the margins might be higher from continuing to produce an alternative product (see also Chapter 2 on how supply-side substitution may be overstated in these circumstances). Hence the CC also considered market shares in terms of sales value. Indeed, it is often useful to compare a number of different market share metrics to gain an understanding of the degree of market power.

---

[23] *Chester City Council and Chester City Transport Limited v Arriva PLC* [2007] EWHC 1373 (Ch), at [191]. We acted for the defendants in this case.

[24] Competition Commission (2006), 'Cott Beverages Ltd and Macaw (Holdings) Ltd Merger Inquiry', 28 March, at [5.3]. PET (polyethylene terephthalate) is what most plastic bottles are made from these days. We advised the merging parties in this inquiry.

3.2.5 Market shares over time

A further consideration is how frequently the market shares are measured and over what **3.28** time period. Competition authorities often use annual market shares, mainly for pragmatic reasons. This may give a good picture of relative market positions over the relevant time period, but may not be appropriate where there are infrequent and large orders, resulting in volatile annual market shares that are uninformative. In this situation, market shares over a longer time period (e.g. three or five years) may be appropriate. One sector characterized by large and infrequent orders is the aircraft industry. In the merger between Boeing and McDonnell Douglas in 1997, the European Commission examined ten years of market share data, measured in terms of the order backlog for aircraft still in production, new orders, and net orders.[25] In the *General Electric/Honeywell* merger, which related to the manufacturing of large jet aircraft engines, the Commission calculated market shares over five and ten years.[26]

In any case, a snapshot of market shares in one year is normally insufficient. You need to **3.29** know how market shares change over time to understand market power and the ability to behave independently. Over a number of years you can see whether companies have been jockeying for position or whether the leading positions have remained stable. The ECJ's decision on AKZO's dominance illustrates this point:

> AKZO's market share is not only large in itself but is equivalent to all the remaining producers put together . . .
>
> AKZO's market share (as well as that of the second and third placed producers Interox and Luperox) has remained steady over the period under consideration and AKZO has always successfully repulsed any attacks on its position by smaller producers.[27]

Stability of market shares is a particularly important indicator in high-tech indus- **3.30** tries characterized by rapid innovation—a theme we return to in section 3.7. In such industries, the dynamics of market shares can often be decisive in a finding of market power. For example, the combined market share for cardiac ultrasound machines in the *Philips/ATL* merger in 2001 would have been above 40 per cent in a number of national markets. Yet the European Commission concluded that there was no concern because the parties' post-merger market share could be expected to be challenged by innovative competitors:

> [T]he cardiac ultrasound market is R&D intensive and largely driven by technological innovations which take place at relatively rapid pace, on average every 4–5 years . . . The rapid innovation rate of ultrasound allows competitors, who manage to place a new product on the market, to gain market shares relatively quickly, while established products might lose out. HSG (then HP, Hewlett-Packard) prior to 1998 was by far the market leader in Europe in cardiac ultrasound. Later on, GE and Acuson managed to improve their position significantly . . . These developments have resulted in a significant price decrease for top-end equipment but also in a change of market shares of the main competitors (HP lost ground on GE and Siemens/Acuson).[28]

---

[25] *Boeing/McDonnell Douglas* (Case IV/M.877), Decision of 30 July 1997.
[26] *General Electric/Honeywell* (Case COMP/M.2220), Decision of 3 July 2001.
[27] Case C-62/86 *AKZO Chemie BV v Commission*, [1991] ECR I-3359; [1993] 5 CMLR 215.
[28] *Philips/Agilent Healthcare Solutions* (Case COMP/M.2256), Decision of 2 March 2001, at [31].

3.2.6 Concentration measures

3.31 In assessing market power, the market share of the company under investigation is not the only statistic of interest. You also want to know the relative size and strength of its competitors, and how many there are. All these aspects can be captured in various measures of concentration—the most common being the number of competitors, Cn measures, and the Herfindahl–Hirschman Index (HHI). The first of these—the number of competitors—is the simplest measure of concentration: the fewer the competitors in a market, the higher the concentration. While easy to dismiss as uninformative (it doesn't tell you anything about the relative strength of these competitors), this measure can be helpful in cases that involve localized markets and where consumer choice matters. In its groceries market investigation, the CC focused on the number of supermarket 'fascias' (i.e. brands of competing shops) in each local market:

> The number of competing fascias in a local market provides another indication of the extent of the competitive constraint faced by particular stores within that market. The greater the number of fascias, the greater the number of alternatives to which customers can switch following any weakening of the retail offer at a store. Where a grocery store faces zero, one or two competitor fascias (i.e. monopoly, duopoly or triopoly stores), and the retailer operating that store has a high market share, that retailer is likely to face little to no competitive constraint in that market.[29]

3.32 This fascia count as a concentration measure is based on the assumption that consumers choose to go to a supermarket because of its overall offering, and then do all their shopping there. They rarely split any one shopping visit across multiple supermarkets. Therefore it is the loss of an option that is important in reducing the competitive constraint on neighbouring supermarkets.

3.33 Cn measures of concentration give the combined share of the 'n' largest firms in a market (they were widely used by IO economists in the 1950s and 1960s but less so now). For example, C4 gives the combined market share of the largest four firms in a market. When assessing the *Cott/Macaw* merger, the CC considered C2 measures in the market for PET-bottled own-label CSDs: the pre-merger C2 ratio was 65 per cent, rising to 89 per cent post-merger, indicating a highly concentrated market (although the CC cleared the merger because it found that buyer power and supply-side substitution would prevent any potential exercise of market power).[30]

3.2.7 The Herfindahl–Hirschman Index

3.34 The most commonly used concentration measure is the HHI, which is calculated by adding the squares of market shares of all the companies in a market. The effect of this squaring is that the index gives more weight to the larger companies. The higher the HHI, the more concentrated the market. An HHI of close to zero indicates a market with many firms, each having a tiny market share. The maximum HHI is 10,000 (the square of 100), which indicates a monopoly. The mechanics of calculating the HHI are presented in Table 3.1. The table shows two industries, each with nine firms, but with quite different distributions

---

[29] Competition Commission (2008), 'The Supply of Groceries in the UK—Market Investigation', 30 April, at [6.10]. We advised one of the retailers during this investigation.

[30] Competition Commission (2006), 'Cott Beverages Ltd and Macaw (Holdings) Ltd merger inquiry', 28 March, at [7.2].

Table 3.1 Concentration measures: an illustration

	Industry A		Industry B	
	Market share (%)	Squared shares	Market share (%)	Squared shares
Firm 1	35	1,225	20	400
Firm 2	35	1,225	20	400
Firm 3	5	25	20	400
Firm 4	5	25	20	400
Firm 5	5	25	4	16
Firm 6	5	25	4	16
Firm 7	4	16	4	16
Firm 8	3	9	4	16
Firm 9	3	9	4	16
Total/HHI	100	2,584	100	1,680
C4	80		80	

of market shares. The C4 measure is actually the same in both industries—80 per cent. But which of them is the more concentrated? Industry A is dominated by two main suppliers with 35 per cent each, followed by a fringe of much smaller firms. Competition in industry B seems more evenly balanced between four firms with 20 per cent each. You can see that the high market shares of 35 per cent, when squared, have a big impact on the HHI. As a result, the HHI for industry A is 904 points higher than for industry B.

The HHI is a good summary measure of the size distribution of firms. It reflects both the distribution of the market shares of the larger firms and the composition of the part of the market served by smaller firms. In theory you need information on the shares of all the firms in the market to calculate the HHI, but firms with small market shares have little effect on the overall HHI. For example, if you don't have precise information on the sales of fringe firms 7 to 9, you can combine them in a residual category or assume some average market share for each—either way the result does not change much. Another useful way of interpreting the HHI is that when you divide 10,000 by the HHI you get the equivalent number of equally sized firms in the market. An HHI of 2,500 gives you 10,000/2,500 = 4, so the structure of industry A (HHI = 2,584) is roughly equivalent to having four equally sized companies in the market (if all four have 25 per cent, the square of that is 625, and the sum of the squares is 2,500). Industry B (HHI = 1,680) is roughly equivalent to a structure with six equally sized firms (10,000/1,680 = 5.95). Finally, we note that the HHI has a theoretical property that economists find particularly interesting. In the standard Cournot model of oligopoly there is a direct positive relationship between the HHI and the price–cost margins in the industry—the higher the concentration, the greater the margins earned by the oligopolists, which is an intuitive result (see also below on the Lerner index). **3.35**

3.2.8 When is a market too concentrated?

We have now defined the various measures of market power and concentration. But how high is too high? This is in essence a matter of judgement. There are no bright lines. In any event, given that market shares and concentration do not tell you the whole story on market power, thresholds may be useful only as an initial filter or safe harbour. The EU Merger Regulation states that a merger does not 'impede effective competition' if the combined **3.36** market share of the merging parties is below 25 per cent.[31] In terms of the HHI, the EU approach is that a post-merger HHI of below 1,000 (e.g. ten firms each having 10 per cent of the market) would not normally be of concern. A post-merger HHI of between 1,000 and 2,000 and a delta (an increase in the HHI as a result of a merger) below 250 would also generally be allowed. However, a post-merger HHI above 2,000 would require further scrutiny if the delta is in excess of 150 (an HHI of 2,000 reflects a market with five equally sized firms). In the United States, concentration in merger cases is also measured using the HHI. A post-merger HHI of below 1,500 would result in an approval of the merger, whereas a merger resulting in an HHI above 1,500 that involves a delta of more than 100 points is said to 'often warrant scrutiny', and a merger resulting in an HHI above 2,500 with a delta of more than 200 points is presumed to be likely to lessen competition.[32]

3.2.9 The Lerner index

3.37   If you recall Figure 2.4 showing how a monopolist sets price, you can see a potential direct test of market power. Because the key economic element of market power is the ability to price above cost, a seemingly obvious measure is the extent to which prices do indeed deviate from marginal costs. For this, economists have the Lerner index, which is defined as price minus marginal cost, divided by price. This is more commonly referred to as the price–cost margin—indeed this is the margin that is of relevance to the formula for critical loss analysis explained in Chapter 2 and the one for merger simulation analysis discussed in Chapter 7. There is a well-known relationship in economic theory, known as the Lerner condition, which captures the link between the demand conditions facing a company and the extent to which it prices above marginal costs (Lerner, 1934). The less elastic the demand a company faces, the higher it will set price above its marginal costs. Specifically, the condition states that at the profit-maximizing price, the price–cost margin (Lerner index) is equal to –1 divided by the elasticity. So if the elasticity is –2 (meaning that if the firm raises its price by 10 per cent, it will lose 20 per cent of its demand), we would expect to observe margins of 50 per cent (–1 divided by –2).

3.38   As with the logic of the hypothetical monopolist, a company with market power will make a trade-off between raising price to earn higher margins on all products, and the fact that the increase in price will reduce sales. The margin it chooses is therefore related to the likelihood of customers switching (and the likelihood of its competitors responding). Where a company has some market power to earn margins and is profit-maximizing, it will not operate on the inelastic portion of its demand curve (we also saw this in Chapter 2).

3.39   In IO theory, the Lerner index is a prime indicator of market power. However, this measure may not be directly applicable to competition cases. It focuses on marginal cost as the benchmark, but there are many reasons why companies price above marginal costs even in markets that are effectively competitive. In most industries there are fixed costs that need to be recovered and therefore require a positive price–cost margin. Earlier we saw the example of monopolistically competitive markets, where margins are positive because companies have some differentiated pricing power, but where in the long run those margins

---

[31]   Council Regulation (EC) No 139/2004 of 20 January 2004 on the control of concentrations between undertakings (the EC Merger Regulation), at [32].

[32]   Department of Justice and Federal Trade Commission (2010), 'Horizontal Merger Guidelines', 19 August, p. 19.

are competed down to the level where they cover average total costs. Instead of comparing prices with marginal costs, you therefore need a longer-term perspective. In section 3.4 we discuss how profitability over a longer time period can be used as an indicator of market power. Like the Lerner index, it has the benefit of directly capturing the essence of the definition of market power: the ability to keep price above the competitive level for a sustained period of time without being undermined by consumers switching or competitors entering the market.

The Lerner condition is sometimes used to sense-check other economic evidence on elas- **3.40** ticities and consumer responsiveness to price. For example, if you observe that a company has a price–cost margin of around 67 per cent, the Lerner condition would imply that this company faces an elasticity of –1.5 (because –1/–1.5 = 0.67). If the economists produce evidence that the elasticity is much higher or much lower than this, you can ask some critical questions about how this can be reconciled with the basic Lerner condition. There are some good reasons why the condition may not hold, and the economists would need to make these explicit. One is that the Lerner condition reflects a long-run profit-maximizing equilibrium. Prices at any point in time may deviate from the optimum, because of factors such as the uncertainty surrounding demand conditions and pricing frictions. Companies may also have chosen not to price that particular product at the profit-maximizing level—for example, if they want to increase market penetration or promote a complementary product. At times, economists have used the Lerner condition in merger cases as a substitute for elasticity evidence (so as more than just a sense-check)—they look at the price–cost margin, and from this derive a direct conclusion on price-responsiveness (the higher the margin, the less elastic the demand). We believe that this may be taking the theoretical relationship a step too far.[33]

3.3 Entry and Exit Barriers

3.3.1 Definition of entry barrier

Potential competition can be as significant as current competition. Entry barriers are an **3.41** important determinant of the extent and persistence of market power. When assessing entry barriers you ask the question: What is the market failure that allows a company to sustain market power without this being undermined by new competitors? The failure could relate to the way customers purchase the product—e.g. informational problems, or transactional frictions—or to some aspect of production—for example, economies of scale or scope. What constitutes a barrier to entry, and how can we judge whether entry barriers are high or low? There is no theory or precedent that sets out the exact height of entry barriers that lead to market power. In the economics literature, two definitions of entry barriers have been most prominent. The first, by Bain (1956), states that barriers to entry are 'the advantages of established sellers in an industry over potential entrants, these advantages being reflected in the extent to which established sellers can persistently raise their prices above a competitive level without attracting new firms to enter the industry.'

---

[33] This use of the Lerner condition in merger cases (specifically in the context of critical loss analysis) has been the subject of a heated debate. See Katz and Shapiro (2003).

3.42   Bain identified three features of the market that could hinder entry: economies of scale, product differentiation, and absolute cost advantages. Economies of scale mean that costs fall as volumes rise. They represent an entry barrier if a new competitor can enter only at a smaller than optimal scale and hence would be at a cost disadvantage relative to the incumbent. Product differentiation means that incumbents may occupy market niches that are hard for entrants to challenge. Absolute cost advantages allow incumbents to sell profitably at prices below the cost of potential entrants. A narrower definition of barriers to entry was proposed by Stigler (1968): '[A] cost of producing (at some or every rate of output)…which must be borne by a firm which seeks to enter an industry but is not borne by firms already in the industry.'

3.43   This definition does not include economies of scale as a barrier to entry because an incumbent faces (or faced) the same requirement to achieve and maintain economies of scale.

3.44   In practice, competition authorities tend to consider a wide range of factors that could constitute barriers to entry, and do not necessarily make the distinction between the above two definitions. The focus is usually on any barriers that prevent entry that is 'timely, likely, and sufficient in its magnitude, character, and scope to deter or counteract the competitive effects of concern'.[34] The term 'likely' reflects the fact that entry inevitably concerns future market developments (any evidence of past instances of entry would add some weight to such forward-looking analysis). For entry to be 'significant', it must be of sufficient scope and magnitude to prevent the exercise of market power by incumbents. Whether entry can be considered 'timely' depends on the characteristics of the market in question. It also depends to some extent on the competition authority's stance on the relevant timeframe for analysing competition problems—in the same way as the interpretation of the term 'non-transitory' does when applying the hypothetical monopolist test. In its Guidance on Article 102, the European Commission states that: 'For expansion or entry to be considered timely, it must be sufficiently swift to deter or defeat the exercise of substantial market power.'[35] In its Merger Guidelines the Commission specifies that entry is 'timely' if it is achieved within two years.[36]

3.45   In this section we do not explicitly discuss exit barriers. An exit barrier, such as laws on minimum redundancy payments, can affect a company's entry decision as much as an up-front investment requirement. When entering a market, a company assesses all its risks, including the costs of failure. Likewise, a company that has made significant up-front investments to gain a market position will not abandon these investments lightly. We also do not draw an explicit distinction in this chapter between barriers to entry faced by new competitors and barriers to expansion faced by existing competitors. Both have many features in common.

3.3.2 Absolute entry barriers

3.46   Patents, supply licences, planning laws, and other types of legislation can constitute absolute barriers to entry. In the case of IP law and certain statutory functions,

---

[34] This wording is from Department of Justice and Federal Trade Commission (2010), 'Horizontal Merger Guidelines', 19 August, p. 28.

[35] European Commission (2009), 'Guidance on the Commission's Enforcement Priorities in Applying Article 82 EC Treaty to Abusive Exclusionary Conduct by Dominant Undertakings', 2009/C 45/02, February, at [19].

[36] European Commission (2004), 'Guidelines on the Assessment of Horizontal Mergers under the Council Regulation on the Control of Concentrations Between Undertakings', 2004/C 31/03, at [74].

monopolies are granted by design. Patents do not only block competitors from making the same product (as they are supposed to do), but can also hinder entry in related products. In the 2005 *AstraZeneca* abuse of dominance case, patents were considered to be a significant barrier to entry into a market for Losec, an anti-ulcer medicine.[37] The abuse related to AstraZeneca seeking to extend the patent protection for Losec's active ingredient, omeprazole, by presenting misleading evidence before patent offices in various EU countries. In the *Tetra Pak/Alfa-Laval* (1991) merger, the Commission found there to be significant entry barriers into the market for aseptic carton packaging machines, one of the reasons being that Tetra Pak owned many patents for the production of these machines.[38] In other areas of law the entry barrier may be an unintended or unfortunate by-product of some other policy objective or government activity. Competition authorities can sometimes intervene in these instances—in their advocacy role or in some countries under specific statutory powers. For example, the CC found that the local planning rules in the United Kingdom—created to meet economic and social objectives of local governments—constrained entry into local grocery retailing markets.[39] Competition authorities have also scrutinized the use of public sector information that is collected by monopoly government agencies such as the Ordnance Survey (mapping), the Met Office (weather), and Companies House (companies).[40] Such information has substantial commercial value in downstream markets, and restricting access to it constitutes a barrier to entry for private entities wishing to compete with the government agencies.

3.3.3 Strategic entry barriers

Strategic entry barriers form a broad category of advantages enjoyed by the incumbents. **3.47** These include economies of scale or scope, reputation, an established distribution network, sunk costs, informational barriers, and customer switching costs. These factors can result from the nature of the market or from a historical position of incumbency. We discuss them further below. In addition, incumbents can create strategic barriers themselves. A common commercial strategy is brand proliferation, where an incumbent puts a range of brands in the market so as to leave little space for entrants to find a niche—the equivalent of a chain of ice cream vendors occupying all the strategic locations along the beach. Incumbents can also raise strategic barriers by engaging in practices such as predatory pricing and tying—these practices could in themselves be found to be illegal, as discussed in Chapter 4.

3.3.4 Informational entry barriers

There are various types of informational barriers. One is where the entrant needs access **3.48** to certain product or technical information, such as information on the interface with an operating system for developers of new software and apps. Another is where the entrant requires access to information on customers. For example, new providers of

---

[37] *AstraZeneca* (Case COMP/A.37.507/F3), Decision of 15 June 2005.
[38] *Tetra Pak/Alfa-Laval* (Case IV/M068), Decision of 19 July 1991.
[39] Competition Commission (2008), 'The Supply of Groceries in the UK Market Investigation', 30 April, at [7.44]. In Chapter 8 we discuss the remedies imposed by the CC in this case.
[40] See, for example, Office of Fair Trading (2006), 'The Commercial Use of Public Information', December.

loan products would benefit from access to information on consumers' credit history that existing credit institutions have collected.[41] A new type of such informational entry barrier is 'big data' on customer behaviour gathered by providers of online services. This data can become an essential input into the provision of related services. Rivals of Google complain of such a data barrier to entry, as Google gathers enormous amounts of information on consumer preferences through their search behaviour. Similar issues arise in other sectors from mobile phones to cars (cars becoming like computers on wheels, continuously transmitting information about your driving behaviour and whereabouts).

3.49   A further type of informational barrier refers to the consumer side. In section 3.6 we discuss the insights from behavioural economics into informational barriers and consumer biases. Information on products may be hard to acquire, or the product may be fully understood only once it is purchased (such products are known as experience goods). These characteristics may make customers more likely to continue to purchase from their current supplier, or from one that has a well-known brand. Such informational barriers can therefore make it difficult for new entrants to grow. Transactional frictions may lead to customer inertia and other customer choice biases. These frictions can be as simple as having to learn the functions on a new smartphone or as complex or costly as digging up the front garden to lay a new cable to one's home. Too much information can be just as bad as too little. Presented with too much information, consumers may decide not to decide. For example, if three types of pension plan are offered, consumers can select the most attractive one, but they may fail to make a purchase at all if they have a choice of twenty plans. Notably, information overload makes both perception and consciously processing options difficult. Consumers tend to adopt the line of least resistance, and may procrastinate, or simply select the default or recommended option. You can see how this can also result in inertia and lack of switching in markets such as electricity supply, mobile phones, and current accounts. Inertia can make consumers conservative in their purchasing behaviour. It has become received wisdom that people are more likely to get divorced than to change their bank (though keen statisticians have refuted this claim).

3.3.5 Economies of scale and scope

3.50   Economies of scale have been explained in Chapter 1. To recap, markets with this feature exhibit unit costs that fall as output increases. This means that there are some fixed or semi-fixed components of cost. Take a law firm that is expecting to grow and therefore moves into an office building that is bigger than currently required. As the firm employs more staff, the average costs of the building per employee will fall since the costs of the building are fixed. This type of scale economy is exhausted when capacity is reached. Where this occurs at relatively low levels of output it does not constitute a major barrier (even the fanciest law firm offices tend to cost only a fraction of firms' total revenues). However, in other markets significant economies of scale mean that there is room for only a limited number of suppliers (in Chapter 1 we discussed the examples of nuclear plants and aircraft manufacturing). Economies of scale can act as a barrier to entry in two ways. First, if the entrant can operate only below the minimum efficient scale, it would have a significant cost disadvantage

---

[41]   There are often arrangements through which banks share credit data on customers, reducing the informational advantages for incumbents.

relative to the incumbent, limiting the degree to which it can compete effectively. Second, even if a potential entrant can enter at the minimum efficient scale, it may be deterred by the knowledge that its entry could lead to excess capacity and consequent price decreases in the market, making the entry unprofitable.

Economies of scope arise where it is cheaper to produce a range of products from a com-   **3.51**
mon cost base. Banking products are an example. Once a financial institution has set up its credit-scoring facility to assess the creditworthiness of potential customers, it can supply a wide range of loan products using this facility, such as overdrafts, credit cards, and personal loans. Additionally, if the bank supplies the main current account to a customer, it has access to crucial information about that customer (income, regular outgoings, location) to feed into its credit-scoring model. An entrant wishing to offer only one product line (e.g. just credit cards) would face higher per-product costs for credit-scoring, because it would be more difficult to get the relevant information on a potential customer's credit history and because it cannot spread the fixed costs over different products.

3.3.6 Sunk costs

Costs are sunk when they have been incurred and cannot be recovered on exit—that is, the   **3.52**
items invested in have no alternative value. Some sunk costs may be absolute barriers, in that it is essential to undertake that investment to enter. This might include building a reservoir to serve a factory's water demand, or the costs of meeting regulatory requirements to be granted a licence to operate in a given market. Sunk costs may also be of a strategic nature, in that an incumbent can choose how much of these costs to 'sink' and thereby affect the costs of new competitors entering the market. A classic example is advertising and brand investment. Brand values tend to be lost after exit (although successful brands can some-times be sold, so this type of investment may not always be completely sunk). In the abuse of dominance case brought against The Coca-Cola Company (TCCC), the Commission found advertising to be an important barrier:

> [T]he strong position of TCCC and its respective bottlers (due to high market shares, unique brand recognition and the must stock nature of TCCC's strongest brands and the exceptional breadth of the [carbonated soft drinks] portfolio) is protected from competition by barriers to entry in the form of sunk advertising costs preventing any significant market entry.[42]

Thus, new entrants must spend significant sums on advertising to get a rival cola brand   **3.53**
established alongside Coke and Pepsi, knowing that this investment is not recoverable if the brand fails (remember RC Cola, Virgin Cola, and Classic Cola?). Another example of sunk costs acting as an entry barrier is in the pharmaceuticals industry. Even after a patent has expired, generic drug producers sometimes have to spend substantial amounts on advertising and marketing in order to establish themselves in a marketplace as effective competitors to the incumbent, which may have a strong reputation built in the years of monopoly supply while still under patent.

3.3.7 Contestable markets

Sunk costs are an important determinant of whether markets are contestable. As dis-   **3.54**
cussed earlier, high market shares do not necessarily equate to market power. A contestable

---

[42] *Coca-Cola* (Case COMP/A.39.116/B2), Decision of 22 June 2005, at [25].

market is one where even an apparent monopolist has little market power, because sunk costs do not exist and barriers are so low that the threat of entry is sufficient to constrain the incumbent.

3.55 The intuition behind contestable markets is simple: the threat of competition may be sufficient to drive prices to the competitive level. Since Baumol (1982) first presented the theory of contestability it has attracted considerable debate in terms of both its theoretical rigour and its applicability. Contestability requires there to be no sunk costs, as otherwise the potential loss from writing off the sunk costs on exit would have to be weighed against the profits derived from entry, and would act as a significant deterrent. The absence of barriers to entry and exit allows for 'hit-and-run' entry—any profit opportunity that arises because an incumbent raises its price above costs, no matter how short-lived, can be fully and costlessly exploited by a new entrant. It is also necessary that there is some period of time in between a new entrant arriving and a response by the incumbent to reduce its price back to the competitive level. It is during this time that the entrant makes the profit that gives it the incentive to enter. Once the incumbent lowers its prices, profits are reduced to the normal level and the entrant costlessly leaves the market with its accumulated profits.

3.56 The initial proponents of the theory suggested that its clearest application was in airline markets, where aircraft could be transferred from one route to another at negligible extra costs. Indeed, the theory was used to justify several high-profile horizontal mergers in the US airline sector in the early 1980s. However, some of the evidence gathered since then shows that fares in fact rose sharply post-merger on routes where market shares were high, and suggests that the sunk costs required in setting up ground support for a new route were overlooked (Shepherd, 1988). Competition cases in the airline industry now tend not to treat airline markets as contestable.

3.57 Perhaps a clearer example is the provision of local bus services, as also discussed in Chapter 2 under supply-side substitution. If an operator has a bus depot nearby, adding services to an existing route or opening new routes can be done swiftly. Any investment in additional buses is not sunk since there is often a reasonably liquid market for second-hand buses should the operator decide to exit the route, or a multi-route operator can shift unwanted capacity elsewhere. Even entry on a small scale can have a strong competitive impact on a particular bus route—for example, if the entrant runs its service only on the busiest part of a route or during the busiest times of the day.

3.58 An example of where contestability was relied upon to clear a merger is the acquisition by CHC Helicopter Corporation (CHC) of Helicopter Services Group ASA (HSG) in 2000.[43] Even though this deal created a duopoly in the market for the supply of helicopter services to oil and gas installations on the UK continental shelf, the CC found that this did not have a detrimental effect since the helicopter services market remained contestable. Entrants did not suffer any cost disadvantage compared with the incumbents, regulatory barriers were low, and there were no issues around the availability of airport or heliport capacity. Helicopter firms operating in other geographic markets were thus considered to

---

[43] Competition Commission (2000), 'CHC Helicopter Corporation and Helicopter Services Group ASA', January.

be potential hit-and-run entrants. The CC also found that the long-term price contracts that incumbents were tied into meant that they could not adjust their prices rapidly in response to any hit-and-run entry. Interestingly, this case was reviewed five years later as part of an ex post evaluation of merger decisions (Office of Fair Trading, 2005). This review indicated that the original clearance may have been over-optimistic in its assessment of the low barriers to entry. Post-merger prices did rise and customers found the quality of service to be lower. One new entrant did emerge, but one large customer incurred significant costs to facilitate this (a form of sponsored entry). With this entrant active in the market, prices fell and quality of service rose again. If the market were truly contestable, this actual entry would not have been required as the mere threat of entry would have kept prices low. In all, while the conditions for a finding of a fully contestable market may be rare, caution should be exercised in assuming that high market shares imply market power. Where barriers to entry are low, the threat of entry can be a strong constraint on incumbents.

3.3.8 Network effects as an entry barrier

Network effects are akin to economies of scale, but driven by the demand characteristics of a product rather than the supply side. A network effect arises where the benefit that one user receives from a network depends on how many other users that network has. Economists call this a positive demand-side externality—positive because users enhance each other's demand; externality because each user does not take into account that positive effect on others when making an individual decision on whether to join the network.

3.59

Network effects can sometimes be exhausted at modest levels of demand. Take the example of a restaurant. Your demand for a restaurant can be positively influenced by the number of people already eating there. First, it is an information signal about the quality of the place, and second, the atmosphere is better. However, such network effects do not lead to significant market power. The positive benefits you receive from the presence of others quickly turn to negative if the restaurant is too crowded. There is a natural limit to the capacity of the restaurant, which is normally well below the total demand for restaurant services in a given area. There is plenty of room in the market for other restaurants.

3.60

Now let's take the example of social networking sites. The benefit of being a member of such a site depends on how many others there are—the more members, the greater the benefits as you can link up with more friends (new and old). Social networking sites took off in the middle of the last decade. MySpace was the early market leader, reaching 76 million users in 2008. However, that same year Facebook overtook MySpace as the usage of social networking sites kept rising. In 2013 Facebook had more than 1.2 billion users, which is a significant proportion of the world's internet users (71 per cent of internet users use Facebook at least once a month). Meanwhile, MySpace is down to a paltry 36 million users. Facebook's critical mass of users is a serious barrier to entry and expansion for other sites wishing to offer a similar service. Instead, sites such as LinkedIn (300 million users), Twitter (255 million active users), and Pinterest (70 million users) have managed to grow because they have differentiated themselves from Facebook rather than compete head-to-head, providing a different type of social networking service (MySpace's offering has also changed substantially from the early days).[44]

3.61

---

[44] These statistics are from various online sources (www.pewinternet.org, *Digital Marketing Ramblings*, and *Facebook Newsroom*) which we have not been able to verify, but even if they are approximations the picture is clear.

3.62 Markets with industry standards can also exhibit significant network effects resulting in barriers to entry. Microsoft Windows is the classic example. Its success in the market for PC operating systems has effectively made it into the global standard: PC users found they could communicate with most other users through Windows-compatible software, and software developers were attracted to the Windows standard as that was what most users had on their PC. As the European Commission stated in its 2004 investigation: 'Microsoft's dominance presents extraordinary features in that Windows (in its successive forms) is not only a dominant product on the relevant market for client PC operating systems, but it is the *de facto* standard operating system product for client PCs.'[45]

3.3.9 Do network effects mean the end of all competition?

3.63 The answer to this question is 'not necessarily'. Network effects may be exhausted well below the total market size—as in the restaurant example above. But even where networks extend almost globally—as in PC operating systems and social networking sites—entry may still occur. Microsoft Windows never achieved a 100 per cent share of all PCs in the world, as other operating systems, such as Apple Mac OS and Linux, have continued to exist alongside it, mainly because they have to some extent differentiated themselves (as have LinkedIn and Twitter in the social networking market). In other markets, several platforms can coexist—and compete—despite the presence of network effects. Smartphones, in sharp contrast with PCs, currently see a fierce battle for supremacy between a number of different operating systems (often referred to as 'ecosystems', more a business than an economics term)—Apple iOS, Android, Blackberry 10, and Windows Phone 8—and it is not clear who will win or even whether there will be only one winner.

3.64 Competition can also still work if networks interconnect or standards are made interoperable. In this way, different producers can compete with each other within the confines of that common network or standard. Manufacturers of Blu-ray disc players can compete with each other as Blu-ray has become the accepted new industry standard for high-definition video, so all discs operate on this standard (as is often the case in these dynamic markets, these manufacturers now face the threat of online distribution of films). Sometimes interoperability or interconnection can be achieved through commercial negotiation (see also Chapter 5), and sometimes it requires government intervention. The main point here is that interoperability, however achieved, means that competing companies can benefit from the same network effects. Significant parts of the IT sector are now based on 'open source', which means that access to the source code and other proprietary information is open to others, who can further modify and develop the software or hardware. Prominent examples include the Linux operating system, the Apache web server, and the Mozilla Firefox internet browser. Thus, the presence of network effects does not always result in insurmountable entry barriers.

3.3.10 Two-sided markets with network effects

3.65 Two-sided network effects are a specific form of network effect (we explained this concept in Chapter 2), arising where platforms bring together two different types of user in some form

---

[45] *Microsoft* (Case COMP/C-3/37.792), Decision of 24 March 2004, at [472].

of common pursuit. Examples are dating agencies and nightclubs bringing together men and women, payment systems bringing together retailers and customers, and newspapers bringing together advertisers and readers. As with other networks there is a chicken-and-egg problem for new entrants as they need to achieve critical mass, but here the challenge is that both types of customer must be attracted.

Entry barriers of this type were found in printed classified directory advertising, which requires businesses to advertise and end-users to look for services. Yell long had the largest classified directory in the United Kingdom (its name derived from the 'yellow pages'). It had been subject to price regulation, and in 2006 the CC concluded that this price regulation needed to continue, despite the growing importance of the internet. Within classified directory advertising, Yell was found to have a market share of 75 per cent and to benefit from strong barriers to entry and expansion arising from two-sided network effects: **3.66**

> [T]he incumbency position of the largest player is reinforced by the network effects present in this market. Other providers wishing to expand have to build usage in order to attract advertisers. This requires investment, particularly in usage advertising, and acts as a barrier to expansion.[46]

A few years later, the Dutch competition authority approved a merger between the only two providers of paper-based classified directories in the Netherlands because the provision of such advertising services over the internet was considered a close substitute.[47] In 2013 the UK authorities also decided that regulation of Yell (which had changed its name to Hibu) was no longer needed, as the company's directory business had declined by more than 60 per cent since 2006 and the internet had overtaken the printed directory as the main platform for classified advertising. Indeed, the CC considered it to be likely that 'this network effect may now be operating in reverse for Yellow Pages as both consumers and advertisers move to the Internet, each making Yellow Pages less attractive to the other group'.[48] **3.67**

3.4 Profitability as a Measure of Market Power

3.4.1 Profitability captures the essence of market power

The most direct means of measuring market power is to look at the gap between prices and costs. After all, the essence of market power is the ability to charge high prices and earn high profits for a sustained period of time without being undermined by customers or competitors. In perfect competition, prices equal marginal cost. In the real world there are fixed costs which must be recovered through mark-ups over and above marginal cost. In addition, prices and costs may fluctuate over time. So rather than a price–cost comparison at a particular point in time you measure profitability over a longer period. In competitive markets, companies are expected to make profits in the long run that are broadly in line with the minimum return required by investors—called the cost of capital. Profits above **3.68**

---

[46] Competition Commission (2006), 'Classified Directory Advertising Services Market Investigation', 21 December, at [54(a)]. We advised Yell during this inquiry.

[47] Nederlandse Mededingingsautoriteit (2008), 'European Directories—Truvo Nederland', Zaaknr. 6246, 28 August.

[48] Competition Commission (2013), 'Review of Undertakings Given by Hibu Plc (formerly Yell Group Plc) in Relation to its Yellow Pages Printed Classified Directory Advertising Services Business', 15 March, at [1.12].

the cost of capital would invite entry by new competitors, and profits below would induce exit. Hence returns that are persistently and significantly above the competitive level reflect the essence of market power. It tells you that there is a profitable opportunity that is not being exploited by new entrants, and hence that entry barriers are significant.

3.69 Profitability analysis can usefully supplement other indicators of market power. For the best part of two decades BSkyB has had a market share of more than 70 per cent in the premium sports and film pay-TV markets in the United Kingdom. Does that by itself indicate market power? Or has BSkyB achieved its success in the face of strong competition, demand uncertainty, and technological change? We show in this section how profitability analysis has shed light on this question in the pay-TV market investigations in the United Kingdom.[49] Profitability analysis can also shed light on the degree of competition in a market where other indicators are not clear-cut. For example, in oligopolistic markets you may see competitors following each other's prices—but does this reflect fierce competition (in perfect competition suppliers also set the same price) or some form of tacit collusion or price leadership? Profitability analysis can help tell the difference between the two (see Morris, 2003). Likewise, several market investigations in the United Kingdom have been triggered in part by concerns (and public outrage) that profits are very high and hence competition is not working effectively—most recently the energy supply market where the regulator, Ofgem, found that: 'Profit increases and recent price rises have intensified public distrust of suppliers and highlight the need for a market investigation to clear the air.'[50]

3.4.2 Who uses profitability analysis?

3.70 Profitability analysis has been used in competition cases in the United Kingdom for decades. The CMA's market investigation guidelines consider there to be prima facie evidence of significant entry barriers where profitability is persistently and substantially above the competitive benchmark for a company that constitutes a significant proportion of the market.[51] The use of profitability analysis for market power by other competition authorities has been more limited. We saw in Chapter 2 that the US Supreme Court referred to Du Pont's profits as an indicator of its monopoly power in the cellophane case of 1956, but the use of profitability analysis has not been fashionable in the United States since.[52] The European Commission conducted a profitability analysis as part of its review of the extent of competition in the payment cards and retail banking industries in the European Union.[53] The Dutch competition authority has measured profitability in a number of cases, but this was to show an abuse of dominance, not as an indicator of market power (see Chapter 4, where we will also explain that there is an important difference between these two uses of profitability analysis).

---

[49] Ofcom (2010), 'Pay TV statement', 31 March; and Competition Commission (2011), 'Movies on Pay TV Market Investigation—Provisional Findings Report', 19 August.

[50] Ofgem (2014), 'Ofgem proposes a reference to the CMA to investigate the energy market', press release, 27 March.

[51] Competition and Markets Authority (2013), 'Guidelines for Market Investigations: Their Role, Procedures, Assessment and Remedies', April, at [119].

[52] *US v EI du Pont de Nemours & Co* 351 US 377 (1956).

[53] European Commission (2006), 'Interim Report I: Payment Cards', 12 April and 'Interim Report II: Current Accounts and Related Services', 17 July.

The techniques of profitability analysis are used not just, or even mainly, in competition **3.71** investigations. They are employed around the world on a daily basis by companies, investors, financial analysts, and credit rating agencies for a myriad of business and investment purposes. Financial information is abundant—in company accounts, financial statements, stock market announcements, analyst reports, financial media—so why not use it in competition cases as well? Profitability analysis can be of relevance to a wide range of competition law issues. We present it here as part of the economics toolkit for assessing market power. Other aspects of competition investigations where profitability may play a role include the assessment of predation, margin squeeze, and excessive pricing (see Chapter 4); failing-firm analysis in a merger context (Chapter 7); ability to pay fines (Chapter 8); and the quantification of damages (Chapter 9).

3.4.3 Measures of economic profitability: NPV and IRR

The conceptually correct measures of economic profitability are net present value (NPV) **3.72** and the internal rate of return (IRR).[54] These reflect the way in which companies make investment decisions: an initial cash outflow (investment) is assessed against the net cash inflows from that investment in subsequent periods, taking account of the time value of money (€1 today is worth more than €1 tomorrow). NPV and IRR are the standard theoretical methods of investment appraisal.[55] They are also the most commonly used profitability measures in the business world. The NPV of a stream of earnings into the future tells you how much those earnings are worth today. The value will differ depending on how risky those earnings are and how patient the investor is. Risk and patience are reflected in the discount rate used to calculate the NPV (the NPV approach is also often referred to as the discounted cash flow, DCF, method). As the CC noted in its market investigation into store cards:

> Financial theory underlying investment decision making, valuation and related matters focuses on the amounts and timing of the cash flows of the activity and leads to the conclusion that the most satisfactory basis for assessing rate of return is a calculation of the IRR on a DCF basis.[56]

Take a simple example where, in exchange for an initial investment, you are promised a **3.73** stream of earnings for five years of €100 per year, with each payment to arrive at the end of the year. Your discount rate is assumed to be 10 per cent—another way of saying this is that your next-best alternative for the money would generate a 10 per cent return per year. The time value of money means that today an amount of €100 is worth that to you, but your first payment of €100 at the end of the year is worth only €90.91 today (€100 discounted by 10 per cent). The fifth and last payment of €100 you receive is worth only €62.09 in today's money.[57] The NPV of the promised income over five years is €379.08. This means that you would be prepared to invest at most €379.08 today to receive the five annual payments of €100 as a reward for the investment. Any higher investment (or lower returns) and you

---

[54] See, for example, Kay (1976), Edwards et al. (1987), Morris (2003), and Oxera (2003).
[55] A leading corporate finance textbook is Brealey et al. (2011).
[56] Competition Commission (2006), 'Store Cards Market Investigation', 7 March, Appendix 8.4, at [14].
[57] Investing €62.09 today and earning five years of 10 per cent return on it again gives you €100 at the end of year 5. This return is compound, which means you reinvest it each year and earn 10 per cent on the return as well as on the original investment (just like in a savings account where you earn compound interest, i.e. interest on interest).

wouldn't make the 10 per cent return that you could earn with the next-best alternative—10 per cent is your opportunity cost of capital.

3.74 The IRR is related to the NPV. It represents the discount rate that makes the NPV equal to zero. Take a retail chain that is considering investing in an own-brand ready-meal product. There will be a period of initial investment while the product is being developed and marketed, followed by a series of net cash inflows in subsequent periods when it is on sale. In the above example, an investment of €379.08 followed by five years of net cash inflows of €100 would result in an IRR of 10 per cent. The retail chain would choose to undertake this investment if the IRR is greater than its cost of capital or hurdle rate for new projects. The cost of capital reflects the minimum return required by investors in the company's activities.

3.75 This investment appraisal principle can be applied to the notion of competitive markets. Free entry and exit should eventually lead to a market outcome in which suppliers make returns equal to the cost of capital. In the case of the retail chain above, if the NPV of the investment in the ready-meal product is positive—or, what amounts to the same thing, the IRR is greater than the cost of capital—it would be profitable to enter this market. In a competitive market other suppliers would make the same decision. With each additional entrant the market returns fall because of increased price competition, until the point at which the IRR equals the cost of capital (or the NPV equals zero). By contrast, an IRR persistently and substantially above the competitive benchmark would indicate the existence of entry barriers and hence market power.

3.4.4 Truncating the period of analysis

3.76 In competition cases there is usually a need to measure the IRR over a specific period during the lifespan of an economic activity, rather than over the entire period of a project or business activity. You won't have data for the entire lifetime of the company (e.g. if the retail chain was established in the distant past, and shows no signs of exiting the market in the near future). More importantly, in a competition case you are normally interested in current market power, so you want to assess profitability for only a limited number of past and future years (yet long enough to take account of year-on-year fluctuations in profit that are unrelated to market power). In practice, therefore, a 'truncated' IRR can be calculated, which is like the IRR explained above but covering only part of the full lifetime of the activity or business. The initial asset value of the business is treated as a cash outflow (as if buying the business were the initial investment), and the residual value at the end of the period is treated as an inflow (as if the business were sold off at the end). So you assess the company's assets at two points in time, and then calculate the returns within that time period. The analysis thus captures the net operating income during the period, and any changes in the company's asset base between the start and end of the period (like a house price increase, an increase in the value of the asset over the period can be seen as a profit, and a decrease as a loss).

3.77 The truncated IRR and NPV are not straightforward to measure. The key information required includes cash flow data for the activity in question over a reasonable length of time, and estimates of the value of assets employed in that activity at the start and end of the period. Cash flow data is normally available from a company's audited accounts. It might be more difficult to obtain if the competition concern relates to a particular line of business

Table 3.2 Truncated IRR and NPV

	Year 0	Year 1	Year 2	Year 3	Year 4	Year 5
Cash flow	−800	100	100	100	100	100 + 1,100
Present value at 10%	−800	90.91	82.64	75.13	68.30	62.09 + 683.01
NPV at 10%	262.09					
IRR	17.8%					

that is not separately reported in accounts, in which case cost and revenue allocation is required; you usually need access to internal management accounts for this. Valuing assets may be complicated if, for example, the business employs a lot of intangible assets. These problems can often, but not always, be resolved.

Say ten years down the line our successful retail chain is accused of abusing a dominant **3.78** position in the market for ready-meal products. It has developed a strong brand and retained a 60 per cent market share for several years, with rivals struggling to gain ground. But has it been able to sustain profits above the competitive level? Table 3.2 shows the profitability of the ready-meal business division in the form of the truncated IRR over the last five years. For the sake of this example, five years is a sufficiently long period to obtain insight into potential market power, as demand and supply conditions for ready-meal products have been relatively stable. The business division's value at the start of the five years ('year 0') is the opening asset value and can be interpreted as the initial investment in this activity for the IRR calculation. It is estimated at 800. In each of the five years ready-meals have generated operating profits of 100, which are cash inflows. In the last year you also count the closing asset value as a cash inflow. This is estimated at 1,100—so the value of the business division has grown over the five years, perhaps reflecting the fact that additional capital investments were made during the period (so the cash flows in years 1 to 5 are net of this investment). As in the earlier example, the cash flow of 100 at the end of year 1 has a present value of 90.91 at the 10 per cent cost of capital. The present value of the cash flow of 100 in year 5 is 62.09, and that of the closing asset value of 1,100 is 683.01. The sum of all the discounted cash flows minus the initial investment equals 262.09, so over the period the activity has had a positive NPV at a 10 per cent cost of capital. The truncated IRR is 17.8 per cent—if you discount all cash flows from year 1 to 5 at 17.8 per cent you get an NPV of zero. This IRR is well above the cost of capital of 10 per cent, indicating that the retail chain's ready-meal division has been highly profitable over the five-year period. This is consistent with it having market power.

3.4.5 Accounting versus economic measures of profitability

The IRR and NPV are economic measures of profitability. It requires some careful effort **3.79** to derive these measures from company accounts. In any set of company accounts you will find a figure in the profit and loss account for the profit (earnings) before interest and tax—EBIT. In the balance sheet figures you can observe the capital employed, which is usually taken as fixed assets less net liabilities. Divide the EBIT for the year by average capital employed over that year and you get the return on capital employed (ROCE). A variant is the return on equity (ROE), where instead of EBIT you take earnings after interest and tax (removing the earnings that go to creditors and the taxman leaves you with the earnings for the equity holders) and divide this by the equity-funded part of the capital employed. The ROCE or ROE calculations produce percentage figures that represent the annual return achieved as a proportion of the capital employed. In order to determine whether these returns are reasonable, these percentages can be benchmarked against the cost of capital of the company in question. For the ROCE the relevant cost of capital is a mix of cost of equity and cost of debt, for ROE it is the cost of equity—we explain this further below.

3.80 However, the ROCE may not be particularly informative about the underlying economic profitability of a business. The annual ROCE measures are likely to differ from the IRR. The reason is that the numerator and the denominator in the calculation of ROCE are sensitive to the selected accounting methods—the same activity with one particular IRR or NPV can show many different values for the ROCE. The EBIT figure in the ROCE numerator can be affected by accounting choices made with respect to accruals—these are costs incurred (or revenues earned) in one period but paid for (or received) in cash in another period. Accruals can cause a significant wedge between the actual cash flows in a period and the profits assigned to that period. The denominator in the ROCE estimate is highly sensitive to depreciation schedules. In the IRR calculation the initial investment or opening asset value is counted as a cash outflow in the first period. In contrast, in the ROCE calculation the asset base is the denominator which is depreciated year on year over the life of the investment. This means that the asset base decreases every year, and hence the ROCE increases, even when annual profits are the same. In addition, there are many different depreciation methods that one can apply (e.g. the straight-line, sum-of-the-years'-digits, and declining-balance methods), each leading to different ROCE outcomes. As noted by the CC in its inquiry into train leasing:

> [B]ecause [the train lessors] operate asset-intensive businesses, accounting returns are very sensitive to the accounting depreciation applied to those assets, which may not reflect their economic value. We also noted that as an asset ages, its NBV [net book value] declines and where the rental remains constant this will lead to an increase in ROCE, which may not accurately reflect the economic profitability of the asset.[58]

3.4.6 Margins and return on sales

3.81 In industries with relatively few fixed assets (such as professional services and the retail parts of the gas and electricity supply chains), it may useful to consider return on sales (ROS), gross margins, or operating margins as measures of profitability. These are all ratios with sales value in the denominator, rather than a measure of capital employed. The ROS represents EBIT divided by sales. The numerator for the gross margins is gross profit (sales minus the direct cost of goods sold), while for operating margins it is the operating profit (sales minus direct and indirect operating costs). Different companies may account differently for direct and indirect costs, so comparisons of margins across companies must be made with care. Data on margins and ROS is often easier to obtain than for IRR and ROCE, particularly where it is difficult to estimate the capital employed, or for companies that have relatively limited capital employed (such as law firms, and train operators which lease rather than own their assets). However, margins in themselves do not give much useful

---

[58] Competition Commission (2009), 'Rolling Stock Leasing Market Investigation', 7 April, Appendix 6.4, at [2]. We advised one of the parties in this inquiry.

information for the purpose of assessing market power since they do not take into account the capital and risk that is involved in the activity.

In its inquiry into retail banking, the European Commission looked at annual revenue and cost data over the period 2000–04 for the payment card activities of 203 issuing and acquiring banks across the Member States.[59] Issuing banks issue cards to cardholders; acquiring banks deal with the merchants that accept the cards for payment. The profitability measure used was the cost mark-up (revenue minus costs, divided by costs), which is closely related to profit margins (revenue minus costs, divided by revenues). The analysis led the Commission to conclude that profitability in the issuing of payment cards was high and sustained over time, suggesting a lack of competition. However, the variation in estimated cost mark-ups for card issuers was very large—from negative to 132 per cent—raising questions about comparability.[60] Also, since capital costs are excluded from the cost mark-up, it is difficult to compare results across different banking activities. Capital costs would be likely to be higher in issuing than on the acquiring side, as a result of banks' need to make provision against default by cardholders. Profitability assessments based on margins, mark-ups, or ROS should be interpreted with care.

3.82

In its inquiry into statutory audit services, the CC considered various profitability measures for the Big Four audit firms—PwC, KPMG, EY, and Deloitte—including ROS and profit per partner.[61] This helped the CC find that within the Big Four firms the margins for audit and non-audit services are broadly similar (as are the risks), such that it could not be said that there was cross-subsidy between these services. However, in relation to market power the CC eventually considered that it was too difficult to draw any conclusions from the profitability analysis, in part because of the challenge of finding meaningful benchmarks: 'Dividing any remaining return by sales to give a percentage metric is only helpful if there is a benchmark against which to compare it.'[62] Possible benchmarks that were considered, but rejected as too different, included the profit per partner in law firms, and the remuneration of financial directors and CFOs of large listed companies.

3.83

3.4.7 Asset valuation

Profits reflect the returns that companies gain from investing in productive assets, such as buildings, machinery, and brands. The most readily available estimates of asset values are in the audited accounts. Here you find figures based on depreciated historical costs—the amount originally spent on the asset, adjusted for age through a specific depreciation schedule. Another available estimate for listed companies is the market capitalization—the share price multiplied by the total number of shares outstanding. Unfortunately neither book value nor market value forms the right basis for valuing assets when trying to assess the state of competition in a market. The book value may not reflect the current economic value of the assets (what would it cost to replace these assets today?) and may exclude relevant intangible assets (see below). The market value, on the other hand, reflects investors' expectations

3.84

---

[59] European Commission (2007), 'Communication From the Commission: Sector Inquiry Under Article 17 of Regulation 1/2003 on Retail Banking', COM (2007) 33 final, 31 January. We advised one of the banks in this inquiry.

[60] European Commission (2007), 'Commission Staff Working Document Accompanying the Communication from the Commission', SEC (2007) 16, 31 January, p. 126.

[61] Competition Commission (2013), 'Statutory Audit Services for Large Companies—Market Investigation', final report, 15 October. We advised third parties in this inquiry.

[62] Ibid., Appendix 7.3, at [106].

of future returns, and may therefore encapsulate future monopoly profits. If you include these monopoly profits in the initial asset base this will result in a lower IRR and ROCE and thus systematically underestimate the company's market power.

3.85 In the context of economic profitability analysis, the value-to-the-owner principle, as defined by Edwards et al. (1987), provides the correct basis for asset valuation. This principle requires an asset to be valued at the minimum loss that a firm would incur were it deprived of the use of that asset. The basis for this rule is that economic profitability relates to the cost of entry into a market and, therefore, it is appropriate to value assets according to the lowest cost of entry. If profitability is still persistently and substantially above the cost of capital when measured on this basis, this is indicative of limitations in the competitive process, as otherwise there would have been new entry to compete away the excess returns. The value-to-the-owner principle therefore forms the basis for the opening and closing asset values that you need for the truncated IRR calculation. You can also use it to adjust the ROCE calculations (where asset values are in the denominator). This will generally improve the usefulness of the ROCE compared with accounting values of assets, and may bring the ROCE estimates more in line with the IRR.

3.86 The value-to-the-owner principle usually prescribes the modern equivalent asset (MEA) value as the correct metric for the asset base. The MEA is defined as the lowest cost of purchasing assets today that can deliver the same set of goods as the existing assets. This is also sometimes referred to as the depreciated replacement cost value. MEA valuation answers a straightforward question: if the same output were to be produced by a modern asset using the best available technology, what is the cost of providing that asset? Effectively, this approach allows technical efficiency to be built into the valuation, taking into account the fact that a new entrant would make use of the latest technology. The historical cost of an asset, as reported in the accounts, may bear little resemblance to the MEA value of that asset, especially in industries with rapid technological development such as telecoms.

3.4.8 Valuing intangible assets

3.87 Intangible assets such as brand value and human capital are typically not included in the balance sheet of companies—accounting rules tend to be cautious. Yet from an economic perspective they are productive assets that the company has invested in. Failing to account for such intangible assets could overstate profitability and result in incorrect conclusions on market power. According to the value-to-the-owner principle, a company's intangible assets should be valued as capitalized costs—what did the company actually spend on the brand, rather than what the brand would be worth if sold in the market. In order for costs to be capitalized (i.e. treated as capital expenditure to create an asset rather than ongoing operating costs), they need to involve an upfront commitment of capital with some risk of it not being recovered. There are three criteria for recognizing intangible assets used by the CMA (and its predecessor, the CC), as first established in the inquiry into banking services to small- and medium-sized enterprises (SMEs): the cost must be incurred now, but primarily to obtain earnings in the future; the cost must be additional to those necessarily incurred in running the business; and it must be identifiable as creating an asset separate from any that arises from the general running of the business.[63]

---

[63] Competition Commission (2002), 'The Supply of Banking Services by Clearing Banks to Small and Medium-sized Enterprises', 14 March.

Applying these criteria in the home credit inquiry, the CC identified four possible categories **3.88** of intangible assets: an experienced and trained workforce; the customer base; knowledge of customers' creditworthiness; and IT systems.[64] So, for example, the costs of training the workforce are treated as an investment and added to the asset base (at the same time, these costs must be removed from the operating profit and loss calculation for the particular year to avoid double counting). The CC rejected the inclusion of corporate reputation (or brand) and start-up losses as intangible assets. It used the concept of deprival value, which is in line with the principle of the value to the owner. It valued each of these intangible assets by identifying what parts of the operating costs in these areas should be capitalized, and then depreciating them over the estimated economic lifetime of the asset. In home credit the lifetime of the intangible assets was taken as three years—so the assumption was that any investment in, for example, training the workforce generates productive assets for three years. In the end, the CC found that, even in scenarios with high estimates of intangible asset values, the profitability of the larger home credit providers was significantly above the cost of capital.

3.4.9 Cost allocation issues

For a company that produces only one line of products it is straightforward to identify the **3.89** relevant costs: all costs incurred are directly attributable to the product in question (hence they are called direct costs). Yet most companies make more than one product or provide more than one service, often using shared production facilities and overheads. The costs of these shared facilities are called indirect costs, and may have to be allocated if you are interested in the profitability of individual products or services. There are two distinct types of indirect cost: joint and common. Joint costs are incurred when the production of one good simultaneously involves the production of another. Examples are the slaughter of a sheep which produces both a sheepskin and mutton, and the processing of crude oil which results in derivatives such as fuel oil, petrol, and various petrochemicals. Common costs arise when two or more goods are produced together, but could in principle also be produced separately (e.g. a law firm with a corporate and a litigation practice).

Economic theory has it that there is no single correct way of allocating indirect costs. All **3.90** results of cost allocation exercises should therefore be treated with some caution. Yet in practice there are some reasonably coherent principles of cost allocation you could follow. The allocation could be based on three types of cost drivers. The first is input-based drivers, where indirect costs are apportioned based on known inputs. An example is allocation according to a single cost driver such as labour input or floor space used. If the corporate department of a law firm occupies four floors and the litigation department two, you might allocate twice as much of the office and overhead costs to the former. Another example is to use so-called equi-proportionate mark-ups across all products based on the direct costs of each product. If €500,000 of overhead costs had to be allocated across the two practices in the law firm, and one practice had €400,000 of direct costs (paralegals and associates) and the other €600,000, 40 per cent of the overhead (€200,000) would be allocated to the first practice and 60 per cent (€300,000) to the second. This approach thus attributes indirect costs in proportion to the underlying direct costs of each product. A more sophisticated allocation method is activity-based costing (ABC). It allocates overhead costs to individual

---

[64] Competition Commission (2006), 'Home Credit Market Investigation', 30 November.

products in stages; first to the underlying activities that give rise to the overheads, and then to the products for which those activities are undertaken.[65]

3.91 The second type of cost-driver is output-based—that is, proportionate to production or sales volumes. The third type is value-based, such as prices and revenues. If the litigation department achieves double the fees of the corporate department, you allocate twice as much of the overhead costs to it. For competition law purposes, value-based cost drivers should be used with caution, as a circularity problem may arise. If revenue is used as an allocator for costs, market power may be overlooked, since higher prices lead to higher levels of cost allocated to that line of business and, consequently, lower estimates of profitability. Equally, in a predation case, lower prices lead to lower levels of cost allocated to the product in question, potentially distorting the comparison of prices and costs.

3.4.10 What is the competitive benchmark?

3.92 In its investigation into the classified directory advertising services market the CC noted that:

> Effective competition should put pressure on the profit levels of these companies so that they move towards their cost of capital in the medium to long run. In comparing profits to the weighted average cost of capital (WACC) we applied two profitability measures; return on capital employed (ROCE) and internal rate of return (IRR).[66]

3.93 As noted earlier, in competitive markets, characterized by free entry and exit, companies are expected to make profits in the long run that are in line with the minimum returns required by investors. The final step in the profitability analysis is therefore to compare the estimated IRR (or a series of annual ROCE estimates) with the cost of capital. The cost of capital is, as the name suggests, an estimate of the price the company must pay to raise the capital that it has employed. Profits above the cost of capital should encourage entry by new competitors, and profits below it should induce exit. Hence, returns that are persistently and significantly above the cost of capital are an indication of barriers to entry.

3.94 The cost of capital is typically expressed as the weighted average cost of capital (WACC)—that is, a weighted average of the cost of equity and the cost of debt, as companies are usually funded through a mix of equity and debt. The WACC is most commonly calculated using the capital asset pricing model (CAPM). The cost of debt can be taken from observed yields on traded debt. The cost of equity is more complex. At the heart of the CAPM is an average measure of the returns achieved by holders of equity over a relatively long period of time, compared with the alternative investment in a risk-free bond—usually taken as government bonds in the jurisdiction concerned. This calculation produces a return for the stock market as a whole, and is a proxy for the return on investment that is normal in a competitive market. To make a comparison with an individual company, a correction factor is needed to compensate investors for any difference in the risk profile between the stock market as a whole and the company in question. This relative risk coefficient is known as the beta. The higher the beta, the higher the cost of capital, as investors require a greater return for the higher risk of that company relative to the overall stock market. Utilities tend

---

[65] A leading textbook on ABC is Kaplan and Anderson (2007).
[66] Competition Commission (2006), 'Classified Directory Advertising Services Market Investigation', 21 December.

to have a beta lower than 1 as income streams are relatively stable and fluctuate less than in the overall stock market. On the other hand, companies in sectors such as shipbuilding and homebuilding tend to have betas in excess of 1 as they are particularly sensitive to fluctuations in the economy.

In the CC's inquiry into the supply of banking services to SMEs, the ROE was considered **3.95** the appropriate measure of profitability due to the nature of the industry (the total capital on banks' balance sheets includes deposits from account holders, which is not relevant investment capital for the purpose of profitability analysis). The cost of equity rather than the WACC was used as the benchmark to ensure a like-for-like comparison with the ROE. A profitability gap of 9–12 percentage points over the years 1998 to 2000 between the ROE and cost of equity of the four largest banks in SME lending activity was considered to indicate a lack of competition in the market.[67] A further example is the home credit market investigation in which the CC concluded that a 5–13 percentage point profitability gap between the ROCE and the cost of capital of the main providers indicated that prices were higher than they would be in a competitive market.[68]

Over relatively short time periods, profits may diverge from the cost of capital for a variety **3.96** of reasons, not all of which are related to market power—for example, economic cycles, windfall gains, or temporary success in innovative markets. Therefore, in addition to the cost of capital, the returns made by appropriate comparator companies which operate in a competitive environment can also be considered as benchmarks for the profitability assessment. If the profits of the company under investigation are in line with those of comparators there may not be a competition problem, even if profits are above the cost of capital. Comparators should be selected so that they are subject to a reasonable degree of competitive pressure and operate in industries with similar cost structures and risks. For example, in its investigation into classified directory advertising services, the CC's benchmarking analysis involved a comparison of Yell's returns with a sample of more than 4,000 publicly listed companies, but also with smaller sub-sets of companies derived on the basis of their similarity in terms of selected quantitative risk metrics (including cost structure, revenue volatility, and the beta).[69]

3.4.11 Case study: Sky-high profits in the pay-TV market

BSkyB has been the major force in the UK pay-TV market for twenty years. Its satellite- **3.97** based platform has long retained more than two-thirds of pay-TV subscribers. At the wholesale level (content and channel production) its Sky Sports and Sky Movies channels represented the main premium content in the country—showing Premier League football and the major Hollywood films. Other retail competitors, in particular cable operators, have been dependent on this content for their own pay-TV offerings. Over the years BSkyB has attracted a good deal of scrutiny by competition authorities, including over concerns that it used its control of premium channels to restrict competition at the retail pay-TV level. In 2002 the OFT cleared BSkyB of margin squeeze allegations, having analysed

---

[67] Competition Commission (2002), 'The Supply of Banking Services by Clearing Banks to Small and Medium-sized Enterprises', 14 March.

[68] Competition Commission (2006), 'Home Credit Market Investigation', 30 November.

[69] Competition Commission (2006), 'Classified Directory Advertising Services Market Investigation', 21 December, Appendix 7.1.

whether the company's retail operations made sufficient profits at the prevailing whole-sale channel prices charged to cable operators (they did, just).[70] In 2007 Ofcom, the communications regulator, opened another market inquiry and looked in detail at BSkyB's profitability as an indicator of market power. The premium film part of the pay-TV market was referred to the CC for a further investigation, but this was dropped in 2012 in light of the emergence of competitors such as Netflix and LOVEFiLM (now owned by Amazon), which show premium films via internet-based streaming or 'over-the-top' (OTT) services in direct competition with Sky Movies.[71]

3.98   The analysis during Ofcom's investigation considered the profitability of BSkyB as a whole and of its separate activities (wholesale and retail, basic and premium, sports and movies).[72] It covered different time periods: from 1995 (the first year after 20 per cent of the company's shares were floated on the stock market) to 2009 (the year of the analysis) to capture the period of growth and market leadership, and from 2005 to 2009 to assess more current market power. The metric used was the truncated IRR, with the ROCE as a cross-check. Cash flow data was obtained from BSkyB's internal accounts (the regulator had access to the company's confidential data). To give an indication of the orders of magnitude involved, BSkyB's reported EBIT was between £700m and £900m in the years 2005 to 2009. Asset valuation raised some complex questions, in particular as regards intangible assets. The analysis identified three types of possible intangibles for BSkyB that were not observable in its accounts: the subscriber base, contractual obligations, and losses made in the early years.

3.99   As regards the first type, customers who subscribe to premium pay-TV packages typically stay for a number of years. It is reasonable for an operator to expect subscription revenues over this period. Therefore, BSkyB's subscriber base—which grew from 2.5 million in 1995 to 9 million in 2008—represents an intangible asset, and BSkyB's costs of acquiring subscribers can be regarded as investments in this asset. In line with the criteria for intangible assets discussed above, only those marketing costs that the company itself classed as customer acquisition costs were capitalized to create the asset value. Other marketing costs, such as retention marketing, and subscriber management costs were treated as ongoing costs incurred to maintain the existing subscriber base, not as investments. The capitalized costs were then depreciated over a number of years, reflecting the average lifetime of subscribers (approximately ten years, calculated on the basis of observed subscriber churn rates—that is, customers leaving and joining each year). This determined the depreciated replacement value of BSkyB's subscriber base. In 2008 it amounted to £1.3 billion, equivalent to around 30 per cent of the company's asset base as recorded in the accounts for that year (£4.1 billion).

3.100 As to the second type of intangible asset, BSkyB acquires certain content—such as Premier League football rights—through long-term contracts in which it commits to making future payments before the content is available for transmission (e.g. football matches in forthcoming seasons). Under accounting rules this content is not recognized as part of

---

[70] Office of Fair Trading (2002), 'BSkyB Investigation: Alleged Infringement of the Chapter II Prohibition', CA98/20/2002, 17 December. We advised one of the cable operators in this inquiry.

[71] Competition Commission (2012), 'Movies on Pay TV Market Investigation—Final Report', 2 August.

[72] Our firm carried out the profitability analysis for Ofcom. The figures provided here are based on information published in Oxera (2009 and 2010).

inventories on the balance sheet, but from an economic perspective it constitutes a productive asset. The value of this asset was determined by capitalizing the future payments as set out in the relevant contracts. This amounted to around 20 per cent of the asset base reported in the accounts. Start-up losses are the third type of possible intangibles. Before 1993 BSkyB incurred significant losses (in excess of £1.5 billion). To the extent that these losses are linked to profits made by the company in later years (e.g. they represented costs of programming and building the subscriber base), there is a case for incorporating them into the opening asset base. Losses excluded from this category were the write-off of an old satellite system and the write-off of goodwill associated with a previous acquisition. The remaining past losses, when capitalized and depreciated, amounted to between 10 per cent and 20 per cent of the reported asset base.

Cash flows and asset values provided the basis for calculating the truncated IRR for BSkyB. **3.101**
In the central scenario the IRR was around 21–8 per cent (other scenarios tested the sensitivity of the results to various assumptions). For the period 2005–09 the IRR was at the lower end of the range, and for 1995–2009 at the higher end. This reflects the fact that, in later years, per-subscriber acquisition costs increased, possibly reflecting enhanced competition and the move to digital TV. The average nominal pre-tax WACC for BSkyB was estimated at 12.4 per cent for 2005–09 and 13.2 per cent for 1995–2009. Hence the profitability gap between the IRR and the WACC was significant over these periods: between 8 and 15 percentage points. This would be consistent with a high degree of market power: BSkyB's customers stay for a long time and generate healthy revenues for the company relative to the investments it has made. The company's profitability also seemed high relative to a large number of comparator companies active in pay-TV and other TV and content-based markets. At the disaggregated level, BSkyB's returns seemed higher at the wholesale level (premium content and channels) than at the retail level where it competed with cable and other providers that rely on its premium content. The CC endorsed most of the analysis carried out for Ofcom and, after its own assessment, concluded that: 'We have looked in some detail at Sky's profitability and our initial assessment is that Sky has persistently earned profits substantially in excess of its cost of capital…Sky's high profitability is consistent with other evidence showing a lack of effective competition.'[73]

3.4.12 Interpretation of the results of profitability analysis

Profitability analysis frequently raises interpretation issues. Are high profits due to a lack **3.102**
of competition or to superior efficiency? Likewise, profits that do *not* exceed the competitive benchmarks may not necessarily imply a lack of market power, since they may reflect 'X-inefficiencies' (inefficiencies from a monopoly position).

Temporary high profits are common in well-functioning markets. If they reflect superior **3.103**
efficiency there may not be an immediate competition problem, even if this superior efficiency gives the company a degree of market power. Yet this does not rule out the possibility that once achieved, this market power may be abused through exclusionary practices. In this regard there is an important distinction that competition authorities and practitioners sometimes fail to make: that between condemning high profits per se, and using high

---

[73] Competition Commission (2011), 'Movies on Pay TV Market Investigation—Provisional Findings Report', 19 August, at [6.104]. As noted earlier, in the final report the CC considered there to be no more competition concerns (because of new entry, not because the profitability analysis had changed).

profits as an indicator of market power. Here we are discussing the latter. From an economic perspective, high profitability is a useful indicator of market power, but that does not mean that those high profits should be prohibited directly (a theme we return to in Chapter 4 when we discuss excessive pricing as an abuse of dominance). In line with this, a well-established principle in competition law is that market power itself is not prohibited; only the abuse of it is.

3.104 BSkyB argued that the profitability gap described above could be explained by the company's continual successful risk-taking and innovation. These idiosyncratic risks are not properly reflected in the WACC, which captures only systematic risk relative to the stock market. Conceptually BSkyB's argument was valid and merited further consideration. Successful innovation can lead to high returns, providing healthy incentives and compensation for the risk of failure taken at the time of the investment. Consider a stylized example of a risky investment with the following characteristics:

- in the successful (upside) scenario, the company earns a high return (30 per cent);
- in the unsuccessful (downside) scenario, it earns a low return (0 per cent);
- the expected return (i.e. the average of different scenarios) is 15 per cent;
- the expected return is assumed to be in line with the ex ante cost of capital (15 per cent).

3.105 If the upside scenario occurred, the ex post analysis of this stylized example would show a significant profitability gap—that is, 15 percentage points (30 per cent ex post return versus 15 per cent ex ante WACC). Given that the expected returns were in line with the cost of capital, high actual returns in this example merely provide compensation for bearing risks at the time of the investment.

3.106 In specific cases you can test whether you are in a situation similar to the stylized example. The main condition is that the company's investments require a significant upfront commitment of capital for a long time period to counter the prospect of uncertain future demand. In the event that such investments prove successful and the realized demand is high, ex post returns could significantly exceed the cost of capital. In contrast, if the investment fails, the capital committed up front could be lost with no return. Where investments are scalable to changes in demand, or demand uncertainty is low, you would not expect a significant difference between actual returns and the cost of capital. In these latter circumstances the downside risks are relatively low, as the company would be able to scale back its investments in response to a demand shock.

3.107 How does the above apply to BSkyB? A comparison with other media companies suggested that BSkyB had a relatively low asset intensity (defined as total assets divided by operating costs). Satellite signals automatically 'pass' nearly every home such that adding a new customer or upgrading to digital media requires little extra investment (no need to dig up the road as in the case of cable). Contemporaneous analyst reports also indicated that the payback period on new subscribers was relatively short (eighteen to twenty-five months). The contractual commitment to pay for the Premier League rights was for a period of only three years. Contractual arrangements with the major film studios were largely proportionate to demand. Finally, demand uncertainty was relatively limited as well. In the early years there was some uncertainty about the growth of pay-TV and digital TV, but after that BSkyB's subscriber base grew steadily with little volatility. Analyst reports over the last five to ten years of the analysis also perceived the demand and subscriber base to be stable, citing its low churn rates and strong market position vis-à-vis competitors (in fact a key risk perceived by the analysts was regulatory intervention). Overall, in light of these characteristics the profitability gap for BSkyB could not be explained by risk-taking and innovation. The most plausible interpretation was still that over this period BSkyB enjoyed a position of significant market power that new entrants could not easily challenge. The CC reached the same conclusion:

> We recognize that it is possible for a firm to earn profits in excess of its cost of capital within a competitive market particularly where significant investment risks have been taken. However, we would not expect such profits to persist for a significant period of time. Although Sky has taken significant risks in the past, we found that its most risky investments were many years ago and achieved short payback periods. Therefore it appears to us that Sky's profitability can no longer be explained by the risk of its earlier investments.[74]

3.4.13 Is profitability analysis 'too difficult'?

The reluctance of many competition authorities to use profitability analysis is often put down to conceptual and measurement issues. While caution should indeed be exercised when measuring profitability and drawing conclusions from it, this is no different from other economic techniques used in competition cases. We believe that the difficulties of profitability analysis are overstated. The theoretical framework for such an analysis has been developed (centred around the truncated IRR and asset valuation on a replacement cost basis, explained in this section). Measuring the IRR is feasible if good data on cash flows and MEAs is available. This is often the case in established industries with historical data over a long period of time, but also sometimes for companies operating in a dynamic environment such as BSkyB. In other industries it may be more difficult. Measurement problems can also arise with other economic tools such as econometrics. Sometimes these tools can be used and sometimes they cannot. Profitability analysis should be seen as part of the economics toolkit for competition cases. **3.108**

3.5 Buyer Power and Bidding Markets

3.5.1 What happens when buyers have the power?

So far we have used the term market power to mean seller power. We now consider the opposite case of buyer power. Just as a strong seller can restrict output to increase price, a strong buyer can restrict its demand in order to pay a lower price. We will also look at countervailing buyer power, where buyer strength can offset supplier strength, including in the specific context of bidding markets. Supermarkets are often used as an example of buyer power, and have been scrutinized in many jurisdictions over the way they treat their suppliers, both under competition law and in wider policy debates. Other examples of buyer power include those of large broadcasters negotiating TV rights with content producers, and governments procuring defence and pharmaceutical products. **3.109**

Buyer power has been characterized in two ways. The first is monopsony power as the mirror image of monopoly power. Monopsony can have the same detrimental effects as **3.110**

---

[74] Competition Commission (2011), 'Movies on Pay TV Market Investigation—Provisional Findings Report', 19 August, at [6.84].

monopoly. A monopsonist restricting its demand in order to lower the price results in a deadweight loss, as production is lower than it would be in the competitive situation.[75] The other characterization is bargaining power—rather than the powerful buyer lowering the market price overall, it negotiates greater individual discounts than less powerful buyers are able to achieve.[76] The indicators of buyer power that you can use are similar to those of market power. Market definition is a useful starting point (sometimes you may need to define the market from the perspective of a hypothetical monopsonist rather than monopolist). You can then measure buyer market shares and concentration. Another relevant factor is the size of the buyer relative to suppliers. Where buyers are able to resist the market power of strong sellers, this is known as countervailing buyer power.[77] In order for a buyer to place strong competitive pressure on a large supplier, it must pose a credible threat in terms of switching to an alternative supplier. This will be enhanced if the buyer is able to enter the upstream market itself or sponsor upstream entry by a third party.

3.111 There are some differences between buyer and seller power. Recall from Chapter 1 that demand curves tend to slope downwards but supply curves are often horizontal. Downward-sloping demand means that a monopolist that restricts output can be guaranteed to raise price. In contrast, if supply curves are flat (which occurs when the same production technology is available to many competitors and economies of scale are limited), the monopsonist may gain little from restricting demand as it will not result in a significant decrease in price. This may mean that in some situations there is relatively little benefit to a strong buyer from 'monopsonizing' the market. Another difference relates to the effects on producer and consumer welfare. Unlike seller market power, buyer power may not necessarily reduce consumer welfare. If retailers have buyer power over suppliers and thus obtain lower input prices, but at the same time they face effective competition in downstream markets, they will pass on the lower input prices to consumers to some extent. In this situation, while there is some detriment to welfare from restricted volumes in the upstream market, consumer welfare downstream is enhanced through lower prices.

3.5.2 Theories of harm from buyer power: Squeezing suppliers

3.112 When assessing buyer power it is important to be explicit about the theory of harm: how is the possible buyer power being used and what effects does it have on competition and market functioning? There are various potential theories of harm, and it is worthwhile exploring if these apply in any specific case. The most obvious theory of harm is that of straightforward exploitation of bargaining power. Here the main question to ask is equivalent to that of seller market power: what is the degree of buyer power and how likely is it to be exploited? You are more worried about high degrees of buyer power, especially if it borders on monopsony power. For example, mergers that create a strong degree of buyer power are likely to be anti-competitive, just like mergers that create a strong degree of market power.

3.113 A theory of harm occurring in the upstream market is that the use of buyer power to extract large discounts or offer onerous terms can damage the long-term incentives of suppliers to invest and innovate, and result in the exit of suppliers. If this happens, the product range on offer to consumers might decrease. On the other hand, incentives for suppliers to innovate

---

[75] Blair and Harrison (1993) provide an extensive treatise on monopsony power.
[76] For a useful overview, see Doyle and Inderst (2007).
[77] This theory was developed in Galbraith (1952).

might increase when they face strong buyers, as this is one way of gaining bargaining power in negotiations. Also, more far-sighted buyers will realize that squeezing suppliers so hard that they exit the market will reduce choice and hence can be self-defeating. In its grocery market investigation the CC found that the large retailers transferred excessive risks and unexpected costs to their suppliers.[78] The main mechanism for doing so was by making retroactive adjustments to the terms of supply. The CC considered that such practices are likely to diminish suppliers' incentives to invest in the development of new products, and thus ultimately affect consumer choice. It did not find that the financial viability of food and drink manufacturers was under threat because of retailers exercising buyer power, and nor was there evidence of declining product innovation. Yet the authority was concerned that innovation would be affected longer term if these practices continued. A new code of practice was implemented describing how retailers 'are expected to fairly manage the relationships with suppliers'.[79]

3.5.3 Case study: Cable consolidation and buyer power

The cable market provides another example of where buyer power concerns have arisen. In a number of countries, including Germany, the United Kingdom, and the United States, small municipal cable networks have over the years been consolidated into larger regional ones. In the Netherlands the process was completed in 2014 when the last two of the large regional operators formed a national cable company. These mergers raised few horizontal competition concerns because the cable networks served non-overlapping geographic areas. However, the last two mergers—taking the industry from three to two and then from two to one—raised vertical concerns about buyer power vis-à-vis content producers and channel providers. **3.114**

In 2006 the NMa investigated the merger between the second- and third-largest operators, Essent Kabelcom and Casema/Multikabel, which together covered around 55 per cent of all Dutch households.[80] At the time, more than 85 per cent of households subscribed to TV via cable. Broadcasters were therefore dependent on having their channels included in the cable TV packages. One theory of harm that the NMa explored was that the merged entity's buyer power over broadcasters would lead to poorer TV offerings, with fewer channels being included in the basic packages. However, the NMa found that broadcasters and cable operators were mutually dependent. Payments could flow in either direction (the broadcaster paying the cable operator for including a particular channel, or vice versa), and often a 'zero tariff' was agreed where neither party paid the other. The authority also found that there was no significant relationship between size of the cable operator and payment received from (or paid to) the broadcaster, and that with the increased capacity after the move to digital TV the number of channels actually offered would only increase. Another theory of harm rejected by the NMa was that the merged entity would use its enhanced buyer power to set retail TV prices at predatorily low levels. Content costs represented less than 5 per cent of retail prices, and as such could not have a major competitive effect downstream. Finally, the concern that enhanced buyer power would result in more exclusive **3.115**

---

[78] Competition Commission (2008), 'The Supply of Groceries in the UK—Market Investigation', 30 April, at [9.37] to [9.87].
[79] The Groceries (Supply Chain Practices) Market Investigation Order 2009.
[80] Zaaknr. 5796/Cinven—Warburg Pincus—Essent Kabelcom, 8 December 2006. We advised the merging parties on this case.

contracts with broadcasters at the expense of rival retail TV operators was dismissed since such contracts had not been common practice, and broadcasters themselves had indicated that exclusivity would not be of interest to them. The merger was cleared unconditionally.

3.116   In 2014 the merged entity, renamed Ziggo, was itself acquired by the only other remaining large operator, UPC (owned by Liberty Global). This time the deal was reviewed by the European Commission.[81] The market had changed significantly since the previous merger, with KPN, the incumbent telephony operator, having become a major player in the pay-TV market through its internet-based service. KPN and the cable operators compete strongly in triple-pay services (TV, internet access, and telephony). Again there were few horizontal concerns about the merger (the Commission did explore potential coordination between KPN and the merged cable entity, and also whether there existed a chain of indirect competition between the two regional cable operators via KPN's national offering, a possibility we discussed in Chapter 2). The two cable operators together controlled around 60 per cent of pay-TV households. One argument considered was that of 'pivotal buyer power'. TV channels that rely on advertising revenue need reach ('eyeballs'), though some need more than others. High-reach channels (around half of the 175 or so channels in the Netherlands) need access to both cable platforms as they need to reach more than 60 per cent of all viewers. But that was already the case before the merger, so the merger itself would not change bargaining positions. Low-reach channels need access to only one of the cable platforms, or KPN's platform. For this group the merger would not change much either. Only for a (relatively small) group of medium-reach channels would the merged cable entity become a pivotal buyer.

3.117   The Commission focused more on the effect of buyer power on the emergence of innovative pay-TV services, in particular internet-based OTT services offered by broadcasters, which have the potential to compete directly with pay-TV over cable (we also saw the importance of OTT services in the context of the UK pay-TV inquiry in section 3.4). Negotiations between cable operators and broadcasters often cover both TV channel distribution and OTT services, and the concern was that the merged entity would use its buyer power as a TV platform to impose restrictive conditions on the roll-out of OTT services. In addition, the Commission was concerned that the merged entity would use its position in the retail broadband market (where it would control around 40 per cent of the market) to impose technical restrictions on OTT services. A condition for clearance of the merger was for Liberty Global to commit to terminate clauses in carriage agreements with broadcasters that restrict, by direct or indirect means, the ability of broadcasters to offer their channels and their content via OTT services. Another condition was that Liberty Global maintain adequate interconnection capacity for OTT services through uncongested routes via its internet network.

3.5.4 Theories of harm from buyer power: The waterbed effect

3.118   Another theory of harm in the downstream market arising from bargaining power is known as the 'waterbed effect'. The concern is that if suppliers get squeezed by the large buyers, they are forced to charge higher prices to the smaller buyers so as to maintain profits (just like when you press down one end of a waterbed the other end goes up). This may force

---

[81] *Liberty Global/Ziggo* (Case COMP/M.7000), Decision of 10 October 2014. We advised the merging parties also on this investigation.

the smaller buyers out of the downstream market because they cannot compete with the larger ones that have bargaining power. The waterbed effect theory has not been universally endorsed by economists. One logical problem with it is that if suppliers could really increase prices to smaller buyers they would do so in any event, regardless of what they charge larger buyers. Inderst and Valetti (2011) have developed a theoretically sound framework for identifying the circumstances in which the waterbed effect may harm consumers. In essence, suppliers must be able to price-discriminate between buyers, size differences between buyers must be very large, and discounts granted to large buyers must be variable rather than lump-sum payments (variable reductions in upstream prices are more likely to be passed on to downstream prices, and thus put competitive pressure on smaller buyers).

The waterbed effect was a major concern raised by independent convenience store operators in the 2008 grocery market investigation in the United Kingdom.[82] The CC analysed a large dataset of prices, volumes, and costs for 141 different product items, from twenty-nine suppliers over a period of five years. The results indicated that the four largest retailers— Asda, Morrisons, Sainsbury's, and Tesco—paid on average between 4 per cent and 6 per cent less for their products than the mean (and indeed Tesco paid lower prices than the other three). Mid-size retail chains such as the Cooperative Group, Somerfield, and Waitrose on average paid supply prices around the mean; larger wholesalers paid 2–3 per cent above the mean; and smaller wholesalers paid 8–9 per cent above the mean. Econometric analysis carried out by the CC also confirmed an overall negative relationship between retailer size and supply prices, reflecting scale effects (cost efficiencies) and a degree of buyer power. Yet the CC did not attribute this to a waterbed effect. Over time the larger retailers had grown relative to smaller ones, but this had not led to a greater price differential. In addition, the price differences were not always systematic—there was a lot of variation not reflected in the averages mentioned above. Also, the larger wholesalers and buyer groups were able to offer convenience stores competitive wholesale prices. The CC found that convenience stores had entered the market in substantial numbers in recent years, indicating that they were not disadvantaged vis-à-vis the larger retailers through a waterbed effect. **3.119**

3.5.5 Countervailing buyer power in bidding markets

A particular form of countervailing buyer power that has become a common defence in competition cases—especially mergers—is that arising in 'bidding markets'. In such markets, competition is *for* rather than *in* the market. Bidders compete, and the winner gets to be the sole supplier for the duration of the contract. This means that large market shares— even 100 per cent—do not necessarily imply market power, and the presence of two or three potential bidders can be enough to keep prices in check for the next bid. **3.120**

The concept of the bidding market played a central role in the much-debated *General Electric (GE)/Honeywell* merger.[83] This concerned the supply of jet engines to aircraft manufacturers, which was typically awarded through competitive tenders. The European Commission took as evidence of GE's market power the fact that it had won ten out of the last twelve bids to supply platforms for which airframe manufacturers offered exclusive positions. The Commission also argued that current market shares are a good proxy for **3.121**

---

[82] Competition Commission (2008), 'The Supply of Groceries in the UK—Market Investigation', 30 April, at [5.19] to [5.43].
[83] *General Electric/Honeywell* (Case COMP/M.2220), Decision of 3 July 2001.

present and future market power because winning contracts allows companies to invest in R&D, and because incumbency can play a role in buyers' future purchasing decisions. This example highlights the difficulty of assessing market power in a bidding market: if a company wins an auction for a large contract, it may become a monopolist for the duration of that contract. However, if the market is contestable, the company may not necessarily win the next contract. The DOJ, which also reviewed the merger, took a different view from the European Commission. It considered static market shares to be a weak indicator of competitive conditions, and found that GE's high market share was mainly due to one particularly large contract that it had recently won (Majoras, 2001).

3.5.6 Criteria for bidding markets

3.122 What are the criteria for judging the nature of a bidding market? Strong countervailing buyer power requires that the buyer has some form of credible threat to remove its business from the supplier. There must be sufficient other suppliers capable of bidding. Four main criteria determine whether a bidding process is likely to deliver a contestable market (Klemperer, 2005):

(1) competition is winner-takes-all—the bidder wins all or none of the contract;
(2) demand is lumpy—each contract is large relative to a bidder's total sales;
(3) competition begins afresh for each auction—there is no 'lock-in' of customers and the incumbent supplier has no major advantages; and
(4) entry is easy.

3.123 There is a spectrum from 'ordinary' markets with no bidding aspects to 'pure' bidding markets. Figure 3.1 organizes the above criteria along two dimensions. The first dimension encompasses criteria 1 and 2, and can be summarized as the 'size of contract' (the horizontal line in the figure). This involves various aspects of the bidding process, such as its frequency (if auctions are frequent, the relative importance of each contract decreases); the size of the contract relative to the overall market and market participants; and the number of contracts awarded within each auction. The second dimension encompasses criteria 3 and 4, and can

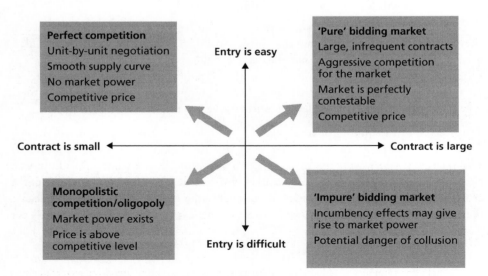

Figure 3.1 The economic characteristics of bidding markets

be described as the 'ease of entry' (the vertical line in the figure). This dimension covers not only entry barriers (e.g. sunk costs), but also the incumbency advantages of the existing supplier that won the last contract (e.g. reputation or know-how).

In bidding markets the buyer can seek to encourage entry through the design of the bid- **3.124** ding process itself. This design should take into account the above dimensions. There is a trade-off as regards the optimal size of the contract to be tendered in cases where a buyer is unsure of the ease of entry: for bigger contracts (which have a large value and long duration) you will get keener bidding if entry is easy, but if entry is difficult it is probably preferable to have smaller contracts in order to prevent incumbency advantages embedding the position of one supplier. If a bidding market is 'impure', the number of bidders will affect the competitiveness of the market—the more bidders the better. However, adding further bidders may not contribute significantly to competition if they are weak. If the market has the characteristics of a 'pure' bidding market, one credible alternative bidder might already be enough to ensure vigorous competition. For this to be the case there must be no significant incumbency advantages—this is captured by criterion 3. Evidence for this would be where more than one company have won contracts in the past or where there is not much specific knowledge acquired in fulfilling previous contracts that new bidders cannot obtain. Part of the reason why there may actually be few markets that meet the bidding market defence in full is that if the first and second criteria hold (i.e. contracts are large and of a winner-takes-all kind), the third criterion is less likely to hold: incumbency advantages may be more significant for large contracts that leave only one supplier in the market. Once the supplier gains a clear advantage in a market, other companies may stop trying to bid against it. Economies of scale in large contracts may also make it more difficult for new bidders to displace an incumbent. This was the case in the second contest to operate the National Lottery franchise in the United Kingdom in 2000. By that time Camelot, the incumbent operator that had won the first contest in 1994 against seven other bidders, had developed substantial learning-by-doing and reputational advantages. Only one other bidder took part, and lost (see Klemperer, 2005).

Some of the characteristics that will make a bidding process contestable and give the buyer **3.125** strong countervailing power may also make a market more prone to collusion. There is a spectrum along the 'size of contract' dimension in Figure 3.1: at one extreme are very large, infrequent tenders for the whole market and at the other are very small, frequent tenders for single units. In the middle of this spectrum there is a greater risk of collusion than in ordinary markets, especially if entry is not easy. The bidding process makes the market more transparent and gives companies the opportunity to communicate; the more frequent the auctions, the more credible punishment strategies become, which again favours collusion.

3.5.7 Examples of the bidding market defence: Soft drinks and fresh eggs

Two mergers in the food and drinks sector are instructive in seeing how the line can be **3.126** drawn for the bidding market defence. Both mergers were between suppliers that faced countervailing buyer power by large supermarkets. In *Cott/Macaw* (2006), the CC cleared the merger even though the merging parties had a combined market share of nearly 70 per cent in the production of own-brand carbonated soft drinks.[84] The CC considered that this

---

[84] Competition Commission (2006), 'Cott Beverages Ltd and Macaw (Holdings) Ltd merger inquiry', 28 March. We advised the merging parties in this inquiry.

market did not meet the criteria of a pure bidding market, but nonetheless had a number of the underlying structural features. Retailers controlled the nature of the tendering process. They determined when the soft drinks supply business is tendered, which tender mechanism is used, the size and composition of the tender, and the length of the contract. Retailers also had the ability to shift to alternative suppliers of their own-brand soft drinks, as they owned the rights associated with the product flavour. Suppliers, in turn, were found to be highly dependent on volume throughput in their plants and hence had strong incentives to bid competitively for both large- and small-volume contracts. Even smaller retailers therefore had a degree of buyer power. There had also been several examples of sponsored entry in this market in the past, with retailers facilitating new investment by giving assurances over purchase prices and volumes for a number of years. All these factors led the CC to conclude that the merger was not problematic. A subsequent appraisal of this merger decision confirmed that the CC's assessment was correct and that it may even have underestimated the incentives for new entry into this market (Deloitte, 2009).

3.127   In contrast, the completed merger of Clifford Kent (owners of Stonegate Farmers) and Deans Food Group (trading as Noble) was unwound after the CC found that there was a substantial lessening of competition.[85] The two parties were direct competitors in the supply of eggs to retailers—their post-merger market share was 60–70 per cent in shell eggs. Because of the nature of egg production, barriers to entry were significant as a supplier would need to build up its stock of egg-producing hens. Retailers, despite their important position as buyers, could not easily switch to alternative egg suppliers. The merger further reduced their choice of suppliers and hence their bargaining power. Sponsored entry was deemed difficult, and threatening not to purchase any eggs would not be credible. The CC considered the profitability of a selection of Deans' customer accounts and found no systematic differences between large and small retail customers, suggesting that the former had no significant buyer power. Rather than a bidding market, the relationship between suppliers and retailers was found to be one of mutual dependence, with both sides exerting a degree of bargaining power. The merger had significantly increased the bargaining power of the two suppliers.

3.6 Behavioural Economics and Market Power

3.6.1 Understanding the consumer

3.128   Buyer power in the previous section referred to large corporate and government buyers: supermarkets, aircraft manufacturers, cable operators, defence departments, and the like. What about consumer markets? What effect do consumers, individually or collectively, have on market power? In competition cases consumers are typically represented by a downward-sloping demand curve, as we saw in Chapter 2. The demand curve has an extensive theoretical framework behind it, in which consumers rationally maximize their utility in line with their preferences, but in the end what matters is that demand goes up when prices go down and vice versa. The analysis then focuses on exactly how sensitive consumers are to price.

---

[85] Competition Commission (2007), 'Clifford Kent Holdings Limited and Deans Food Group Limited', 20 April.

Thanks to behavioural economics there is now much richer insight into how consumers **3.129**
actually behave and form their preferences, and what effect this has on market outcomes.
In this section we explain behavioural economics and its relevance to competition law.
Consumers have (some would say, suffer from) cognitive biases and bounded rationality,
and this in turn may give suppliers a greater and more persistent degree of market power
than would follow from traditional models of competition (see Oxera, 2013). Yet we'll also
see (limited) instances where psychological factors give consumers more rather than less
buyer power.

Behavioural economics applies psychological principles to explain observed behaviours and **3.130**
market outcomes. It is perhaps more accurately referred to as 'psychology and economics'.
Behavioural economics is not especially new. It dates back to the 1950s and became a field in
its own right in the late 1970s with the work of psychologists Daniel Kahneman and Amos
Tversky (1979) and the economist Richard Thaler (1980). What is more recent is the attention it has received from the wider public, helped by popular books such as *Nudge* (Thaler
and Sunstein, 2008) and *Predictably Irrational* (Ariely, 2008), and by Kahneman winning
the Nobel Prize for Economics in 2002. Traditional consumer theory relies on stringent
assumptions of rationality and consistently ordered preferences. Behavioural economics
provides a framework for exploring systematically how interactions between demand and
supply are affected when less stringent assumptions are made about consumers.

3.6.2 How consumers form preferences and make choices

Traditional models assume that consumers have stable preferences and learn from past **3.131**
experiences. They use all available information to make fully rational judgements, with
the ultimate aim of maximizing their utility. Given these assumptions, it is possible to
make fairly straightforward predictions about how consumers will behave, based on their
preferences, their budget, and the prevailing prices of different goods. In this framework
it is not necessary to explore in any detail *why* they make these decisions (in the same way
that you don't need to know the workings of the internal combustion engine to be able
to drive a car).

Behavioural economics seeks to integrate theory and practice from psychology with eco- **3.132**
nomics. It provides a framework for understanding why people face a variety of problems
in processing information and making decisions. To illustrate this, it is useful to consider
some of the core psychological processes involved when people make choices. The top half
of Figure 3.2 displays processes that will be familiar to psychologists: how people perceive

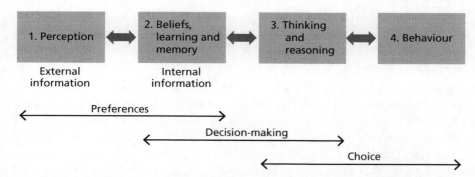

Figure 3.2 Cognitive and behavioural processes involved in consumer choices

information presented to them; how they draw on their internal information, such as beliefs, goals, and experience; how they then think about the best course of action; and finally, how they behave. The bottom half of the figure matches these to concepts that are familiar to economists: consumers' preferences, their decision-making process, and the choices they make.

3.133　Working from left to right, traditional economic models make a number of implicit or explicit assumptions. The first is that preferences do not depend on context—they are not affected by the way in which information is presented or 'framed', or by social comparisons. The second assumption is that decision-making involves fully rational deliberation. People use all available information and are able to remember their past experiences in full. It is also assumed that consumers engage in rational, conscious reasoning to determine the best course of action. The third assumption is that choices are time-consistent. Consumers do not put off making decisions that they know are in their long-term interest, and are able to resist short-term behaviours that go against their long-term interest. These assumptions, while stringent, are often good enough in terms of predicting in general how consumers are likely to behave—for example, in response to price changes (knowing the slope of the demand curve or the price elasticity of demand can be sufficient). Yet there are situations where the simplicity of the assumptions is evident and the traditional models fail to predict or reflect observed behaviour.

3.134　Behavioural economics adopts more specific assumptions about consumer preferences, decision-making, and choice. It takes account of a cornerstone of psychology: that people rely on two cognitive systems. The first is system I processing, undertaken by the older (in evolutionary terms) parts of the human brain, and involves instinctive processing rather than conscious 'thinking'. The other is system II processing, undertaken by the 'newer' parts of the brain, and facilitates conscious, rules-based processing. This distinction calls into question whether consumers always make conscious and fully deliberative choices. The three assumptions of traditional models discussed above are substantially altered in the behavioural economics framework. We discuss this below.

3.6.3 Types of consumer bias: Context-dependent preferences

3.135　As regards the first assumption in Figure 3.2, a main theme in behavioural economics is that preferences do depend on how the information is framed. If a bottle of wine is initially priced at €20 and then reduced to €15, you may perceive that you are getting a better deal than if the wine were offered at €15 in the first instance. Consumers may perceive an option at the top of a search or price-comparison website list as being better value than one towards the bottom, even when there is no real difference between the two. Moreover, people dislike losing what they perceive they already own more than they like making gains. Therefore, whether information is presented, or framed, to consumers in terms of gains or losses can affect their preferences.

3.136　In a famous study Kahneman and Tversky (1984) presented a group of physicians with two hypothetical dilemmas. In the first, 600 people are expected to die following the outbreak of a rare disease. Adopting treatment programme A would lead to 200 lives being saved, and adopting programme B would lead to a one-third probability that 600 lives would be saved and two-thirds probability that no lives would be saved. Hence both programmes produce the same expected value of the number of lives saved (200). 72 per cent of the physicians chose programme A (the safe option), and only 28 per cent chose programme

B (the risky gamble). Thus the physicians expressed 'risk-averse' preferences (preferring known outcomes to risky ones). But the dilemma was then reframed: if programme C is adopted, 400 people will die, whereas with programme D there is a one-third probability that no one will die and a two-thirds probability that 600 people will die. Here, 22 per cent of the physicians chose programme C (the safe option), while 78 per cent chose programme D (the risky option). In fact, the two dilemmas posed are identical in terms of outcomes (outcome A = C and outcome B = D). Yet when the information was reframed from gains (200 saved lives) to losses (400 deaths) the physicians reversed their choices and became risk-taking. This reversal breaches a fundamental assumption in traditional economics that preferences are invariant. That preference orders do change when the description of outcomes changes is an insight from behavioural economics (more precisely, a strand of it called prospect theory).

3.6.4 Types of consumer bias: Heuristics and time-inconsistency in decision-making

As regards the second assumption in Figure 3.2, behavioural economics takes into account the fact that decision-making involves taking shortcuts. Conscious, fully rational deliberation of every single decision would be exhausting to apply to all day-to-day tasks. Instead, many decisions are made subconsciously. This relies on system I processing. In addition, between conscious and subconscious decision-making lies a series of shortcuts known as heuristics. For example, consumers may make quick decisions based on a selection of the information provided in the marketplace, their memories of recent experiences, looking to what others are doing, or focusing on what they think are salient aspects of the information. This can lead to miscalculations. A common example is that of the bat and the ball which together cost €110. The bat costs €100 more than the ball. How much is the ball? With some time to think, you will work out that the answer is €5, but heuristics—in this case the shortcut for working out a price difference—may suggest €10. Using heuristics saves a lot of time and effort, in particular when dealing with complex problems, but can be imperfect and open to exploitation by sellers. **3.137**

As to the third assumption, choices can be time-inconsistent. Consumers can face a conflict between their short-term urges (system I processing) and what would be best for them in the long term (system II processing). In economic terms, their preferences can be 'present-biased' or 'time-inconsistent'. As the time for action draws nearer, optimal plans can be put off. Procrastination bias is all too familiar—even the most rational lawyers and economists benefit when their clients set them tight deadlines, as it helps them actually focus and organize the work (as did the deadline set by Oxford University Press for this book). **3.138**

A familiar example of time-inconsistency, and an effort to do something about it, is discussed in an article called 'Paying not to go to the gym' (Della Vigna and Malmendier, 2006). Those who incur monthly gym membership fees can end up paying significantly more than if they had simply paid per visit (in the article the average cost of gym membership was $75 per month, the average number of visits four per month, and the per-visit charge $10). This suggests that people treat gym membership as a form of commitment, with the intention to go to the gym regularly and get value for money. Alas, once this amount is paid and the time comes to go to the gym, they fail to do so. Gyms know how to exploit this bias. (Yet before you begin to wonder if your gym membership was such a good **3.139** idea, note that some of those joining might not have gone to the gym at all had they not pre-committed themselves.)

3.6.5 How biases influence the interaction between demand and supply

3.140 Behavioural economics demonstrates that consumers are sensitive to the way in which information is framed and have limits to their decision-making ability, and that this has implications for their preferences, decisions, and behaviour. In turn, the way in which suppliers present their offerings to consumers can affect market outcomes. Companies may have incentives to exploit consumer biases systematically. A framework first established by the OFT sets out how consumers interact with the supply side in three stages. In well-functioning markets, consumers: (i) access information about the various offers available in the market; (ii) assess these offers in a well-reasoned way; and (iii) act on this information and analysis by purchasing the product or service that gives the best value (Office of Fair Trading, 2010). Behavioural economics has shown how this virtuous circle between the demand side and supply side may be broken because of consumers' cognitive processes and bounded rationality—Figure 3.3 illustrates how this can occur at each of the three stages.

3.141 Suppliers may go a step further and seek to take advantage of consumer biases in each of the three stages. At the stage of accessing information, suppliers can make it more difficult for consumers to perform searches. Because consumers do not always look at pricing terms that are not provided up front, suppliers may exploit this by using drip pricing. You may have experienced this when buying online: you get a headline price up front, and then as you engage in the buying process, additional charges are 'dripped through' by the seller. The endowment effect is involved here: having been through several steps on the website, your point of reference (the anchor) shifts and you feel to some extent that you already own the product, so you are more inclined to pay not to lose it. Another sales tactic is to put more of the price into add-on services, sometimes referred to as partitioned pricing. A study into eBay auctions of CDs (Hossain and Morgan, 2006) found that auctions with lower opening-bid reserve prices but higher shipping charges attract more bidders and more

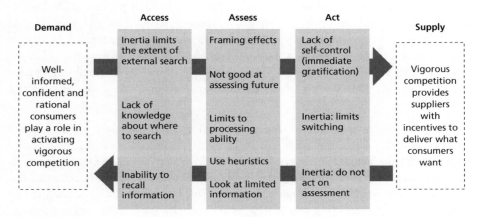

Figure 3.3 Interactions between demand and supply: where the virtuous circle may break down

Source: Based on Office of Fair Trading (2010)

revenues than those with higher opening-bid prices and lower shipping charges. This suggests that potential bidders focus more on the reserve price and less on the add-on price. Consumers' perception and computation may be affected by the characteristics of the partitioned price. Another factor that has been shown to be influential is the degree to which the surcharge language conveys whether the add-on is within or outside the company's control (e.g. 'tax', 'fee', 'additional charge'). Ott and Andrus (2000) find that consumers treat expenses that are presented as being beyond the control of the seller more forgivingly than other add-ons.

At the second stage in Figure 3.3, suppliers can make it more difficult for consumers to **3.142** assess the best deal. Where consumers find it difficult to compare offers that are structured differently, suppliers may exploit this by making their prices less clear, increasing the number of options on offer, or raising the degree of complexity (you may have noticed this when comparing mobile phone packages). Finally, at the stage of acting on information and analysis, suppliers can make it more difficult for consumers to get the best deals. Consumers may display more inertia than traditionally thought, perhaps due to procrastination bias or overconfidence in their capacity to improve their situation at a later time. Suppliers, knowing this, may raise switching costs—for example, by requiring existing customers to use registered post to cancel a subscription, applying defaults and automatic renewals, or using time-limited offers.

3.6.6 Market power and disciplining by consumers

We have seen that consumers have biases and suppliers may exploit this. But is this a con- **3.143** cern for competition law? Markets can correct themselves over time, even when there are biases. Positions of market power can be eroded through disciplining by consumers and competitors. Consumers can learn over time about practices such as drip pricing and partitioned pricing. Companies that are straightforward in their communication with customers can gain market share at the expense of those that seek to confuse and exploit—the 'good' drive out the 'bad'. So the existence of consumer biases does not automatically result in significant distortions to the virtuous demand–supply interaction in Figure 3.3. Yet disciplining by consumers and competitors is not always effective, as we explore in this section and the next.

Disciplining by consumers can be hindered by inertia: consumers may not switch between **3.144** products even if they can gain financially. Therefore, even with many competitors in the market, a lack of switching may give each of them a degree of market power. An example is the CC investigation into the personal banking market in Northern Ireland. On the basis that consumers did not frequently switch current-account providers, the CC concluded that all banks had 'unilateral market power', including those with a market share of less than 5 per cent.[86]

Different consumers will be willing to search for low prices to varying degrees. The behav- **3.145** ioural economics literature has analysed the impact of the presence of so-called 'naive' consumers on market outcomes. These consumers are unable (or unwilling) to learn or compare prices, which affects their purchasing and searching behaviour. In contrast, 'sophisticated'

---

[86] Competition Commission (2007), 'Personal Current Account Banking Services in Northern Ireland Market Investigation', 15 May. We advised one of the banks in this case.

consumers are well informed and purchase from the firm offering the best deal.[87] Suppliers recognize the presence of sophisticated and naive consumers, and realize that they may exert market power over the latter but not the former. In many markets the sophisticated consumers protect the naive consumers, especially if suppliers cannot distinguish or discriminate between the two groups (we discussed this in Chapter 2 in the context of price discrimination markets). However, where partitioned or drip pricing is feasible, some studies suggest that average prices in the market tend to go up in line with the proportion of naive consumers: the more naive consumers there are, the higher the prices, and hence the greater the degree of market power. Sophisticated consumers may even benefit from the naive, rather than protect them. Suppliers using partitioned pricing set low prices for the primary product, and then make a profit by selling secondary or add-on products for high prices. Naive consumers fall into this 'trap'. Sophisticated consumers are likely to anticipate the trap, purchasing the primary products for the low price, while purchasing secondary products through a different channel. In this situation, the normal disciplining of market power by sophisticated consumers does not work, and the naive consumers end up cross-subsidizing the sophisticated ones.

3.146 Finally, in certain circumstances consumers may have a degree of power over suppliers. As we mentioned before, countervailing buyer power, in the traditional sense of fully offsetting seller market power, is unlikely to exist in consumer markets. Nonetheless, behavioural economics provides some insight into why disciplining of sellers by consumers may sometimes be effective. It has long been recognized that people care not only about their own material welfare, but also about, first, their immaterial welfare, and second, the welfare of other people. Fairness and reputation considerations may directly enter consumers' preferences. Likewise, consumers can grow accustomed to products being offered free of charge. For example, in a number of countries it has been common for current accounts to be free of charge to bank customers who are in credit. The label 'free' can trigger a strong emotional response. When customers are used to this 'free-in-credit' banking, they may regard it as unfair and undesirable when banks start to charge for the current account and payment services, and this can result in negative publicity and reputation effects. This could then be one factor preventing banks from unilaterally changing to a different charging model. The same can hold for 'free handsets' with a mobile phone contract. In 2002, mobile operators in the Netherlands could not get rid of handset subsidies unilaterally and instead colluded to reduce payments to retailers; they were fined €88 million by the NMa.[88]

3.6.7 Market power and disciplining by competitors

3.147 Suppliers employing desirable practices may discipline those employing undesirable practices (the 'good' driving out the 'bad', as we said above). Behavioural economics has shown that this self-correcting mechanism may not always function. If markets work well, and consumers are fully informed and rational, sellers would not hide (or 'shroud') add-on information from their customers. However, this may not be the case if there are both sophisticated and naive consumers. Studies have shown that if the proportion of naive consumers is high enough, all suppliers—including those with low market shares and hence

---

[87] Naivety and sophistication in this context are not necessarily related to intelligence.
[88] Zaaknr. 2658-344/Mobiele operators, 30 December 2002.

not usually thought of as having market power—choose to shroud the add-on price information (Gabaix and Laibson, 2006). Why is this? In the situation described, sophisticated consumers buy the base good but not the add-on. They receive a subsidy from naive customers who pay the add-on fees (as we saw in the previous section). Competition between suppliers fails to unwind this, since any attempt by any one supplier to educate naive consumers about the add-on market will—if there are close substitutes for the add-on product—lead to a loss of those profitable naive consumers. At the same time, sophisticated consumers, who are not profitable to the supplier, prefer to buy from suppliers that offer loss-leader prices on the base good, and would rather that the status quo of shrouded add-ons be retained. All suppliers exploit the biases, and no individual supplier has an incentive to correct its behaviour in consumers' overall interests.

Studies such as these question the received wisdom that more competition (a larger number of suppliers) will drive out poor practices. The market may become stuck in a sub-optimal equilibrium for consumers. Some behavioural economics studies go even further: not only may competition not resolve the shrouding issue, it may actually exacerbate it—competition can make things worse rather than better (Spiegler, 2006). In these studies, suppliers adopt complex, multi-component pricing strategies. In the face of information overload, consumers find it difficult to grasp this structure in its entirety, so they resort to heuristics, sampling a small number of dimensions and choosing the best-performing supplier along these dimensions. This heuristic saves considerable cognitive resources, and is applicable to many market settings, but suppliers may then have an incentive to increase complexity. As competition increases, suppliers in these studies react by making pricing even less clear and exploiting consumers, rather than engaging in more competitive pricing. **3.148**

We note here that many of these studies are theoretical—not much real-world evidence has been gathered yet beyond lab experiments. Therefore the (rather controversial) notion that more competition may actually be harmful to consumers does not carry too much practical weight. Yet the notion that having more suppliers does not always resolve sub-optimal outcomes in consumer markets is useful to bear in mind in competition cases. **3.149**

3.6.8 Add-ons, partitioned pricing, and drip pricing: Creating market power in narrow markets?

We have seen that, in consumer markets, suppliers engaging in practices such as partitioned and drip pricing may enjoy a greater and more persistent degree of market power than would follow from traditional models of competition. What does this mean for competition law? Is this the kind of market power you should be concerned about? Can these practices be considered an abuse of dominance? Precedent on competition enforcement against these practices is rare, with the exception of the market investigations regime in the United Kingdom (in which the CMA, and before it the OFT and CC, can intervene in markets where competition is deemed not to be working effectively, but suppliers are not dominant or colluding). Abuse of dominance cases involving the direct exploitation of customers are rare. Issues arising from add-ons, partitioned pricing, and drip pricing are more commonly dealt with through consumer protection laws, or sector regulation such as in financial services. Still it is worth exploring how the competition rules might apply in principle, starting with the assessment of market definition and market power. **3.150**

3.151 Applying the principles of market definition as discussed in Chapter 2, add-ons and drip pricing may well give rise to narrowly defined relevant markets, and hence findings of market power or dominance. For example, with add-ons, what is the starting point for the SSNIP test to which a hypothetical increase is applied? Should it be the headline (primary) price which attracted the consumer to the product in the first place, or should it be the total price that the consumer ends up paying? Behavioural economics would suggest that consumers may be more sensitive to increases in the price of the primary product than in the prices of add-ons. Suppliers can use add-on pricing and drip pricing to benefit from the lower price sensitivity of consumers to prices of add-ons and secondary products. If all suppliers in the market apply the same pricing practices and consumers compare overall prices between suppliers over a longer time period (e.g. when making repeated purchases), a SSNIP test applied to the total price is still relevant. However, if consumers persistently and systematically focus only on the primary price when comparing competing offerings, that may be the focal point for market definition. Add-ons would then be in separate relevant markets, covering individual consumers who, at that point, are to a large extent captive to the selected supplier.

3.152 As in the case of price discrimination markets (discussed in Chapter 2), the contribution of behavioural economics is to highlight that there can be pockets of market power in markets characterized by drip pricing and add-on sales. Some caution should be exercised in these cases. Defining narrow markets and establishing market power or dominance this way runs a risk of over-intervention. In the next section we discuss a case where the relevant market for a secondary product was defined narrowly.

3.6.9 Case study on market power in narrow markets: Payment protection insurance

3.153 Payment protection insurance (PPI) is sold to consumers who take out credit, and provides cover against events that may prevent them from keeping up with their repayments. Policies tend to pay out following unemployment, accident, or illness (depending on the specific terms). PPI is considered a secondary product because it is purchased only once the primary product (in this case, a credit facility) has been bought. When the CC initiated its investigation in 2007, PPI had developed into a popular retail insurance product, sold alongside personal loans, credit cards, and mortgages.[89] Mis-selling allegations in relation to PPI were investigated in parallel by the financial regulator. Why do people buy primary and secondary products from the same provider? While in some markets there may be benefits of enhanced compatibility (in buying computer hardware and software, for example), in many other cases consumers may simply find it more convenient to buy the primary and secondary product at the same time, in the same place. In the case of credit card PPI, the purchase of insurance from the same firm providing the credit card would protect repayments on any balance outstanding at any point in time. Other, third-party PPI providers would not have access to the cardholder's account details and would typically offer protection for a fixed amount.

3.154 From a competition perspective, problems arise with secondary products where consumers are deterred from shopping around for the product that is most appropriate for them.

---

[89] Competition Commission (2009), 'Market Investigation Into Payment Protection Insurance', 29 January. We advised one of the PPI providers during this investigation.

Although consumers may do so for the primary product, a failure to research the secondary product thoroughly may result in a lack of competition for the latter. This can lead to poor quality or high prices—particularly if neither quality nor prices can easily be observed or understood by consumers prior to the purchase. This was the issue examined in the PPI case.

To define the relevant market, the CC assessed whether consumer behaviour in the market for the secondary product constrained the behaviour of providers. If consumers are sufficiently aware of the secondary product, and if it is also offered by alternative providers separately from the primary product, they may shop around and choose to buy the primary and secondary product from the same supplier or from different ones. This should result in a competitive market for secondary products. The CC found that most lenders offered a PPI product only in combination with the credit product sold. In other words, it was not possible to obtain a loan from bank A and then purchase the PPI from bank B. While a number of stand-alone PPI products had been launched, their sales volumes were relatively limited. Alternative insurance products were available, but evidence on competitive pressure from these products was mixed. One of the most important options available to consumers was in fact not taking the PPI product—in other words, opting for no insurance. The CC found that 60 per cent of consumers who took personal loans and 80 per cent of those who took credit cards did not purchase PPI. **3.155**

The CC also assessed whether consumer behaviour in the market for the primary product constrained providers in the market for the secondary product. Even if consumers do not shop around for the secondary product separately, competition concerns do not necessarily arise. If, when shopping around, consumers compare the total cost of the products they wish to buy, the secondary product may be subject to competitive constraints (we discussed systems markets in Chapter 2s). Consumer surveys undertaken by the CC and credit providers indicated that a proportion of consumers do indeed think about buying PPI before applying for a loan, and that some consumers look at various PPI products when shopping around for a loan. However, the CC found that the number of consumers who compare the costs of combined credit and PPI products was insufficient to place genuine competitive pressure on PPI providers. It also found that informational factors were a major entry barrier for stand-alone PPI providers: **3.156**

> The second barrier we found was poor consumer awareness of PPI. We found that a significant number of consumers did not consider PPI before approaching their lender for credit; moreover, a significant number of customers did not know that they could take out PPI from someone other than their credit provider. This low consumer awareness and poor understanding of options restricts the ability of providers of stand-alone PPI successfully to enter or expand into PPI markets.[90]

The CC concluded that the relevant product market was limited to an individual distributor's sales of a particular type of PPI policy. In other words, each distributor held an effective monopoly over the sale of PPI to its own credit customers. This case is therefore an example of where consumer biases are taken into account and tested empirically, and market power is explicitly established in narrowly defined markets. **3.157**

---

[90] Ibid., at [57].

3.6.10 How can you use behavioural economics in assessing market power?

3.158 The rise of behavioural economics has triggered extensive debate about its usefulness. Competition practitioners (officials, lawyers, judges, and economists) have expressed many different views on this. The more sceptically minded would say that, just as traditional economic models can explain some of the phenomena associated with behavioural economics, competition practitioners have always had some awareness of consumer biases, and past competition cases have sometimes taken these biases into account without any explicit reference to behavioural economics. In addition, bounded rationality and consumer biases typically have greater relevance where individual consumers, as opposed to companies, are concerned, and competition law often deals with company behaviour and business-to-business disputes, which can be analysed with the more traditional instruments and tools. It has also been argued that the adverse outcomes resulting from bounded rationality are best dealt with under consumer protection rather than competition law, and that well-intentioned policy-makers and regulators inevitably suffer from biases as well. Finally, the sceptics argue, behavioural economics is reasonably well developed theoretically but not yet empirically. The theory has not been sufficiently proven, and practical policy implications are difficult to test.

3.159 On the other side of the debate, it is clear from the discussion in the previous sections that there are certain types of competition problem that can be better understood with reference to insights from the behavioural economics literature. This is not to say that behavioural economics has, or should have, a radical impact on competition law (contrary to what some proponents of 'behavioural antitrust' would like to see). Indeed, behavioural economics still has only a modest part in this book (albeit slightly larger than in the first edition). Instead, behavioural economics can be seen as providing useful additional insight; a further instrument in the economist's toolkit (just like profitability analysis). There are certain market situations and outcomes that are driven by consumer biases and bounded rationality, and that can best be understood or explained through behavioural economics. Phenomena such as search costs, switching costs, and product differentiation have long been understood in competition law. The added value of behavioural economics is that it can cast further light on what drives search costs and switching costs, and on how product differentiation affects consumer behaviour, in each of the access, assess, and act stages of the consumer decision-making process illustrated in Figure 3.3. Behavioural economics has also provided a good deal of insight into the design of remedies, a theme we return to in Chapter 9. One cannot really classify competition cases according to whether behavioural economics is relevant or not; sometimes consumer biases and bounded rationality will be a major factor in the investigation, and other times they will be just one aspect among others that need to be considered, or will not be relevant at all. There is no reason to discard behavioural economics altogether.

3.7 Market Power, Investment, and Innovation

3.7.1 A difficult trade-off

3.160 We now return to one of the most difficult trade-offs for competition law: how to assess market power in markets where investment is risky but potentially lucrative when successful? There is a long history of competition enforcement in dynamic industries where successful innovation has led to companies having very strong market positions. Think of IBM in the 1970s and 1980s, Microsoft in the 1990s and 2000s, and Google this decade. Innovation is a strong driver of long-run economic welfare. There has been much debate about which type of market structure is most conducive to innovation. At one end is the Schumpeterian view that monopolies give rise to 'creative destruction': each new innovation destroys the monopoly rents generated by previous innovators (Schumpeter, 1942). At the other end is Arrow's theory that highly competitive markets are most likely to yield innovation: a monopolist might innovate less than competitive firms because it has more to lose from radical change (Arrow, 1962). The more recent empirical literature has found an 'inverted U'-shape relationship between the degree of competition and the degree of innovation: oligopolistic markets tend to be more innovative than either monopoly or highly competitive markets. Too much competition will dissipate the post-innovation profits and hence reduce the rewards from trying to escape intense competition by innovation. Too little competition allows for the quiet life of the monopolist. Which effect dominates depends on the technological characteristics of a sector or industry (Aghion et al., 2005).

Where there is a significant risk of failure, high returns are necessary to reward those willing to take such risks. The award of IP rights for innovation recognizes this: because it is costly and risky to research and develop a new product, an innovator is given monopoly rights over the commercialization of the idea for a period of time. In fact, having a patent or an IP right is no guarantee of an actual monopoly. Designing a new type of kitchen tap may be patent-protected, but because it competes with a wide range of other taps that are sufficiently close substitutes, the patent may confer only limited pricing power. Equally there are innovations that are not protected by IP rights but that may still yield market power. The communication protocols in dispute in one of the *Microsoft* cases were not protected by IP; yet Microsoft had been able to prevent others from interoperating with its systems and thus strengthen its market position.[91] While there is not always a one-to-one mapping between IP and true monopoly, a clear tension exists between competition and IP law, as successful innovation, protected by IP, may erect absolute entry barriers that reduce competition in existing or new markets. We return to this in Chapter 4 on abuse of dominance and Chapter 8 on the design of remedies. The complex trade-off between competition and innovation is also touched upon in other places, including in Chapter 5 in the context of technology and licence agreements. **3.161**

3.7.2 Dynamic rivalry: Lessons from past interventions

We have emphasized in a number of places that price is not the only parameter of competition. This is particularly the case in dynamic markets where companies tend to compete mainly through innovation. By offering the most innovative products, companies aspire to gain a competitive edge over their rivals, or indeed to create whole new markets for themselves. The benefits of such advantageous market positions can then be reaped, up to the point when rivals catch up or create new products that render the existing ones obsolete. With such dynamic rivalry, the standard tools for market definition and dominance need to be applied with caution. In assessing market power, a company with a very high market share, or even 100 per cent, today may not be in the same position in a year's time—strong **3.162**

---

[91] *Microsoft* (Case COMP/C-3/37.792), Decision of 24 March 2004, at [432].

market positions can be eroded quickly. Likewise, companies may currently be competing fiercely with each other to develop products and services that have not yet fully made it to market, again making it difficult to define markets based on current product features. Within a few years it may be that one company has exited the market while the other has captured a large proportion of demand.

3.163 It is difficult for anyone, including competition authorities and judges, to evaluate future developments in dynamic markets. Competition authorities should therefore exercise caution when assessing dominance based on current market positions or product features. The 1995 inquiry by the Monopolies and Mergers Commission (MMC) into game consoles serves as a healthy reminder of this.[92] Investigating the game console market between January 1994 and March 1995, the MMC found that it was dominated by Nintendo and Sega, which held a combined market share of nearly 100 per cent for consoles (hardware) and around 40 per cent for games (software). The MMC concluded that 'Nintendo and Sega remain well placed to retain their dominant position in the market and derive profit from it.'[93] However, the report was outdated almost from the time of its publication. In the same year, Sony launched its highly successful PlayStation game console, which represented a whole new 'generation' of consoles at the time (e.g. it had CDs containing the necessary software, rather than cartridges). Microsoft successfully entered the fray in 2001 with its Xbox, while Sega, one of the two 'dominant' companies in 1995, exited the market in that same year. Several further generations of game consoles have been developed since, with the current rivalry being between Nintendo's Wii U and 3DS, Sony's PlayStation 4, and Microsoft's Xbox One and 360. The console market is a good example of 'creative destruction' at work: new generations of products frequently making the existing ones obsolete. The MMC case illustrates how the durability of market power can be overestimated in such innovative markets.

3.164 Leading high-tech firms have long histories of disputes with competition authorities. IBM is a famous case in point (see, for example, Pugh, 1995). Post-World War II, IBM's product line consisted of tabulators, card punch machines, accounting machines, scales, typewriters, and time-recording systems, and it had a strong market position in many of these. In 1946 it began developing a new technology—computing. In 1956 it signed a consent decree with the DOJ regarding a range of restrictive practices, particularly in relation to the sales of tabulators and card punches. At that point these markets were in decline. IBM was then scrutinized again from 1969 to 1984, in both the United States and Europe, over concerns about interoperability of its CPUs (central processing units) and its bundling practices in the mainframe market. The case was dropped in the United States in 1982 and settled in Europe in 1984, with IBM agreeing to offer access to its interface protocols and not to bundle other products with its CPU.[94] By that time, however, IBM's market position had already diminished, and the company suffered a serious decline through the 1980s and 1990s, finding itself outflanked by the innovations in PCs and servers that were the source of market power for the likes of Microsoft and Intel. IBM, through some renewed innovative efforts, managed to regroup and moved into software and IT services. Perhaps

---

[92] Monopolies and Mergers Commission (1995), 'Video Games: A Report into the Supply of Video Games in the UK', March.

[93] Ibid., at [1.4].

[94] Bull EC 7/8-1984, point 1.1.1 *et seq.*

to come full circle, in 2010 the European Commission again opened proceedings against IBM in relation to anti-competitive practices in the mainframe maintenance market (the case closed a year later after IBM committed to make spare parts and technical information available to independent maintenance providers on reasonable terms).[95]

Were the concerns about IBM's durable market power founded? Doesn't the IBM case **3.165** demonstrate that all positions of market power will one day be eroded? Microsoft became the next regular suspect in competition investigations (and so did Intel, the other part of the so-called 'Wintel monopoly' that ruled the PC world after IBM's demise). As noted earlier, the European Commission found Microsoft to be super-dominant on the basis of a strong and enduring near-monopoly position in the market for PC operating systems. The network effects are stronger with Microsoft Windows than, for example, games consoles. Yet today Microsoft's position doesn't seem as powerful as it once did. In PC operating systems it faces competition from the likes of Apple Mac OS and Linux. More importantly, in devices that increasingly compete with PCs, such as set-top boxes, tablets, and smartphones, Microsoft is not the major player: Apple and Google are. As it happens, these last two companies have received their fair share of competition law scrutiny in recent years, and in particular Google's position in online search is now perceived by many to be as unassailable as that of IBM and Microsoft in the past. Will we see a decade of competition investigations into Google?

To what extent, and at what stage of development, should competition authorities inter- **3.166** vene in these dynamics markets? Economics would suggest that the long-term benefits of dynamic efficiency can easily outweigh any short-term losses of allocative inefficiency from high pricing. Judging when to intervene to support dynamic rivalry—for example, by obliging dominant companies to make their products interoperable with those of rivals, or to include rivals' offerings in search results—or when to allow market forces to run their course is inherently difficult. In Chapters 4 and 8 we discuss some economic principles that may assist in making such judgements. In any event, the principle that market power as such is not prohibited, but the abuse of it is, remains a sound one.

---

[95] European Commission (2011), 'Commission Makes IBM's Commitments Legally Binding to Ensure Competition in Mainframe Maintenance Market', press release, IP/11/1539, 14 December.

4

ABUSE OF DOMINANCE

4.1 Successful Competitor or Bull in a China Shop?

4.1.1 A matter of philosophy and policy judgement

4.01 Market power is a matter of degree, as we saw in Chapter 3. The local corner shop has market power, but not enough to be of any concern. Competition authorities have been more worried about companies such as Coca-Cola, United Brands, Deutsche Post, Sky, and Microsoft. We also saw that market power has a temporal dimension: the umbrella salesman sees his market power diminish as soon as the sun comes out, but even the very strong market positions of IBM, Microsoft, and (eventually, no doubt) Google tend to get eroded over time. How concerned you are about market power depends on your philosophy about market functioning: do you trust the process of competition to do its work over time, or do you think some state intervention can speed up the process? Philosophies and policy judgements also matter when it comes to concerns about the abuse of market power (usually labelled abuse of dominance, unilateral conduct, or monopolization). We saw in Chapter 1 that US and EU competition law come from very different traditions. While there has been convergence in the last ten to fifteen years, the differences remain marked in the approaches to unilateral conduct.

4.02 A guiding principle in US antitrust law that we referred to before is that '[t]he successful competitor, having been urged to compete, should not be turned upon when he wins'.[1] Recall the analogy of the boxing match in Chapter 1. By holding back or punishing the winner, the referee can actually dampen the intensity of the fight and leave spectators (consumers) worse off. In Europe, the approach to abuse of dominance under Article 102 was originally influenced by ordo-liberalism. This school of thought sees a strong role for the state in keeping markets competitive and protecting individual freedom. The presence of dominant companies is seen as weakening the competitive process and reducing the economic freedom of other market participants. Rather than being admired, as they often are in the United States, dominant companies tend to be viewed with suspicion in the ordo-liberal tradition. They are like the proverbial bull in a china shop. They must be restrained to prevent further damage to their already fragile surroundings. As formally established in *Michelin I* in 1983, a dominant company has a 'special responsibility not to allow its

---

[1] *US v Aluminum Co of America* 148 F 2d 416, 430 (2nd Cir. 1945).

conduct to impair genuine undistorted competition on the common market'.[2] We believe that the ordo-liberal view on how competition works is rather outdated. Economic theory and practical experience have shown that competitive dynamics can function well even in markets with some very large suppliers. Indeed, temporary positions of market power can improve competitive dynamics and provide incentives to innovate. The European Commission has recognized this, and sought to introduce some significant changes to the treatment of abuse of dominance through its 2008 Guidance on Article 102 (although the EU courts have endorsed these reforms only in part).[3] As discussed in this chapter, the reforms focus the application of Article 102 more on protecting the process of competition than on maintaining a competitive market structure as such, and on the effects rather than the form of business practices.

What is the optimal degree of intervention? Competition policy on both sides of the Atlantic, and elsewhere in the world, has largely moved away from dogmatic approaches. Instead, most competition authorities and courts try to assess allegations of anti-competitive practices by considering whether there is harm to competition. In this chapter we discuss the approaches to predation, price discrimination, rebates, margin squeeze, bundling, and refusal to supply. These approaches are reasonably similar across jurisdictions. Nevertheless, where a particular assessment of the facts does not provide a clear-cut answer (and this will happen frequently in abuse of dominance cases), differences in philosophy do still matter. The way an authority or court views dominant companies and market forces—favourably, with suspicion, or somewhere in between—will often influence its ultimate decision of whether to intervene or leave the market to do its job. **4.03**

4.1.2 Form versus effect

EU case law on abuse of dominance has historically followed a two-step approach: first determine dominance, and then assess the form or nature of the conduct. Once a company was found dominant, its 'special responsibility' not to impair competition meant that it could not engage in certain forms of behaviour, such as pricing below variable cost, tying its products, and offering loyalty and exclusivity rebates. This virtual per se prohibition, combined with a low (and mainly market-share-based) threshold for dominance, led to a rather interventionist abuse of dominance regime in Europe. Little consideration used to be given to the likely effects of these practices on competition and consumer welfare in the circumstances of a given case. **4.04**

This has now changed, up to a point. The Guidance on Article 102 endorses an approach that focuses on examining the economic effects of practices. It also builds on the principle—long accepted in US antitrust—that competition law should protect the competitive process in the market, not individual competitors. Aggressive commercial behaviour by dominant companies should not be ruled illegal merely because it makes life difficult for competitors. Rather, the analysis should focus on the effects of the behaviour on competition and consumers. If a particular business practice is unlikely to foreclose competition in a significant part of the market, or if it generates efficiencies that benefit consumers, intervention may not be required, even if individual competitors are harmed by the practice. In this regard, **4.05**

---

[2] Case 322/81 *Nederlandsche Banden-Industrie Michelin NV v Commission* [1983] ECR 3461 (*Michelin I*).
[3] European Commission (2008), 'Guidance on the Commission's Enforcement Priorities in Applying Article 82 EC Treaty to Abusive Exclusionary Conduct by Dominant Undertakings', December.

US case law requires there to be proof of a 'dangerous probability of success' in monopolizing the market. It is not sufficient to provide evidence of the form and the intent of the exclusionary conduct. This follows the Supreme Court ruling in *Spectrum Sports* (1993), a dispute between a sports goods distributor and the owner of a patent on a polymer used in athletic goods.[4]

4.06 The ECJ seemed to give the European Commission's reform efforts a boost when it referred to the importance of effects analysis in its *Post Danmark I* ruling in 2012.[5] This concerned a disputed determination by the Danish competition authority that the postal incumbent had abused its dominant position by offering targeted discounts to specific customers. There was evidence that these discounted prices were discriminatory and below average total cost (ATC). Yet the court held that this in itself was not yet sufficient to establish an abuse:

> Thus, not every exclusionary effect is necessarily detrimental to competition…Competition on the merits may, by definition, lead to the departure from the market or the marginalisation of competitors that are less efficient and so less attractive to consumers from the point of view of, among other things, price, choice, quality or innovation.[6]
>
> …Article 82 EC [now 102 TFEU] must be interpreted as meaning that a policy by which a dominant undertaking charges low prices to certain major customers of a competitor may not be considered to amount to an exclusionary abuse merely because the price that undertaking charges one of those customers is lower than the average total costs attributed to the activity concerned, but higher than the average incremental costs pertaining to that activity… In order to assess the existence of anti-competitive effects in circumstances such as those of that case, it is necessary to consider whether that pricing policy, without objective justification, produces an actual or likely exclusionary effect, to the detriment of competition and, thereby, of consumers' interests.[7]

4.07 However, the Article 102 pendulum has not swung as far towards an effects-based approach as the Commission and many practitioners (lawyers as well as economists) had wished. Indeed, the pendulum received a strong pull in the other direction in the General Court judgment in *Intel* in 2014.[8] Intel had long been the dominant chip-maker worldwide and controlled more than 70 per cent of the global market for central processing units (CPUs). In its 2009 decision the Commission carried out a detailed assessment of the effects of Intel's rebates to major computer manufacturers (referred to as original equipment manufacturers, OEMs).[9] In line with its Guidance on Article 102, the Commission assessed whether an as-efficient competitor would be able to match these rebates, and concluded it could not (we discuss this in section 4.6). The Commission also followed the more form-based case law condemning rebates that are conditional on exclusivity. Thus, both effects and form of the rebates pointed to the same conclusion in the Commission's assessment in this case. However, the General Court held that the Commission's analysis of effects was unnecessary: 'The question whether an exclusivity rebate can be categorized as abusive does not depend on an analysis of the circumstances of the case aimed at establishing a potential foreclosure effect.'[10]

---

[4] *Spectrum Sports, Inc. v McQuillan*, 506 U.S. 447 (1993).
[5] Case C-209/10 *Post Danmark A/S v Konkurrencerådet*, Judgment of 27 March 2012 (*Post Danmark I*).
[6] Ibid., at [22].
[7] Ibid., at [44].
[8] Case T-286/09 *Intel Corp v Commission*, Judgment of 12 June 2014.
[9] *Intel* (Case COMP/C-3/37.990), Decision of 13 May 2009.
[10] Case T-286/09 *Intel Corp v Commission*, Judgment of 12 June 2014, at [80].

Reminiscent of the ordo-liberal view of the world, the court held that 'exclusivity rebates **4.08** granted by an undertaking in a dominant position are by their very nature capable of restricting competition'.[11] It does not matter whether these rebates result in foreclosure of a significant or only a small part of the market. Nor does it matter that competitors are free to sell to other customers, since they 'must be able to compete on the merits for the entire market and not just for a part of it'.[12] The court also stated that even if as-efficient competitors are able to match the rebates, there could still be foreclosure effects since access to the market is made more difficult. Equally irrelevant in the General Court's view was the fact that AMD, Intel's main competitor, was commercially highly successful and grew its market share during the period of abuse. The *Intel* judgment favoured a form-based approach, unlike *Post Danmark I* before it, and went against the grain of the Commission's Guidance on Article 102.[13]

The pendulum keeps moving. The ECJ's *Post Danmark II* ruling of 2015—concerning a **4.09** rebate scheme—left greater scope for effects-based analysis than *Intel*.[14] The ECJ considered it necessary to take into account the extent of Post Danmark's dominant position, and the fact that the rebates applied to most of the incumbent's largest customers:

> the fact that a rebate scheme, such as that at issue in the main proceedings, covers a majority of customers on the market may constitute a useful indication as to the extent of that practice and its impact on the market, which may bear out the likelihood of an anti-competitive exclusionary effect.[15]

One theme in the debate about form versus effects is that of legal certainty. Everyone will **4.10** agree that sound legal criteria must give certainty to businesses and their advisers about what is allowed and what is not. We can see how it would be a lawyer's nightmare if each abuse of dominance case required an exhaustive economic analysis of all the positive and negative effects on competition and consumers. However, that is not what the more sensible proponents of an effects-based approach (both lawyers and economists) have in mind. US antitrust law has developed a set of effects-based criteria for unilateral conduct cases, and these cannot be said to create any more legal uncertainty than exists in other jurisdictions. If anything, the *Intel* ruling itself has created legal uncertainty in the EU by dismissing the as-efficient competitor test for exclusivity rebate cases, while for other price-based abuses the EU courts have endorsed it.

Nor does an effects-based approach have to be overly complex. As we set out in this chap- **4.11** ter, it can sometimes be sufficient to ask a few simple effects-based questions that take the analysis beyond dominance and form: what is the degree of dominance? What is the degree of foreclosure? Is the exclusionary strategy likely to succeed? Form-based approaches are not necessarily straightforward either. We cannot help but notice that the *Intel* judgment contains a long discussion, running over many pages, of emails, internal presentations, and other factual evidence to establish whether Intel's customers actually understood the form

---

[11] Ibid., at [85].

[12] Ibid., at [132].

[13] The *Intel* judgment generated much debate among commentators, revisiting many of the arguments on form versus effects that were used ten years earlier at the start of the Commission's reform process. See Wils (2014) and Rey and Venit (2015).

[14] Case C-23/14 *Post Danmark A/S v Konkurrencerådet*, judgment of 6 October 2015 (*Post Danmark II*).

[15] Ibid., at [46].

of the rebates—that is, that they were conditional on exclusivity. These pages could have been devoted to the question of whether the rebates led to significant foreclosure effects. We accept that a 'special responsibility' falls on the economics profession to contribute to clear and workable criteria for assessing economic effects under Article 102. Throughout this chapter we discuss the main economic criteria that have been developed, and you can judge for yourself how practical or uncertain they are.

4.1.3 The remainder of this chapter

4.12 Section 4.2 further sets out the main economic principles for assessing exclusionary conduct. It continues the discussion on form versus effects, and describes various tests to identify anti-competitive effects. Section 4.3 is also of general application, explaining the cost benchmarks that can be used to assess exclusionary conduct in the context of the as-efficient competitor test. Section 4.4 deals with predatory pricing, a classic type of abuse. Section 4.5 addresses price discrimination, a practice that is very common and often welfare-enhancing, but may sometimes have exclusionary effects. Section 4.6 discusses quantity, loyalty, and exclusivity rebates. The next sections explore margin squeeze (section 4.7), bundling and tying (section 4.8), and refusal to supply and essential facilities (section 4.9). While interventions under the abuse of dominance rules tend to focus on exclusionary behaviour, the competition rules in the EU and elsewhere (though not the United States) also condemn exploitative conduct that is directly at the expense of customers. Article 102 covers 'directly or indirectly imposing unfair purchase or selling prices or other unfair trading conditions'. There is little clarity about the criteria for exploitative abuse (and the Guidance on Article 102 does not cover it). In section 4.10 we take you through the relevant economic principles of excessive pricing as a specific form of exploitative abuse.

4.2 General Principles for Assessing Exclusionary Conduct

4.2.1 Why the effects-based approach is different

4.13 We saw that the debate on form versus effects is still in full swing in EU competition law. Here we give some more detail on the main features of an effects-based approach. First, the degree of dominance matters. Practices such as below-cost pricing and refusal to supply are more likely to have an anti-competitive effect if the perpetrator has a very high degree of dominance (or even 'super-dominance') than if it just passes the threshold for dominance.

4.14 Second, the degree of foreclosure matters. It is not just the nature or form of the conduct, but also its incidence—the extent to which the dominant company is applying it in the market. For instance, in the case of selective price cuts (e.g. targeted discounting or 'fighting brands'), the direct link between dominance and the likelihood of success of predation breaks down. The dominant company is not using the full weight of its market power to exclude rivals, so the existence of dominance in itself would not be sufficient to infer a high likelihood of success of the exclusionary strategy. Instead, what matters is whether these selective price cuts or rebates foreclose a significant or only a small proportion of all customers. Competition is clearly more likely to be harmed if a significant part of the market is foreclosed (contrary to what the General Court said in *Intel*: in the form-based approach it does not matter whether the exclusivity rebates are offered to a large or small proportion of customers).

Third, only conduct that would exclude as-efficient competitors is abusive. This princi-   **4.15**
ple seeks to draw the line between exclusionary conduct that simply reflects 'competition on the merits' and exclusionary conduct that is harmful to consumers. Fourth,
exclusionary behaviour can still be justified on the grounds of necessity, meeting competition, or efficiency.

The cases brought by Virgin Atlantic against BA illustrate how an effects-based approach   **4.16**
to abuse of dominance can result in a different outcome to a form-based approach. In 1993,
Virgin lodged a complaint before the European Commission, and in 1994 before a US
court, claiming that BA had used incentive schemes to foreclose the market and impede its
growth.[16] Using an effects-based test, the US court concluded that BA's discount schemes
had not harmed competition and it therefore rejected the complaint. The Commission
reached the opposite conclusion, focusing its analysis on the form of the incentive schemes
rather than their effects on competition.

Under the schemes, travel agents could qualify for 'performance rewards' and other   **4.17**
bonuses, and for funds from BA for marketing and staff training courses. The schemes
were generally linked to the yearly growth in the sales of BA tickets by the travel agent, and
were structured to pay rewards retroactively on all ticket sales once the performance target
was met, not just on the incremental sales above the target. In 1997, BA held 40 per cent of
Heathrow Airport's slots and operated around 60 per cent of all international routes from
the airport. Virgin was a smaller operator, with 2 per cent of slots at the same airport and
5.5 per cent of airline sales in the United Kingdom. The US court considered that Virgin
had failed to demonstrate that BA's behaviour harmed overall competition. It also stated
that BA's discounts had not prevented Virgin from becoming a successful airline; it had
even become the leading operator on the London–New York route in 1995. Furthermore,
the schemes could have only a marginal impact on the competition between travel agents
since 'truly loyal' agents (defined as those who booked more than 80 per cent of their UK–
US ticket sales with BA) represented less than 5 per cent of the total sales. The court also
held that rewarding customer loyalty promotes competition on the merits. In contrast, the
Commission focused on the form of the incentive structures offered by BA. Of particular
concern was the retroactive nature of the discounts, which might induce travel agents who
are close to the sales target to promote BA rather than rival airlines. In condemning these
schemes, the Commission highlighted the irrelevance of effects: 'Such commission schemes
carried out by a firm enjoying a dominant position as a purchaser of services from travel
agents are illegal, regardless of any possibility for the travel agents or competing airlines to
minimize or avoid their effects.'[17]

This reflects the principle in EU case law that a dominant company is allowed to offer dis-   **4.18**
counts that relate to efficiencies only (e.g. cost savings for large orders), but not to encourage
loyalty. It ignores the potential reductions in the prices of tickets offered to final consumers
or improvements in the quality of the service offered by sales agents. In contrast with the US
judgment, the commercial success of rivals was not given much weight in the Commission's
decision. Although the Commission recognized that rival airlines had been gaining market

---

[16] *Virgin/British Airways* (Case IV/D-2/34.780), Decision of 14 July 1999; and *Virgin Atlantic LTD v British Airways PLC* 257 F 3d 256 (2d Cir. 2001).
[17] *Virgin/British Airways* (Case IV/D-2/34.780), Decision of 14 July 1999, at [102].

share in the United Kingdom, it stated that 'it can only be assumed that competitors would have had more success in the absence of these abusive schemes'.[18]

4.2.2 Relevance of the degree of market power

4.19 The first stage in any abuse of dominance investigation is to define the relevant market and assess whether the company in question has a dominant position. These topics were covered in Chapters 2 and 3. The assessment of the degree of dominance is always a useful first step in the analysis of the effects of an alleged abuse. EU case law states that a dominant undertaking can act to an appreciable extent independently of competitors, both actual and potential. This should imply that the undertaking has current and future market power. Often the dominance analysis focuses on the current market position. Yet it is also important to examine the dynamic structural features of the market, so as to assess whether an abuse of a current position of market power is in fact likely to result in future market power. Dominant positions acquired through aggressive actions are of less concern if they are likely to be eroded by new entry. The analysis of entry barriers therefore matters here as well.

4.20 EU case law has focused very much on market share thresholds for dominance, with 40–50 per cent market share being the rule of thumb. In *AKZO* (1991), the ECJ ruled that a company with a stable market share of more than 50 per cent would be presumed dominant unless there were exceptional circumstances.[19] The rule of thumb also appeared in the 2005 Coca-Cola undertakings with respect to exclusivity, rebates, and tying, which applied to those countries where Coca-Cola's soft drinks represented more than 40 per cent of national sales (and more than double the share of the nearest competitor).[20] Such thresholds have a useful policy function as a safe harbour—we won't go after you if you have less than 40–50 per cent of the relevant market. However, they are not very informative for the analysis of effects. An aggressive price cut is more likely to be detrimental to competition if the company has 80 per cent of the market than if it has 40 per cent. The relevance of the degree of dominance has to some extent been recognized in EU case law, which has developed the concept of 'super-dominance'. The Guidance on Article 82 also states explicitly that 'in general, the stronger the dominant position, the higher the likelihood that conduct protecting that position leads to anti-competitive foreclosure'.[21]

4.21 This principle was reflected in *Post Danmark II* (2015), where the ECJ considered it necessary to take into account the extent of dominance.[22] Bring Citymail, a subsidiary of the Norwegian postal incumbent, had entered the Danish market for business mail, including direct mail, in 2007. It was the only serious competitor to Post Danmark, but exited the market in 2010 after suffering heavy losses. The ECJ noted that Post Danmark had a market share of more than 95 per cent in bulk mail, and that barriers to entry and expansion were high due to economies of scale and the national coverage of Post Danmark's delivery network. In addition, the ECJ considered it relevant that more than 70 per cent of the bulk mail

---

[18] Ibid., at [107].

[19] Case C-62/86 *AKZO Chemie BV v Commission*, [1991] ECR I-3359, [1993] 5 CMLR 215.

[20] *Coca-Cola* (Case COMP/A.39.116/B2), Decision of 22 June 2005.

[21] European Commission (2008), 'Guidance on the Commission's Enforcement Priorities in Applying Article 82 EC Treaty to Abusive Exclusionary Conduct by Dominant Undertakings', December, at [20].

[22] Case C-23/14 *Post Danmark A/S v Konkurrencerådet*, judgment of 6 October 2015 (*Post Danmark II*).

market was subject to statutory monopoly at the time, which meant that Bring Citymail could compete for only 30 per cent of the market (we discuss the concept of contestable share in section 4.6 on rebates).

4.2.3 Assessing effects: The welfare, profit-sacrifice, and no-economic-sense tests

It is broadly accepted that the rules on abuse of dominance should address harm to competition, not harm to competitors. But how do we know whether the competitive process is harmed? Where do we draw the line between fierce but healthy competition and exclusionary conduct? Various economic tests to assess effects and set thresholds for intervention have been proposed over the years.[23] **4.22**

Perhaps the most natural way of judging an alleged anti-competitive practice is to assess whether on balance it causes more harm than good to economic welfare. The competitive process delivers higher welfare, so if the process is harmed you would expect to see a reduction in welfare. The test would therefore ask whether the conduct reduces competition to the detriment of consumers, without creating efficiencies that are sufficient to offset this detriment. This is similar to the substantial lessening of competition criterion used in merger control (see Chapter 7). Such a test has the attractive property of fitting with competition policy's general objective of maximizing welfare (whether total welfare or consumer welfare). Its downside is that assessing the full effects on welfare is complex. Evaluating all possible anti-competitive effects and offsetting efficiencies would be a laborious exercise for courts and competition authorities. It would also be rather costly for businesses to do this in respect of all their conduct in markets where they may exceed or come close to the dominance threshold. It could result in legal uncertainty and overly cautious behaviour, dampening aggressive but desirable competitive actions. The welfare test should therefore be seen as a guiding principle for other, more practical, tests for assessing abusive behaviour. **4.23**

One of the practical approaches proposed is the profit-sacrifice test. This asks whether the conduct in question is commercially irrational 'but for' the expectation that rivals are excluded or disciplined. Practices such as below-cost pricing would be condemned under this test unless they generate higher profits in the absence of the exclusionary effect. A variant of this is the 'no-economic-sense' test. These tests are most suitable in the context of predation and similar practices which involve a temporary sacrifice of profits in the expectation of greater future profits. The advantage of the profit-sacrifice test is that it is conceptually simpler than assessing consumer welfare. The focus is on the financials of the dominant company, not on the ultimate effects on consumers. It is a fairly straightforward test to apply if the challenged conduct has an unambiguous exclusionary rationale. However, if the conduct has the effect of generating legitimate profits as well as profits from excluding competitors—that is, the conduct makes 'some' rather than 'no' economic sense—the test is less clear-cut. Think of an exclusive-dealing case where the dominant company wants retailers to stock its product but not those of its rivals, and has to pay those distributors additional commission in exchange for exclusivity. Or consider a predation case in which **4.24**

---

[23] Useful discussions on the various tests can be found in Elhauge (2003), Vickers (2005), Werden (2006), and Department of Justice (2008), 'Competition and Monopoly: Single-firm Conduct under Section 2 of the Sherman Act', September, Ch 3. The DOJ withdrew this report in 2009, but the chapter on standards for exclusionary conduct remains a useful contribution to the debate.

the company is dominant in one market and engages in below-cost pricing in a new market where network effects are important. Here the profit-sacrifice and no-economic-sense tests may not work well, since the conduct can be commercially rational with or without an exclusionary effect. An additional point to make here is that not all types of abuse involve a profit sacrifice or outright losses. A dominant company can make its competitors' lives difficult through practices that are not necessarily costly or loss-making, such as certain forms of refusal to supply and loyalty rebates. Economists place these practices under the heading 'raising rivals' costs' (Salop and Scheffman, 1987). The profit-sacrifice test would not work in these instances.

4.2.4 Assessing effects: The as-efficient competitor test

4.25 Another practical approach is the 'as-efficient competitor' test (or equally-efficient competitor test), which has gained much traction in the EU and elsewhere. This asks whether the conduct would exclude a rival that is as efficient as the dominant company. It usually assesses whether the prices charged by the dominant company cover its own costs or, in the case of margin squeeze, whether the dominant company's downstream business would be profitable if it had to pay the wholesale price charged by its upstream business. The as-efficient competitor principle seeks to draw a line between conduct that reflects competition on the merits and exclusionary conduct that is harmful to consumers. Conduct that involves the dominant company cutting its prices down to, but not below, its own costs is beneficial to consumers and will tend to exclude only rivals that are less efficient—that is, rivals with higher costs. The test works best in pricing cases, but can also be used for certain types of bundling, as discussed in this chapter.

4.26 The idea behind the as-efficient competitor test has been reflected in EU case law on predatory pricing since *AKZO* (1991), which referred to average variable cost (AVC) and ATC as the relevant benchmarks.[24] Other cost floors have since been proposed and used. The Guidance on Article 102 refers to average avoidable cost (AAC) and long-run average incremental cost (LRAIC). All these cost concepts fit within the framework of the as-efficient competitor test. We explain them in more detail in section 4.3. If prices are above the chosen cost benchmark, equally efficient companies—those with similar costs—can still compete in the market. As stated in the Guidance:

> Vigorous price competition is generally beneficial to consumers. With a view to preventing anti-competitive foreclosure, the Commission will normally only intervene where the conduct concerned has already been or is capable of hampering competition from competitors which are considered to be as efficient as the dominant undertaking.[25]

4.27 The EU courts have accepted the Commission's use of the as-efficient competitor test in a number of margin squeeze cases—*Deutsche Telekom* (2010), *TeliaSonera* (2011), and *Telefónica* (2012).[26] Yet we saw that in the *Intel* judgment the test was not accepted in relation to exclusivity rebates.

---

[24] Case C-62/86 *AKZO Chemie BV v Commission*, [1991] ECR I-3359, [1993] 5 CMLR 215.

[25] European Commission (2008), 'Guidance on the Commission's Enforcement Priorities in Applying Article 82 EC Treaty to Abusive Exclusionary Conduct by Dominant Undertakings', December, at [23].

[26] Case C-280/08 P *Deutsche Telekom AG v Commission*, Judgment of 14 October 2010; Case C-52/09 *Konkurrensverket v TeliaSonera Sverige AB*, Judgment of 17 February 2011; Case T-398/07 *Kingdom of Spain (Telefónica) v Commission*, Judgment of 29 March 2012.

A practical problem with the as-efficient competitor test can arise in markets where an **4.28** incumbent company faces competition from new entrants that do not enjoy the same scale advantages, and are therefore not as efficient, or at least *not yet* as efficient. The Guidance recognizes situations where strong network or learning effects exist, and competitors that are currently less efficient than the dominant company may be foreclosed by particular pricing practices. The implication is that even prices above ATC could be deemed anti-competitive. Yet this raises difficult policy questions since it could lead to the protection of inefficient companies. It also seems impractical from a compliance perspective—how is a dominant company to know its competitors' costs in order to benchmark whether its prices fall below that level? One area where this 'not-yet-as-efficient' competitor standard has been implemented is in liberalized markets, where a former monopolist is still dominant and new entrants are expected to gain scale advantages over time. We return to this in section 4.7 on margin squeeze.

4.2.5 Abuse of collective dominance

Article 102 refers to abuses by 'one or more undertakings', and is therefore not necessarily **4.29** only a matter of single-firm conduct. Nonetheless, abuse cases based on collective domi-nance are rare. This has a logical reason: collective dominance is more commonly associated with collusion (explicit or tacit) than with exclusionary practices. Explicit collusion among competitors is caught under Article 101. This includes collective boycotts, which in effect are similar to a refusal to supply by an individually dominant company. For an abuse of col-lective dominance, you need two or more independent companies that are united by strong economic links such that they adopt the same conduct in the market. In *Cewal* (1992), the Commission found an abuse of dominance by a shipping conference which tried to elimi-nate its main independent competitors on routes between northern Europe and Zaire (now Democratic Republic of the Congo). It signed exclusive agreements with the port authorities, established loyalty arrangements with clients, and employed so-called 'fighting ships'.[27] The role of these ships was to target competitors with selective price cuts, avoiding the need to lower the incumbent shipping companies' prices across the board. The shipping conference established a 'Special Fighting Committee' which ensured that freight tariffs were modified with respect to the prevailing conference tariffs, in order to offer lower rates than competitors for vessels sailing on the same date. The difference between the fighting tariff and the prevail-ing tariff was absorbed by all conference members.

Yet shipping conferences are a rather exceptional type of organization—their members **4.30** can act almost as one entity while benefiting from a block exemption from Article 101 (this privilege was removed in 2006).[28] As stated by the ECJ on appeal, by its very nature and objective a liner conference 'can be characterised as a collective entity which pre-sents itself as such on the market vis-à-vis both users and competitors'.[29] For collective dominance in other sectors you can see that parallel conduct motivated by economic links (and yet without amounting to a concerted practice falling foul of Article 101) is likely to be rare, and found only where there are contractual links between the companies

---

[27] *Cewal* (Case IV/32.448 and IV/32.450), Decision of 23 December 1992.
[28] European Commission (2006), 'Competition: Commission welcomes Council agreement to end exemption for liner shipping conferences', press release, 26 September.
[29] Joined Cases C-395/96 P and C-396/96 P, *Compagnie Maritime Belge and Dafra-Lines A/S v Commission*, Judgment of 16 March 2000, at [48].

involved which give them shared economic interests. For example, consider clubs organizing a sports league which behave in parallel when selling TV rights, or companies that may behave in parallel as a consequence of cross-shareholdings. For the most part, such arrangements are treated under Article 101 or as joint ventures under merger control. Where collective dominance issues do arise under Article 102, it is important to establish the link between dominance and the effects on competition: are all the collectively dominant companies adopting the same conduct at the same time, such that the full force of their dominant position is utilized?

4.2.6 Dominance and abuse in related markets

4.31 Leveraging of market power from one market to another is a topic that has been extensively dealt with in economic theory. It is also recognized in EU case law, which states that a dominant position in one market can be abused in a related market. The principle was set out by the ECJ in the *Tetra Pak II* case. This concerned the markets for aseptic and non-aseptic cartons. Tetra Pak, a major food packaging company, had a market share in aseptic cartons of nearly 90 per cent, and was accused of predatory pricing in the market for non-aseptic cartons. The ECJ referred to the concept of 'associative links' between the two markets:

> The relevance of the associative links which the Court of First Instance thus took into account cannot be denied. The fact that the various materials involved are used for packaging the same basic liquid products shows that Tetra Pak's customers in one sector are also potential customers in the other. That possibility is borne out by statistics showing that in 1987 approximately 35% of Tetra Pak's customers bought both aseptic and non-aseptic systems. It is also relevant to note that Tetra Pak and its most important competitor, PKL, were present on all four markets. Given its almost complete domination of the aseptic markets, Tetra Pak could also count on a favoured status on the non-aseptic markets. Thanks to its position on the former markets, it could concentrate its efforts on the latter by acting independently of the other economic operators.[30]

4.32 Markets can be related vertically or horizontally. Vertical leveraging is perhaps most common. Where a company has control of a key input into a downstream market in which it is competing with other suppliers, this might enable it to foreclose the downstream market. In *Tetra Pak II* the markets for the different types of carton involved were linked horizontally. Another example of horizontally related markets would be those for the delivery of general letters and for business-to-business mail services. In the *De Post-La Poste* case, the Belgian postal incumbent, which was dominant in the market for the delivery of general letters, was found by the European Commission to have abused that position with the aim of eliminating a competitor in the neighbouring market for business-to-business mail services.[31] When discussing practices such as margin squeeze, bundling, and refusal to supply, we will see several examples of vertical and horizontal leveraging. A general principle worth bearing in mind in these cases is that leveraging can be a rational strategy, but is not as straightforward as exercising market power in the same market. You cannot assume that a dominant position in one market automatically gives a company the ability to eliminate competition in another market. It is important to identify the mechanism through which the position in one market can be used to gain advantage in the other.

---

[30] Case C-333/94 *Tetra Pak v Commission* [1996] ECR 1-5951 at [29].
[31] *De Post-La Poste* (Case COMP/37.859), Decision of 5 December 2001.

4.3 Cost Benchmarks for Exclusionary Conduct

4.3.1 The logic of cost benchmarks

Cost benchmarks can help you distinguish between situations in which the dominant com- **4.33**
pany's pricing would force the exit of as-efficient rivals, and situations in which that pricing
would exclude only less efficient rivals. The basic logic of the tests for below-cost pricing was
first proposed by Areeda and Turner (1975, p. 712):

> Marginal-cost pricing by a monopolist should be tolerated even though losses could be
> minimized or profits increased at a lower output and higher price, for the reasons, among
> others, that marginal-cost pricing leads to a proper resource allocation and is consistent
> with competition on the merits. Neither reason obtains when the monopolist prices below
> marginal cost.

So marginal cost is the basic reference for cost-based benchmarks. Marginal cost pricing **4.34**
is efficient, so the logic goes, and therefore prices at or above marginal cost cannot be considered too low. Note that pricing at marginal cost can still involve a profit sacrifice since
any company with a bit of market power could do better than set price at that level. Areeda
and Turner themselves proposed AVC as a practical approximation of marginal costs. The
AVC test gained rapid acceptance in the US courts at the time.[32] Other cases referred to
variants of marginal cost: '[M]odern antitrust courts look to the relation of price to "avoidable" or "incremental" costs as a way of segregating price cuts that are "suspect" from those
that are not.'[33] EU case law has referred to AVC and ATC since *AKZO*.[34] The European
Commission's Guidance on Article 102 expresses a preference for two cost benchmarks
that are variants of marginal cost: AAC and LRAIC.[35] Below we explain the various cost
concepts, starting with marginal cost.

4.3.2 Marginal cost

Marginal cost is the cost of producing the last unit of output. As long as price exceeds **4.35**
marginal cost, each additional sale will make a contribution to profit. What is the marginal
cost of a seat on your flight from Berlin to Brussels at 7.05 a.m.? There is no 'right' answer to
this question. It depends on two dimensions: the relevant marginal (or incremental) unit of
output, and the relevant time period. The more you expand these two dimensions, the more
costs are included in your measure of marginal cost. If the plane is about to take off and has
an empty seat, the marginal cost to the airline of filling that seat is close to zero (the weight
of the extra passenger and luggage will add a fraction to the fuel costs, and they may get a
free snack). If the relevant increment is the scheduled 7.05 a.m. flight as a whole, you include
the costs of flying the plane, consisting of fuel, crew, and variable airport charges. If the
relevant increment is the whole Berlin–Brussels service, yet more costs become part of the
marginal (incremental) cost, including the costs of setting up additional service facilities at

---

[32] Early cases included *International Air Indus., Inc. v American Excelsior Co.*, 517 F.2d 714 (5th Cir.
1975); *Hanson v Shell Oil Co.*, 541 F.2d 1352 (9th Cir. 1976); and *Janich Bros., Inc. v American Distilling Co.*,
570 F.2d 848 (9th Cir. 1977).

[33] *Barry Wright Corp v ITT Grinnell Corp* 724 F 2d 227, 232 (1st Cir. 1983).

[34] Case C-62/86 *AKZO Chemie BV v Commission* [1991] ECR I-3359, [1993] 5 CMLR 215.

[35] European Commission (2008), 'Guidance on the Commission's Enforcement Priorities in Applying
Article 82 EC Treaty to Abusive Exclusionary Conduct by Dominant Undertakings', December, at [26].

either airport. In any abuse case where cost benchmarks are used, it is therefore crucial to identify the increment and time frame that would be most informative about whether an as-efficient competitor can effectively compete in the market.

4.36 We return later to the variants of marginal cost that involve larger increments and longer time periods. In Table 4.1 we first illustrate short-run marginal cost. Suppose that an incumbent airline operates four flights a day from Berlin to Brussels, and four flights in the other direction. For this operation it uses two aircraft with 150 seats. A smaller rival is about to enter the route. In response, the incumbent adds two additional flights a day in both directions, using a third aircraft. Fares on the route drop as a result. Is this a healthy competitive response or a predatory act? Cost benchmarks can help inform the assessment. We start with marginal cost. The airline now operates twelve flights a day, using three 150-seater aircraft, thus offering a total of 1,800 seats (900 in either direction). The direct variable costs of flying the plane from one airport to the other totals €5,700. This includes fuel, crew, and variable airport charges (assuming for simplicity that crew are paid per flight, and airport fees are charged per plane). In addition, there is a small variable cost of €3 per passenger, which reflects extra fuel required and the free snack they get. There are fixed costs of the operation as well, but these are not yet relevant here. The short-run marginal cost of carrying an extra passenger if the flight is already scheduled and has seats available is €3. The other variable costs are incurred regardless of whether the empty seats get filled.

4.37 In manufacturing industries the marginal cost of producing an additional unit is normally equal to AVC if the plant is below full capacity. Because capacity is more quickly exhausted in a plane, in aviation the marginal and variable costs can be lumpy, since putting on an extra aircraft comes with multiple seats.[36] If the aircraft has empty seats the cost of carrying an extra passenger is €3. But if the aircraft is full, carrying an additional passenger would require putting on an extra plane. You can see that short-run marginal cost is somewhat unsatisfactory as a benchmark for the current case. Comparing price with marginal cost tells us only whether the incumbent airline is losing money on the very last seat sold. It

Table 4.1 Short-run marginal cost

Flights per day (Berlin–Brussels, Brussels–Berlin)	12
Number of aircraft (150-seaters)	3
Total seats (12 × 150)	1,800
Variable costs (€)	
Direct cost per flight (fuel, crew, variable airport charges)	5,700
Variable cost per passenger (extra fuel, snack)	3
Fixed costs (€)	
Not relevant	
Cost benchmark (€)	
Short-run marginal cost (plane about to take off with empty seat)	3

---

[36] Alfred Kahn, a pioneer in the field of regulatory economics and a driver of airline deregulation in the United States in the 1970s, famously referred to aeroplanes as 'marginal costs with wings'. See McCraw (1984).

would be more relevant to assess whether the airline's alleged exclusionary strategy makes sense across the whole increment of potentially exclusionary output, not merely on the last unit of that output. Choosing the relevant increment is therefore important. We return to this when discussing AAC and LRAIC.

4.3.3 Average variable cost

AVC is the sum of all the costs that vary with the quantity of a particular good, divided by the total quantity. Typical variable costs are materials, fuel, and labour. The AVC benchmark is usually applied in a short-term context, taking production capacity as given and excluding all fixed costs. But it can also have a time dimension—as time passes, a higher proportion of a company's fixed costs tend to become variable. Therefore, using AVC requires (sometimes difficult) determinations of whether a particular cost is fixed or variable. AVC was suggested by Areeda and Turner (1975) as a more workable proxy for marginal cost. Information on variable cost is easier to obtain from a company's accounts. Continuing with our airline example, Table 4.2 shows the incumbent's AVC. The direct costs per flight are €5,700. Each flight offers 150 seats, so the AVC per seat equals €38. Add to this the €3 in variable cost per passenger and you get an overall AVC of €41. **4.38**

One issue to watch is that AVC normally measures the average over the product's entire output (here all twelve flights), not just the incremental output that is the focus of the exclusionary conduct. In this example there is no difference since the costs per flight are the same for the eight flights that the incumbent offered previously and the four additional flights. In other situations the additional services may have different costs—for example, if a different type of aircraft is used. An example is the response by Cardiff Bus, an incumbent operator of local bus services in Cardiff, Wales, to a new entrant, 2 Travel.[37] Cardiff Bus launched the so-called 'white services' to compete directly on 2 Travel's routes, using buses that were older than on its main routes and that did not have the Cardiff Bus livery. These white services were effectively the relevant increment of potentially exclusionary output, **4.39**

Table 4.2 Average variable cost

Flights per day (Berlin–Brussels, Brussels–Berlin)	12
Number of aircraft (150-seaters)	3
Total seats (12 × 150)	1,800
Variable costs (€)	
Direct cost per flight (fuel, crew, variable airport charges)	5,700
Variable cost per passenger (extra fuel, snack)	3
Fixed costs (€)	
Not relevant	
Cost benchmark (€)	
Short-run marginal cost (plane about to take off with empty seat)	3
Average variable cost (5,700/150 + 3)	41

---

[37] Office of Fair Trading (2008), 'Abuse of a Dominant Position by Cardiff Bus', CA98/01/2008, 18 November.

and had costs that differed from the existing services. In this case the costs were lower, but the white services were still found to be loss-making and the OFT considered the conduct to be predatory.

4.3.4 Average avoidable cost

4.40   According to the Guidance on Article 102, prices below AAC indicate that the dominant company is sacrificing profits in the short term, and an equally efficient competitor cannot match this without incurring a loss.[38] The dominant company would be better off producing nothing and avoiding these costs altogether. AAC covers all variable costs and product-specific fixed costs that could have been avoided had the company not produced a particular amount of additional output. Normally this refers to the amount that could have been avoided by not engaging in the exclusionary strategy. The absence or presence of avoidable losses is a test for whether the dominant company is making or losing money on this increment. Unlike LRAIC (discussed next), AAC omits all fixed costs that were already sunk before the time of the exclusionary conduct—that is, costs that can no longer be avoided, such as previous brand advertising. Consequently, AAC will generally be lower than LRAIC.

4.41   Continuing with the above example, the incumbent airline stands accused of having launched the four extra flights in response to new entry, resulting in a fall in fares. Which costs could have been avoided by not introducing these extra flights? Clearly this includes all variable costs, as these are by definition not incurred when not producing the output. There are also some fixed costs that can be avoided. Table 4.3 shows all the fixed costs involved in running the Berlin–Brussels service. For simplicity these are shown in terms of daily costs, where annual costs are in reality more common. This does

Table 4.3 Average avoidable cost

Flights per day (Berlin–Brussels, Brussels–Berlin)	12
Number of aircraft (150-seaters)	3
Total seats (12 × 150)	1,800
Variable costs (€)	
Direct cost per flight (fuel, crew, variable airport charges)	4,800
Variable cost per passenger (extra fuel, snack)	3
Fixed costs (€ per day)	
Cost of aircraft (€4,200 per aircraft)	12,600
Airline service costs at airports	3,000
Route marketing costs	4,200
General overhead	3,600
Cost benchmark (€)	
Short-run marginal cost (plane about to take off with empty seat)	3
Average variable cost (5,700/150 + 3)	41
Average avoidable cost (one aircraft, four flights as increment)	48

---

[38] European Commission (2008), 'Guidance on the Commission's Enforcement Priorities in Applying Article 82 EC Treaty to Abusive Exclusionary Conduct by Dominant Undertakings', December, at [26].

not really matter for the illustration of cost concepts, as AAC, LRAIC and ATC are all calculated as averages—we effectively divide the annual fixed costs by the number of operational days to get the daily fixed costs, and work out the averages from there. The first category of fixed cost is the aircraft (whether leased or owned by the airline). This is €4,200 per aircraft (€12,600 in total for the three aircraft, although only one is avoidable in this case). The second category is that of the airline's service facilities at the two airports (staff, ticket desks, etc.), totaling €3,000. These costs are fixed and do not vary with the number of flights operated each day. Third are the route-specific marketing costs, at €4,200. This is for advertising the Berlin–Brussels, Brussels–Berlin route. Assume that it has doubled since the additional services were launched in response to new entry. Finally, the airline allocates some general overheads to each of its routes, so Berlin–Brussels gets €3,600.

Which of these fixed costs are avoidable? Overhead costs and the fixed service costs at the airport cannot be avoided by going back from twelve to eight flights per day. Marketing costs for the route are sunk, and cannot be recovered by reducing frequencies on the route. They fall outside AAC. That leaves the cost of the aircraft. The airline launched the four extra services by adding another aircraft to the route. This cost of €4,200 can be avoided—the plane can be used for other routes (or the lease contract terminated). So AAC associated with the four extra flights and one extra aircraft equals the AVC of €41 (€38 per seat and €3 per passenger), plus €7 per seat for the cost of the aircraft (€4,200 divided by 600 seats)—a total of €48. **4.42**

4.3.5 Long-run average incremental cost

LRAIC is the change in total costs resulting from the production of a relevant increment in the quantity of output. It is also commonly known as LRIC (there is no real difference; LRIC is also usually expressed as an average per unit, so effectively LRAIC). The relevant increment can be the whole output of the product in question or just the incremental output associated with the exclusionary conduct. The Commission's Guidance refers to LRAIC as 'the average of all the (variable and fixed) costs that a company incurs to produce a particular product'.[39] However, if we want to understand the profitability of the exclusionary conduct it is also informative to calculate the LRAIC of just the additional output associated with exclusion. You can see here that the increment matters. Unlike AAC, LRAIC includes product-specific fixed costs even if these were sunk before the period of exclusionary pricing. In other words, LRAIC includes both recoverable and sunk fixed costs. **4.43**

What about LRAIC in our airline example? If we take the exclusionary output as the increment (i.e. the four extra flights), the main difference with AAC is that now sunk marketing costs are included as well. We mentioned earlier that half of these marketing costs were incurred with the launch of the four flights. So that is €2,100 of incremental cost, or €3.50 on average per incremental seat offered (€2,100 divided by 600 seats). LRAIC on this basis equals €51.50. Table 4.4 shows the calculation of LRAIC on a different basis, namely where the whole Berlin–Brussels operation is taken as the relevant increment. The fixed costs that are incremental to the whole route include all marketing costs (€4,200) and the fixed **4.44**

---

[39] Ibid., at n 2.

Table 4.4 Long-run average incremental cost

Flights per day (Berlin–Brussels, Brussels–Berlin)	12
Number of aircraft (150-seaters)	3
Total seats (12 × 150)	1,800
Variable costs (€)	
Direct cost per flight (fuel, crew, variable airport charges)	4,800
Variable cost per passenger (extra fuel, snack)	3
Fixed costs (€ per day)	
Cost of aircraft (€4,200 per aircraft)	12,600
Airline service costs at airports	3,000
Route marketing costs	4,200
General overhead	3,600
Cost benchmark (€)	
Short-run marginal cost (plane about to take off with empty seat)	3
Average variable cost (5,700/150 + 3)	41
Average avoidable cost (one aircraft, four flights as increment)	48
Long-run average incremental cost (whole route as increment)	52

service costs at the two airports (€3,000). These equal €4 per seat offered (€7,200/1,800), so LRAIC comes to €52 on this basis.

4.45 Pricing below LRAIC can be economically rational. As LRAIC includes all product-specific sunk and fixed costs, a company pricing below that level of cost, say at a price of €50, can still generate a positive cash flow—that is, it would cover its variable costs and hence make a contribution to the recovery of its already-sunk fixed costs. Such sales, which a LRAIC or ATC standard might condemn as exclusionary, could be profitable and hence might reflect commercially rational behaviour. In its Guidance on Article 102, the European Commission has proposed that prices above AAC but below LRAIC indicate that an equally efficient competitor might be foreclosed from the market—there is no presumption of foreclosure as is the case with prices below AAC.[40] LRAIC serves in most cases as a threshold above which concerns about exclusionary pricing are unlikely to materialize.

4.46 LRAIC (or LRIC) has been deemed to be of particular relevance to network industries. In its 1998 notice on the application of the competition rules to the telecommunications industry, the Commission indicated that LRIC could be an appropriate cost floor for predation cases:

> In the case of the provision of telecommunications services, a price which equates to the variable cost of a service may be substantially lower than the price the operator needs in order to cover the cost of providing the service. To apply the AKZO test to prices which are to be applied over time by an operator, and which will form the basis of that operator's decisions to invest, the costs considered should include the total costs which are incremental to the provision of the service. In analysing the situation, consideration will have to be given to the

---

[40] European Commission (2008), 'Guidance on the Commission's Enforcement Priorities in Applying Article 82 EC Treaty to Abusive Exclusionary Conduct by Dominant Undertakings', December, at [26].

appropriate time frame over which costs should be analysed. In most cases, there is reason to believe that neither the very short nor very long run are appropriate.

In these circumstances, the Commission will often need to examine the average incremental costs of providing a service, and may need to examine average incremental costs over a longer period than one year.[41]

In *Deutsche Post* (2001), the Commission found the incumbent postal operator in Germany **4.47** guilty of predatory pricing, cross-subsidy and granting fidelity rebates. The Commission referred to incremental cost in the medium term, including network capacity costs:

> In the period 1990 to 1995 DPAG's revenue from mail-order parcels was below the incremental costs of providing this specific service . . . This means that in the period 1990 to 1995 every sale by DPAG in the mail-order parcel services business represented a loss which comprises all the capacity-maintenance costs and at least part of the additional costs of providing the service. In such circumstances, every additional sale not only entailed the loss of at least part of these additional costs, but made no contribution towards covering the carrier's capacity-maintenance costs. In the medium term, such a pricing policy is not in the carrier's own economic interest. This being so, DPAG had no economic interest in offering such a service in the medium term. DPAG could increase its overall result by either raising prices to cover the additional costs of providing the service or—where there is no demand for this service at a higher price—to discontinue providing the service, because revenue gained from its provision is below the additional costs incurred in providing it. However, DPAG, by remaining in this market without any foreseeable improvement in revenue restricted the activities of competitors which are in a position to offer this service at a price that covers their costs.[42]

4.3.6 Average total cost

ATC is the sum of fixed and variable costs, divided by total output. Prices above ATC are not **4.48** exclusionary under the as-efficient competitor test since they allow any efficient competitor to make a profit. There are possible exceptions—although from an economic perspective you should be careful in condemning a company that covers its total costs. One is in the case of loyalty rebates, where prices can exceed ATC if measured against all units sold to a customer, but are below cost (even below AAC) if measured against the 'contestable' units only. We explain this in section 4.6. Another possible exception is where the dominant company enjoys positive network effects or economies of scope that a competitor cannot currently replicate. In this case, while the competitor's costs are higher than those of the dominant company, a competition authority may take a dynamic view on costs, that is, whether the rival could overcome its disadvantage and become as efficient as the incumbent. In our airline example the incumbent's total cost for the route add up to €97,200 per day—€73,800 of variable costs and €23,400 of fixed costs, the latter also including allocated overheads. Dividing this by the 1,800 seats offered gives an ATC of €54. See Table 4.5.

What is the conclusion in this example? We saw five potential cost benchmarks. Marginal **4.49** cost (€3) and AVC (€41) are not that informative in the current context since the question was whether the airline's expansion of capacity and resulting drop in fares on the route was exclusionary. Our measures of AAC (€48) and LRAIC (€52) are more closely related to the alleged exclusionary conduct. AAC shows the avoidable costs associated with the

---

[41] European Commission (1998), 'Notice on the application of competition rules to access agreements in the telecommunications sector—Framework, Relevant Markets and Principles' [1998] OJ C265, at [114–15].
[42] *Deutsche Post AG* (Case COMP/35.141), Decision of 20 March 2001, at [36].

Table 4.5 Average total cost

Flights per day (Berlin–Brussels, Brussels–Berlin)	12
Number of aircraft (150-seaters)	3
Total seats (12 × 150)	1,800
Variable costs (€)	
Direct cost per flight (fuel, crew, variable airport charges)	4,800
Variable cost per passenger (extra fuel, snack)	3
Fixed costs (€ per day)	
Cost of aircraft (€4,200 per aircraft)	12,600
Airline service costs at airports	3,000
Route marketing costs	4,200
General overhead	3,600
Cost benchmark (€)	
Short-run marginal cost (plane about to take off with empty seat)	3
Average variable cost (5,700/150 + 3)	41
Average avoidable cost (one aircraft, four flights as increment)	48
Long-run average incremental cost (whole route as increment)	52
Average total cost	54

expansion by four flights—if the average ticket price on these four flights falls below €48, the incumbent airline is not making a profit on those additional flights. LRAIC is indicative of whether an as-efficient competitor could compete on the route; at a price below €52 the entrant would find it difficult to cover the same marketing and fixed airport service costs as the incumbent. The example has shown that the relevant increment must be determined carefully, relating as closely as possible to the alleged exclusionary conduct. Moreover, cost benchmarks in this type of pricing abuse case must be considered in conjunction with other evidence on market structure and conduct, as we shall see in the remainder of this chapter.

4.3.7 Profitability tests for below-cost pricing

4.50 One specific issue as regards predation and margin squeeze is the allocation of costs over time—the question being what costs are within the alleged period of below-cost pricing. Where genuine investment is required in a particular year, it would be incorrect to assume that losses in that year represent below-cost pricing, since that investment is also relevant to revenues in future years. The treatment of costs should reflect these conditions. Rather than price–cost comparisons you can analyse the profitability of the product over a longer time frame, using the techniques of profitability analysis described in Chapter 3. For example, when assessing a potential margin squeeze by BSkyB in premium pay-TV services, the OFT included as a relevant cost in the profitability calculation the investment in supplying set-top boxes to new subscribers.[43] Such up-front investments should be amortized or depreciated according to their economic use—for example, operational costs (marketing or promotional costs) that are front-loaded within a project lifetime, but will be recovered over a number

---

[43] Office of Fair Trading (2002), 'BSkyB Investigation: Alleged Infringement of the Chapter II Prohibition', CA98/20/2002, 17 December, at [463].

of years. The OFT amortized the set-top box cost over an average subscriber lifetime of ten years. However, alternative amortization periods might also have been valid, including the useful lifetime of a set-top box (which was less than ten years due to changing technology). The assumption regarding the lifetime of the investment can have an appreciable impact on the results of a margin squeeze or predation test. If the set-top box were instead amortized over five years, the relevant costs for the benchmark would have been higher and profitability lower. A potential problem of profitability analysis in exclusion cases is that it does not easily distinguish between future profits arising from normal competition, and recoupment of losses following a successful predatory strategy. We turn to predation now.

4.4 Predation

4.4.1 What is predation, from an economic perspective?

Predatory pricing was for a long time one of the most debated business practices in competition law. Intuitively, there seems nothing wrong with a low price since that is exactly what competition is supposed to bring about. Still, ever since the enactment of the first competition laws, the concern has persisted that a company might unduly force its rivals out of the market by setting low prices. An early predation case was that against Standard Oil, which eventually resulted in the break-up of the company in 1911 (as discussed in Chapter 8). One accusation levied against Standard Oil was that 'it frequently cuts prices to a point which leaves even the Standard little or no profit, and which more often leaves no profit to the competitor, whose costs are ordinarily somewhat higher'.[44]   **4.51**

From an economic perspective, predatory pricing involves a dominant company deliberately incurring short-term losses to eliminate competitors, in order to be able to charge monopoly prices in the long term. This is difficult to distinguish from fierce but healthy price competition. Pricing low, and even below cost, is a common commercial practice—for example, when companies enter a new market, launch a new product, or wish to gain market share. Predatory pricing is to some extent a self-deterring practice. Predation pays off only if the predator can subsequently raise prices sufficiently to recover the previous losses, making enough extra profit thereafter to justify the risks. These risks are not small, since even the exit of a rival may not by itself destroy the rival's assets. Those assets might be acquired by new entrants. As such, while complaints about predation may be frequent—companies often cry foul when they see a rival undercutting them—actual prohibitions of predatory pricing are not. According to the Canadian Predatory Pricing Enforcement Guidelines of 1992:   **4.52**

> in the period 1980 to 1990 the Director [of Investigation and Research] received some 550 complaints alleging an offense under the predatory pricing provisions. Of those complaints, only 23 resulted in formal inquiries under the [Competition] Act, four were referred to the Attorney General, and only three resulted in the laying of charges.[45]

How can you distinguish predatory pricing from instances of aggressive but desirable low pricing? Predatory pricing can be conceptualized as a three-stage process, as shown in   **4.53**

---

[44] *Standard Oil Company of New Jersey v United States* 221 US 1 (1911).
[45] Director of Investigation and Research (1992), 'Predatory Pricing Enforcement Guidelines'. An updated version of these guidelines was published in 2008.

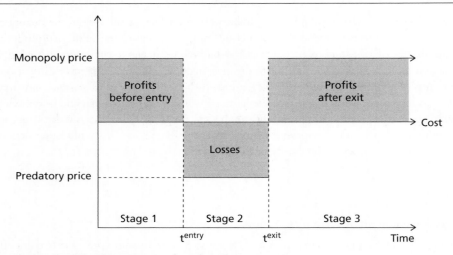

Figure 4.1 The three stages of predatory pricing

Figure 4.1. In the first stage you have a monopolist (or a dominant company that is happy to tolerate some smaller rivals in the market). The second stage is where the dominant company engages in below-cost pricing against a new or existing competitor. In the third and final stage, the rivals have been forced out of the market and the dominant company can reap monopoly profits. Any standard for assessing predatory pricing needs to take into account these three stages. The dominance criterion in essence relates to the first stage: does the alleged predator have a dominant position in the market? This makes economic sense and may seem obvious. However, in some cases the predation allegation concerns a new or related market where the predator is not (yet) dominant, and in these situations the likelihood of successfully completing the three stages may be lower. The cost benchmarks that we discussed earlier focus on the second stage. Is the alleged predator pricing below cost and hence incurring losses?

4.54   Another set of criteria that we discuss in this section focuses on the third stage, where the losses of the second stage are being recovered. If the concern about abuse of dominance is harm to consumers and not harm to competitors, it makes sense to ask if this third stage is likely to be reached and, if so, whether it will last. In other words: is successful predation feasible? If not, there should be no presumption of consumer harm (in fact, consumers benefit from low prices in the second period), and the practice usually deters itself, even if some harm may have been done to competitors in the second period. This logic is reflected in the recoupment test, which we discuss below. One advantage of this focus on the third stage is that complex price–cost comparisons for the second stage may be avoided if it is clear that the third stage is unlikely to be reached. A disadvantage is that it can be speculative as it typically refers to future market developments—most predation complaints are made during the second stage.

4.4.2 Legitimate reasons for below-cost pricing

4.55   As illustrated in Figure 4.1, what you observe in cases of predation is a period of below-cost pricing, followed by a period of high prices. The trouble is that this pricing pattern can be consistent with normal commercial behaviour—for example, in the case of the introduction of a new product or where a product exhibits strong network effects. New products are often introduced at a discount, or even given away for free—according to *The Complete MBA for Dummies*, 'Giving your products away can be a great pricing strategy' (Allen and Economy, 2000). With network effects the case for doing so is even stronger. A new network product needs to reach critical mass, and one way to achieve this is by setting very low prices, giving the product away for free, or even paying early adopters (Ten Kate and Niels, 2003). Prices are raised once critical mass has been achieved. Consumers are better off compared with the situation where the network does not get established at all. This economic logic might apply even if the network product faces no competition; in other words, monopolists may have legitimate reasons to price below cost. You can see that AVC or other cost and profitability benchmarks may not be very informative in such cases.

If the new product does face competition—say, from a rival network that seeks to achieve critical mass at the same time—the rational pricing strategy might provoke allegations of predatory pricing. When two new network products compete in this way, not only are price–cost tests of limited assistance, but it is also difficult to establish whether either is dominant since they are new to the market. Instead you could consider whether one of the providers has a dominant position in a related market which it can use to gain an undue advantage over its rival (e.g. through cross-subsidy or bundling), but you would need to be explicit about the link between dominance and abuse in the two markets. In contrast, in a situation where a company already has a dominant position in the market itself, loss-leading a new product in that market seems less likely to be justifiable. A non-dominant company has more reasons to price below cost—switching costs make it rational to persuade customers to change supplier by offering an attractive discount. **4.56**

Another rational reason to price below AVC or AAC may arise with multi-product offerings. It can be efficient to set different mark-ups for different products due to product complementarities. In restaurants, for example, the main meal can be good value but the side orders and drinks expensive. Similarly, when you buy a new car, the basic model can be priced competitively, but the optional extras such as heated car seats and metallic paint can be costly. With respect to aftermarkets, where a customer buys a product that results in follow-on purchases in a related market, it is common practice to subsidize the initial expenditure in order to acquire the customer. In supermarkets, so-called known-value items (KVIs, such as eggs or bread) may be priced as loss-leaders to attract customers to the store where high-margin products are also available. In all these situations you may observe a pattern such as that in Figure 4.1, except that the profits are not made in stage 3 on the same product but rather simultaneously in stage 2 on other products. Pricing one of the products below the relevant cost floor is in itself not harmful in these situations. Incidentally, we note that countries such as Austria, Belgium, Germany, France, and Ireland, have (or had) specific laws that prohibit below-cost pricing by retailers per se. These are not competition laws as such, but they rule out loss-leading on KVIs if it involves selling below the purchase price. This is a rather protectionist measure. It may shield smaller retailers from competitive pressures, but has been shown to have resulted in higher overall retail prices and impaired competitive dynamics.[46] **4.57**

---

[46] See Oxera (2005a) and Collins and Oustapassidis (1997).

4.4.3 Recoupment, and the feasibility of predation

4.58   From an economic perspective, a useful starting point when trying to distinguish legitimate price competition from predatory pricing is to examine the market structure. From this it may be evident that the market in question does not lend itself to successful predation. In many markets, stage 3 of Figure 4.1 may never be reached, or may be very short-lived as new entrants come in. Analysing market structure first can be an efficient way of dealing with predation complaints. This logic can be seen in the US Supreme Court's *Brooke Group* judgment of 1993, which established the 'recoupment test' as the primary standard for predatory pricing cases, relegating cost-based tests and inquiries into intent to a second stage:

> Recoupment is the ultimate object of an unlawful predatory pricing scheme; it is the means by which a predator profits from predation. Without it, predatory pricing produces lower aggregate prices in the market, and consumer welfare is enhanced. Although unsuccessful predatory pricing may encourage some inefficient substitution toward the product being sold at less than its cost, unsuccessful predation is in general a boon to consumers... That below-cost pricing may impose painful losses on its target is of no moment to the antitrust laws if competition is not injured.[47]

4.59   The recoupment test means that intervention is required only if the 'predatory' prices are likely to be offset (i.e. recouped) at a later stage through monopoly profits. In terms of Figure 4.1, the recoupment test comes down to measuring whether the losses in stage 2 are likely to be outweighed by the subsequent profits in stage 3. It is a matter of comparing the size of the rectangle in the middle to that on the right (although the profits in stage 3 are later in time and therefore need to be discounted). In this sense, predation strategies may be compared to a financial investment decision: below-cost pricing is the initial 'investment', followed by payback once market power is achieved or restored (Elzinga and Mills, 1989).

4.60   The recoupment test can be applied more pragmatically. Rather than regarding it as a rigid mathematical exercise, the DOJ has referred to the recoupment test as 'a valuable screening device to identify implausible predatory-pricing claims'.[48] In EU competition law, the feasibility of recouping losses is now also recognized as a relevant factor in predatory pricing cases, although it is not given the same importance as in the United States. EU case law has usually assumed that recoupment is feasible once dominance is established. In the 2009 *France Télécom* ruling, the ECJ acknowledged for the first time that recoupment may be relevant in the assessment, but it rejected the earlier opinion of the Advocate General in this case that recoupment should be a necessary condition to establish predation.[49]

4.61   Incidentally, the logic of recoupment (aligned with a certain scepticism regarding predation complaints) is not new. In 1904, the economist A.C. Pigou made the following comment in the context of 'dumping', a practice in international trade that has some similarities with predation:

> Destructive dumping into England from abroad does not take place, and for a very simple reason. The only purpose of that policy is to secure the control of the supply, and therewith the power to extract monopoly prices... In the British market, if a German Kartel or an

---

[47]   *Brooke Group Ltd v Brown & Williamson Tobacco Corp* 509 US 209 (1993).
[48]   Department of Justice (2008), 'Competition and Monopoly: Single-firm Conduct Under Section 2 of the Sherman Act', September, p. 69.
[49]   Case C-202/07 P *France Télécom v EC Commission*, Judgment of 2 April 2009.

American Trust kills British competitors, what advantage has it? It is still prevented from reaping its reward by the presence of sellers from other foreign countries. It will not, therefore, be worth its while to 'dump' unless it has not merely an American or a German, but a world-embracing monopoly.[50]

4.4.4 Determinants of the feasibility of predation

In what circumstances is it likely that the stage 3 monopoly profits would outweigh the losses from the predatory pricing stage? From the perspective of the predator, stage 2 must be short and stage 3 must be long—predation must be 'quick and dirty'. If stage 2 drags on, the dominant company keeps building up losses and the prospect of ever recouping these losses diminishes. Driving out competitors through low prices is usually more costly for the predator than for its victims because it has a higher market share. In the *Deutsche Post* case the below-cost pricing period was six years (albeit that in this case the incumbent may have been able to enjoy higher profits in related markets during this period—a different type of recoupment).[51] At the other extreme, in *Aberdeen Journals*, the OFT formally found predation during only one month, which seems on the short side (indeed predation was apparently not successful as the competitor remained in the market).[52] We discuss this case in more detail below. Another factor of importance is the proportion of customers who are offered low prices. The ability to exclude rivals from the market and ultimately affect consumer welfare depends on the proportion of the market that is foreclosed. If a dominant company with 60 per cent of the market targets only 10 per cent of its customers with a discount, the foreclosure effect may be weaker than if it offered the discount to its entire customer base (although in some circumstances targeting the discounts at those customers who could potentially switch to a rival can be an effective predatory strategy if other customers cannot easily switch—we return to the issue of 'contestable share' of the market in the discussion about rebates in section 4.6). **4.62**

Next you would consider the structural features of the market. Successful predatory pricing requires having market power now (during the predation period) and in the future (during the recoupment period). As to current market power, the dominant company must expand output in order to depress the overall market price and put pressure on its rivals. To have a strong impact on market price, it needs a substantial market share from the start. A company with 80 per cent of the market will find this easier than a company with only 40 per cent market share. Moreover, if market demand is elastic, the dominant company must take on further sales at a loss in order to satisfy the new demand that is created at the lower price, in addition to the sales it gains from its victims as they exit. A company planning to initiate a predatory campaign must therefore have sufficient capacity to expand output beyond current levels. Finally, just as the dominant company needs a source of funds for predation, so an intended victim can withstand and prolong the price-cutting period by using its own reserves, obtaining outside financing, or engaging in long-term relationships with clients. **4.63**

As to future market structure, the costs of predation must be offset by recoupment via future monopoly profits. Such profits depend on an expectation of enhanced market power via the exclusion of rivals. As noted above, even if current competitors are forced to exit, **4.64**

---

[50] Quoted in Viner (1923), p. 120.
[51] *Deutsche Post AG* (Case COMP/35.141), Decision of 20 March 2001.
[52] Office of Fair Trading, *Predation by Aberdeen Journals Ltd*, No CA98/5/2001, [2001] UKCLR 856.

a monopoly price cannot always be sustained for long enough because of new entry or re-entry by former rivals. Recoupment is thus possible only if there are high barriers to entry. However, driving rivals out of the market simultaneously requires low barriers to exit for actual competitors. Such asymmetry between entry and exit conditions may not be typical. If barriers to entry are high because it requires significant investment in highly specific assets, exiting the market may be unattractive as there is value to the option of the assets remaining in the market, either by riding out the predatory attack, or by selling the assets to another competitor.

4.4.5 Reputation effects: Achieving recoupment by deterring future entrants

4.65 In predation cases there is a further relevant entry barrier: the predatory strategy may send a signal that the dominant company will price aggressively in response to any future entry. This provides another means to achieve recoupment. The point is intuitive. Even when it is easy to open the door to a house and step inside (there are no entry barriers), you may think twice if you see the pathway to the house littered with corpses. Economics, and in particular game theory, has formalized this logic, and identified the circumstances in which it is most likely to apply.[53] This is therefore the point at which to introduce some basic game theory.

4.66 Figure 4.2 shows a game tree. There are two players—the incumbent and a potential entrant—and they move sequentially. The entrant moves first, and decides whether to enter or stay out. Then, if the entrant comes in, the incumbent decides whether to 'fight' by pricing low and expanding output, or simply to 'share' the market. The pay-offs to the two players are shown at the bottom of the tree for each possible outcome. Consider the left branch first. Here the entrant faces a 'normal' incumbent. For this incumbent, fighting the entrant is costly, that is, it requires below-cost pricing. There are three outcomes of this branch. To the left, the entrant stays out and the incumbent reaps monopoly profits of 10 (the entrant's pay-off is 0). In the middle, the incumbent fights the entrant and both make a

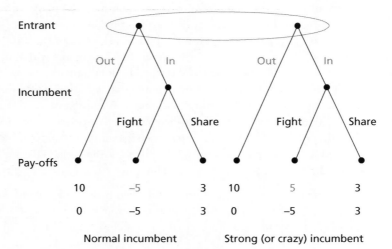

Figure 4.2 A game tree: reputation effects in predation

---

[53] The leading works are Selten (1978), Kreps and Wilson (1982), and Milgrom and Roberts (1982).

loss of 5. In the outcome to the right, the incumbent accommodates entry and both players make a profit of 3.

If this game on the left-hand side of the figure were played by itself and only once, the incumbent would never fight, because fighting is always more costly than sharing the market with these pay-offs. Knowing this, the entrant will always enter. Predation does not work. However, what if the entrant does not know whether it faces a 'normal' incumbent or a 'strong' incumbent? As shown on the right-hand branch, by strong incumbent we mean one that has an efficiently low cost base and spare capacity. This strong incumbent can successfully fight entry by just undercutting the entrant's costs, while still covering its own costs. In the figure it gets a positive pay-off of 5 from fighting. Other models feature an incumbent that is 'crazy'—that is, it gets some positive utility from picking a fight. The effect is the same as for the strong incumbent. The entrant's lack of information regarding whether the incumbent is strong or weak is denoted by the ellipse at the top of the figure. The entrant does not know on which side of the game tree it is playing. Such imperfect information is not an unrealistic assumption; entrants may generally not know whether the incumbent has a significant cost advantage. Importantly, in this situation, 'normal' incumbents can create a false reputation—or essentially bluff—that they are strong (or crazy), and thereby deter future entrants. **4.67**

It is in the incumbent's interest, therefore, to try to signal to all entrants that it is strong. Imagine that the incumbent is a multi-product firm. Predating in one market can bring wider benefits if it establishes the incumbent's reputation as a strong competitor who will always fight predation across its other key markets. Recoupment is no longer just about future profits for the product that is subject to predation, but also about protecting profits earned in other markets in which the incumbent is dominant. This logic of reputation effects has been given some weight in the assessment of entry barriers in a number of abuse and merger cases (i.e. it is not restricted to predation). The European Commission's 2007 merger decision on *Ryanair/Aer Lingus* stated the following: **4.68**

> The Commission's investigation showed that Ryanair has a reputation of engaging in aggressive competition in case of new entry to Ireland, notably by temporarily lowering prices and expanding its capacity in order to drive out the new entrant on routes to or from Ireland. The likelihood of aggressive retaliation is relevant because it has the factual consequence that potential entrants are likely to be deterred from entry and that it is less likely that a dominant firm will be constrained by the threat of new entry.[54]

The logic can also be seen in one of the US court rulings in the *Microsoft* monopolization case: **4.69**

> Most harmful of all is the message that Microsoft's actions have conveyed to every enterprise with the potential to innovate in the computer industry. Through its conduct toward Netscape, IBM, Compaq, Intel, and others, Microsoft has demonstrated that it will use its prodigious market power and immense profits to harm any firm that insists on pursuing initiatives that could intensify competition against one of Microsoft's core products. Microsoft's past success in hurting such companies and stifling innovation deters investment in technologies and businesses that exhibit the potential to threaten Microsoft. The ultimate result is that some innovations that would truly benefit consumers never occur for the sole reason that they do not coincide with Microsoft's self-interest.[55]

---

[54] *Ryanair/Aer Lingus* (Case COMP/M.4439), Decision of 27 July 2007.
[55] *US v Microsoft*, Civil Action No 98-1232 (TPJ), US District Court for the District of Colombia, Court's Findings of Fact, 5 November 1999.

4.70 Thus, the incentives to deter entrants are enhanced if the predator is active in several markets—either sequentially in time, or in a number of geographic or product markets. However, bear in mind that the predator may be bluffing if it is using predation in one market to signal strength in other markets. Ultimately, in the game-theoretical logic, bluffing works only if weakness is never revealed (i.e. entry is always fought). Even Microsoft has not managed to fight off entrants for some of its products, and has thereby revealed that it is not always the 'strong' or 'crazy' incumbent of the theoretical models. Another question is whether the act of bluffing itself should be considered abusive. Any aggressive act might in theory add to a company's reputation, and in game theory the predatory acts do not necessarily involve below-cost pricing (any undercutting of the entrant may do). From this perspective the cost benchmarks discussed previously seem more suitable for identifying practices that exclude as-efficient competitors. Reputational effects may be useful additional indicators when assessing recoupment or entry barriers more generally.

4.4.6 The (limited) relevance of intent

4.71 Intent is a subjective concept. Sometimes intent is inferred if an incumbent reduces its price after entry, forcing the new competitor to exit. However, such behaviour may also occur in competitive circumstances. After all, new entry has the effect of increasing overall market output, and confronts the incumbent with the choice of reducing price or ceding market share. If the incumbent's price decrease is down to the level of its own cost, only entrants with higher costs will leave the market. So rather than intent, it is the cost benchmarks discussed in section 4.3 that help identify instances where an as-efficient competitor is excluded. In addition, aggressive boardroom talk and internal memos revealing intentions to marginalize rivals may also be entirely consistent with fierce but healthy competition. A situation where competitors talk about each other using combative language is clearly preferable to one where they have a cosy relationship and veer towards tacit collusion.

4.72 Thus, factual evidence of an intentional predatory strategy is of limited relevance from an economic point of view. Naturally it adds some colour to the picture that the claimant or competition authority is presenting when bringing a predation case. It may also be used to confirm suspicions or to point to further areas of investigation. As noted earlier, the *AKZO* test in EU case law states that prices in the range between AVC and ATC can be predatory if set in the context of a plan aimed at eliminating a competitor, so evidence of intent is considered to be important.[56] In contrast, in *Brooke Group* the US Supreme Court held that no matter how strong and unambiguous the evidence of intent, predation could not be established unless objective market factors showed that recoupment is possible.[57] An earlier lower court decision, *AA Poultry Farms* (1989), had already rejected intent as a basis for liability in predatory pricing cases:

> Firms 'intend' to do all the business they can, to crush their rivals if they can... Entrepreneurs who work hardest to cut their price will do the most damage to their rivals, and they will see good in it... If courts use the vigorous, nasty pursuit of sales as evidence of forbidden 'intent', they run the risk of penalizing the motive forces of competition.[58]

---

[56] Case C-62/86 *AKZO Chemie BV v Commission*, [1991] ECR I-3359, [1993] 5 CMLR 215.

[57] *Brooke Group Ltd v Brown & Williamson Tobacco Corp* 509 US 209 (1993).

[58] *AA Poultry Farms, Inc. v Rose Acre Farms, Inc.* 881 F 2d 1396 (7th Cir. 1989), cert. denied, 494 US 1019 (1990).

Evidence on intent was considered in the OFT's investigation into alleged predatory pric-   **4.73**
ing by Flybe, a regional airline.[59] Flybe had entered the Newquay–London Gatwick route
in 2009. The incumbent on that route, Air Southwest, accused it of predatory pricing. If it
strikes you as odd that the entrant should be accused of predation rather than the incumbent,
you are right, but the theory of harm was that Flybe intended to cause Air Southwest losses
on its main route so as to drive it out of business altogether. Air Southwest had its main base
at Plymouth Airport, and was a regional competitor to Flybe's base at Exeter Airport (the two
airports being about one hour's drive from each other in the south-west of England). There
was some evidence from internal Flybe documents that appeared to be in line with such a
theory of harm. Flybe saw Air Southwest's Plymouth operations as a threat, and wished to
prevent other airlines from acquiring Air Southwest. Flybe believed Air Southwest to be in
a financially vulnerable position, with the Newquay–Gatwick route being its only profitable
route, and considered that Air Southwest would not survive Flybe's aggressive entry on that
route. However, the OFT also noted that 'there is a danger that statements simply indicating
legitimate strong rivalry between competitors may be incorrectly interpreted as evidencing
a clear and unlawful intention to eliminate a competitor'.[60] Instead, the OFT carried out
detailed analysis of the likely effects on competition. It rejected the predation complaint,
emphasizing that Flybe was the new entrant on the route and therefore not dominant. Flybe
had projected losses (prices below AAC) for the first two years of operation on the route,
but this was no different from recent instances of new entry on other routes. As to the links
between the Newquay–Gatwick route and the wider south-west market, the OFT considered that these were not sufficient to support the theory of harm that predation in the former
would strengthen a dominant position in the latter.

4.4.7 Newspaper wars: The predation principles illustrated

The *Aberdeen Journals* (2001) case provides a useful illustration of several of the economic   **4.74**
principles discussed in this section.[61] The evidence collated by the OFT seemed to paint a
clear picture. Aberdeen Journals, previously a monopolist in the local newspaper market in
Aberdeen, sought to get rid of a new entrant which had introduced a free-of-charge weekly
newspaper, the *Aberdeen & District Independent*. Internal memos revealed that Aberdeen
Journals' parent company had specifically set aside funds to fight the entrant. Management
was told to 'please keep your foot on their neck'. Its own free newspaper, the *Herald & Post*,
was 'pitched against the *Independent*', 'with a view to denying the *Independent* all commercial oxygen', and 'to neutralise them'. Aberdeen Journals even considered acquiring its rival,
while trying to convince it 'that we will not allow the *Independent* to break even'. Hence
there was plenty of evidence on intent. But what about the analysis of economic effects?

Aberdeen Journals published three local newspapers in the Aberdeen area, two of which   **4.75**
were paid-for daily titles, and one, the *Herald & Post*, was a free-of-charge weekly title. It

---

[59] Office of Fair Trading (2010), 'No Grounds for Action Decision: Alleged Abuse of a Dominant Position
by Flybe Limited', Case No. MPINF-PSWA001-04, December. We advised Flybe on this case.
    [60] Ibid., at [6.78].
    [61] Office of Fair Trading (2001), 'Predation by Aberdeen Journals Ltd', Case No. CA98/5/2001, 16 July.
At first this decision was reversed on appeal by the Competition Appeal Tribunal (CAT) because of the way
the OFT had treated market definition, but a subsequent decision in which the OFT reinstated its finding of
predation was ultimately upheld by the CAT. *Aberdeen Journals Limited v Office of Fair Trading*, [2003] CAT
11, 23 June 2003. These subsequent stages do not alter our discussion of the case here.

was the only publisher of paid-for newspapers in the area. The *Herald & Post* had faced competition from the *Independent* since 1996. Including both paid-for and free newspapers, Aberdeen Journals had a local market share of over 70 per cent by value and over 60 per cent by volume. The OFT determined that Aberdeen Journals was dominant in the market of supply of advertising space in both paid-for and free local newspapers, and that it had sold advertising space in the *Herald & Post* below AVC. Thus, the OFT considered paid-for and free local newspapers to be in the same relevant market. However, it also stated that its finding of predation would hold even if separate markets were defined for the two types of newspaper. Aberdeen Journals would still have abused its dominant position in the paid-for market (where it had a monopoly) by behaving predatorily in the 'associated' market for advertising space in free newspapers.

4.76 Does this accord with economic theory? It is clear from the evidence that Aberdeen Journals 'pitched' only its own free newspaper, the *Herald & Post*, against the *Independent*. It reduced prices of advertising space in the *Herald & Post*, but not in its two paid-for newspapers. The OFT described the *Herald & Post* as a 'fighting title'—a reference to the 'fighting brands' and 'fighting ships' we mentioned earlier. However, from an economic point of view, there is something inherently implausible about 'fighting brand' allegations that involve predation in only a segment of a broader market. If the two types of newspaper were really close substitutes, the reduction in price of advertising space in the *Herald & Post* would be expected to depress the advertising prices for paid-for titles as well. The fact that apparently no such substitution took place is an indication that the two products were actually in separate markets.

4.77 If predation takes place only in one segment, the relationship between the predator's market share and the competitive effects of predation breaks down. With fighting brands, the predator does not use the full weight of its market share in the combined market— Aberdeen Journals was not using its full 60–70 per cent share of the overall market to fight the *Independent*, since only prices for its free newspaper were lowered. Therefore, the general principle that a high market share means a high likelihood of success of predation cannot be applied to this case. If anything, Aberdeen Journals was the smaller supplier in the separate market for free newspapers, with a share of around 30 per cent, while the *Independent* had 70 per cent. In order to make the case that predation is enabled by leveraging market power from a neighbouring market, it is necessary to show explicitly how linkages between the two markets facilitate such predation.

4.78 Using monopoly profits in one market to subsidize losses in the other market would be an example of such a link. The OFT noted that Aberdeen Journals was part of a major newspaper group. This is a 'deep-pockets' argument. The fact that it could fund the losses made on the *Herald & Post* for four years was taken by the OFT as evidence of Aberdeen Journals' (or its parent company's) deep pockets. However, the relevance of the deep-pocket argument is limited. For an assessment of the economic impact of predatory pricing, it is in principle irrelevant where the predator's losses are funded from. Indeed, internal memos suggested that Aberdeen Journals was somewhat disappointed about the 'stalemate' after four years of fighting: 'Our response to [the owner of the *Independent*] was very vigorous and most publishing entrepreneurs would not have been able to fund these losses over four years.' This seems to suggest that the *Independent* may have had some deep pockets of its own.

4.79 From the evidence presented by the OFT, it appears that the *Aberdeen Journals* case does not really fit the requirements for feasible predation. The internal memos show that Aberdeen

Journals had repeatedly been over-optimistic about its chances. In mid-1996 it believed that the *Independent* would cease publication by Christmas that year. In May 1998 it expected to be successful in closing down its rival over the next 18 months to two years. Yet by March 2000, the *Independent* still had a share of more than two-thirds in the free newspaper market. All this does not point to significant economic effects or a high likelihood of success of predation, despite the factual evidence that such a strategy was intended.

4.5 Price Discrimination

4.5.1 What is price discrimination?

Price discrimination is defined as the sale of different units of the same product at price differentials that do not correspond to any cost difference. The most common form is the sale of identical products to different customers at varying prices. The definition also includes the sale of identical units to the same buyer at different prices (e.g. electricity suppliers charging a customer lower tariffs for each additional block of demand), and charging the same price for transactions entailing different costs (e.g. uniform geographic pricing in postal services). Charging customers different prices that reflect differences in costs is not discriminatory. We discussed price discrimination in Chapter 2 on market definition, showing that it can sometimes give rise to separate price discrimination markets. A potential concern about price discrimination under the abuse of dominance rules is that charging one customer more than another may distort competition between those customers if they compete with each other in a downstream market. **4.80**

There are three basic requirements for price discrimination to be feasible. First, the seller must have some control over price. For this reason, the fact that a company is able to price-discriminate is sometimes taken as an indication of a degree of market power (but not necessarily a high degree, given how common price discrimination is in many markets and industries). Second, the seller must be able to divide its customers into groups or markets with different price elasticities of demand—that is, groups that react differently to a price change. It must therefore have enough information about customers' willingness to pay so that it can segment the market. Finally, there must be very limited scope for arbitrage—that is, low-price customers reselling the product to high-price customers, or purchasing it on their behalf. Any arbitrage would undermine the ability to price-discriminate. **4.81**

Economics textbooks distinguish three types of price discrimination. First-degree (or perfect) price discrimination occurs where the seller charges each buyer the maximum amount they are willing to pay. The seller thus captures the entire consumer surplus. This practice is rare because it requires perfect information about each customer. However, it may be approximated in some bargaining situations, such as haggling for a second-hand car. Savvy sales people may extract each customer's full willingness to pay during the bargaining process. (You may have heard the advice 'never pay the sticker price on a car', but this is what facilitates price discrimination: the actual price is set as a variable discount on the sticker price.) First-degree price discrimination may also be on the rise in online markets. For many online products, information on customers has improved radically as search engines, social networking sites, and other online service providers follow your and other internet users' every click and thereby observe demand patterns in real time (to the point of raising privacy concerns). Personalized pricing in online markets is becoming more common as a result. **4.82**

4.83   Second-degree price discrimination (sometimes more generally called non-linear pricing) occurs when a company offers a selection of deals and allows each customer to choose the one that most suits them. This is a very common business practice. Carnets—books of ten single tickets on the Paris Metro—have a lower unit price than buying single tickets individually. Mobile phone users can choose from a variety of price packages. Volume discounts and loyalty rebates are also forms of second-degree price discrimination. The last type is third-degree price discrimination. Usually a company does not have sufficient information to price-discriminate perfectly; instead, it may be able to segment its market and price each segment differently. This is also frequently observed across many markets. Student discounts and regional variation in pricing are examples of this. The company charges different prices to consumers with different observable characteristics (such as gender, age, or location).

4.5.2   What are the benefits of price discrimination?

4.84   Price discrimination is a very common business practice, as we saw from the examples above. Economists also see it as usually a good thing. Economic theory shows that in many circumstances price discrimination enhances economic welfare and efficiency by increasing total market output compared with a situation of uniform pricing. It allows sales to customers or markets that would not be served if price was the same everywhere. This output expansion is welfare-enhancing in its own right. In Chapter 1 we explained the principle that any transaction between a willing buyer and a willing seller is inherently desirable from an economic welfare perspective.

4.85   Price discrimination may also offer an effective means for suppliers to recover the fixed costs of production. In a market with many small suppliers producing a homogeneous product, the most efficient outcome is achieved if price equals marginal cost. However, in many industries such pricing would not allow companies to recover their fixed costs. In these circumstances, charging non-uniform prices can expand the market that is served and allow suppliers to recover fixed costs more effectively than by raising prices across the board. It is well established in economic theory that the most efficient departure from marginal cost pricing is a 'Ramsey' form of price discrimination—named after the economist Frank Ramsey—where customers with greater willingness to pay and less elastic demand are charged higher prices.[62] The Ramsey pricing logic originally referred to taxation (Ramsey, 1927), but applies to pricing generally: by charging higher prices to the less elastic customers, the distortion of such high pricing (or taxation) is minimized because the negative effect on output is smallest. If you charged the higher price to the elastic customers instead, the negative effect on output would be greater.

4.86   The benefits of price discrimination can be explained by reference to the standard monopoly representation (recall Figure 2.4), where the monopolist sets the same price for all customers. Compared with a situation of perfect competition there is a deadweight loss that benefits no one. Customers who are willing to pay the cost of the product but not the monopoly price are not being served. What happens if the monopolist is able to price-discriminate? Take first-degree discrimination. The savvy monopolist is able to bargain with its customers one by one and extract their maximum willingness to pay. Customers with a willingness

---

[62]   See, for example, Baumol and Bradford (1970).

to pay equal to the single monopoly price pay the same as before. Customers to the left of this point on the demand curve, with a higher willingness to pay, now pay more. They still benefit from buying the product at a price they are willing to pay, but the monopolist has extracted their consumer surplus. However, the monopolist does not stop there. It can still profitably sell to customers further to the right on the demand curve, with a lower willingness to pay, in the safe knowledge that it can keep prices for the other customers unchanged (thanks to the ability to engage in first-degree price discrimination). Indeed, the monopolist can sell all the way down to where the price just covers its marginal cost. Therefore, under first-degree price discrimination by a monopolist, output and total welfare are exactly the same as under perfect competition—there is no deadweight welfare loss. The catch is that this total welfare now ends up entirely in the monopolist's pockets. However, if you are indifferent to how welfare is distributed between consumers and producers (as economists are in theory), this is still the preferred outcome. If it seems unfair, think of those customers to the right of the monopoly output who now get to buy the product when previously they could not afford it.

Second- and third-degree price discrimination can have similar output-expanding effects. **4.87** Just think about how many mobile phone contracts would be sold if everyone had to buy exactly the same price package. Or ask yourself whether airlines would offer as many flights as they currently do if every passenger had to pay the same fare. When publishers try to extract more revenues from a book by first issuing a hardcover edition at a high price (those keenest to get their hands on the book will purchase it at that price), followed by a cheaper paperback edition, the result may be an increase in the total quantity of the book sold compared with a strategy of a single price.[63] There is even greater flexibility to price-discriminate over time with e-books. Hollywood studios do the same by issuing their films sequentially in different 'windows': cinemas, premium pay-TV channels and online streaming, DVD rental and sale, and finally free-to-air TV.

Another example of third-degree price discrimination having positive output effects is the **4.88** supply of medicines at different prices to different countries. Countries with a lower willingness or ability to pay, or stricter government procurement and pricing rules, can be charged a lower price and still be served, while price remains high in the other countries. This output expansion is efficient and it may perhaps also be said to be fair—the poorest countries get their medicines cheap (at marginal cost, say), while the high profit margins in the rich countries allow the pharmaceutical companies to recover their fixed R&D costs. Under a single price, some of those poorest countries might not be served at all. These strategies of price discrimination across national markets give intermediary companies the incentive to exploit arbitrage opportunities by engaging in parallel trade (also known as grey imports), thus undermining price discrimination. Attempts by pharmaceutical companies to deter such parallel trade have given rise to a different type of abuse of dominance case, as discussed below.

Finally, we note that from a competition law perspective, price discrimination has an additional benefit in oligopolistic markets: it can scupper attempts at tacit and explicit collusion. It is difficult for cartel members to detect cheating in a market where companies can offer secretive discounts to their customers. Given that collusion is one of the prime concerns of

---

[63] Knowing this, what do you make of the pricing strategy for this book?

competition law, such discounting practices are quite desirable. In all, economists see price discrimination as a benign phenomenon in many circumstances.

4.5.3 So what are the concerns about price discrimination?

4.90 The beneficial effects of price discrimination explain why competition law does not normally condemn the practice by dominant companies per se, but rather assesses its effects on welfare and competition. There are four main reasons why competition law may make such assessments. First, charging excessively low prices to some but not all customers may have the effect of excluding competitors from the market—a form of predatory pricing. Second, charging one customer more than another may distort competition between those customers if they compete with each other in a downstream market. The US Robinson–Patman Act of 1936, which specifically addresses price discrimination, calls this secondary-line injury to competition (the first effect, predatory pricing, is called primary-line injury). Third, a dominant company may be seen to be exploiting the group of customers to which it charges the higher price. Finally, segmenting markets and engaging in price discrimination along national boundaries is seen in the European Union as going against the objective of creating a 'single market'. This concern has been central in a number of actions by the European Commission and policy-makers against attempts by companies to carve out national markets and prevent parallel imports in products ranging from pharmaceuticals and new cars to mobile roaming and the geo-blocking of online content.

4.91 How can each of these concerns be addressed? For the first and the third, the answer to this question can be given swiftly. Complaints about exclusion of competitors through price discrimination can normally be assessed as predatory pricing. Whether the investigated company charges higher prices to other customers or markets is usually not of major importance in the assessment of economic effects of such discounting; the relevant question is whether the low prices charged are excessively low, not whether they are discriminatory as such. Likewise, if the concern is about the exploitation of some customers you can deal with this along the lines of an excessive pricing inquiry.

4.92 From an economic perspective, secondary-line injury is the main concern about price discrimination, and indeed non-price forms of discrimination, such as discriminatory access conditions. Article 102 itself also seems to emphasize this concern. Paragraph (2)(c) states that an abuse of dominance may consist of 'applying dissimilar conditions to equivalent transactions with other trading parties, thereby placing them at a competitive disadvantage'. This implies that the favoured and the disadvantaged customers must be competing with each other in a downstream market. In its *United Brands* (1978) and *Hoffmann-La Roche* (1979) judgments, the ECJ established secondary-line injury as the relevant criterion for applying Article 102(2)(c).[64] In *United Brands*, it found that price discrimination between national markets by the dominant supplier of bananas in Europe placed certain downstream distributors at a competitive disadvantage. In *Hoffmann–La Roche* it was certain purchasers of vitamins that were disadvantaged vis-à-vis other purchasers.

---

[64] Case 27/76 *United Brands v Commission* [1978] ECR 207; and Case 85/76 *Hoffmann-La Roche & Co AG v Commission* [1979] ECR 461.

Price discrimination with downstream effects will be of greatest concern if the relevant **4.93** product is an essential input for downstream producers and if the favoured customer is a subsidiary of the provider of the essential input. This situation commonly arises in network industries such as telecoms, rail, gas, and electricity. Often these concerns are addressed through sector-specific regulation, which addresses undue discrimination in prices and other terms and conditions. Under competition law, price discrimination is assessed more narrowly than under sector regulation, as competition authorities consider the economic effects on consumers and competition, while sector regulators often have to consider social or distributive effects as well. In Chapter 8 we discuss the main insights from regulation for the design of remedies in competition law, including the regulation of access. An important concept in access regulation is that of FRAND—terms must be fair, reasonable, and non-discriminatory.

So are price discrimination cases under EU competition law limited to situations where **4.94** downstream competition is hindered? The answer is no. In a case against the organizers of the 1998 Football World Cup in France, the Commission imposed a symbolic fine of €1,000 for discrimination against residents outside France in ticket sales.[65] The main mechanism through which this was achieved was the requirement on purchasers of tickets to provide a postal address in France. Arguably there is no downstream competition between the favoured football fans in France and the affected fans elsewhere—at least not in the commercial sense—and hence no competition was distorted. The organizer, the Comité français d'organisation de la Coupe du monde de football 1998, used this argument in its defence. The Commission disagreed, stating that price discrimination can be abusive in a broader set of circumstances:

> The Commission rejects such an interpretation of Article 82 [now 102]. While the application of Article 82 often requires an assessment of the effect of an undertaking's behaviour on the structure of competition in a given market, its application in the absence of such an effect cannot be excluded. Consumers' interests are protected by Article 82, such protection being achieved either by prohibiting conduct by dominant undertakings which impairs free and undistorted competition or which is direct [sic] prejudicial to consumers. Accordingly, and as has been expressly recognised by the Court of Justice, Article 82 can properly be applied, where appropriate, to situations in which a dominant undertaking's behaviour direct prejudices the interests of consumers, notwithstanding the absence of any effect on the structure of competition.[66]

4.5.4 Price discrimination and parallel trade

Anyone who regularly travels abroad will have observed that there are often significant price **4.95** differentials between countries. This is true for all kinds of products, including beverages, electronic goods, designer-label goods, and pharmaceuticals. A natural market response to such price discrimination is to try to undermine it through arbitrage. In the context of international trade this can be done in the form of parallel or grey imports. In turn, a natural response to parallel imports is to take measures to stop them, through commercial or legal means. The question of whether such measures are anti-competitive or welfare-enhancing

---

[65] *1998 Football World Cup* (Case IV/36.888), Decision of 20 July 1999.
[66] Ibid., at [100]. A similar issue arose in France in 2015, when the European Commission opened an investigation into Disneyland Paris for charging British and German visitors more than French residents. Agence France Presse (2015), 'EU probes Disneyland Paris for alleged price discrimination', press statement, 28 July.

has been the subject of various competition cases, and is closely linked to the welfare effects of price discrimination.

4.96 Formally, parallel imports are goods brought into a country without the authorization of the copyright, patent, or trademark owner, after those goods have legitimately been placed into circulation in another country by that owner or an authorized distributor. A relevant IP law principle here is that of exhaustion. Once trademarked goods are 'put on the market', the trademark owner is no longer allowed to control their further distribution. It is said to have 'exhausted' its distribution right by the first sale of the goods. A controversial issue is whether the exhaustion should be national, international, or regional. The first type means that rights are exhausted only with respect to the countries in which the goods were put on the market by the trademark owner. If the applicable law recognizes only national exhaustion, a parallel importer would infringe the relevant trademark right in the importing country. Thus, the ability of IP owners to prevent parallel trade remains intact under national exhaustion. International exhaustion means that rights are exhausted when goods are first sold in a market anywhere in the world. If a jurisdiction adopts this rule on exhaustion, IP owners cannot stop parallel imports into the jurisdiction. Regional exhaustion is adopted by the EU as an intermediate policy. Rights are exhausted when goods are first sold in any market in the European Economic Area (EEA).

4.97 In the *Silhouette* case (1998), the ECJ ruled on the legitimacy of parallel imports of branded sunglasses.[67] An Austrian discount chain, Hartlauer, had bought a consignment of Silhouette sunglasses from a company in Bulgaria (then outside the European Union and EEA), which had previously bought them from Silhouette International in Austria. Hartlauer was charged in an Austrian court on the grounds that the trademark rights for the sunglasses had not been exhausted by the act of selling the consignment to the Bulgarian company, and that Silhouette therefore could prohibit Hartlauer from selling them in Austria. The ECJ ruled that community-wide—i.e. regional—exhaustion of rights was the proper interpretation of the 1989 EU Trade Marks Directive. Several subsequent cases have followed this principle, including one where a number of supermarkets in the United Kingdom (including Tesco and Costco) had bought perfumes and jeans that Davidoff and Levi Strauss had placed on markets outside the EEA.[68]

4.98 The economic arguments against parallel trade are closely linked to those of protecting IP rights in general. Arguments for limiting exhaustion derive from the belief that this provides a higher economic reward to companies that invest in the quality or image of their products, and that this incentive is necessary to maintain the range and quality of goods. Parallel importers may undermine this by free-riding on the marketing and service efforts of authorized distributors, thereby reducing the incentive to make those efforts in the first place. We return to this free-rider theme in Chapter 6 on vertical restraints.

4.99 Another issue highlighted by these parallel trade cases relates to the desirability of price differences between markets. Parallel trade arises only because prices in one country are lower than in another. Sometimes this may be due to transient phenomena such as exchange-rate

---

[67] Case C-355/96 *Silhouette International Schmied GmbH & Co KG v Hartlauer Handelsgesellschaft mbH* [1998] ECR I-4799.
[68] Cases C-414/99 to C-416/99 *Zino Davidoff SA v A & G Imports Ltd and Levi Strauss & Co and Others v Tesco Stores Ltd and Others* [2001] ECR I-8691.

movements, where parallel traders are able to react more quickly than the trademark holders or authorized distributors. A more fundamental cause, however, is that the trademark holder wishes, as a matter of commercial policy, to sell goods at different prices in different markets—it wishes to exploit opportunities to engage in price discrimination, made possible by differences in the ability or willingness of consumers to pay for the product, or differences in wealth or tastes. We saw above that price discrimination is often benign and that it can enhance welfare. The *Silhouette* principle, by imposing certain restrictions on parallel trade, implicitly recognizes that price discrimination by an IP holder is a legitimate business practice. However, where parallel trade *within* the European Union (or EEA) is concerned, the EU's stance changes because the internal-market objective comes into play. Parallel imports are immediately seen in a much more favourable light (and geographic price discrimination is regarded unfavourably). This has been reflected in a number of abuse of dominance cases against pharmaceutical companies that took actions to prevent parallel trade of their products between Member States. One of the main cases is that against GlaxoSmithKline (GSK) Greece, which went through various judgments and lasted many years (from 2000 to 2008).[69]

4.5.5 Parallel trade and competition law: The *GSK Greece* case

Parallel importers buy medicines under patent in countries where wholesale prices are relatively low, and sell them at a higher price in other countries—a form of international arbitrage. Parallel trade in pharmaceuticals in the EU was worth approximately €4.3 billion in 2006, around the time of the GSK case (European Federation of Pharmaceutical Industries and Associations, 2008). You can see why pharmaceutical companies have an incentive to try to prevent it. A Greek wholesaler complained about GSK's refusal to supply it with three patented products: Imigran (for migraines), Lamictal (an anti-convulsant treatment for epilepsy), and Serevent (for asthma). The Greek competition authority initiated an investigation and subsequently referred several questions to the ECJ. Advocate General Jacobs advised that the patent holder would not automatically infringe Article 102 by refusing to supply because the conduct might be justified in light of sector-specific factors. His advice motivated the Greek competition authority's decision in favour of GSK. At a subsequent stage of the legal proceedings, Advocate General Colomer expressed his opinion that GSK's conduct did infringe Article 102 because of GSK's failure to justify its actions economically. The argument that parallel trade has negative effects on R&D investments was in principle accepted, but GSK's conduct was considered to be disproportionate. The final ruling of the ECJ, in 2008, determined that a producer of pharmaceuticals must be in a position to protect its own interest if orders from international distributors are 'out of the ordinary'.[70] The court ruled that GSK's actions to prevent parallel trade within the EU would constitute an infringement of Article 102 when orders were at 'ordinary' levels, but left it to national courts to ascertain whether the orders in this particular case would be ordinary in relation to the requirements of the market.

4.100

---

[69] Case C-53/03 *Synetairismos Farmakopoion Aitolias & Akarnanias (Syfait) and Others v GlaxoSmithKline plc and GlaxoSmithKline AEVE* [2005] ECR I-4609; and Joined Cases C-468/06 to C-478/06, *Sot. Lélos kai Sia EE and Others v GlaxoSmithKline AEVE Farmakeftikon Proïonton, formerly Glaxowellcome AEVE* [2008] ECR I-7139.

[70] Joined Cases C-468/06 to C-478/06, *Sot. Lélos kai Sia EE and Others v GlaxoSmithKline AEVE Farmakeftikon Proïonton, formerly Glaxowellcome AEVE* [2008] ECR I-7139, at [76–7].

4.101 So is price discrimination by pharmaceutical companies desirable or should parallel trade be allowed? Price-setting mechanisms in the pharmaceutical sector are different from those in many other industries. New medicines brought to the market are afforded patent protection which confers a temporary monopoly on its holder (often for twenty years). Patent holders are thus not constrained by competition when setting prices during this period (although they may still be constrained by national price regulations). The rationale behind patent protection is that for there to be sufficient incentives to invest in pharmaceutical research, the costs of R&D and drug testing need to be recovered. Thus returns from successful drugs must be sufficient to compensate for the costs of unsuccessful drug developments. Wholesale prices for pharmaceutical products have traditionally differed within the EU—for example, they are typically higher in Germany, the Netherlands, and the United Kingdom than in Greece and Spain. This is a situation of third-degree price discrimination. An important question is why manufacturers are able to charge higher prices in some Member States than in others. Is it due to differences in the price elasticity of demand or willingness to pay, as in the standard theory of price discrimination? In the case of pharmaceuticals, wholesale price differentials for patented drugs mainly reflect differences in the way countries regulate their pharmaceutical markets and how prices are determined in negotiations between governments and the industry. The importance of regulatory pricing restrictions driving increased opportunities for arbitrage via parallel trade was also acknowledged in the ECJ judgment:

> Although the degree of price regulation in the pharmaceuticals sector cannot therefore preclude the Community rules on competition from applying, the fact none the less remains that, when assessing, in the case of Member States with a system of price regulation, whether the refusal of a pharmaceuticals company to supply medicines to wholesalers involved in parallel exports constitutes abuse, it cannot be ignored that such State intervention is one of the factors liable to create opportunities for parallel trade.[71]

4.102 Parallel imports thus create a tension between the principle of autonomy of Member States in influencing pharmaceutical prices in the context of their national healthcare system, and the creation of a single European market. Price differentials in the EU are largely due to the Member States each setting their own regulations that influence pharmaceutical prices, while the principle of free movement of goods within the EU allows traders to arbitrage those differences.

4.103 These abuse cases involving parallel trade in pharmaceutical products tend to be complex because they are judged under several different criteria. There is an IP law angle: should IP holders be entitled to exploit their rights as they see fit? There are various political angles: should each Member State be allowed to influence its own price levels? Is it right that some countries get the medicine cheap while others end up paying the bill for the R&D costs? Is it appropriate for the rules to be different depending on whether the trade is inside or outside the EU? The economic test for short-term welfare effects is relatively simple in this context: are total sales of medicines higher under price discrimination or with parallel trade? Another relevant question for the analysis of dynamic effects in these cases relates to R&D investment: is price discrimination between countries an efficient mechanism for pharmaceutical companies to recover their R&D costs, and would they invest less in R&D

---

[71] Joined Cases C-468/06 to C-478/06, *Sot. Lélos kai Sia EE and Others v GlaxoSmithKline AEVE Farmakeftikon Proïonton, formerly Glaxowellcome AEVE* [2008] ECR I-7139, at [67].

if such discrimination were undermined by parallel trade? Economic analysis can shed some light on these questions and assist courts and competition authorities in weighing up the various legal arguments that are often put forward in these disputes.

4.6 Quantity, Loyalty, and Exclusivity Rebates

4.6.1 Different types of rebate: Form versus effect

Price discounts and rebates are ubiquitous. Most companies, small and large, offer them in one way or another. Discounts enhance sales, and dissuade customers from switching to competitors. Buyers rarely complain about discounts because they get a lower price. Selective discounting can also make coordination between competitors more difficult, as we mentioned in section 4.5. So what's the problem? Aren't discounts a feature of how competitive markets are supposed to work? At one level the answer to this question is yes. You could treat a discount or rebate in the same way as any price cut: mostly desirable for competition and consumers, occasionally anti-competitive if it excludes as-efficient competitors. In that regard, you could apply the same standards to discounts and rebates as for predatory pricing, focusing on whether foreclosure is significant and feasible, and on whether prices are below a certain cost benchmark. This is in essence how the US courts assessed Virgin Atlantic's loyalty rebates claim against BA, in sharp contrast with the way the European Commission and courts dealt with the case, as discussed before.[72] **4.104**

Yet there is more to discounts than just predatory or discriminatory pricing. Some forms of discount and rebate scheme may foreclose rivals from gaining access to customers or distribution channels, even when no outright predation is involved. Note that we use the term *forms* of discount scheme here. Whether a scheme also has foreclosure *effects* is something that must still be analysed on a case-by-case basis, at least if you apply an effects-based approach. EU case law does not currently prescribe such an approach for rebate schemes: establishing the form of the scheme is sufficient. For this purpose the case law distinguishes between three forms or categories of rebate scheme.[73] **4.105**

The first category is quantity rebates, also known as unconditional rebates. These are solely linked to the quantity of purchases. Rather than determining which customers will be charged which prices, the supplier offers a menu of prices at different volume levels, and customers 'self-select' their preferred volume/price combination. Quantity rebates are generally deemed benign even if offered by a dominant company, since they tend to reflect gains in efficiency at higher volumes. Yet in some circumstances quantity rebates have been considered anti-competitive, as we will see in this section. **4.106**

The second and third categories of rebate scheme are the problematic ones: loyalty rebates and exclusivity rebates. The General Court in *Intel* described loyalty rebates as 'rebate systems where the grant of a financial incentive is not directly linked to a condition of exclusive or quasi-exclusive supply from the undertaking in a dominant position, but where the mechanism for granting the rebate may also have a fidelity-building effect'.[74] **4.107**

---

[72] *Virgin/British Airways* (Case IV/D-2/34.780), Decision of 14 July 1999; and *Virgin Atlantic LTD v British Airways PLC* 257 F 3d 256 (2d Cir. 2001).
[73] As summarized in Case T-286/09 *Intel Corp v Commission*, Judgment of 12 June 2014, at [74–8].
[74] Ibid., at [78].

4.108 Loyalty rebates are granted to customers according to their purchasing behaviour. The percentage rebate given to a customer increases, usually in discrete jumps, when its purchase volumes exceed a certain target level. Often these target levels are set specifically for that customer, and are based on an increment above its purchases in a previous reference period. The form of loyalty rebate that has received most attention in competition law is the retroactive rebate, which applies not only to the customer's incremental purchases above the target, but retroactively to all purchases. This has also been referred to as a 'back to dollar one' or 'rollback' rebate scheme. The *Virgin/British Airways* case concerned retroactive rebates offered to travel agents. The other classic EU case is *Michelin II* (2003), which concerned the loyalty rebates that Michelin offered to specialist dealers on replacement tyres for heavy vehicles.[75]

4.109 Retroactive rebates can have exclusionary effects even if they don't involve selling at a loss, hence making them different from predatory pricing. They make it very tempting for customers to also purchase any incremental requirements from the dominant company as that generates large additional rebates—a loyalty-enhancing mechanism called the 'suction effect'. We explain this below. The Guidance on Article 102 sought to establish an effects-based test for loyalty rebates, assessing the strength of the suction effect and whether as-efficient competitors can match the rebates.[76] However, the EU courts have not fully endorsed this effects-based approach to loyalty rebates. In *Tomra* (2012), involving a company that controlled 70–95 per cent of the European market for automatic recovery machines for empty beverage containers (also called reverse vending machines), the ECJ held that retroactive rebates offered by dominant undertakings constitute an abuse because they are capable of excluding rivals through the suction effect.[77] There was no need to assess the actual strength of the suction effect or the ability of as-efficient competitors to match the rebates.

4.110 Exclusivity rebates are closely related to loyalty rebates (in the classic *Hoffmann-La Roche* case of 1979 they were called fidelity rebates).[78] They are conditional on the customer obtaining all or nearly all of its requirements from the dominant company. In the extreme version the rebates are explicitly conditional on full exclusivity. In softer versions the condition refers to some majority proportion of the customer's requirements. There is therefore a continuum between exclusivity rebates and other forms of loyalty rebates. The *Intel* case was about exclusivity rebates.[79] Intel offered rebates on its CPUs to various OEMs. Some of these were conditional on the manufacturer obtaining all its CPUs from Intel—this was the case for Dell, and for Lenovo's notebooks. Some were conditional on the manufacturer obtaining a certain percentage of its CPUs from Intel—95 per cent for HP's corporate desktops, and 80 per cent for NEC's PCs. As discussed in section 4.1, the Commission analysed whether an as-efficient competitor would be able to match Intel's rebates in line with the test developed in its Guidance, but the General Court then prescribed a form-based prohibition of exclusivity rebates by dominant companies. An effects-based approach was not required.

---

[75] Case T-203/01 *Manufacture Française des Pneumatiques Michelin v Commission* [2003] ECR II-4071.
[76] European Commission (2008), 'Guidance on the Commission's Enforcement Priorities in Applying Article 82 EC Treaty to Abusive Exclusionary Conduct by Dominant Undertakings', December, at [37–45].
[77] Case C-549/10 P *Tomra Systems and others v Commission*, Judgment of 19 April 2012.
[78] Case 85/76 *Hoffmann-La Roche & Co AG v Commission* [1979] ECR 461.
[79] Case T-286/09 *Intel Corp v Commission*, Judgment of 12 June 2014.

4.6.2 Foreclosure and 'suction' effects of loyalty rebates

An effects-based approach to loyalty rebates can focus on the same questions as in predatory pricing and other exclusion cases: what is the degree of market power of the dominant company? Is a significant part of the market foreclosed by the rebates? What is the likelihood of success of the foreclosure? Two loyalty rebate cases against South African Airways (SAA) before the South African Competition Tribunal, in 2005 and 2010, illustrate how asking such effects-based questions can shed additional light on the analysis.[80] SAA had signed 'override agreements' with travel agents which established a system of retroactive rebates. The Tribunal found that with a market share of 65–70 per cent SAA was 'overwhelmingly dominant' in the market for scheduled domestic flights. For comparison, BA had a share of only 39.7 per cent when the European Commission ruled against its loyalty rebates. The Tribunal also assessed the degree of foreclosure. It found that 70–85 per cent of airline tickets were sold through travel agents in the relevant period (similar to the United Kingdom in the period of the BA case), and that SAA's agreements covered travel agents representing close to 90 per cent of all airline sales. The European Commission found that BA's rebates covered 'the most important travel agents in the UK' but it did not quantify the degree of foreclosure, and this did not feature in its assessment of abuse. Finally, the Tribunal carried out an extensive review of evidence that SAA's retroactive rebates did indeed have a strong effect on individual travel agents' behaviour. The European Commission performed no such analysis under its form-based approach.

4.111

After the general effects analysis of the degree of market power and foreclosure, you can turn to an assessment that is specific to loyalty rebates: measuring the strength of the suction effect. We illustrate this through a stylized example based on the *Intel* case (the real figures were excised from the published version of the Commission's decision). The Commission applied the as-efficient competitor test to analyse whether competitors could match Intel. This involved determining whether a competitor that was as efficient as Intel (i.e. had the same level of production costs), but without as broad a sales base, could profitably operate in the market in the presence of Intel's rebate schemes. As mentioned before, the General Court in fact considered this effects analysis to be redundant since the Intel rebates were conditional on exclusivity. However, it is still a useful illustration of the mechanics of the suction effect.

4.112

See Figure 4.3. Suppose that Dell's total requirement for CPUs is 100 units, and that Intel and AMD can both fulfil this need. Intel's undiscounted unit price is €5. It offers Dell a rebate of 20 per cent if the computer maker purchases 100 per cent of its CPU requirements from Intel. So Dell would pay a unit price of €4 instead of €5 for 100 units. This is a conditional exclusivity rebate. It could also have been formulated as a retroactive rebate: you've purchased sixty CPUs so far for €5; if you buy the remaining forty from Intel you get 20 per cent off not just on those forty but also on the first sixty. The effects are similar. Suppose that Dell is in principle willing and able to buy up to 40 per cent of its CPUs (forty units) from AMD, but for technical reasons it needs sixty units from Intel. The 40 per cent is the 'contestable share' of Dell's demand for which AMD can compete (we discuss the assessment of the contestable share in the next section). What would you do if you were Dell? Or AMD?

4.113

---

[80] Competition Tribunal South Africa (2005), '*Competition Commission vs South African Airways (Pty) Ltd*', Case 18/CR/Mar01, 28 July; and Competition Tribunal South Africa (2010), '*Nationwide Airlines (Pty), Comair Ltd vs South African Airways (Pty) Ltd*', Case 80/CR/Sep06, 17 February. We advised the claimants in both cases.

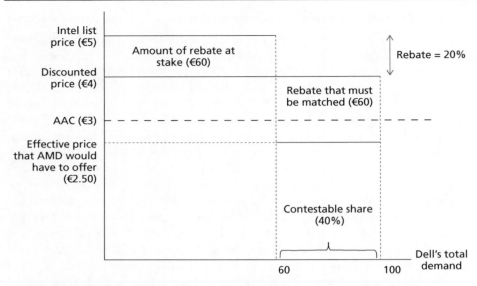

Figure 4.3 Stylized example of the as-efficient competitor test for loyalty rebates

4.114 Dell would miss out on the Intel rebate of 20 per cent or €1 per unit if it went ahead and switched to AMD for those forty units. On the sixty units that it still buys from Intel, Dell would pay €5 per unit rather than €4, thus forgoing a rebate of €60. In order to attract Dell, AMD would have to at least compensate for these lost rebates when offering a price for the forty units. This compensation would need to be €1.50 per unit. The highest price that AMD can therefore charge to win Dell's business on the forty units would be €1.50 lower than Intel's price of €4, so €2.50. Another way of putting this is that Intel's effective price for the last forty units is not €4 but €2.50, as Dell now gets the first sixty units for a cheaper price too. This is the suction effect of loyalty rebates. This effective price in the contestable share of the market is the one that AMD has to match in order to compete with Intel on the contestable part of Dell's business. The effective price can also be calculated using the following formula: effective price = (discounted price − (undiscounted price × non-contestable share)) / contestable share = (€4 − (€5 × 60 per cent)) / 40 per cent = €2.50.

4.115 The final step in the test is to assess whether AMD can compete at this price, that is, whether it can match Intel's rebates without incurring losses. This is where the cost benchmarks come in. According to the Guidance on Article 102, effective prices above LRAIC are usually acceptable, while effective prices below AAC are deemed harmful. For prices between AAC and LRAIC, the Commission would investigate whether there are 'counterstrategies' available to rivals—for example, their ability to use a non-contestable portion of their own buyers' demand as leverage to decrease the effective price for the contestable part of the market. In this example, the AAC of Intel—and any as-efficient competitor—equals €3 per unit. An effective price below €3 implies that AMD would not be able to compete for Dell's contestable business, as illustrated in Figure 4.3. You can conclude that the Intel rebate forecloses an as-efficient competitor that has access to only 40 per cent of the market.

The Commission used the framework of the stylized example above to assess the suction **4.116** effect in the *Intel* case, but in an extended form. Instead of calculating the effective price and then comparing it to LRAIC and AAC, it applied a version of the test where the focus was on market shares rather than price. The aim was to work out the extent of potential foreclosure of as-efficient competitors on a customer-by-customer basis. This worked as follows. First, the Commission determined the share of an OEM's demand that would be required by AMD to price just at AAC and at the same time compensate the customer for the loss in rebates from Intel. This was termed 'the commercially viable share'. Obtaining this is simply a matter of rearranging the effective price formula above: commercially viable share = (undiscounted price – discounted price) / (undiscounted price – AAC). In Figure 4.3, the commercially viable share would be (5 – 4) / (5 – 3) = 50 per cent. This commercially viable share was then compared with the contestable share to determine the foreclosure effect. If the contestable share of an OEM's demand was lower than the commercially viable share, an as-efficient competitor could not viably compete. So in our stylized example we reach the same conclusion as before: the contestable share of 40 per cent is lower than the commercially viable share of 50 per cent, and hence AMD is foreclosed. The Commission followed these steps for each OEM and, in most cases, found the contestable share to be below the commercially viable share.

4.6.3 Unavoidable trading partners and the contestable share of the market

The strength of the suction effect depends on a number of factors. One is the level and struc- **4.117** ture of the threshold above which the rebate applies. If this is set above the amount that a customer would normally purchase from the dominant company, the rebate should induce it to purchase more. Thresholds that are set for each customer individually based on the purchases made in the previous period have a stronger suction effect than thresholds that apply across the board, as the latter will not target customers' loyalty so effectively. Likewise, the higher the rebate as a proportion of the total price and the higher the threshold as a proportion of a customer's purchases, the greater the loyalty-enhancing effect. A further factor is the length of the reference period—that is, the period over which volumes are assessed for the purposes of calculating the rebate. Reference periods of one or several years have a greater loyalty-enhancing effect than a monthly or quarterly reference period, because customers can switch less frequently.

The size of the contestable share of the market (also known as the 'relevant range') is a cru- **4.118** cial factor in assessing the strength of the suction effect. We saw this in the stylized Intel example in Figure 4.3. The mere fact that such a contestable share is considered is based on the premise that competitors can compete only for a subset of customers—that is, their addressable market is smaller than the whole market. The non-contestable share is effectively assumed to be in the pocket of the dominant company. This is a strong assumption and will not always apply—even dominant companies must normally compete for their customers. Below we discuss the factors that may make a dominant company an 'unavoidable trading partner' or 'must-have' in this sense, and that determine the size of the contestable share. But first we illustrate the effect of the contestable share on the outcome of the as-efficient competitor test for loyalty rebates.

Table 4.6 follows on from the Intel example. If the entire market were contestable—i.e. **4.119** Intel and AMD compete for every customer—the effective Intel price that AMD would have to compete with is the same as the actual Intel price: €4. There is no suction effect.

Table 4.6 Loyalty rebates: relationship between contestable share and effective price

Contestable share (%)	Non-contestable share (%)	Effective unit price in contestable share (€)
100	–	4.00
60	40	3.33
50	50	3.00
40	60	2.50
30	70	1.67
20	80	0

In this case the as-efficient competitor assessment becomes like a normal predatory pricing assessment: how does the actual price compare with the relevant cost benchmark? There is no predation because the price of €4 exceeds the AAC of €3. If the contestable share were 60 per cent of the market, the effective unit price in this contestable part of the market would be €3.33, which is still above AAC. If the contestable share were 50 per cent, the effective price would be €3 and equal to AAC. As we saw above, this 'break-even' level of contestable share is referred to as the commercially viable share. At a 40 per cent contestable share the effective price would be €2.50 as in Figure 4.3. Interestingly, if the contestable share were only 20 per cent of the market, the retroactive discount from €5 to €4 implies that Intel is effectively giving away the last twenty units for free. This would mean a strong suction effect.

4.120   What determines the contestable share? There are no clear-cut criteria. The first step is usually to assess whether a dominant company is an unavoidable trading partner. This will not be the case for all dominant companies, and has to be analysed rather than assumed. An example would be where the product in question is a 'must-stock' item for a retailer because customers expect it to be on offer. The European Commission considered BA to be an 'obligatory business partner for travel agents' given its position in the air travel market, as 'agents have to deal with BA and accept that a large portion of their income from these services will be that generated by the sale of BA tickets'.[81] Likewise, in *Michelin II* the Commission found that '[a] dealer that did not sell new Michelin tyres or did not send its carcasses for retreading to Michelin or Pneu Laurent (Michelin's subsidiary) would run the risk of weakening its commercial credibility'.[82] In *Post Danmark II* the ECJ noted that 70 per cent of the bulk mail market was uncontestable due to statutory monopoly, making Post Danmark an unavoidable trading partner.[83] The suction effect from Post Danmark's retroactive rebates was enhanced by the fact that they applied across the contestable and non-contestable parts of the market.

4.121   In *Intel* the Commission carried out a more detailed analysis of whether the dominant chipmaker was an unavoidable trading partner for OEMs:

> Intel's brand equity resulting from its investment in product differentiation and its installed base have given it 'must-stock' status at the OEM level, in other words, it is an unavoidable trading partner for OEMs. All the main OEMs offer predominantly or exclusively

---

[81]   *Virgin/British Airways* (Case IV/D-2/34.780), Decision of 14 July 1999, at [92].
[82]   *Michelin* (Case COMP/E-2/36.401/PO), Decision of 20 June 2003, at [201].
[83]   Case C-23/14 *Post Danmark A/S v Konkurrencerådet*, judgment of 6 October 2015 (*Post Danmark II*).

Intel-based products. Intel's must-stock status provides it with significant leverage over its OEM customers because a switch to an all- or majority-AMD product line-up would be unrealistic for them.[84]

There may also be factors which are specific to an OEM which may also serve to limit how quickly an OEM can ramp-up non-Intel based products and therefore how much of its x86 CPU requirement is contestable at any given point in time. For example, these may relate to the fact that an OEM could have a range of different computer platforms based on a particular x86 CPU which it renews on a staggered, rolling basis, and which hence means that in a given period, it will only be seeking to source a limited share of its overall x86 CPU requirements.[85]

To get from a confirmation of unavoidable trading partner status to the actual contestable **4.122** share is not straightforward. The Guidance on Article 102 describes the contestable share ('relevant range') as follows:

> If it is likely that customers would be willing and able to switch large amounts of demand to a (potential) competitor relatively quickly, the relevant range is likely to be relatively large. If, on the other hand, it is likely that customers would only be willing or able to switch small amounts incrementally, then the relevant range will be relatively small. For existing competitors their capacity to expand sales to customers and the fluctuations in those sales over time may also provide an indication of the relevant range. For potential competitors, an assessment of the scale at which a new entrant would realistically be able to enter may be undertaken, where possible. It may be possible to take the historical growth pattern of new entrants in the same or in similar markets as an indication of a realistic market share of a new entrant.[86]

Sometimes the non-contestable share is approximated by the actual market share of **4.123** the dominant company or the share of customers covered by exclusivity rebates. This may not always be appropriate as it effectively assumes that the dominant company no longer has to compete for its current share. It may also introduce some circularity in the reasoning: rival suppliers may well have been able to compete for at least some of the dominant company's current customers, and the fact that they did not win does not mean that the business of those customers was non-contestable. In *Intel* the Commission considered on a customer-by-customer basis how much business could realistically be shifted to AMD:

> The contestable share of the OEMs and the PC retailer covered by this Decision (Dell, HP, NEC, Lenovo and MSH) is relatively low. This is based on submissions provided by the companies in question as well as contemporaneous documentary evidence from each undertaking (as well as from AMD) which details in particular the rates at which the companies considered it was feasible to 'ramp up' their supplies from AMD were they to choose to go down such a path.[87]

In any event, good practice would be not to assume from the outset that a dominant com- **4.124** pany is an unavoidable trading partner, and to test the sensitivity of the results of the as-efficient competitor test to variations in the assumed contestable share.

[84] *Intel* (Case COMP/C-3/37.990), Decision of 13 May 2009, at [870].
[85] Ibid., at [1011].
[86] European Commission (2008), 'Guidance on the Commission's Enforcement Priorities in Applying Article 82 EC Treaty to Abusive Exclusionary Conduct by Dominant Undertakings', December, at [42].
[87] *Intel* (Case COMP/C-3/37.990), Decision of 13 May 2009, at [2012].

4.6.4 Quantity rebates

4.125 With quantity rebates, a supplier offers a menu of prices at different volume levels, and customers 'self-select' the volume/price combination they desire. Quantity rebates are a form of second-degree price discrimination, as described in section 4.5. Unlike with loyalty rebates, the 'depersonalized' rebate threshold will be too high for some buyers and too low for others. In other words, it will be insufficiently specific to keep all purchasers loyal to the dominant company. Smaller customers may never reach the required threshold, while the larger buyers may purchase considerably more. In these circumstances the rebate system is unlikely to have a significant foreclosure effect since a large buyer would not lose the rebate by switching to an alternative supplier for part of its demand, and small buyers would be unaffected by the whole scheme. Competition law usually considers unconditional quantity rebates to be benign.

4.126 But not always. In 2000, Oftel (the telecoms regulator before the creation of Ofcom in 2003) in the United Kingdom condemned the volume discounts offered by Vodafone to mobile service providers and resellers.[88] These were based on a stepped structure, increasing in accordance with subscriber levels. Oftel was concerned that the thresholds for discounts were set very high and that a company offering mobile telephony services over Vodafone's network could make a reasonable return only if it secured the maximum discount. Oftel closed the case after Vodafone changed the terms on which the wholesale service was supplied. This was effectively a case about margin squeeze and discrimination, where the affected party was a downstream rather than a horizontal competitor.

4.127 From an economic perspective the concern about volume discounts arises only if they are not cost-reflective *and* if they are designed to mimic the structure of a loyalty rebate scheme. This may occur if most customers purchase more or less the same amount of output, and the threshold at which the discount kicks in is set close to this output level. Say that 90 per cent of an incumbent postal operator's bulk-mail customers each send around 5 million items per year, and that the incumbent offers a 10 per cent discount to customers sending precisely this quantity of items every year. In this case, rivals could be excluded for the same reasons outlined above in relation to loyalty rebates. Similar effects can occur if the discounts are stepped and customers can be classified into groups depending on the volume of output purchased. Figure 4.4 provides a stylized example of this type of scheme. There are three steps in the discount structure: at 1 million, 5 million, and 10 million mail items per year. Customers which send fewer than 1 million mail items—such as customer A in the figure—are not really affected by the discount scheme. However, customers such as B and C, which are close to the higher discount thresholds (of 5 million and 10 million items, respectively), may have an incentive to stay with the incumbent operator and indeed enhance their volumes so as to hit the target and receive a bigger discount. Whether this has any foreclosure effect depends on an analysis similar to that which we saw above in relation to loyalty rebates. The difference is that assessing the discount scheme has a precondition: you first need to know the distribution of customer demand, and hence check whether the discount scheme gets close to mimicking the individualized thresholds commonly used in loyalty rebates.

---

[88] Case BX/633/141 *Pre-pay Services on the Vodafone Network*. See Oftel (2000), 'Competition Bulletin', Issue 15, March.

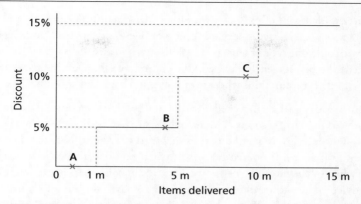

Figure 4.4 Illustration of stepped quantity rebates with potential foreclosure effects

4.6.5 More examples of rebate cases: From boat engines to chocolate bars

Loyalty rebate cases have been less common in the United States than in Europe, but they do arise from time to time. We saw above how the US courts rejected the claim by Virgin Atlantic against BA. In *Concord Boat Corp v Brunswick Corp* (2000), twenty-four builders of recreational boats challenged Brunswick's discount programme on boat engines.[89] Brunswick had about 75 per cent of the market for such engines. Boat builders that agreed to buy a certain percentage of their engine requirements from Brunswick for a certain period received a discount on the list price for all engines purchased—a retroactive loyalty rebate. Because some of the boat builders' customers apparently preferred Brunswick engines, it was claimed that they had to purchase a significant percentage of their engine needs from Brunswick. Note that, somewhat unusually, the plaintiffs in this case were the customers of Brunswick, not its competitors. The boat builders felt that Brunswick had monopolized the engine market, ultimately resulting in higher prices. The court concluded that the plaintiffs had not offered sufficient evidence to determine that Brunswick's conditional discounts were anti-competitive. They were free to walk away from the discounts offered by Brunswick at any time. At least two customers, which previously had purchased more than 80 per cent of their engines from Brunswick, had in fact switched to a competitor for more than 70 per cent of their purchases—an indication that the contestable part of the market was large. **4.128**

One successful complaint in the United States was *Masimo v Tyco* in 2006.[90] This related to sales to hospitals of pulse oximetry sensors, which are used to monitor the oxygenation of a patient's blood. Tyco had a market share above 65 per cent. Its typical offer involved a 40 per cent discount if customers bought at least 90 per cent of their requirements from Tyco, but only a 16–18 per cent discount otherwise. The US court ruled that the possible loss of Tyco's higher discounts on all of a hospital's sensor purchases effectively forced hospitals to deal exclusively with Tyco. There were indications that Tyco was an unavoidable trading partner. It had an established position in the industry whereas Masimo was a new entrant. **4.129**

---

[89] *Concord Boat Corporation v Brunswick Corporation* 207 F 3d 1039 (8th Cir. 2000), 24 March 2000.
[90] *Masimo Corp v Tyco Health Care Group, LP*, No CV 02-4770 MRP, 2006 WL 1236666 (CD Cal. 22 March 2006).

Tyco had an installed base of oximetry monitors that it had previously sold to hospitals. These monitors were expensive, had a useful life of five to seven years, and were typically compatible with only one type of sensor. Hospitals that had already acquired Tyco monitors therefore needed to buy its sensors as well. The contestable share of the market for sensors was therefore limited to situations where hospitals purchased new monitors.

4.130 A Dutch court case in 2013 concerned a complaint by Nestlé against Mars in relation to incentives offered to petrol stations.[91] Mars had a share of 67 per cent in the sale of chocolate bars through petrol stations (the parties disputed whether this channel constituted a separate relevant market). It offered owners of petrol stations a so-called entrepreneurial programme whereby they would receive free boxes of chocolate bars in exchange for following Mars's advice on how to arrange shelf space and displays. These free products effectively amounted to a discount. Nestlé, which had a 25 per cent share, claimed that this had the effect of foreclosing it from the petrol station sales channel. The court agreed that Mars was dominant and that the programme could have exclusionary effects. In its judgment it stated the need for a court-appointed expert to assess the foreclosure effects in more detail, but the parties did not continue the case. Still, it is interesting to consider the economic features of the incentives and compare them with other forms of rebate.

4.131 The commercial context in which Mars offered the programme was relevant to understanding the incentive scheme. First, Mars did not sell to independent petrol stations directly but rather through wholesalers, the largest of which, Lekkerland, controlled more than 60 per cent of sales to this channel. This is why Mars could not offer any discounts to petrol stations as an incentive to comply with the programme, and instead offered them free products (although, in financial terms, free products and discounts are equivalent). Second, the programme could be seen as a variant on category management, which is a common practice in fast-moving consumer goods. The retailer appoints one of its suppliers as the 'category captain', which then uses its expertise to advise the retailer on how best to present the products. The objective of category management is to promote sales for the entire category, including products of the captain's competitors. The entrepreneurial programme was in part aimed at incentivizing petrol stations to place extra sales displays in their shops (e.g. in close proximity to the coffee machine) to promote the overall sale of chocolate bars. Only 3 per cent of customers of petrol stations actually bought a chocolate bar when paying for the petrol, so there was scope to enhance sales. Yet the programme would also give Mars's chocolate bars a more prominent place on the main shelves near the tills. This was Nestlé's main concern, as it felt that customers paying at the till purchased chocolate bars on impulse, and would therefore select those bars that were displayed most prominently on the shelves. So rather than rebates conditional on exclusivity as in *Intel*, the rebates (or free products) offered by Mars where conditional on prominent but non-exclusive shelf space. How does an effects-based test work in this case?

4.132 The degree of foreclosure played a role in the analysis. The entrepreneurial programme covered only independent petrol stations and not those operated by the large oil companies. The independents were generally smaller petrol stations: they represented around three-quarters of all stations in the Netherlands but only around 40 per cent of all chocolate sales

---

[91] *Nestlé/Mars*, Court of Oost-Brabant, ECLI:NL:RBOBR:2013:4356, Judgment of 7 August 2013. We acted as experts for the defendant.

through this channel. Hence a significant part of the overall channel was not affected by the programme. There were also indications that a significant proportion of the independents actually rejected the Mars programme, often because they wished to arrange their own shelves or had already signed up to a rival programme with the wholesaler Lekkerland or indeed Nestlé. Mars was thus not necessarily seen as an unavoidable trading partner. There was also debate about the contestable share of the market. Some of Mars's chocolate bars were popular and could be seen as 'must-stock' items, including Mars, Snickers, Twix, and M&Ms. However, the same could be said of some of Nestlé's products, in particular Kit Kat, Lion, and Nuts.

How was the as-efficient competitor test applied? Nestlé put forward an analysis of the **4.133** effective price in the contestable share of the market along the lines presented in Figure 4.3 above. However, there were some question marks about this, including the contestable share that was proposed. Importantly, the free products offered were in effect simple quantity rebates. They were not individualized, and nor were they retroactive. There was therefore no suction effect. That in essence left one theory of harm: that Nestlé would be unable to match the programme merely because its share in this sales channel was 2.7 times smaller than that of Mars (i.e. 25 per cent versus 67 per cent). If Mars offered a 10 per cent discount, Nestlé would effectively have to offer 27 per cent in order to match this. Take a petrol station that purchases €67 worth of Mars bars and €25 worth of Kit Kat bars each month. The 10 per cent discount offered by Mars amounts to €6.70. In order to match this, and persuade the petrol station owner to sign up to its programme rather than that of Mars, Nestlé would have to offer at least €6.70 in discounts as well, which is 27 per cent of €25. This may indeed be an unattractively high discount. However, is this really the right way of assessing this type of quantity rebate? A company with a low market share will always have to offer a proportionately higher discount than a competitor with a high market share; that's a matter of arithmetic. Yet the discount scheme here had no loyalty-inducing suction effect. In such cases we suggest that the net price after the discount can simply be compared against a relevant cost benchmark, that is, treating the discounts in the same way as predatory pricing.

4.7 Margin Squeeze

4.7.1 What is margin squeeze, and why is it of concern?

Margin squeeze is a form of leveraging whereby a vertically integrated company uses a **4.134** dominant position in an input market to restrict competition in a downstream market. The company lowers its downstream price or raises the price of the input. These actions, either on their own or together, squeeze the margin earned by downstream rivals. In the last ten years there have been several high-profile margin squeeze cases in Europe involving telecoms operators, in particular *Deutsche Telekom* (2010), *TeliaSonera* (2011), and *Telefónica* (2012).[92] The earliest margin squeeze cases dealt with by the European Commission involved commodity markets where a company with a near-monopoly upstream left

---

[92] Case C-280/08 P *Deutsche Telekom AG v Commission*, Judgment of 14 October 2010; Case C-52/09 *Konkurrensverket v TeliaSonera Sverige AB*, Judgment of 17 February 2011; Case T-398/07 *Kingdom of Spain (Telefónica) v Commission*, Judgment of 29 March 2012.

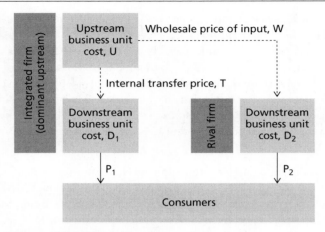

Figure 4.5 Illustration of a margin squeeze

insufficient margin for producers downstream. National Coal Board, which controlled 95 per cent of the UK coal market, was found guilty of margin squeeze in a 1975 decision.[93] In 1988, the Commission found a margin squeeze in the United Kingdom by British Sugar, which historically had a legal monopoly in the production of beet sugar and a market share of 58 per cent of granulated sugar at the time of the investigation.[94] A UK case of 2004, *Genzyme*, involved the drug Cerezyme (used to treat Gaucher disease) and its associated home-delivery service.[95]

4.135 As illustrated in Figure 4.5, the basic conditions of a margin squeeze are that the company is vertically integrated and dominant in the upstream market, such that downstream competitors have a degree of reliance on the company's input. One way of abusing its position would be for the integrated company to discriminate in favour of its own downstream business, setting upstream price W above the internal transfer price T. This type of abuse has been discussed in section 4.5. However, even in the absence of price discrimination as such—i.e. even if W equals T—there can be harm to competition through margin squeeze. This occurs if the dominant company sets a margin between the wholesale price W and its retail price P_1 that is so low that a downstream competitor relying on the wholesale input is unable to compete, even if it has a unit cost D_2 equal to unit cost D_1—that is, even if it is an as-efficient downstream competitor. Note that in this assessment only the margin between P_1 and W matters, as this is what defines the scope for the downstream rivals to make a profit. The internal transfer price T within the dominant company as such is irrelevant for the assessment of margin squeeze.

4.136 Figure 4.6 shows the margin squeeze concept a different way. On the left-hand side there is no margin squeeze. The difference between the wholesale price charged to the entrant and the incumbent's retail price is sufficient to cover the costs of an as-efficient entrant. Since

---

[93] *National Coal Board, National Smokeless Fuel Limited and National Carbonising Company Limited* (76/185/ECSC), Decision of 29 October 1975.

[94] *Napier Brown-British Sugar* (Case IV/30.178), Decision of 18 July 1988.

[95] *Genzyme Limited v The Office of Fair Trading*, [2004] CAT 4, 11 March 2004.

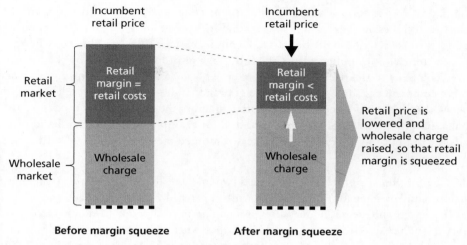

Figure 4.6 A different illustration of a margin squeeze

these costs are, by definition, the same as those of the incumbent (they are equally efficient), the above statement is equivalent to saying that the costs of the incumbent's downstream arm are adequately covered by the retail margin. The downstream arm is not making any losses at the given prices. Compare this with the right-hand side, where the incumbent has squeezed the entrant from two directions, lowering its retail price and increasing its wholesale price. The as-efficient entrant can no longer compete, as the incumbent's retail margin above the new wholesale charge is now below its retail costs.

While the concept of margin squeeze is easy to grasp, the mechanics of margin squeeze **4.137** tests and their practical application by regulatory and competition authorities raise some complex economic issues. Some of these relate to identifying and measuring the appropriate prices and costs. Another is the trade-off between the objective of promoting efficient entry, and providing incumbent companies with sufficient flexibility and incentives to compete and invest. This is a trade-off that regulators and competition authorities may approach differently, as discussed below.

4.7.2 Assessing margin squeeze under competition law

Prior to the telecoms margin squeeze cases in the last ten years there had been lit- **4.138** tle guidance in EU case law on how to assess margin squeeze—even on whether it constituted a distinct form of abuse under Article 102, separate from predation, excessive pricing, and refusal to supply. In the 2008 *Deutsche Telekom* ruling the CFI confirmed that margin squeeze was indeed a distinct pricing practice that can constitute an abuse of dominance, and endorsed the conceptual and practical approach followed by the Commission.[96] This approach revolves around the as-efficient competitor test. First, the dominant company must be vertically integrated and active in both wholesale and retail markets. It has to be dominant in the wholesale market, but does not need to be dominant in the affected retail market. Second, the as-efficient

---

[96] Case T-271/03 *Deutsche Telekom AG v Commission*, Judgment of 10 April 2008.

competitor test is applied using the dominant company's own retail costs, and its retail and wholesale charges. This determines the profitability of its retail operating arm. Retail costs will usually be estimated on the basis of LRAIC. Third, the margin squeeze test will be applied across the full range of products offered by the investigated company in the relevant retail market. This is an important point in telecoms where companies tend to sell bundles (e.g. broadband, telephone, and television). It means that the retail price will be calculated across the full range of products, and that a margin squeeze would not be found if, for example, only the broadband price fails the test but the full range of products combined meets it (bundling is discussed further in section 4.8).

4.139 The Commission's approach also recognizes two methods for measuring the profitability of the dominant company's downstream arm—a period-by-period approach and a DCF or NPV approach. The former measures profitability in each period (a month, quarter, or year). It is better suited to mature and stable markets where year-on-year profitability measures may be a reasonable guide for economic profitability. The latter measures profitability across the lifetime of an investment, and is better suited to growing or dynamic markets where initial investments are expected to be recovered by a future stream of profits. In the BSkyB case that we saw in section 4.3, concerning a potential margin squeeze in premium pay-TV services, the OFT included as a relevant cost in the DCF calculation the investment in supplying set-top boxes to new subscribers.[97] In the *Telefónica* case, the Commission applied both approaches and reached the same conclusion.[98]

4.7.3 Whose costs should be used? As-efficient versus reasonably efficient competitors

4.140 There are several variants of the tests for margin squeeze. They all assess whether the retail margin of the dominant company's downstream business is unreasonably low, but do so in different ways. As mentioned above, the main test is to use the costs of the dominant company's downstream business—this is in line with the as-efficient competitor test. It is also called the 'imputation test' because you 'impute' the costs of the as-efficient competitor from the costs of the dominant company. A margin squeeze exists where the margin between the retail price and the wholesale price is lower than the dominant company's downstream cost. This is the standard test for margin squeeze in competition law. It provides the conditions for efficient entry by rival companies.

4.141 An alternative test is based on the costs of a 'hypothetical reasonably efficient downstream operator'. Under this test, a margin squeeze exists where the margin between the retail price and the wholesale price is below the hypothetical reasonably efficient operator's downstream cost. This variant has been used primarily in markets that are in the process of liberalization. In such markets the incumbent company may have a lower downstream unit cost due to economies of scale that cannot easily be replicated by smaller entrants. Where this occurs—typically in network industries such as telecoms—the use of this test promotes the entry of operators that are 'not yet' as

---

[97] Office of Fair Trading (2002), 'BSkyB Investigation: Alleged Infringement of the Chapter II Prohibition', CA98/20/2002, 17 December, at [463].

[98] *Wanadoo España v Telefónica* (Case COMP/38.784), Decision of 4 July 2007.

efficient as the incumbent. From a consumer welfare perspective, the justification for applying this test is that using the entrants' cost may deliver long-term gains. Using the higher cost base of the entrant initially leads to inefficiency and potentially higher prices, but as the entrants establish themselves and begin to compete in the downstream market, allocative efficiency increases because downstream competition delivers more cost-reflective prices.

In a competition investigation in 2004 into BT's pricing of a line-rental product (BT **4.142** Together), Ofcom applied various cost tests, including both the imputation test and the hypothetical reasonably efficient operator test.[99] Although it rejected the use of the reasonably efficient operator test, Ofcom did modify its imputation test to exclude structural cost advantages derived from BT's inherited customer base. This case suggests that where a dominant company's unit cost is lower than that of its rivals due to scale or scope economies arising from its former legal monopoly status, it is reasonable to adjust its cost base for features that are not due to 'competition on the merits'. This sets up a counterfactual market structure under 'normal' competitive conditions—that is, without the legacy advantages. In line with this, Ofcom modified BT's downstream costs by adding in a 'local calls disadvantage', to take account of the scale economies and lower interconnection costs enjoyed by BT at the local exchange level.

In a regulatory context the hypothetical reasonably efficient operator test is often regarded **4.143** favourably. Unlike competition authorities, sectoral regulators often have a statutory duty to promote competition, and may therefore seek to shield entrants to some degree. In reviewing the ex ante margin for BT's wholesale broadband access product in 2008, Ofcom described this difference as follows:

> [I]n terms of a margin squeeze analysis ex post competition law would tend to start from a presumption that the appropriate standard against which the dominant firm should be assessed is one of equally efficient competitors i.e. analysing the margin such that an equally (or more) efficient competitor to BT could enter and compete effectively with BT in the relevant downstream services markets. However . . . the context for the setting of a margin for [wholesale broadband access] is one of ex ante regulation which has as its objective the promotion of competition. Given this objective, Ofcom has concluded that a modification of this conceptual approach is warranted.[100]

Hence, relying largely on the objective of promoting competition, Ofcom decided to uplift **4.144** BT's costs to capture the impact of a reasonably efficient entrant's lower market share; to employ ATC as the relevant cost standard to account for an entrant's inability to benefit from the same economies of scale as BT; and to implement an ex ante margin squeeze test on each product supplied by BT so as to avoid an entrant having to replicate BT's product mix in order to be viable. These adjustments were intended to provide potential entrants with a sufficiently large margin on a product-by-product basis to ensure that they would have the incentives and ability to enter the market. Competition law is usually somewhat less kind towards 'not yet' as-efficient competitors.

---

[99] Ofcom (2004), 'Investigation Against BT about Potential Anti-competitive Exclusionary Behaviour', Decision of the Office of Communications, Case CW/00760/03/04, 12 July.

[100] Ofcom (2008), 'Complaint from Energis Communications Ltd about BT's Charges for NTS Call Termination', 1 August.

4.8 Bundling and Tying

4.8.1 Some definitions first

4.145 Bundling and tying have been extensively debated in economic theory and in competition law. They are very common business practices and not always associated with competition concerns. A new car comes with a set of tyres and seatbelts. Under some definitions you would not even call this bundling but rather the sale of a product consisting of several components. Yet until the late 1950s seatbelts were sold separately. Many cars now have built-in multimedia players and sat navs. Are these also intrinsic components of a new car? Independent producers of portable music players and sat navs may disagree and complain (just like they may complain about smartphones now having these functionalities built in). When Microsoft was first investigated for bundling in the United States in the 1990s, it argued that Internet Explorer was simply a part of the PC operating system, and that integrating it with Windows was technologically justified.[101] But what about its subsequent bundling of Media Player with Windows?[102] Is a media player also an intrinsic part of an operating system (it had not been before the second edition of Windows 98, launched in 1999)? And what to make of Hilti bundling its nail guns, cartridge strips, and nails into what it considered to be an integral system for powder-actuated fastening, or Nespresso bundling its successful espresso machines with Nespresso capsules?[103] You can see how bundling and tying raise complex questions. Trying to resolve these through an assessment of product characteristics is often inconclusive, as in the Microsoft cases. Instead, competition law, informed by economics, has developed a framework for analysing the effects of bundling and tying. This includes the potential theories of harm to competition. However, it also includes the assessment of potential efficiency benefits from bundling and tying, which must be weighed against the anti-competitive effects. Economics has provided useful insights into such benefits. This starts with the simple notion that, as a buyer, you save transaction costs when your new car comes with tyres, seatbelts, a multimedia player, and a sat nav.

4.146 Before discussing the economic principles behind the efficiency and competition effects, we describe some of the main types of bundling and tying. There are no precise definitions. A distinction is often made between three types: pure bundling, mixed bundling, and tying. Bundling itself can be defined as follows: products A and B are bundled if the price of the two products sold together is less than the sum of their individual purchase prices. With pure bundling, the products are offered only as a package. You cannot buy the sports section of a newspaper separately from the other sections. With mixed bundling, the individual components are offered separately as well as in a bundle. Microsoft Office comes as a suite of software packages, which you can usually also purchase separately at a higher price. With tying, product B is tied to product A if a supplier will not sell product A (the 'tying good') unless the customer also purchases product B (the 'tied good').

---

[101] *US v Microsoft*, Civil Action No 98-1232 (TPJ), US District Court for the District of Colombia, Court's Findings of Fact, 5 November 1999.

[102] *Microsoft* (Case COMP/C-3/37.792), Decision of 24 March 2004.

[103] *Eurofix-Bauco v Hilti* (Cases IV/30.787 and 31.488), Decision of 22 December 1987; Case C-53/92 P *Hilti AG v Commission*, Judgment of 2 March 1994; and Autorité de la concurrence (2014), 'Single-portion espresso coffee machines', press release, 4 September.

Technical tying occurs when the tying product is designed such that it works only with the   **4.147**
tied product and not with alternatives offered by competitors. Contractual tying is where
the customer is committed by contract to purchase the tied product as well. The Nespresso
case involved a combination of technical and contractual tying, as discussed below. Tying
can be in variable proportions, in which case the amount of product B purchased varies
with the intensity of use of product A—the number of razor blades purchased depends on
how often the razor is used; the number of coffee capsules purchased depends on usage of
the coffee machine. Or tying can be in fixed proportions between products A and B—a
new car will come fitted with four tyres; shoes come in pairs. Bundling is usually in fixed
proportions (though not always, such as when you get unlimited text messages with your
mobile phone contract). Tying in fixed proportions is equivalent to pure bundling, since
the outcome for the consumer is the same (you cannot buy the car without the four tyres,
or a left shoe without a right shoe). Given the similarities between bundling and tying, and
the lack of precise definitions, we discuss the economics of bundling and tying for the most
part without drawing a distinction between the two.

For the analysis of competition effects it is useful to identify whether bundling is horizontal   **4.148**
or vertical, and whether it takes place within a market or across markets. Horizontal bundling within one product market occurs when the two bundled products form part of the
same relevant market. The products can be substitutes, such as a six-pack of beer bottles or a
bag of oranges. In this case bundling is like a volume discount and the competition analysis
can be undertaken accordingly. The bundled products can also be complements, which
may result in competition in the market being between bundles. Examples include package
holidays and 'triple play' packages of telephony, broadband internet, and TV services. We
discussed market definition in the presence of bundles or 'systems' in Chapter 2. Bundling
over two different product markets is more common, and can be horizontal (a car and a sat
nav) or vertical (a coffee machine and coffee capsules). The competitive concern with such
bundling is that it leverages market power in one of the markets into the other, or that it
protects existing market power in one or both markets. We discuss these theories of harm
below, but first set out the potential efficiency benefits of bundling and tying.

4.8.2 Supply-side efficiencies of bundling and tying

There are several possible efficiency reasons for bundling. We discuss these below under the   **4.149**
headings of supply-side and demand-side efficiencies, though the distinction is not clear-
cut. On the supply side, bundling can lead to a reduction in production and distribution
costs through economies of scale and scope. Technical bundling is the clearest example: it
saves production costs to fit seatbelts and tyres as part of the assembly process for new cars.
Likewise, in distribution, it is cheaper to deliver a suite of goods to a wholesale or retail
outlet than to send out each good separately. Bundling can also save marketing and billing
costs: with triple play packages including telephony, broadband, and TV, the provider can
advertise the three products jointly and needs to send only one bill to the customer. Apart
from cost savings in production and distribution, bundling is commonly used as a marketing and selling tool. Think of shrink-wrapped packages of shampoo and conditioner, or a
newspaper and magazine. Another example is tour operators, whose core business it is to
bundle travel, accommodation, and leisure activities and sell them as package holidays.

A further reason for suppliers to engage in tying is to protect their reputation by maintain-   **4.150**
ing control of the quality of the product. Tying a maintenance contract to a complex piece

of machinery or IT system is common practice. It ensures that maintenance or upgrades are carried out by trained personnel, giving the supplier confidence to offer its customers a longer warranty. With this form of tying, the supplier does not have to worry that a complementary good outside its control (maintenance) will damage customers' perceptions of the quality of its main product (the machinery or IT system).

4.151 One of the first cases to address the issue of quality as a justification for tying was *Jerrold Electronics* in the United States, which resulted in a Supreme Court ruling in 1961.[104] Back in the 1950s Jerrold made community antenna systems for towns located remotely from TV transmitting stations. The system had originally been developed by a friend of Jerrold's founder for private use, and became hugely successful following national press coverage of its first commercial use in a borough in Pennsylvania in 1951. By 1954 Jerrold had installed 80 per cent of all community antenna systems in the United States. It recognized that its system was new, technically complex, and potentially sensitive and unstable. There had been some negative experiences early on with independent installers. To ensure the proper functioning of the systems, Jerrold therefore would not sell separate parts but only whole systems, and on the condition that it installed and serviced the system itself. Jerrold also required exclusive purchase of its own equipment whenever capacity was added. The ruling by the lower court (as affirmed by the Supreme Court) stated that Jerrold's tying of the sales of cable TV systems to installation and maintenance services was justified on quality-control grounds. Jerrold's contracts with customers protected not only its own reputation but also that of community antenna systems. A separate justification accepted by the lower court was that in many contracts the payment to Jerrold was made contingent on the success of the system. In all, an important consideration for the court was that tying by Jerrold took place in the context of the launch of a new business with a highly uncertain future. The court did find that the justification for selling only complete systems and on an exclusive basis had diminished over time, as antenna systems became more established and customers and independent suppliers developed the required technical knowledge.

4.152 In one of the first major EU cases involving bundling and tying, Hilti also argued that its tying practices were motivated by concerns about the reliability, operation and safety of its powder-actuated fastening systems. Dr Martin Hilti developed the original nail guns in the late 1950s and they quickly became popular. When Hilti was investigated in the 1980s it had a market share in nail guns in Europe of around 55 per cent. Operating nail guns required special training. Sub-standard cartridges and nails could damage the nail gun, endanger the person operating it, and result in unreliable fastenings. Hilti considered the cartridges and nails made by independent producers to be unfit for purpose. The Commission was sceptical about these arguments since it found no evidence that Hilti had actually put in writing its concerns about safety and reliability, either to its customers or to the independent producers. Instead, the Commission considered that Hilti's actions were driven mainly by a desire to foreclose independent producers of cartridges and nails, as most of Hilti's profits came from those products rather than the nail guns themselves.[105]

---

[104] *United States v Jerrold Electronics Corp.*, 187 F Supp. 545 (E.D. Pa. 1960); and *Jerrold Electronics Corp. et al. v United States*, 365 US 567 (1961).
[105] *Eurofix-Bauco v Hilti* (Cases IV/30.787 and 31.488), Decision of 22 December 1987, at [87–9].

4.8.3 Demand-side efficiencies of bundling and tying

Customers benefit from bundling if it reduces the total price they pay and the transaction costs they incur in the process of product search and purchase. Beyond these direct savings to customers, there is a large body of economic literature on how bundling may be used as a price discrimination tool that reduces inefficiencies in pricing.[106] Recall from section 4.5 that price discrimination requires the producer to have some control over prices, to restrict arbitrage, and to be able to distinguish between consumers with different willingness to pay. Bundling can improve matters for suppliers with respect to this last condition. One mechanism is through using bundling as a 'metering device'. By bundling its coffee machines and capsules, Nespresso was able to extract higher total margins from frequent users of the machines than from those who use them less often. Hilti did the same with its nail guns, cartridges, and nails. This discrimination through bundling allows the seller to increase profits, but like other forms of price discrimination it also tends to enhance output and thereby overall welfare (although not necessarily consumer welfare). **4.153**

The other mechanism through which bundling facilitates price discrimination is by addressing the diversity—or heterogeneity, in economics jargon—in preferences across customers. Take the case of pay-TV packages that commonly include a range of channels, many of which you would never watch. TV viewers have very diverse preferences for different types of channel. Selling packages of channels allows pay-TV operators to increase sales without having to identify each customer's willingness to pay. They make use of the fact that demand for a bundle will be less heterogeneous than demand for individual channels. See the stylized example in Table 4.7. There are two types of viewer: those with a preference for sports channels and those who value watching films more. These preferences tend to be mutually exclusive (economists say that preferences are inversely correlated). The sports fan is willing to pay €9 per month for the sports channel but only €3 for the film channel. The film fan values the film channel at €10 and the sports channel at €2. How should the pay-TV operator set prices for the channels? Without bundling, the operator could price the sports channel at €9 per month. Only the sports fan would buy at that price. Alternatively, it could set the price at €2 per month and sell to both types of viewer, but you can see how this would be very unattractive to the operator. The film channel could be priced at €10 per month, and bought only by the film fan. With these prices of €9 and €10, total revenue would be €19, and a total of two channels would be sold (one of each). The operator can do better than this—by bundling. It can sell the two channels in a bundle for €12. Now both **4.154**

Table 4.7 Efficiency benefits of bundling: pay-TV package

	Sports fan	Film fan
Willingness to pay for sports channel (€)	9	2
Willingness to pay for film channel (€)	3	10
Willingness to pay for both sports and film (€)	12	12

[106] See, for example, Bowman (1957), Adams and Yellen (1976), Schmalensee (1982), and Bakos and Brynjolfsson (1999). For an accessible overview see Nalebuff (2003).

the sports fan and the film fan will buy both channels, since the combined price matches the sum of their willingness to pay. The operator's revenue is now €24, up from €19 when offering the products separately. In addition, total output has increased: four channels are sold, as both viewers purchase the two channels. This increase in output will normally enhance overall welfare.

4.155 The output-enhancing effect of bundling may represent a pure market expansion effect, which happens when bundling attracts new customers who were previously not purchasing any product. Alternatively, bundling may enhance sales to existing customers who were previously purchasing only a subset of the products included in the bundle, as in the above example of the sports and film channels. Bundling may also come at the expense of existing sales. In this context it is useful to distinguish between the impact on rivals' sales (business stealing) and a company's own sales (cannibalization). Bundling will to some extent cannibalize existing revenues because bundles are priced below the sum of the stand-alone prices. The business-stealing effect is where the incumbent's output grows at the expense of its competitors. Clearly the risk of harm to competition is greater when business-stealing effects are prevalent.

4.8.4 An illustration of welfare and foreclosure effects of bundling

4.156 The various effects of bundling are illustrated in Figure 4.7. This shows consumers spread out over a willingness-to-pay field for broadband and TV services. A consumer near the top-left corner of the field has a low willingness to pay for TV and a high one for broadband; a consumer near the bottom-right values TV highly but broadband less so. The maximum valuation that any consumer has for either product is €25 per month. The figure shows two situations. On the left-hand side there is no bundling, and each product is sold at €20 per month. On the right-hand side there is mixed bundling: consumers can purchase each product separately at a unit price of €20 per month, or both products in a bundle at a discounted price of €32 per month. Consider the left-hand side first. At the separate prices of €20 there are four categories of consumer, as represented by the four rectangles: consumers in the bottom-left rectangle buy nothing because their willingness to pay for either

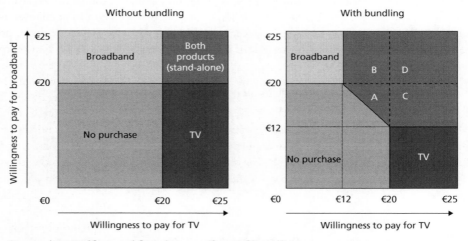

Figure 4.7 **Welfare and foreclosure effects of bundling**

service is below €20; those in the top-left rectangle purchase only broadband; those in the bottom-right only TV; and those in the top-right buy both products.

The overall market expansion effect of bundling is represented by areas A, B, and C. Before **4.157** the introduction of the bundle, consumers in area A did not buy any of the products at a price of €20 because they valued them less. However, their combined valuation for broadband and TV is above €32, and they are therefore willing to purchase the bundle. Examples of consumers in area A are those who value broadband at €19 and TV at €13, and those who value both services at €16. Similarly, areas B and C represent consumers who previously purchased only one product on a stand-alone basis, and now purchase both products in a bundle. Their willingness to pay for the product they favour least is between €12 and €20; for the product they value most it is €20 or more. From the operator's perspective, selling to consumers in area A represents additional revenues of €32 per consumer, and in areas B and C €12 per consumer. Area D, on the other hand, shows the cannibalization effect that may arise from bundling. These consumers were spending €40 in total when purchasing both products on a stand-alone basis, and now spend €8 less by purchasing them in a bundle. The profitability of bundling to the operator depends on whether the cannibalization effect is outweighed by the increase in profits from the new sales. On the whole, again, this bundling enhances output and this in turn will normally increase overall welfare.

One effect of bundling that we have not yet discussed is the business-stealing or foreclosure **4.158** effect. Say the operator competes with stand-alone providers of broadband and TV services. Without bundling, all providers are in the same position in that they can compete for the same consumers. By bundling, the multi-product operator can make life difficult for the stand-alone providers. Take a stand-alone provider of TV services (say, a satellite-based operator). At a price of €20, it can compete for all consumers to the right of the €20 mark in the situation without bundling. However, the stand-alone TV provider sees its addressable market significantly reduced if the multi-product operator bundles TV with broadband. Consumers in areas C and D are lured into purchasing the bundle, which leaves only consumers to the bottom-right of the figure interested in purchasing TV from stand-alone providers. In essence these are consumers who value broadband very little (at less than €12). Thus, by bundling, multi-product operators can foreclose single-product rivals from a significant part of the market. Note that this can be achieved through both mixed bundling and pure bundling (if anything, under pure bundling none of the consumers in the bottom-right of the figure would buy from the multi-product operator, leaving that bit of the market to single-product providers). In the extreme, if one of the products in the bundle is a must-have product, the addressable market for stand-alone providers of the other product becomes very small. If there are economies of scale in production of the other product, the effect can be the foreclosure of existing single-product rivals and the creation of entry barriers for new rivals. The latter may have to enter in both products simultaneously in order to circumvent the bundling effect. This may be more costly than entering one product, and may not always be feasible. You would have to analyse this foreclosure effect on a case-by-case basis. In some markets, rivals can effectively compete by creating their own bundles (satellite TV operators now also commonly offer broadband over fixed networks). In addition, you should bear in mind that providers may have reasons for bundling other than the foreclosure of rivals, as discussed above. Furthermore, foreclosure through bundling is not always a profitable strategy, a theme we turn to now.

4.8.5 Bundling and tying to leverage market power: The Chicago critique and responses to it

4.159 The notion that bundling or tying is a means to leverage market power is intuitive, but was forcefully criticized by the Chicago School in the 1970s (see Bork, 1978). This critique was based on the economic logic that in any vertical supply chain or combination of complementary products there is 'only one monopoly profit to be had'. It is closely linked to the concept of double marginalization, which we explain in Chapter 6 in the context of vertical restraints. If a company enjoys a monopoly in one of the complement products, the full monopoly rent can be extracted by pricing that product at the monopoly level. Attempting to leverage that market power into a related product through bundling (or indeed through any other means) may shift some of the profit to the market for the bundled product, but will not raise total profits. Take the example of a privately owned ski resort that has no rival resorts nearby. Skiing lessons are a competitive activity within the resort, as there are many instructors willing to offer their services. Say the owner of the resort decides to bundle the ski resort pass with skiing lessons, visitors can still buy a pass separately, but if they want lessons they need to purchase those together with the pass (lessons are the tied product; the pass is the tying product). This form of tying forecloses independent instructors from offering their services in the same way as illustrated in Figure 4.7. But does it enhance the resort owner's profits? The answer is no. The resort owner cannot increase the price for skiing lessons, once monopolized, without negatively affecting sales of ski passes. To put it the other way round, it cannot extract higher rents than in the situation in which it charges the monopoly price for the ski resort pass and leaves skiing lessons at the competitive price. From a profit perspective the resort owner should be indifferent to whether these competitive lessons are offered by its own instructors or by independents. Indeed, in such situations the monopolist of the tying good (here the resort) usually benefits most if there is effective competition in the complementary product market (skiing lessons) as this will tend to increase demand for the monopoly product as well. Therefore, so the Chicago School logic goes, if bundling or tying is observed in these circumstances, it must be motivated by efficiency or quality considerations rather than attempted monopolization. In our example, the owner of the ski resort may have introduced tying in order to maintain the reputation of the resort by ensuring that lessons are provided only by qualified instructors.

4.160 The Chicago critique has been influential in helping competition authorities and courts understand the rationale for bundling and tying. It provides an analytical benchmark: if the assumptions of the Chicago critique hold, the bundling or tying practice in question is probably not of concern. If the assumptions do not hold, you should inquire further. This approach follows the insights on bundling by Whinston (1990), who showed that the Chicago critique depends on a number of key assumptions: the tied market is perfectly competitive, and there are no economies of scale in production. The incentives to adopt a foreclosure-based bundling strategy are different when the tied good market is oligopolistic. When a monopolist in the tying market faces a competitor in the tied market offering a product subject to strong scale economies and imperfect competition (e.g. switching costs), bundling can be used to monopolize the tied market. This reduces the addressable market for competitors of the tied product, as illustrated previously in Figure 4.7, and may prevent them from reaching an efficient scale.

A hypothetical example of such a situation is provided in the 2008 DOJ report on single-firm conduct:[107] the only hotel on a holiday island may tie accommodation and meal packages. If there are insufficient island residents to support a second restaurant, the hotel may be able to extract greater profit through its tie of accommodation and meals because the tie enables it to also monopolize restaurant services. The hotel would thus extract monopoly profits from not only its guests (the purchasers of the monopoly product—accommodation) but also island residents (who would buy only the second product—restaurant food). The hotel's tie prevents competition from independent restaurants, which, but for the tie, would be able to achieve efficient scale by selling meals to both hotel guests and island residents. With the tie, hotel guests obtain meals in the hotel at zero marginal cost, having paid for the combination of full-board meals and accommodation, which discourages them from trying out an independent restaurant. You can see that tying in this situation is similar to loyalty rebates, where the effective price of the tied good faced by consumers is below the costs of an as-efficient competitor that can supply only the tied product (meals) but not the tying product (accommodation). The hotel guests will not be thrown out of the hotel if they have a meal elsewhere, but they have a strong price incentive to remain loyal to the hotel's restaurant. Below we discuss how a price–cost test may be applied to such bundling cases.

4.161

A recent case of leveraging of market power through bundling involved Nespresso coffee machines.[108] The French competition authority received complaints from two rival coffee-makers—D.E. Master Blenders 1753 and the Ethical Coffee Company—that Nespresso hindered their sales of capsules for Nespresso machines. In 2012, Nespresso had a share of 73 per cent of the market for single-portion espresso coffee machines in France. Its own capsules represented 85 per cent of sales of capsules compatible with Nespresso machines—that is, it faced some competition from third-party capsules. Nespresso was found to have engaged in technical and contractual tying. At the technical level, it made four modifications to its machines between 2007 and 2013 that had the effect of rendering competing producers' capsules incompatible with the new models. At the contractual level, it linked the warranty for the machines to the exclusive use of Nespresso capsules. Nespresso further promoted the use of its own capsules through the text on its packaging and in its instructions, and through product information provided to the press and retail outlets (George Clooney almost certainly helped too). Following concerns expressed by the authority, Nespresso agreed to remedies whereby it would notify its competitors of technical modifications and provide them with a prototype four months in advance. It would also delink the warranty from the exclusive use of Nespresso capsules, and refrain from making any public comments about competitors' capsules. It is not clear from the available information on the case whether there may have been any efficiency justifications for Nespresso's bundling practices, or to what extent a more competitive capsule market will benefit consumers more than the previous situation. Separately, you can see the close link between bundling and refusal to grant access to competitors where IP is involved—a theme we turn to in section 4.9.

4.162

---

[107] Department of Justice (2008), 'Competition and Monopoly: Single-firm Conduct Under Section 2 of the Sherman Act', September, p. 83. The DOJ withdrew this report in 2009.

[108] Autorité de la concurrence (2014), 'Single-portion espresso coffee machines', press release, 4 September.

4.8.6 Bundling and tying to protect an existing market position

4.163   Bundling and tying may protect an existing market position in the tying product if it creates new entry barriers. Pure bundling commits a company to a stronger price and investment reaction. This is because a failure to sell in the tied product market will also entail losing a sale in the tying product market. This commitment to a stronger price or investment reaction may deter potential competitors. When rivals cannot match the supply of the bundle or tie, they will attract only those consumers who prefer one product instead of the bundle. If the products are strong complements, this entry barrier might be significant since potential competitors have to offer a whole bundle where consumers strongly prefer the two products together. We saw this logic illustrated in Figure 4.7. Entrants must either seek out the small number of consumers who do not value the tying product, or must compete bundle for bundle, which may be costly or infeasible.

4.164   A dynamic version of such bundling to protect an existing market position can be seen in the *Microsoft* browser case in the United States.[109] The DOJ and the court found evidence that Microsoft had engaged in bundling in order to protect its Windows PC operating system—not from a competing PC operating system, but rather from Netscape's new internet browser, which had the potential of becoming a new gateway to online software applications that might undermine PC-based applications. If successful, Netscape Navigator could overcome what the DOJ and court referred to as the 'applications barrier to entry' that embedded the strong position of Windows—that is, rival operating systems could not develop because Microsoft had a critical mass of applications compatible with Windows (a network effect that we also discussed in Chapter 3). As stated by the court:

> As soon as Netscape released Navigator on December 15, 1994, the product began to enjoy dramatic acceptance by the public; shortly after its release, consumers were already using Navigator far more than any other browser product. This alarmed Microsoft, which feared that Navigator's enthusiastic reception could embolden Netscape to develop Navigator into an alternative platform for applications development. In late May 1995, Bill Gates, the chairman and CEO of Microsoft, sent a memorandum entitled 'The Internet Tidal Wave' to Microsoft's executives describing Netscape as a 'new competitor "born" on the Internet.' He warned his colleagues within Microsoft that Netscape was 'pursuing a multi-platform strategy where they move the key API into the client to commoditize the underlying operating system.' By the late spring of 1995, the executives responsible for setting Microsoft's corporate strategy were deeply concerned that Netscape was moving its business in a direction that could diminish the applications barrier to entry.[110]

4.165   Microsoft spent significant resources on developing its own browser, Internet Explorer, and at some stage decided to include it for free with Windows. While Microsoft sought to argue that Internet Explorer had become an integral part of Windows, the court held that Microsoft would not have made such significant development efforts and forgone profits by including Internet Explorer for free but for the aim of protecting the Windows applications barrier to entry:

> Neither the desire to bolster demand for Windows, nor the prospect of ancillary revenues, explains the lengths to which Microsoft has gone. For one thing, loading Navigator makes

---

[109] *US v Microsoft*, Civil Action No 98-1232 (TPJ), US District Court for the District of Colombia, Court's Findings of Fact, 5 November 1999.

[110] Ibid., at [72].

Windows just as Internet-ready as including Internet Explorer does. Therefore, Microsoft's costly efforts to limit the use of Navigator on Windows could not have stemmed from a desire to bolster consumer demand for Windows.[111]

4.8.7 The as-efficient competitor and attribution tests for bundling

We have seen from various examples that bundling has some similarities with discounting. After all, bundling is defined as the sale of two or more products at a total price that is less than the sum of the individual product prices. The logic of the as-efficient competitor test as applied to discounts and rebates may therefore be of relevance to bundling as well. This is particularly the case where the rebates are explicitly linked to buying the bundle—a combination of bundling and loyalty rebates, as discussed in section 4.6. US antitrust law has developed the discount attribution test for such cases, as proposed by the Antitrust Modernization Commission (2007) and applied in *Cascade Health Solutions v PeaceHealth* (2008).[112]

4.166

We first consider the *LePage's v 3M* bundled rebates case of 2003.[113] 3M's Scotch brand dominated the transparent tape market with a market share above 90 per cent. LePage's successfully entered the market producing private-label tape for retailers. In response, 3M introduced bundled rebates whereby customers would obtain significant rebates if they purchased across six of 3M's product lines, which besides tape include other stationery products, healthcare, homecare, and home improvement products. This was effectively a bundling strategy to protect 3M's existing position in the tape market. The court found that the bundled rebates created a strong incentive for customers to meet the targets across all product lines. In finding against 3M, the court considered evidence of significant anti-competitive effects on LePage's: the company had been growing healthily, but when the bundled rebates were introduced it lost sales to key customers such as Kmart, Sam's Club, and Staples, and began to make losses. A buyer for Kmart, LePage's largest customer representing 10 per cent of its sales, told LePage's: 'I can't talk to you about tape products for the next three years', and 'don't bring me anything 3M makes'. The court found there to be sufficient evidence that the long-term effects of the bundled rebates were anti-competitive, and that 3M had not put forward any legitimate business justifications for the bundling.

4.167

The *LePage's v 3M* case did not apply a price–cost test, which caused some confusion as 3M's overall prices were above ATC. The Antitrust Modernization Commission therefore proposed the attribution test, which is akin to the as-efficient competitor test applied to loyalty rebates. In essence this test attributes the entire discount to the competitive products and then compares the price with the relevant cost benchmark (the Commission proposed incremental cost, but you could also use AAC or LRAIC). Consider the example we saw in Figure 4.7, where broadband and TV were priced separately at €20 each, and the bundle cost €32. If TV is the competitive product where a stand-alone provider tries to enter, you would allocate the entire discount of €8 to it, resulting in an effective price of €12. This is the price you then compare against the relevant cost benchmark.

4.168

---

[111] *US v Microsoft*, Civil Action No 98-1232 (TPJ), US District Court for the District of Colombia, Court's Findings of Fact, 5 November 1999, at [141].

[112] *Cascade Health Solutions v PeaceHealth* 515 F 3d 883 (9th Cir. 2008).

[113] *LePage's Inc. v 3M Co.*, 324 F 3d (3d Cir. 2003).

4.169   The attribution test was accepted by the court in *Cascade Health Solutions v PeaceHealth*, involving hospital care in Lane County, Oregon. PeaceHealth had a high market share in tertiary-care services, approaching 90 per cent in certain specialities. In the related local markets for primary and secondary acute-care hospital services, PeaceHealth competed with McKenzie (later named Cascade). McKenzie did not provide tertiary services, which included more complex services such as invasive cardiovascular surgery and intensive neonatal care. It complained about PeaceHealth's offers of bundled service packages to certain customers (insurance companies). These bundled offerings provided discounts on all services if insurance companies made PeaceHealth their sole preferred provider for primary, secondary, and tertiary care. Thus the discount on tertiary care was offered only if a customer also purchased primary and secondary care from PeaceHealth. The court agreed that 'it is possible, at least in theory, for a firm to use a bundled discount to exclude an equally or more efficient competitor and thereby reduce consumer welfare in the long run'.[114] It wished to establish a test that was consistent with case law on predation, requiring that prices be set below an appropriate measure of cost. However, rather than considering the overall price, the court favoured the attribution test. It stated that:

> The discount attribution standard provides clear guidance for sellers that engage in bundled discounting practices. A seller can easily ascertain its own prices and costs of production and calculate whether its discounting practices run afoul of the rule we have outlined... under the discount attribution standard a bundled discounter need not fret over and predict or determine its rivals' cost structure.[115]

4.170   Thus, the court ruled that for a bundled discount to be exclusionary or predatory, the plaintiff must establish that prices are below incremental cost after allocating to the competitive product the discount given by the defendant on the entire bundle of products. The attribution test is informative for the as-efficient competitor test but does not in itself prove anti-competitive effects. As with loyalty rebates you must also consider other factors such as the degree of foreclosure and the likelihood of successful exclusion.

4.9 Refusal to Supply and Essential Facilities

4.9.1 A difficult trade-off

4.171   Refusal to supply covers a broad range of practices, such as refusal to deal with customers or distributors, refusal to license IP rights, and refusal to grant access to an essential facility. It can include offering a product under such unreasonable conditions (e.g. a very high price) that they amount to a constructive refusal to supply. The main theory of harm from refusal to supply is that a dominant company can disadvantage its rivals in a downstream or otherwise related market by not supplying them with an important input or service. There is an inherent policy trade-off in these cases: forcing a company to provide its competitors with access to an input or facility may diminish the company's incentives to invest in that input or facility. Intervention in these cases thus involves balancing short-run gains in competition in the related market against potential long-run harm to investment and innovation in the input market. Different jurisdictions have different philosophies about how to strike

---

[114] *Cascade Health Solutions v PeaceHealth* 515 F 3d 883 (9th Cir. 2008), at [896].
[115] Ibid., at [907–8].

such a balance. US antitrust law has traditionally placed strong emphasis on the freedom of market participants to choose who they do business with. The Supreme Court emphasized this freedom in a 1919 ruling on Colgate, a manufacturer of soap and other toiletries, which had refused to supply certain retailers.[116] This '*Colgate* doctrine' was referred to again in *Trinko* (2004), where the Supreme Court found nothing wrong with the refusal by Verizon Communications to share its local telephone network with competitors:

> Firms may acquire monopoly power by establishing an infrastructure that renders them uniquely suited to serve their customers. Compelling such firms to share the source of their advantage is in some tension with the underlying purpose of antitrust law, since it may lessen the incentive for the monopolist, the rival, or both to invest in those economically beneficial facilities. Enforced sharing also requires antitrust courts to act as central planners, identifying the proper price, quantity, and other terms of dealing—a role for which they are ill suited. Moreover, compelling negotiation between competitors may facilitate the supreme evil of antitrust: collusion. Thus, as a general matter, the Sherman Act 'does not restrict the long recognized right of [a] trader or manufacturer engaged in an entirely private business, freely to exercise his own independent discretion as to parties with whom he will deal'.[117]

The issue in *Trinko* was AT&T's lack of access to the local telephony loop and associated facilities operated by Verizon, the incumbent local exchange carrier in New York State. The case began in 2000 when Curtis V. Trinko, a lawyer and customer of AT&T, filed a class action suit against Verizon on behalf of all AT&T customers in the area, on the basis that Verizon was blocking access in a manner designed to deter customers from buying their telephony services from other companies. He alleged that this constituted a breach not only of the US Telecommunications Act 1996—which sets out sector-specific regulations—but also of Section 2 of the Sherman Act. The Supreme Court ultimately rejected the case. Thus, when it comes to the trade-off between requiring access to facilitate competition and maintaining a dominant company's commercial freedom and incentives to invest, the Supreme Court tends to have more sympathy for the latter. **4.172**

However, even in the United States the right to deal with whoever you please is not unqualified. The *Colgate* doctrine itself states that it applies 'in the absence of any purpose to create or maintain a monopoly'.[118] A much-debated case in which the Supreme Court did find fault with a refusal to deal with a competitor was *Aspen Skiing Co* (1985).[119] This concerned a company that owned three of the four mountain areas in the Aspen skiing region and refused to continue a joint-ticketing arrangement with a rival that owned the fourth mountain area. The two companies had operated the 'all-Aspen' ticket arrangement for several years, but then disagreed on how to run the scheme and divide revenues. The court considered the discontinuation of the arrangement to be exclusionary, and found that the operator of the one mountain area could no longer compete effectively as skiers had developed a preference for tickets giving access to multiple mountains. In a case from 1897, *Trans-Missouri Freight Association*, the Supreme Court had stated that while private traders and manufacturers had the right to sell to whom they pleased, this did not apply to a railroad **4.173**

---

[116] *United States v Colgate & Co* 250 US 300 (1919).
[117] *Verizon Communications Inc. v Law Offices of Curtis V Trinko, LLP* 540 US 398 (2004), at [407–8] (quoting *United States v Colgate & Co* 250 US 300, 307 (1919)).
[118] *United States v Colgate & Co* 250 US 300, 307 (1919).
[119] *Aspen Skiing Co v Aspen Highlands Skiing Corp* 472 US 585 (1985).

business, given its public and natural monopoly character, and its obligation to transport all persons and goods on a reasonable and non-discriminatory basis.[120] Thus the court was of the view back then that the antitrust laws also apply to railroads and other network and utility companies.

4.174 What about the other problem identified by the Supreme Court in *Trinko* as quoted above: that if a court orders a dominant company to supply a rival, it must say something about the terms of supply, and thereby risks becoming like a regulator? We return to this in Chapter 8, where we show that the insights and experiences from the field of regulation can be of assistance in competition law, and that competition authorities in Europe and elsewhere do not necessarily shy away from using competition law to address problems of access to network and infrastructure bottlenecks. The Supreme Court's hands-off position in *Trinko* leaves these bottleneck problems unaddressed. We'll also see an example of an access case where the court's finding of abuse of dominance was sufficient for the parties to agree to a new access deal, without the court having to prescribe access terms.[121]

4.9.2 The concept of essential facility

4.175 Like its US counterpart, EU competition law does not grant access to competitors lightly. It has developed an effects-based approach building on the concept of essential facility, although refusal to supply has sometimes been applied more broadly than this concept. The Guidance on Article 102 summarizes the approach as follows: a refusal to supply is likely to constitute an abuse if: (i) it relates to a product or service that is objectively necessary to be able to compete effectively in a downstream market; (ii) the refusal is likely to lead to the elimination of effective competition in the downstream market; and (iii) the refusal is likely to lead to consumer harm.[122] The conditions under which a service or facility will be deemed essential were developed by the ECJ in *Oscar Bronner v Mediaprint* in 1998.[123] An Austrian court asked the ECJ whether the refusal by a newspaper group, Mediaprint, to allow the publisher of a competing newspaper access to its home-delivery network constituted an abuse of dominance. Mediaprint was the leading publisher of daily newspapers in Austria, with its *Neue Kronen Zeitung* and *Kurier* titles representing 46.8 per cent of newspapers in circulation and 42 per cent of advertising revenue. Mediaprint had invested in establishing and administering a nationwide distribution network delivering newspapers directly to subscribers' homes in the early hours of the morning. Oscar Bronner, a rival publisher, had asked Mediaprint to include its newspaper *Der Standard* in the home-delivery service in exchange for a reasonable payment. *Der Standard* represented 3.6 per cent of newspapers in circulation. Mediaprint refused, arguing that it was not obliged to assist a competitor, and that its home-delivery network would not have sufficient capacity to also deliver *Der Standard*. Mediaprint did in fact deliver another third-party newspaper, *Wirtschaftsblad*, but it argued that the publisher of *Wirtschaftsblad* also used Mediaprint for distribution services to other points of sale, such as kiosks.

---

[120] *United States v Trans-Missouri Freight Association* 166 US 290, 320 (1897).
[121] *Arriva The Shires Ltd v London Luton Airport Operations Ltd* [2014] EWHC 64 (Ch), [2014] UKCLR 313.
[122] European Commission (2008), 'Guidance on the Commission's Enforcement Priorities in Applying Article 82 EC Treaty to Abusive Exclusionary Conduct by Dominant Undertakings', December, at [81].
[123] Case C-7/97 *Oscar Bronner v Mediaprint* [1998] ECR I-7791.

The ECJ held that the refusal to grant access to a distribution facility would constitute an **4.176** abuse only if there was no real or potential substitute for it. In other words, it is not sufficient that the dominant undertaking's control over the facility gives it a competitive advantage. Rather, duplication of the facility must be impossible or extremely difficult owing to physical, geographical, or legal constraints. An essential facility therefore shares economic characteristics with a natural monopoly where the total revenue generated in the market in question would not make investment in two facilities profitable. The ECJ concluded that the newspaper home-delivery service was not an essential facility because the market could potentially support another nationwide distribution system. Moreover, it did not consider it material that it would be uneconomic for a newspaper with limited circulation, such as *Der Standard*, to establish its own nationwide distribution system. Rather, for the system to be deemed an essential facility, it would have to be demonstrated that the market as a whole could not sustain a competing system at all. The ECJ also pointed out that there were alternative, even if less convenient, means of distributing newspapers, such as postal deliveries and conventional newspaper retail outlets. In sum, the ECJ did not consider access to the newspaper home-delivery network to be essential, but rather a nice-to-have. In this regard, the stance of the ECJ in *Bronner*, and the resulting essential facilities doctrine in EU case law, is not dissimilar to the approach in the United States.

The concept of essential facility played a central role in two cases involving Deutsche Bahn **4.177** AG (DB), the railway infrastructure manager and main train operator in Germany. In 2003 the German competition authority initiated proceedings against DB on account of its refusal to include timetable and fares information in its information systems on two long-distance routes operated by the Connex group (Gera–Berlin–Rostock and Zittau–Berlin–Stralsund). Until then, DB had been the sole provider of long-distance passenger rail services in Germany. Connex was the first competitor to enter this market. DB's refusal was directed specifically at Connex because the timetables of rail companies competing in the short-distance rail passenger sector did get included in DB's information systems. Since Connex had also brought proceedings against DB before the civil law courts, the case was ultimately resolved by a decision of the Berlin Court of Appeals in 2003.[124] The court concluded that DB had a dominant position in the market for the provision of services to railway undertakings, notably in respect of the provision of customer information via timetables. DB was not permitted to discriminate against competitors by refusing to include their services in the timetables. However, the court also concluded that Connex had no right to ask DB to publish its fares in addition to the timetable information. It was not considered essential for fare information to be supplied via DB's information systems—such information could also be communicated to customers by the new operator itself. Thus, the court made a careful distinction between information access services that were truly essential and those for which there were viable alternatives.

In a second timetable case in 2004, the Regional Court of Berlin confirmed DB's obliga- **4.178** tion to include train services of competitors in its timetables.[125] The court confirmed that DB had a dominant position in the market for customer information via timetables. In light of the expectations of the general public as regards the exclusivity and completeness

---

124 Decision of the Kammergericht [KG] (Berlin) of 26 June 2003, 2 U 20/02 Kart.
125 LG Berlin, Judgment of 27 April 2004, 102 O 64/03 Kart.

of the timetables provided by the former monopolist, the service that DB offered could not be replaced by competitors' own services. Furthermore, the court found that there was no objective justification for DB to exclude the train services of competitors. It did acknowledge that a dominant undertaking could not be obliged to implement measures in favour of competitors that would be uneconomical and to its own detriment. However, according to the court, in this context a balance needed to be struck between the parties' competing interests. This balancing of interests had to take account of, among other things, whether the dominant company bore considerable entrepreneurial risks in creating the infrastructure in question, or whether the infrastructure was created in the context of a legally protected monopoly. The latter was considered to apply to DB.

4.9.3 The *IMS Health* case: The tension between competition law and IP rights

4.179 The inherent trade-off between requiring access to facilitate competition, and maintaining incentives to invest, arises frequently in the area of access to IP. Patents and copyrights, which are designed to protect IP, at the same time confer monopoly rights to the owner for a defined period. This may not always sit well alongside policy aims to promote competition and open markets. One question that arises is whether a dominant undertaking should be required to offer its IP to its rivals. EU case law indicates that a refusal to license IP would be objectionable only if competition in a secondary, related, market is eliminated, and the refusal prevents the emergence of a new product for which there is potential consumer demand. One of the key cases in this area is *IMS Health* (2004).[126]

4.180 The case involved two American companies, IMS Health and NDC Health, which collected data on sales of pharmaceutical and healthcare products in Germany. This information was sold on to pharmaceutical manufacturers, which used the data in the development of their sales and marketing strategies. At the heart of the issue was a specific geographical structure used to provide data to the pharmaceutical companies. This structure was originally designed by IMS Health. It presented the data to customers in 'bricks' that corresponded to a designated geographic area. IMS held the copyright over the original brick structure, but NDC acquired knowledge of the design through the acquisition of a venture, PII, which had been set up by a former manager of IMS. PII had encountered considerable difficulty in marketing regional data on pharmaceutical products using a different brick structure. Customers were not willing to buy information based on a different structure, given the investment they had made in helping to design the original structure and the switching costs they would have to incur. PII therefore reverted to a brick structure that was very close to that designed and owned by IMS. The latter brought legal proceedings under IP law before a German court, which prohibited PII and NDC from using any kind of brick structure that was derived from the IMS version. The question then turned to NDC being able to obtain a licence from IMS for the use of the brick structure. IMS refused. Having established itself as the de facto market standard, it saw no benefit in allowing access to its IP, even for a fee. It preferred to earn its monopoly rent through its own direct sales in the retail market rather than through IP licence fees.

4.181 The German court referred three questions to the ECJ. Is refusal by the dominant undertaking to grant a licence to use the brick structure abusive if potential customers will reject

---

[126] Case C-418/01 *IMS Health GmbH & Co OHG v NDC Health GmbH & Co KG* [2004] ECR I-5039.

any product not based on that system (i.e. if the brick structure is essential)? Is it relevant to consider the extent to which IMS Health involved customers in the design of the brick structure (and in so doing, may have helped create dependency on its system)? Are switching costs faced by customers of the data service relevant to the question of abusive conduct by a dominant undertaking? The ECJ addressed the second and third questions first, so as to clarify the criteria for assessing whether access to the brick structure was essential for potential competitors. It determined that both the degree of participation by the users in the development of the brick structure, and the potential switching costs that customers would face were they to move to a rival brick system, were relevant factors in the assessment.

With respect to the first question, the ECJ held that a refusal to license IP constitutes an **4.182** abuse of dominance only in exceptional circumstances. Referring to *Magill*, a case from 1995 concerning the licensing by broadcasters of TV listings to an independent TV guide, the ECJ articulated three cumulative conditions that must be satisfied for a refusal to license to constitute an abuse.[127] First, the refusal to license must prevent the emergence of a new product for which there is potential consumer demand; that is, the new product must not merely duplicate the products already offered by the IP owner in the secondary market. Second, the refusal must be unjustified. Third, the refusal must eliminate any competition in the secondary market, thus restricting that market to the IP owner. The first and third conditions both relate to the secondary (or downstream) market, for products that use the IP. The first condition focuses on promoting products that are different from that of the IP owner. This seeks to strike the balance between protecting the IP owner from its products being copied, and allowing customers to benefit from the emergence of new products. The third condition focuses on preventing the elimination of competition in the secondary market. There may be some tension with the first condition. If the product must be sufficiently different from the IP owner's product (as per the first condition), is it actually in the same relevant secondary market as the IP owner's product? If the new product is in a different secondary market, the refusal cannot be said to restrict that secondary market to the IP owner (as per the third condition). Thus, the *IMS Health* conditions seem to require access to IP where a new downstream product is sufficiently distinct from that of the IP owner, but still sufficiently substitutable to be in the same market.

Comparing the US *Trinko* and *Aspen* rulings with *IMS Health* suggests that courts will con- **4.183** tinue to take different views on these issues. In *Trinko*, the US Supreme Court stated that:

> *Aspen Skiing* is at or near the outer boundary of [Section 2] liability. The Court there found significance in the defendant's decision to cease participation in a cooperative venture... The unilateral termination of a voluntary (and thus presumably profitable) course of dealing suggested a willingness to forsake short-term profits to achieve an anticompetitive end...
>
> The refusal to deal alleged in the present case does not fit within the limited exception recognized in *Aspen Skiing*. The complaint does not allege that Verizon voluntarily engaged in a course of dealing with its rivals, or would ever have done so absent statutory compulsion...
>
> In *Aspen Skiing*, what the defendant refused to provide to its competitor was a product that it already sold at retail—to oversimplify slightly, lift tickets representing a bundle of services to skiers... In the present case, by contrast, the services allegedly withheld are not otherwise marketed or available to the public.[128]

---

[127] Joined Cases C-241/91 P and C-242/91 P *Radio Telefis Eireann and Independent Television Publications Ltd v Commission* [1995] ECR I-743 (the *Magill* case).
[128] *Verizon Communications Inc. v Law Offices of Curtis V Trinko, LLP* 540 US 398, 416 (2004).

4.184   Thus, the US Supreme Court saw in *Aspen* that refusal to supply an *existing* product suggested a willingness to forsake short-term profits in order to exclude competition, whereas in *Trinko* there was no forsaking of existing profits since the Verizon access had not previously been supplied. As such, a line could potentially be drawn between *Trinko* and *Aspen* to say that a withdrawal of supply would be worse than never supplying. However, the ECJ's *IMS Health* conditions point in the opposite direction: a refusal to supply is more likely to be condemned when it prevents the emergence of a new product, which by definition has never had access before. From an economic perspective, it does not necessarily matter whether access is withdrawn or never granted. What matters most is the effect of the refusal on competition and efficiency in the round, that is, in both the IP and the downstream markets, and in both the short and long run.

4.9.4 Effects on downstream competition: The airport bus and parking cases

4.185   The UK courts have dealt with a number of cases involving refusals by airports to grant access to their premises to competing car park and bus operators. These are competitive services that operate 'downstream' from the airport, in that they require access to the airport's facilities, in particular to drop off and pick up passengers. The two biggest cases, which both resulted in the High Court establishing an abuse of dominance, are *Purple Parking and Meteor Parking v Heathrow Airport* (2011) and *Arriva v London Luton Airport* (2014).[129] In the first, Heathrow Airport was found to have favoured its own 'meet and greet' parking service (where you drop off and collect your car at the terminal entrance, with someone else looking after the parking) by not granting Purple Parking and Meteor Parking, two independent operators, access to the terminal forecourt. In the second case, Luton Airport had stopped providing Arriva with access to the bus station, which is located just outside the terminal building at the airport. Both cases were therefore about access to infrastructure that was deemed necessary for providing downstream services. They were not strictly placed under the heading of essential facility cases; as the court noted in *Purple Parking*:

> I therefore find that the case against [Heathrow Airport Limited] does not have to fit into the category of essential facilities or fail. Even if the subject of the Facilities Market can be described as essential facilities, Purple and Meteor are entitled to put their case on abuse in another way; and even if they rely on the 'essential facilities' type of abuse I doubt if elimination of competition, as opposed to a significant enough distortion, is required.[130]

4.186   The *Arriva v Luton Airport* case raised a number of economic questions. Arriva had operated bus services between the airport and central London for thirty years, carrying over 1 million passengers per year. Arriva paid Luton Airport 2–2.5 per cent of turnover on this route in exchange for the use of the bus station. In 2013, the airport granted another bus operator, National Express, an exclusive concession to run bus services between the airport and London for seven years. This was in exchange for a significant proportion of National Express's passenger revenue on this route, which amounted to between 20 per cent and 25 per cent over the duration of the contract. The agreement also granted National Express the right of first refusal over the operation of new routes between the airport and other

---

[129]   *Purple Parking Ltd, Meteor Parking Ltd v Heathrow Airport Ltd*, [2011] EWCH 987 (Ch); and *Arriva The Shires Ltd v London Luton Airport Operations Ltd*, [2014] EWHC 64 (Ch). We acted as experts for the claimant in the second case. See also Granatstein and Niels (2015).

[130]   *Purple Parking Limited, Meteor Parking Limited v Heathrow Airport Limited*, [2011] EWCH 987 (Ch), at [105].

destinations in London. The High Court determined that these terms constituted an abuse of dominance.

Luton Airport controls access to the bus station, which is located on its premises. No economic alternatives were available. For a period after Arriva was excluded, it used drop-off/pick-up points at some distance from the airport, with passengers being transported by a shuttle bus. However, this coincided with a significant drop in passengers and revenue (when you travel to an airport with luggage, you want to be dropped off near the terminal and not change bus on the journey). Arriva was thus found to have been significantly disadvantaged by not having access to the bus station. Luton Airport argued that it was objectively justified in refusing access due to capacity constraints at the airport. The question of available capacity at the bus station was disputed between the parties, and expert traffic management evidence was employed to address this issue. Regardless of whether there was a capacity constraint at the time of the trial, the court held that there was unlikely to be such a constraint for the seven-year duration of the contract with National Express. Luton Airport had plans to improve the airport, including adding capacity to the bus station. At that point there could no longer be any objective justification to refuse access on the basis of capacity constraints. **4.187**

As with other refusal-to-supply cases, there was a trade-off in the *Arriva v Luton Airport* case between promoting competition in the downstream market and providing a company with sufficient commercial freedom to organize access as it sees fit. Airports compete to an extent with other airports to attract both passengers and airlines, and could be expected to have the right incentives to ensure efficient transport links to and from the airport. In this case, the court gave more weight to the negative effect on the downstream market for bus services. It determined that there were a sufficient number of passengers who did not regard rail as a good substitute to bus, and who would benefit from competition between bus services. This was in part because Luton Airport operates in the 'budget airline' market segment and tends to attract a high proportion of passengers for whom the cost of access to the airport is a material factor. The court also considered evidence that competition in the downstream bus market could work effectively if both National Express and Arriva were granted access to the bus station. There were no indications that the route to London was too 'thin' to allow space for more than one operator—that is, it was not a natural monopoly route, particularly given the future expansion plans of the airport and its stated objective to increase the proportion of passengers travelling to and from the airport by public transport. Head-to-head competition between bus operators can in general produce good outcomes for passengers in terms of fares, quality, and choice. The market is usually better placed than the airport to determine how many companies should operate the route. Indeed, following the judgment, Arriva regained access to the bus station, allowing it to operate services between Luton Airport and London in competition with National Express. **4.188**

A further point considered by the court was whether the upstream company needed to be dominant, or even have a presence, in the downstream market for there to be an abuse. In *Purple Parking* the distortion to downstream competition was between Heathrow Airport's own parking service and those of the independent operators, which fitted the usual vertical leveraging theory of harm. In contrast, Luton Airport was not itself active in the provision of bus services to and from the airport. However, through the award of an exclusive concession the airport raised its commercial stake in the downstream market: it derived **4.189** commercial benefit from the terms of the concession since the fee it received was related to the expected revenue on the route, and was much higher than in the previous, non-exclusive arrangement. With such a stake in the downstream service, Luton Airport would have sufficient incentive to favour one downstream provider over another. As the court put it, Luton Airport was 'not a neutral or indifferent upstream provider of facilities'.[131]

4.10 Excessive Pricing

4.10.1 Should excessive prices be controlled, and is competition law the right tool?

4.190 The previous sections have dealt with practices that have the effect of excluding competitors. The harm to consumers from these practices is indirect: they weaken competition, and may thus result in higher prices and reduced quality and choice. The rules on abuse of dominance in many jurisdictions also cover practices that directly exploit consumers, including excessive pricing. If the main objective of competition law is to promote consumer welfare, prohibiting excessive prices surely makes sense. Or does it? This question is surprisingly complex and controversial for a host of practical, economic, and ideological reasons. US antitrust law does not prohibit excessive pricing by dominant companies. It is concerned with exclusionary conduct only. But even in the EU and other jurisdictions, excessive pricing cases have been rare. In this section we present some economic insights on excessive pricing and explain why these cases pose some problems, but perhaps not the problems that many commentators normally focus on.

4.191 To start with, we note that a prohibition of excessive pricing can be economically sound. Even the most free-market-minded economists would accept that monopoly poses a problem. If there is no prospect of that monopoly being removed or undermined through market forces—for example, because it is a natural or statutory monopoly—welfare and efficiency can be improved through capping prices. This is why many countries, including the United States, have set up elaborate price regulation mechanisms for monopolies in network and utility industries such as rail, telecoms, energy, water, and postal services. There is extensive experience of price regulation, as we discuss in Chapter 8 in the context of designing remedies. Arguments that price controls are always inappropriate or impossible to implement are therefore overstated. Rather, the two main policy questions are, first, where to draw the line between regulating and not regulating prices and, second, if a price control is deemed appropriate, whether sector-specific regulation is required or if competition law can do the job. Setting up a specific regulatory structure for price control is costly, but it is the path most chosen in network industries because it has several advantages: companies have greater certainty ex ante about whether their price will be regulated, and a regulator with detailed knowledge of the sector can perform the difficult balancing act between capping prices at competitive levels and allowing sufficient returns to preserve incentives to invest and provide good quality. How does competition law fare in comparison?

4.192 Competition law certainly doesn't do well in terms of providing legal certainty on how excessive pricing will be treated. There is a prohibition, but it has no clear criteria and is

---

[131] *Arriva The Shires Ltd v London Luton Airport Operations Ltd*, [2014] EWHC 64 (Ch), at [100].

not often enforced. What should a dominant company do? Act contrary to its commercial instincts (and to economic textbooks) by not setting prices at the profit-maximizing level? Or act as usual and hope no competition authority will come after it? EU case law is not very enlightening, and the European Commission's Guidance on Article 102 expressly ignores the topic.[132] Article 102 itself states that abuse may include 'directly or indirectly imposing unfair purchase or selling prices or other unfair trading conditions'. In *General Motors* (1975), the ECJ determined that an abuse might exist if the price imposed is 'excessive in relation to the economic value of the service provided'.[133] The case related to the price charged for the inspection of imported vehicles, an activity for which the Belgian authorities had granted a legal monopoly. This was expanded upon in *United Brands* (1978), the bananas case we saw before, where the ECJ related 'economic value' to production costs and prices of competing products:

> In this case charging a price which is excessive because it has no reasonable relation to the economic value of the product supplied would be such an abuse.

> This excess could, inter alia, be determined objectively if it were possible for it to be calculated by making a comparison between the selling price of the product in question and its cost of production, which would disclose the amount of the profit margin; however the Commission has not done this since it has not analysed UBC's costs structure.

> The questions therefore to be determined are whether the difference between the costs actually incurred and the price actually charged is excessive, and, if the answer to this question is in the affirmative, whether a price has been imposed which is either unfair in itself or when compared to competing products.[134]

The concepts of 'economic value' and 'unfair' have caused a good deal of confusion. **4.193**
(Incidentally, in both *General Motors* and *United Brands* the ECJ overruled the finding of excessive pricing by the European Commission.) In *United Brands*, the ECJ stated that alternative ways may be devised to determine what is economic value or an unfair price (adding that 'economic theorists have not failed to think up several'). A number of national competition authorities and courts, in particular in the United Kingdom, the Netherlands, and South Africa, have tried to come up with ways to interpret these concepts and apply them in cases of excessive pricing. Below we set out the economic considerations that played a role in these cases. Perhaps the main conclusion that can be drawn from these cases is that they have provided greater clarity on what excessive pricing is *not* than on what it is.

4.10.2 Relying on the market instead of intervening: From tampons to condoms

We have seen that monopoly pricing creates allocative inefficiency in the form of a dead- **4.194** weight welfare loss to society—prices are too high and output is too low. Forcing the dominant company to set prices at the competitive level reduces the welfare loss. However, you can see that from a longer-term perspective prohibiting excessive pricing can be counterproductive. While allocative efficiency may be improved, dynamic and productive efficiency could be affected. High prices signal to entrants where new business opportunities lie. The very prospect of high profits is what drives companies to reduce costs and introduce new

---

[132] European Commission (2008), 'Guidance on the Commission's Enforcement Priorities in Applying Article 82 EC Treaty to Abusive Exclusionary Conduct by Dominant Undertakings', December, at [7].
[133] Case 26/75 *General Motors Continental NV v Commission* [1975] ECR 1367, at [12].
[134] Case 27/76 *United Brands v Commission* [1978] ECR 207, [1978] 1 CMLR 429, at [250–2].

products and technologies. The prospect of those profits being regulated once a dominant position is obtained may distort these incentives. Hence, the crucial question in each specific case is whether new competitors are indeed likely to enter the market, and in what time frame. Economics can help here. However, the question of whether to regulate or not to regulate is also to some extent a matter of policy judgement and philosophy. It depends on how much faith you have in the ability of market forces to erode positions of market power, and how long you are prepared to wait for that process to happen.

4.195   There are several past cases where competition authorities considered intervening against excessive pricing by dominant companies, but ultimately decided not to in order to give market forces a chance. In a 1986 report on the tampons market, the MMC found prices to be excessive.[135] Two producers—Tambrands and Southalls (with the Tampax and Lil-lets brands, now owned by Procter & Gamble and Premier Foods, respectively)—controlled more than 95 per cent of the market. However, the MMC did not recommend price controls because it expected effective competition to develop as new competitors entered the market. These included major consumer goods companies such as Johnson & Johnson and Kimberly-Clark, and own-brand tampons from retailers such as Boots and Sainsbury's. In the markets for pest control and credit card services, the MMC investigated concerns about excessive pricing, but then focused its remedies on removing the structural market imperfections that facilitated the excessive pricing (including the lack of customer information and the presence of regulatory entry barriers), rather than controlling those prices directly.[136] In 1998 the Dutch competition authority investigated the introduction of rental charges for post office boxes by PTT Post, as the postal incumbent was called then (post office boxes were outside the regulated postal services).[137] It concluded that the charges would in fact enhance competition in this market by attracting entry. In an inquiry into the market for scientific publishing in the United Kingdom, the OFT found indications of high prices and profits, but decided not to intervene 'for now' because a number of market developments pointed to potentially increased competition and new entry.[138]

4.196   In 2002 the OFT opened an abuse of dominance investigation into excessive pricing by the makers of Durex condoms (then SSL International).[139] Condoms (also referred to by the authorities as 'contraceptive sheaths') had been the subject of various monopoly inquiries and price regulation during the 1970s and 1980s. The last such inquiry by the MMC, in 1994, had resulted in price liberalization in light of new entry and the reduction in Durex's market share from 95 per cent to around 75 per cent during the 1980s.[140] The OFT closed the new case in 2005 without finding an abuse, noting that it (like the MMC previously) found 'evidence of emerging competition'. Durex's market share had fallen further (if slowly) to around 60 per cent by 2002, and several new brands had entered the UK market, including Trojan, the market leader in the United States. The OFT observed that in such

---

[135] Monopolies and Mergers Commission (1986), 'Tampons', January.

[136] Monopolies and Mergers Commission (1988), 'Pest Control Services', February; and Monopolies and Mergers Commission (1989), 'Credit Card Services', August.

[137] *Case 13/Complaints against PTT Post.* See NMa (1999), 'NMa Annual Report 1998'.

[138] Office of Fair Trading (2002), 'The Market for Scientific, Technical and Medical Journals', September.

[139] Office of Fair Trading (2005), 'Competition Case Closure Summaries', Issue 19, June. We advised the defendant in this investigation.

[140] Monopolies and Mergers Commission (1994), 'Contraceptive Sheaths', March.

circumstances, 'any potential remedies such as a price cap could stifle such entry and hinder rather than help the competitive process.' The OFT also highlighted a methodological problem with determining excessive pricing in this case: in order to judge whether there was an abuse, it would have needed to develop an estimate of the value of the Durex brand. Brand is one of the intangible assets employed by the company, and therefore forms an important part of the analysis of the economic returns made on its investment. As discussed in Chapter 3, in competitive markets, investing in intangible assets such as customer acquisition and workforce skills can be as important as investing in tangible assets, but valuing intangibles can be difficult. The OFT considered that 'a robust valuation would require substantial additional time and expense'.

4.10.3 Comparisons with other prices: Bananas, funeral services, and morphine

As noted above, one interpretation of *United Brands* is that an assessment of excessive pricing may be based on a comparison with prices of other products. There was evidence that United Brands set prices for its Chiquita bananas that were 20–40 per cent higher than prices of unbranded bananas (although only 7 per cent higher than the brands of its main rivals). The European Commission placed great weight on the fact that prices in Germany, Denmark, and the Benelux countries were up to twice as high as in Ireland. It considered Ireland to be a valid benchmark since United Brands still seemed to make profits there. The Commission considered that United Brands should drop prices by 15 per cent. However, the ECJ ruled that the Commission had failed to analyse the cost of production of bananas when determining the economic value, and therefore considered its price comparisons insufficient in this case. **4.197**

In a case in 1988 involving funeral services in France, the ECJ did accept price comparisons between regions as a basis for assessing excessive pricing.[141] In the town of Charleville-Mézières in the north of France, the local commune had granted an exclusive concession to the defendant to provide 'external' funeral services—defined as 'the carriage of the body after it has been placed in the coffin, the provision of hearses, coffins and external hangings of the house of the deceased, conveyances for mourners, the equipment and staff needed for burial and exhumation and cremation'. This excluded 'internal services' (religious services) and 'unregulated services' ('non-essential' funeral services such as the supply of flowers and marblework). Such exclusive concessions were allowed under French law, and had been granted by around 5,000 of the 36,000 communes in France. The exclusivity itself was not challenged, but the ECJ considered that, in principle, the behaviour of the concessionaires could distort competition. One complaint in this case related to excessive pricing. The ECJ found that because over 30,000 communes did leave the provision of funeral services to market forces, it must be possible to compare prices between communes with and without exclusive concessions and to use this as the basis for determining whether prices by concessionaires were unfair in the context of Article 102. **4.198**

In *NAPP*, the OFT determined that a pharmaceutical company had charged excessive prices for its sustained-release morphine product, MST, in the 'community' (pharmacy) market. This was in combination with predatory pricing in the hospital market. The finding **4.199**

---

[141] Case 30/87 *Corinne Bodson v SA Pompes funèbres des régions libérées* [1988] ECR 2479, [1989] 4 CMLR 984.

was upheld by the CAT in 2002.[142] The OFT found that NAPP's gross profit margin on MST sales (80 per cent) was more than 10 percentage points higher than the margin earned by its next most profitable rival (after allowing for cost differences), and also much higher than the margins that NAPP made on other drugs (which were on average between 30 per cent and 50 per cent). Furthermore, NAPP's MST price was 40 per cent higher than that of the highest-priced rival. The OFT also highlighted the persistency of excessive pricing. MST prices had not fallen since the expiry of NAPP's patent in 1992, and effective competition from new entrants had not developed. However, the *NAPP* case did not subsequently set a trend for more excessive pricing cases by the OFT (we saw the example of the condoms inquiry that was abandoned). This may be because *NAPP* was not a pure excessive pricing case as such. Rather, the OFT found excessive pricing in the community market in combination with predatory pricing by NAPP in the hospital market. According to the OFT, one of the main reasons why entry in the community market did not take place despite excessive pricing was because NAPP charged excessively low prices in the hospital market, where sustained-release morphine products are usually prescribed first.

4.10.4 Excessive pricing based on excessive profits: Debit cards in the Netherlands

4.200 We have said before that rather than compare unit prices with unit costs, it may be more informative to look at profitability over a longer time period. This can give a better picture of how profits relate to investments and risk. We discussed this in the context of assessing market power in Chapter 3, and in the context of cost benchmarks for predatory pricing earlier in this chapter. In 2004 the Dutch competition authority (NMa) imposed a fine of €30 million on Interpay, then the sole provider of network services for PIN debit card transactions, for excessively charging retailers for these services.[143] The PIN network had achieved a strong position among the various payment methods in the Netherlands. The NMa commissioned an accounting firm to measure the ROCE for PIN services over the period 1998–2001. The conclusion was that the annual ROCEs over this period were well in excess of the cost of capital, and therefore that an abuse had taken place. However, the Appeals Advisory Committee subsequently agreed with the criticisms raised by the parties against the NMa's finding of excessive pricing. The NMa eventually withdrew the fine, although the Committee did uphold the NMa's finding that some of the PIN system arrangements constituted restrictive agreements between banks, and changes to the system were made.

4.201 As to the assessment of excessive pricing, the main shortcoming of the NMa's approach was that the returns over the period 1998–2001 did not provide an accurate picture of the economic profitability of the PIN network services. The test set out by the NMa for excessive pricing was that the difference between prices and costs should be disproportionate, such that capital providers will have sustained excessive returns on the capital they have invested and the risks they have incurred. This test should take account of any investments and risks incurred by the capital providers—in this case the banks that owned the PIN system before 1998. The system was set up in 1989 under conditions of uncertainty, and it

[142] *Napp Pharmaceutical Holdings Limited and Subsidiaries v Director General of Fair Trading* [2002] CAT 1, 15 January 2002.
[143] NMa (2004), 'Besluit van de directeur-generaal van de Nederlandse Mededingingsautoriteit als bedoeld in artikel 62 van de Mededingingswet, nummer 2910/638', 28 April. We advised the defendant in these proceedings.

was not guaranteed that it would be successful until the mid-1990s. It had to gain a critical mass of users among both retailers and consumers, and faced some competition from rival card networks. Start-up losses were made for a number of years. From an economic (as opposed to accounting) perspective, these start-up losses should also be treated as investments. It could be shown that an appropriate return on these investments had not yet been achieved by 1998, which was the start of the period assessed by the NMa. An analysis of profitability over the whole period 1989–2001, incorporating the earlier start-up losses, demonstrated that the PIN network services had achieved an IRR in line with the cost of capital. (As discussed in Chapter 3, it is more appropriate to use the IRR rather than the ROCE as the measure of economic profit in an analysis of this type.) This indicated that the excessive pricing test set out by the NMa was not met, and hence that no abuse could be established.

To illustrate this point, consider Figure 4.8, which shows a stylized investment project **4.202** over fifteen years, with start-up losses (negative cash flows) in the early years and higher returns (positive cash flows) in later years, once the project has become successful. This investment project has a cash-flow profile similar to the PIN system, but the figures are hypothetical. Overall the project makes an IRR of 10 per cent—that is, discounting all the cash flows of the project at 10 per cent gives an NPV of exactly zero. This is a 'truncated' IRR over the fifteen-year period; after year fifteen the activity still continues, but the investor 'sells off' the assets in year fifteen (the high cash inflow in that year that can be seen in the figure reflects the closing asset value). Assume that the cost of capital is also 10 per cent. This means that the project overall makes a 'normal' return. But consider the annual ROCEs: these fluctuate from very negative in the early years to very positive in the later years, reflecting the profile of the project's cash flows which are initially low and then increase. Looking only at the ROCEs in the later years—the NMa effectively considered only years eleven to fourteen—does not give the correct answer. It points to very high

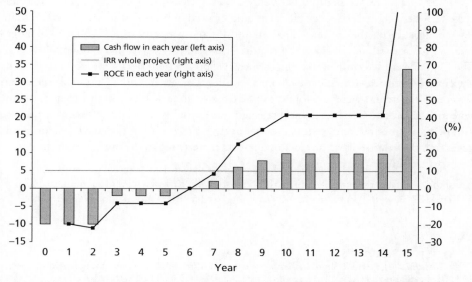

Figure 4.8 Profitability of a stylized investment project—IRR versus ROCE

227

profits in those four years, but overlooks the fact that the activity incurred risks and start-up losses in the previous years.

4.10.5 Economic value to downstream purchasers: Ports and horseracing data

4.203 Several of the cases discussed above sought to determine excessive prices through a price–cost comparison or profitability analysis. Other cases have rejected this approach as too narrow an interpretation of 'economic value'. One example is the case involving the Port of Helsingborg in Sweden in 2004.[144] Ferry operators accused the port of setting excessive charges. The European Commission rejected the complaint. It considered that excessive prices could not be established through a simple cost-plus approach. In attempting to assess price–cost margins and profitability of the port, the Commission encountered some practical problems with the allocation of the port's large fixed costs between ferry and other services. It also considered that there would be 'insuperable difficulties' with finding valid benchmarks for profitability.[145] We believe that this overstates the point, since the financial tools to estimate such benchmarks are well established—see Chapter 3. In the end the Commission concluded that prices did appear to exceed costs by a significant margin, but it then proceeded to assess whether these prices were also 'unfair'. It drew a comparison with the prices charged for other services at the port and with prices charged to ferry operators at other ports, and found on this basis that prices were not excessive. A final step in the Commission's assessment of economic value was to take into account the fact that the land used by the port for the ferry operations was very valuable in itself. It stated that ferry operators 'benefit from the fact that the location of the port meets their needs perfectly', and that 'this represents an intangible value in itself, which could be taken into account as part of the economic value of the services provided'.[146] Hence, the Commission attached weight to the economic value that the product represented to customers, rather than considering only the cost to the supplier. This is a theme that was also central in the following case concerning the pricing of horseracing data.

4.204 The British Horseracing Board (BHB)—then the regulatory authority for horse racing in Great Britain—was accused of charging excessive prices to Attheraces (ATR), a broadcaster. This concerned pre-race data that could be used in broadcast services overseas (data for broadcasting in the United Kingdom and Ireland was subject to a different arrangement). Broadcasters and bookmakers required this data, and BHB had a monopoly over it. The High Court determined that the competitive price would be one where BHB recoups the cost of producing its database (about £5 million) together with a reasonable return on that cost. The actual price was found to be excessive because it was higher than this cost-reflective price. The Court of Appeal rejected this cost-plus approach to excessive pricing. Following a line of reasoning similar to that in *Port of Helsingborg*, the court took into consideration the value that the product in question represented to the purchaser of the data:

> [W]e conclude that, in holding that the economic value of the pre-race data was the cost of compilation plus a reasonable return, the judge took too narrow a view of economic value in Article 82 [now 102]. In particular he was wrong to reject BHB's contention on the relevance

---

[144] *Scandlines Sverige AB v Port of Helsingborg* (Case COMP/A.36.568/D3), Decision of 23 July 2004.
[145] Ibid., at [156] and [225].
[146] Ibid., at [209].

of the value of the pre-race data to ATR in determining the economic value of the pre-race data and whether the charges specified by BHB were excessive and unfair.[147]

ATR's new broadcast service intended to make a commercial profit and it had shown a **4.205** willingness to pay substantial amounts for other media rights for the service. The pre-race data had value to ATR because it was related to British horseracing, which represented a core part of the content of the broadcast service. In contrast, BHB's production costs of the data as such were relatively low because it becomes available as a by-product of the organization of horseracing (it is not a product that is created for its own sake). There was therefore a wide gap between the costs of producing the data and the commercial value of the data to the purchaser, which used it as an input to a commercial downstream service. In essence, therefore, the dispute was over who would get the bigger share of the downstream pie—BHB or ATR—rather than about the total size of the pie. Consumers would get the end-service regardless of how the pie was divided higher up the supply chain (unless ATR decided not to buy the data at all, in which case there would be no more pie). The Court of Appeal considered that in these circumstances the upstream provider is entitled to charge a price that reflects the value to (and willingness to pay of) the intermediary purchaser downstream:

> We appreciate that this theoretical answer leaves the realistic possibility of a monopoly supplier not quite killing the goose that lays the golden eggs, but coming close to throttling her. We do not exclude the possibility that this could be held to be abusive, not least because of its potential impact on the consumer. But Article 82, as we said earlier, is not a general provision for the regulation of prices. It seeks to prevent the abuse of dominant market positions with the object of protecting and promoting competition. The evidence and findings here do not show ATR's competitiveness to have been, or to be at risk of being, materially compromised by the terms of the arrangements with or specified by BHB.[148]

From an economic perspective, saying that economic value means the value to the pur- **4.206** chaser comes close to saying that no price can ever be excessive. Recall from Chapters 1 and 2 that the price that customers pay reflects their willingness to pay. If prices are very high, some customers may no longer buy the product, and those who still do get less consumer surplus out of it, but purchasers would—by definition—never pay more than what they are willing to pay. Hence, they never pay more than the economic value—to them—of the product. In the context of pricing in intermediary markets, such as in *Port of Helsingborg* and *Attheraces*, this may be sensible because end-consumers are not always harmed by disputes over the sharing of the pie upstream. But too broad an interpretation of economic value as customer willingness to pay would make the excessive pricing prohibition rather superfluous. The Court of Appeal acknowledged this tension and made the following comment (using the 'on the one hand, on the other' expression that is so often associated with economists):

> On the one hand, the economic value of a product in market terms is what it will fetch. This cannot, however, be what Article 82 and section 18 [of the Competition Act 1998] envisage, because the premise is that the seller has a dominant position enabling it to distort the market in which it operates... On the other hand, it does not follow that whatever price a seller in a dominant position exacts or seeks to exact is an abuse of his dominant position.[149]

---

[147] *Attheraces v British Horseracing Board* [2007] EWCA Civ 38, at [218].
[148] Ibid., at [217].
[149] Ibid., at [205–6].

4.10.6 Economic value through free interaction of demand and supply: Steel in South Africa

4.207 Yet another interpretation of economic value was put forward by the South African Competition Tribunal in the *Mittal* case (2007), although this was subsequently overturned by the Competition Appeal Court (2009).[150] Mittal represented around 80 per cent of steel production in South Africa, a legacy from previous ownership and support by the state. Its production exceeded total demand in the South African market, and it exported its surplus production at low prices in order to remain competitive in overseas markets (transport costs are high). At the same time it set its domestic prices at 'import parity', that is, the level at which imports were priced (which includes the high transport costs). The difference between the domestic and export prices was 50–60 per cent. Two customers in the gold mining sector filed a complaint before the Tribunal. Section 8(a) of the Competition Act in South Africa prohibits excessive pricing by a dominant company to the detriment of consumers. The Act defines an excessive price as one that is higher than the economic value (echoing EU case law). Mittal argued that its prices could not be excessive because its profitability was not high. The Tribunal was reluctant to determine what the right or wrong price level was. It said that it 'should at once dispel the notion that the term "economic value" is intended to impute a cost-based theory value, much less one that is rooted in any particular version of cost'.[151] Instead, it interpreted economic value as having been determined by the free interaction of demand and supply in a competitive market, and set out a market structure test for excessive pricing: the market must be 'uncontested' (with a position of monopoly or super-dominance), 'incontestable' (subject to insurmountable entry barriers), and unregulated (not subject to price regulation). The Tribunal considered Mittal to be 'one of those rare firms endowed with sufficient market power to charge excessive prices'.[152] It then focused on Mittal's arrangements with its exporting affiliate, which obtained the steel at the lower export price, but was prevented from selling it in the domestic market. It was this conduct that the Tribunal deemed abusive (calling the economics behind the conduct 'disarmingly elementary'—'the first principle of monopolistic conduct').[153] Because of this approach, the Tribunal considered it unnecessary to assess the 'volumes of expert evidence' on the relationship between prices and costs. The Competition Appeal Court found this structural test to be unsatisfactory and noted that:

> The erroneous approach of the Competition Tribunal also explains why Mittal ends up in the anomalous and wholly impractical position of having been found guilty of and heavily fined for excessive pricing, without any finding of which prices for which of the variety of products were excessive, nor of the period in which the excessive prices were charged, nor of what a non-excessive price would have been, nor of the amount of the excess which it was found to have charged, nor any indication of how—in changing market conditions, eg where production costs may have risen, or supply and/or demand may have changed—an 'excessive price' would in future be determined.[154]

4.208 The Appeal Court sent the case back to the Tribunal, but it was then settled between the parties. Hence, having received widespread international attention following the Tribunal

---

[150] *Mittal Steel South Africa Limited and ors v Harmony Gold Mining Limited and Durban Roodeport Deep Limited* (Case No 70/CAC/Apr07) Competition Appeal Court of South Africa, 29 May 2009.

[151] Ibid., at [21] (Competition Tribunal as cited by the Competition Appeal Court).

[152] Ibid., at [17].

[153] Ibid., at [54].

[154] Ibid., at [18].

decision, in the end the *Mittal* case did not shed much further light on how competition law can assess excessive pricing.

4.10.7 Common misperceptions: What economics can and cannot say about excessive pricing

As you can tell from this section, the current state of affairs of the excessive pricing pro- **4.209**
hibition under competition law is not a happy one. There is no clarity on the criteria to determine whether prices are excessive. There is no consensus on the fundamental question of whether 'economic value', the test established by the ECJ and followed elsewhere, means the costs of production incurred by the seller or the value of the product to the buyer. Competition authorities bring these cases only sporadically, or not at all. Dominant companies find it difficult to assess whether they should maximize profits as usual or exercise some self-restraint. Most legal and economic commentators would agree that interventions against excessive pricing under competition law should be rare, and some would advocate removing the prohibition of excessive pricing altogether (thus mirroring the situation in the United States). This may well be an appropriate policy choice, but we believe that such a choice should be made for the right reasons. Some of the arguments against the prohibition are based on misperceptions of what economics can and cannot say about excessive pricing.

As we noted earlier, a prohibition of excessive pricing can be economically sound if there **4.210**
is no prospect of market forces removing or eroding a monopoly position. Economics can assist with identifying the circumstances in which this arises (e.g. does the activity have natural monopoly characteristics; are there significant entry barriers?). Many countries, including the United States, have extensive experience with regulating prices of particular activities, using well-established economic tools. Arguments that price regulation is always inappropriate or impossible to implement are overstated. The main point to be aware of—and this may well be a decisive factor in any cost–benefit analysis of intervention—is that such regulatory structures are costly to set up and maintain.

A further misperception is that excessive pricing cannot be prohibited because it is too dif- **4.211**
ficult to measure. Many commentators—and some of the cases discussed in this section—point to the conceptual and practical difficulties of measuring economic profits, of allocating costs, and of determining the competitive benchmark. However, as discussed in Chapter 3, a theoretically sound framework for assessing economic profitability in competition law exists, and addresses most of the conceptual and practical problems. The framework is not straightforward to apply, and in some cases it cannot be applied, but that is no reason to reject it outright. The same holds for other economic techniques discussed in this book. In those cases where it is feasible to apply the framework for profitability analysis it can provide useful insight. Interestingly, the ECJ said pretty much the same in *United Brands*:

> While appreciating the considerable and at times very great difficulties in working out production costs which may sometimes include a discretionary apportionment of indirect costs and general expenditure and which may vary significantly according to the size of the undertaking, its object, the complex nature of its set up, its territorial area of operations, whether it manufactures one or several products, the number of its subsidiaries and their relationship with each other, the production costs of the banana do not seem to present any insuperable problems.[155]

---

[155] Case 27/76 *United Brands v Commission* [1978] ECR 207, [1978] 1 CMLR 429, at [254].

4.212 In other words, it's only bananas. In the condoms and debit card cases mentioned above, a detailed profitability analysis was undertaken in line with the economic framework we have outlined, and played a central role in the ultimate outcome. Some conceptual issues arose but these could be resolved within the framework. In the condoms case the main difficulty was the valuation of the brand which could be done in different ways, while in the debit card case the main dispute centred around the relevant time period for the profitability analysis. In all, therefore, it is correct to say that *if* the relevant test for excessive pricing is taken as 'cost-plus' or profitability in excess of the competitive level, economics provides the relevant tools for applying the test.

4.213 The real problem with measuring economic profitability—and this is also often misunderstood—is not that it is too difficult to do. It is that the method for measuring economic profitability is not meant to determine excessive prices as such, but rather to assess the existence of entry barriers and market power (that is why we explained it in Chapter 3, not here). The method determines profitability with reference to replacement costs and the cost of entry. If profits are found to be higher than the costs that an entrant would face, this indicates that entry barriers exist (profitable opportunities are not taken up by entrants). While this can be a powerful tool to assess market power, it does not in itself determine that prices are too high. That is ultimately a policy or legal judgment. Only if profits are in line with the benchmark (as they were in the debit card case) could one draw the conclusion that there is no competition problem, and hence infer that there is no excessive pricing. In this regard profitability analysis provides a one-way test. Again, therefore, the case law and the economics can provide greater clarity on what excessive pricing is *not* than on what it is. There is no excessive pricing when profits are in line with the competitive level. But when profits are excessive, the economics tells you only that you have a problem of market power, not that you should prohibit those excessive prices as an abuse of dominance.

5

CARTELS AND OTHER
HORIZONTAL AGREEMENTS

5.1 Are All Cartels Bad?

5.1.1 A long-standing concern

Consider the following cases:

5.01

(a) senior and junior managers of three producers of methionine, an amino acid that is used in chicken feed, regularly meet in different European cities to agree price rises and exchange commercially sensitive information;

(b) the chairmen of Sotheby's and Christie's, the art auction houses, meet at their private residences in London and New York and agree to raise the commissions charged to sellers at the auctions;

(c) Ford and Volkswagen, rival car manufacturers, get together and form a joint venture for the production of multi-purpose vehicles;

(d) a number of supermarket chains reach individual agreements with tobacco companies linking the retail prices of competing tobacco brands;

(e) a branded and a generic pharmaceutical company enter into a settlement agreement with respect to an IP dispute, where the generic company is paid to drop its patent validity suit and delay its entry into the market;

(f) the member banks of a payment card scheme agree the fee to be paid by the bank that acquired the retailer to the bank that issued the card to the customer, every time a payment is made.

5.02 These are real-world examples of explicit horizontal agreements between competitors. The odd one out in this respect is agreement (d), which is vertical rather than horizontal, but like the others it has been scrutinized by competition authorities for its potential to enable horizontal collusion. Which of these agreements would you consider to be in breach of competition law per se? What does economics have to say about them?

5.03 Competition law has always looked unfavourably upon agreements among competitors, especially when they come in the form of price fixing, market sharing, or bid rigging. The US Supreme Court has referred to such 'hardcore' cartels as the 'supreme evil of antitrust'.[1] The then EU Commissioner for Competition stated in 2009 that, 'under any analysis, cartels cause terrible damage' (Kroes, 2009). The concern about competitors getting together to discuss prices is not new. Back in 1776, Adam Smith made this famous observation: 'People of the same trade seldom meet together, even for merriment and diversion, but the conversation ends in a conspiracy against the public, or in some contrivance to raise prices.'[2]

5.04 In other words, business people can't help themselves. Put two competitors together in a room (smoked-filled or otherwise) and the temptation to fix prices or share markets will prove too much. Less well known is the comment that Smith made immediately following the above quote: 'It is impossible indeed to prevent such meetings, by any law which either could be executed, or would be consistent with liberty and justice.'[3]

5.05 Two-and-a-half centuries after Adam Smith we obviously do have a law that prohibits business people from meeting with their competitors and conspiring against the public: competition law. This law can be 'executed' effectively—most jurisdictions prohibit hardcore cartels per se, and competition authorities have enforced this prohibition with vigour, dawn-raiding premises, imposing billions of euros in fines, and sending some executives to jail (see also Chapter 8). This tough enforcement action has no doubt had a strong deterrent effect on many other would-be cartelists, in a way that—to allay Smith's fear—would nonetheless seem 'consistent with liberty and justice'.

---

[1] *Verizon Communications Inc v Law Offices of Curtis V Trinko, LLP* 540 US 398, 408 (2004).
[2] Smith (1776), Book I, Ch X.
[3] Ibid.

The per se prohibition of hardcore cartels has economic merit. By restricting output   **5.06**
and raising prices, a cartel aims to achieve the same negative effects as a monopoly: it
distributes welfare from consumers to producers and reduces allocative, productive, and
dynamic efficiency. A cartel is in many ways worse than a full merger between competing producers, because a merger normally brings with it some efficiencies in the form of
integration of production processes and elimination of duplicate resources. Cartels usually produce no (or limited—see below) efficiencies that could offset the negative effects
on competition. By prohibiting such agreements per se, competition law has created a
good deal of legal certainty—many business people are fully aware that they had best
steer clear of talking to competitors about prices. The one important caveat here is that
the above applies to hardcore cartels only. The line between hardcore cartels and other
horizontal agreements must be drawn carefully. That this is not always straightforward
is a theme we turn to now.

5.1.2 'Hardcore' cartels and 'naked' restrictions versus other horizontal agreements

There is significant debate among legal and economic commentators about the boundary   **5.07**
between hardcore cartels and other horizontal agreements. Of the above examples, you
might place agreements (a) and (b) in the first category. They involved price fixing supported by information sharing, and not much else. But what about (c), (d), (e), and (f)? These
are also agreements among competitors, and relate to price or production, but they arise in
a specific market context that would be relevant to take into account. Even the most fervent
proponents of a non-interventionist competition policy would agree that cartels are bad
and merit a per se treatment, but some would prefer to see the class of hardcore cartels to be
narrowly circumscribed. Robert Bork, a leading proponent of the Chicago School, argued
that only 'naked' cartel agreements should be illegal per se:

> The rule should be restated so that it is illegal per se to fix prices or divide markets (or to
> eliminate rivalry in any other way) only when the restraint is 'naked'—that is, only when the
> agreement is not ancillary to cooperative productive activity engaged in by the agreeing par-
> ties. Only then is the effect of the agreement clearly to restrict output. Many price-fixing and
> market-division agreements make cooperative productive activity more efficient, and these
> should be judged, according to the circumstances, by the standards applicable to internal
> growth or by horizontal merger rules.[4]

Bork cited the Supreme Court ruling in *Sealy* (1967) as an example of a per se cartel prohi-   **5.08**
bition under Section 1 of the Sherman Act 1890—which prohibits 'every contract, combination in the form of trust, or conspiracy, in restraint of trade'—where in reality the
agreement involved co-operative productive activity.[5] A number of manufacturers of bed-
ding products and mattresses across the United States decided that there was commercial
benefit in advertising nationally, and together set up the Sealy trademark for that purpose.
This was then used to license other producers, fix retail prices, and allocate exclusive territories among the licensees. Bork argued that this arrangement was capable of producing
efficiencies and therefore the Supreme Court should not have ruled it illegal per se. It enabled economies of scale in national advertising, helped standardize products, and prevented

---

[4] Bork (1978), p. 263.
[5] *United States v Sealy, Inc* 388 US 350 (1967).

manufacturers from free-riding on each other's local sales efforts (a common justification in vertical restraint cases, as discussed in Chapter 6).

5.09 Competition law tends to define the category of hardcore cartels more broadly than Bork proposed through his classification of 'naked' versus 'ancillary' restraints. The per se prohibition in US antitrust law often refers to 'naked' restraints in line with Bork, but is sometimes applied more broadly (as it was in *Sealy*). Article 101(1) TFEU prohibits 'all agreements between undertakings, decisions by associations of undertakings and concerted practices which may affect trade between Member States and which have as their object or effect the prevention, restriction or distortion of competition'. EU case law under Article 101(1) has identified a class of 'obvious restrictions of competition such as price-fixing, market-sharing or the control of outlets'.[6] One leading legal text identifies the following horizontal agreements as falling within the 'restrictions by object box': price fixing; exchanging information that reduces uncertainty about future behaviour; market sharing; limiting output (including the removal of excess capacity); limiting sales; collective exclusive dealing; and paying competitors to delay the launch of competing products (Whish and Bailey, 2015, p. 132).

5.10 There is consensus in competition law that a per se prohibition is not always warranted. Horizontal agreements such as on R&D, joint production, and technology licensing— including example (c) at the start of the chapter—may generate benefits in terms of technological progress, efficiencies, and greater choice for consumers. The traditional mechanism in Europe is to assess the efficiency benefits under Article 101(3) and see if they outweigh any restrictive effects identified under Article 101(1). To achieve an exemption under Article 101(3) the burden is on the parties to show that any restriction of competition is justified through meeting all of the four following conditions. The agreement must: (i) contribute to improving the production or distribution of goods or contribute to promoting technical or economic progress; (ii) allow consumers to receive a fair share of the resulting benefits; (iii) include only restrictions that are indispensable to the attainment of these objectives; and (iv) not afford the parties the possibility of eliminating competition in respect of a substantial part of the products in question. For hardcore restrictions by object, these exemption criteria under Article 101(3) are unlikely to apply, but other horizontal agreements may meet them. Some types of horizontal agreement may not actually constitute restrictions of competition at all, and therefore fall outside Article 101(1), as discussed in this chapter.

5.1.3 Object versus effect: A clear dichotomy?

5.11 A principle in EU competition law is that once an anti-competitive object has been established, it is not necessary to examine the actual or potential effects of the agreement.[7] This clearly reduces the burden on the competition authority when bringing an Article 101(1) case. In recent years an increasing number of horizontal agreements outside the hardcore cartel category have been classed as object infringements, despite evidence that agreements of that type may achieve efficiency benefits. The question therefore arises whether such prohibitions by object are warranted for horizontal agreements other than hardcore cartels.

---

[6] Cases T-374/94 etc *European Night Services v Commission* [1998] ECR II-3141; [1998] 5 CMLR 718.
[7] Case 56/65 *Société Technique Minière* (*LTM*) *v Maschinenbau Ulm GmbH* (*MBU*), [1966] ECR 234, [1966] 3 CMLR 244.

In fact, the object test under Article 101(1) does contain at its heart a requirement to con-   **5.12**
sider the effect of the practice. The dichotomy between object and effect is therefore not so
clear-cut. Considering economic effects under the object assessment is not cast as a balance
to any restrictive effects, but rather as an assessment of whether the agreement restricts
competition in the first place. As set out in the Commission's Guidelines on Horizontal
Agreements, in order to assess whether an agreement has an anti-competitive object, consideration must be given to the content of the agreement, the objectives it seeks to attain,
and the economic and legal context of which it forms part.[8] This requires counterfactual
analysis: if the competitive situation would be worse in the absence of the agreement, you
can conclude that the agreement in itself does not have the object of restricting or distorting competition. In determining this counterfactual it is necessary to adopt a realistic view
of what is feasible and practical. This follows the CFI judgment in *Métropole Télévision*
(2001), which refers to the operations being 'difficult or even impossible to implement' in
the absence of the agreement.[9] This case involved six French broadcasters and telecommunications companies that were jointly launching a new satellite TV service to compete with
the incumbent, Canal+, and had agreed on certain exclusivity and non-compete restrictions. The CFI held that under Article 101(1) (then Article 81(1)) the test is whether such
ancillary restrictions were objectively necessary to implement the main agreement (here the
new satellite TV service), but without this amounting to a full balancing of pro- and anti-
competitive effects, which is done under Article 101(3).

Counterfactual analysis may show that an agreement is not restrictive because without it   **5.13**
the recognized benefits would not be achieved—for example, a new product would not be
launched at all, or the underlying product (say, a payment card scheme) would not work. In
this case, the agreement does not infringe Article 101(1). In 2001, two mobile telephony operators in Germany—T-Mobile and O2—entered into an agreement to share 3G infrastructure
and allow national roaming. The European Commission considered that the infrastructure
sharing did not restrict competition, but that the national roaming agreement did.[10] The
Commission agreed that without sharing infrastructure with T-Mobile, O2 would not be able
to launch a 3G service with sufficient breadth to compete effectively. 3G services were new at
the time, and O2 was a smaller competitor in the prevailing 2G services, with a market share
of around 8 per cent (T-Mobile had 42 per cent). However, the Commission concluded that
the roaming agreement would restrict O2's efforts to expand its own network, particularly in
urban areas. The CFI found that the Commission had failed to carry out an objective analysis
of the competition situation in the absence of the agreement. It considered that without the
roaming agreement O2 would not be able to launch a viable service, and therefore that this
agreement did not infringe Article 101(1) (then Article 81(1)):

> It follows from the foregoing that the Decision, in so far as it concerns the application of
> Article 81(1) EC…suffers from insufficient analysis, first, in that it contains no objective
> discussion of what the competition situation would have been in the absence of the agree-
> ment, which distorts the assessment of the actual and potential effects of the agreement on
> competition and, second, in that it does not demonstrate, in concrete terms, in the context of

---

[8] European Commission (2011), 'Guidelines on the Applicability of Article 101 of the Treaty on the
Functioning of the European Union to Horizontal Co-operation agreements', OJ (2011/C 11/01), at [25].
[9] Case T-112/99 *Métropole Télévision (M6) v Commission* [2001] ECR II-2459, at [109].
[10] *T-Mobile Deutschland/O2 Germany: Network Sharing Rahmenvertrag* (Case COMP/38.369), Decision
of 16 July 2003.

the relevant emerging market, that the provisions of the agreement on roaming have restrictive effects on competition.[11]

5.1.4 Object versus effect: A moving boundary

5.14 Sceptics may see the increasing number of cases that are put into the 'object box' as being driven by competition authorities' desire to avoid the difficult task of establishing the effects of agreements. The ECJ's *T-Mobile Netherlands* ruling in an information-exchange case in 2009 is suggestive of a very low hurdle for establishing an anti-competitive object (we discuss this case in more detail in section 5.3):

> [A] concerted practice pursues an anti-competitive object for the purpose of Article 81(1) EC where, according to its content and objectives and having regard to its legal and economic context, it is capable in an individual case of resulting in the prevention, restriction or distortion of competition within the common market. It is not necessary for there to be actual prevention, restriction or distortion of competition or a direct link between the concerted practice and consumer prices. An exchange of information between competitors is tainted with an anti-competitive object if the exchange is capable of removing uncertainties concerning the intended conduct of the participating undertakings.[12]

5.15 The *Cartes Bancaires* ruling of 2014 is more restrictive in terms of what can go into the 'object box'.[13] The Groupement des cartes bancaires (CB) was created in 1984 in France so that the holders of a payment card issued by a member of CB could make payments to affiliated merchants and withdrawals from cash machines operated by members. Pricing (or fee transfer) arrangements were agreed between members, akin to interchange arrangements in four-party credit and debit card schemes (see also section 5.4). The European Commission concluded in 2007 that the pricing measures adopted by CB were an infringement by object and effect. On appeal, the General Court supported the Commission's finding that the pricing measures restricted competition by object, and therefore stated that there was no need to examine the effects of the measures. The ECJ overturned this ruling: 'The concept of restriction of competition 'by object' can be applied only to certain types of coordination between undertakings which reveal a sufficient degree of harm to competition that it may be found that there is no need to examine their effects.'[14]

5.16 The General Court had inferred that the object of the CB pricing measures was to impede new entry into the market for issuing payment cards in France, since entrants had no choice but to pay the fees or limit their card-issuing activities. The ECJ considered that the General Court had set out the reasons why the measures were capable of restricting competition, but had not explained how that restriction of competition led to a sufficient degree of harm in order to be characterized as a restriction by object. The ECJ found the object of the fee structure to be the imposition of a financial contribution on the members of CB, to reflect the fact that each member benefited from efforts of other members to get merchants to accept the card. Given that the General Court had taken the view that preventing free-riding by members in the CB system was a legitimate objective, the ECJ did not agree that the structure could be regarded as being harmful by its nature. The Opinion of Advocate General

---

[11] Case T-328/03 *O2 (Germany) GmbH & Co, OHG v Commission* [2006] ECR II-1234, at [116].
[12] Case C-8/08 *T-Mobile Netherlands and Others v Commission*, Judgment of 4 June 2009, at [43].
[13] Case C-67/13 P *Groupement des cartes bancaires (CB) v Commission*, Judgment of 11 September 2014.
[14] Ibid., at [58].

Wahl in this case recognized the danger that the object test under Article 101 could close off potentially welfare-enhancing agreements:

> [T]he method of identifying an 'anticompetitive object' is based on a formalist approach which is not without danger from the point of view of the protection of the general interests pursued by the rules on competition in the Treaty...
>
> Only conduct whose harmful nature is proven and easily identifiable, in the light of experience and economics, should therefore be regarded as a restriction of competition by object, and not agreements which, having regard to their context, have ambivalent effects on the market or which produce ancillary restrictive effects necessary for the pursuit of a main objective which does not restrict competition...
>
> To hold otherwise would effectively deny that some actions of economic operators may produce beneficial externalities from the point of view of competition...
>
> Because of these consequences, classification as an agreement which is restrictive by object must necessarily be circumscribed and ultimately apply only to an agreement which inherently presents a degree of harm.[15]

Thus, in many horizontal agreement cases it is relevant to understand the economic context **5.17** and the actual or likely effects on competition, even if the focus is on the object of the agreement. As implied by Advocate General Wahl, 'experience and economics' are at the heart of such assessments.

5.1.5 The remainder of this chapter

In this chapter we discuss both cartels and other horizontal agreements. Because, as noted **5.18** above, economic theory supports the per se prohibition of hardcore cartels, there is not that much more to say on the topic here. The main economic theory of collusion is addressed in Chapter 7 in the context of co-ordinated effects—the conditions under which collusion is likely to be sustained do not differ much between tacit and explicit collusion. We also discuss hardcore cartels in Chapter 8 in the context of setting fines, and in Chapter 9 on quantifying damages. Section 5.2 reviews the main economic characteristics of cartels—what makes them tick, and in which sectors of the economy do they arise most frequently? Section 5.3 addresses information-sharing arrangements, including 'hub-and-spoke' co-ordination, which differ from hardcore cartels but have received extensive scrutiny from competition authorities.

We then turn to the economic questions that arise when assessing the pros and cons of non- **5.19** hardcore horizontal agreements, where counterfactual analysis is crucial and a balance must be struck between any restrictive characteristics and the efficiency-enhancing aspects of an arrangement. We start in section 5.4 by discussing various forms of co-operation among competitors, including joint purchasing and selling—the joint selling of sports rights being one example—and the participation of banks in four-party payment card schemes. In section 5.5 we turn to R&D and technology licensing agreements, and settlement agreements in the pharmaceutical industry. How should the balance between competition and IP law be struck in these areas? Finally, in section 5.6 we explore how economics can assist competition authorities with cartel enforcement. Economists have developed quantitative tools that can spot trends and patterns in data, and these can also be applied to identify cartel behaviour. Recent inquiries into price fixing in financial markets have been triggered by such analysis.

---

[15] Opinion of Advocate General Wahl, Case C-67/13 P *Groupement des cartes bancaires (CB) v Commission*, 27 March 2014, at [54–8].

5.2 Economic Characteristics of Hardcore Cartels

5.2.1 What makes cartels tick?

5.20 As you can see from the quote by Adam Smith, cartels existed long before economics began as a discipline. Over the centuries business people have devised a wide variety of methods to form cartels—both before and after they were prohibited under the first competition laws (the difference being that ever since the prohibition, the methods have required more creativity to avoid detection). In Chapter 7 we describe the basic economic principles of collusion, including the tension that cartel members face between sticking together (the course most profitable for all) and cheating on each other (very profitable for the cheat in the short run, but not for the others). There we discuss it in the context of tacit collusion and co-ordinated effects resulting from mergers, but the principles are similar for explicit collusion. In a nutshell, the attractiveness of collusion is influenced by two forces. On the one hand, there are the benefits of collusion in the form of higher profits compared with a competitive outcome—the higher these profits, the stronger the incentives to form and maintain a cartel. On the other hand, there are immediate benefits from deviating from the collusive agreement—the higher the benefits of cheating to individual cartel members, and the longer it goes undetected, the more difficult it is to sustain the cartel. Compared with the tacit variant, an explicit cartel arrangement may make it easier to agree on the joint profit-maximizing price and to monitor any cheating. However, because they know that explicit agreements fall foul of the law, cartel members must trade off the benefits of collusion against the risk of being caught and the punishment that follows.

5.21 Cartels have different forms of agreement to choose from. These can be broadly classified as price fixing, output restriction, market or customer sharing, and bid rigging. The harmful effects of cartels are broadly the same for each type. You would expect a cartel to select the form that suits the industry best. Where cartels target quantities directly rather than prices, this will often be because it is easier or more effective to monitor quantities (any restriction in output normally results in a corresponding rise in price). Where cartel members operate in different geographic markets or where customers are diverse, some form of market or customer sharing may be most effective, again because it may be easier to implement the cartel in this way. Such customer-allocation cartels give each cartel member a degree of monopoly power over its allocated customers, allowing it to restrict output and increase price (again causing similar harm to other cartel arrangements). Bid rigging is a specific type of cartel agreement that you see in markets where contracts are awarded through some form of bidding process. If all cartel members agree on bid prices, co-ordinate cover prices (bidding a high price designed not to be successful), or allocate tenders, the effect may be similar to that of a price-fixing cartel.

5.22 Bid-rigging 'rings' sometimes organize subsequent private auctions ('knockouts') among the members to determine who gets the product.[16] One example is the *Seville Industrial Machinery* (1988) case in the United States, where a group of bidders formed a ring at a bankruptcy auction of equipment previously owned by a company that had gone bust.[17]

---

[16] See Marshall and Marx (2012) for an extensive discussion.
[17] *United States v Seville Industrial Machinery Corp.*, F. Supp. 986 (D.N.J. 1988).

After acquiring the items at artificially low prices, the members of the ring conducted their own private auction. The proceeds from the private auction over and above those bid at the public auction were divided among the ring members. As noted by the court, '[t]he pursuit of greed did not end there however'. Some of the ring members proceeded to hold a second, secret, private auction, having excluded some of the others, thereby cheating on their own partners. They in turn divided the additional proceeds derived at the second private auction among the remaining members. The court made it quite clear what it thought of this conduct: 'If the evidence presented in this case is indicative of the ethics of this or any segment of the business community, then we should weep for its existence and fear for its future.'[18]

5.2.2 Where do we find cartels?

Are there any common patterns in the market characteristics of the many cartels that have been uncovered by competition authorities? Economic theory indicates that cartels are easiest to sustain in concentrated industries with a small number of suppliers that have similar cost structures, homogeneous products, stable and inelastic demand, and limited technological change. Collusion is also easier if there is a degree of transparency in market prices and sales, such that any deviations from the agreement can be detected quickly. **5.23**

The usual suspects that tend to meet the above description are basic industrial goods and commodities. Many cartels have indeed been found in these industries: synthetic rubber, vitamins, lysine, methionine, bitumen, paraffin wax, sugar, cement, and hydrogen peroxide are but a few examples. Take methionine—our example (a) at the start of this chapter. Three companies—Aventis (formerly Rhône-Poulenc), Nippon Soda Company, and Degussa—controlled most of the European production of this homogeneous good. The cartel, fined by the European Commission in 2002, was in place from 1986 to 1999, with participants meeting in secret three to four times a year.[19] There were 'summit meetings' among top-level managers, and 'technical meetings' at the more junior manager level. The cartel members exchanged information on sales volumes and production capacity and used this to determine fixed target prices and minimum prices for methionine in each national market. They also agreed specific price increases. The target prices were based on the cartel members' assessment of the willingness to pay in each market (just the thing a textbook monopolist would do). The cartel members on occasion agreed to limit imports from outside Europe to support the price level in Europe. **5.24**

Yet cartels are not limited to basic industries. There are several examples of cartels in markets where customers have highly specific requirements and put their orders out for tender, including lifts and escalators, and gas-insulated switchgear.[20] In this category, the construction industry seems to be particularly prone to bid rigging, with cartels having been uncovered in the Netherlands, Japan, the United States, and the United Kingdom, among other countries. Bid rigging has also occurred in industries such as defence, **5.25**

---

[18] Ibid., at [993].

[19] *Methionine* (Case C.37.519), Decision of 2 July 2002.

[20] *Elevators and escalators* (Case COMP/E-1/38.823—PO), Decision of 21 February 2007; and *Gas insulated switchgear* (Case COMP/F/38.899), Decision of 24 January 2007.

agricultural products, and pharmaceuticals. Other cartels have been formed in service sectors as diverse as driving schools, supermarkets, insurance, air cargo, and art auction houses—see the Sotheby's and Christie's case we mentioned as example (b) at the start of this chapter.[21] In recent years there have been several high-profile cartel investigations in financial markets, with enormous fines and criminal convictions, in particular those concerning LIBOR and foreign exchange. A cartel case concerning local waste collection in New York City illustrates that competition law enforcement sometimes strays into the murkier parts of society as well: the convicted cartelists were 'captains' in the Gambino and Genovese crime families.[22] It would seem that organized crime not only produces drug cartels but runs some commercial ones too.

5.26   Cartels may seek to put in place certain mechanisms to try to stabilize the agreement while avoiding the need for regular communication (and hence reduce the risk of being caught). A particularly inventive mechanism was that of the famous US 'electrical conspiracy' in the 1950s, through which General Electric, Westinghouse, and other rivals rigged bids for government and private procurement contracts for heavy electrical equipment. The DOJ found that the cartel members held meetings and agreed to rotate the prices of their bids to correspond with the phases of the moon. Each manufacturer would thus periodically be the lowest bidder and get its agreed share of the market, while keeping ongoing communication between the cartel members to a minimum.[23]

5.27   This degree of inventiveness in sharing information was matched by the bidders in the auctions for radio spectrum organized by the US Federal Communications Commission (FCC) in 1996–97. These were for more than 1,000 spectrum licences covering 493 cities and regions across the United States. Three bidders—21st Century Telesis, Omnipoint, and Mercury PCS—were found to have colluded through coded bids.[24] The scheme worked as follows. Each of the regions had a three-digit code assigned by the FCC. If one of the companies wanted the licence in market 302, for example, and another had bid on it, the first company would submit a bid in another market known to be important to the second company, and end the bid price with the numbers 302 (e.g. it would bid something like $2,500,302). The message was clear: if you stop bidding in my market, I'll stop bidding in yours. The scheme allowed the bidders to share information without direct communication. In fact it turned the FCC into an unwitting participant, since at the end of each bidding round the authority would announce both the identity and the amount of the highest bidders, thus divulging the information relevant to the collusive arrangement. In sum, it would seem that few industries are immune to hardcore cartel formation, and the manners in which cartels operate are as diverse as the industries in which they are formed.

---

[21] US Department of Justice (2001), 'Former Chairmen of Sotheby's and Christie's auction houses indicted in international price-fixing conspiracy', press release, 2 May; and European Commission (2002), 'Commission rules against collusive behaviour of Christie's and Sotheby's', press release, 30 October.

[22] See 'Trash Haulers Plead Guilty In Cartel Case', *New York Times*, 23 July 1997.

[23] See the coverage of this cartel in 'Business: Rigging the Bids?', *Time Magazine*, 9 February 1960, and 'Corporations: The Great Conspiracy', *Time Magazine*, 17 February 1961.

[24] Federal Communications Commission (1997), 'Notice of Apparent Liability for Forfeiture, In Re Applications of Mercury PCS II LLC', FCC-97-388, 28 October. The companies in question breached the FCC auction's anti-collusion rule 47 CFR, s 1.2105(c).

5.3 Concerted Practices and Information Sharing

5.3.1 The economics of information sharing

Explicit cartel agreements are clearly prohibited. Tacit collusion is more difficult to address **5.28** under competition law since, in the absence of proof of communication or intent, it can be difficult to distinguish from normal business conduct. In between these two forms of collusion lies a range of behaviours and practices that can have the effect of enabling collusion. Competition law has long struggled to draw the line between what can be prohibited and what cannot. Article 101 also applies to cases where there has not necessarily been a formal agreement, but price fixing or market sharing has been achieved through more informal means. These are often placed under the heading 'concerted practices', defined by the ECJ as: 'a form of coordination between undertakings which, without having reached the stage where an agreement properly so-called has been concluded, knowingly substitutes practical co-operation for the risks of competition'.[25]

The wording 'knowingly substitutes practical cooperation for the risks of competition' can **5.29** be found in many cartel decisions by the European Commission and national competition authorities. Economics can assist in explaining the rationale and effects of such concerted practices, and hence provide some guidance as to the circumstances in which they are likely to be anti-competitive.

There has been an increasing focus on the sharing of commercial information between **5.30** competitors as an infringement by object. The theory of harm is that the information exchange facilitates co-ordinated outcomes and reduces market uncertainty, thus dampening competition. However, as a differentiator between harmful and efficiency-enhancing information exchanges, 'reducing uncertainty' is problematic. Almost by definition, any exchange of information will reduce some uncertainty. The key question is whether that reduction significantly restricts competition. As with the assessment of explicit agreements, the legality of any exchange will depend not only on what is communicated, but also on the market context. Economists are often involved in such cases to analyse the counterfactual and the likely impact on market outcomes of the information exchange under scrutiny. This also involves analysing price and volume data to see if the exchange of information had any observable effects in the market (see Chapter 9 for an overview of the methods that can be used for this).

Sometimes there will be little doubt that information is shared with the aim of forming or sup- **5.31** porting a cartel (as in the methionine and auction house examples). However, in other situations information exchanges may have more benign motives—for example, the monitoring of industry developments generally, or the provision of information to customers to enable them to plan purchases. Evidence from businesses themselves suggests that communications are frequent: in a recent UK survey, 44 per cent of companies said that they communicated with competitors on a weekly basis, and 9 per cent said that these communications related to prices (IFF Research, 2015). Not all of these communications have anti-competitive motives. Businesses may share certain information to improve performance through benchmarking, or to diffuse industry best practice or a new technology. Sharing information about market

---

[25] Cases 48/69 etc *ICI v Commission* [1972] ECR 619, [1972] CMLR 557, at [64].

demand can allow for better planning of capacity expansion and inventories; many trade associations collect and publish information on market size and trends.

5.32 There are sectors where a certain degree of transparency is required for the industry to work effectively. In the banking and insurance industries, information sharing on individual consumers' risks can reduce problems of information asymmetry. Businesses share information about credit and claims history to overcome the problem that they cannot tell the risk characteristics of a new customer (known as adverse selection), and to prevent the customer from behaving in a more risky manner once insured (known as moral hazard). In these circumstances, information-sharing mechanisms allow the industry to operate efficiently, increasing output and enabling new entry. The advent of mobile technology in Kerala, India, yields a further example of the positive results from sharing information on future behaviour. Communicating through mobile calls, fishermen were able to co-ordinate their daily fish deliveries to the fish markets along the coast. Compared with the situation before they had the possibility of communication, wastage decreased from 5–8 per cent of the catch to zero, and prices fell on average by 4 per cent (Jensen, 2007). This shows that even exchanges that would appear highly problematic on the face of it— co-ordinating future sales and prices, clearly 'reducing uncertainty'—can have efficiency benefits and improve market functioning.

5.3.2 Defining harmful information exchange

5.33 The examples above show that rules on when information exchange will be harmful are difficult to define. Yet businesses want to have guidance on what they can and cannot talk about. Competition authorities are increasingly putting exchanges of information about prices in the 'object box', even in situations where the exchange might in theory have efficiency benefits, or have no material negative effect. Yet even in object cases it is worth asking some economic questions to identify the types of information exchange that are more likely to be harmful and have limited efficiency benefits. These questions are also reflected in the European Commission's Guidelines on Horizontal Agreements.[26] How frequent is the exchange of information? The less frequent, the less likely it is to have anti-competitive effects. What is the degree of disaggregation of the information? The more aggregated across suppliers it is, the better, as less information is revealed about the behaviour of individual suppliers. Does the information exchange relate to historical, current, or future pricing or output decisions? Historical is not that bad; current potentially is; future is highly problematic. Exchanges that raise competition concerns also include disaggregated, commercially sensitive, or strategic information that cannot be found in the public domain. Exchanges between those operating in transparent, concentrated markets involving products that are not particularly complex and in which market shares are relatively stable and symmetric are most likely to be problematic, as these conditions facilitate co-ordinated behaviour. However, industries not traditionally associated with collusion should not consider themselves at lesser risk if such exchanges take place.

5.34 Consider the 2013 case of banana producers that exchanged weekly information on prices and volumes in advance of agreeing contracts with customers, and that were found guilty

---

[26] European Commission (2011), 'Guidelines on the Applicability of Article 101 of the Treaty on the Functioning of the European Union to Horizontal Co-operation Agreements', OJ (2011/C 11/01), section 2.

of an object infringement.[27] Chiquita, Dole, and Weichert co-ordinated their quotation prices for bananas marketed in northern Europe from 2000 to 2002. The companies engaged in bilateral pre-pricing communications prior to setting their quotation prices (distributed to customers) for their brands each week. Communications included volumes and market information, price trends, and likely future quotation prices. Actual prices were in general agreed directly with customers in weekly negotiations, after the quotation prices had been shared with customers. In most cases, actual prices paid by retailers and distributors for bananas were not linked explicitly to the shared quotation prices, but in some cases these quotations did feed through into actual prices through long-term contracts. There was a need for banana producers to share information to comply with requirements under the Common Agricultural Policy, but the General Court found that this did not require them to share forward-looking price and output information that was likely to affect actual prices paid. In addition, there was no plausible efficiency rationale for the extensive information exchange that occurred. Given its finding on object, the court did not consider it relevant to assess evidence that suggested that there had been no effect on market outcomes.

The bananas case is an example of the type of exchange that seems likely to affect **5.35** future prices and where no strong efficiency rationale was forthcoming. Private, direct exchanges of information relating to future pricing and output decisions are considered object restrictions. But it is not just these types of exchanges that are frowned upon. Sharing of strategic information can be found to be problematic even if not related to prices, and not done on a regular basis. Just being present when a competitor decides to reveal that information can sometimes be sufficient to constitute an object infringement, even if no subsequent action is taken. Two cases in the mobile industry illustrate this. The *T-Mobile Netherlands* case referred to earlier related to sharing confidential information on potential future strategies.[28] On 13 June 2001, T-Mobile, Vodafone, and KPN were present at a meeting that was one-off and otherwise lawful, but one topic that came up was that of reductions in standard dealer remunerations for certain contract subscriptions, to take effect from a certain date later that year. The ECJ confirmed that the information exchange that occurred at this meeting was a restriction of competition by object. Discussing dealer commissions was seen as being capable of affecting end-user prices indirectly because these commissions are an important factor in the end-user price. Despite the fact that there had been only one meeting and it was not clear to what extent those present acted upon that information subsequently, the ECJ found that one meeting was sufficient and that there should be a presumption that information shared in this way would be acted upon. Furthermore, even though the information shared was designed to reduce dealer remunerations and therefore reduce the prices paid by consumers, it was still judged to be a restriction of competition to discuss these confidential matters with competitors. In 2014, the Dutch competition authority, ACM, ruled against the same three mobile operators for making public statements relating to future changes to contract prices and individual companies' expansion plans.[29] The operators did so while

---

[27] Joined Cases T-587/08 and 588/08 *Del Monte and Dole v Commission*, Judgment of 14 March 2013.
[28] Case C-8/08 *T-Mobile Netherlands and Others v Commission*, Judgment of 4 June 2009.
[29] Autoriteit Consument en Markt, Case 13.0612.53, 'Commitments Decision with Mobile Operators', 7 January 2014.

speaking on a panel at a conference and through interviews with the trade press. The ACM found this to infringe competition law by object, and agreed commitments with the operators that such communications would no longer be made.

5.3.3 Communicating with customers: Price announcements

5.36   Direct communications with rivals may understandably give a competition authority a reason to investigate, but when can communicating pricing information to customers be problematic? Being transparent about prices will usually facilitate the competitive process; however, authorities are also pursuing cases where price announcements to customers are seen as a means of signalling strategic intent to competitors. The European Commission has opened formal proceedings against a number of container liner shipping companies regarding regular public announcements about price increase intentions, through press releases on their websites and in the specialized trade press.[30] The Commission was concerned that this practice 'may allow the companies to signal future price intentions to each other and may harm competition and customers by raising prices on the market for container liner shipping transport services on routes to and from Europe'. This case is ongoing, but one relevant consideration is the potential beneficial aspects that arise from signalling prices in advance to customers in terms of ensuring efficient use of container capacity. This was recognized by the ECJ in the wood pulp information exchange case of 1993.[31] The system of price announcements in this industry was found to constitute a rational response to the long-term and cyclical nature of the pulp market and the desire of both suppliers and customers to limit commercial risks. Originally it was the customers (paper manufacturers) that had required the introduction of the system of price announcements. Since pulp accounted for between 50 per cent and 75 per cent of the cost of paper, those customers wished to have certainty about their costs.

5.37   Two examples from the UK market investigation regime—energy and cement—are also instructive. By the nature of this regime, the CMA takes an effects-based approach to any potential competition concern, including information sharing. In the energy supply market, price announcements were found to be consistent with competitive behaviour, whereas in cement they were found to be an important enabler of market share co-ordination between the suppliers. In the energy inquiry, the industry practice of trailing changes to standard tariffs some weeks in advance, through press releases and discussions in the trade press, was investigated to see if it facilitated collusion and thereby raised prices.[32] The CMA concluded provisionally that, while there was evidence that price announcements were followed by parallel movements in standard tariffs by the major energy companies, these seemed to be driven by unilateral considerations relating to cost changes and regulatory obligations. The announcements were not a mechanism to facilitate tacit collusion. This illustrates that treating such announcements as object infringements would remove a useful means of disseminating information to customers that has limited harmful effects.

---

[30]   European Commission (2013), 'Antitrust: Commission Opens Proceedings Against Container Liner Shipping Companies', press release, 22 November. We advised one of the parties on this case.

[31]   Joined Cases C-89/85, C-104/85, C-114/85, C-116/85, C-117/85, and C-125/85 to C-129/85, *A. Ahlström Osakeyhtiö and Others v Commission*, [1993] ECR I-01307.

[32]   Competition and Markets Authority (2015), 'Energy Market Investigation: Provisional Findings Report', 7 July. We advised one of the energy companies in this case.

In its aggregates inquiry in 2014, the CMA did find evidence of tacit co-ordination through **5.38** price announcements.[33] The market structure seemed conducive to co-ordination: homogeneous products; high concentration; a significant degree of transparency; and frequent interactions between the main cement producers—Cemex, Hanson, and Lafarge (now Lafarge Tarmac). The CMA concluded that the main cement producers had co-ordinated to keep market shares stable, one of their mechanisms being through making general pricing announcements in advance of price negotiations with customers. While prices were agreed individually with customers, the CMA found that the letters sent to all customers announcing indicative price rises contributed to price parallelism and to softening customer resistance to price increases. To verify whether price parallelism was not simply a reflection of strong competition in the market, the CMA measured the profitability of the cement producers (we explain profitability analysis in Chapter 3). It concluded that returns were somewhat above the cost of capital for the previous six years, and that margins had been stable. However, given the spare capacity and significant fall in demand due to the global recession, the CMA noted that it would have expected to observe more fluctuations in margins and lower overall profits had the industry been operating in a competitive manner. The CMA thus concluded that successful co-ordination was prevalent in the cement market. As a remedy, it required divestment of a cement plant by the largest producer so as to disrupt the focal nature of existing market shares, and implemented two measures aimed at reducing transparency: restricting the speed at which cement market data is published in order to reduce its usefulness in monitoring rivals' performance; and prohibiting generic price announcement letters.

5.3.4 Communicating via customers or suppliers: Hub-and-spoke arrangements

Co-ordination between horizontal competitors can also take place indirectly through **5.39** communication or vertical agreements with a supplier or a customer. Examples of vertical mechanisms with a potential horizontal effect are meeting-the-competition (price-match promise) clauses and most-favoured-nation (MFN) clauses. These have been investigated in vertical restraints cases, most recently those involving online distribution (e-books, online travel booking). We discuss MFNs in Chapter 6. A related practice discussed here is where information is exchanged between competing retailers indirectly, via a common supplier, or between competing suppliers via a common retailer. These are called hub-and-spoke arrangements. One retailer (A) transfers commercially sensitive information to a supplier (B), with the intention that the information be transferred to a competing retailer (C), in circumstances where C knows that the information had been provided by A to B, and where it uses that information.

The concern is that these vertical price and information-sharing agreements facilitate hori- **5.40** zontal collusion. Sometimes the hub is a manufacturer, and through its vertical agreements with competing retailers (the spokes) it can facilitate collusion between them. In other cases the hub is a retailer and the concern is about collusion between manufacturers. There can also be combinations of these two. Evidence from the business world shows that customers and suppliers are an important source of information on competitors' prices: in one

---

[33] Competition and Markets Authority (2014), 'Aggregates, Cement and Ready-Mix Concrete Market Investigation: Final Report', 14 January.

survey, 44 per cent of companies that monitor prices said that customers or other businesses informed them about rivals' prices, and a further 13 per cent said that they asked customers directly for such information (IFF Research, 2015).

5.41 An example of a hub-and-spoke case is the retailing of replica football kit in the United Kingdom.[34] The OFT investigated agreements between manufacturer Umbro and a number of retailers. It concluded that the retailers (the 'spokes') would signal to each other via Umbro (the 'hub') that they would not cut prices (e.g. it was thus established that a Manchester United replica shirt should sell at £39.99 across all retailers). When the European football championship in 2000 was approaching, JJB Sports, the largest sportswear retailer in the United Kingdom at the time, was keen to avoid a price war for the England replica shirt, in particular with Sports Soccer, a discount retailer. A series of telephone conversations took place between JJB Sports and Umbro, and between Umbro and Sports Soccer, during which confidential price information was exchanged. There was no direct communication between JJB Sports and Sports Soccer. However, as a result of their respective discussions with Umbro, the two retailers avoided discounting the England replica shirts. By the start of Euro 2000 it was very difficult to purchase such shirts for less than £39.99. (Incidentally, after England's premature exit from the championship, Sports Soccer swiftly reverted to discounting the shirts.)

5.3.5 The UK tobacco hub-and-spoke case

5.42 In a case involving tobacco sales, the OFT determined that the bilateral agreements between ten retailers and the two main tobacco manufacturers—Imperial Tobacco and Gallaher, which jointly held around 90 per cent of the market—infringed Chapter I of the Competition Act 1998 (the equivalent of Article 101):

> The Infringing Agreements comprised in each case an agreement and/or concerted practice between each Manufacturer and each Retailer whereby the Manufacturer co-ordinated with the Retailer the setting of the Retailer's retail prices for tobacco products, in order to achieve the parity and differential requirements between competing tobacco brands that were set by the Manufacturer, in pursuit of the Manufacturer's retail pricing strategy. The Infringing Agreement between each Manufacturer and each Retailer restricted the Retailer's ability to determine its retail prices for competing tobacco products.[35]

5.43 The parallel vertical agreements with retailers allowed the manufacturers to maintain certain desired pricing relativities between their own and each other's brands—these were referred to as parity and differential agreements (P&Ds). The OFT found that the P&Ds restricted competition at the horizontal level, and would be expected to increase retail prices. The concern that a series of bilateral vertical agreements was thus used to facilitate horizontal collusion is reminiscent of resale price maintenance (RPM), which we discuss in Chapter 6. In this case, the P&Ds did not restrict the level at which the retailer could sell tobacco products, but rather affected the price differentials between specific sets of competing brands. The OFT did not rely on effects analysis, instead establishing an infringement by object.

---

[34] Office of Fair Trading (2003), 'Decision of the Office of Fair Trading No. CA98/06/2003: Price-fixing of Replica Football Kit', 1 August, Case CP/0871/01.
[35] Office of Fair Trading (2010), 'Decision of the Office of Fair Trading: Case CE/2596-03 Tobacco', 15 April, at [1.4]. We advised one of the retailers in these proceedings.

On appeal, the OFT withdrew its case when factual evidence came to light that showed that **5.44** its understanding of how the P&Ds actually operated had been incorrect. It had assumed that the agreements required a fixed parity or differential to be adhered to regardless of the wholesale price set by the manufacturer. The OFT relied on a theoretical model showing that in such circumstances retail prices increase. However, in reality, the desired parity or differentials were often adjusted when wholesale prices changed, which meant that the OFT's model prediction of price rises was no longer valid. The CAT quashed the decision.[36] Given the correct factual interpretation of how the agreements affected pricing incentives, the economic analysis showed that their likely horizontal effect was to reduce rather than increase prices. A detailed assessment of the market context and functioning of the P&Ds was therefore important in understanding their competitive effects, which in turn sheds light on their object as well. This case illustrates the risks in pursuing an object infringement without any evidence of harmful effects.

5.4 Co-operation Among Competitors: Joint Purchasing, Joint Selling, and Other Forms of Collaboration

5.4.1 Joint purchasing and selling

Sometimes competitors join forces to collectively negotiate the prices of an input. An exam- **5.45** ple is a co-operative of retailers jointly purchasing products from suppliers. Joint purchasing can bring benefits of economies of scale or other efficiencies, which in turn can lead to lower prices for consumers. Is that sufficient reason to allow such agreements? Joint purchasing may be of concern if the co-operating parties have a high degree of buyer power in the input market and market power in their own product markets. In this situation, any lower purchase prices or other efficiencies that are achieved through joint purchasing may not benefit consumers much. Buyer power in the purchasing market may also give rise to foreclosure of competing purchasers.

The Dutch bitumen cartel is one example where joint purchasing was judged to have **5.46** amounted to price fixing and where the claimed efficiency benefits were refuted.[37] The European Commission concluded that eight of the nine suppliers of bitumen (including BP, Shell, and Total), and the six largest road-construction companies, had an arrangement whereby the suppliers and the purchasers jointly agreed on prices and rebates for the bitumen in a series of meetings during the period 1994–2002. The purchasers of the bitumen argued that these price agreements were a case of joint purchasing, falling within the scope of Article 101(3), which states that restrictive agreements may nonetheless be allowed if they produce efficiencies that benefit customers. The Commission rejected this for a number of reasons. One was that the suppliers did not in fact purchase anything collectively, but merely agreed on prices—no real efficiencies in joint purchasing were achieved.

Like joint purchasing, joint selling agreements can be beneficial for consumers in cer- **5.47** tain circumstances. Arguments concerning the pro-competitive nature of such agreements played an important role in the European Commission's investigation in 2002

---

[36] *Imperial Tobacco et al. v Office of Fair Trading* [2011] CAT 41, 12 December 2011.
[37] *Bitumen–NL* (Case COMP/38.456), Decision of 13 September 2006.

into producers of gas from the Norwegian continental shelf.[38] Since 1989, the Norwegian gas producers had sold their gas through a single seller, the Gas Negotiation Committee (Gassforhandlingsutvalget, GFU). The Commission concluded that these producers were in breach of Article 101(1) since they fixed the prices and quantities of the gas sold. This signalled an end to the GFU agreement, although a fine was not imposed.

5.48 The GFU had two permanent members—Statoil and Norsk Hydro, Norway's largest gas producers—and was occasionally extended to other producers. It engaged in a joint operating and selling agreement, and negotiated the terms of all supply contracts with buyers on behalf of all natural gas producers in Norway. A number of studies have shown that, in certain circumstances, such joint operating and selling agreements in the gas industry can be efficient.[39] The development of any gas field entails significant long-term investment with associated risks in the construction costs, added to which are the considerable price and volume risks associated with the marketing of the gas itself. These risks imply that investors in such projects will be looking for a relatively high return. Joint selling arrangements, in conjunction with joint operating arrangements, allow the burden of these risks to be shared. This reduces financing costs and can ensure that the investment actually takes place.

5.49 This therefore raises the question of what would happen in the counterfactual with a joint operating agreement but no joint selling agreement. Would the gas producers still have developed the gas field? The answer is possibly not. A joint operating agreement provides each participant in the agreement with a veto over the development of the field. Consequently, if there is too much uncertainty for any one participant regarding the future sales of the gas from the field, the whole development could be threatened. In this situation, the additional joint selling arrangement reduces the degree of volume uncertainty by ensuring that every participant has a means of selling the gas. Another factor to consider in the economic analysis of this case—whether under Article 101(1) or 101(3)—is that the Norwegian producers in the GFU sold a large proportion of their gas to the European market, in which they represented less than 15–20 per cent of all capacity, and faced competition from gas producers from other countries. In all, this case illustrates that joint purchasing and selling agreements do not warrant a per se prohibition. The economic effects of such agreements can be assessed on a case-by-case basis through counterfactual analysis under Article 101(1) or through the analysis of efficiencies under Article 101(3).

5.4.2 Joint selling of sports rights

5.50 Sports rights are an example of where joint selling arrangements have been found to be consistent with competition law in certain circumstances. High-profile cases concerned the joint and exclusive selling of the broadcast rights for premium football events, including the UEFA Champions League, the German Bundesliga, and the English Premier League.[40] These joint selling arrangements have been exempted under Article 101(3), often subject to

---

[38] European Commission (2001), 'Commission Objects to GFU Joint Gas Sales in Norway', press release, 13 June; and European Commission (2002), 'Commission Successfully Settles GFU Case with Norwegian Gas Producers', press release, 17 July. We advised the main parties in this inquiry.
[39] See, for example, Dinnage (1998).
[40] *Joint Selling of the Commercial Rights of the UEFA Champions League* (Case COMP/C.2-37.398), Decision of 23 July 2003; *Joint Selling of the Media Rights to the German Bundesliga* (Case COMP/C-2/37.214), Decision of 19 January 2005; and *Joint Selling of Media Rights to the FA Premier League* (Case COMP/C-2/38.173), Decision of 22 March 2006.

certain commitments, on the grounds that they bring important benefits: (1) the creation of a single point of sale, generating efficiencies for sports organizers and media content operators; (2) the ability to enhance the quality and brand of the league, thereby improving recognition and distribution; and (3) through principles of financial solidarity, improving the competition in the league as a whole rather than just individual clubs. The commitments in these cases related to the way in which the broadcast rights must be sold, so as to ensure that competition between broadcasters is enhanced. The commitments limit the duration of the exclusive contracts to three years. They also limit them in scope, ensuring that there are several different rights packages of varying sizes, and that there are separate packages earmarked to support the development of different media besides TV. Furthermore, commitments were expanded to include a 'no single buyer' rule, with the aim of increasing competition between channel providers carrying these sports. Many football leagues now structure their rights auctions in line with these principles.[41]

The collective and exclusive selling of sports rights was also addressed in *BAGS v AMRAC* **5.51** (2008).[42] This case concerned the broadcasting of British horseracing into betting shops, which was worth around £100m per year at the time. The claimants were major bookmakers and the associated media rights buyer, BAGS, which alleged that the new broadcaster, AMRAC, had restricted competition. AMRAC was a joint venture involving around half of all British racecourses and a media company, Alphameric. The allegation was that AMRAC had acquired the media rights on a collective and exclusive basis (we discuss the exclusivity aspects of this case in Chapter 6). The High Court found that neither the collective nor the exclusive nature of the arrangement restricted competition. Counterfactual analysis was at the heart of this finding. There had been a monopoly—SIS—in the provision of horseracing broadcasting services to bookmakers for twenty years when AMRAC entered the fray. The racecourses acting collectively was considered necessary for successful entry, and not restrictive of competition in these circumstances.

The bookmakers argued that SIS and AMRAC were both 'must-have' broadcast services, **5.52** since each had exclusive access to around half of all horseracing events, and bookmakers wish to show all events in their shops. According to this view, the advent of AMRAC had not created a competitor but rather a second monopolist. The court did not agree, since competition in this market took place in different forms: ex ante competition for media rights; competition in technology; and competition in secondary content. The ex ante competition between SIS and AMRAC for media rights was found to be a legitimate form of competition, enabling the racecourses to realize the value of their content and invest in their sport, even if it resulted in higher costs to the bookmakers that had to subscribe to both services. Note the similarities between this complaint by the bookmakers and recent grumblings about the costs of pay-TV football packages in the United Kingdom. The 'no single buyer' rule and the split of Premier League rights into different packages has been successful in enabling a new competitor, BT Sports, to establish itself as a rival to Sky in the broadcast

---

[41] Various national competition authorities have also dealt with the collective selling of media rights for their national football leagues and other sports. For an overview, see Organisation for Economic Co-operation and Development (2013b).

[42] Case 161/84 *Bookmakers Afternoon Greyhound Services Limited & Ors v Amalgamated Racing Limited & Ors* [2008] EWHC 1978 (Ch), 8 August 2008. We acted as economic experts for the defendants in these proceedings.

market (a number of predecessors to BT had failed). This has resulted in very competitive bidding for the Premier League live TV rights: the 2015 auction generated £5.2 billion of revenues—70 per cent more than in 2012—with Sky buying five packages for £4.2 billion and BT the other two packages for £960 million. Yet because the two broadcasters show different matches exclusively, there are many consumers and commercial premises who regard both as 'must-have' services. Ofcom launched a further investigation into the sale of Premier League rights to address this issue.[43]

5.53 Collective selling in *BAGS v AMRAC* was further considered at the Court of Appeal, which agreed with the High Court that the racecourses had not restricted competition, but in addition found in favour of the racecourses on the issue of whether they were competitors.[44] The racecourses had argued that they did not compete with each other in the sale of media rights and therefore collective selling could not be anti-competitive. The British horseracing calendar is set such that all races take place at different points in time, without overlap. In addition, the nature of the betting market means that bookmakers want to show all races in their shops, rather than a partial schedule, as this generates betting. Therefore the media rights are complements rather than substitutes. The Court of Appeal agreed with this reasoning. It also applies to certain other sports. Individual Formula One races do not compete with each other since they take place on different weekends. UEFA Champions League matches are competing events when they are scheduled to kick off at the same time, but UEFA is now in the habit of spreading matches in the later stages of the tournament as much as it can over weekdays.

5.54 In an earlier case involving media rights for horseracing—*RCA and BHB v OFT* (2005)—collective purchasing and selling was also considered necessary for the launch of a new venture.[45] A group of British racecourses sold media rights collectively to a new service for interactive TV and internet betting on horseracing. This required a critical mass of horseracing content for a successful launch (in the end the service was never actually launched). The OFT found an infringement because it considered that, in a counterfactual without the agreement, the venture could have assembled a critical mass of rights by negotiating individually with each racecourse. The CAT disagreed, and found that from a practical point of view collective selling was the only realistic way to achieve a sale and purchase of the rights. These rights had never been sold before, and interactive betting was a new service at the time. We come back to this case in Chapter 10, in the context of the discussion about theory versus commercial reality.

5.4.3 Co-operation among banks in payment card schemes: The interchange fee cases

5.55 Payment and clearing systems in the banking sector are examples of activities that require co-operation and co-ordination between competitors in order to function properly. This need for co-operation makes these systems different from a hardcore cartel, but there are still concerns about an elimination of competition among the banks in related markets.

---

[43] Ofcom (2014), 'Ofcom Investigation into Premier League Football Rights', press release, 18 November.

[44] *Bookmakers Afternoon Greyhound Services Limited & Ors v Amalgamated Racing Limited & Ors* [2009] EWCA Civ 750, 28 July 2009.

[45] *The Racecourse Association and the British Horseracing Board v Office of Fair Trading* [2005] CAT 29, 2 August.

The fine balance between co-operation and competition has been extensively explored in the various investigations into interchange fees set by payment card schemes. Visa and MasterCard are the two major global card schemes. Thousands of banks around the world participate in them. Known as four-party schemes, they involve two types of bank and two types of customer—issuing banks that have a direct relationship with cardholders, and acquiring banks that have a direct relationship with merchants that accept the card for payments in their shops. This contrasts with three-party schemes such as American Express, which traditionally deal directly with both merchants and cardholders and therefore have not attracted the same level of competition law scrutiny (although American Express now also uses independent banks to issue its cards).

Every card transaction involves a cardholder and a merchant. Say you use your credit card **5.56** to make a payment of €100 in a shop. The acquiring bank credits the merchant's account with €100 minus a merchant service charge—say 2 per cent (so the merchant receives €98, having sold a product for €100). The issuing bank adds the full €100 to your balance, a statement of which is sent to you periodically (you can then choose to pay the balance in full or to take up the option of extended credit, which will incur interest). Still in relation to the same transaction, the issuing bank credits the acquiring bank for €100, minus the so-called interchange fee—say 1 per cent. So the acquiring bank receives €99, of which €98 is paid on to the merchant. This interchange fee is set by the scheme and the participating banks—hence it is called the multilateral interchange fee (MIF).

The MIF is not new to competition law. The *NaBanco* ruling (1986) in the United **5.57** States gave the principle of MIF a clean bill of health.[46] But decades later the tide has turned. Australia was one of the first jurisdictions to tackle interchange fees, through combined action by the Reserve Bank of Australia and the Australian Competition and Consumer Commission in 2001.[47] The European Commission prohibited the MasterCard cross-border MIF in 2007, a decision upheld by the ECJ in 2014, while agreeing settlements with Visa at different stages.[48] The European Commission also introduced an Interchange Fee Regulation in 2015, which prescribes caps on debit and credit card MIFs for domestic and cross-border transactions.[49] Why these concerns? The most direct allegation is that the MIF constitutes price fixing by banks at the expense of merchants. One problem with this argument is that the MIF does not really fit the description of a standard price-fixing cartel. Some sort of agreement between issuing and acquiring banks is necessary for the scheme to operate. The MasterCard and Visa schemes have an 'honour-all-cards' rule, which means that merchants who agree to accept MasterCard must accept all payments with cards carrying the MasterCard logo, regardless of who the issuing bank is. Merchants can do this in the certainty that their payment will be guaranteed, and the acquirer in turn can do this because of the existing agreement with the issuer (multilaterally via the scheme). Without such an agreement, the scheme would not function.

---

[46] *National Bancard Corp v VISA USA Inc* 779 F 2d 592 (11th Cir. 1986).

[47] Reserve Bank of Australia (2001), 'Reform of Credit Card Schemes in Australia', December.

[48] *MasterCard* (Case COMP/34.579), Decision of 19 December 2007; and Case C-382/12 P *MasterCard and Others v Commission*, Judgment of 11 September 2014; *Visa International—Multilateral Interchange Fee* (Case COMP/29.373), Decision of 24 July 2002.

[49] European Commission (2015), 'Regulation (EU) 2015/751 of the European Parliament and of the Council of 29 April 2015 on Interchange Fees for Card-based Payment Transactions', 19 May.

5.58 It is commonly accepted—including by the European Commission—that payment card schemes are two-sided platforms: there are two types of user, cardholders and merchants, with positive externalities between them (we also saw this in Chapters 2 and 3). The more consumers with a MasterCard card in their wallet, the more attractive it is for retailers to accept MasterCard, and vice versa. The ECJ also recognized this two-sided nature of payment card schemes in its *Cartes Bancaires* ruling of 2014, where it found that the fee transfer between banks (similar to an interchange arrangement) had as its object to prevent free-riding between issuers and acquirers.[50]

5.59 Two-sided platforms face the commercial imperative to get, and keep, both types of user on board. A new platform faces the challenge of attracting a critical mass of users on both sides. An established platform that competes with other platforms faces the challenge of keeping sufficient users on both sides. This commonly results in a skewed pricing structure, with one side paying a relatively lower price than the other—some newspapers are free of charge to readers, raising their circulation and hence becoming more attractive to advertisers. The reason is that one side may have an inherently lower willingness to pay, or may be more important to attract users on the other side. Payment card schemes tend to charge more on the merchant side than on the cardholder side. This has the effect of increasing the size of the scheme, as more cardholders use the card and more merchants accept it.

5.60 From an economic perspective, practices that enhance output will generally be pro-competitive. In a well-functioning market, suppliers are expected to try to gain market share from their rivals by making themselves attractive to customers. This contrasts with the standard concern about cartels, which is that they artificially *restrict* output. Indeed, one of the main concerns about the MIF was precisely that it leads to an excessive use of credit cards, at the expense of other payment methods, not that output was artificially restricted. By recovering more of their costs through the merchants, issuers can make the card 'artificially' attractive to cardholders through loyalty points, cashback, and other benefits. This way, so the allegation goes, the economy ends up with too many credit card transactions, with merchants, and ultimately end-consumers, footing the bill. Whether this concern fits naturally under Article 101 is an open question.

5.61 Proponents and opponents of the MIF thus agree that its effect (and object) is to increase usage of the card scheme, by recovering some of the issuer costs through merchants rather than cardholders. This is in line with the economic theory of interchange. Baxter (1983) was the first to provide an economic explanation of interchange fees, and showed that four-party payment systems dating back to the nineteenth century have tended to set inter-bank fees of this type—that is, well before the advent of credit cards.[51] He also showed that setting the interchange fees multilaterally tends to be more efficient than a system of bilateral agreements between issuers and acquirers, in particular because of the large number of banks involved. Baxter gave various reasons why the optimal MIF in credit card schemes is more likely to flow from acquirers to issuers than the other way round—mainly because a greater proportion of the scheme's costs fall on issuers (processing costs, protection against cardholder default, and the costs of the interest-free credit

---

[50] Case C-67/13 P *Groupement des cartes bancaires (CB) v Commission*, Judgment of 11 September 2014.
[51] This is the same William Baxter who, in 1982, as the DOJ Assistant Attorney General, was behind the break-up of AT&T—see Chapter 8.

period offered to cardholders), and because cardholders typically have a low willingness to pay (cash and other payment methods are often 'free' at point of use). Indeed, three-party schemes such as American Express also tend to recover more of their costs from merchants than from cardholders, but do not require an interchange fee to balance costs and revenues between the two sides because of their proprietary nature—and hence they are not caught under Article 101.

5.4.4 Multilateral interchange fees: Counterfactual analysis

The Commission's finding of restriction in the 2007 *MasterCard* decision referred to competition *within* the scheme (intra-system competition), and on only one side: competition between acquiring banks: 'The MasterCard MIF therefore creates an artificial cost base that is common for all acquirers and the merchant fee will typically reflect the cost of the MIF. This leads to a restriction of price competition between acquiring banks, to the detriment of merchants (and subsequent purchasers).'[52]   **5.62**

The restriction of competition did not refer to competition *between* payment systems (inter-system competition). Given that, as noted above, the skewed pricing structure facilitated by the MIF is aimed at enhancing the competitiveness of MasterCard vis-à-vis other payment systems, it would be hard to argue that the MIF would restrict competition at this inter-system level—indeed, the MIF promotes inter-system competition. What about the restriction of competition between acquirers? First, a higher common cost floor does not necessarily affect the nature of competition between acquirers (just like an increase in wholesale petrol prices does not necessarily affect the nature of competition between petrol stations). Second, when assessing concerns about high prices on one side of a two-sided platform, you should explore whether this is driven by the commercial imperative on the platform to keep both sides on board. You cannot consider one side in isolation.   **5.63**

This raises the question of the counterfactual. In determining whether a MIF restricts competition under Article 101(1), you need to consider the competition that would exist without the MIF. An obvious potential counterfactual is where all transaction settlements between acquirers and issuers within the scheme require a bilateral agreement on interchange. In such a situation, once a transaction takes place, the acquirer effectively has no choice but to settle the payment with the issuer in question, since the payment was made by one of that issuer's cardholders. Thus each acquirer faces multiple 'monopoly' issuers. Economic models commonly find that a situation with a series of bilateral interchange fees and no MIF tends to result in higher interchange fees overall than a situation with a MIF. This is a version of the problem of double marginalization (explained in section 6): complementary producers with market power (here issuers) set higher prices individually (in bilateral contracts) than they would if set collectively through the MIF.   **5.64**

This matters for the analysis of restriction of competition under Article 101(1): if the concern is that the MIF restricts competition and raises prices to merchants, how is this consistent with the fact that, without the MIF, prices to merchants would be *higher*? In other words, in a counterfactual with bilateral arrangements the competitive outcome would be worse for merchants. This is one reason why interchange fees do not naturally fit within the   **5.65**

---

[52] *MasterCard* (Case COMP/34.579), Decision of 19 December 2007, at [410].

assessment under Article 101(1). Indeed, one of the main reasons why an earlier OFT case against MIF in the United Kingdom was set aside by the CAT in 2006 is that the OFT decision had put forward bilateral interchange fees as the relevant counterfactual.[53] When this counterfactual was criticized on the above grounds, the OFT sought to change this position during the appeal but ultimately could not sustain its case.

5.66 The European Commission relied on a different counterfactual in its 2007 decision: 'a rule that imposes a prohibition on ex post pricing on the banks in the absence of a bilateral agreement between them'.[54] It considered that such a rule would protect acquirers from issuers exploiting their bargaining power in bilateral negotiations, and would be less restrictive of competition than a MIF. Quite apart from the question of how realistic such a hypothetical rule would be, the difficulty with this alternative counterfactual is that the prohibition on ex post pricing would effectively establish a default MIF as well; it is simply a MIF of zero. In that sense it is a restriction of competition in the same way as the MIF is seen as a restriction: an agreement (or scheme rule) that issuers will not charge acquirers. This would be a restriction of competition in the issuing market, just like the Commission considered the MIF to be a restriction of competition in the acquiring market. It would be analogous to newspaper publishers agreeing that they would all adopt the free-of-charge model, thus no longer charging readers and instead recovering all their costs on the advertising side.

5.67 Finally, the Commission raised a concern that inter-system competition does not constrain the level of interchange fees, but rather exerts an upward pressure on it. This is indeed a commonly recognized mechanism in the competition between payment card schemes: a high interchange fee is one way in which a scheme can attract issuing banks which have the option of issuing other schemes' cards to their customers. There are several national markets where one of Visa, MasterCard, or American Express has gained significant issuer business from the other schemes by offering more attractive interchange fees. This is an inherent feature of how competition between payment systems works—it has the effect of raising fees on one side of the platform (merchants end up paying for the higher interchange fees), but competition on the other side (between issuers) and between platforms is enhanced.

5.68 On the whole, from an economic perspective, interchange fees cannot easily be classed as restrictions of competition under Article 101(1). In many respects they have a pro-competitive purpose and effects, and competition in the counterfactual without a MIF would result in a worse outcome (higher bilateral interchange fees). The concern about high interchange fees seems to be more of a policy or regulatory nature: credit card schemes growing too much, at the expense of cheaper payment methods, with merchants and, ultimately, consumers paying for this. From this perspective, to the extent that one shares this concern, addressing it under a specific regulation—such as Regulation (EU) 2015/751 on Interchange Fees for Card-based Payment Transactions that came into force in 2015—would seem more appropriate than dealing with interchange fees under competition law.

---

[53] *MasterCard UK Members Forum Limited and others v Office of Fair Trading*, [2006] CAT 14, Judgment on setting aside the Decision, 10 July 2006. We advised MasterCard on this case.
[54] *MasterCard* (Case COMP/34.579), Decision of 19 December 2007, at [554].

5.5 Technology and Intellectual Property Agreements: Beneficial or Anti-competitive?

5.5.1 R&D agreements

R&D is a costly and time-consuming activity aimed at bringing new products or processes   **5.69**
to the market. It suffers from a well-known market failure problem: once public, the fruits
of the R&D may be used by other parties without additional cost, making it difficult for the
innovator to reap the benefits. IP rights have been created to address this problem: innovators are granted patents for a sustained period (typically around twenty years) to allow them
to earn returns on their R&D efforts and hence incentivize them to make such efforts in
the first place. Companies may also seek collaboration with their competitors to share these
risks. In other instances, companies seek to prevent others from using their IP through litigation, and may enter into agreements to settle such disputes. In all these cases, Article 101 will
be relevant in assessing how R&D agreements and settlements in IP dispute are structured.

One potential competition problem from R&D agreements relates directly to the R&D   **5.70**
market itself. In Chapter 2 we saw that innovation capability may be treated as a separate relevant market in its own right, and hence an agreement to share R&D activity may
limit competition in that market. An example we mentioned was the proposed merger
of General Motor's Allison Division and ZF Friedrichshafen, a German company, which
together controlled most of the worldwide innovation market for the design, development,
and production of transmissions.[55] Another concern is that R&D co-operation could affect
competition in the final product market, even where the agreement is strictly limited to the
R&D component and not to subsequent commercialization of the products. Because of
their common interest in the joint venture, companies may be more amenable to limiting
rivalrous behaviour in final product markets as well.

However, competition law has in general viewed R&D agreements between competitors   **5.71**
favourably, especially if there is sufficient remaining competition in the innovation and
final product markets. An example of R&D co-operation between competitors is the *Ford/
Volkswagen* case (1992), concerning a joint venture agreement to develop and produce a
multi-purpose vehicle (MPV) in Portugal, in which the European Commission concluded
as follows:

> The cooperation between Ford and VW will not lead to an elimination of competition in the
> MPV segment. Having regard to the leading position of the Renault 'Espace', it will, on the
> contrary, stimulate competition through the creation of an additional choice in this area and
> lead to a more balanced structure in the MPV market segment. There will also be increased
> competition concerning price and quality over the next five to ten years with the further
> penetration of the segment by Japanese producers as well as other new entrants.[56]

5.5.2 Technology licensing agreements and the block exemption

Once successfully developed, new technologies are often exploited by licensing the IP   **5.72**
rights to other suppliers, including competitors. Such licence agreements frequently

---

[55] *United States v General Motors Corp* Civ No 93-530 (D. Del) filed 16 November 1993.
[56] *Ford/Volkswagen* (Case IV/33.814), Decision of 23 December 1992, at [37].

fall under Article 101, and the rules on which type of agreements meet the conditions for exemption are clarified in the Technology Transfer Block Exemption Regulation—commonly referred to as the TTBER—and its accompanying Guidelines, which were updated in 2014.[57] The TTBER establishes the principle that IP holders should be free to exploit their rights as they wish, but that they should not distort competition in doing so (we saw this principle in abuse of dominance cases involving IP in Chapter 4). Another principle recognized by the European Commission is that IP licensing is generally pro-competitive. The rules make a distinction between agreements involving competitors and non-competitors. In order for the TTBER to apply, the combined market share for the parties if they are competitors must not exceed 20 per cent; if they are not competitors the share for each of the parties must not exceed 30 per cent. For the latter type, the criteria are similar to those applied to vertical restraints (see Chapter 6). As to agreements between competitors, a number of 'hardcore' restrictions cannot be exempted: price fixing; output restriction; customer and market allocation; and non-compete restrictions. In terms of restrictive effects in innovation markets, the Guidelines seek to provide some legal certainty by stating that Article 101 is 'unlikely to be infringed where there are four or more independently controlled technologies in addition to the technologies controlled by the parties'.[58] This threshold would seem conservative, as it is not often that there will be four different technologies competing directly in the same innovation market.

5.73 With technology agreements there is often a difficult line to be drawn between customer and market allocation clauses, which are deemed anti-competitive, and 'field of use' restrictions. The latter are commonly included in technology licences. They serve the legitimate purpose of preventing the licensee from exploiting the IP for uses other than those specified in the licence. Exclusivity in licences is usually accepted, but in agreements between competitors there is greater concern if the exclusivity is reciprocal than if it is non-reciprocal. Reciprocity creates mutual commitments not to supply third parties, and may facilitate collusion.

5.74 The 2014 TTBER has removed all exclusive grant-back obligations, where the licensee is required to assign or license back to the licensor on an exclusive basis any improvements made to the technology. Previously, a safe harbour had existed for such exclusivity clauses where they related to non-severable improvements (i.e. improvements that required a licence for the original technology as well). This change in the Commission's approach was based on studies showing that such restrictions had similar effects on severable and non-severable improvements, and were responsible for limiting licensees' incentives to innovate. This was because exclusive grant-back obligations weakened the scope for licensees to extract sufficient value for their improvements. From an economic perspective, the previous distinction between severable and non-severable improvements remains important. In the case of non-severable improvements (i.e. those that cannot be used without infringing the

---

[57] Commission Regulation 316/2014 of 21 March 2014 on the Application of Article 101(3) of the 'Treaty on the Functioning of the European Union to Categories of Technology Transfer Agreements', [2014] OJ L93/17; and European Commission (2014), 'Guidelines on the Application of Article 101 of the Treaty on the Functioning of the European Union to Technology Transfer Agreements', 2014/C 89/03, 28 March.

[58] European Commission (2014), 'Guidelines on the Application of Article 101 of the Treaty on the Functioning of the European Union to Technology Transfer Agreements', 2014/C 89/03, 28 March, at [157].

initial technology), the original licensor directly benefits from these improvements (e.g. via royalties). Conversely, the licensor may not benefit at all from severable improvements and, in such a case, a grant-back obligation that is non-exclusive means that the licensee can license its technology to others without any contribution to the original innovation. This may reduce the licensor's initial incentive to license its technology.

Another change in the 2014 TTBER relative to the previous version concerns 'no-challenge' clauses. The TTBER excludes termination clauses in non-exclusive licensing agreements from its safe harbour. Such clauses would allow the licensor to terminate the agreement if the other party challenges the validity of the licensed technology. The overall impact of such clauses in terms of encouraging innovation and technology diffusion depends on the negotiating balance between the licensor and the licensee. It is not the case that licensors are always the large technology or pharmaceutical companies. Licensors may be small start-ups and licensees may be the larger companies. The degree of market power and strength of competitors should therefore play a role in the assessment. The market share thresholds and the current strict approach in the guidelines may not capture the full complexity of the parties' respective bargaining power, and clauses that may now fall outside of the TTBER safe harbour may be important to facilitate efficient technology sharing. **5.75**

5.5.3 Technology licensing agreements: Patent pools and standards

The main changes to the TTBER Guidelines relate to reverse payment settlements and multi-party licensing, neither of which in fact benefit from any safe harbour under the 2014 TTBER. The Commission has sought to give guidance on these two complex areas. We discuss reverse settlement payments in the next sub-section. The two main mechanisms through which multi-party licensing can be achieved are technology (or patent) pools and standard-setting organizations (SSOs). These multi-party arrangements are very common in the high-tech and telecoms industries, as products such as smartphones, memory chips, and digital video equipment require common technology standards which usually incorporate a large number of patented technologies. Competitors must license their technologies to each other in order for the market to function effectively. Counterfactual analysis is again called for: are more competitive outcomes achieved with or without the licensing agreements? The Guidelines recognize that technology pools can be pro-competitive, in that they reduce transaction costs and limit the problem of double marginalization by keeping the cumulative IP royalties in check.[59] Such positive effects must be weighed against the possible restrictive effects on competition. The creation of a technology pool necessarily implies joint selling. Moreover, technology pools may affect innovation by foreclosing alternative technologies, since the existence of a standard may make it more difficult for new and improved technologies to enter the market. **5.76**

The Guidelines cover the creation of the pool and its subsequent licensing out. The intention is that by structuring a pool in compliance with the conditions in the Guidelines, the parties can be certain of the outcome of any competition law assessment—this is intended to encourage the creation of pro-competitive patent pools. The conditions for exemption are: open participation; only essential (and thereby complementary) technologies are pooled, and on a non-exclusive basis; exchange of sensitive information (such as pricing **5.77**

---

[59] Ibid., at [245] *et seq.*

and output data) is restricted to what is necessary; licensing is on fair, reasonable, and non-discriminatory (FRAND) terms (we discuss FRAND in Chapter 8 on remedies); and the parties contributing technology to the pool and the licensees are free to challenge the validity and the essentiality of the pooled technologies, and remain free to develop competing products and technology.[60]

5.5.4 Pay for delay: Reverse settlement agreements between branded and generic pharmaceutical companies

5.78 Originator (branded) and generic pharmaceutical companies are frequently in dispute over the validity or infringement of the branded company's patents. These are often 'process patents' related to the commercial manufacture of the medicine, which typically expire after the patent on the underlying chemical entity (the development of the process by which a new chemical entity can be commercialized comes some time after its initial discovery). In those situations, generic firms may search for new ways of manufacturing a chemical entity, in order to take advantage of the expiry of the underlying product patent as soon as possible. Disputes then arise over whether a generic firm's process is genuinely new, or whether it uses some of the patented technological know-how of the originator company. As litigation proceeds, the originator and generic firm may settle, and this can involve a 'reverse payment' to the latter in exchange for dropping the litigation and delaying entry into the market. Also known as 'pay-for-delay' agreements, such settlements have attracted significant attention from competition authorities. The payments look like hardcore market sharing infringements: one pharmaceutical company paying a potential rival to stay out of the market. But is that an accurate picture?

5.79 The FTC has challenged several pay-for-delay agreements since the early 2000s.[61] In 2015 it settled a lawsuit against Cephalon (which had begun in 2008) after the company promised to pay $1.2 billion in reimbursements to buyers of Provigil (a narcolepsy medicine) who had been overcharged, and to avoid certain reverse payments to generic firms in the future.[62] In Europe, a burst of activity by competition authorities began after the European Commission's inquiry into the sector in 2009.[63] In 2013 the Commission imposed a fine of €93.8m on Lundbeck, and €50.2m on eight generic firms, for agreeing to delay generic competition in the market for Citalopram, an antidepressant.[64] In July 2014 the Commission imposed fines totalling €427.7 million on Servier and five generic firms for agreeing reverse payment settlements with respect to Perindopril, an inhibitor used to treat high blood pressure and heart failure.[65] There are some differences in the treatment of pay-for-delay agreements between the United States and Europe. As set out in *Lundbeck*, the Commission treated the agreements as anti-competitive by their very nature. In contrast, the US Supreme Court ruled in the 2012 *Actavis* case that, in light of the many factors and

---

[60] Ibid., at [261].

[61] For example, *In re. Cardizem CD Antitrust Litigation*, 332 F.3d 896 (6th Cir. 2003); and *Schering-Plough Corp. v Federal Trade Commission*, 402 F.3d 1056 (11th Cir. 2005).

[62] Federal Trade Commission (2015), 'FTC Settlement of Cephalon Pay for Delay Case Ensures $1.2 Billion in Ill-Gotten Gains Relinquished; Refunds Will Go To Purchasers Affected By Anticompetitive Tactics', press release, 28 May.

[63] European Commission (2009), 'Pharmaceutical Sector Inquiry: Final Report', 8 July.

[64] *Lundbeck* (Case AT.39226), Decision of 19 June 2013. We advised one of the generic firms in this case.

[65] *Perindropil (Servier)* (Case AT.39612), Decision of 9 July 2014. We advised one of the generic firms in this case.

complexities that determine the competitive effects of reverse payment settlements, the FTC must still prove its case on a rule-of-reason basis, and cannot presume these settlements to be illegal.[66] Counterfactual analysis is required in these circumstances to take into account these factors and complexities, as we explain below.

5.5.5 Pay for delay: Counterfactual analysis

The economics of pay-for-delay agreements would point to the same conclusion as that of the US Supreme Court: these agreements are not necessarily harmful to competition. In certain circumstances, settlement agreements may facilitate more rapid entry by generic firms rather than delay it. The underlying assumption of the Commission's treatment of pay-for-delay agreements as object infringements is that, in the counterfactual, the generic firm would be in a position to supply the market in the very near future. This may not always be the case. Pay-for-delay agreements relate to an underlying dispute over IP. If the disputed patent were found to be valid, the generic firm would in fact not be able to enter the market, and is therefore not a competitor in the correct counterfactual. The settlement agreement will by definition reduce the generic firm's incentive to continue the existing litigation. However, it is not certain that these agreements will delay entry compared with an appropriate counterfactual. **5.80**

Consider Figure 5.1, which shows a stylized timeline of a patent litigation. The originator enjoys a monopoly position granted by the patent, which is valid until time T. However, at an earlier date t_1, the generic firm challenges the validity of the patent, or claims that its own product does not infringe it. Thus the IP litigation process begins. With the litigation under way, the originator and generic firm have two options: settle the litigation (at time t_2 in Figure 5.1) and agree that the generic firm will enter only at time T; or not settle and continue to litigate until a court decision. The generic firm has a third option, which is to discontinue the litigation at some time before T and simply wait until patent expiry. **5.81**

Of these options, the first and third—settle at time t_2; or discontinue litigation—involve no or limited uncertainty once selected. However, if the originator and generic firm continue to litigate (the second option), the outcome of the litigation and the timing of entry **5.82**

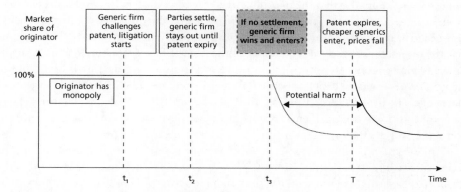

Figure 5.1 Timeline in a patent litigation case

---

[66] *Federal Trade Commission v Actavis Inc*, No. 12–416, 17 June 2013.

are uncertain. To begin with, the date of the court decision is usually uncertain, and the litigation may not in fact be resolved before the originator's patent expires at time T. Even if the litigation is resolved before T (e.g. at time t_3 in Figure 5.1), there is no guarantee that the generic firm would ultimately win the litigation. If the generic firm wins, entry would occur at t_3, and prices would be expected to fall as the generic firm gains market share—as shown by the downward-sloping line after t_3 in the figure. If, however, the originator wins the litigation, the market continues without any entry until patent expiry at time T. Price reductions would occur only after time T, just like in the case of a pay-for-delay agreement (the first option).

5.83 Thus, banning settlement agreements will facilitate entry only if three conditions hold: the generic firm decides to litigate in the absence of a settlement; the litigation is resolved before the patent expiry date; and the generic firm wins the litigation. The treatment of these agreements as an object infringement effectively assumes that these conditions do all hold. However, there are significant uncertainties and complexities inherent in the process of patent litigation, as noted above. The outcome of the patent dispute itself would depend on factors such as the strength or necessity of the originator's patent, the precise process used by the generic firm, and properties of the generic firm's product.

5.84 In its infringement decisions the European Commission pointed to the fact that the settlement values in question were large, and were linked to the generic firm's forgone profits. The Commission saw this as evidence of an anti-competitive object. However, an economic assessment of the uncertainties and incentives of the two parties casts these payments in a different light. In theory, a settlement will occur only if the offered payment is acceptable for both parties, and reflects the expected benefits and costs that both parties face if they continue litigating. The profits expected by the generic firm and the originator (with and without entry) are relevant to this, as are their individual expectations of the strength of their case and the costs of the litigation process. It is legitimate for the originator to expect to earn higher profits in the scenario where its patent is found to be valid. If it is not valid, the generic firm will enter and the originator will suffer a significant reduction in profits. Linking the settlement value to the level of forgone profits therefore has a business rationale.

5.85 An example shows how the difference in benefits and expectations of success can drive settlement values. Suppose that the overall market size for a drug is 100,000 units per year, the price of the product on patent is €1, and marginal production costs are (for simplicity) assumed to be near zero. The originator earns revenue of €100,000 in one year. Now assume that the originator's perceived probability of the generic firm successfully challenging its patent's validity is only 10 per cent, so its expected loss from the litigation is €10,000, and the originator would be happy to settle for any payment less than €10,000. Now assume that the generic firm also perceives its challenge to be weak (though slightly less so): a 20 per cent probability of winning. If entry occurs, the generic firm expects to price its generic version of the drug at €0.20 and capture the whole market (abstracting from any price response from the originator)—thus, its expected profit (again assuming marginal production costs to be near zero) is 20 per cent × 100,000 × €0.20 = €4,000. The generic firm would settle for any payment higher than €4,000. Thus an offer between €4,000 and €10,000 will be accepted, and the costs and uncertainties of litigation will be avoided. You can see that the generic firm's expected profits are, by definition, part of the consideration of the level of any reverse payment in these cases.

An additional feature of the impact of these agreements on entry arises when multiple   **5.86**
generic firms are involved in litigations concerning the same patent (as is often the case).
The incentive for one generic firm to challenge a patent of the originator may be weakened
if it fears that rival generic firms will benefit by free-riding on the litigation. If the patent is
found to be invalid, other firms can enter without bearing any of the litigation costs. This
risk of additional generic entry will lower the benefits to the original generic firm from
winning the litigation, and thereby make it less likely it will take this risk. Settlement agreements between the originator and some generic firms can make continued litigation by one
generic firm more likely. This was the situation in the *Servier* case, where the generic firm
Apotex did not reach an agreement with Servier and continued to litigate.

In all, the economic incentives regarding R&D in the pharmaceuticals industry are com-   **5.87**
plex, and competition law should be careful that interventions are genuinely welfare-
enhancing. An effects-based or rule-of-reason approach would be more appropriate than
an object or per se approach, so as to capture the specific market context and uncertainties
relevant to each case, and to ensure that short-term price reductions for existing medicines
do not come at the expense of the discovery of new ones.

5.6 Finding Cartels: Can Economics Help?

5.6.1 Leniency: Incentive theory at work

In 2007, ABB, one of several companies involved in the gas-insulated switchgear cartel,   **5.88**
escaped a €215 million penalty by blowing the whistle.[67] Its ten co-conspirers were fined
a total of €750 million by the European Commission. From 1988 to 2004 they had been
rigging bids for procurement contracts. You may conclude that ABB got a good deal: it
reaped the benefits of the cartel for many years, and then confessed in time to qualify for
immunity from fines under the leniency rules while making its competitors pay. To an
economist this is incentive theory at work. Companies respond to incentives (see also the
discussion on optimal fines in Chapter 8). This is why the leniency programmes in several
competition regimes have been so successful as a means of uncovering cartel activity. In
most of the European Commission cartel decisions in the last ten years there has been
some form of leniency for one or more of the cartel members. The catch is that you have to
be the first to report the cartel and provide sufficient evidence to the authorities (although
subsequent whistleblowers may get some reduction in the fine too if they co-operate with
the investigation). When Spain introduced its leniency rules in 2008 there were queues of
business people (or rather the competition lawyers representing them) outside the offices of
the national competition authority, hoping to be the first to report their particular cartel.[68]

Potential and actual cartelists will trade off the benefits of collusion against the risk and   **5.89**
severity of punishment. Leniency programmes have a significant impact on this calculation. They substantially increase the risk of punishment: secret meetings may be possible
to organize without the authorities ever finding out, but it takes quite a bit of mutual trust
among cartel members for them not to be constantly worried about one of them running

---

[67] *Gas insulated switchgear* (Case COMP/F/38.899), Decision of 24 January 2007.
[68] 'El primer chivato de un cártel aguarda a las puertas de la CNC', news story on <http://www.cincodias.
com>, 28 February 2008.

off to the authorities in exchange for immunity. Many companies have made the trade-off and decided to report their cartel to the authorities in exchange for leniency. From a policy perspective, leniency programmes are very attractive. Cartels are notoriously diffi-cult to detect without a whistleblower. Significant investigative powers and resources are required. Leniency means that a substantial part of the detection and evidence gathering is made easier by the information provided by the whistleblower. This is also an argument for allowing leniency applications *after* investigations have started, as occurs in the EU, as this still has the benefit of enabling the authority to achieve a successful outcome more efficiently. Whistleblowers such as ABB may escape the fine, but they are not immune to subsequent damages claims by those who have suffered harm from the cartel. From an incentives perspective, therefore, the European Commission's policy of promoting such private actions for damages—discussed in Chapter 9—does run somewhat counter to the leniency policy.

5.90   Economists have sought to develop theoretical and empirical analysis to explore how the leniency rules are working and how they may be improved. One suggestion has been that the first party applying for leniency should receive not just immunity from fines but also a financial reward, to be paid out of the fines collected from the other cartel members (Spagnolo, 2004). The intuition behind this is that such rewards make leniency applica-tions even more attractive. This may be particularly relevant for individual whistleblowers, given the potentially detrimental effects that their actions can have on their careers or personal circumstances. However, aside from the ethical questions that this raises about rewarding collusive activities, there may be a risk of encouraging speculative applications that could waste authorities' time. Another theoretical point made is that leniency can actu-ally result in some undesirable effects—because it lowers the expected costs of participating in cartels, leniency may, perversely, make it more attractive for companies to form a cartel (Motta and Polo, 2003). On the other hand, the possibility of leniency may encourage companies to keep evidence of cartel involvement that they might otherwise be tempted to destroy. A company with limited documentation of its cartel participation will risk being unable to secure leniency, or obtaining it on less favourable terms.

5.91   Empirical analysis of the effects of leniency policy is made difficult by the covert nature of cartels. What would have happened in the absence of the policy is not directly observable since the effects are on an unknown number of current and prospective cartels. What you can observe is the number of cartels that are discovered. If only a few cartels are discovered, this could be due to effective deterrence; however, it is also consistent with poor detection and a large number of undiscovered cartels. One hypothesis might be that, following the introduction of leniency, the number of cartels detected will rise, but then fall again after a period as the increased detection rate leads to deterrence of new cartel activity. A num-ber of empirical studies have analysed the effects of the 1996 introduction of the leniency programme by the European Commission (Brenner, 2009; Stephan, 2009). There is some evidence that the duration of investigations, which is a proxy for their cost, has decreased as a result of leniency—this is consistent with the point made earlier that the information provided by whistleblowers saves the competition authorities time and effort. Fines in cartel cases that made use of the leniency programme have been found to be higher, which could be because leniency allows the Commission to construct a more robust case. Another find-ing is that the duration of cartels involving full immunity was longer than those involving partial immunity, suggesting that leniency helps uncover the more durable cartels. The number of new cartel investigations per year has increased substantially since the introduction of leniency. However, nearly three-quarters of cartel cases opened by the European Commission between 1996 and 2005 as a result of leniency applications had already been under investigation in the United States.

5.6.2 Experimental economics: Leniency and cartel stability

Another set of empirical studies on leniency makes use of experiments, a tool that is increasingly popular among economists, especially where real-world situations are difficult to analyse. Participants in experimental studies make decisions in a controlled setting in return for some reward. The results are monitored electronically. The controlled environment enables multiple trials of the same scenario, allowing a picture to be built up of typical behavioural responses. The participants (often students, or other types of people with time on their hands) are tested to ensure that they understand the rules of the experiment, and they get a financial reward to ensure that they have a stake in the outcome (apparently students can be effectively motivated in this way). An experimental setting allows the creation and stability of cartel behaviour to be monitored under different types of enforcement policy. In experimental cartel studies, participants usually take the roles of the companies setting prices at intervals over time. They are able to discuss price setting among themselves in a structured way so as to allow for the possibility of collusion. The role of the competition authority is reflected in the introduction of a certain probability of detection and a fine. This is then supplemented by offering the opportunity of leniency, where a proportion of the fine will be waived. Over many experimental trials this gives a picture of how prices and cartel formation differ according to the probability of detection and the scale of the fine, with or without leniency.

5.92

These experimental studies show that introducing leniency does indeed have the expected effect of reducing cartel stability and prices (Apesteguia et al., 2006; Hinloopen and Soetevent, 2006; Oxera, 2008). Leniency was found to reduce cartel formation, to increase defection by cartel members, and to increase the price cuts implemented by defectors after leaving the cartel. According to Hamaguchi and Kawagoe (2005), the likelihood of a leniency application is higher the more companies there are in the cartel, but the stability of cartels is not affected by whether the fine reduction is available only to the first company coming forward, or to subsequent ones as well. This suggests that creating a race to be the first leniency applicant may not have much added benefit over and above simply having the leniency policy in the first place. It provides some support for the Commission's policy of giving the greatest fine reduction to the first applicant but then also granting some reductions to latecomers who agree to co-operate fully with the inquiry.

5.93

5.6.3 Economists as detectives?

Thanks to economists such as Steven Levitt, the economics profession has gained some reputation among the wider public for having an ability to spot trends and patterns in data that no one else can see. In the popular economics book *Freakonomics* (Levitt and Dubner, 2005), Levitt described the academic research in which he systematically analysed a large database of test results from the Chicago public school system, revealing that teachers had cheated in around 5 per cent of cases by changing answers on the students' test forms (Jacob and Levitt, 2003). Teachers had an incentive to cheat because they were rewarded according

5.94

to their students' performance. Another of his studies analysed results from sumo wrestling in Japan and confirmed suspicions of match rigging (Duggan and Levitt, 2002). Such economic studies are only just starting to have an impact on competition law. However, there is increasing interest in using quantitative tools to help detect cartels.[69]

5.95 The techniques used for this type of analysis are similar to those for quantifying cartel damages—discussed in Chapter 9—except that here you employ them to detect a cartel in the first place. One important distinction in cartel spotting is that between structural and behavioural features of the market. Focusing on structural features, such as high concentration, homogeneous goods, and inelastic demand, may help identify markets that are more prone to cartelization than others, but it does not get you much closer to identifying actual cartel behaviour, especially since cartels may arise in a wide variety of markets (as we saw in section 5.2). Analysing behaviour seems more promising in this regard. There are two main stages to this. The first is analysing whether something odd is going on, such as company behaviour not being in line with competitive behaviour, or structural breaks in prices or bidding patterns for which there is no apparent 'normal' explanation (such as a change in costs). In competitive industries prices tend to respond to cost and demand shocks; a finding to the contrary could be indicative of cartel behaviour. The second stage is then verifying that the oddity can indeed be ascribed to collusion. One way of testing this is to explore whether the behaviour of the suspected colluding suppliers is different from that of suppliers that are not in the cartel (e.g. suppliers in other geographic markets). Another is to assess whether theoretical models of collusion fit the data more closely than models of competition.

5.96 One prominent study based on the comparator method was that by Porter and Zona (1993), of bid rigging in highway construction contracts tendered by the New York State Department of Transportation. The authors had data on 116 auctions between 1979 and 1985. There were five suspected members of the bidding ring. A model of 'normal' bidding behaviour was estimated using variables such as a company's backlog of projects won in the past but not yet completed, other indicators of available capacity, and location. This model did pretty well in explaining the bidding behaviour by the non-cartel companies. In contrast, the suspected colluders showed a statistically significant deviation from this competitive behaviour. It was also found that the suspects' bid prices had no systematic relationship with their costs, which indicated that they often put in artificially high bids (rather than not bid at all), just to create an appearance of competitive bidding. Another study by the same authors analysed bid rigging in the supply of school milk in Ohio (Porter and Zona, 1999). This used data relating to costs, such as the distance between the milk-processing plant and the school, to explain competitive bidding behaviour (bids can normally be expected to increase with the distance to the school, since transport costs are higher). Three suppliers in one particular area were suspected of bid rigging. Other suppliers (mostly in more distant regions) were not. The study indicated that the bidding behaviour differed systematically between the suspected colluders and the others—the colluders' bids bore no systematic relationship with costs, while those of the unsuspected suppliers did. Harrington (2008) notes that it was ironic that the cartel members' decision to make 'phantom' bids rather than not bid at all ultimately provided the relevant data to help demonstrate the existence of collusion.

---

[69] For an overview, see Harrington (2008).

A main conclusion that can be drawn from these studies is that cartel detection through   **5.97**
economic analysis of data seems most promising in auction markets. The rules of the game
are reasonably clear in these markets, such that competitive and collusive behaviour can be
readily identified and distinguished. Good data on the relationship between bids and the
underlying costs is also usually required. Another conclusion is that the most informative
studies seem to have been those where there was already a suspicion of collusion, such that
the behaviour of the suspects could be compared with that of suppliers not suspected of collusion. Economists will have greater difficulty detecting a cartel from scratch.

Another area where economic and statistical analysis has triggered competition investi-   **5.98**
gations in recent times is in the financial services sector. On 29 May 2008, the *Wall Street
Journal* first flagged unusual patterns in LIBOR (the London Interbank Offered Rate, an
interest rate benchmark that is widely used in financial instruments around the world).[70]
Several global banks reported LIBOR quotes significantly lower than those implied by
prevailing credit default swap rates, which would not normally occur. Empirical economic studies confirmed that the patterns were unusual. Research by Rosa Abrantes-
Metz and others examined in detail the data on LIBOR and the daily submissions by
banks used to determine LIBOR, to investigate whether there were any anomalies.[71] The
authors used two screening techniques: searching for improbable events, and using a control (another financial instrument) to compare against. They concluded that, while the
average level of LIBOR did not appear to be lower than expected, the clustering of bids
was abnormal, particularly in 2007, and the LIBOR submissions made by banks were
inconsistent with other financial performance benchmarks for a number of these banks.
The authors were careful to highlight that this type of statistical analysis cannot yield
conclusive evidence of anti-competitive activity or market manipulation. However, they
concluded that there was 'statistical evidence of patterns that appear to be inconsistent
with those expected to occur under conditions of market competition for certain periods
under study'.[72]

Manipulation of financial market benchmarks such as LIBOR is not necessarily the same   **5.99**
as price fixing. LIBOR is not a market clearing price as such on which the banks compete,
but rather a reference rate, and whether a particular bank desires a higher or lower rate
depends on its particular financial position at that point in time. One can therefore question whether the manipulation of LIBOR is actually a restriction of competition for the
purpose of competition law, since there is no competition as such that is being restricted.
Nevertheless, competition authorities and financial regulators in several jurisdictions have
successfully prosecuted the banks and individual traders involved in the fixing of LIBOR
and related interest rate benchmarks.[73] The use of economic data analysis has proven its
worth in these cases.

---

[70] 'Study Casts Doubt on Key Rate; WSJ Analysis Suggests Banks May Have Reported Flawed Interest
Data for Libor', *Wall Street Journal*, 29 May 2008.

[71] As published later in Abrantes-Metz et al. (2012). Another empirical study is Snider and Youle (2010).

[72] Abrantes-Metz et al. (2012), p. 149.

[73] In the United States, several banks have agreed to plead guilty in connection with manipulation
of LIBOR and to paying significant penalties. The European Commission has also imposed significant
fines. See, for example, Department of Justice (2015), 'Deutsche Bank's London Subsidiary Agrees to Plead
Guilty in Connection with Long-Running Manipulation of LIBOR', press release, 23 April; and European
Commission (2013), 'Antitrust: Commission Fines Banks €1.71 billion for Participating in Cartels in the
Interest Rate Derivatives Industry', press release, 4 December.

5.100 This leaves the policy question of whether competition authorities should apply economic techniques to systematically screen markets for cartel behaviour. We mentioned above that a review of the structural features of markets would be insufficient and therefore any such screening would have to focus on behavioural patterns. Tax authorities systematically analyse data to identify fraudulent tax returns. Financial regulators do the same for insider trading on stock markets. Should competition authorities follow their example? One difference is that competition authorities do not collect data in the same systematic and comprehensive manner. Another is that tax and financial authorities usually know a fraudulent tax return or an instance of insider trading when they see one, or at least they know when to investigate a case further. When odd patterns in pricing and bidding data are detected, there are still many other possible explanations besides cartel behaviour that must be explored before competition authorities can open a formal investigation on this basis. It is not clear whether economists will ever play a prominent role as cartel detectives. Yet in some cases—such as the LIBOR manipulation and the bid rigging in New York highway construction and Ohio school milk contracts—a sophisticated economic analysis showing that cartel behaviour is the most likely explanation for observed patterns in the data can be powerful evidence for competition authorities.

6

VERTICAL RESTRAINTS

6.1 Business Practices, the Law, and the Economics

6.1.1 It's verticals, not cartels

When Apple launched its iPad and iBookstore in 2010, it had signed agreements with five **6.01** major publishers enabling it to match any retail price for e-books that was offered by other book retailers. Dentsply, the leading manufacturer of false teeth in the United States (sold under the Trubyte brand), refused to supply its products to independent dental-product dealers if they sold competing dentures. Pronuptia de Paris, the French maker of wedding dresses and accessories, granted its franchisees in Germany exclusivity in their territories, but did not allow them to open other shops or sell competing wedding dresses. Volkswagen did not allow its dealers in Italy to sell cars to people living outside Italy. To a business person these may seem like everyday examples of producers trying to organize and control their distribution channels. To competition practitioners they are potentially harmful vertical restraints that have been scrutinized in high-profile competition cases.[1]

6.02 There has always been tension between competition law and business arrangements that span vertical supply chains. Section 1 of the US Sherman Act of 1890 prohibits 'every contract, combination in the form of trust, or conspiracy, in restraint of trade', without making the distinction between horizontal contracts between competitors and vertical contracts between companies at different layers of the supply chain. The same is true for Article 101(1) TFEU, which prohibits 'all agreements between undertakings, decisions by associations of undertakings and concerted practices which may affect trade between Member States and which have as their object or effect the prevention, restriction or distortion of competition'. In US antitrust it was recognized early on that horizontal price-fixing agreements are harmful and merit a per se prohibition. But for a long time vertical agreements also received hostile treatment. Per se prohibition of territorial and customer restrictions is found in the Supreme Court's ruling in *Arnold, Schwinn & Co* (1967), which concerned the distribution of bicycles.[2] This changed with the 1977 Supreme Court ruling in *Continental TV v GTE Sylvania*.[3] Sylvania, a manufacturer with a 1–2 per cent share of colour TV sales in the United States, had adopted a new distribution strategy reducing the number of franchisees and not allowing them to sell outside their franchise area. The court viewed this favourably, and overruled the earlier per se prohibition of exclusive territories. It cited a number of economists who had demonstrated that such restrictions can enhance efficiency, including Richard Posner of the Chicago School (Posner, 1976).

6.03 In Europe, recognition that vertical agreements are inherently different from horizontal ones also took some time. In *Maschinenbau Ulm*, a 1966 ruling, the ECJ accepted that an exclusive deal between a manufacturer and a distributor does not infringe Article 101(1) (then 85(1)) by object where it is necessary to penetrate new markets.[4] MBU, a German manufacturer of bulldozers, had granted LTM exclusive distribution rights in France, subject to certain restrictions on LTM regarding the sale of rival bulldozers. A year into the contract a dispute arose over the quality of the bulldozers, and in the ensuing litigation in the French courts LTM argued that the exclusive agreement was void under EU competition law. The question was referred to the ECJ, which ruled that while Article 85(1) covered both horizontal and vertical agreements, the economic context and effect of this type of exclusive agreement needed to be considered when assessing whether competition is restricted:

> The competition in question must be understood within the actual context in which it would occur in the absence of the agreement in dispute. In particular it may be doubted whether there is an interference with competition if the said agreement seems really necessary for the penetration of a new area by an undertaking.[5]

---

[1] *United States v Apple Inc.* No. 13-3741 (2d Cir. 2015); *United States v Dentsply International, Inc* 399 F 3d 181 (3d Cir. 2005); Case 161/84 *Pronuptia de Paris GmbH v Pronuptia de Paris Irmgard Schillgallis* [1986] ECR 353, [1986] 1 CMLR 414; and *VW* (Case IV/35.733), Decision of 28 January 1998.

[2] *United States v Arnold, Schwinn & Co* 388 US 365 (1967).

[3] *Continental TV Inc v GTE Sylvania, Inc.* 433 US 36 (1977).

[4] Case 56/65 *Société Technique Minière (LTM) v Maschinenbau Ulm GmbH (MBU)*, [1966] ECR 234, [1966] 3 CMLR 244.

[5] Ibid., at p. 250.

Thus the ECJ set the scene for counterfactual analysis under what is now Article 101(1): what **6.04** would competition be like in the absence of the agreement? This is where economists come in. In *Pronuptia de Paris*, a 1986 ruling, the CFI accepted that some, but not all, restrictions in franchise agreements are necessary for legitimate commercial purposes such as protection of the brand.[6] We return to this case below. The economic approach to vertical agreements received a boost in 1999 and 2000 when the European Commission issued a Block Exemption Regulation and Guidelines on Vertical Restraints.[7] These recognized explicitly that vertical agreements can have efficiency benefits, and that they are usually of little concern if the parties involved have low market shares. Both the Regulation and Guidelines were further reformed in 2010.[8]

6.1.2 Efficiencies and competition concerns

The changes in the treatment of vertical agreements reflect an increased understanding of **6.05** the economic rationale for, and effects of, such agreements. Economists have highlighted with formal analysis what business people have known for ages: if you want your products to reach consumers efficiently, it makes sense to enter into agreements with your distributors, and such agreements necessarily contain certain mutual commitments and restrictions. Vertical agreements do not necessarily have anti-competitive motives. Nor, more importantly, do they always have negative effects on consumers; quite the opposite in fact— economics has shown that vertical agreements often contribute to greater efficiency and consumer welfare, and indeed there can be a presumption that a vertical agreement is likely to be pro-competitive, as is reflected in the 2010 Guidelines:

> Vertical restraints are generally less harmful than horizontal restraints...In vertical relationships...the activities of the parties to the agreement are complementary to each other. This means that the exercise of market power by either the upstream or downstream company would normally hurt the demand for the product of the other. The companies involved in the agreement therefore usually have an incentive to prevent the exercise of market power by the other.[9]

The aim of an upstream manufacturer is generally to encourage its retailers to sustain and **6.06** increase sales of its products, and one of the main ways of doing this is to sign agreements with retailers which provide for low retail prices. Vertical agreements can also be aimed at promoting a high quality of service; this is consistent with promoting high volumes. Thus, in general, the interests of buyers and sellers are aligned in expanding sales to end-customers rather than in seeking to restrict sales. This is unlike a horizontal restraint, where the parties are competitors and will directly benefit from co-ordinating decisions to increase prices or reduce output. Moreover, it is obviously necessary for vertically related firms to communicate, and enter into agreements, with one another because they are engaged in a direct commercial supply relationship.

---

[6] Case 161/84 *Pronuptia de Paris GmbH v Pronuptia de Paris Irmgard Schillgallis* [1986] ECR 353, [1986] 1 CMLR 414.

[7] Regulation 2790/99 on the application of Article 81(3) of the Treaty to Categories of Vertical Agreements and Concerted Practices, [1999] OJ L336/21, [2000] 4 CMLR 398; and European Commission (2000), 'Guidelines on Vertical Restraints', 13 October.

[8] Regulation 330/2010 of 20 April 2010 on the application of Article 101(3) of the Treaty on the Functioning of the European Union to Categories of Vertical Agreements and Concerted Practices; and European Commission (2010), 'Guidelines on Vertical Restraints', 2010/C 130/01.

[9] European Commission (2010), 'Guidelines on Vertical Restraints', 2010/C 130/01, at [98].

6.07 The *Sylvania* ruling relied heavily on such insights from the Chicago School and other contemporaneous economists. It held that even if the reduction in the number of Sylvania retailers affected intra-brand competition—between sellers of Sylvania TVs—any market power by retailers was still constrained by inter-brand competition from other TV brands. RCA was the leading TV manufacturer, with a market share of 60–70 per cent. Sylvania had used its aggressive franchise plan to grow its market share from 1–2 per cent to 5 per cent. Moreover, the court acknowledged that vertical restraints can promote inter-brand competition by allowing the manufacturer to achieve efficiencies in the distribution of its product. Sylvania used the restraints to induce the more competent and aggressive retailers to engage in promotional activities and provide service and repair facilities, while at the same time preventing free-riding on these efforts by rival retailers.

6.08 Since the heyday of the Chicago School, economists have developed further theoretical and empirical understanding of vertical restraints. Newer theories are often rooted in principal–agent theory, where the supplier is the principal and the distributor is the agent. Vertical contracts are used in this context to align incentives and resolve information asymmetries between the two. This literature has in fact identified a greater variety of circumstances where the economic efficiency justifications for vertical restraints may *not* hold. Indeed there are some types of vertical agreement that are deemed to constitute hardcore 'object' infringements, such as RPM. Nevertheless, many economists would still agree that vertical restraints generally serve the purpose of making the distribution of goods more efficient, and that they are of concern only when inter-brand competition is weak. Most industries tend to do a reasonable job at organizing their vertical supply chains effectively, and vertical agreements and restraints are an integral part of this. A number of empirical economic studies have shown that where competition authorities or governments *have* intervened in the prevailing vertical relationships, the resulting market outcomes have not always made consumers better off (Lafontaine and Slade, 2008).

6.09 In the last few years, vertical restraints have received renewed attention in the context of online markets. Classic vertical restraints such as exclusive dealing, territorial restrictions and pricing restrictions abound in the online world. Not only has the internet become an alternative sales channel for physical products, it has also enabled the creation and spread of entirely new digital products. Do the economic insights on vertical restraints apply in the same manner to the digital world as they do to the physical distribution of products?

6.1.3 The remainder of this chapter

6.10 Competition law faces the challenging task of assessing whether the efficiency effects of vertical agreements outweigh the anti-competitive effects. In this chapter we set out the basic economic principles. We start in section 6.2 by explaining the main efficiency rationales for vertical restraints. These are important in understanding the economic context of a vertical agreement, and in EU competition law often come in under Article 101(3) which deals with exemptions for restrictive agreements. Not all vertical restraints cases require a comprehensive balancing exercise. In section 6.3 we discuss how counterfactual analysis can often provide insight into whether there is actually a restriction of competition in the first place—in Europe this assessment fits under Article 101(1). Section 6.4 discusses the foreclosure effects of vertical restraints; these were also dealt with in Chapter 4 on abuse of dominance, and here we discuss whether the assessment under Article 101 should be any different. Section 6.5 considers two types of vertical restraint that continue to receive hostile treatment from competition authorities: RPM, where a supplier imposes the price at which the distributor can sell the product; and territorial restrictions along national boundaries, which in Europe are seen as violating the single-market objective. RPM in vertical agreements may have the effect of enabling horizontal co-ordination, a theme we saw in Chapter 5 where we discussed hub-and-spoke agreements. Finally, in section 6.6 we deal with vertical restraints in online markets and explore the extent to which these raise new or different challenges for competition law. One particular type of vertical restraint that has come under scrutiny in this context is the MFN clause, the *Apple* e-books case mentioned at the start of this chapter being one example.

6.2 Economic Rationales for Vertical Restraints

6.2.1 The problem of double marginalization

Economists in the nineteenth century not only developed formal models showing the prob-   **6.11** lem of monopoly, they also discovered what is worse than a monopolist: a succession of monopolists. If, on its way from producer to end-consumer, a product passes through a series of intermediaries, and each intermediary wishes to earn a profit margin on top of the costs incurred, you get a situation known as double (or multiple) marginalization—a problem first identified by French mathematician/economist Antoine Augustin Cournot.[10] Vertical agreements can be used as a means to overcome the double marginalization problem, as we explain here. Vertical mergers are another way of dealing with the problem (as discussed in Chapter 7), as are bundling and tying, when double marginalization arises in the context of horizontal or vertical complement goods (as discussed in Chapter 4).

The pepper trade in the fifteenth century illustrates the problem. Peppercorns travelled a   **6.12** long way from the fields of southern India to north-west Europe. This trade route had existed since at least the time of the Romans, but in medieval Europe there was a very strong demand for pepper and other spices from the East. Arab and Indian ships would take peppercorns up the Red Sea and Persian Gulf. They would then be transported over land to important trading hubs in the Levant and Egypt, such as Damascus and Alexandria, controlled (interchangeably) by local rulers or bigger powers, such as the Mamluk Sultanate and the Ottomans. Access to Europe was controlled by Venice (or from time to time by one of its rival city states such as Genoa). Every time the peppercorns changed hands, the price went up, as each trader wanted to earn a healthy profit margin. And so did each local ruler imposing a duty on trades. By the time they reached the kitchens of (rich) consumers in the Low Countries, France, and England, the price was about fifteen times higher. What was essentially a basic commodity in South Asia became a luxury good in Europe (used as currency and a status symbol as much as for culinary purposes). Too many middlemen all wanted their slice, and all would have liked the others to reduce prices to increase demand.[11]

---

[10] Cournot (1838). The 'Cournot effect' refers to a situation in which complementary goods are sold separately, which is analytically similar to having the same good sold by successive intermediaries. The first paper to formalize the double marginalization problem in the context of a vertical chain was Spengler (1950).

[11] You can find accounts of the spice trade not only in history or culinary books. Economic history has developed as a separate branch of economics (with a Nobel Prize in 1993 for two leading proponents, Robert Fogel and Douglass North). Economists have extensively studied fifteenth-century prices of pepper and other spices from contemporary sources. The exact price differential for pepper between Asia and Europe is difficult to pin down, and prices fluctuated wildly over the century, but a factor of fifteen has been suggested. See Lane (1968) and O'Rourke and Williamson (2006).

6.13 An important finding in economics is that such a situation of multiple profit margins on top of each other is bad for everyone involved. End-consumers face a very high price, which only some are willing and able to pay. Because of this high price, the last intermediary—the local merchant in Antwerp or York—sells only a small amount of the product, and by implication purchases only a small amount from the previous merchant. And so it goes all the way back to the original producer. The producer and every intermediary in the chain sell less pepper than they would like. Consumers would already be better off if only one, or a few, of the intermediaries kept any price rise limited to the level of costs incurred (marginal cost), without charging a monopoly premium on top. As to the intermediaries, economics shows that collectively they would be best off if only one of them charged a monopoly price and the rest passed the product on at cost. This 'single marginalization' would maximize the total profits in the chain. It would also benefit consumers since the final price is lower—they pay only one monopoly premium, not multiple ones. Obviously, for the single marginalization approach to work, the intermediaries need some mechanism to co-ordinate their pricing and share the monopoly rents—this is where vertical agreements (and vertical integration) come in. In the fifteenth century, the scope for such co-ordination among the rivalrous traders and rulers would have been rather limited. The best attempt at achieving a single monopoly was when the Portuguese bypassed the whole overland trading route by reaching South Asia by sea (Columbus had sailed the wrong way in 1492, but Vasco da Gama was successful in sailing east round the Cape of Good Hope in 1498). The Portuguese did not manage to establish a lasting monopoly—the overland route via Venice remained active, and later the Spanish, Dutch, and English weighed in with their naval power. This rivalry did eventually succeed in making pepper and other spices more affordable to the average European consumer.

6.14 Co-ordination between the vertical partners in a supply chain can overcome double marginalization. The most direct and complete form of co-ordination is vertical integration. A looser form is through vertical agreements. Producers may restrain their distributors from setting prices above a certain level, possibly in return for a side payment (reflecting a share of the greater total profits) or some other concession. Another method is quantity forcing, whereby the producer requires the distributor to purchase or sell a minimum number of products that corresponds to the single marginalization output. A third type of vertical restraint to avoid double marginalization is for the supplier to set a two-part charge to the distributor—a fixed and a variable charge. This method has some sophisticated economic theory behind it, but the principle is commonly applied in practice. The producer sells the product to the distributor (say, a franchisee) at a price per unit that equals marginal cost. This way the franchisee still buys the optimal quantity of the product, avoiding the output-reducing effect of double marginalization. The franchisee is then the one in the chain that gets to set a profit margin on top of its costs, but the supplier extracts the profits thus earned (in part or in full) through the fixed franchise fee.

6.2.2 Free-rider problems: Other manufacturers

6.15 A basic justification for vertical restraints centres round the free-rider problem. There are two categories of free-riders in this context: rival producers and rival distributors. Economists often express the problem in terms of an externality: one party makes an effort, thereby benefiting another party that does not contribute to the effort itself. In economics jargon, vertical restraints are a means to internalize the externality, and align the interests of the parties along the supply chain.

As to the first free-rider category—rival producers—a manufacturer may wish to promote **6.16** the effective distribution of its products by investing in the distribution channel. It may provide general training to the sales staff, or invest in the look and feel of the distribution outlets. Ice cream producers may provide retail stockists with a freezer cabinet; Pronuptia de Paris may assist franchisees with the interior design of the sales outlets. The value of this investment would be diminished if rival producers then used the same outlets without contributing to the investment—they would be free-riding. As a result, the first producer may not wish to make the investment. Consumers are worse off if this affects the distribution channel: fewer shops would sell ice cream; the experience of buying a wedding dress would not be the same. Vertical restraints can be used to prevent this free-rider problem. The supplier may require the distributor not to sell rival products. This is commonly referred to as exclusive dealing or single branding. Unilever imposed such restraints on the retail outlets to which it had provided freezer cabinets free of charge—no competing ice cream brands were allowed in the cabinets.[12] A softer variant of exclusive dealing is where the manufacturer requires that its products represent a minimum percentage of the retailer's sales. Pronuptia de Paris imposed this on its franchisees—they had to purchase 80 per cent of their wedding dresses and accessories from Pronuptia, together with a specified proportion of cocktail and evening dresses, and could purchase the remainder only from suppliers approved by Pronuptia.

6.2.3 Free-rider problems: Other distributors

As to the second free-rider category—rival distributors—a producer may want its distribu- **6.17** tors to provide pre- and after-sales services to consumers if it believes that this enhances the sales or the reputation of its products. You may value the retailer giving you a demonstration of the technical features of the latest tablet computer or smartphone, or allowing you to test-drive a new car. This service has a cost (sales staff time is money) which the retailer will want to recover. Now suppose that after the product demonstration or test drive you go to the discount dealer next door or online, where no such pre-sale service is provided, and you buy the same product at a lower price. The discount dealer is effectively free-riding on the full-service retailer's efforts. This can lead to a situation where the latter is unwilling to provide any pre-sales services at all. Again, the effectiveness of the producer's distribution network would be diminished, and consumers would be worse off. To avoid such an outcome, the producer may grant each distributor an exclusive territory such that there are no discount dealers next door (Sylvania and Pronuptia de Paris both used milder variants of exclusive territories in their franchise systems). Alternatively, the supplier may impose a minimum retail price (known as RPM) such that any discounting by dealers is ruled out. More recently, some manufacturers have sought to prevent online distribution of their products on the grounds that a face-to-face sales element is necessary for appropriate use of the product or to maintain brand or product quality perceptions. We discuss this in more detail in section 6.6.

---

[12] Case C-552/03 P *Unilever Bestfoods (Ireland) Ltd, formerly Van den Bergh Foods Ltd v Commission* [2006] ECR I-9091.

6.18 All these vertical restraints addressing the second free-rider problem are intended to reduce intra-brand competition between distributors. Note that there is some tension with the double marginalization rationale that we saw earlier: reducing intra-brand competition means giving each distributor a bit more market power, which may bring you back to the problem of having too many profit margins taken throughout the chain. The free-rider justification for vertical restraints may also be a bit outdated in some industries. Now when you buy a new tablet or smartphone you can access a number of pre-sales services online— product demonstrations, reviews, user guides—even if some manufacturers and consumers still prefer product demonstrations by sales staff, and test-driving a new car is difficult to do online. Likewise, post-sales services (repairs, maintenance) can be charged for directly by retailers. Market dynamics in distribution channels change over time, and economic arguments for and against vertical restraints must be applied carefully to the specific facts of the case at hand. The free-rider problem must be shown to be of some importance first, and then weighed against the possible anti-competitive effects of the restraint.

6.19 One US case where the relevance of the free-rider argument was tested involved the vertical restraints imposed by a retailer, Toys 'R' Us, rather than a manufacturer.[13] The FTC had found that Toys 'R' Us, a 'giant in the toy retailing industry', had orchestrated a horizontal agreement among toy manufacturers through the creation and enforcement of multiple vertical agreements in which each manufacturer promised to restrict supply of its products to low-priced warehouse club stores on the condition that other manufacturers would do the same. The court upheld the FTC's findings, and dismissed the free-rider argument put forward by Toys 'R' Us in defence of the restraints. Until the late 1980s, Toys 'R' Us accounted for approximately 20 per cent of all toy sales in the United States, but enjoyed a particularly strong position because it was the only specialist retailer that offered a full range of toys in its stores (around 11,000 individual toy items). As stated by Judge Diane Wood (a well-known commentator on antitrust law):

> The toys customers seek in all these stores are highly differentiated products. The little girl who wants Malibu Barbie is not likely to be satisfied with My First Barbie, and she certainly does not want Ken or Skipper. The boy who has his heart set on a figure of Anakin Skywalker will be disappointed if he receives Jar-Jar Binks, or a truck, or a baseball bat instead. Toy retailers naturally want to have available for their customers the season's hottest items, because toys are also a very faddish product, as those old enough to recall the mania over Cabbage Patch kids or Tickle Me Elmo dolls will attest.[14]

6.20 This market position came under threat in the early 1990s when warehouse clubs also began to offer a greater range of toys. As the name suggests, warehouse clubs provided only very basic retail services and sold at low prices, albeit only to members who paid an annual fee of around $30. This competitive threat prompted Toys 'R' Us to impose vertical restraints on manufacturers. These were somewhat different from standard vertical restraints in that they were driven mainly by the retailer rather than the manufacturer. Toys 'R' Us was seen as a critical outlet for toy manufacturers, even for the large ones such as Hasbro and Mattel. One of the defences presented by Toys 'R' Us was that its actions were a legitimate response to free-riding by the warehouse clubs. The court rejected this argument:

> The manufacturers wanted a business strategy under which they distributed their toys to as many different kinds of outlets as would accept them: exclusive toy shops, [Toys 'R' Us],

---

[13] *Toys 'R' Us, Inc v Federal Trade Commission* 221 F 3d 928 (2000). See also Scherer (2009).
[14] *Toys 'R' Us, Inc v Federal Trade Commission* 221 F 3d 928 (2000), at [2].

discount department stores, and warehouse clubs...The manufacturers did not think that the alleged 'extra services' [Toys 'R' Us] might have been providing were necessary. This is crucial, because the most important insight behind the free rider concept is the fact that, with respect to the cost of distribution services, the interests of the manufacturer and the consumer are aligned, and are basically adverse to the interests of the retailer (who would presumably like to charge as much as possible for its part in the process)...Furthermore, we note that the [FTC] made a plausible argument for the proposition that there was little or no opportunity to 'free' ride on anything here in any event. The consumer is not taking a free ride if the cost of the service can be captured in the price of the item. As our earlier review of the facts demonstrated, the manufacturers were paying for the services [Toys 'R' Us] furnished, such as advertising, full-line product stocking, and extensive inventories...On this record, in short, [Toys 'R' Us] cannot prevail on the basis that its practices were designed to combat free riding.[15]

6.2.4 The hold-up problem: Relationship-specific investments

The hold-up problem is another classic rationale for vertical restraints. Sometimes **6.21** new business ventures require close co-ordination and combined efforts between two parties at different layers of the vertical chain. Take the example of a low-cost airline approaching an under-utilized regional airport and convincing it that there is a commercial opportunity to develop and grow the airport. Low-cost airlines have done this successfully across Europe in the last ten to fifteen years. The two parties sign a ten-year agreement that contains certain commitments and restrictions on both sides. While somewhat different to the standard manufacturer–retailer relationship, the airport and the airline are in a vertical relationship (the former provides an input to the latter), and this is therefore a form of vertical agreement. For the venture to succeed, the airport first needs to invest significantly in upgrades to its passenger terminal and handling facilities. Before it makes the investment, it requires some guarantees that the airline is indeed going to use the airport. The airline therefore commits to base a minimum number of aircraft at the airport for the duration of the agreement (a base is the airport where an aircraft stays overnight and is maintained). The airline even agrees to not fly from the main rival airport in the vicinity for the ten years—a form of exclusive dealing. In the absence of these upfront commitments by the airline, the airport would run the risk of being held to ransom by the airline after the completion of the investment, since the airline can threaten to walk out at that point. Economists call this a hold-up problem— like the free-rider problem, it is an externality that can be internalized by means of a vertical restraint. At the same time, to make the venture a success, the airline must invest significantly in setting up the base and in promoting the airport as a new destination or departure point. This investment is highly specific to the new venture, and would have to be written off if the airport didn't stick to its part of the deal (the investment in the terminal). To reassure the airline, the airport guarantees that the airline will get substantial discounts on its landing and handling charges. This avoids a hold-up of the airline's investment.[16]

---

[15] Ibid., at [7–8].
[16] There is some confusion regarding terminology: does hold-up refer to the investment being held up (as in obstructed or delayed), or to the party making the investment subsequently being held up by the other party (as in robbed at gunpoint)? It does not really matter. Both interpretations capture the essence of the problem: the relationship-specific investment would not be made in the absence of the vertical restraint.

6.22   Thus, the hold-up problem has two main characteristics: the required investment is highly specific to the vertical relationship, and it is sunk (i.e. not recoverable upon exit). Both these characteristics are usually a matter of degree. The investment by the airport in its terminal and handling facilities is largely sunk—the full value cannot be recovered should the airport cease to operate, and must therefore be compensated through operating profits over a sufficient period of time. However, it is not necessarily relationship-specific, since the facilities can also be used to serve other airlines (if other airlines can be attracted to the airport). The airline's investment in advertising the new flights from the airport is both sunk and relationship-specific, but is lower in magnitude and can therefore be earned back more quickly. Given these characteristics, the investments by both parties require some mutual assurances, and vertical restraints are a common means to provide these.

6.23   A more extreme example of relationship-specific investments resulting in hold-up problems would be where the airport organizes a competitive tender for a new railway service to be set up between the airport and the nearest city. The owner of the railway would want some guarantees from the airport about minimum usage of the service before building it (possibly by means of the airport taking on some of the volume risk). It may also seek to restrain the airport from promoting other rail, bus or taxi services that compete directly with the railway. For its part, the airport would want assurance that the railway, once established, does not charge monopoly prices and thereby reduces the number of passengers (a combination of the hold-up and double marginalization problems). Again, an ex ante vertical agreement between the airport and the rail operator can solve these problems.

6.2.5 The hold-up problem: Required contract duration

6.24   Once an investment has been identified as relationship-specific, financial analysis can help identify what a reasonable duration for the exclusivity or other restraints would be. Over what period can the party making the investment be expected to make a sufficient return to cover the investment and risk? We discussed the techniques for profitability and investment analysis in Chapter 3. As in damages cases (discussed in Chapter 9), this analysis of expected profitability must be carried out on an ex ante basis, from the position that the investor was actually in at the time of investment.

6.25   The required contract duration is again a matter of degree. The European Commission's 2010 Guidelines on Vertical Restraints do not view exclusive supply agreements favourably if they last longer than five years, on the basis that 'agreements lasting longer than five years are for most types of investments not considered necessary to achieve the claimed efficiencies or the efficiencies are not sufficient to outweigh the foreclosure effect of such long-term exclusive supply agreements'.[17] However, while five years may be a useful indication of the threshold that competition authorities are likely to apply, it is in essence an arbitrary number. The optimal payback period depends on the size of the initial investment, the profile of the expected returns over time, and the required cost of capital.

6.26   In some cases long contract durations have been accepted in light of the nature of the investments made. In its 2014 ruling in *Estación de Servicio Pozuelo*, the ECJ stated that an exclusive purchase agreement with a thirty-year duration could be lawful.[18] This agreement

---

[17] European Commission (2010), 'Guidelines on Vertical Restraints', 2010/C 130/01, at [195].
[18] Case C-384/13 *Estación de Servicio Pozuelo 4 SL v GALP Energía España SAU*, Judgment of 4 December 2014.

involved Galp, a fuel supplier, building a fuel service station on land owned by Pozuelo in Spain, and subsequently letting the operation of the station to Pozuelo. As part of the agreement, Pozuelo was required to purchase fuel products exclusively from Galp for thirty years. This arrangement involved relationship-specific investments since the station was built on a specific site and could not easily be used for other purposes. It would also seem clear that such an investment cannot easily be earned back in a short period. The ECJ did not consider thirty years excessive given that exclusive purchase agreements of twenty to thirty years were common in this industry. Another important factor to the ECJ was that Galp had a market share in petrol products of less than 3 per cent, while it faced three major competitors which between them had more than 70 per cent. The court determined that in these circumstances there was no appreciable restriction of competition under Article 101(1).

6.2.6 Other distribution efficiencies achieved through vertical restraints

There are other efficiencies in distribution that vertical restraints may seek to achieve. **6.27** Producers may want to restrict the number of distributors in each area if there are economies of scale in distribution. Car manufacturers tend to limit the number of dealers in a town to one or two—market demand would be too small to justify ten or fifteen dealers, each with their own showroom and service facilities. A vertical restraint imposing some form of exclusive territory for each distributor makes commercial sense in these situations. An additional efficiency is that such a restraint can provide distributors with greater incentives to promote the product. This is especially important when a producer seeks to enter a new geographic market, as recognized by the ECJ in the 1966 *Maschinenbau Ulm* judgment that we saw previously.[19] The distributor with the exclusivity has the right incentives to do its best to promote the product, and will share in the rewards if it succeeds. This means that the interests of the principal and the agent are aligned.

Restraints that limit intra-brand competition may also induce distributors to maintain **6.28** optimal (from the supplier's perspective) stock levels. A publisher launching a new title, supported by an advertising campaign, will want bookshops to keep a sufficient number of copies in stock in order to avoid disappointed customers in the event of the book becoming a bestseller. Bookshops, however, may be reluctant to order too many copies—should the title not be successful, they would run the risk of other bookshops beginning to discount, and their inventory ending up in the bargain basement. RPM and exclusive territories can prevent such early discounting and hence reduce the inventory risk to distributors. Against this, you might say that in many countries the scrapping of minimum book prices has led to a vast expansion of outlets that sell books at accessible prices, including supermarkets and Amazon (e-books have further undermined the traditional book distribution model, as we discuss in section 6.6).

Finally, a well-known justification for vertical restraints is that they can assist in protect- **6.29** ing the producer's brand and reputation. We saw earlier that the *Pronuptia de Paris* ruling accepted that certain restrictions in franchise agreements are necessary in order to achieve legitimate commercial purposes such as protection of the brand.[20] Suppliers like Pronuptia

---

[19] Case 56/65 *Société Technique Minière (LTM) v Maschinenbau Ulm GmbH (MBU)*, [1966] ECR 234, [1966] 3 CMLR 244.
[20] Case 161/84 *Pronuptia de Paris GmbH v Pronuptia de Paris Irmgard Schillgallis* [1986] ECR 353, [1986] 1 CMLR 414.

want to be associated with a certain image, and it matters to them how the retail outlets convey this image in terms of design, decoration, and other products being sold. Such a defence was rejected by the ECJ in the *Pierre Fabre* online selective distribution case, which we also discuss in section 6.6.[21] Likewise, manufacturers of products such as cars and washing machines may want to control which spare parts are used in their products, or who provides repairs and maintenance for them, if they perceive a risk to their reputation should something go wrong with a third-party supplier. You can see how this kind of restraint may lead to concerns about foreclosure of the spare parts and maintenance markets (aftermarkets). We discussed this under bundling and tying in Chapter 4.

6.2.7 Vertical restraints as a bargaining outcome: Sharing the pie, and 'jilted distributors'

6.30 Another, more prosaic, rationale for vertical restraints is that they may simply reflect a bargaining outcome between producer and distributor. Fights over how the pie is shared occur all the time. The outcome usually depends on who has greater bargaining power. As explained above, the total pie in the chain would be largest if only one party charged the monopoly price—but which party will achieve this? At one extreme are markets where very large suppliers deal with very small distributors (large airlines and small travel agents may be an example, albeit one that is becoming less common). The supplier keeps the monopoly profit; the distributors recover only their marginal costs. At the other extreme are markets with very small suppliers that deal through very large retailers (farmers and supermarket chains are an example). Here the retailer gets to keep the profits and the suppliers recover only their marginal costs. In between are situations where the bargaining power is more balanced, either because both parties have a strong market position (in which case vertical restraints can be used to avoid the otherwise inevitable double marginalization), or because both operate in very competitive markets (in which case there are fewer competition concerns).

6.31 If a vertical restraint has an impact only on who gets the biggest share of the pie, it does not necessarily have a negative effect on the consumer. What ultimately matters, from an economic perspective at least, is the effect of the restraint on consumers and on competition in the market overall. If there is one layer in the chain that earns a monopoly rent, it does not matter much to end-consumers which layer it is—final prices and quantities are the same. This is not to say that all vertical restraints are of this nature. Sometimes the interests of the supplier and distributor are more aligned, and the two may conspire against the interest of the consumer. Even if the complaint is indeed motivated by a struggle over the rents, or appears opportunistic as one party wishes to get out of an agreement that it signed voluntarily, there may still be negative effects on competition and consumers. In any event, when you are presented with a complaint by one of the parties about a vertical agreement, it is worth checking whether it is motivated by a dispute over the rents in the vertical chain. If so, it should not be automatically assumed that there is a competition problem. The European Commission recognized this principle in the context of the food supply chain, where disputes between suppliers and supermarkets over vertical contracts are common:

> Contractual imbalances associated with unequal bargaining power are tackled through policy tools other than competition law instruments, such as, for example, contract law,

---

[21] Case C-439/09 *Pierre Fabre Dermo-Cosmétique SAS v Président de l'Autorité de la concurrence* [2011] ECR I-9447.

common agricultural policy, SME policy, or unfair commercial practices laws... EC anti-trust law is not concerned with particular outcomes of contractual negotiations between parties unless such terms would have negative effects on the competitive process and ultimately reduce consumer welfare. It is not the aim of EC competition rules, as currently devised, to interfere in the bargain struck between contractual parties, in the absence of proven competitive harm.[22]

6.32 In the United Kingdom a code of practice was introduced in 2001 to govern the relations between the major supermarkets and their suppliers. Over the next few years there continued to be many complaints by suppliers and smaller retailers that supermarkets were using their bargaining position unfairly. In 2008 the CC completed another market investigation, and proposed a strengthened and extended Groceries Supply Code of Practice, to be overseen and enforced by an independent ombudsman.[23] This independent body is now up and running and in the last year has opened one investigation and participated in two arbitrations; however its main focus is on encouraging the large retailers to comply with the Code.[24]

6.33 US antitrust law has developed the principle of the 'jilted distributor', 'who loses a manufacturer's franchise and accuses the manufacturer and the new suitor of attempting to monopolize something'.[25] In US case law it is usually considered reasonable for manufacturers to terminate contracts with distributors and choose their own business partners, a principle that goes back to the '*Colgate* doctrine', discussed in Chapter 4.[26] In *Dunn Mavis* (1975), Chrysler replaced the company that had transported trucks from its plant in Warren, Michigan, for thirty years. The court found that transport of Chrysler trucks was not a relevant market (or 'relevant line of commerce', as it was referred to then), and that there was no harm to inter-brand competition since Chrysler did not dominate the market for trucks:

> Since the complaint does not allege facts suggesting that Chrysler's refusal to deal had any significant anti-competitive effect on the market, there is no rule of reason case alleged. Chrysler's substitution of one auto transport company for another at its Warren plant does not limit competition in any substantial sense. A contrary decision would limit without reason the normal principle that a buyer is entitled to choose among various sellers who offer competing products or services.[27]

6.34 In an earlier case, *Burdett v Altec Corp* (1975), involving a contract for carrying out sound engineering services on behalf of Altec, a manufacturer of sound equipment, the court sent out a warning to 'jilted distributors':

> Lest any other former distributors succumb to the temptation of treble damages, we reiterate that it is simply not an antitrust violation for a manufacturer to contract with a new

---

[22] European Commission (2009), 'Competition in the Food Supply Chain', staff working document accompanying the Communication from the Commission to the European Parliament, the Council, the European Economic and Social Committee and the Committee of the Regions on 'A Better Functioning Food Supply Chain in Europe', COM(2009) 591, p. 18.
[23] Competition Commission (2008) 'The Supply of Groceries in the UK—Market Investigation' 30 April, at [46–47].
[24] Groceries Code Adjudicator (2015) 'Annual Report and Accounts', 20 July, p. 22.
[25] *Dunn Mavis, Inc. v Nu-Car Driveaway, Inc.*, 691 F.2d 241 (6th Cir. 1982).
[26] *United States v Colgate & Co* 250 US 300 (1919).
[27] *Dunn Mavis, Inc. v Nu-Car Driveaway, Inc.*, 691 F.2d 241 (6th Cir. 1982).

distributor, and as a consequence, to terminate his relationship with a former distributor, even if the effect of the new contract is to seriously damage the former distributor's business.[28]

6.3 Is a Restraint a Restriction? Counterfactual Analysis under Article 101(1)

6.35 Vertical restraints can have positive effects on competition and efficiency. A legal question that arises is at what stage of the analysis you take these positive effects into account and weigh them up against the possible anti-competitive effects. The EU competition rules have a structure where vertical agreements that restrict competition are prohibited under Article 101(1), but may be exempt under Article 101(3) if they contribute to greater efficiency and consumers receive a fair share of the benefits. This two-part structure allows efficiencies to be taken into account in the second stage, thus potentially offsetting the restrictive effects found under the first part. The economic rationales of vertical restraints may also be taken into account under Article 101(1) itself, not as a balancing exercise as such, but to better understand the economic context of the agreement. In many circumstances a vertical restraint on one party's freedom is not a restriction of *competition* as such. This occurs when the competitive situation in the absence of the restraint is worse than with the restraint. Counterfactual analysis is called for here (we also discussed this in Chapter 5 in the context of horizontal agreements). As summarized by the English High Court in the *BAGS v AMRAC* judgment concerning exclusive broadcast rights for horseracing:

> When considering the alleged effect on competition, an economic approach is called for. The approach must be realistic. There must be a proper market analysis of the position with the relevant restriction and the position in the absence of the relevant restriction. Not every restriction on conduct amounts to a restriction on competition, much less to a significant restriction on competition.[29]

6.36 We saw an early example of this approach in *Maschinenbau Ulm*, in which the ECJ accepted that an exclusive deal between a manufacturer and a distributor may not infringe Article 101(1) where it is necessary to penetrate new markets.[30] In *Pronuptia de Paris*, the CFI stated that 'the provisions of franchise agreements for the distribution of goods which are strictly necessary for the functioning of the system of franchises do not constitute restrictions of competition for the purposes of Article 85(1)'.[31] The court found this to apply to provisions that prevent the know-how and assistance provided by the franchisor from benefiting its competitors (akin to the free-rider problem discussed earlier), and to provisions that establish the control necessary for maintaining the identity and reputation of the franchisor. However, customer or location restrictions in the franchise agreement were considered to restrict competition. The *Pierre Fabre* ruling gives further clarity on the grounds for finding

---

[28] *Burdett v Altec Corp.*, 515 F.2d 1245, 1249 (5th Cir. 1975).

[29] Case 161/84 *Bookmakers Afternoon Greyhound Services Limited & Ors v Amalgamated Racing Limited & Ors* [2008] EWHC 1978 (Ch), 8 August 2008, at [452]. We acted as economic experts for the defendants in these proceedings.

[30] Case 56/65 *Société Technique Minière (LTM) v Maschinenbau Ulm GmbH (MBU)*, [1966] ECR 234, [1966] 3 CMLR 244.

[31] *Pronuptia de Paris GmbH v Pronuptia de Paris Irmgard Schillgallis* [1986] ECR 353, [1986] 1 CMLR 414, summary, at [2].

selective distribution arrangements to be an object infringement (discussed further in section 6.6). The ECJ stated that:

> the organisation of such a network is not prohibited by Article 101(1) TFEU, to the extent that resellers are chosen on the basis of objective criteria of a qualitative nature, laid down uniformly for all potential resellers and not applied in a discriminatory fashion, that the characteristics of the product in question necessitate such a network in order to preserve its quality and ensure its proper use and, finally, that the criteria laid down do not go beyond what is necessary.[32]

While Pierre Fabre had maintained that its cosmetics needed to be sold by a qualified phar- **6.37** macist, they were not prescription-only products; hence the court rejected the claim that it was necessary for them to be sold by a pharmacist. Furthermore, it found that: 'The aim of maintaining a prestigious image is not a legitimate aim for restricting competition and cannot therefore justify a finding that a contractual clause pursuing such an aim does not fall within Article 101(1) TFEU.'[33]

The *BAGS v AMRAC* judgment found that Article 101(1) did not apply because a degree **6.38** of exclusivity over broadcast rights was necessary for a new entrant (AMRAC) planning to take on an incumbent broadcaster (SIS), which had controlled the market for live horserac- ing broadcasting for twenty years:

> The evidence clearly showed that a course would receive less revenue from granting nonex- clusive rights to two operators as compared with granting exclusive rights to one operator. What was happening in that period was that competition between BAGS/SIS on the one hand and AMRAC on the other took the form of competition to take exclusive licences. That activity was how a competitive market worked, not anti-competitive behaviour...
>
> It is commonplace for media sports rights to be sold on an exclusive basis. When there is competition for the purchase of such rights, exclusivity is favoured by the purchaser and by the seller, for proper commercial reasons. Exclusivity gives the purchaser the ability to dif- ferentiate his service downstream. Exclusivity gives the seller greater revenue. Where there is competition, the grant of exclusive rights is the natural form for that competition to take.[34]

From an economic perspective, considering the counterfactual situation in the absence of **6.39** the vertical restraint makes sense as part of the assessment under Article 101(1). It allows you to ask whether a restraint is a restriction in the first place. The answer to this question is no if the competitive situation would be worse in the absence of the restriction. There was a monopoly for twenty years in the provision of horseracing broadcasting services to bookmakers before AMRAC entered on the back of exclusive contracts with roughly half of the British racecourses. Competition was not found to be restricted in these circumstances. Carrying out such a counterfactual analysis under Article 101(1) gives greater weight to the inherent efficiencies and competition-enhancing effects that vertical restraints can bring about. The balancing approach under Article 101(3) also acknowledges efficiencies, but it implicitly assumes that vertical agreements are inherently restrictive—after all, Article 101(1) comes before Article 101(3). The burden of proof under Article 101(3) is on the defendant

---

[32] Case C-439/09 *Pierre Fabre Dermo-Cosmétique SAS v Président de l'Autorité de la concurrence* [2011] ECR I-9447, at [41].

[33] Ibid., at [46].

[34] Case 161/84 *Bookmakers Afternoon Greyhound Services Limited & Ors v Amalgamated Racing Limited & Ors* [2008] EWHC 1978 (Ch), 8 August 2008, at [465] and [468].

and can be a high hurdle in practice. The burden of proof under Article 101(1) is on the claimant or competition authority.

6.4 Foreclosure Effects of Vertical Restraints

6.4.1 Vertical restraint or abuse of dominance?

6.40 The main competition concern about vertical restraints is that they may be used to foreclose access of competitors to inputs or distribution channels. Dentsply was accused of foreclosing the access of rival false-teeth manufacturers to independent dental-product dealers; Unilever of shutting out rivals from the impulse ice cream market by denying them access to freezer cabinets in retail outlets. Hence, is this foreclosure concern not exactly the same as that relating to abuse of dominance? And if so, should the analysis of the economic effects of vertical restraints be the same as that for abuse of dominance? From an economic perspective, the answer to this is probably yes. An exclusive distribution arrangement between a supplier and distributor is more likely to foreclose competition the greater the degree of market power of the producer, and the greater the distributor's importance relative to other sales channels.

6.41 Dentsply had a stable market share of 75–80 per cent for a number of years and its dealer network represented 80 per cent of all laboratory dealers, so the US court ruled in 2005 that its exclusivity requirements were anti-competitive.[35] Unilever's freezer cabinet exclusivity was condemned under both Articles 101 and 102. Unilever had a market share in Ireland of close to 80 per cent for several years, and around 40 per cent of retail outlets were effectively foreclosed to competitors. These restrictive effects were found to outweigh the possible efficiency benefits. The Commission considered that the freezer exclusivity did not promote inter-brand competition, and that without it there would still be plenty of freezer cabinets left in the market.[36] Arnold, Schwinn & Co, whose exclusive distribution system was prohibited per se in 1967, had been the leading bicycle manufacturer in the United States, with 22 per cent of the market in the early 1950s, and selling through twenty-two bicycle wholesalers which, in turn, supplied a large number of specialized dealers with whom Arnold, Schwinn & Co had a franchise arrangement.[37] In subsequent years it lost market share to other manufacturers and to alternative distribution channels such as the large retail chains. Sylvania had only 1–2 per cent of the colour TV market, growing to 5 per cent, as we saw before. In these last two cases, significant foreclosure would seem unlikely. All these factors are no different from those that are considered in abuse of dominance cases. We therefore refer you to Chapter 4 for the economic principles that are relevant to the foreclosure effects of vertical restraints.

6.42 There are few competition statutes that explicitly treat vertical restraints and abuse of dominance under the same standard. The first statute to do so was Mexico's Federal Law

---

[35] *United States v Dentsply International, Inc* 399 F 3d 181 (3d Cir. 2005).

[36] Under some pressure from the European Commission during the investigation stage, Unilever offered retailers the option to hire the freezer cabinet instead of getting it free of charge (thus reducing the scope for free-riding), but not many retailers took up this option. *Van den Bergh Foods Limited* (Cases IV/34.073, IV/34.395, and IV/35.436), Decision of 11 March 1998; and Case C-552/03 P *Unilever Bestfoods (Ireland) Ltd, formerly Van den Bergh Foods Ltd v Commission* [2006] ECR I-9091.

[37] *United States v Arnold, Schwinn & Co* 388 US 365 (1967).

of Economic Competition, enacted in 1992 and amended in 2006 and 2014.[38] Articles 54 to 56 of this law place all business practices that are not hardcore cartels, so vertical and unilateral practices, in the category of 'relative monopolistic practices'. These are then prohibited if the responsible party has substantial market power (comparable to a dominance test) and if competition is unduly foreclosed (an effects-based test). EU policy regarding vertical restraints also identifies foreclosure as one of the main consequences of concern. The 2010 Guidelines on Vertical Restraints stress that foreclosure is more likely the greater the degree of market power of the supplier and the distributor.[39] In line with this emphasis on the degree of market power to assess foreclosure, the block exemption for certain types of vertical agreement applies where the producer or distributor has a market share below 30 per cent.[40] The guidelines also state that 'if inter-brand competition is fierce, it is unlikely that a reduction of intra-brand competition will have negative effects for consumers', and that 'single branding obligations are more likely to result in anti-competitive foreclosure when entered into by dominant companies'.[41] Yet the Commission stops short of equating the analysis of foreclosure under Article 101 to that of abuse of dominance:

> Appreciable anticompetitive effects are likely to occur when at least one of the parties has or obtains some degree of market power and the agreement contributes to the creation, maintenance or strengthening of that market power or allows the parties to exploit such market power…The degree of market power normally required for a finding of an infringement under Article 101(1) is less than the degree of market power required for a finding of dominance under Article 102.[42]

The reason why the required degree of market power is less for appreciable effects than for dominance is not given. From an economic perspective, if foreclosure is the concern, the same criteria are relevant. One formalistic difference is that Article 101 is about agreements between two parties, while Article 102 is about unilateral conduct. However, the means by which a practice arises—by mutual agreement or by one party imposing it, or some combination of the two—should not really matter when it comes to assessing the effects on competition. Under the current legal framework in the European Union, if there happens to be an agreement between two parties a lower threshold for intervention is applied than if the conduct were unilateral. **6.43**

6.4.2 Networks of agreements: The beer cases

One situation in which competition authorities may want to intervene without there being an abuse of dominance is where distribution channels are foreclosed by a 'network' of vertical agreements. If there are, say, ten producers each with a 10 per cent market share (so no one is dominant), and every distributor in the market deals exclusively with one of the ten producers, the distribution channel is as foreclosed to a new producer wishing to enter as in a situation where a monopoly producer has such exclusive deals. The ECJ confirmed this **6.44**

---

[38] Ley Federal de Competencia Económica, *Diario Oficial de la Federación*, 23 May 2014.

[39] European Commission (2010), 'Guidelines on Vertical Restraints', 2010/C 130/01.

[40] Commission Regulation (EU) 330/2010 of 20 April 2010 on the application of Article 101(3) of the Treaty on the Functioning of the European Union to categories of vertical agreements and concerted practices.

[41] European Commission (2010), 'Guidelines on Vertical Restraints', 2010/C 130/01, at [102] and [133].

[42] Ibid., at [97].

principle of cumulative foreclosure in *Delimitis* (1991), a case concerning a vertical agreement between a brewery and the owner of a pub in Frankfurt:

> A beer supply agreement is prohibited by Article 85(1) [now 101(1)] if two cumulative conditions are met. The first is that, having regard to the economic and legal context of the agreement at issue, it is difficult for competitors who could enter the market or increase their market share to gain access to the national market for the distribution of beer in premises for the sale and consumption of drinks. The fact that, in that market, the agreement in issue is one of a number of similar agreements having a cumulative effect on competition constitutes only one factor amongst others in assessing whether access to that market is indeed difficult. The second condition is that the agreement in question must make a significant contribution to the sealing-off effect brought about by the totality of those agreements in their economic and legal context. The extent of the contribution made by the individual agreement depends on the position of the contracting parties in the relevant market and on the duration of the agreement.[43]

6.45 Concerns about distribution channels being foreclosed (or 'sealed off') through the cumulative effect of separate exclusivity deals were also at the heart of the UK government's intervention in the vertical structure of the beer market in 1989. This followed a report by the MMC which found that 75 per cent of pubs in the United Kingdom were owned by brewers and sold their beer exclusively.[44] Another 12.5 per cent of pubs were tied to a particular brewer through an arrangement that granted exclusivity in exchange for a loan at below market rates of interest. There were six national brewers that represented 75 per cent of the beer market (Allied, Bass, Courage, Grand Metropolitan, Scottish & Newcastle, and Whitbread)—none of them had a dominant position. The brewers argued that the exclusivity allowed them to control the product quality from the producer through to the consumer, and that it allowed thousands of small entrepreneurs into the pub business with minimal capital expenditure. Yet as the MMC noted, 'Eloquently though the industry's case has been put, we are not persuaded that all is well.'[45] It considered that the exclusivity restricted consumer choice and foreclosed independent brewers and wholesalers from access to the pub distribution channel. Over time, the MMC found, the vertical structure served to 'keep the bigger brewers big and the smaller brewers small'.

6.46 As a remedy it recommended a ceiling of 2,000 on the number of pubs or other beer-selling premises which any brewery may own, and the elimination of all loan ties. The government then issued the 'Beer Orders' in 1989 in order to enforce the vertical separation in line with the MMC recommendations. Eventually around 14,000 premises were divested by the national brewers. While not reviewed under Article 101, the UK beer case is an example of where a competition authority intervened because a series of vertical agreements had the cumulative effect of foreclosing the distribution channel, without there being a dominant producer. The vertical separation and untying of exclusivity between brewers has been shown to have produced mixed results: some increase in consumer choice, but also in beer prices. In part this is because the new market structure saw the development of large pub chains that began to act as intermediaries between brewers and pubs, which in itself created problems of bargaining power and exclusivity (Waterson, 2009; Slade, 1998).

---

[43] Case C-234/89 *Stergios Delimitis v Henninger Bräu AG* [1991] ECR I-935 [1992].
[44] Monopolies and Mergers Commission (1989), 'The Supply of Beer', March.
[45] Ibid., at [1.18].

6.5 'Hardcore Vertical Restraints': Resale Price Maintenance and Exclusive Territories

6.5.1 Resale price maintenance

We saw above that RPM can have positive effects on efficiency in distribution, just as   **6.47**
other types of vertical restraint can. Preventing distributors from discounting may provide
them with better incentives to promote the product, to offer pre-sales services, or to keep
optimal stock levels. You can also see the difference with horizontal price fixing: cartels
eliminate inter-brand competition; RPM eliminates only intra-brand competition, and
does not directly affect inter-brand competition (though it may dampen it indirectly, as
discussed below).

Yet competition law has invariably treated RPM with hostility, at least until very recently.   **6.48**
The US Supreme Court outlawed the practice in its 1911 *Dr Miles* judgment.[46] Dr Miles
Medical Company produced proprietary medicines by means of 'secret methods and for-
mulas', and determined the prices at which wholesalers and retailers could sell them. The
justifications put forward by Dr Miles were not unlike those discussed in section 6.2: independent pharmacists needed a fair profit in return for promoting the products; the big
department stores had begun a cut-price system which created 'much confusion, trouble,
and damage' and 'injuriously affected the reputation' of Dr Miles's medicines; and without
RPM the majority of pharmacists would be unwilling to keep the medicines in stock. The
Supreme Court rejected this defence and imposed a per se prohibition, because it considered that RPM had as its sole purpose the restriction of competition and fixing of prices.
However, a century and much criticism from economists later, the Supreme Court over-
ruled *Dr Miles* in the 2007 *Leegin* judgment.[47] Leegin was a designer and manufacturer of
women's leather accessories (such as belts, handbags, and shoes), which it sold to independent small boutiques and speciality stores across the United States under the Brighton brand.
Leegin had implemented the 'Brighton Retail and Promotion Policy', which involved
refusing to sell Brighton products to retailers that discounted below its 'suggested retail
prices'. The justification for such a policy was to provide retailers with a margin that allowed
them to offer top-quality customer service. Leegin also expressed concern that discounting
harmed Brighton's brand image and reputation. A few years later it introduced the 'Heart
Store Program', through which it offered a number of incentives to retailers in exchange
for selling at its suggested prices. One 'jilted' retailer—Kay's Kloset—sued Leegin when
its supply contract was suspended because it had sold below the suggested price. A lower
court awarded damages to Kay's Kloset under the *Dr Miles* per se prohibition. However,
the Supreme Court determined that vertical price restraints are to be judged under a rule of
reason, recognizing economic principles:

> Economics literature is replete with procompetitive justifications for a manufacturer's use
> of resale price maintenance, and the few recent studies on the subject also cast doubt on the
> conclusion that the practice meets the criteria for a per se rule. The justifications for vertical
> price restraints are similar to those for other vertical restraints.[48]

---

[46] *Dr Miles Medical Co v John D Park & Sons Co* 220 US 373 (1911).
[47] *Leegin Creative Leather Products, Inc v Psks, Inc, dba Kay's Kloset...Kay's Shoes* 551 US 877, 127 S
Ct 2705 (2007).
[48] Ibid., at [2] Syllabus/[2708].

6.49 In Europe, RPM is considered a 'hardcore' vertical restriction that cannot qualify for a block exemption.[49] However, the 2010 Guidelines on Vertical Restraints do acknowledge its potential efficiency benefits, such that individual exemptions may be granted under Article 101(3).[50] The main potential harmful effect of RPM that is now emphasized in the guidelines is that it may facilitate collusion among suppliers or distributors, in a similar way to hub-and-spoke arrangements, as discussed in Chapter 5. This theory of harm is different from the emphasis in *Dr Miles*, which was on the fixing of resale prices in its own right, without reference to horizontal collusion concerns.

6.5.2 Maximum, recommended, and communicated retail prices

6.50 Two variants of this vertical restraint are maximum resale prices and recommended resale prices. These practices raise fewer competition concerns than standard RPM where minimum prices are set, and they are generally treated more favourably under competition law. In terms of efficiencies, maximum resale prices may be a useful mechanism to address the problem of double marginalization—distributors are prevented from raising prices beyond a certain level. As to potential negative effects, you could verify whether the maximum resale prices serve as a focal point to facilitate horizontal collusion among suppliers or distributors in the same way that RPM may. The boundaries between recommended and fixed retail prices may not always be clear-cut—Leegin also started with 'suggested retail prices'. In these cases the key is to analyse the extent to which recommended prices are in fact adhered to, or are functioning as a focal point for price setting.

6.51 Nor does every communication between manufacturer and retailer about prices necessarily amount to RPM. Such communications may serve useful business purposes—for example, the manufacturer may want to give the retailer some guidance on what price levels are sustainable as it knows the market for its product better; or the retailer may require some assurance from the manufacturer before stocking the product that rival retailers are not getting the product at a cheaper price. You can see that it is not easy to determine where such communications become anti-competitive. A prohibition per se, or by object, may not be suitable in these circumstances. Considering the actual effects of the practices may be more insightful. We saw the example of the 2010 tobacco hub-and-spoke case in the United Kingdom in Chapter 5.

6.52 In another UK case the OFT investigated communications about price between DBA, makers of the Shock Absorber sports bra, and three major department store chains (Debenhams, House of Fraser, and John Lewis).[51] Extensive email and other documentary evidence was gathered on such communications, and the concern was that these were aimed at fixing minimum retail prices for Shock Absorber products. The parties maintained that these communications were part of normal commercial dealings between manufacturer and retailer. The actual effects on price levels were also considered by comparing prices in other periods and for similar products. The CMA, the OFT's successor, closed the investigation

---

[49] Commission Regulation (EU) 330/2010 of 20 April 2010 on the application of Article 101(3) of the Treaty on the Functioning of the European Union to categories of vertical agreements and concerted practices, Article 4(a).

[50] European Commission (2010), 'Guidelines on Vertical Restraints', 2010/C 130/01, at [225].

[51] Competition and Markets Authority (2014), 'Sports Bras Resale Price Maintenance Investigation; Case Closure Summary', 13 June. We advised one of the department stores on this case. See also Oxera (2014).

in 2014 after finding that the parties had provided credible alternative explanations for their email exchanges and that there were no clear effects on price levels.

6.5.3 Exclusive territories in the EU

Prices of new cars have always varied significantly across EU Member States, much to the chagrin of consumers, and of the European Commission. In the 1990s, savvy VW and Audi drivers in Germany decided to order their new cars from dealers in northern Italy, where prices were 20–30 per cent lower. Volkswagen clamped down hard on its Italian VW and Audi dealers through its vertical agreements in order to prevent such cross-border selling. Their sales were closely monitored; their bonuses cut if they were caught selling to non-residents; and scripts handed out on what they should say to German customers as to why they could not possibly buy their car in Italy. The Commission considered this to be a restriction of competition by object under Article 101(1)—placing it in the same category as hardcore cartels and RPM—and fined the car maker €102 million (reduced to €90 million on appeal).[52] Other car manufacturers, including Opel, Mercedes-Benz, and Peugeot, were targeted for similar practices.[53] The Commission's actions against such export restrictions in vertical agreements have covered a wide range of products, from consumer electronics and sports equipment to alcoholic beverages and pharmaceuticals. Why this strict approach, especially since in section 6.2 we discussed how exclusive territories for distributors may provide the right incentives and improve distribution efficiencies? Was Volkswagen not entitled to shield its German car dealers, which were understandably disgruntled by this unplanned intra-brand competition from their Italian counterparts?

6.53

The answer lies not so much in the economics of vertical restraints as with the objective in the EU Treaty of creating a single market. Restrictions on dealers that prevent the movement of goods across borders do not sit well with this broader European policy objective, even if they have some efficiency rationale. This does leave the European Commission with a conundrum: it does not wish to rule out territorial restrictions per se and therefore has to draw the line somewhere. The way it has sought to do this is by reference to 'active' and 'passive' sales.[54] Active sales are defined as actively approaching individual customers through means such as direct mail and other targeted advertising methods. Passive sales means responding to unsolicited requests from individual customers, or engaging in general advertising. Restrictions on active sales may qualify for the block exemption under certain circumstances, but restrictions on passive sales may not. You can see how this line may not always be clear-cut. Presumably, VW may legally prevent its Italian dealers from distributing leaflets in Germany, but not from selling to Germans who happen to walk into their showroom. And what about the growth of sales over the internet? According to the 2010 Guidelines, using a website to advertise and sell products is a form of passive sales, but territory-based banners on third-party websites are a form of active sales into the territory where these banners appear. However, the internet has moved on since, and the distinction

6.54

---

[52] *VW* (Case IV/35.733), Decision of 28 January 1998; Case T-62/98 *Volkswagen AG v Commission* [2003] ECR II-2707, [2000] 5 CMLR 853; and Case C-338/00 *Volkswagen AG v Commission* [2003] ECR I-9189, [2004] 4 CMLR 351.

[53] *Opel* (Case COMP/36.653), Decision of 20 September 2000; *Mercedes-Benz* (Case COMP 36.264), Decision of 10 October 2001; and *SEP et autres/Automobiles Peugeot SA* (Case COMP/36.623), Decision of 5 October 2005.

[54] European Commission (2010), 'Guidelines on Vertical Restraints', 2010/C 130/01, at [51] *et seq.*

between active and passive sales is becoming ever more blurred. We return to this in the next section.

6.55 The cases against export restrictions in car distribution agreements have highlighted another issue where the current legal treatment of vertical restraints is not necessarily consistent with the economics. Article 101 covers agreements between undertakings. It does not cover vertical restraints between companies that share a degree of legal ownership, that is, where producer and distributor are vertically integrated, or where the distributor acts as an 'agent' for the supplier. The 2010 Guidelines on Vertical Restraints contain a detailed explanation of when a vertical agreement can be considered an agency agreement—in essence, distributors are considered agents if they bear very limited financial and commercial risk in relation to the agreement in question.[55] Again, from an economic perspective, the effects on efficiency and competition are in principle the same, and yet the legal treatment is different. An example of where this leads to a somewhat odd result is the *DaimlerChrysler/Mercedes-Benz* case.[56] The restrictions imposed on Mercedes-Benz dealers in Germany were in essence the same as those in the *Volkswagen* and other cases, but the CFI annulled the fine imposed on Mercedes because it was established that the German dealers acted as agents of the car maker. Mercedes bore the principal risk. The dealers did not buy the cars for resale, were not required to hold a stock of new vehicles, and did not set the resale price. Some economists have been a bit puzzled by these legal distinctions, and have wondered whether they may lead companies to adopt certain forms of vertical relationship purely because they receive a more favourable treatment under competition law, and not for efficiency reasons.

6.6 Vertical Restraints in Online and Digital Markets

6.56 Online retailing has grown significantly in the last decade. With it has come increasing competition law scrutiny of arrangements between retailers and suppliers over pricing and availability of products online and in bricks-and-mortar outlets. Online shopping venues and price-comparison websites give consumers access to a wide variety of suppliers, enable suppliers to reach many more customers, and enhance market transparency and growth. The internet itself increasingly functions as a distribution channel for digital products such as e-books and media streaming services. Online and digital markets give rise to the same challenges that suppliers face in traditional distribution channels: How can suppliers prevent free-riding by online discounters on the customer service offered in a face-to-face environment? How can hold-up problems be resolved when launching new online products? We consider a number of recent cases involving selective distribution and MFN in online markets.

6.6.1 Selective distribution: Cosmetics (not) online

6.57 Pierre Fabre Dermo-Cosmétique, a French company selling cosmetics and personal care products under the Klorane, Ducray, Galénic, and Avène brands, came under scrutiny for blocking sales of its products over the internet. Pierre Fabre's products are not classified as medicines, but its distribution contracts stipulated that sales must be made in

---

[55] Ibid., at [12–21].
[56] Case T-325/01 *DaimlerChrysler AG v Commission* [2005] ECR II-3319, [2007] 4 CMLR 559.

the presence of a qualified pharmacist. It wished to ensure that consumers were well-informed about the appropriate product to purchase given their specific health or beauty concerns, and that they understood the technical and scientific characteristics of the products. In addition, Pierre Fabre considered the face-to-face aspect of the sales process to be important to its brand positioning, underlining the luxury, high-quality nature of its products. These vertical restraints had the effect of preventing all forms of selling of Pierre Fabre products over the internet. In 2008, the French competition authority ordered Pierre Fabre to allow online sales of its products, and on appeal the case was referred to the ECJ.[57]

In its 2011 judgment, the ECJ confirmed the authority's finding that the selective distribution arrangements of Pierre Fabre infringed Article 101 by object.[58] Although Pierre Fabre had a market share of only 20 per cent, its arrangements did not benefit from the safe harbour of the Vertical Block Exemption because the restriction on online sales was seen to affect both active and passive sales. The ECJ recognized that there could be a justification for selective distribution restrictions where they enhance competition on factors other than price, including quality and technology. However, it rejected Pierre Fabre's efficiency arguments relating to quality, customer service, and brand in this particular case. It did not consider that the products required the presence of a pharmacist, given that they were not medicines and the pharmacist was not generally involved in the sale process. The ECJ also rejected brand enhancement as a legitimate efficiency justification for a manufacturer to refuse online distribution. **6.58**

This approach was in line with earlier rulings—for example, the ECJ's *Ker-Optika* judgment of 2010 regarding the online distribution of contact lenses in Hungary.[59] Such rulings may open up a broader range of channels for customers to source products from, but they may also limit the ability of suppliers to organize the distribution of their own products in the way they consider most efficient. As we noted before, a strict approach towards vertical restraints in distribution contracts may encourage companies to adopt certain forms of vertical relationship purely because they receive more leniency under competition law, rather than for efficiency reasons. In this case, a business may decide to integrate vertically and supply only through its own retail outlets (online and physical), so as to be able to control its brand image, the customer experience, and pricing. **6.59**

6.6.2 Most-favoured-nation clauses: The online hotel bookings cases illustrating the principles

When companies promise you that they 'will match any price' if you find the product cheaper elsewhere, you may wonder what the catch is. Is it just some clever marketing ploy that assumes that most customers will not bother to compare prices so actively? Sometimes it is, and you can benefit as a customer if you do make the effort. But meeting-the-competition policies are also a means by which competitors signal to each other that **6.60**

---

[57] Autorité de la concurrence (2008), 'Internet sales of parapharmaceuticals: the Conseil de la concurrence orders Pierre Fabre Dermo-cosmétique to amend its contracts to allow distributors to sell its products online', press release, 29 October.

[58] Case C-439/09 *Pierre Fabre Dermo-Cosmétique SAS v Président de l'Autorité de la concurrence* [2011] ECR I-9447, Judgment of 13 October 2011.

[59] Case C-108/09 *Ker-Optika bt v ÀNTSZ Dél-dunántúli Regionális Intézete* [2010] ECR I-0000, Judgment of 2 December 2010.

any price cut by one of them will be matched (after it has been duly reported by a customer), thus reducing the incentive to offer discounts in the first place.

6.61 The same applies to MFN clauses (also referred to as most-favoured-customer clauses). The term is borrowed from the World Trade Organization rules, which establish the principle of the most-favoured nation in international trade agreements: any trade privileges (such as lower import tariffs) offered to a third party must be extended to the counterparty, so that the counterparty remains a 'most-favoured nation' at all times. MFN clauses are commonly used in vertical distribution agreements, including in online markets. They stipulate that a seller will offer its good or service to the distributor or retailer on terms that are as good as the best terms offered to third parties. Scrutiny of these terms under competition law has increased with the advent of online retailing and price-comparison websites, and the concern is that these clauses may dampen competition and provide a price floor in the market.

6.62 A prominent example is MFNs in the online hotel bookings market, which have been investigated in many jurisdictions. Through an MFN, a hotel guarantees to an online travel agent (OTA) that it will receive the best room prices among those offered to all OTAs. In some cases, the clauses also prevent the hotels themselves from offering better deals through their own websites or to last-minute 'walk-in' customers. The main concern of competition authorities is that these clauses can dampen competition among OTAs and increase prices to consumers. In several jurisdictions MFNs in hotel bookings have now been banned or the hotels and OTAs have agreed to remove them.[60]

6.63 To understand the authorities' concerns, it is useful to first set out the two main business models under which MFNs typically operate. The first is the merchant or wholesale model. Here the hotel offers the product to an OTA on wholesale terms (say €200 per room per night), and the OTA sets the retail price to customers (e.g. €210, thus making a profit of €10). A wholesale MFN agreement in this case would typically stipulate that the hotel cannot provide the same room to a different OTA at a 'wholesale' cost of less than €200. However, OTAs are free to set the final price to consumers at any level (for example, a competing OTA may set a retail price of €205, undercutting the other OTA while making a lower profit margin). Such wholesale MFNs, in isolation, maintain the freedom of retailers to set prices and hence are usually not considered problematic.

6.64 The second business model is the agency model. Here an OTA is considered to be an 'agent' of the hotel and has no involvement in price-setting decisions. Thus, competing OTAs would advertise rooms of the same hotel at the respective prices which are set by the hotel itself (e.g. the hotel sets a price of €210, which is then advertised by the OTAs). For every booking the OTA receives a commission, which may depend on the price of the room (e.g. 5 per cent, so a commission of €10.50). In this case, an MFN clause between an OTA and the hotel may stipulate that the hotel cannot advertise the same (or a similar) room for a lower price through any alternative OTA or any other sales channel, including the hotel's

---

[60] See, for example, Bundeskartellamt (2013), 'Online hotel portal HRS's "best price" clause violates competition law—Proceedings also initiated against other hotel portals', press release, 20 December 2013; and Autorité de la concurrence (2015), 'Online hotel bookings sector: the Autorité de la concurrence, in coordination with the European Commission and the Italian and Swedish authorities, has obtained particularly extensive commitments from Booking.com aiming to boost competition between online booking platforms and give hotels more freedom in commercial and pricing matters', press release, 21 April.

own website—that is, the hotel guarantees to the OTA that no other OTA or website advertises below the price of €210.

In online hotel bookings, the concern has been primarily about the latter business model: retail MFN clauses under agency agreements. A retail MFN that covers a large proportion of sales channels will prevent the hotel from 'rewarding' low-commission OTAs through setting lower prices for their offerings. OTAs that are protected by such an MFN will not be concerned about being undercut by rival OTAs when negotiating an increase in their commission (because the hotel will be bound by the MFN not to reflect the higher commission in the price advertised through this OTA). Thus, there is likely to be a lower incentive for agents to reduce commission rates (and therefore prices). MFNs may also undermine market entry. For example, a new OTA wishing to advertise lower prices to consumers will not be able to do so in the presence of MFN clauses between existing agents and sellers.

6.65

6.6.3 Balancing the effects of most-favoured-nation clauses

MFN clauses were also scrutinized in the 2014 investigation into the motor insurance market in the United Kingdom.[61] The CMA found that certain types of MFN between motor insurance providers and price-comparison websites restricted competition between these websites. Two types of MFN existed in this market. The first was 'wide' MFNs, where the insurance provider had to offer prices to a price-comparison website that were no higher than those offered through any other price-comparison website, or through the provider's own website. The other type was 'narrow' MFNs, which stipulate that the price advertised through a specific price-comparison website cannot be higher than that offered through the provider's own website, but make no reference to other price-comparison websites. The CMA found that the wide MFNs restricted competition between price-comparison websites, dampening the incentive to lower commissions. It also found that the narrow MFNs did not raise substantial concerns, mainly because they did not restrict prices advertised through other price-comparison websites. This case therefore drew another useful distinction between types of MFN—wide and narrow—in addition to the distinction between wholesale and retail MFNs described above.

6.66

Given the recent scrutiny and negative views of MFN clauses, should they not be regarded as anti-competitive per se? From an economic perspective the answer is no. MFNs can deliver benefits similar to those of other vertical restraints. Perhaps most obviously, MFN clauses can benefit consumers directly. By allowing retailers to advertise 'lowest-price offers', consumers are assured that they will find the best available price on a single platform. This, in turn, can significantly reduce search costs. MFNs also assist in overcoming hold-up problems. By preventing the supplier from offering better terms to other retailers, and from undercutting the retailer via the supplier's own sales channels, MFNs can prevent free-riding on a retailer's investment.

6.67

The extent to which an MFN clause is likely to harm competition will depend on a combination of factors, including the type and scope of the clause—wholesale and narrow MFNs are deemed less problematic overall compared with retail and wide MFNs. The competitive

6.68

---

[61] Competition and Markets Authority (2014), 'Private Motor Insurance Market Investigation: Final Report', 24 September. We advised one of the insurance providers in this investigation.

effect also depends on the extent of use of similar clauses by other suppliers and agents in the market; the payment arrangements in place (e.g. the structure of the commission rates); and the market structure and positions of the respective suppliers and retailers. Use of MFNs by smaller retailers is likely to be of less concern, as these clauses may enable them to become competitive. Recent findings in the academic literature also show that MFNs can assist market entry—for example, when the payment to the retailer is based on profit-sharing rather than revenue-sharing arrangements, and when the potential entrant has a less differentiated and higher-cost business model than the incumbent.[62] On the whole, a per se prohibition of MFNs seems unwarranted.

6.69   A US court dealing with a case against MFNs in the online hotel bookings market in 2014 considered that the effects of MFNs on intra-brand competition were not of concern.[63] The court regarded MFNs in this sector simply as the result of hotels and OTAs defending their own market position independently by rationally adopting similar vertical distribution agreements. Concerns about the effects of MFNs on inter-brand competition do play a role on US antitrust law, especially where there is evidence of collusive behaviour. We turn to this now in discussing the *Apple* e-books case.

6.6.4   The most favoured one: The *Apple* e-books case

6.70   The *Apple* case nicely illustrates the mechanics of an MFN and the effects it has on competitive dynamics. The district court in 2012, and later the appeals court in 2015, found Apple guilty of conspiring to raise the retail price of e-books through its agreements with five major publishers which contained an MFN provision.[64] Before Apple came on the scene, Amazon had been the dominant force in e-book retailing, with nearly 90 per cent of the market, following the successful launch of its Kindle e-reader in 2007. Amazon's strategy was to charge $9.99 for many new and bestselling titles. The major publishers—Hachette, HarperCollins, Macmillan, Penguin, Random House, and Simon & Schuster—'abhorred' this pricing model, as it eroded their profits. The prevailing distribution model for books at the time was the wholesale model, whereby the retailer (Amazon in this case) would receive a discount (often 20 per cent) on the actual retail price it set. With a retail price of $9.99, and a discount of 20 per cent accruing to the bookseller, there was not much margin left for the publisher. Yet the publishers could not do anything individually against Amazon's 'bullying behaviour', and could not prevent the 'wretched $9.99 price point becoming a de facto standard'.[65]

6.71   This is when, in the words of the court, 'Apple seized the moment and brilliantly played its hand.'[66] In late 2009, Apple was close to launching its iPad, which was to include an e-reader, and started discussions with the major publishers. Apple conveyed the message that it was willing to sell e-books at prices up to $14.99, and did not want to compete directly with Amazon's pricing model. It signalled to the publishers that this was their 'once-in-a-lifetime opportunity to eliminate Amazon's control over pricing'. An agency

---

[62]   See Johnson (2014) and Boik and Corts (2013).

[63]   *In re Online Travel Company (OTC) Hotel Booking Antitrust Litigation*, Case 3:12-cv-3515-B (N.D. Tex., 18 February 2014).

[64]   *United States v Apple Inc. et al.*, 12 Civ. 2826 (DLC) (SDNY 2012); *United States v Apple Inc.* No. 13-3741 (2d Cir. 2015).

[65]   *United States v Apple Inc. et al.*, 12 Civ. 2826 (DLC) (SDNY 2012), p. 16 and p. 19.

[66]   Ibid., p. 11.

model was proposed to replace the wholesale model, giving the publishers the power to set retail prices, with Apple acting as an agent receiving a commission (30 per cent, the same as in its App store). Both Apple and the individual publishers rather liked the sound of this new model, but the main challenge was still Amazon's $9.99 strategy. Amazon would have to be moved from the wholesale model to an agency model like Apple, otherwise it would continue to set e-book prices at $9.99. This is where the MFN clause came into play. The publishers guaranteed to Apple that the e-books in its e-bookstore would be sold for the lowest retail price available at any other reseller. For Apple this eliminated the risk that it would have to compete on retail prices with Amazon, and allowed it instead to rely on the attractiveness of its devices as the main selling point. For the publishers it provided a commitment mechanism: having to match any retail price would be so costly to publishers that they effectively committed themselves to avoiding such an outcome by changing the deal with Amazon. As the court noted:

> To change the price of e-books across the industry, however, the Publishers would have to raise Amazon's prices. This is where the MFN became such a critical term in Apple's contracts with the Publisher Defendants. It literally stiffened the spines of the Publisher Defendants to ensure that they would demand new terms from Amazon. Thus, the MFN protected Apple from retail price competition as it punished a Publisher if it failed to impose agency terms on other e-tailers.[67]

Amazon opposed the agency model when it found out what the publishers were up to. It threatened the publishers with disintermediation—that is, signing deals with authors directly. However, as the publishers one by one put Amazon on notice that they were joining forces with Apple, it became clear to Amazon that it was facing a 'united front'. In the final days before signing the agency agreement with Apple in January 2010, the publishers still sought reassurance that they would not be alone in signing such an agreement. Apple gave them this reassurance (Random House was the only major publisher not to sign). Even after signing, the publishers individually were still wary of confronting Amazon: **6.72**

> [T]he Publishers recognized that any one of them acting alone would not be able to compel Amazon to move to agency. Five of them had now agreed to join forces, but none of them was eager to be the first to meet with Amazon . . . Macmillan, the smallest of the five Publishers, did the honorable thing and delivered its message in person. [The Macmillan executive] did not expect the meeting to go well. As he put it, he was 'on [his] way to Seattle to get [his] ass kicked by Amazon.' He was right.[68]

Yet Macmillan knew that it would not stand alone. Amazon realized this, and eventually capitulated, accepting the agency model (although it also complained to the FTC about this, triggering the subsequent investigations).   **6.73**

Steve Jobs, Apple's legendary CEO, launched the iPad on 27 January 2010 (and inadvertently revealed the agreement with the publishers following awkward journalist questions about why a customer would pay $14.99 for an e-book that cost $9.99 on Amazon).[69] In April 2010 Apple opened the iBookstore. The immediate outcome was higher retail prices, not just for e-books but also for hardcover titles. Bestsellers went up in price by more than   **6.74**

---

[67] Ibid., p. 55.
[68] Ibid., pp. 86–7.
[69] The general counsel of one of the publishers wrote in an email to her CEO that she could not believe that Jobs had made that statement, calling it 'incredibly stupid'. Ibid., p. 86.

40 per cent on average; new releases by 14 per cent. The court considered that 'without the collective action that Apple nurtured, it is unlikely any individual Publisher would have succeeded in unilaterally imposing an agency relationship on Amazon', and that 'Apple participated in and facilitated a horizontal price-fixing conspiracy.'[70] The court also made clear that the MFN clause in its own right was not anti-competitive, but its use in facilitating the conspiracy was.

6.75 This finding of per se illegal price fixing was upheld by the appeal court in 2015.[71] Yet one of the three judges dissented, arguing that the agency agreement was the only way in which Apple could realistically have entered the market, and that its entry broke down the Amazon monopoly and hence enhanced competition and innovation. This case illustrates how MFNs in a vertical agreement can function as a powerful commitment device facilitating horizontal co-ordination. Yet the dissenting opinion also highlights how vertical restraints in dynamic markets such as e-books are difficult to judge, even when the facts of the case are clear.

6.76 In Europe, the e-books case is not over yet. The European Commission reached a settlement with Apple and the five publishers in 2012 and 2013.[72] This led to the removal of MFNs from the Apple agency agreements. But now the MFNs in the Amazon agency contracts have triggered complaints by certain publishers (Hachette and Bonnier). The Commission has recently opened an investigation into these parity clauses that cover price and non-price aspects.[73] While the original wholesale MFNs used by Amazon may have restricted the entry of a rival such as Apple (which was overcome only by Apple agreeing its own retail MFNs with the publishers), the current retail MFNs also do not find favour. Vertical restraints cases in online markets—similar to e-books, hotel bookings, and price-comparison websites for motor insurance—will continue in years to come.

---

[70] Ibid., p. 119 and p. 120.

[71] *United States v Apple Inc.* No. 13-3741 (2d Cir. 2015).

[72] European Commission (2012), 'Antitrust: Commission accepts legally binding commitments from Simon & Schuster, Harper Collins, Hachette, Holtzbrinck and Apple for sale of e-books', press release, 13 December.

[73] European Commission (2015), 'Antitrust: Commission Opens Formal Investigation into Amazon's E-Book Distribution Arrangements', press release, 11 June.

7

MERGERS

7.1 Mergers Under Scrutiny

7.1.1 What's the competition concern?

7.01 Mergers and acquisitions routinely make the financial headlines. They take place around the world and across different industries, and often involve big names and big numbers: Facebook acquired WhatsApp for $22 billion in 2014; Berkshire Hathaway and 3G Capital acquired H.J. Heinz Company for $28 billion in 2013; Inbev merged with Anheuser-Busch in a $52 billion transaction in 2008; Glaxo Wellcome merged with SmithKline Beecham in a $76 billion deal in 2000. Several of the world's largest law firms—including Dentons, Norton Rose Fulbright, Freshfields Bruckhaus Deringer, and Hogan Lovells—have been through one merger or more to reach their current size. Mergers and acquisitions are part and parcel of a market economy. Companies are forced to consolidate or reposition when an industry goes through fundamental changes on the supply side or the demand side—for example, market liberalization, technological developments, changes in consumer preferences, or a recession. Mergers are often aimed at improving efficiency through economies of scale and synergies. Ambitious companies (and their managers) see mergers and acquisitions as a means to achieve rapid expansion or to enter new markets more quickly than through organic growth. Some mergers are defensive, protecting a market position in the face of new entry. Some are designed outright to eliminate competition and create market power.

7.02 Whatever the rationale for the merger, deal-makers nowadays are well aware that they may require clearance from the competition authorities. Over the years many high-profile deals have been scuppered on competition law grounds. For example, AT&T abandoned its plans to buy T-Mobile USA for $39 billion in 2011 when the DOJ challenged the deal.[1] The European Commission blocked the $21 billion acquisition of Honeywell by General Electric in 2001 (even though the US authorities had cleared it), and the $9.5 billion merger between Deutsche Börse and NYSE Euronext in 2012.[2] Around 130 jurisdictions now have a competition regime, typically including rules on merger control, from Albania and Barbados to Yemen and Zimbabwe.[3] The need for regulatory clearance is now often built into the deal preparations and negotiations, sometimes with explicit provisions for what happens if competition authorities object to the merger. The more far-sighted among deal-makers also consider at an early stage which divestments or other remedies may need to be offered to the authorities.

7.03 Why are competition authorities concerned? Because a horizontal merger may eliminate competition between the merging parties, create market power for the merged entity, or dampen competition between the remaining suppliers in the market. A vertical merger may give a company control over bottlenecks in the supply chain. Across many jurisdictions, these concerns are now codified as a test asking whether the merger will lead to a substantial

---

[1] *United States v AT&T Inc., T-Mobile USA Inc., and Deutsche Telekom AG*, Civil Action No. 11-01560, (ESH) (D.D.C. filed 30 September 2011).

[2] *General Electric/Honeywell* (Case COMP/M.2220), Decision of 3 July 2001; and *Deutsche Börse/NYSE Euronext* (Case COMP/M.6166), Decision of 1 February 2012.

[3] The FTC has a list on its website; https://www.ftc.gov/policy/international/competition-consumer-protection-authorities-worldwide.

lessening of competition (SLC). The term SLC is used in the United States, Australia, New Zealand, and the United Kingdom. Canada and South Africa refer to a substantial prevention or lessening of competition (SPLC), and in the EU the test is phrased as significant impediment to effective competition (SIEC). In China the test is whether a merger eliminates or restricts competition. Yet the substantive test is similar across jurisdictions. How do you determine whether a merger will result in an SLC? One challenge is that the analysis is necessarily forward-looking. Competition authorities must assess how the market will evolve with and without the merger—that is, a combination of forecasting and counterfactual analysis. This is where economics comes in.

7.1.2 Other policy questions

Before turning to the economics of merger analysis, it is worth exploring a number of other **7.04** policy questions in relation to merger control. First, why not simply prohibit all mergers? Companies that want to grow would have to do so organically, earning success on their own account. Such a policy would stimulate healthy competitive effort, and save enforcement costs. Yet outright prohibitions of mergers are relatively rare. Competition authorities recognize that mergers and acquisitions are an inherent part of how markets work and often have efficiency rationales. Instead of a prohibition, what often happens is that mergers that risk reducing competition are cleared with remedies to address the competition concerns, often in the form of divestments.

A second policy question is whether there should be a limit on how much companies can **7.05** grow through mergers. Increasing consolidation has long been of concern. In 1966, during a wave of conglomerate mergers in the United States, humorist Art Buchwald wrote the following in a newspaper column (which was reproduced that same year in a Supreme Court judgment concerning a brewery merger):

> It is 1978 and by this time every company west of the Mississippi will have merged into one giant corporation known as Samson Securities. Every company east of the Mississippi will have merged under an umbrella corporation known as the Delilah Co. It was inevitable that one day the chairman of the board of Samson and the president of Delilah would meet and discuss merging their two companies...
>
> The Antitrust Division of the Justice Department studied the merger for months. Finally the Attorney General made his ruling. 'While we find some drawbacks to only one company being left in the United States, we feel the advantages to the public far outweigh the disadvantages. Therefore, we're making an exception in this case and allowing Samson and Delilah to merge.'[4]

Consolidation has not turned out to be as inevitable as feared in past decades. Companies **7.06** have discovered that growth through mergers has its limitations, conglomerates have become less popular, and divestments of businesses are now almost as common as acquisitions. In any event, it has been generally accepted that competition authorities should not judge mergers and acquisitions by their size, but rather by reference to their effects on competition.

A third policy question is whether competition authorities should take into account the fact **7.07** that mergers often fail. Received wisdom in the business literature seems to be that merger

---

[4] Buchwald (1966), as reproduced in *United States v Pabst Brewing Co.*, 384 U.S. 546 (1966).

and acquisition activity has an overall success rate of at most 50 per cent. Several economics and finance studies have shown that mergers on average destroy more value for shareholders than they create.[5] Case studies abound of post-merger integration failing due to a range of strategic and cultural differences (famous examples are Daimler Benz/Chrysler, AOL/Time Warner, and Mattel/The Learning Company). From this perspective, by prohibiting a merger the competition authority might in fact be doing the merging parties and their shareholders a favour. Yet the merger rules are not normally applied with such paternalistic considerations in mind. While the question of whether a merger is likely to succeed or fail is in principle not considered during the competition assessment, to the extent that efficiencies from the merger become an important part of the assessment, the authority will need to judge how realistic it is that the claimed efficiencies will be achieved. The prevalence of merger failures may have generated some scepticism among competition authorities about such claims (we turn to the assessment of merger efficiencies later in this chapter).

7.1.3 The remainder of this chapter

7.08 If you got to this chapter having read Chapters 2 and 3 you will already have a good understanding of many of the economic concepts used in merger cases: market definition, market concentration, barriers to entry, and countervailing buyer power. In Chapter 8 we deal with the design of merger remedies. In this chapter we explain the additional economic principles and analyses that are of relevance to merger control. We start in section 7.2 by exploring the principles behind the SLC test and its variants—which types of competition concern are addressed, and should the focus be on consumer welfare or total welfare? We go on in section 7.3 to discuss counterfactual analysis, which is used to assess what would happen in the absence of the merger. This includes situations where one of the merging parties is a failing firm. In section 7.4 we discuss unilateral effects, in particular the analysis of closeness of competition. We explain the diversion ratio as an indicator of closeness of competition, and describe best practice in designing consumer surveys to obtain diversion ratios. In section 7.5 we continue with unilateral effects and discuss the various techniques for simulating price effects from mergers. These range from simple illustrative price rise analysis to full merger simulation. Section 7.6 deals with co-ordinated effects. We explain static and dynamic oligopoly theory and the circumstances in which tacit collusion can arise. Section 7.7 explores the theories of harm arising in non-horizontal mergers, in particular vertical mergers, but also those that are diagonal or have portfolio effects. In section 7.8 we discuss the assessment of minority shareholdings, which sometimes raise competition concerns. Finally, in section 7.9 we deal with merger efficiencies: how they arise, how they can be measured, and in which situations they benefit consumers sufficiently to offset any anti-competitive effects of the merger.

7.2 The Substantive Test: SLC, SIEC, and Other Variants

7.2.1 Dominance, and unilateral and co-ordinated effects

7.09 The SLC, SIEC, and other substantive tests have evolved over time. There have been extensive debates about the scope of these tests. US antitrust law established one of the earliest

---

[5] For example, Mitchell and Stafford (2000), Moeller et al. (2005), and Malmendier et al. (2012).

frameworks for merger control. Section 7 of the Clayton Act of 1914 prohibits mergers where 'the effect of such acquisition may be substantially to lessen competition, or to tend to create a monopoly'. Thus there are two criteria for judging whether a merger is anti-competitive: it gives the merged entity market power, or it substantially lessens competition. US merger control has traditionally placed great importance on concerns about tacit collusion or co-ordinated effects between the remaining competitors in the market. Such co-ordinated effects are difficult to address directly under competition law (in the absence of explicit collusion; see Chapter 5). Merger control is a tool to prevent market structures that are prone to co-ordination. In contrast, EU merger control originally focused on the first criterion, that is, the creation or strengthening of a dominant position. This led to some confusion during the 1990s as to whether situations of tacit collusion were also covered by the EU merger rules. The answer was yes, and in a number of cases the EU courts confirmed that concerns about tacit collusion could be made part of the dominance test by calling it collective (or joint) dominance.[6] The SIEC test that was adopted under the 2004 EU Merger Regulation and accompanying Commission Guidelines captures co-ordinated effects explicitly.[7]

A dominance or monopoly test focuses on the market position of the merged entity. The SLC and SIEC tests allow for a wider range of competition distortions to be considered, covering both co-ordinated and unilateral effects. The distinction between co-ordinated and unilateral effects is not clear-cut, either in theory or in practice. In merger control it is usually interpreted as follows. Co-ordinated effects involve both the merged entity and the remaining competitors, and refer to situations in which the post-merger market structure is such that these companies can more easily engage in tacit collusion. Unilateral effects, in contrast, result directly from the loss of competition between the merging parties. With this direct rivalry removed, the merged entity can profitably raise its own prices, regardless of the response of its remaining competitors. In reality such price increases are not purely unilateral, as suppliers do not normally ignore their competitors' responses. Yet it can be useful to make the distinction between co-ordinated and unilateral effects, as it requires the competition authority to be explicit about the theory of harm from the merger—is it co-ordination between the remaining suppliers, or a unilateral price increase by the merged entity? The theoretical distinction—which is also not pure—is that unilateral effects are based on static oligopoly theory, where prices and outputs change from one competitive outcome to the next as the number of suppliers is reduced. Co-ordinated effects relate to dynamic oligopoly theory, where suppliers seek to avoid competitive outcomes by tacitly colluding. **7.10**

The creation of dominance through a merger is one type of unilateral effect, but the concept is broader. Unilateral effects may arise, for example, if the merger is between the second- and third-largest competitors in the market and these two competed more vigorously with each other than with the market leader. This type of unilateral effect arose in the *Heinz/Beech-Nut* case in 2001, which we discuss in section 7.4.[8] Such mergers were **7.11**

---

   [6] For example, Case T-102/96 *Gencor v EC Commission* [1999] 4 CMLR 971.

   [7] Council Regulation (EC) No 139/2004 of 20 January 2004 on the control of concentrations between undertakings (the EC Merger Regulation) (Text with EEA relevance); and European Commission (2004), 'Guidelines on the Assessment of Horizontal Mergers Under the Council Regulation on the Control of Concentrations Between Undertakings', [2004] OJ C31/03.

   [8] *Federal Trade Commission v HJ Heinz Co* 246 F 3d 708 (US Ct of Apps (District of Colombia Cir.), 2001).

believed to have been outside the scope of the old dominance test in EU merger control (this was termed the 'unilateral effects gap'), but now come under the remit of the SIEC test. Another type of merger that is caught under the SLC and SIEC tests but not necessarily the dominance test is where a large company acquires a small but very aggressive competitor. An example is the acquisition of tele.ring by T-Mobile Austria in 2006.[9] This deal combined the second- and fourth-largest mobile operators in Austria. At 30–40 per cent, their post-merger market share would be smaller than that of the largest provider, Mobilkom, which had 35–45 per cent. tele.ring itself had a market share of 10–20 per cent. According to the HHI (explained in Chapter 3), the market was concentrated and the increase in the HHI by 500–600 points would be enough to raise concerns under the SIEC test. The European Commission found that the merged entity would not be dominant because of Mobilkom's presence, and nor would the nature of the mobile telephony market be conducive to tacit collusion between T-Mobile and Mobilkom. The Commission did, however, establish an SIEC on the basis of tele.ring's competitive behaviour before the merger. It noted that 'tele.ring, as a maverick, has a much greater influence on the competitive process in this market than its market share would suggest'.[10] Using an aggressive entry strategy, tele.ring had cut prices and doubled in size in just a few years. The merger would reduce the intensity of competition by integrating the maverick competitor into one of the larger incumbents. The deal was eventually cleared, with remedies in the form of divestments of spectrum and mast sites. The aim of these remedies was to allow H3G, one of the other smaller operators, to grow, and thereby to reproduce the pre-merger competitive dynamics.

7.2.2 Consumer or total welfare?

7.12 Another aspect of the substantive merger test is whether it should focus on consumer welfare or total welfare. As we discussed in Chapter 1, there can be a tension between protecting consumer welfare and using a total welfare standard that encompasses producers and consumers. This is most clearly seen in the treatment of merger efficiencies. If weight is attached to producer surplus as well as consumer surplus, merger efficiencies are regarded as beneficial in and of themselves. With a consumer welfare standard, only those efficiencies that are passed on to consumers are considered relevant. This can make an important difference. Figure 7.1 presents a (somewhat hypothetical) situation of a merger to monopoly from a starting point of perfect competition.

7.13 The price P_1 equals marginal costs in the starting situation. The merger generates efficiencies: marginal costs decrease. Yet because the merger also gives market power to the new entity, the price increases in the end, from P_1 to P_2, which is the new profit-maximizing price. From a total welfare perspective, only the triangle marked 'welfare loss' would be of concern in this merger—recall from Chapters 1 and 2 that this is the deadweight welfare loss resulting from market power. You can undertake a simple welfare analysis based on this figure (as first introduced by Williamson, 1968). The welfare loss must be balanced against the efficiencies rectangle marked 'welfare gain'. If the area of the welfare loss triangle is greater than the welfare gain rectangle, the merger harms total welfare. If the efficiencies rectangle is larger, total welfare increases. However, the result is different if the authority

---

[9] *T-Mobile Austria/Tele.ring* (Case COMP/M.3916), Decision of 26 April 2006.
[10] Ibid., at [129].

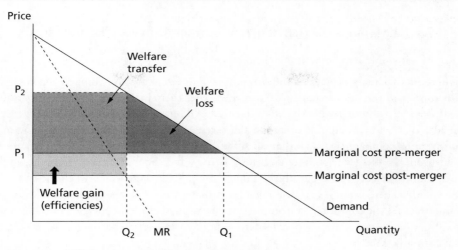

Figure 7.1 Efficiencies versus market power in mergers

applies the consumer welfare standard. The concern would be that the price increases post-merger despite the cost efficiencies, and that there is a welfare transfer from consumers to the merging companies—the upper rectangle in Figure 7.1. In this framework the fall in marginal cost would have to be very large for there to be no net price increase after the merger. Otherwise, the efficiency gains would be considered insufficient, even if they compensated for the deadweight welfare loss in the triangle. This means that the consumer welfare standard can result in the blocking of mergers that would lead to higher prices but that would also ultimately enhance total welfare.

Most competition authorities place greater emphasis on consumer welfare than on total **7.14** welfare. Canada is an exception. Under the Competition Act 1985, two standards can be applied. The first is the total surplus standard, which involves quantifying the dead-weight welfare loss (the triangle in Figure 7.1). Equal weight is given to producer and consumer surplus. Any welfare transfers from producers to consumers are considered to be neutral. The second is the balancing weights standard, under which the effect on consumer surplus may be given greater weight (in the extreme, this test becomes the same as the consumer welfare test). The burden of quantifying the anti-competitive effects lies with the authority. In 2015 the Canadian Supreme Court ruled on a merger between three of the four secure landfill sites for hazardous waste in Northeastern British Colombia.[11] The Competition Bureau, Competition Tribunal, and Federal Court of Appeal all found this merger to be anti-competitive. However, the Supreme Court determined that the Bureau had not properly quantified the anti-competitive effects of the merger—a tentative estimate had suggested a 10 per cent price increase, but was not carried out in a robust and verifiable manner. The court determined that the anti-competitive effects should therefore not be given any weight in the welfare trade-off. This meant that the efficiencies that had been quantified by the merging parties outweighed the anti-competitive effects. The original decision to block the merger was therefore overturned.

---

[11] *Tervita Corp v Canada* (Commissioner of Competition), 2015 SCC 3 [SCC Decision].

7.3 The Counterfactual: Current Market, Entry, or Failing Firm?

7.3.1 What would happen without the merger?

7.15 Counterfactual analysis plays an important role in different areas of competition law—in horizontal and vertical agreements to assess whether there is a restriction of competition (see Chapters 5 and 6); and in the quantification of damages (Chapter 9). In merger cases, the idea of a counterfactual is to isolate and assess the specific effects of the transaction. You need to compare two hypothetical situations: the market outcome that is likely to result from the merger (which requires forecasting), and the market situation as it would be in the absence of the merger (the counterfactual). The difference between the two tells you whether there is an SLC post-merger. Fortunately, in most cases you can take as the counterfactual the conditions of competition prevailing before the merger. In these cases the SLC assessment boils down to considering the likely impact of the merger on the market as it currently stands.

7.16 However, the current situation is not always a good guide for what would happen in the absence of the merger. There can be potential imminent changes in the market structure. The EU Horizontal Merger Guidelines recognize this:

> In assessing the competitive effects of a merger, the Commission compares the competitive conditions that would result from the notified merger with the conditions that would have prevailed without the merger. In most cases the competitive conditions existing at the time of the merger constitute the relevant comparison for evaluating the effects of a merger. However, in some circumstances, the Commission may take into account future changes to the market that can reasonably be predicted. It may, in particular, take account of the likely entry or exit of firms if the merger did not take place when considering what constitutes the relevant comparison.[12]

7.17 We consider two situations where future competitive conditions without the merger differ from the prevailing conditions: one in which new entry is expected, and one in which the target may exit (i.e. it is a 'failing firm').

7.3.2 Entry in the absence of the merger: Anti-viral drugs, steel drums, and concert tickets

7.18 The following cases illustrate how the counterfactual may differ from the pre-merger situation as a result of changing market dynamics and entry. In the *Glaxo Wellcome/SmithKline Beecham* merger in 2000, the European Commission explored whether the counterfactual should include products that were expected to enter the market in the short term regardless of the merger:

> In the pharmaceuticals industry, a full assessment of the competitive situation requires examination of the products which are not yet on the market but which are at an advanced stage of development (normally after large sums of money have been invested). These products are called pipeline products.[13]

---

[12] European Commission (2004), 'Guidelines on the Assessment of Horizontal Mergers Under the Council Regulation on the Control Of Concentrations Between Undertakings', [2004] OJ C31/03, at [9].
[13] *Glaxo Wellcome/SmithKline Beecham* (Case COMP/M.1846), Decision of 8 May 2000, at [70].

This new entry in the counterfactual is subtly different from the general entry analysis **7.19** that you carry out in the market power stage (see Chapter 3), since it is entry that does not depend on, or is not triggered by, the merger. In *Glaxo Wellcome/SmithKline Beecham* this issue arose in relation to anti-viral medicines. Although there was a pipeline of products from other companies, the Commission did not consider this to be sufficiently strong to constrain the merged entity. Indeed, there were concerns that the merger would make it more difficult for the pipeline products to achieve their market potential. In the end the parties agreed to make divestments in this product category.

In 2007 the CC investigated the completed acquisition by Greif—the largest manufac- **7.20** turer of industrial steel containers in the United Kingdom—of the steel drum and closures business of Blagden Packaging Group.[14] The merged entity's market share in large steel drums was 85 per cent. The CC found that, of all the competitors in the relevant market pre-merger, Blagden had posed the most significant competitive constraint on Greif. The CC's analysis of switching showed that Greif and Blagden had lost more customers to each other than to any other competitor. Furthermore, there was limited competitive constraint from smaller producers or imports. However, this pre-merger market situation did not tell the whole story. The CC found that the merged entity would be constrained in future by a new steel drum manufacturing line run by Schütz Group, a competitor, at its new industrial packaging facility in the Netherlands. Schütz Group stated that the manufacturing line would have been installed in the absence of the merger—i.e. in the counterfactual—but that it brought forward the installation by eighteen months because of the merger. This new rival plant was capable of supplying large orders from UK customers, and the CC's analysis showed that imports from Schütz Group could be competitive for some types of steel drum and for some UK customers. The merger was therefore cleared without remedies.

The third example is the 2010 merger between Ticketmaster Entertainment, a ticketing **7.21** agent, and Live Nation, a venue owner and promoter. The deal was scrutinized in both the United States and United Kingdom. The CC cleared the deal unconditionally, but had initially raised concerns in relation to horizontal and vertical effects.[15] This was predominantly a vertical merger in the supply chain for live music events. One theory of harm specific to the United Kingdom was that the merger would have a horizontal effect through a loss of potential competition in the supply of tickets for live music events. Before the merger, Live Nation had entered into an agreement with another ticketing agent, CTS Eventim, a strong player in the German market but new to the United Kingdom. The potential horizontal harm was that the merger could prevent CTS's planned entry, as Live Nation might use only Ticketmaster as a partner going forward. Hence the counterfactual was not the pre-merger situation but the future market with competition from CTS, in partnership with Live Nation. The CC carried out a detailed analysis of this counterfactual, assessing whether the contract with Live Nation was a necessary stepping stone for CTS to enter the UK market. It also explored whether the merger would remove the rationale for that contract (both Live Nation and CTS publicly expressed their intention to honour the contract irrespective of the former's merger with Ticketmaster). Live Nation's ultimate commercial aim was to sell tickets directly to consumers using its own website, powered by CTS's ticketing

---

[14] Competition Commission (2007), 'Greif Inc and Blagden Packaging Group', 17 August.
[15] Competition Commission (2010), 'Ticketmaster and Live Nation', 7 May. We advised a third party in this inquiry.

platform. As part of the agreement, CTS would be allocated a proportion of the tickets to events promoted by Live Nation. However, this in itself would not be sufficient to make CTS capable of constraining the two larger companies, Ticketmaster and See Tickets. The CC noted that CTS becoming a large-scale ticket retailer in the United Kingdom would depend mainly on its own efforts and abilities. The agreement between Live Nation and CTS was neither necessary nor sufficient to ensure the successful large-scale entry of CTS, and therefore there was no SLC from the merger in this regard.

7.3.3 The failing-firm defence

7.22 The failing-firm (or exiting-firm) defence can be relevant when the target firm is in distress. If in the counterfactual it would go out of business and therefore no longer be a competitor to the acquirer, you may conclude that the merger changes little about the competitive landscape. However, the fact that a target company would be unlikely to survive is not in itself sufficient. Competition authorities also consider what would happen to its productive assets. The failing-firm defence applies if the proposed merger is the only, or least anticompetitive, way of maintaining the assets of the failing firm in the market. The US Merger Guidelines highlight the importance of the final whereabouts of the failing firm's assets:

> [A] merger is not likely to enhance market power if imminent failure . . . of one of the merging firms would cause the assets of that firm to exit the relevant market. This is an extreme instance of the more general circumstance in which the competitive significance of one of the merging firms is declining: the projected market share and significance of the exiting firm is zero. If the relevant assets would otherwise exit the market, customers are not worse off after the merger than they would have been had the merger been enjoined.[16]

7.23 In the absence of the merger, would the target firm really exit the market? Would its assets be bought by another firm? Would it not recover and become a viable business again? As noted by one authority, failing-firm counterfactuals 'are easily the subject of self-speculation—relatively easily alleged but difficult, given the informational asymmetries, to verify independently'.[17] Not surprisingly, therefore, the requirements for qualifying as a failing firm are stringent. Most jurisdictions explicitly spell out the necessary conditions for a successful application of the failing-firm defence. While the detailed conditions may differ, they can broadly be grouped under the following two criteria: exit of the target business and its assets is inevitable in the near future; and there is no realistic and less anti-competitive alternative outcome than the proposed merger.

7.24 The first criterion—exit is inevitable in the near future—is usually the result of businesses in financial difficulties, although it can also be due to a change in corporate strategy (e.g. an otherwise healthy company pulling out of a particular market). Evidence on a company's viability should be evaluated in the context of the prevailing economic and market conditions—for example, a recession affects both the financial health of the target and the availability of alternative purchasers. Furthermore, it should be shown that the assets of the target business will exit the market as well, and that the financial difficulties cannot be easily rectified by restructuring the business. This will involve examining the company's

---

[16] Department of Justice and Federal Trade Commission (2010), 'Horizontal Merger Guidelines', August, p. 32.
[17] Office of Fair Trading (2008), 'Restatement of OFT's Position Regarding Acquisitions of "Failing Firms"', December, p. 3.

accounts, board minutes, and strategic plans. Another way of looking at this is that the evidence must show that there is no investor willing to provide the necessary capital for the business to remain a going concern.

This analysis can be based on a number of well-established financial metrics and ratios. **7.25** A common metric is the estimated likelihood of default as reflected in the credit rating of the business. Credit rating agencies use financial tests to assess the risk of creditors not receiving the interest and principal in a timely manner, as these factors typically lead to default. As an example, in one survey AA-rated debt had a default rate of only 0.03 per cent, while for CCC-/C-rated companies this was 25.7 per cent (Altman and Narayanan, 1997). Other metrics relate to profitability, liquidity, and solvency. The relevant profitability measure would reflect a firm's ability to generate economic value by realizing the returns required by debt and equity investors. For liquidity, the relevant financial ratios indicate a firm's ability to meet its short-term obligations, such as interest payments, from current cash flows. An illiquid but potentially solvent firm (i.e. one that cannot obtain funding for short-term liabilities, but whose overall liabilities do not outweigh its assets) might not be able to survive as a going concern if investors are unwilling to commit additional funding. For solvency, the relevant measures would capture a firm's ability to repay its fixed financial obligations, including the principal on its debt (the credit rating is relevant here).

As noted above, the rationale for the failing-firm defence is that the proposed merger allows **7.26** productive assets to be retained in the market in a way that does not substantially impair competition. The second overall criterion requires that there is no realistic and substantially less anti-competitive alternative means of achieving this. If in the absence of the merger the target business would have been sold to one or more other purchasers (even if potentially for a lower price), this would represent a realistic counterfactual. In some cases there will have been a formal bidding process to sell the failing business, which the authorities can use to assess the most likely counterfactual. These other purchasers could be existing competitors or new entrants. In the case of a sale to a new entrant, the counterfactual is likely to be similar to the pre-merger competitive conditions (the assets in question simply change hands, with no change in the number of competitors). If instead the assets are dispersed across several existing firms, this could suggest a counterfactual with one less competitor, but with each remaining competitor getting slightly stronger (with more assets). To satisfy this second overall criterion, the merging parties need to show either that these alternatives are not feasible, or that the competitive situation will not be better in these scenarios.

7.3.4 Failing-firm examples: From solvents to Greek airlines

A European Commission case where the failing-firm defence was successful is the acquisi- **7.27** tion in 2001 by BASF of Eurodiol and Pantochim.[18] These were two Belgian chemicals producers owned by the SISAS Group from Italy, and both the subsidiaries and parent company were in the process of liquidation. Even though this merger enhanced BASF's strong position in a number of solvents markets, the Commission considered that it met the conditions of the failing-firm defence. The target companies were going to exit the market and, despite the best efforts by the Tribunal de Commerce of Charleroi to find suitable buyers under the Belgian pre-bankruptcy regime, only BASF had made an offer. The

---

[18] *BASF/Eurodiol/Pantochim* (Case COMP/M.2314), Decision of 11 July 2001.

criterion regarding the exit of the assets of the target business was also satisfied since the two plants operated as a single unit and could not have been sold independently. Hence the Commission concluded that these assets would have exited the market had BASF not made the offer to acquire Eurodiol and Pantochim.

7.28 A high-profile case where the failing-firm defence was ultimately rejected is the acquisition by Lloyds TSB of HBOS in 2008.[19] Lloyds TSB was one of the large UK banks. HBOS also had a significant presence in retail banking, itself the product of an earlier merger between a large building society, Halifax, and the Bank of Scotland. HBOS was in distress as a result of liquidity issues and exposure to toxic assets that reached a critical point at the start of the global financial crisis. Aware of the potential systemic risks (one bank failure leading to others), the Secretary of State for Business intervened in the public interest, taking control of the ultimate decision of whether to approve the merger. He asked the OFT for a report on the competitive effects of the transaction. The OFT found that the HBOS acquisition resulted in an SLC that was not easily remediable. Central to this conclusion was the chosen counterfactual. The OFT agreed that using pre-merger competitive conditions was not appropriate given the unprecedented volatility in the financial markets. However, it considered that in the counterfactual the competitive constraints from HBOS would not be completely eliminated. Rather, the OFT judged the appropriate counterfactual to be that the government would step in to ensure that HBOS did not collapse (as indeed the government did soon thereafter with Lloyds TSB itself). In the medium term, when that support was no longer required, the government could sell HBOS to another bank with no existing strong position in the United Kingdom, or return it to viability. Thus the OFT did not consider this case to meet the requirements for treating HBOS as a failing firm with no alternative, less anti-competitive options. Nevertheless, the acquisition was cleared by the Secretary of State on the basis of its benefits to the financial stability of HBOS and the UK financial system as a whole.

7.29 In a bus merger in the United Kingdom in 2009, the failing-firm argument was acknowledged but not considered to be the relevant counterfactual because it was alleged that the target was failing due to predatory actions by the acquirer.[20] The CC found that there had been an SLC from Stagecoach's completed acquisition of Preston Bus, a rival bus operator in Preston in the north of England. The authority required Stagecoach to divest a reconfigured Preston Bus business. The decision was appealed to the CAT, which upheld the CC's finding of an SLC, but questioned the counterfactual.[21] The background to the case was that Stagecoach first approached Preston Bus in 2006 with an offer to purchase the business. The offer was rejected. Following this, Stagecoach developed a plan for expansion in the Preston area, and launched a number of local bus services in direct competition with Preston Bus. Both Stagecoach and Preston Bus incurred losses as a result of this competition. After a year of unprofitable services, Preston Bus suffered financial difficulties, and decided to sell. It approached a number of major bus companies. Stagecoach made an

[19] Office of Fair Trading (2008), 'Anticipated Acquisition by Lloyds TSB plc of HBOS plc', 24 October; and Department for Business, Enterprise and Regulatory Reform (2008), 'Decision by Lord Mandelson, the Secretary of State for Business, not to refer to the Competition Commission the merger between Lloyds TSB Group plc and HBOS plc under Section 45 of the Enterprise Act 2002', 31 October.
[20] Competition Commission (2009), 'Stagecoach Group plc/Preston Bus Ltd', 11 November. We advised the acquiring party in this case.
[21] *Stagecoach Group PLC v Competition Commission* [2010] CAT 14, 21 May 2010.

offer in October 2008 which Preston Bus accepted. Stagecoach submitted that Preston Bus was a failing firm and that, on liquidation, it was highly unlikely that any other company would purchase its assets to provide local bus services in Preston. The CC concluded that the counterfactual should be based on the most recent period of 'normal' competition, that is, before Stagecoach entered. Therefore, the counterfactual would be that of Preston Bus profitably running the local services and Stagecoach running inter-urban services outside Preston—in essence, the situation that existed about eighteen months before the merger. The CAT rejected the CC's decision to ignore the events of the June 2007–September 2008 period for the purposes of constructing the counterfactual. The CAT agreed with the CC that the counterfactual would not have been a complete exit by Preston Bus. However, it concluded that the alternative counterfactual put forward by the CC—the competition prevailing before Stagecoach's entry—was incorrect. As a result the CAT found the CC's remedy to be disproportionate.

A failing-firm case that did get accepted by the UK authorities was *Optimax/Ultralase* in 2013, involving providers of refractive eye surgery.[22] The merging parties were the second- and third-largest competitors in the market, with Optical Express being the market leader with national presence, and Optegra and Accuvision as other notable providers. Refractive eye surgery is often considered a luxury purchase, and hence demand for such services fell considerably during the recession. This drop in demand, coupled with the significant installed laser eye treatment capacity in the United Kingdom, meant that many clinics were under-utilized. There was ample evidence that Ultralase was expected to run into funding problems towards the end of 2012, and that its previous restructuring programmes had been unsuccessful. The sale process of Ultralase started in April 2012, and a number of potential buyers expressed interest. However, Ultralase received only one offer in the end, from Optimax. Faced with the alternative prospect of going into administration, the company accepted this offer. Economic modelling of Ultralase's likely future profitability in a range of scenarios showed that a private equity or other non-trade purchaser would not be able to achieve a sufficient return to justify the initial investment. The CC confirmed that there was no credible alternative purchaser that would have acquired Ultralase as a going concern, or its assets on a piecemeal basis. As to other possible alternatives, the CC carried out a consumer survey which found high diversion ratios from Ultralase to both Optical Express, the largest supplier, and Optimax, the acquirer. As a result, it concluded that Ultralase's exit would not have led to a substantially less anti-competitive outcome than the merger, as Optical Express and Optimax would have picked up most of Ultralase's customers. Note the somewhat counterintuitive implication of this last part of the test: high diversion ratios between the acquirer (Optimax) and the target (Ultralase) are normally of concern as they indicate closeness of competition, but here they were actually favourable to the merger as they indicated that exit by Ultralase would not result in a much more competitive situation than the merger itself.

7.30

Prevailing economic conditions also played a role in the European Commission's approval in 2013 of the acquisition of Olympic Air by its main domestic rival in Greece, Aegean Airlines, on failing-firm grounds.[23] This was less than three years after the Commission had

7.31

---

[22] Competition Commission (2013), 'Optimax Clinics Limited and Ultralase Limited', 20 November. We advised the merging parties in this case.

[23] *Aegean/Olympic II* (Case Comp M.6796), Decision of 9 October 2013.

blocked the same deal on competition grounds, rejecting the failing-firm defence.[24] The merger would lead to a quasi-monopoly on the main domestic routes in Greece. In the 2011 decision the Commission did not accept that Olympic would inevitably exit the market, and considered that some form of restructuring or less anti-competitive sale was still possible. However, in the 2013 decision the Commission approved the renewed bid by Aegean without conditions. Olympic was facing even greater financial difficulties, as was the Greek economy as a whole. Domestic air travel had fallen by 26 per cent, several routes had been closed, and there seemed to be no other credible purchaser of the assets. Accordingly, the Commission accepted the failing-firm defence this time round.

7.4 Unilateral Effects: Assessing Closeness of Competition

7.4.1 Homogeneous versus differentiated products

7.32   If the products of the two merging companies are reasonably homogeneous, adding up their market shares can give a useful indication of the strength of the merged entity. The assessment of mergers in homogeneous product markets focuses on market definition, market shares, and entry barriers, in line with the principles set out in Chapters 2 and 3. The greater the concentration resulting from the merger and the higher the entry barriers, the more likely it is that there will be a competition case to answer. This traditional framework for merger analysis is still widely used internationally.

7.33   In most markets there is a degree of product differentiation. We discussed in Chapter 2 that market definition works best as an intermediate tool for merger analysis when products are homogeneous. You can test whether one group of products competes with another (e.g. apples with bananas, or cellophane with other wrapping materials). With product differentiation there is a spectrum of products that are close but imperfect substitutes. Drawing the line between products that are inside and outside the relevant market, and adding up market shares, may be less informative in these circumstances. Yet as we also noted in Chapter 2, market definition can still be useful in differentiated product markets. In many of these markets you can find meaningful groups of products that are reasonably similar, such that you can group them together and hypothetically monopolize them to test the competitive constraints from other groups—for example, top-of-the-range sports cars, high-quality chocolates, or children's breakfast cereals. An element of judgement will be required. If the degree of product differentiation is very high you may be better off focusing directly on the competitive effects of the merger and place less emphasis on market definition. This is where unilateral effects analysis comes in.

7.34   Unilateral effects analysis involves an assessment of expected post-merger prices. Would the merger give the new entity additional incentives and ability to raise prices? This depends on whether the merging parties are close competitors. The closer they are to each other on the spectrum of differentiated products or geographic areas—e.g. they produce very similar top-of-the-range sports cars, or their stores are located very near to each other—the more intense the competition between them, and hence the higher the likelihood of a significant price increase after the merger. The key measure of closeness of competition used in merger analysis is the diversion ratio. We saw the diversion ratio in Chapter 2 in the context of

---

[24]   *Olympic/Aegean Airlines* (Case Comp M.5830), Decision of 26 January 2011.

market definition, where it is used to rank substitutes for inclusion in the hypothetical monopolist test. In this section we explain the main economic features of the diversion ratio, and how to estimate it in practice.

First, however, we show two examples of merger cases where the closeness of competition **7.35** turned out to be more important than the position of the merged entity in the overall market. One is Heinz's proposed acquisition of Beech-Nut in the market for baby food in the United States.[25] Heinz and Beech-Nut were the second- and third-largest suppliers in the US baby food market, far behind market leader Gerber. The Court of Appeals upheld the FTC's injunction to halt the transaction (thereby rejecting an earlier district court judgment which had over-ruled the FTC). Although the merging parties were relatively small—Heinz had a 17.4 per cent market share; Beech-Nut 15.4 per cent—the FTC found that each was the other's closest competitor. Competition between the parties mainly took place in vying for shelf space at retail outlets, including offering lower prices and promotions. Most retailers stocked two baby food product ranges—Gerber, plus either Heinz or Beech-Nut. Gerber's products were sold in over 90 per cent of all supermarkets in the United States, while for Heinz this was only 40 per cent and for Beech-Nut 45 per cent. The competition between the two smaller rivals led to pressure on Gerber's pricing as well. The FTC was concerned that this competition would be removed after the merger. In addition, entry barriers were found to be high. The court concluded that:

> the merger will eliminate competition at the wholesale level between the only two competitors for the 'second shelf' position. Competition between Heinz and Beech-Nut to gain accounts at the wholesale level is fierce with each contest concluding in a winner-take-all result...

> Heinz's own documents recognize the wholesale competition and anticipate that the merger will end it. Indeed, those documents disclose that Heinz considered three options to end the vigorous wholesale competition with Beech-Nut: two involved innovative measures while the third entailed the acquisition of Beech-Nut. Heinz chose the third, and least pro-competitive, of the options.[26]

The issue of the closest competing products also arose in LOVEFiLM's acquisition of **7.36** Amazon's online DVD rental service in the United Kingdom.[27] Online DVD rental involved customers paying a fixed monthly fee entitling them to select and receive DVDs via the post. This was a relatively new type of business model at the time (although streaming of films would overtake this model within a few years). The merged entity would have a share of online DVD rentals of 92 per cent. Despite this strong position, the OFT approved the merger unconditionally. Survey evidence showed that customers saw other methods of accessing DVDs as close substitutes, in particular renting DVDs from bricks-and-mortar shops (now virtually extinct) and downloading films. Internal documents indicated that the merging parties regularly monitored activities relating to these other products, as opposed to monitoring each other, thus confirming the competitive constraint from these other products. This evidence was consistent both with online DVD rentals forming part of a wider relevant market, and with each merging party not being the other's closest competitor. Either way, the conclusion was that no SLC would result from the merger.

---

[25] *Federal Trade Commission v HJ Heinz Co* 246 F 3d 708 (US Ct of Apps (District of Colombia Cir.), 2001).
[26] Ibid., at [23] and [15].
[27] Office of Fair Trading (2008), 'Anticipated Acquisition of the Online DVD Rental Subscription Business of Amazon Inc. by LOVEFiLM International Limited', ME/3534/08, 8 May. We advised the acquiring party in this transaction. Through this deal Amazon became a minority shareholder in LOVEFiLM, and in 2011 it took full control of the company.

7.4.2 Diversion ratios as a measure of closeness of competition

7.37 Diversion ratios seek to capture a basic economic logic: if the price of a product is raised, some consumers will switch away from that product and spend their money elsewhere. The alternative product that captures most of this diverted expenditure will have the highest diversion ratio, and can be regarded as the closest substitute of the first product. In general, the higher the diversion ratio between two products, the greater the competition is between them, and the more concerned you should be if they merge. The diversion ratio in its own right gives useful information on closeness of competition. It is also the key parameter used in the simulation of price effects of mergers, as discussed in section 7.5.

7.38 There are various definitions of the diversion ratio. The differences between these definitions are subtle, and sometimes do not matter. We illustrate them through a numerical example, which we try to keep simple by using the ubiquitous apples and pears (based on ten Kate and Niels, 2014). As an indicator of the closeness of competition between products, any of the diversion ratios shown in this example will do a reasonable job. However, if the diversion ratio is used to simulate the price effects of a merger, not all these ratios are suitable, as we discuss later.

7.39 Say there are 10,000 customers in an area, buying on average 10 kg of apples per year, at €3 per kg. The total sales of apples amount to 100,000 kg, worth €300,000. Now the price of apples is increased by 10 per cent. This leads to 2,000 customers (20 per cent of all customers) ceasing to buy apples. 800 of them turn to pears, 600 to other fruits, and 600 give up consuming fruit altogether (i.e. they spend their money elsewhere in the economy). Assume that the 8,000 non-switching customers were buying 10.5 kg of apples on average before the price increase; the 800 customers switching to pears were buying 9 kg of apples on average; the 600 customers switching to other fruits 8 kg; and the 600 customers giving up fruit 6.67 kg. This leads to the situation shown in Table 7.1.

Table 7.1 Diversion ratios: an apples and pears example

Apple purchases	Before price increase	After price increase	Loss after price increase	Switching to pears	Switching to other fruits	Give up fruit
Customers	10,000	8,000	2,000	800	600	600
Initial apple sales to those customers (kg)	100,000	84,000	16,000	7,200	4,800	4,000
Initial apple sales to those customers (€)	300,000	252,000	48,000	21,600	14,400	12,000
New pear sales to those customers (kg)				6,400		
New pear sales to those customers (€)				22,400		
Switching-customers diversion ratio	800/2,000 = 40%					
Lost-sales diversion ratio	7,200/16,000 = 45% (volume); 21,600/48,000 = 45% (value)					
Volume capture ratio	6,400 kg of pears/16,000 kg of apples = 4 kg of pears/10 kg of apples					
Value capture ratio	22,400/48,000 = 46.7%					

You may have worked out that the own-price elasticity of demand for apples is –1.6: the 10 **7.40** per cent price increase resulted in a 16 per cent volume loss (16,000 out of 100,000 apples). However, here we are interested in diversion ratios. A frequently used definition illustrated in this example is the fraction of customers switching away from A that is diverted to B. Of the 2,000 apple customers who switch after the 10 per cent price increase, 800 turn to pears. So in this case the diversion ratio from apples to pears would be 800/2,000 = 40 per cent. We call this the switching-customers diversion ratio. Another way of defining the diversion ratio is in terms of loss of sales, either in volume or value terms. We call this the lost-sales diversion ratio. In volume terms this ratio is 7,200/16,000 = 45 per cent. The 800 apple customers switching to pears used to buy 7,200 kg of apples, while the total volume loss of apples is 16,000 kg. In value terms the lost-sales ratio is the same in this example, since apple prices are uniform at €3 per kg—that is, 21,600/48,000 = 45 per cent. The 800 switchers used to spend €21,600 on apples, while the total loss of apples sales is €48,000.

So far this example has considered diversion from the perspective of the apples. Now we **7.41** turn to the pear side to define the diversion ratio. A more accurate term would be 'capture ratio', as it is about the pear side capturing a share of the lost apple sales. Assume that the 800 former apple customers buy on average 8 kg of pears at a price of €3.50 per kg (recall that they used to buy on average 9 kg of apples at €3 per kg). So they buy 6,400 kg of pears for a total amount of €22,400. If we define the diversion ratio as the volume capture ratio it is equal to 6,400/16,000 = 4 kg of pears/10 kg of apples. This cannot be expressed as 40 per cent, because (literally and technically) you cannot divide kilos of pears by kilos of apples. If we define the diversion ratio in value terms—the value capture ratio—it equals 22,400/ 48,000 = 46.7 per cent. The increased expenditure on pears is €22,400, while the total loss of sales of apples is €48,000. Altogether this example gives four different diversion ratios: a switching-customers ratio of 40 per cent, a lost-sales ratio of 45 per cent, a volume capture ratio of 4 kg pears/10 kg apples, and a value capture ratio of 46.7 per cent.

7.4.3 Which diversion ratio?

Which of these ratios is the right one to use? That depends on the purpose of the diversion **7.42** ratio. As mentioned before, any of the four ratios will do a reasonable job as an indicator of the closeness of competition between products. In the above example they had broadly similar values. However, if the diversion ratio is used to simulate the price effects of an apples-and-pears merger (or for the hypothetical monopolist test), only the two capture ratios on the pear side are strictly correct. This is because you need to assess the effect of the price increase on the merged entity's profitability. This depends on the relationship between lost profits and captured profits—that is, how do the lost profits from the price increase in apples compare with the profits captured by pears following the switching from apples to pears? Neither of the ratios defined on the apple side—the switching-customers ratio and the lost-sales ratio—is capable of establishing such a relationship. The ratios defined on the pear side do perform the task, as discussed further in section 7.5. Hence, the ratios of 4 kg pears/10 kg apples (volume capture ratio) and 46.7 per cent (value capture ratio) are the most relevant diversion ratios from apples to pears when considering likely merger price effects.

Still, in practice the switching-customers ratio (here 40 per cent) and lost-sales ratios **7.43** (45 per cent) are often used. In part this is because these ratios are intuitive—they represent the fraction of apple customers or apple sales that is diverted away to the other product. In part it is also because these ratios may be easier to estimate. In consumer surveys—as discussed below—it is straightforward to obtain the switching-customers ratio and the lost-sales ratio by first identifying the total base of customers who would switch away from the product (2,000 apple customers), and their total expenditure (€48,000), and then to ask where they would switch to (800 to pears, 600 to other fruits, and 600 giving up fruit). While theoretically incorrect for price rise analysis, this practical approach can still yield meaningful insight if a number of conditions hold. One is that all customers who switch must reduce their purchases of the base product by the same amount. This condition was met in the example above, as all switching apple customers were buying the same amount of apples before the price increase, and switched away from apples completely. Another condition is that all switching customers buy the same quantity of the new product as they previously bought of the base product. In some circumstances this is plausible. If switching is between near-identical products at different geographic locations—think of ice-cream sellers on the beach, or petrol stations—it is not unreasonable to assume that a switching customer buys the same quantity of the product at the other location. The same may hold for switching between different brands of a product that is otherwise nearly homogeneous—for example 2-litre bottles of soft drinks of different brands. In the above example this condition was not met, as the 800 switchers used to buy 9 kg of apples each but now buy only 8 kg of pears. These and other conditions must hold in order for the switching-customers and lost-sales ratios on the apple side to be the same as the capture ratios on the pear side. When designing a survey, you should ideally try to obtain the right diversion ratio. However, if that makes the survey too complicated (capture ratios are more difficult to identify in one question), it is still useful to obtain the switching-customer or lost-sales ratio. The presentation of the survey results should state explicitly that these ratios are used as approximations of the capture ratios, and discuss why this assumption is reasonable in the case at hand.

7.4.4 Consumer surveys to estimate demand responsiveness and diversion ratios

7.44   Consumer surveys are a tool that can be used to estimate demand elasticities and diversion ratios. They can be used to ask the SSNIP question directly—how would customers react if prices were raised by a small amount? And they can be used to obtain information on diversion ratios—if prices were raised, or the product were no longer available, which products would customers switch to? Surveys focused on diversion ratios are often preferred over surveys which try to gauge consumer reactions to a hypothetical price increase. Instead of asking what consumers would do if faced with a SSNIP, a diversion survey asks what their second choice would be if the first choice were no longer available. Forced-choice questions of this type require (somewhat) less hypothetical thinking by the respondents than the SSNIP question, and can be asked to all survey respondents rather than just to those who said they would switch after a price increase, thus generating a larger response base. This allows you to infer diversion ratios, which you can use to simulate price rise effects resulting from the merger.

7.45   Surveys provide information on consumers' 'stated preferences'—that is, what they say they would do after a price increase or if forced to select an alternative product. This contrasts with 'revealed preferences' reflecting what they actually did (or would do). Clearly this raises an important question about the use of surveys: can you rely on the results to show how consumers would actually respond when faced with a price increase or forced choice between options? There is a good deal of literature on how to undertake consumer research in a robust manner. Some common understanding on best practice in the use of surveys for competition cases has developed. A significant contribution in this regard was the guidance document issued by the UK authorities in 2011.[28] Surveys that are suitably designed and executed can provide useful evidence complementing that from other sources, such as internal documents showing which competitors a company focuses on most, or data on where new customers came from and lost customers went. As noted in the 2010 US Horizontal Merger Guidelines:

> The Agencies consider any reasonably available and reliable information to evaluate the extent of direct competition between the products sold by the merging firms. This includes documentary and testimonial evidence, win/loss reports and evidence from discount approval processes, customer switching patterns, and customer surveys.[29]

The UK guidance puts it as follows.   **7.46**

> Amongst other things, consumer survey evidence may be used for market definition or for the assessment of the closeness of competition between firms. We welcome this type of evidence and believe that the use of statistically robust consumer survey research can help us reach informed decisions.[30]

We give some flavour of what good practice looks like in the next sub-section. First we   **7.47** return to the *LOVEFiLM/Amazon* case, in which a consumer survey was carried out focusing on both market definition and diversion.[31] The transaction created a near-monopoly in online DVD rentals. Hence the question was whether LOVEFiLM and Amazon were each other's closest competitors, which in this case (effectively a two-to-one merger) was similar to asking whether the relevant product market was limited to online DVD rentals. Internet-based surveys were commissioned on behalf of the acquiring party, canvassing the views of approximately 2,000 customers of online DVD rental services. First, questions about current behaviour and choice were asked, such as which provider they currently rent online DVDs from, and how much they pay per month. The survey then asked the SSNIP question: say that your online DVD provider decided to increase its prices, so that instead of paying £x per month, you had to pay 10 per cent more, that is, £y (£x + 10 per cent) per month to receive the same service, what would be your most likely response? The 'x' was shown as the price that the respondent actually paid for online DVD rentals, as answered in an earlier question. The online survey question also showed what £y was in money terms.

Finally, questions about switching and diversion were asked: were you to cancel your online   **7.48** rental contract, how would you meet your demand for films? The survey results showed that 30–40 per cent of respondents said they would switch after a 10 per cent price increase. Since the critical loss threshold of 20–30 per cent was below this actual loss, the relevant market was deemed to be wider than online DVD rental services. There was no clear nearest substitute. Instead, alternatives such as renting DVDs from bricks-and-mortar shops,

---

[28] Competition Commission and the Office of Fair Trading (2011), 'Good Practice in the Design and Presentation of Consumer Survey Evidence in Merger Inquiries', March.

[29] Department of Justice and Federal Trade Commission (2010), 'Horizontal Merger Guidelines', August, p. 20.

[30] Competition Commission and the Office of Fair Trading (2011), 'Good Practice in the Design and Presentation of Consumer Survey Evidence in Merger Inquiries', March, at [1.2].

[31] Office of Fair Trading (2008), 'Anticipated Acquisition of the Online DVD Rental Subscription Business of Amazon Inc. by LOVEFiLM International Limited', ME/3534/08, 8 May.

downloading films, and watching fewer films, were all given frequent mentions by switchers. In the end, while there was some discussion about the interpretation of the survey results, the OFT cleared the merger because it found internal business and strategy documents confirming that the parties saw other products as their closest competitors, which was consistent with the market being broader than online DVD rentals.

7.49 Another case where diversion ratio evidence from consumer surveys played an important role is the *Co-op/Somerfield* (2008) supermarket merger, which was cleared at phase one by the OFT.[32] The authority based its decision on what it described as 'probably the largest consumer survey ever conducted in a merger case'.[33] More than 40,000 customers were surveyed in over 400 Co-op and Somerfield stores. Customers were asked where they would do their grocery shopping if the store where the survey was conducted were to close (this was posed as a hypothetical closure, simply to get respondents' views on what they considered to be their next-best alternative; Co-op did not actually intend to close one of the two stores after the merger). Higher diversion ratios between merging stores imply more intense competition between them pre-merger, and hence higher predicted price rises after the merger. On this basis, potential competition concerns were identified for 126 local markets, and divestment remedies were agreed for those markets.

7.4.5 Good practice in consumer survey design

7.50 The literature on marketing, psychology, and more recently, behavioural economics, provides useful lessons for the design of surveys.[34] A survey used for the hypothetical monopolist test or diversion ratio analysis should normally be directed at existing customers of the product in question. Even so, there are various consumer biases that can raise doubts about the reliability of survey responses. If you have ever been asked to respond to a survey of this nature (by telephone, on the street, or online), you may agree that it helps if it is not too long and follows a logical structure. Framing the questions such that the real-world choice situation is approximated as closely as possible is of critical importance.

7.51 A survey must be representative of the relevant population in order to provide statistically meaningful results. Representativeness means that the sample has been selected randomly from the appropriate population. If you are looking for information on apple consumption, the whole population is probably reasonable. If it is underwired bras, you might sample randomly from women. You need similar proportions of geographic, income, and other demographic characteristics in your sample as exist in the underlying population. For example, data from a survey may be biased if it is conducted in a location that tends to have different types of people passing through it at different times. Carrying out a survey at a railway station on a weekday morning will yield a different sample of travellers (commuters) than if the same survey were carried out during the weekend (leisure travellers). Established statistical tests can help determine representativeness.

7.52 Having designed your sampling process to ensure a representative sample, the next task is to decide on the size of the sample so as to ensure that the results will be statistically valid.

---

[32] Office of Fair Trading (2008), 'Anticipated Acquisition by Co-operative Group Limited of Somerfield Limited', 17 November. We advised the acquiring party in this transaction.
[33] Office of Fair Trading (2008), 'OFT considers grocery store divestments in Co-op/Somerfield Merger', press release, 20 October.
[34] See, for example, Tourangeau et al. (2000), Bradburn et al. (2004), and Lucey (2005).

There are no hard and fast rules and there will always be a margin of error, but the larger the sample size, the narrower (and more acceptable) the confidence interval around the survey results.[35] Rules of thumb have been developed from statistical theory, known as the law of large numbers, indicating that you ought to have at least thirty responses in the smallest group you wish to examine. To give an indication from the examples we saw earlier, in *Co-op/Somerfield* around 100 shoppers were surveyed at each of the 400 stores. The survey in *LOVEFiLM/Amazon* was among around 2,000 online DVD rental customers. This was considered sufficient to ensure at least thirty responses for most of the plausible diversions categories (e.g. pay-TV movies, bricks-and-mortar rental), while also allowing the results to be segmented by existing purchasing behaviour of the respondents (e.g. do they currently subscribe to pay-TV?).

Formulating the questions is probably the trickiest part of survey design. The language **7.53** used should be clear, unambiguous and neutral. Complexity should be avoided—for example, many people have difficulties understanding percentage changes, and are more likely to understand questions about price increases if these are framed in terms of absolute amounts, or in both absolute and percentage terms. The survey should start by asking some 'warm-up' questions—about the respondents themselves, their current behaviour and habits, why the customer chose the given product, and whether alternative products were considered. These questions reveal certain characteristics of customers and help bring respondents towards the actual product choice situation that they would be in. Then you can ask the SSNIP or diversion questions. A SSNIP question for a customer who pays €3 for a kilo of apples could be phrased as follows: 'Suppose that the price of apples increases by 10 per cent, from €3 per kilo to €3.30 per kilo, what would you do?' In the first instance respondents could be given options capturing whether they would continue buying or switch (partially or fully), and the likelihood of doing so (e.g. a scale from very likely to continue buying to very likely to switch).

The next question is to ask the switchers which alternative they would buy instead—the **7.54** diversion question. In merger cases where the focus is on unilateral effects rather than market definition, the diversion question is usually asked directly to all respondents, omitting the SSNIP question. It could be phrased in terms of forced diversion. In the supermarket example above, the wording was along the following lines: 'If this store had not been available, which, if any, of these types of store would you have used instead?' In some cases respondents could be shown a list of generic alternatives (e.g. a same-size supermarket, an out-of-town supermarket, and a convenience store), or a list of specific alternative stores in the area. The proportion of customers choosing a particular alternative provides the diversion ratio from the original store to that alternative. This is what we referred to as the switching-customers ratio, or, if weighed by the volumes or value of their purchases, the lost-sales ratio.

7.4.6 Conjoint analysis

Conjoint or discrete-choice surveys are a more sophisticated and potentially more robust **7.55** type of survey. Instead of asking respondents what they would do in a hypothetical situation

---

[35] See, for example, Mazzocchi (2008).

of a price increase or forced diversion, a conjoint survey asks them to choose among products with different characteristics, including price. This process more closely resembles the actual choice-making situation that customers may find themselves in. Given the time involved, conjoint analysis is not frequently used in the context of merger cases. It is more common in other types of competition inquiry. For completeness we briefly set out the basics of conjoint analysis here.[36]

7.56 A conjoint survey presents customers (or potential customers) with a menu of products that differ slightly from each other in their 'attributes', including price, functionality, and different aspects of quality. Two options are presented each time, and the respondent has to express a preference. By varying the product attributes in each option, a picture emerges of how customers trade off price and other attributes against each other. Econometric analysis can then be applied to the responses in order to estimate a price elasticity (or indeed to estimate an elasticity of demand with respect to any of the product attributes).

7.57 Conjoint analysis was used in Ofcom's review of the pay-TV market in the United Kingdom.[37] The regulator sought to understand whether channels containing premium content, such as Football Association Premier League (FAPL) matches, constituted a separate market. The conjoint survey sought to test the importance of different sports when deciding to subscribe to premium sports channels, and to evaluate the degree of substitution between sports. It covered 1,904 respondents who subscribed to pay-TV and watched sports at least once a week (85 per cent of this sample were male, which was apparently deemed representative of the sports viewing population). Respondents were presented with a series of pay-TV sports packages and in each case were asked which of two options they would prefer. Figure 7.2 shows a stylized example of one of these choice situations: two sports packages where the main differences are the price and whether they include FAPL matches. The survey, combined with other evidence, led Ofcom to

Package A	Package B
- price: £15 per month	- price: £13.50 per month
- brand: Sky Sports	- brand: Sky Sports
- live FAPL games: Yes	- live FAPL games: NO
- other football competitions: NO	- other football competitions: YES
- international cricket: YES	- international cricket: YES
- cricket featuring England: NO	- cricket featuring England: YES
- other sports: motor racing, darts	- other sports: rugby, golf, tennis, motor racing, darts, many others

Which of these options would you prefer?

Figure 7.2 Stylized example of the choices presented in a conjoint survey

Source: Based on the sports bundles conjoint survey in Ofcom (2008), 'Pay TV second consultation—Access to premium content', 30 September, Annex 10.

---

[36] Textbooks on conjoint analysis include Raghavarao et al. (2010) and Rao (2014).
[37] Ofcom (2008), 'Pay TV Second Consultation—Access to Premium Content', 30 September.

conclude that channels containing premium football content did indeed constitute a separate market. Setanta Sports, then a new (but ultimately unsuccessful) entrant that had purchased a package of premium football rights, was found to be the closest competitor to Sky Sports, the incumbent channel provider. Channels without this premium football content were not seen as sufficiently close substitutes, even when offering lower prices and other attractive content.

7.4.7 Other evidence on closeness of competition

There are other sources of information on closeness of competition besides consumer surveys. Internal strategy or board documents may give an indication of which of its rivals a company monitors or reacts to most. In some markets companies keep data on lost and gained customers, including where they came from or which competitor they switched to. Such data can be useful to construct a picture of which competitors target each other's customers most. In bidding markets it can be useful to collect data on tender participation. How often was one of the merging parties a bidder in tenders won by the other? **7.58**

The European Commission looked at several of these information sources in the *Baxter/Gambro* merger in 2013.[38] The deal involved two producers of medical equipment, with an overlap in various renal replacement therapy products (used for kidney failures). At the European level, the parties would have a combined market share of 30–40 per cent in a group of products for haemodialysis (HD) treatments, and in some countries this share would be above 50 per cent. In another group of products, for continuous renal replacement therapy (CRRT), the parties would have 60–70 per cent at European level, and even more in some countries. The Commission focused on the closeness of competition, given that Baxter was a relatively small supplier and the parties faced at least one other strong competitor, Fresenius. One source of information was a questionnaire that the Commission sent to customers. In HD, a large majority of these customers named Fresenius as Gambro's closest competitor, describing Baxter as weaker in terms of quality and product range. A questionnaire given to competitors revealed a similar picture for HD. In CRRT, customers and distributors saw Gambro, Baxter, and Fresenius all as close competitors. Such questionnaires undertaken by the Commission in merger inquiries are not usually as robustly designed as the consumer surveys described in the previous section, but can nonetheless give some indication of closeness of competition. **7.59**

The Commission also obtained switching information from the questionnaires. In HD, there were twice as many instances of switching between one of the parties and Fresenius as there were between the parties themselves. In CRRT, switching was found to be less common. Finally, the Commission obtained bidding data at the national level in a number of countries. The overall picture that emerged for HD was similar, with Fresenius participating in most of the high-value tenders won by Gambro, and also winning most of the tenders in which Gambro participated but did not win. More limited bidding data was available for CRRT, but in many cases all three providers were invited to bid. In the end, the Commission cleared the merger on condition that Baxter divest its CRRT business. **7.60**

---

[38] *Baxter International/Gambro* (Case Comp/M.6851), Decision of 22 July 2013.

7.5 Unilateral Effects: Simulating Price Rises

7.5.1 From simple to complex merger simulation

7.61 Diversion ratios tell you whether products are close competitors. But the question remains: how close is too close? To answer this you need to consider diversion evidence within a framework of how prices are set before and after the merger. A range of tools is available for this kind of analysis, with varying levels of complexity. At one end are models with simplifying assumptions on company behaviour and demand; at the other are full-blown merger simulations based on complex estimates of demand systems and competitive interaction. In between are various tools which relax some of the assumptions of the simplest approaches, without being as comprehensive and time- and data-intensive as merger simulations.

7.62 We set out these approaches below, but first we go through the basic economic framework. This begins with the pricing logic of a profit-maximizing company after it has acquired a close, but differentiated, competitor. The thought process is very similar to that for the SSNIP test. Product differentiation gives the supplier a degree of monopoly power. In unilateral effects analysis you have the same demand system as for the hypothetical monopolist test, except that every product or brand is already a monopoly. You can therefore focus the analysis on competition between products or brands. With control over two products, the merged entity will have an incentive to raise the price of the new product portfolio (in the same way that the hypothetical monopolist sets prices in the second iteration of the SSNIP test, where it controls both the focal product and the nearest substitute). Pre-merger, if a company tried to raise the price of its existing product, it would earn higher profit margins on the remaining sales, but would forgo the margins on sales that are lost as a result of the price rise. Owning both products post-merger, the company will no longer be concerned about losing sales to the recently acquired product. Whether it is profitable to raise prices will therefore depend on the company's margins on the existing and newly acquired products, and on the diversion between the two. If it is rational to raise prices post-merger in this framework, the merger may result in an SLC. There are no clear thresholds, but 5 per cent is often used for judging a price increase to be of concern.

7.5.2 Illustrative price rise analysis

7.63 Full merger simulation is often not practical. There are simpler models of competition that are less data-intensive and can be used to calculate indicative or illustrative price increases post-merger. An established approach is to take the Bertrand oligopoly model (see also Chapter 3 and section 7.6 below). In this model companies compete on price, and capacity is not constrained. With homogeneous products, the Bertrand oligopolists behave as if the market were perfectly competitive and prices are in line with marginal costs. With differentiated products, which is the relevant model here, raising the price of one product does not lead to the entire market switching to the cheapest supplier. Customers have differing preferences for the various product characteristics and this gives each company some market power. In this model, price will be above marginal cost in equilibrium—by how much will depend on the degree of differentiation and the number of competitors. To 'simulate' the effect of the merger, you put the merging products together under common ownership and you get a new equilibrium of prices and outputs. By comparing the pre- and post-merger outcomes, you get an indication of the price effect of the merger. All you need for the simplest version of this simulation exercise are estimates of the diversion ratios (e.g. from a survey) and data on existing price–cost margins.

How does this work in practice? Consider a merger between products A and B. Assume **7.64** that they have the same price–cost margin (m). The diversion ratios (d) from A to B and from B to A are symmetric. A further assumption relates to the shape of the demand curve. Two common specifications are linear demand (as in most of the charts presented in this book) and isoelastic demand (where the own-price elasticity is equal along the whole of the demand curve). Based on all these assumptions, the differentiated Bertrand model generates a formula for the post-merger price increase which depends on two factors: m and d. For linear demand the predicted price increase equals $md / 2(1 - d)$. For isoelastic demand it is $md / (1 - m - d)$. Table 7.2 takes you through these formulae and shows the sensitivities of the simulated price rises to different assumptions on demand and different values for m and d.

The results in Table 7.2 should be intuitive. In both formulae, the predicted price increase **7.65** is larger the higher the margin and the higher the diversion ratio. With linear demand, the price increase is 5 per cent if the margin is 40 per cent and the diversion ratio 20 per cent (see the second column). The price increase is 7.5 per cent if the margin is 60 per cent, for the same level of diversion (third column). The higher the margin on product B, the greater the profit on the sales captured by product B from customers diverted away from product A, and hence the more attractive it becomes to raise the price of A after the merger. In the fourth column, with low diversion, the predicted price rise is lower (2.2 per cent with linear demand). Low diversion means that consumers do not see products A and B as close substitutes, and therefore the unilateral effect of the merger is weaker.

Table 7.2 also demonstrates the sensitivity with respect to the demand curve assumptions. **7.66** Across all three examples, the difference between isoelastic and linear is marked. If the competition authority were to use a 5 per cent threshold for the price rise, in one of these scenarios (low diversion) the merger would be cleared if the linear specification is used, but it would be blocked under isoelastic demand. The linear specification reflects a self-correction mechanism in demand: as the price rises, demand becomes more elastic and therefore consumers are more likely to switch away (we explained this in Chapter 2). This makes the merged entity less keen to raise prices beyond some optimal point. By contrast, in the isoelastic formulation the responsiveness to prices does not change, regardless of the

Table 7.2 Illustrative price rises based on simple assumptions

Description	Moderate margin and diversion	High margin	Low diversion
Margin (m)	40% = 0.4	60% = 0.6	40% = 0.4
Diversion ratio (d)	20% = 0.2	20% = 0.2	10% = 0.1
$m \times d$	0.08	0.12	0.04
$1 - d$	0.8	0.8	0.9
$1 - m - d$	0.4	0.2	0.5
Price rise, linear demand: $md / 2(1 - d)$	0.05 = 5%	0.075 = 7.5%	0.022 = 2.2%
Price rise, isoelastic demand: $md / (1 - m - d)$	0.2 = 20%	0.6 = 60%	0.08 = 8%

price level. This can result in very high, and rather unrealistic, predicted price increases. In the *Somerfield/Morrisons* supermarket merger in the United Kingdom, the CC found a price rise in one local area exceeding 1,900 per cent, based on the assumption of isoelastic demand.[39] The diversion ratio between two stores in this area was 72 per cent, and the average profit margin 27 per cent (the corresponding price rise based on linear demand was 35 per cent, as you can work out from the formula).

7.5.3 Illustrative price rises with efficiencies and asymmetric diversion

7.67 The framework for illustrative price rises can be extended by incorporating other features and relaxing some of the assumptions. One extension is to account for cost reductions resulting from the merger. We discuss in section 7.9 how merger efficiencies in general can be analysed in merger cases. Here we discuss the narrower point of how to incorporate any variable cost reductions into the price rise analysis. As we discuss in Chapter 9 (in the context of the pass-on of cartel overcharges), if the variable or unit cost of production decreases, even a profit-maximizing monopolist will have an incentive to pass on part of this cost reduction. Thus, if the merger delivers such cost efficiencies (e.g. by giving the merged entity greater buyer power and therefore an ability to purchase inputs more cheaply), this will reduce the predicted price rises. If large enough, this efficiency improvement could cancel out the price rise or even reduce prices, as we also saw in Figure 7.1.

7.68 In the case of linear demand, there is a simple adjustment to the price-rise formula that takes into account such efficiencies. The price rise formula becomes equal to $md/2(1-d) - \Delta m/2$. As above, m is the pre-merger margin and d is the diversion ratio. Δm reflects the increase in the product margin due to cost reductions from efficiencies. It is assumed that half of the cost savings will be passed on in the form of a lower price increase. As an illustration, using the final scenario in Table 7.2 (40 per cent margin, 10 per cent diversion ratio), if merger efficiencies are forecast to deliver a 3 per cent decrease in marginal costs, we would expect a 0.7 per cent price increase with linear demand. Without efficiencies this was 2.2 per cent. An example of where merger efficiencies were considered as part of the price-rise analysis was the South African Competition Tribunal assessment of the *Masscash/Finro* merger in the groceries wholesale sector.[40] Assuming linear demand, the Tribunal accepted that a 1 per cent efficiency improvement would lead to a reduction in the predicted price rise by half a percentage point.

7.69 Another assumption that can be relaxed is that of symmetric diversion. In practice, one product may constrain the other product's pricing more strongly than the other way round. For example, in a merger where location is key, it may be that one of the stores has a number of other competitors close to it, but that they are too far away to affect the other store. This is likely to result in different diversion ratios between the stores, since customers at one store have more choice than customers at the other. With asymmetry, you have to carry out the simulation for both products separately, and the resulting price rises will be different. The

---

[39] Competition Commission (2005), 'Somerfield plc/Wm Morrison Supermarkets plc', September, Appendix E.

[40] *Masscash Holdings (Pty) v Finro Enterprises (Pty) Ltd t/a Finro Cash and Carry* (04/LM/Jan09) [2009] ZACT 66 (Competition Tribunal in South Africa). We assisted the South African Competition Commission which brought the case originally.

price-rise formula becomes a bit more complicated with asymmetric diversion. Rather than describing it here we show how the results in Table 7.2 may change. Looking at the second column, instead of a symmetric 20 per cent diversion between the two products, we assume that the diversion from A to B is 30 per cent and the diversion from B to A is 10 per cent. This means that B places more of a constraint on A than the other way round. With symmetric diversion, the simulated price rise was 5 per cent. With asymmetric diversion the model predicts that the price of A will rise by 6.7 per cent after the merger and the price of B will rise by only 3.3 per cent. The intuition is that product B is more of a constraint pre-merger on product A than A is on B, and therefore post-merger the price of A will rise more as the constraint from B is removed.

7.5.4 UPP and GUPPI

A variant of illustrative price rise analysis gained prominence at the time of the 2010 US Horizontal Merger Guidelines: the upward price pressure (UPP) test. A related concept introduced around the same time is the gross upward price pressure index (GUPPI). The economists proposing these tests certainly chose labels that caught on.[41] The basic logic of UPP is captured in the Guidelines: **7.70**

> Adverse unilateral price effects can arise when the merger gives the merged entity an incentive to raise the price of a product previously sold by one merging firm and thereby divert sales to products previously sold by the other merging firm, boosting the profits on the latter products. Taking as given other prices and product offerings, that boost to profits is equal to the value to the merged firm of the sales diverted to those products. The value of sales diverted to a product is equal to the number of units diverted to that product multiplied by the margin between price and incremental cost on that product. In some cases, where sufficient information is available, the Agencies assess the value of diverted sales, which can serve as an indicator of the upward pricing pressure on the first product resulting from the merger.[42]

The UPP and GUPPI tests in fact sit somewhere in between just looking at diversion ratios and the illustrative price rise analysis discussed above. UPP starts with assessing the diversion from the original product to the acquired product. We saw that before. But it then assesses the profitability of those sales diverted to (or rather, captured by) the acquired product. The more profitable they are, the more attractive it is to raise price on the original product; hence, the greater the upward pricing pressure. In essence, the UPP test takes the diverted sales and multiplies these by the margin, so $d \times m$ in terms of the price rise formulae we saw earlier. In Table 7.2, $d \times m$ equaled 0.08, 0.12, and 0.04 in the three scenarios. It is important to be precise which d and which m we are talking about. Recall that in the illustrative price rise analysis in Table 7.2 we first assumed that the margins were the same for both products and diversion was symmetric in both directions (we then relaxed these assumptions). Applying the UPP test to product A, the relevant diversion ratio is that from product A to product B. So A increases price, and the diversion ratio reflects the lost sales in A that are captured by B. The relevant profit margin is that of product B. Multiplying the two then gives the profitability of the sales captured by B after the price increase in A. The higher this profitability, the greater the upward pricing **7.71**

---

[41] Leading proponents included Salop and Moresi (2009) and Farrell and Shapiro (2010).
[42] Department of Justice and Federal Trade Commission (2010), 'Horizontal Merger Guidelines', 19 August, p. 21.

pressure on product A. Applying the UPP test to product B, you use the diversion ratio from B to A, and the margin on A, to measure the profitability of the sales captured by A after the price increase in B.

7.72 The UPP measure still doesn't tell you how high is too high. One proposed approach is to compare the UPP estimate with any cost reductions in product A that result from the merger. This comparison seeks to capture the net effect of two opposing forces following a merger: the elimination of competition pushes the price of product A up; a reduction in marginal costs of product A tends to drive its price down. A merger creates a net upward price pressure if the UPP effect ($d \times m$) outweighs the cost efficiency effect. You should perform the same analysis from the perspective of product B (i.e. taking into account diversion from B to A, the margin on A, and cost savings on B).

7.73 Another approach is to take GUPPI rather than UPP. GUPPI is given by UPP ($d \times m$) multiplied by the ratio of prices of the two products. This simply relates the UPP to the initial price levels (though GUPPI does not yet represent a percentage price change either). An advantage of both UPP and GUPPI is that they do not rely on assumptions regarding the shape of the demand curve (in contrast with the illustrative price rise approach). However, there are no clear thresholds for when a GUPPI or UPP is too high, as neither represents a price change as such. The GUPPI estimates are usually compared against some 'tolerable' threshold. To give an indication, under certain assumptions GUPPI can be shown to be twice the optimal SSNIP for a hypothetical monopolist, so a GUPPI threshold of 10 per cent is sometimes used as this may be comparable to a 5 per cent threshold for SSNIP. Thus, if the GUPPI measures are larger than, say, 10 per cent, the merger could raise competition concerns. Following this initial screening, consideration can be given to whether any upward pricing pressure might be offset by factors such as efficiencies, entry, innovation, or product repositioning by competitors.

7.5.5 GUPPI in practice: Petrol stations, cinemas, and channel crossings

7.74 The European Commission and the UK authorities have applied UPP and GUPPI analysis in a number of differentiated-product mergers, involving mobile telephony, airlines, cinema chains, petrol stations, supermarkets, and soft drinks, among other products. Two examples are the acquisition by Sainsbury's of petrol stations from Rontec in 2012, and the merger between Cineworld and Picturehouse (City Screen) in 2013.[43] In both cases diversion ratio and GUPPI analyses were carried out in specific local areas where few competitors would remain. Petrol stations are differentiated mainly geographically (though some differentiation occurs at the level of additional services, such as a grocery store in the case of Sainsbury's, and car wash facilities). The two merging cinema chains were more differentiated in their product offering. Cineworld was a large operator with seventy-seven multiplex cinemas (defined as having five screens or more). Picturehouse had twenty-one mainly smaller cinemas located in city centres.

7.75 In the petrol stations case, diversion ratio evidence obtained from a consumer survey in each local area indicated that the merging parties were not each other's closest competitors

---

[43] Office of Fair Trading (2012), 'Proposed acquisition by J Sainsbury plc of 18 Petrol Stations from Rontec Investments LLP', 7 June 2012. We advised the acquiring party on this transaction. Competition Commission (2013), 'Cineworld Group plc and City Screen Limited', 8 October.

in many of these locations. In one area the diversion ratio from one of the petrol stations to another was 80 per cent, but diversion in the other direction was only 7 per cent (this was due to the specific location of these and competing petrol stations, and highlights the fact that one should not too readily assume that diversion ratios are symmetric). Yet even the 80 per cent diversion ratio did not result in a high GUPPI value. This was because the petrol stations concerned made very low profit margins (less than 5 per cent). The GUPPI was therefore less than 4 per cent in this area, and even lower for the other areas. The OFT cleared the merger unconditionally.

In the cinemas case the OFT found high GUPPI levels in the first phase and referred the **7.76** matter to the CC. In one city the diversion ratio was 30–40 per cent and the profit margin 50–60 per cent, resulting in a GUPPI of 17.0 per cent. In other areas the GUPPI varied from 3.2 per cent to 13.6 per cent. The CC largely confirmed these findings on GUPPI, and complemented them with other analyses. It eventually required divestments in three local areas. In one of these, Cineworld had two multiplexes, Vue (a rival chain) had one, while Picturehouse operated a smaller cinema in the city centre. This Picturehouse cinema was clearly differentiated from the multiplexes. It received subsidies from local government in exchange for maintaining a diverse programme of films and events. The survey evidence showed high diversion from the Picturehouse cinema to Cineworld (40–50 per cent), resulting in a GUPPI of 30 per cent for the Picturehouse cinema. Diversion from the two Cineworld multiplexes to Picturehouse was lower (10–30 per cent), reflecting closer competition from the Vue multiplex. These low diversion rates, combined with a low profit margin at Picturehouse, generated modest GUPPI values for the Cineworld sites (5–9 per cent). The theory of harm in this local area was therefore that the merger would result in upward pricing pressure on the Picturehouse cinema, and not that the Cineworld multiplexes would substantially raise prices. The merging parties were required to divest one cinema in the area.

A perhaps more unusual application of GUPPI was in relation to the completed acquisition **7.77** by Eurotunnel of certain assets of SeaFrance, a bankrupt ferry operator, in 2013.[44] Crossing the Channel through the Eurotunnel is clearly different from a crossing by ferry, but to some extent they are substitutable options for cars and lorries. The question was how substitutable? The CC found that Eurotunnel's main rationale for the deal had been to prevent the SeaFrance assets from being acquired by DFDS/LD, another ferry operator that had just entered the Dover–Calais route. The merger was considered to result in the exit of DFDS/LD, leaving only P&O as a competing ferry operator to Eurotunnel. The test was whether Eurotunnel would unilaterally increase prices after DFDS/LD's exit, caring less about sales lost to its own new ferry operations. In the absence of direct evidence of diversion between tunnel and ferry crossings, the CC considered that lost Eurotunnel customers would be captured by the two ferry operators (Eurotunnel's own and P&O) in proportion to their expected market shares. With ferry operator margins for both passengers and freight being in the range of 65–85 per cent, the CC concluded that the merger resulted in strong upward pricing pressure, as reflected in high values for GUPPI. As a remedy it prohibited Eurotunnel from operating its own ferry operations, thus effectively undoing the original acquisition.

---

[44] Competition Commission (2013), 'Groupe Eurotunnel S.A. and SeaFrance S.A. Merger Inquiry', 6 June.

7.5.6 Full merger simulation

7.78 Full merger simulation is the most comprehensive approach to estimating price effects. It involves specifying an IO model that best reflects the nature of competition in the market. This can be the Bertrand model used in the approaches discussed above, but also any other model specifying how firms compete. Unlike the illustrative price rise analysis and UPP and GUPPI, merger simulation can capture price reactions of the remaining competitors. It requires estimating a demand function that reflects consumer preferences and price sensitivity. The model is then calibrated using actual market data (calibration in this context means assigning values to the key parameters of the model so that it fits the actual data). Some of the data used for this purpose, such as pre-merger prices and market shares, may be readily available (e.g. from industry reports or the merging parties' own market intelligence), but parameters such as the elasticity of demand will usually need to be estimated. In the price rise framework we referred to linear and isoelastic demand, but full demand-system modelling often uses other, more flexible, demand specifications. One of these is the logit framework, which treats consumer demand decisions as a series of discrete choices—for example, consumers first decide whether to buy a chocolate bar or other type of snack, and then they choose between different chocolate bars. While potentially generating more robust results than the approaches discussed above, full merger simulation is not very common because of its complexity and data requirements.

7.79 Nevertheless there are cases where such models have been used in the SLC assessment. One of the earliest was *United States v Interstate Bakeries and Continental Baking* in 1995.[45] This concerned a merger between two leading producers of white bread in a number of cities in Illinois and California. To complement its findings of high concentration and entry barriers in local markets, the DOJ carried out a merger simulation exercise. This was based on a Bertrand oligopoly model to reflect the brand-level competition in the market, and a logit specification to represent the demand conditions. It accounted for the competitive constraints imposed by the closest competitors of the merging parties in the two regions. Under this approach, the predicted price increases were around 5–10 per cent for the brands of the merging parties (which included Wonder, Weber's, Butternut, Sunbeam and Mrs. Karl's), and 3–6 per cent in the overall market. In the end, the merger simulation was not relied on in court as the DOJ settled with the parties, resulting in a number of divestments.

7.80 A similar model was considered by the European Commission in the *Volvo/Scania* merger in 2000 between two manufacturers of trucks and buses.[46] The simulation employed a logit demand system and a Bertrand model of price competition, with the parameters estimated from data on prices, market shares and other variables over a two-year period. The model was applied to two types of truck for each of the major truck manufacturers, and in each relevant country. It predicted price increases in excess of 10 per cent in most markets. The model was criticized by the merging parties in relation to data measurement errors, and the mismatch between actual price–cost margins and those estimated by the model. In its final decision, the Commission did not rely on the results, recognizing the novelty of the approach and the level of disagreement relating to the model results. In any event the

---

[45] *United States v Interstate Bakeries Corp and Continental Baking Co*, No. 95 C 4194, 1995 WL 803559 (N.D. Ill. 1995), final judgment, 9 January 1996. See also Werden (2000).
[46] *Volvo/Scania* (Case COMP/M.1672), Decision of 15 March 2000. See also Ivaldi and Verboven (2005).

Commission prohibited the merger on the basis that it would create a dominant position in several national markets for heavy trucks, touring coaches, and buses.

The Commission did rely on a model of this kind in the *Lagardère/Natexis/VUP* merger in the publishing sector.[47] Editis (formerly known as VUP) was the leading publisher of French-language books at the time. Lagardère owned Hachette, the number two, and wanted to acquire Editis. The merger simulation model focused on the market for general literature in paperback and hardcover format, and estimated demand using a nested logit framework. Data on prices and sales volume were obtained from a market research company. Consumers' demand decisions were assumed to be hierarchical (nested): they first choose the genre of book—e.g. crime, romance or humour—and then the specific title. The simulation exercise predicted a price increase for the merging parties' books of 4.5 per cent for paperback and hardcover titles combined. For paperbacks only, the predicted price rise was 5.5 per cent and for hardcover titles it was 1.6 per cent. There were other concerns, such as the strong access that the merged entity would have to key authors and sales channels. The Commission approved the merger on condition of a number of divestments by the parties.   **7.81**

A further example of the European Commission's reliance on merger simulation is Kraft's   **7.82**
acquisition of Cadbury, approved (with conditions) in 2010.[48] In this case a detailed merger simulation was conducted by the merging parties, based on econometric estimations of demand conditions. The chocolate sector was divided into three segments: countlines (chocolate bars), tablets, and pralines. In the United Kingdom and Ireland the merged entity would have market shares of 30–40 per cent in countlines and pralines. They would have 60–70 per cent in tablets, with a number of strong brands (Toblerone, Milka, and Côte D'Or for Kraft; Dairy Milk, Green & Black's, and Bournville for Cadbury). The parties based their merger simulation on a differentiated-goods Bertrand model of price competition and employed a nested logit demand system. As in the publishing case, this allows for a two-stage (nested) structure of consumers' choices: first, the choice between consuming a count-line, tablet, or praline product; and second, the choice of brand within the selected segment. The model predicted a price increase of less than 1 per cent in the UK and Irish markets, without accounting for efficiencies. The Commission requested further sensitivity analyses of these results, but accepted that the merger simulation exercise provided evidence that the proposed operation was unlikely to lead to significant price increases in tablets in the United Kingdom and Ireland. These were Cadbury's main national markets, but Kraft's brands were not as established. The Commission did require divestments in Poland and Romania, where the parties had a strong combined market position.

A very different simulation model, involving auctions, was considered by the European   **7.83**
Commission in *Oracle/PeopleSoft*, a merger between the second- and third-largest vendors of service software products.[49] The case involved 'high-function' enterprise software for human resource and financial planning functions. The parties faced strong competition from SAP, and a number of smaller software companies. In addition, the Commission found that customers are typically sophisticated when purchasing enterprise software,

---

[47] *Lagardère/Natexis/VUP* (Case COMP/M.2978), Decision of 7 January 2004. See also Ivaldi (2005).
[48] *Kraft Foods/Cadbury* (Case COMP/M.5644), Decision of 6 January 2010.
[49] *Oracle/PeopleSoft* (Case COMP/M.3216), Decision of 26 October 2004.

organizing competitive tenders. It analysed data on hundreds of tenders. A sealed-bid auction model was used to represent the competition in procurement, along with possible efficiency gains. The model predicted price increases of 6.8–30 per cent for various products. However, it was later disregarded by the Commission in light of new evidence, and because it was a model of only three suppliers, whereas market definition evidence had indicated that there was a larger number of potential bidders. Instead, based on analysis of bidding data, the Commission found that Oracle's bidding behaviour was not particularly affected by the specific identity of the rival bidders in the final rounds of a given bidding contest. The presence of PeopleSoft as a rival did not give rise to more aggressive discounting by Oracle relative to bids in which it faced SAP or other rivals. The DOJ challenged the merger, having found price effects from a merger simulation exercise that used a different auction format in the model (an English auction with complete information). However, the District Court rejected this simulation on the basis of the uncertainty of the predictions, and the merger was allowed to proceed.[50]

7.5.7 Rivals' reactions: Entry and repositioning

7.84 The merger simulation approaches discussed above—both the simple and more complex ones—assess what happens to prices in the market if two products or brands are joined together. They do so by taking the current degree of product differentiation as given—that is, products do not change the way they are positioned in the market; all that changes is that two previously independent products are brought under common ownership. In reality, however, other suppliers may reposition their products in response to the merger. Capturing such repositioning in merger simulation models is complicated, and to an extent speculative. The US Guidelines suggest that repositioning can be analysed in a similar way to entry

> In some cases, non-merging firms may be able to reposition their products to offer close substitutes for the products offered by the merging firms. Repositioning is a supply-side response that is evaluated much like entry, with consideration given to timeliness, likelihood, and sufficiency.[51]

7.85 The likelihood of repositioning will depend on factors such as the sunk costs and length of time that any such response would take. Repositioning can mitigate the concerns about SLC. Even if each merging party is the other's closest competitor, other rivals may enter their part of the product spectrum. Yet repositioning may also be done by the merged entity. One case that shows both effects is Heinz's acquisition of HP Foods UK in 2006.[52] This deal led to a potential overlap in a number of sauce products, baked beans, and other tinned food products. It was unconditionally cleared by the CC on the basis that the Heinz and HP brands were not close competitors in ketchup and baked beans, although barriers to entry were high for these products. For other sauce products, the CC found that there was a sufficient threat of entry. A 2009 review of past merger decisions by the UK authorities showed that products in this market were subsequently repositioned in a way that was not predicted by the CC (Deloitte, 2009). There was successful entry into the baked beans segment, with the new entrant capturing 10 per cent of the market (supporting the original decision to

---

[50] *United States of America et al. v Oracle Corporation* 331 F 2d 1098 (ND Cal 2004).
[51] Department of Justice and Federal Trade Commission (2010), 'Horizontal Merger Guidelines', August, p. 22.
[52] Competition Commission (2006), 'HJ Heinz and HP Foods', 24 March.

clear the Heinz/HP Foods merger). However, Heinz itself repositioned a number of its sauce brands and entered the brown sauce market, making it more difficult for entrants to fill this space in the product spectrum than envisaged at the time of the merger review.

7.5.8 Price–concentration analysis to infer price effects

An alternative to simulating price rises based on IO models is to assess directly the rela-   **7.86** tionship between prices and changes in market concentration. This can be done by refer-ence to past events, or to similar markets. The US Horizontal Merger Guidelines set this out as follows:

> The Agencies look for historical events, or 'natural experiments,' that are informative regard-ing the competitive effects of the merger. For example, the Agencies may examine the impact of recent mergers, entry, expansion, or exit in the relevant market. Effects of analogous events in similar markets may also be informative.
>
> The Agencies also look for reliable evidence based on variations among similar markets. For example, if the merging firms compete in some locales but not others, comparisons of prices charged in regions where they do and do not compete may be informative regarding post-merger prices.[53]

A well-known example of such price–concentration analysis across local markets is the   **7.87** *Staples/Office Depot* merger of 1997. The FTC looked at how the pricing of these two retail chains of large office supply stores differed pre-merger across local markets.[54] It found evi-dence in internal documents that the two chains saw each other as direct competitors and that they generally set lower prices in those cities in which both chains had a presence than in cities where only one of them had a store. The FTC's econometric analysis confirmed this, showing a statistically significant price difference of more than 5 per cent between cities with just one of these stores and cities with both (after controlling for other factors that may have contributed to the price difference). On this basis, the FTC concluded that the merger would lead to a price increase.[55]

The European Commission pursued this type of econometric evidence in analysing   **7.88** Ryanair's first attempt to acquire Aer Lingus, in 2007.[56] It identified significant overlaps between the two airlines in thirty-five point-to-point markets. In twenty-two markets the merger would create a monopoly and in the other thirteen markets it would lead to market shares above 60 per cent. The Commission highlighted that this was an unusual airline merger case since it involved two airlines based at the same airport (Dublin). Both the Commission and Ryanair carried out a price–concentration analysis. Ryanair undertook a study of 313 city pairs on which it operated, and systematically tested for any price differ-ences between the routes depending on whether Aer Lingus was present. The Commission estimated the impact of the entry of Ryanair on routes operated by Aer Lingus. It considered that the effect on competition of Ryanair's entry on a route in the past was a good natural

---

[53] Department of Justice and Federal Trade Commission (2010), 'Horizontal Merger Guidelines', August, p. 3.

[54] *Federal Trade Commission v Staples Inc* 970 F Supp 1066 (DDC 1997). See also Baker (1999).

[55] In 2015, 18 years after their previous attempt, Staples and Office Depot agreed another merger. At the time of writing the deal was still under review by the FTC.

[56] *Ryanair/Aer Lingus* (Case COMP/M.4439), Decision of 27 June 2007. The Commission undertook similar analysis in the 2013 case, *Ryanair/Aer Lingus III* (Case COMP/M.6663), Decision of 27 February 2013. We advised Ryanair on the 2013 case.

experiment to understand the likely effect of the removal of this competitive constraint after the merger. The Commission used a 'difference-in-differences' regression technique (see Chapter 9 for more detail on this technique), which covers information both over time and across a number of routes. It found that Aer Lingus's prices were 5–8 per cent lower when Ryanair was present on a route, and that the same effect was not observed when other carriers had entered a route. In contrast, Ryanair's approach (which had comparisons only across routes, not over time) found there to be no significant difference in its pricing depending on the presence of Aer Lingus. The Commission rejected Ryanair's approach on the grounds that it lacked robustness and was not a suitable natural experiment for judging the price effect. It concluded that the merger would create or strengthen a dominant position on the overlap routes.

7.6 Co-ordinated Effects

7.6.1 The two dead Frenchmen and their models

7.89 An SLC or SIEC can also arise in the form of co-ordinated effects. The theory of harm is that the merger results in a market structure that lends itself to tacit collusion between the remaining suppliers. They compete less vigorously with each other than before the merger. Co-ordinated effects require oligopoly markets with few competitors. In such markets, no one supplier can act fully independently, and they all know that their individual actions have an impact on the others. The basic models of duopoly (a market with two suppliers) were developed in the nineteenth century by two French mathematicians/economists, Antoine Augustin Cournot (1838) and Joseph Bertrand (1883). These models are easily extendable to a larger numbers of suppliers (oligopoly).

7.90 In the Cournot model suppliers set quantities rather than prices. The model assumes that there are capacity constraints in production. The two suppliers commit in advance to the production quantity and then place their products in the market. The market clears at a price where supply meets demand. Real-world industries that resemble this model include heavy industries where large capacity investments are decided on years in advance and cannot be altered quickly, and tour operators booking charter flights and hotel room capacity for the following holiday period (see the *Airtours* case below). In deciding on the level of output, each supplier recognizes that its profit will depend on the choice made by the other supplier. They both choose an optimal output level on the assumption that the other will not change its output once chosen. Each then effectively behaves like a monopolist on its residual demand, that is, the amount of the demand left after the other supplier's production decision. Because of the capacity constraints, the two suppliers cannot adjust their choices once the behaviour of their rival is revealed.

7.91 Without going into detail on the mathematics of the model, the end result is intuitive: output, price, and profits in Cournot oligopoly lie at a certain point between perfect competition and monopoly. The essence of Cournot is that the two suppliers are still competing with one another but recognize their strategic interdependence. This means that they can achieve prices above the competitive level and exploit some market power. However, this market power falls short of what could be achieved if there were a monopoly. Neither supplier has the incentive to restrict its output to (half) the monopoly level because each knows that the other would then produce more and capture a greater market share. Achieving a jointly profit-maximizing output would require co-ordination (tacit or explicit) between the two—we return to this below. An appealing feature of the standard Cournot model is that as the number of competitors increases, the outcome moves further away from the monopoly outcome, increasing total output until it approaches the competitive level. In terms of the Lerner index of market power (see Chapter 3), the price–cost margin in the Cournot model decreases directly with the number of suppliers in the model, and increases with the HHI (the more concentrated the market, the higher the margin).

Bertrand altered the assumption that there are capacity constraints and in so doing dra- **7.92** matically changed the predictions of market outcomes under duopoly. He posited that instead of choosing output in advance, the duopolists choose their price. Without capacity constraints, price and output will be the same as in perfect competition. This is called the Bertrand paradox: even with only two horses you get a perfectly competitive race. To see why, imagine that one supplier chooses a price that is 5 per cent lower than its rival's. With no capacity constraints, the cheaper supplier captures all the demand for the product. Anticipating this, the other supplier will seek to adjust its price below that of its rival in order to steal back the demand. This (anticipated) interaction continues until the price is at the level of costs and neither supplier can profitably undercut the other. As we saw in the discussion of merger simulation, economists now commonly use Bertrand as their base model, but with differentiated goods. This model is very distinct from the original homogeneous-goods Bertrand model. Product differentiation is one way out of the paradox: the more differentiated the products, the lower the intensity of competition, and the further prices can be raised above marginal cost.

There are many extensions of the Cournot and Bertrand models. One important variant **7.93** relates to the assumption that suppliers see their rivals' choices as fixed, either in quantities (Cournot) or in prices (Bertrand). This assumption can be changed—a feature known as the conjectural variation.[57] In Cournot, rather than assuming that rivals do not react once output has been chosen as in the standard model (conjectural variation equals zero), it can be assumed that rivals either match or offset output decisions. At one extreme, the assumption can be that any quantity changes will be fully matched by rivals. This conjectural variation of 1 will result in a monopoly outcome—suppliers will be reluctant to increase output too far, since they know that the others would match this and prices would fall. At the other extreme, it can be assumed that any changes in output will be fully offset by rivals. If one supplier increases its quantity, it expects others to reduce their quantities proportionately. This conjectural variation of −1 leads to an outcome resembling perfect competition—each supplier thinks it can bully the others and raises output accordingly, but they all end up doing this. Hence, even in Cournot oligopoly you can theoretically obtain any outcome ranging between monopoly and perfect competition once conjectural variations are included.

The Cournot and Bertrand models are static oligopoly models. Like the standard monopoly **7.94** and perfect competition models that we saw previously, they refer to only one time period (also described as one-shot games). The players simultaneously select their output or price, the market clears, and that's it. Even the conjectural variations (which introduce a form of

---

[57] The OFT issued an entire research report on conjectural variations and its use in competition policy. See RBB Economics (2011).

dynamics with predicted reactions to others' decisions) still take place within the context of a one-shot game. These static models have provided significant insight into the outcomes that you can expect in markets that are neither monopolistic nor perfectly competitive. However, when looking at co-ordinated effects we turn to dynamic oligopoly models, based on game theory. These take the Cournot or (more commonly) differentiated Bertrand models as the starting point, but then play these games over and over again. This opens the possibility of signalling, reputation, and retaliation effects between competitors, and hence allows us to analyse tacit collusion. We turn to this topic now.

7.6.2 Oligopolists and the prisoner's dilemma

7.95 Dynamic oligopoly theory provides a good understanding of tacit collusion. For the purposes of competition law, tacit collusion can also be referred to as collective or joint dominance, co-ordinated effects, or conscious parallelism—the economics is essentially the same. Oligopolists may naturally recognize their shared incentive to limit production and raise prices without any communication. Here we do not deal with explicit co-ordination, such as price-fixing and market-sharing cartels (this is covered in Chapter 5), but the economic principles discussed here apply to both tacit and overt collusion. So, if the two oligopolists recognize their interdependence, will they always find a cosy solution that benefits both? A situation where they don't compete too hard but settle on a price and output that maximizes their joint profits? Unfortunately for the oligopolists—and fortunately for consumers and competition authorities—the answer is no. The mere recognition of their interdependence is insufficient. Effective co-ordination requires more than that. This is because oligopolists face a fundamental problem that they cannot easily overcome without some form of collusion: the attractiveness of cheating on each other.

7.96 To understand this point, it is useful to think of a well-known illustration from game theory known as the prisoner's dilemma. Game theory is a branch of mathematics that looks at strategic interactions between players and predicts behaviour according to the structure of the game and its incentives. It is commonly used in economics to understand companies' behaviour and lies at the heart of modern IO theory. Given the set-up of a game, players may have dominant strategies—that is, strategies that give a player its highest pay-off regardless of the strategic choice made by the other. If both players have a dominant strategy, the outcome is predictable and stable. This is a type of Nash equilibrium, after the pioneering work in this area by mathematician John Nash (1950a).

7.97 Figure 7.3 shows this game in the form of a pay-off matrix. The set of strategies available to the two duopolists, firm 1 and firm 2, is to price either 'high' or 'low'. Both firms pick their move simultaneously (we are still in a one-shot game). There are four possible outcomes to this game. If firm 1 decides to price high and firm 2 prices low, firm 1 receives a pay-off of zero while firm 2 gets the whole market for itself and receives €15. We are in the bottom-left cell of the matrix. If it is firm 1 that undercuts firm 2's attempt to price high, we are in the top-right cell and the pay-offs are reversed (both firms have exactly the same size and costs in this example). If both price low, they get €5 each (bottom-right cell). If both price high, they get €10 (top-left). You can see that this (10, 10) cell is the preferred outcome for both firms as combined profits are maximized. The bottom-right cell represents the competitive outcome (which can be Cournot or Bertrand; this does not really matter here). Will they reach the joint desired outcome of (10, 10)?

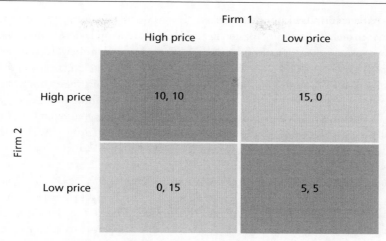

Figure 7.3 The oligopoly (prisoner's) dilemma game: Pay-off matrix

Consider firm 2's preferred choice given each of firm 1's possible strategies. If firm 1 prices **7.98** high, firm 2 will prefer to price low, steal the market, and earn high returns (it gets €15, rather than just €10 if it also prices high). If firm 1 prices low, firm 2 will again prefer to price low, rather than have the market stolen from it and earn nothing if it prices high (the €5 thus obtained is better than zero). This means that firm 2's dominant strategy is always to price low, regardless of what firm 1 does. The game is symmetric, so firm 1 has the same dominant strategy of pricing low. They therefore end up in the bottom-right of the matrix, each obtaining a profit of €5. Clearly not what they had hoped to achieve.

Both companies would like to reach the point where they price high and obtain profits of **7.99** €10 each. However, this is not a stable (Nash) equilibrium because each could gain even more by cheating and pricing low while the other prices high. This incentive to compete and undercut one's rival is present even in a duopoly, and it shows that tacit collusion is not necessarily the natural outcome in an oligopolistic market. The more suppliers there are in the market, the more likely it is that one of them will find the temptation to cheat irresistible. This fundamental oligopolist dilemma should give consumers and competition authorities some reassurance. The original prisoner's dilemma has two prisoners who committed a crime jointly, but are interrogated separately. They get the choice between 'confessing' and 'not confessing'. The game has the same pay-off structure, with confessing being like pricing low and not confessing like pricing high. Ideally they would both like not to confess and walk free, but the temptation for both to confess and get a reward while the other gets locked up proves too tempting, so both end up confessing. You may notice some similarity with the leniency policy for cartel infringements that has been introduced successfully in many competition regimes—the first company to blow the whistle on the cartel gets immunity from fines, and many cartelists have succumbed to the temptation. Leniency policy is another example of the prisoner's dilemma in action (see Chapter 5).

7.6.3 Tacit collusion to escape the prisoner's dilemma

Alas, oligopolists (and economists modelling their behaviour) have a number of ways of **7.100** getting around the prisoner's dilemma. In the real world, they do not play the Cournot or Bertrand game only once. Rather, oligopolists meet each other time and time again in the same market, or indeed in other markets. Dynamic oligopoly theory recognizes that rivalry between oligopolists is not limited to a single game in a single time period. Games are repeated over time, either over a finite number of periods or indefinitely. Dynamic interaction over time allows suppliers to learn about their rivals' behaviour, and between them they could reach an implicit understanding about behaviour that is in their common interest (infinitely repeated games make this easier than games with a finite number of periods). Repeated interactions provide scope for co-ordination, signalling, and reputation building. Importantly, no explicit collusion is required; companies can anticipate the likely reactions of their rivals. For example, if firm 1 always prices low when firm 2 prices low, but responds to an increase in firm 2's price by likewise increasing its price, firm 2 may note this behaviour and continue to price high. In this case the two firms have reached the desired joint profit optimum of (10, 10). But firm 2 will still have an incentive to cheat and diverge from this outcome to earn higher profits of €15 for a while. If firm 1's response is then rapidly to price low as well, both firms gain only €5 in the next period and are unlikely to trust each other again.

7.101   Hence, members of the oligopoly need to devise an effective retaliation mechanism in order for 'high' pricing to be the economically sustainable outcome. A 'low' price reaction to another firm's divergence is a form of retaliation or punishment, even though both firms suffer the consequences. In general, for sustained collusion the cost of the punishment to the deviator needs to exceed its gain from divergence. This will be influenced by the difference in payoffs between the two strategies. Continued co-ordination has a payoff of €10 for a large number of periods. Cheating gives a higher payoff of €15, but only until it is detected. Retaliation brings both firms back to the competitive payoffs of €5, and they may not trust each other to co-ordinate thereafter (a permanent breakdown in trust results from what is known in game theory as the 'grim strategy'). So a key factor is the speed with which cheating is detected and acted upon. This determines how long the cheater can continue earning €15 before retaliation kicks in. Another factor that matters is the discount rate, that is, the degree to which companies value future profits less than current profits. The higher the discount rate, the more the cheater values its short-term gains from undercutting rivals, and the less it cares about future retaliation. Economists have combined these various economic factors—payoff from cheating versus co-ordination; speed of detection; payoff under retaliation; and discount rate—into what is known as the folk theorem or general feasibility theorem. This sets out the conditions for tacit collusion to form a stable Nash equilibrium in infinitely repeated oligopoly games. While dynamic oligopoly models have a range of possible outcomes (sustained tacit collusion being only one of these), they provide useful insight into the conditions required for tacit collusion to be feasible. These conditions have made their way into EU case law on collective dominance and co-ordinated effects—in particular the *Airtours* judgment, to which we turn now.

7.6.4 The *Airtours* conditions for co-ordinated effects

7.102   In *Gencor* (1999) the CFI defined collective dominance as the 'relationship of interdependence' between the parties of an oligopoly that 'encourages them to align their conduct in such a way as to maximize joint profits'.[58] The CFI's ruling in *Airtours* (2002) further confirmed this approach to joint dominance.[59] Under the 2004 EU Merger

---

[58]   Case T-102/96 *Gencor v EC Commission* [1999] 4 CMLR 971, at [276].
[59]   Case T-342/99 *Airtours plc v EC Commission* [2002] 5 CMLR 7.

Regulation and accompanying guidelines the concept of joint dominance is now more commonly referred to as co-ordinated effects.[60] The *Airtours* case was an appeal against the European Commission's decision to block the proposed acquisition of First Choice, a rival tour operator.[61] The Commission was concerned that the UK market for short-haul foreign package holidays was already concentrated, with Airtours, First Choice, Thomson, and Thomas Cook having a combined market share of more than 80 per cent. In coming to its prohibition decision, the Commission had largely relied on a theory of oligopolistic interdependence in a static sense, with tour operators behaving like Cournot oligopolists setting quantities. The CFI found this to be insufficient. It stated that collective dominance arises when the adoption of a long-lasting common policy by the members of an oligopoly is 'possible, economically rational, and hence preferable'.[62] In other words, joint dominance is about tacit collusion, not mere oligopolistic interdependence. The CFI translated this into guidance in the form of three conditions that need to be met to support a concern of collective dominance. First, the members of the 'dominant oligopoly' must have the ability to monitor the other members (transparency). This makes economic sense: the market must be sufficiently transparent such that members can co-ordinate on prices or output without communication, and can easily detect deviations so there is limited opportunity for cheating. Second, suitable retaliation mechanisms must exist should one of the oligopolists cheat. Third, the reaction of current and future competitors, as well as consumers, must be unable to destabilize the outcome of the common policy. This basically means that all major suppliers in the market must participate in the tacit agreement, and entry barriers must be high.

In assessing whether these conditions are met, an understanding of the nature of the market is necessary. As we saw earlier, a wide range of outcomes is possible within these oligopolistic market structures. A number of indicators are of relevance. To some extent taking a 'checklist' approach to assess each of these indicators is inevitable. One indicator is that there are very few competitors in the market (EU case law has called this 'tight oligopoly', a term that does not really exist in economic theory). Another is transparency, which makes it easier to co-ordinate prices and to detect cheating. A further factor is whether products are homogeneous. If they are, co-ordination may be easier as it needs to focus only on price, and the oligopolists will understand each other's cost structures. Co-ordination is generally more difficult in markets with differentiated products, as there are more competitive dimensions than just price on which a common understanding must be reached. Stable demand and low levels of technological change also make tacit collusion easier. **7.103**

Excess capacity is an indicator of the ability to retaliate. It allows oligopolists to increase production quickly and thereby retaliate effectively by lowering the market price in response to cheating. Multi-market contact is another indicator. Retaliation can occur in another market where the companies also compete. The speed with which prices can be adjusted matters too. The ability to retaliate will be restricted if prices or output choices are **7.104**

---

[60] Council Regulation (EC) No 139/2004 of 20 January 2004 on the control of concentrations between undertakings (the EC Merger Regulation) (Text with EEA relevance); and European Commission (2004), 'Guidelines on the Assessment of Horizontal Mergers under the Council Regulation on the Control of Concentrations Between Undertakings', [2004] OJ C31/03.

[61] *Airtours/First Choice* (Case IV/M.1524), Decision of 22 September 1999.

[62] Case T-342/99 *Airtours plc v EC Commission* [2002] 5 CMLR 7, at [61].

committed significantly in advance and cannot be easily altered. High entry barriers reduce the likelihood of outsiders undermining the collusive equilibrium. Note that high switching barriers for customers enhance unilateral market power, but may make retaliation less effective as customers cannot easily be taken away from the cheater by undercutting its price. Unilateral market power and co-ordinated effects often do not go hand-in-hand.

7.105   One of the challenges of analysing oligopoly markets is known as the 'topsy-turvy principle'. Homogeneous goods and stable demand and technology all make the market potentially fiercely competitive, but at the same time make co-ordination easier. Indicators such as excess capacity can signal that the market will be very competitive, as suppliers will have a strong incentive to price low to capture market share and earn revenue to cover the fixed costs of operation. However, as set out above, excess capacity may facilitate retaliation. It is precisely the fact that fierce competition can result in very low prices (because of the excess capacity) that gives an extra incentive to collude and keep the prices high. In terms of Figure 7.3, if the market is fiercely competitive without co-ordination and the (low, low) outcome generates paltry payoffs, this in itself may induce suppliers to seek to achieve and sustain co-ordination. Cheating would be unattractive since retaliation means a return to those low payoffs.

7.6.5   Cases of co-ordination: Platinum, package holidays, and recorded music

7.106   Against this framework we can consider some cases to understand the assessment of tacit collusion. A deal in 1996 between two major mining companies, Gencor and Lonrho, to combine their activities in platinum group metals was blocked on the basis of collective dominance.[63] Although this decision was taken before *Airtours*, it meets the criteria set out therein. The markets for platinum group metals (platinum, palladium, rhodium, iridium, ruthenium, and osmium) were found to be transparent. There was only moderate growth in demand, production technology was mature, and suppliers had very similar cost structures. It was also a 'tight' oligopoly with significant barriers to entry. The two parties, together with Amplats (owned by Anglo American) and Russia (as a national producer), had a combined share of 90 per cent of the global platinum industry. The main producers had financial links and multi-market contacts (geographically and across different metals), so detection of deviation would be relatively swift. Retaliation would be possible because of significant excess capacity and the homogeneous nature of platinum group metals.

7.107   We have set out the economic principles defined in *Airtours*, but what was the result of the application of these principles to the facts in that case? Airtours and First Choice were two of the four major package tour operators in the United Kingdom. The Commission's disputed decision stated that a merger is to be blocked on the grounds of collective dominance when the degree of interdependence between the oligopolists is such that it is rational for them to restrict output.[64] It did not consider the presence of a retaliation mechanism to be a condition for collective dominance. This conclusion was at the core of the CFI's rejection of the prohibition decision: competing oligopolists will always have an incentive to restrict output, but an outcome of tacit collusion is not sustainable if the prisoner's dilemma cannot be overcome. The CFI reassessed the facts and concluded that the merger would not result

---

[63]   *Gencor/Lonrho* (Case No IV/M.619), Decision of 24 April 1996; Case T-102/96 *Gencor v EC Commission* [1999] 4 CMLR 971.
[64]   *Airtours/First Choice* (Case IV/M.1524), Decision of 22 September 1999, at [54].

in a market structure that was amenable to co-ordinated effects. It did not consider the market to be transparent, since flight and accommodation commitments were negotiated on a confidential basis at least one year in advance. Rival tour operators would not necessarily know the full range of locations that others had developed until the brochures for the next holiday season were released. Thus it would be hard to co-ordinate tacitly on output choices. Importantly, retaliation was considered to be difficult. There was limited excess capacity for operators to use for punishment of a rival that deviated from the collusive outcome since capacity choices were made more than a year ahead. Adding extra capacity late in the annual process (once the brochures of rivals had been produced) was found to be expensive, difficult, and generally of lower quality. Hence two of the core criteria to maintain the collusive equilibrium were not met.

In another case that reached the European courts, Sony had sought to acquire the BMG music business, increasing concentration in the market for recorded music. The merged entity would have a market share of 20–25 per cent and the industry would move from five to four major international publishers. The Commission cleared the merger in 2004, rejecting the alleged risk of collective dominance post-merger.[65] The General Court overturned this decision after an appeal by Impala, an association of independent music producers, forcing the Commission to re-examine the case.[66] The court's main reason was that this was indeed a market in which co-ordinated effects were likely to be a concern. The Commission had found that the music products were not homogeneous, as different publishers focused on different genres. While there was reasonable transparency of pricing, there was frequent discounting of list prices that undermined this transparency and would be likely to disrupt attempts to co-ordinate. There was a possible mechanism for retaliation—exclusion of a major's recording artists from compilation albums—but there was little evidence that this had ever been used. **7.108**

The court disagreed with the Commission's assessment. It found that the market was in fact sufficiently transparent for effective monitoring by members of the 'dominant oligopoly' to take place. Even in the absence of direct evidence of transparency in the market, the court considered that the fact that prices were closely aligned and in excess of competitive levels was sufficient, given that there was no alternative reasonable explanation for these features. The General Court's assessment of past pricing behaviour led it to conclude that tacit co-ordination had probably already taken place before the merger. Yet in 2007 the Commission reinstated its clearance, after undertaking further analysis of the *Airtours* criteria for tacit collusion.[67] The Commission did not find online and offline markets for recorded music to be transparent. It also found no evidence of existing price alignment between record companies, either at the level of individual albums or as regards overall pricing policies. **7.109**

This last case illustrates that, even when using the same framework and analysing the same facts, conclusions can differ markedly in terms of whether a market is considered conducive to tacit collusion. Since *Airtours* and *Sony/BMG*, few mergers have been blocked, or **7.110**

---

[65] *Sony/BMG* (Case COMP/M.3333), Decision of 19 July 2004.
[66] Case T-464/04 *Independent Music Publishers and Labels Association* (*Impala association internationale*) *v Commission* [2006] ECR II-2289. See also Pilsbury (2007).
[67] *Sony/BMG* (Case COMP/M.3333), Decision of 3 October 2007.

required remedies, on the basis of a theory of harm from co-ordinated effects. Prominent examples include *ABF/GBI Business* (2008), a merger concerning the production of yeast in France, Spain, and Portugal, reviewed by the European Commission, and the *Anglo American/Lafarge* joint venture (2012) in the bulk cement market, reviewed in the United Kingdom.[68] It seems that competition authorities find the *Airtours* criteria difficult to meet—economically sound as these criteria are. It appears to be more common now to challenge four-to-three and three-to-two mergers under the banner of unilateral effects rather than co-ordinated effects.

7.7 Non-horizontal Mergers

7.7.1 A different concern

7.111   Non-horizontal mergers are between companies that do not compete directly with each other. They often involve complementary goods, in particular when they are vertical mergers between parties in the same supply chain. As we know from Chapter 2, bringing two complementary goods under the control of one company has the opposite effect of combining two substitutes: prices will fall rather than rise. In other words, there is inherent downward pricing pressure after the merger, as opposed to upward pricing pressure (the term DPP has not caught on like UPP has). The logic is that the merged entity is now aware that lowering prices will have a positive impact on both of its goods. The vertical merger removes the problem of double marginalization (explained in Chapter 6): rather than each producer setting its own profit margin, with higher prices and lower output at the end of the supply chain, the merged entity maximizes profits across the two layers of the chain. For this reason, non-horizontal mergers often result in lower prices for consumers. Another reason for welcoming the combination of complementary goods is that it can eliminate inefficiencies in investment decisions, such as co-ordination problems and 'hold-ups' (again, see Chapter 6).

7.112   The concerns about non-horizontal mergers are different. The theories of harm are similar to those in abuse of dominance cases: the ability and incentive to foreclose rivals in upstream or downstream markets, raising rivals' costs, or weakening their offering through practices such as refusal to supply, bundling, and discrimination. In this sense, non-horizontal merger control is trying to prevent such exclusionary practices from materializing post-merger. This may to some extent require a policy choice between ex ante merger control and ex post competition enforcement: is the authority so concerned about the possibility of vertical leveraging that it blocks the merger or imposes behavioural remedies? Or does it allow the merger on the basis that any future attempt at leveraging market power may be caught under the abuse of dominance rules as and when it arises?

7.113   In this section we discuss three types of non-horizontal merger: vertical, diagonal, and mergers with portfolio effects. A vertical merger spans different layers of the supply chain, where one party uses an input from the other. A diagonal merger is between an upstream company and a downstream company that does not use that upstream company's input,

---

[68] *ABF/GBI Business* (Case COMP/M.4980), Decision of 23 September 2008; and Competition Commission (2012), 'Anglo American PLC and Lafarge S.A.', 1 May.

but competes with other downstream companies that do use the input. A merger with portfolio effects is one between complementary goods that may be bundled or tied together. All these non-horizontal combinations produce no immediate change in the level of concentration in any relevant market. They are therefore not caught by the usual market share or HHI thresholds. The theories of harm are based on concerns about foreclosure of rivals post-merger.

The key questions in these cases are: does the merged entity have the ability to foreclose **7.114** rivals? Does it have the incentive to foreclose rivals? Is there a negative effect on competition? Only if all three conditions are met would there be serious concerns. This is in line with the approach set out in the 2008 EU Guidelines on non-horizontal mergers.[69] The ability and incentive to exclude certain competitors does not always equate to the ability to harm competition to the detriment of consumers. The third question, whether competition will be harmed, takes into account efficiencies and the extent of foreclosure of competitors. Foreclosure is a matter of degree and only significant foreclosure would be of concern. Non-horizontal mergers are generally more likely to generate efficiencies than horizontal mergers since, as noted above, they may eliminate double marginalization and investment hold-up. In the legal assessment these efficiencies can be put forward as a 'defence', just as they are in horizontal mergers. Competition authorities must be careful not to use the very efficiencies created by a non-horizontal merger against the parties—we discuss this 'efficiency offence' in section 7.9.

7.7.2 Input foreclosure

The ability to foreclose depends on whether the merged company controls an input that is **7.115** important to downstream rivals, such that a lack of access to it weakens their competitive position. This will depend on the cost of that input as a proportion of the total costs of producing the downstream product. If the input is a relatively small cost item, having to use a more expensive alternative will have little effect on downstream competition. It will also depend on what alternative inputs are available. If an input is essential and has no alternatives, the disadvantage to downstream rivals is absolute (but in this case the upstream company should be constrained by the rules on abuse of dominance, both before and after the merger).

The incentive to foreclose matters as much as the ability. If the merged company stops **7.116** selling its upstream product to rivals, it will forgo profits on those lost sales. Hence, input foreclosure involves a profit sacrifice. Against this, it may generate additional profits downstream as rivals find it more difficult to compete without access to the upstream input. This depends on some degree of imperfect competition downstream. If the downstream market is fully competitive, input foreclosure makes little sense. Even an upstream monopolist that acquires a downstream company will not automatically wish to foreclose the other downstream rivals, since healthy competition downstream can contribute to expanded sales, which in turn enhances demand for the monopoly input and profits upstream. Thus, trying to monopolize the downstream market generates extra profits only if that downstream market is not fully competitive.

---

[69] European Commission (2008), 'Guidelines on the Assessment of Non-horizontal Mergers Under the Council Regulation on the Control of Concentrations Between Undertakings' [2008] OJ C265/07, 18 October.

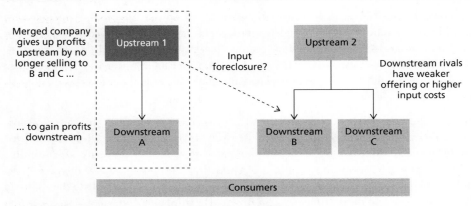

Figure 7.4 Vertical merger: Input foreclosure effect

7.117 The incentive to foreclose depends on the balance of profits upstream and downstream. This is illustrated in Figure 7.4. Upstream firm 1 and downstream firm A merge. The new entity has the option of cutting off downstream firms B and C from the input supplied by upstream firm 1. If it does, it will sacrifice profits upstream on those units formerly sold to B and C. However, at the same time it will earn higher profits downstream as B and C are weakened. These rivals struggle to compete as their offering becomes less varied or they are forced to rely on an inferior or more expensive input supplied by upstream firm 2. Figure 7.4 illustrates a case of total input foreclosure, where upstream firm 1 stops selling to B and C. A variant on this is partial input foreclosure, where upstream firm 1 reduces the quality (or increases the price) of the input sold to B and C, while keeping quality high (or price low) for its newly integrated downstream arm.

7.7.3 Incentives to foreclose: The vertical arithmetic

7.118 The profitability of an input foreclosure strategy reflects a trade-off between profits lost upstream and profits gained downstream. You can analyse this by looking at the arithmetic of profit incentives. Working out the incentives can be a complex exercise since you need to know what drives profits upstream and downstream. For example, the ability to win significant profits downstream will depend on the profit margin downstream and the degree to which the merged company can win additional sales if its rivals are disadvantaged by lack of access to its upstream product. This in turn depends on the extent of the rivals' disadvantage, the diversion from B's and C's products to that of A, and the price elasticity of demand for the downstream product. Table 7.3 looks at this vertical arithmetic in a simple example.

Table 7.3 Input foreclosure incentive: Vertical arithmetic

	Pre-foreclosure	High switching post-foreclosure	Low switching post-foreclosure
Upstream units	8	7	6
Upstream margin (€)	1.50	1.50	1.50
Upstream profits (€)	12.00	10.50 (down by €1.50)	9.00 (down by €3.00)
Downstream units	5	7	6
Downstream margin (€)	1.00	1.20	1.20
Downstream profits (€)	5.00	8.40 (up by €3.40)	7.20 (up by €2.20)
Total profit (€)	17.00	18.90 (up by €1.90)	16.20 (down by €0.80)

Producing 1 downstream unit requires exactly 1 upstream unit. Pre-merger, the upstream business sold eight out of ten units in the upstream market (i.e. its market share was 80 per cent), with profits per unit of €1.50 and hence total profits of €12.00. The downstream business A sold five out of ten units in its market (i.e. a downstream market share of 50 per cent), with profits per unit of €1 and hence total profits of €5.00. What effect does the merger have on the incentive to foreclose?

Consider the situation where the merged company refuses to supply B and C with the input, such that these rivals must rely on an alternative supplier. Say that this rival supplier's input is either inferior or more expensive. Accordingly, B and C become less competitive, and the merged company has an opportunity both to raise prices and to increase its market share (it can still undercut the price of B and C, which face higher costs). If the merged company's downstream sales rise from five to seven (the middle column), the foreclosure strategy works: the merged firm forgoes €1.50 of profit upstream but gains €3.40 downstream. It does so partly by selling more units downstream and partly through increased margins. However, if the merged company's sales rise only from five to six (the right column), the foreclosure strategy is unprofitable. It has lost two units of upstream sales, worth €3.00 in upstream profits, while gaining only €2.20 in downstream profits. In this example the parameter we varied is the extent of downstream switching to the merged firm. Equally, we could vary the profit margins, the market shares, or the pricing reactions. All these factors would influence the incentives outcome, and hence whether the merger is likely to lead to foreclosure.

The European Commission undertook a similar modelling exercise in *TomTom/Tele Atlas* in 2008, a vertical merger between a sat nav manufacturer and a producer of digital maps.[70] The main theory of harm in this case was input foreclosure: would the merged entity foreclose TomTom's competitors in the sat nav market from access to Tele Atlas maps? In order to assess the profitability of such an input foreclosure strategy, the Commission estimated how many sales TomTom would be able to capture downstream (which is similar to working out whether we are in the high or low switching scenario in Table 7.3). It found that the sat nav sales captured by the merged entity downstream by raising its rivals' costs would not be sufficient to compensate for the lost digital map sales upstream. An important factor in this was the remaining upstream competition from NAVTEQ, another producer of maps. The Commission also considered the efficiencies of the vertical integration between TomTom and Tele Atlas. Its model predicted a small decrease in average sat nav prices as a result of the elimination of double marginalization (i.e. downward pricing pressure). The overall price effect depended on the balance of pricing power and merger efficiency. Long-term, higher prices are likely if the foreclosure effect is substantial (and barriers to entry are high), and less likely if the merger leads to significant cost efficiencies. A potential outcome of these dynamics is that one vertical merger prompts another, since rivals that are disadvantaged by foreclosure might compensate by seeking their own vertical partnership. Indeed, around the time of the TomTom/Tele Atlas transaction, rival sat nav maker Garmin agreed a long-term contract with NAVTEQ, and NAVTEQ itself merged with Nokia (which incorporated sat nav services into its mobile devices).[71] Within the space of two months, the Commission cleared both these vertical mergers unconditionally.

7.119

7.120

---

[70] *TomTom/Tele Atlas* (Case COMP/M.4854), Decision of 14 May 2008.
[71] *Nokia/NAVTEQ* (Case COMP/M.4942), Decision of 2 July 2008.

7.7.4 Customer foreclosure

7.121   A different theory of harm from vertical mergers is that of customer foreclosure. This is illustrated in Figure 7.5, where upstream firm 2's access to downstream firm A is cut off or degraded by the merged entity. The analysis of customer foreclosure is similar to that of input foreclosure, and the same vertical arithmetic logic can be applied. An important factor with customer foreclosure is the presence of economies of scale or scope at the upstream level. If downstream firm A is an important route to market for upstream firm 2, cutting off access may make upstream firm 2 a less effective competitor to upstream firm 1. This can arise if downstream firm A is such an important distributor or customer that upstream firm 2's business now falls below the minimum efficient scale for production, such that it becomes uncompetitive. The merged entity will lose those downstream customers who still prefer upstream firm 2's product, but could offset this loss by increased sales and market power upstream.

7.122   Customer foreclosure can be accompanied by input foreclosure—a double whammy. Imagine that, in addition to the customer foreclosure in Figure 7.5, the merged entity refuses to sell upstream firm 1's product to downstream firms B and C. B and C can now buy only from upstream firm 2. If firm 2 is still below efficient scale at that point, the inputs bought by B and C would be inferior to those bought by firm A, and accordingly the merged entity gains market power downstream as well. For the merged entity to have this incentive, downstream firm A has to be a very important distributor, and upstream economies of scale or scope must be significant. Whether this harms consumers still depends on the net effect of merger efficiencies and market power accruing to the merged entity.

7.123   The European Commission assessed both customer and input foreclosure in 2015 when Telenet, a Belgian cable operator owned by Liberty Global, merged with De Vijver Media, producer of two major TV channels in Belgium.[72] The theory of harm regarding customer foreclosure was that Telenet would no longer include rival TV channels in its retail TV offering, particularly those produced by Medialaan and VRT. The Commission first determined that Telenet would have the ability to engage in customer foreclosure, given its

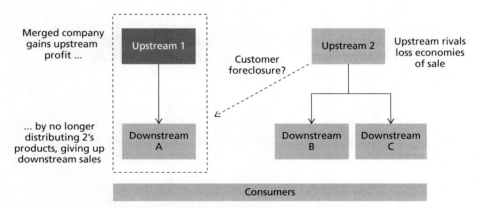

Figure 7.5 Vertical merger: Customer foreclosure effect

---

[72] *Liberty Global/Corelio/W&W/De Vijver Media* (Case COMP/M.7194), Decision of 24 February 2015. We advised the acquirer in this case.

dominant position as a retail TV platform in its footprint (Flanders, part of Brussels, and one municipality in the Walloon Region). As to the incentive to foreclose, it was noted that Telenet would be reluctant to degrade the quality of its retail TV offering by removing popular Flemish TV channels (e.g. Medialaan's VTM channel was the second most popular TV channel in Flanders, with a viewer share of close to 20 per cent). This would affect Telenet's competitive position vis-à-vis Belgacom in the sale of retail multiplay packages (TV, internet, telephony). Vertical arithmetic analysis indicated that switching by only a small percentage of Telenet customers would already undermine a strategy of customer foreclosure. The channels produced by VRT, the Flemish public broadcaster, could in any event not be foreclosed due to their official must-carry status.

The Commission did find an incentive to engage in partial customer foreclosure. This would **7.124** be in the form of degrading the viewer experience of rival TV channels by making them less easily accessible (e.g. through their position in the electronic programming guide), or by hindering their non-linear content offerings, such as video-on-demand. However, new carriage agreements between Telenet and Medialaan and VRT, put in place during the merger investigation, were deemed sufficient to prevent such partial customer foreclosure strategies. As regards input foreclosure, the Commission found that Telenet would have the ability and incentive to refuse to license the newly acquired channels (Vier and Vijf) to rival TV platforms, the largest of which was Belgacom. The Commission imposed a behavioural remedy, requiring Telenet to license Vier and Vijf to other TV platforms on FRAND (fair, reasonable, and non-discriminatory) terms for a period of seven years—see Chapter 8 on FRAND remedies.

7.7.5 Diagonal mergers

A diagonal merger is between an upstream company and a downstream competitor to a **7.125** customer of that upstream company. See Figure 7.6, where downstream company A merges with upstream company 2. This type of merger lacks the co-ordination efficiencies that arise in a vertical merger, since company A does not actually use the products of upstream company 2. The theory of harm is that the merged entity could harm downstream company B by raising the prices it charges for the input used by company B.

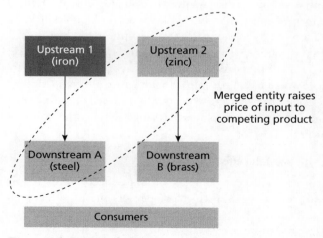

Figure 7.6 Diagonal merger

7.126 The usual analysis of ability, incentive, and effect applies. The merged company has a greater ability to foreclose company B if its upstream input is an important component of B's product, and if B lacks a good alternative to that input. The classic (hypothetical) example of a diagonal merger creating a competition problem involves steel and brass as the downstream products, and iron and zinc as the upstream products. Steel is an alloy of iron and carbon, and brass of copper and zinc. For a number of applications, steel and brass compete in the same relevant market. What happens if the main producer of zinc is acquired by a producer of steel? Although there is no obvious horizontal overlap, a merger between the steel and the zinc producer can have anti-competitive effects if the merged entity can raise the price of zinc and this feeds through to a higher price for brass. Subsequently, customers will switch to steel from brass, benefiting the steel business of the merged company. Thus, a price rise for zinc becomes more profitable than it was before the merger of zinc and steel. This conclusion relies on three conditions. First, the zinc supplier must have a very significant market position, as otherwise brass manufacturers could simply source zinc from other suppliers in response to higher prices. Second, brass and steel must be close competitors, such that customers will rapidly switch to steel when the price of brass rises. Third, zinc has to be a significant input to the production of brass in terms of its share in total production costs. If not, the zinc price increase might be diluted in the total brass costs, and therefore not significantly affect competition between steel and brass.

7.127 This theory of diagonal mergers was invoked in the *Google/DoubleClick* merger in 2008.[73] As this was a complex merger, we stylize the facts here to focus on the diagonal theory of harm. Google was at the time a supplier of text-based internet advertising ('steel'), whereas DoubleClick provided services and technology used as an input ('zinc') for internet display advertising ('brass'). Display advertising consisted of images and other audiovisual content, and competed with text-based advertising. DoubleClick's technology was a necessary input for display advertising, but not for Google's text-based advertising. The theory of harm was that the merged company might raise DoubleClick's prices, which would result in higher input costs for display advertising and therefore ultimately generate switching towards Google's text-based adverts. The European Commission cleared the merger, having concluded that the incentive for a DoubleClick price rise was not consistent with this theory of harm. It found that there were credible alternatives to DoubleClick's technology and services. This would enable display advertisers to substitute away from DoubleClick in the event of the merged entity charging higher prices for DoubleClick. This is equivalent to our brass producers being able to switch to other options for their zinc. The Commission also investigated the dilution effect and found that the cost of DoubleClick's technology represented only a small proportion of the total costs of providing display advertising. Hence, a price rise would have little impact on downstream competition between display advertising and Google's text advertisements. (As it turned out, the DoubleClick acquisition allowed Google to grow in display advertising itself; in other words, it became a steel and brass producer.)

7.7.6 Mergers with portfolio effects

7.128 Portfolio effects—also called conglomerate or range effects—arise if a merged company can offer bundled products against which competitors offering a smaller portfolio cannot

---

[73] *Google/DoubleClick* (Case COMP/M.4731), Decision of 11 March 2008.

compete. The general idea is that a company that is active in various different, but related, markets can exercise market power even without necessarily being dominant in the individual markets. The theory of harm is that having a portfolio of activities in different markets gives the merged entity a degree of market power that is greater than the sum of its parts. The concept of portfolio power was applied by the European Commission in *Guinness/ Grand Metropolitan* in 1997, a deal involving a wide range of alcoholic beverages:

> The holder of a portfolio of leading spirit brands may enjoy a number of advantages. In particular, his position in relation to his customers is stronger since he is able to provide a range of products and will account for a greater proportion of their business, he will have greater flexibility to structure his prices, promotions and discounts, he will have greater potential for tying, and he will be able to realise economies of scale and scope in his sales and marketing activities. Finally the implicit (or explicit) threat of a refusal to supply is more potent.[74]

Is there really a concern here? A broad portfolio may allow a company to offer its customers product bundles or one-stop shopping, or to obtain economies of scope in production and distribution. All of this can be efficient and beneficial for consumers—we explained the efficiency benefits from bundling in Chapter 4. But imagine that the merged company produces two complementary products while all its rivals produce only one (i.e. the merged entity has the greater portfolio). The theory of harm is that the merged entity will increase the price of one product when sold on a stand-alone basis, while keeping constant or lowering the bundled price of the two products. This would give customers an incentive to buy the second product from the merged entity as well, and potentially allow it to exclude competition for that second product. This is the same theory of harm as for bundling and tying as an abuse of dominance. However, as with other non-horizontal mergers, the framework of ability, incentive, and effect applies when analysing portfolio effects. In particular, in the merger context, a portfolio effects theory of harm does not work unless customers have preferences for buying the bundle and there are significant economies of scope in supplying that bundle (which gives the ability to foreclose). Another precondition is that rivals in the second market can be kept at a disadvantage (which gives the incentive to foreclose). If rivals have counterstrategies, such as entering the second market themselves and offering both products, competition will be 'bundle to bundle' and the portfolio concern is diminished. We return to portfolio and range effects when discussing merger efficiencies in section 7.9.

7.129

7.8 Minority Shareholdings

7.8.1 Theories of harm from minority shareholdings

Merger control usually deals with transactions where control of a company changes: one party acquires a controlling stake in another, or the two parties create a new company with a new ownership structure. Competition authorities also increasingly deal with partial acquisitions and minority shareholdings under the merger rules (albeit that not all authorities have jurisdiction to do so). Such shareholdings are common in some countries. They can be pure financial investments, or strategic investments with an eye on future market developments. Economic theory shows that minority shareholdings can have negative effects on competition in certain circumstances. There are two main drivers for this. One

7.130

---

[74] *Guinness/Grand Metropolitan* (Case IV/M. 938), Decision of 15 October 1997, at [40].

is that the minority interest grants the acquirer a limited, non-controlling degree of influence on the company, which can nonetheless affect certain strategic decisions (e.g. through voting or veto rights). The other is that the minority shareholding normally entitles the acquirer to a proportionate share of the profit (through dividends), and this may give it an incentive to dampen competition so as to enhance the profitability of the target company. This gives rise to a number of possible theories of harm, which we discuss here. However, a preliminary observation is that any negative effects on competition from minority shareholdings will logically tend to be an order of magnitude smaller than those from full mergers and acquisitions.

7.131 One theory of harm is that of horizontal unilateral effects. When a company acquires a financial stake in a competitor, this usually brings with it an incentive for the acquiring company to raise its own price (or, more generally, to compete less aggressively). In doing so it may lose customers, but some of these will switch to the target company if the two are close competitors. This increases the target company's sales and profits and, as a result, the value of the acquirer's financial stake. The analysis of such unilateral effects is very similar to the price rise analysis we discussed previously. You can basically apply the same formulae for the illustrative price rise, UPP and GUPPI. The only difference is that the acquirer does not obtain 100 per cent of the profits of the acquired product, but a fraction that is proportionate to its shareholding. The resulting upward pricing pressure will therefore be smaller than for a full merger, but in some cases may still be sufficient to cause SLC concerns. In practice, the acquiring company may not always benefit directly from an increase in the target company's profits. For example, the target may decide to invest its profits in additional production capacity, rather than paying dividends to shareholders. In this case the proportionate price rise analysis will overstate the true unilateral effects.

7.132 Another theory of harm is that of co-ordinated effects. Competitors owning minority shares in each other, or both holding minority shares in a third company, may provide another mechanism to co-ordinate actions, communicate intentions, or retaliate in the event of deviation. Minority or cross-shareholdings are therefore a relevant factor when assessing the criteria for co-ordinated effects. The European Commission raised concerns about co-ordinated effects through minority shareholdings in the *VEBA/VIAG* merger in 2000.[75] This merger, together with another deal (RWE/VEW) that was reviewed in parallel by the German competition authority, would create a strong duopoly in the German wholesale electricity market. In addition, there was a complex web of minority shareholdings held by both VEBA/VIAG and RWE/VEW in various regional and local electricity suppliers. The Commission was concerned that these shareholdings would enhance the likelihood of co-ordination between the duopolists. Both deals were cleared subject to structural and behavioural remedies. These included extensive divestments by both groups of their minority shareholdings in regional and local suppliers. VEBA/VIAG and RWE/VEW were also required to sell the shares they each held in VEAG, another wholesale producer, enabling it to compete more effectively with the two groups.

7.133 A further theory of harm is that of vertical foreclosure. For diverse strategic and commercial reasons, companies sometimes take a non-controlling stake in a distributor (forward shareholding) or a supplier (backward shareholding). As in the case of outright vertical

---

[75] *VEBA/VIAG* (Case COMP/M.1673), Decision of 13 June 2000.

mergers, such shareholdings could in theory give rise to concerns about input or customer foreclosure. An example is the *IPIC/MAN Ferrostaal* merger in 2009.[76] IPIC, an investment company with shares in various industrial companies, sought to acquire MAN Ferrostaal, a contractor company. There were no horizontal overlaps between the parties, but one vertical issue arose involving a minority shareholding. IPIC held a controlling stake in AMI, one of two leading producers of melamine (a chemical compound used across a range of industries). MAN Ferrostaal had a 30 per cent stake in Eurotecnica, which owned essential technology for the production of melamine and licensed this to producers such as AMI. The Commission was concerned that this minority shareholding, while not controlling, was sufficient to exercise influence over certain strategic decisions that required a 'super majority' according to Eurotecnica's governance structure. This influence might be used to disadvantage AMI's rivals. The Commission cleared the deal on the condition that IPIC divest its entire minority shareholding in Eurotecnica.

7.8.2 A minority saga: The *Ryanair/Aer Lingus* case

Ryanair tried to acquire Aer Lingus, the other major airline in Ireland, a number of times, but twice found the European Commission in its way—in 2007 and 2013.[77] From 2006, as part of its (hostile) acquisition move, Ryanair had gradually increased its share in Aer Lingus, reaching 29.82 per cent in 2008. After the Commission's prohibition of the full merger in 2013, the UK authorities challenged the minority shareholding itself (the European Commission had lacked the jurisdiction to do so). The CC found an SLC from the 29.82 per cent shareholding and ordered Ryanair to reduce it to a maximum 5 per cent.[78]

7.134

The CC was not very concerned about unilateral price effects. At the time of the analysis Ryanair had held the minority share in Aer Lingus for several years, so plenty of data was available on the effects of this shareholding on competition in the relevant markets. There was no evidence that Ryanair's own pricing had been affected. The CC accepted that strong competition remained between the two airlines in the period of Ryanair's shareholding (indeed, the evidence suggested that competition had intensified over the years). Moreover, the CC did not expect the shareholding to cause Aer Lingus's management to compete less fiercely with Ryanair in order to avoid antagonizing its largest shareholder. It also rejected the theory of harm of co-ordinated effects between the two airlines, given the well-publicized animosity between them.

7.135

Instead, the CC's concerns focused on potential ways in which Ryanair could affect Aer Lingus's commercial policy and strategy, and thereby weaken it as a competitor. This mechanism would arise through Aer Lingus's governance structure. In particular, the CC was concerned that the shareholding would enable Ryanair to prevent Aer Lingus from combining with another airline (through a merger, acquisition or joint venture), or from other corporate actions such as issuing new shares. Ryanair's minority stake would provide it with sufficient votes to block special resolutions, which required approval by more than 75 per cent of shareholders at a general meeting. The CC was also concerned that having a

7.136

---

[76] *IPIC/MAN Ferrostaal AG* (Case COMP/M.5406), Decision of 13 March 2009.
[77] *Ryanair/Aer Lingus* (Case COMP/M.4439), Decision of 27 June 2007; and *Ryanair/Aer Lingus III* (Case COMP/M.6663), Decision of 27 February 2013. We advised Ryanair on the latter case.
[78] Competition Commission (2013), 'Ryanair Holdings plc and Aer Lingus Group plc', 28 August. We advised Ryanair also on this case.

competitor like Ryanair as a shareholder would in itself make Aer Lingus less attractive to other potential airline partners.

7.137 The CC concluded that its concerns could be addressed only through a (partial) divestment of Ryanair's shares. In order to determine the minimum size of such divestment, it assessed Ryanair's effective voting power—that is, the number of votes available to Ryanair relative to the total number of votes actually submitted at a shareholders' meeting. The CC identified a range of potential voting scenarios that would increase Ryanair's effective voting power beyond its actual share. One scenario was where the Irish government—the other major shareholder in Aer Lingus, with a stake of 25.1 per cent—abstained from voting at a shareholders' meeting. Another scenario was one of limited turnout by shareholders other than Ryanair and the Irish government. The CC also considered it possible that some shareholders ('allies') might vote in line with Ryanair on a particular issue, and that the Irish government might sell its stake at some point in the future, with its shares being dispersed to the general public (thereby potentially reducing the turnout for those shares). A number of scenarios that combined these situations were considered for different levels of voter turnout at Aer Lingus's shareholders' meetings. This is shown in Table 7.4.

7.138 The key threshold in this analysis is the 25 per cent of votes cast that would give Ryanair the ability to block special resolutions. The lower the overall voter turnout, the higher Ryanair's share of total votes cast. For each of its scenarios, the CC calculated the minimum level of actual shareholding that would correspond to an effective 25 per cent blocking minority. Consider the cell top-right: here the assumption is that all shareholders attend the meeting (100 per cent participation). Ryanair would then need 25 per cent of the shares to get 25 per cent of the votes. Staying in the same row, assume that turnout of shareholders other than Ryanair and the Irish government is equal to the historical average of 37.2 per cent. In this

Table 7.4 Ryanair shareholding that would give it 25% effective voting power (%)

Scenario at the shareholder meeting	Turnout of shareholders other than Ryanair and the Irish government (%)			
	Historical low (23.4)	Historical average (37.2)	Historical high (41.4)	Full participation (100)
Ryanair without allies, Irish government votes	13.2	15.7	16.4	25.0
Ryanair with allies, Irish government votes	9.5	12.2	12.9	22.0
Ryanair without allies, Irish government stake dispersed	7.2	11.0	12.1	25.0
Ryanair with allies, Irish government stake dispersed	3.5	7.5	8.6	22.0
Ryanair without allies, Irish government abstains	5.4	8.3	9.1	18.7
Ryanair with allies, Irish government abstains	1.7	4.7	5.6	15.7

Source: Adapted from Competition Commission (2013), 'Ryanair Holdings plc and Aer Lingus Group plc', 28 August, Table 3.

case Ryanair would need only 15.7 per cent of the shares to block resolutions. You cannot reproduce this calculation immediately from the table. In this situation you have Ryanair (with 15.7 per cent), the Irish government (with 25.1 per cent), and 37.2 per cent of the other shareholders turning up at the meeting. These others represent 22.0 per cent of shares (37.2 per cent of 59.2 per cent, which is the proportion of shares not owned by Ryanair or the government in this situation). So 62.8 per cent of shares are represented at the meeting (15.7% + 25.1% + 22.0%), and Ryanair has 25 per cent of the vote. In other scenarios, Ryanair has some allies (defined by the CC as 3 per cent of total shares voting the same way as Ryanair), the Irish government abstains, or the government shares are dispersed.

You can see that the 5 per cent maximum shareholding determined by the CC in its divest- **7.139**
ment remedy is based on one of the more adverse scenarios for Ryanair. It lies in the bottom row of Table 7.4, in the situation where Ryanair has allies, the Irish government abstains from voting, and turnout among the other shareholders is somewhere between the historical average (where 4.7 per cent of shares is sufficient to get 25 per cent of the effective vote) and the historical high (where 5.6 per cent is sufficient). The CC rejected behavioural remedies proposed by Ryanair that would prevent the airline from voting against specific types of decision, thereby addressing the SLC concerns. This framework for analysing voting rights in the corporate governance structure can be applied in other cases. Following the same criteria as the CC would suggest that competition authorities do not look favourably on minority share-holdings in companies that are direct competitors, unless these shareholdings are too small to stand a chance of blocking corporate decisions that require special shareholder approval.

7.9 Merger Efficiencies

7.9.1 A balancing act

Mergers usually give rise to some efficiencies. At the very least they cut out some of the **7.140**
overheads (only one CEO and General Counsel required), but efficiencies are often are more substantive than that. They can potentially outweigh the adverse effects of reduced competition. We saw the basic logic of the trade-off between a lessening of competition and enhanced efficiencies in Figure 7.1. A merger will increase overall welfare if the efficiency gains to the merged entity exceed the deadweight loss from the price increase. We also saw that most competition authorities apply a stricter consumer welfare test: the efficiencies must be so large that they offset any upward pricing pressure. Another way of formulating this test is to require efficiencies to be passed on to consumers. Usually the burden of proof for showing efficiencies is on the merging parties, and the authority's role is to verify these claimed efficiencies and to evaluate whether they are sufficient to offset any price increases. Most merger regimes follow a similar approach. The EU Horizontal Merger Guidelines require that efficiencies 'benefit consumers, be merger specific and be verifiable', with these three conditions being cumulative.[79] Similarly, the US Horizontal Merger Guidelines state that the agencies will:

> consider whether cognizable efficiencies likely would be sufficient to reverse the merger's potential to harm customers...

---

[79] European Commission (2004), 'Guidelines on the Assessment of Horizontal Mergers under the Council Regulation on the Control of Concentrations Between Undertakings', [2004] OJ C31/03, at [78].

credit only those efficiencies likely to be accomplished with the proposed merger and unlikely to be accomplished in the absence of either the proposed merger or another means having comparable anticompetitive effects...

verify by reasonable means the likelihood and magnitude of each asserted efficiency, how and when each would be achieved (and any costs of doing so), how each would enhance the merged firm's ability and incentive to compete, and why each would be merger-specific.[80]

7.141 In most of the merger simulation techniques we discussed earlier, efficiencies came in the form of reduced marginal costs. In reality there any many types of efficiency.[81] Yet not all of these would necessarily be of relevance to the merger review. An important distinction is that between efficiencies based on simple scale economies and genuine merger synergies (Farrell and Shapiro, 1990 and 2001). Scale economies can, at least in principle, also be achieved unilaterally through organic growth. They may therefore not be merger-specific in that sense. A merger synergy involves the combination of assets that were previously owned by different companies, allowing output or cost configurations that would not be feasible or practical without the merger. This still does not make the synergy merger-specific. There may be a means of combining the assets that is less restrictive. For example, there may be other merger candidates that have the required assets to generate efficiencies but trigger fewer competition concerns. In general, the more difficult it is to find the assets, the more likely it is that the synergies are merger-specific. Efficiencies that are not merger-specific tend to carry less weight in the analysis. In the merger between Ticketmaster and Live Nation that we saw before, the CC considered the possible vertical efficiencies between the ownership and operation of live music venues and the business of selling tickets.[82] It concluded that such efficiencies could also be achieved through long-term contracts between Ticketmaster and Live Nation, and therefore were not specific to the merger.

7.142 Cost savings resulting from anti-competitive output reductions following a merger also do not carry much weight. In *FTC v Cardinal Health* (1998), two simultaneous mergers would have replaced competition between the four largest drug wholesalers in the United States with a duopoly controlling nearly 80 per cent of the market.[83] The FTC was concerned that hospitals, pharmacies, and government purchasers would find themselves paying higher prices for drug wholesaling services. The merging parties claimed that the proposed acquisitions would result in significant efficiencies. Their principal argument was that cost savings would result from the consolidation and closing of distribution centres. However, the FTC argued that this was actually not a benefit but rather 'the very anticompetitive effect flowing from the transaction'. It pointed out that the parties themselves had recognized that excess capacity drove down prices, and hence the elimination of this spare capacity after the merger would increase prices to consumers.

7.9.2 Sources of merger efficiencies

7.143 The most obvious merger efficiencies are on the supply side: fixed and variable cost savings. A merger can achieve cost reductions in a number of ways, one being economies of scale. As the scale of the production is increased, average costs per unit fall. Another is economies

---

[80] Department of Justice and Federal Trade Commission (2010), 'Horizontal Merger Guidelines', 19 August, p. 30.
[81] See Organisation for Economic Co-operation and Development (2007 and 2013a).
[82] Competition Commission (2010), 'Ticketmaster and Live Nation', 7 May.
[83] *Federal Trade Commission v Cardinal Health Inc and Others* 12 F Supp 2d 34 (D.D.C. 1998).

of scope—joint production or marketing of different products leading to lower variable or fixed costs. Cost reductions can also be achieved through rationalization of production processes, such as improved capacity utilization; lower transport costs by optimizing production locations or distribution networks; and the shifting of production to facilities with lower costs. As noted above, economies of scale as such are not merger-specific. However, a merger can speed up the process of realizing scale efficiencies, which *is* a relevant merger benefit. In the 2001 merger between AmeriSource Health and Bergen Brunswig, the third- and fourth-largest drug wholesalers in the United States (i.e. another merger case in this market after *Cardinal Health*), the FTC accepted the parties' merger efficiency arguments, partly because the merger would speed up the process of achieving efficient scale relative to a counterfactual where each party sought scale independently:

> Based on our review, the proposed transaction likely will give the merged firm sufficient scale so that it can become cost-competitive with the two leading firms and can invest in value-added services desired by customers. Furthermore, we believe that the combined firm will be able to initiate these improvements more rapidly than either could do individually, and that this timing advantage will be significant enough to constitute a cognizable merger-specific efficiency. The resulting firm, operating in a market increasingly characterized by value-added services, likely will provide customers with greater choices among suppliers and therefore will give customers sufficient leverage to obtain competitive prices.[84]

There can also be merger efficiencies directed at the demand side—for example, product **7.144** repositioning post-merger resulting in greater variety and choice for consumers. In the 2008 merger of Global Radio and GCap, two commercial radio stations in the London area, product repositioning was seen by the OFT as a relevant benefit of the merger.[85] The transaction combined largely complementary assets. In the counterfactual of no merger, the independent radio stations would each target a 'middle-of-the road' music mix in order to appeal to a wide audience. The merged company was better positioned to exploit the advantages of having more narrowly defined target audiences—e.g. younger versus older listeners—which could be complementary. Product repositioning by the radio stations would allow advertisers (the main paying customers of radio stations) to reach their target audiences more effectively. As the OFT explained:

> Global will reposition its now commonly-owned stations to attract listeners, in a way designed to increase total audience size for all stations combined, and increase the demographic focus of the respective station audiences. While directly benefiting end-consumers—who are at no risk of price effects—advertisers also benefit: not only from the ability to reach a greater audience, but also to better target their advertising towards more focused demographics (because many product advertisements are targeted, to greater or lesser degree, towards certain age, gender and income groups), which means less wastage of the message and better value-for-money for the advertising customer. Both types of efficiencies, if realized, will improve the Global/GCap station offer to listeners and advertisers.[86]

Another example of demand-side merger efficiencies is 'one-stop shopping' for customers, **7.145** which may reduce their transaction or search costs. This was also found in *Global Radio/*

---

[84] 'Statement of the Federal Trade Commission: *AmeriSource Health Corporation/Bergen Brunswig Corporation*', File No 011-0122, 24 August 2001, pp. 2–3.
[85] Office of Fair Trading (2008), 'Completed Acquisition by Global Radio UK Limited of GCap Media plc', 27 August.
[86] Ibid., at [18].

GCap. The OFT considered that bundles of radio airtime could be sold to advertisers more efficiently as a result of the merger, since advertisers could opt to purchase only one large bundle instead of several smaller bundles from independent radio stations. Portfolio effects where therefore regarded in a positive light in this case.

7.146 Competition authorities also take into account dynamic merger efficiencies in the form of quality and innovation. These are typically considered over a longer time period than efficiencies resulting from cost reductions. Dynamic merger efficiencies include the diffusion of know-how, more efficient use of IP, and increased R&D. For instance, mergers may help develop new products or reduce costs by combining certain assets and expertise that are not easily transferred between separate companies. A merger could also eliminate the duplication of R&D efforts, or facilitate obtaining finance for R&D projects. In 2010 the European Commission approved the acquisition by Microsoft of Yahoo's internet search business.[87] Both companies had lost significant ground to Google in the online search market, with a combined market share of less than 10 per cent in Europe. The Commission found that Yahoo! lacked the ability to compete effectively through innovation, and Microsoft lacked scale. Together they would achieve efficiencies and be better placed to compete with Google. Advertisers and users were expected to benefit from the improved innovation and services, and from reductions in fixed costs.

7.147 A merger between two hospitals in the Netherlands in 2009 illustrates efficiencies in the form of better service and quality.[88] The transaction was approved by the Dutch competition authority despite the combined market share of the two parties being in excess of 80 per cent in the regional markets for clinical and non-clinical general hospital care. Both hospitals had experienced problems and inefficiencies pre-merger. They had difficulties filling staff vacancies, and neither hospital had 'level-2' accident and emergency facilities or adequate intensive-care units. These issues had led to patients in the region having to travel further afield for surgery or being treated in inadequate facilities. The problems were inter-related. On the one hand, the lack of intensive-care facilities limited the types of surgery that could be performed. On the other hand, their small catchment areas meant a relatively low demand for specialist procedures and intensive-care facilities. Specialists were not attracted to these hospitals since they offered limited specializations and low complexity of procedures. In essence, this was an economic problem—the merging parties were operating below the minimum efficient scale for general hospitals. The aim of the merger was to achieve the required scale of operation by combining the catchment areas. This would allow the merging parties to attract larger teams of medics with greater specialization and thereby improve the quality of service to patients. Thus, the efficiency argument in this case was in terms of quality and service rather than costs. The authority found that the efficiencies outweighed the loss of competition after the merger.

7.9.3 Measuring efficiencies: Data envelopment analysis

7.148 For all their importance in merger analysis, merger efficiencies are only infrequently quantified in a robust manner. Economists have developed various techniques to measure efficiency and productivity, which are used in a range of commercial, regulatory, and policy

---

[87] *Microsoft/Yahoo! Search business* (Case COMP/M.5727), Decision of 18 February 2010.
[88] NMa (2009), *Walcheren Hospital—Oosterschelde Hospitals*, Case 6424, 25 March.

contexts. They can also be used for merger cases. Here we present the basic features of data envelopment analysis (DEA), one of the most widely used techniques for efficiency assessment. DEA measures efficiency by reference to an efficiency frontier, reflecting companies that produce the most output at the lowest cost. It is commonly used for measuring comparative efficiency when there are multiple inputs and outputs that cannot readily be captured in a single input or output measure. In commercial merger analysis, DEA is sometimes used as a planning tool—that is, to assess the potential efficiencies to be realized by merging two units or companies.[89] In this same vein it can be used by competition authorities and merging parties to predict potential efficiency gains from a merger.

Figure 7.7 shows an example of the efficiency frontier and what happens after a merger. The frontier is constructed as linear combinations of efficient (best-practice) companies—that is, those producing the most output at the lowest cost. DEA assumes that two or more companies can be 'combined' to form a composite producer with optimally efficient costs and outputs— a 'virtual company'. The actual companies are then compared with these virtual companies to see how efficient they are. In Figure 7.7 this is shown for two dimensions only: total costs and output. More sophisticated versions of DEA can capture multiple inputs and outputs.[90] The figure shows where ten actual companies in the market—A to J—are located in terms of their total cost (the vertical axis) and their output (horizontal axis). You can see that the further a company is to the bottom or to the right in the chart—low costs, high output—the more efficient it is. The DEA efficiency frontier is drawn by joining together the points representing the most efficient companies: B, C, D, E, and F. These companies expend the least cost to produce a given level of output. An equivalent way of putting this is that they produce the maximum output given the level of cost. Company A is clearly not as efficient. It could achieve its current level of output with much lower costs, like virtual company V which is on the frontier. V is effectively a weighted average of the frontier companies B and C. Companies B and C are referred to as A's peers, with B having a higher weighting than C (as its output level is closer to that of A). DEA gives the following insight to the management of A: you could improve your productive efficiency by adopting best practices from companies B and C.

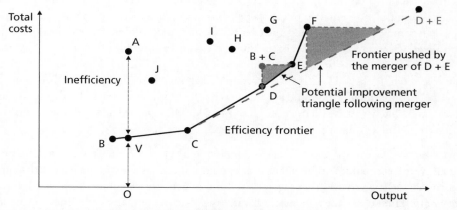

Figure 7.7 An illustration of DEA and merger efficiencies

[89] See, for example, Lozano and Villa (2010).
[90] See Thanassoulis (2001) and Kumbhakar et al. (2015).

7.149

7.150 Now let's consider two mergers, between B and C and between D and E. DEA gives insight into the expected levels of synergy. If the businesses integrate without exploiting any synergies, the outcome would be the points (B + C) and (D + E), which simply add together their existing costs and outputs. DEA can be used to estimate the additional cost savings (or improvements in output) that should be feasible by merging two companies that are already on the efficiency frontier. The possibilities for improvement in the first merger are shown in the smaller shaded triangle, which is obtained by moving to the frontier from point (B + C) horizontally (equally efficient output) and vertically (equally efficient costs). If the merging parties are indicating efficiencies of this magnitude, DEA would confirm that this is consistent with two efficient companies remaining on the frontier. If the merging parties are suggesting significantly higher efficiency gains, this would take them beyond current best practice. A competition authority might thus require additional evidence of these claimed savings, since they would represent a shift in the industry efficiency frontier. As regards the merger between D and E, these companies are also already efficient, and if they achieve no further synergies they reach point (D + E), summing the outputs of D and E into one large company. This point in fact pushes out the efficiency frontier, reflecting economies of scale (there were previously no comparable companies of that size). This changes industry dynamics. Company F, previously the largest supplier and judged to be efficient, now has a larger peer (D + E) showing that additional output growth can be achieved at a lower unit cost (represented by the larger shaded triangle reaching out from point F to the new frontier).

7.151 DEA was used in the context of hospital mergers in Denmark, not under competition law but as part of the policy debates on consolidation. In 2007 the Danish government rolled out a substantial programme centralizing medical services in fewer hospitals, claiming that consolidation of hospitals would increase efficiency. Applying DEA, Kristensen et al. (2010) assessed the government's claim that the consolidations would deliver efficiency gains in the hospital sector. The analysis followed a two-step approach: the cost frontier was identified using DEA analysis; and the efficiency levels of existing and virtual hospitals were measured, thus identifying the potential for efficiency gains. These gains were then decomposed into a number of sources, including learning effects (hospitals adopting best practice from the most efficient ones), scope effects (hospitals focusing on the services that they deliver most efficiently), and scale effects. Because some of these potential gains could be realized without a merger, decomposing the effects in this way allowed identification of those efficiency gains that were actually merger-specific. The results showed that sizeable cost reductions could be realized through learning effects and improved economies of scope. Economies of scale could arise where smaller hospitals merged, but diseconomies of scale were likely to arise if larger hospitals merged. DEA proved a useful tool to test the claimed efficiencies robustly.

7.152 A specific merger context where DEA is relevant is in the water industry in England and Wales. Water companies are regional monopolies but are regulated based on their comparative efficiency—that is, they engage in a form of benchmark competition through the regulatory framework. The regulator, Ofwat, assesses each company's efficiency during its periodic price control reviews, using DEA and other efficiency techniques. It sets price caps and efficiency targets with reference to companies at the efficiency frontier. In recent years there have been several mergers between water companies, reducing their number from over twenty to seventeen at present. These mergers involve no direct competitive overlaps. Instead, the competition question—to be addressed by the CMA, and before it the CC—is whether the remaining number of companies is still sufficiently large in order for Ofwat to carry out a robust comparative efficiency analysis during its price control reviews, and to preserve effective benchmark competition in the industry.[91]

7.9.4 When do merger efficiencies benefit consumers?

From an economic perspective, efficiencies achieved through a merger are beneficial to **7.153** overall welfare. Competition authorities weigh these efficiencies against the negative effects of the merger on competition. We saw that they often apply stringent conditions in doing so: the efficiencies must be merger-specific, verifiable, and passed on to consumers. Sometimes these conditions are too stringent, especially when a consumer welfare test is applied and the efficiencies must be so great that they offset any upward pricing pressure— that is, the efficiency benefits are passed on to consumers. Many types of efficiency cannot easily be assessed against the pass-on test. Moreover, from an economic perspective there will always be a degree of pass-on, even if the merger leads to a degree of market power. We discuss pass-on in Chapter 9 in the context of damages claims, but note here that even a profit-maximizing monopolist will pass on a proportion of any cost savings to lower prices (50 per cent if demand is linear and marginal costs are constant). As to the nature of the efficiencies, variable cost reductions are more likely to benefit consumers in the form of lower prices than fixed cost reductions, since in theory prices are set with reference to variable (marginal) costs. However, fixed cost reductions (e.g. resulting from innovation efforts) can also benefit consumers in the longer term.

The European Commission's assessment in 2004 of the proposed alliance between Air **7.154** France and Alitalia is one example of where the efficiency defence was dismissed because pass-on was not sufficiently established.[92] Air France and Alitalia sought to interconnect their worldwide aviation networks by creating a European multi-hub system at Paris, Rome, and Milan, and by co-ordinating their passenger service operations, including code-sharing, scheduled passenger networks, and sales. The Commission acknowledged that the proposed alliance could generate significant efficiencies in terms of an extensive network that would offer customers more direct and indirect flights. There were also possible cost reductions due to an increase in traffic throughout the network, better planning of frequencies, and other operational efficiencies. The Commission recognized that these efficiencies were merger-specific. However, it was concerned that the expected cost reductions would not result in lower fares:

> The Parties have not, however, shown how such cost savings and synergies would be passed on to the customer and were not able to identify precisely on which routes (trunk routes, other routes within the France-Italy bundle, other routes) price decreases would be applied as a result of the Alliance. If their co-operation results in the elimination of competition in certain markets, there will be no incentive for them to pass on these efficiencies to local passengers.[93]

---

[91] See, for example, Competition Commission (2007), 'South East Water Limited and Mid Kent Water Limited', 1 May; and Competition Commission (2012), 'South Staffordshire Plc/Cambridge Water PLC merger inquiry', 31 May. We advised the merging parties in both cases.
[92] *Société Air France/Alitalia Linee Aeree Italiane SpA* (Case COMP/38.284/D2), Decision of 7 April 2004.
[93] Ibid., at [137].

7.155 The Commission approved the alliance, but subject to remedies on particular routes where the parties faced little or no competition. Note that the Commission's point about there being no incentives to pass on efficiencies is not consistent with economic theory; as we mentioned before, even a monopolist will normally pass on cost savings to some extent (for profit-maximizing, rather than altruistic, reasons).

7.156 Another example is the proposed acquisition of TNT Express by UPS in 2013, which the Commission ultimately prohibited.[94] The deal would have reduced the number of competitors in international small-package deliveries from three to two in fifteen EU Member States. DHL was the only alternative in those countries. FedEx, the fourth of the global 'integrators' had a less well-established position in Europe. UPS presented an extensive analysis of the efficiencies resulting from the merger. Combining the delivery and logistics networks of the two integrators would generate significant economies of density and scope, and improve service quality. UPS estimated these at €400 million–€550 million (for comparison, UPS's turnover in the relevant market was €4.6 billion in 2011, and that of TNT €2.2 billion). It did not have access to data from TNT, this process having started as a hostile takeover bid. The Commission acknowledged that the market for international small-package deliveries is characterized by significant economies of scale and density. However, it did not consider the analysis carried out by UPS to be sufficiently robust and verifiable. The Commission did accept the quantification of the expected cost savings in the European air network. The workings for these were better documented, and originated from UPS's internal network planning model. To estimate pass-on of these cost savings, the Commission used the modelling results from the price–concentration analysis that was carried out to measure unilateral effects—this model had produced a coefficient reflecting the relationship between prices and total average costs, implying 60–70 per cent pass-on. The Commission then analysed the price effects of the merger in each country, and assessed whether the predicted price rise would be offset by the estimated cost savings. In some countries the Commission found that the merger efficiencies were sufficient to prevent an SIEC, but in many countries they fell short. This contributed to the Commission's decision to block the merger.

7.9.5 The 'efficiency offence'

7.157 In Chapter 1 we saw how US antitrust law in the 1960s was not very sympathetic towards large, efficient companies. We gave the example of *FTC v Procter & Gamble* (1967), a merger concerning the household bleach market.[95] The Supreme Court established the 'entrenchment doctrine', whereby mergers could be prohibited if they strengthened the position of merging parties relative to rivals through efficiencies, broader product ranges, or greater financial resources. Becoming too efficient was deemed harmful to competition. This approach changed radically in the United States in the 1970s under the influence of the Chicago School, but not necessarily elsewhere.

7.158 The *General Electric/Honeywell* merger case of 2001 has been much discussed, largely because it illustrates the different approaches of the US and the EU competition authorities—while the former cleared the merger (subject to a number of divestments), the latter blocked

---

[94] *UPS/TNT Express* (Case COMP/M.6570), Decision of 30 January 2013.
[95] *Federal Trade Commission v Procter & Gamble* 386 US 568 (1967).

it.[96] One of the main differences in the assessment of this merger was how efficiencies were treated. General Electric (GE) was a major supplier of large aircraft engines, while Honeywell supplied avionics and other components for commercial aircraft. Thus, there were limited horizontal overlaps between the merging parties (mainly just in certain products, such as US military helicopter engines). This was predominantly a conglomerate merger. A rationale for such mergers can be improved efficiency, resulting from economies of scale and scope.

The case in itself was complex, but in essence the US authorities approved the merger (sub-   **7.159** ject to some conditions in the markets where GE and Honeywell had horizontal overlaps) on the basis that it would enhance efficiency, and thus would foster competition. In contrast, the European Commission blocked the merger because it believed that the more efficient merged entity would have both the incentives and the market power to exclude competitors. The theory of harm in the EU was referred to as range effects, which are in essence similar to the portfolio effects discussed above. The concern was that the merged entity would have the ability and incentive to offer low-priced bundles of aircraft engines and avionics systems which its non-integrated competitors would be unable to match. Thus, the same efficiencies that were seen as desirable in the United States were seen as an unfair advantage in Europe—economies of scope yielding the ability to bundle products and sell them at a lower price. This case gave rise to extensive debate about whether EU merger control was seeking to protect competitors rather than competition, (Majoras, 2001; Kolasky, 2001; and Emch, 2004). These days the 'efficiency offence' does not play a major role in merger control, but that does not preclude the possibility that from time to time some competition authority may be tempted to use it.

---

[96] Department of Justice (2001), 'Justice Department requires divestitures in merger between General Electric and Honeywell', press release, 2 May; Majoras (2001); and *General Electric/Honeywell* (Case COMP/ M.2220), Decision of 3 July 2001.

8

DESIGN OF REMEDIES

8.1 After the Diagnosis, What's the Cure?

8.1.1 Catchers versus cleaners

Most of the scholarly literature on competition law, and most of this book so far, has **8.01** focused on the identification and analysis of competition problems. Much less attention has been paid to the design of remedies for these problems. As one commentator noted, 'Everybody likes to catch them, but nobody wants to clean them.'[1] This gap is increasingly

---

[1] Comment made by Tad Lipsky at the 2007 FTC hearings on s 2 of the Sherman Act (transcript of 28 March, p. 47, at: <http://www.ftc.gov/os/sectiontwohearings/docs/transcripts/070328.pdf>). The quote

recognized among competition officials and practitioners. Remedies matter a great deal for the effectiveness of competition law enforcement. Spending a substantial amount of resources on an investigation and concluding that there is a competition problem is of little value if a suitable remedy cannot be found. As stated by the DOJ, 'Without a proper remedy, winning a judgment of a [Sherman Act] section 2 violation is similar to winning a battle but losing the war.'[2] It quotes the former FTC Chairman William E Kovacic (1999): 'Responsible prosecutorial practice dictates that government agencies begin an abuse of dominance case only after they first have defined their remedial aims clearly and devised a convincing strategy for achieving them if the defendant's liability is established.'

8.02 We use the term remedy here in a wide sense. It includes not only remedial actions to alter the structure of the market or the behaviour of companies, but also the imposition of fines on the perpetrators and the award of financial damages to the victims. Jurisdictions around the world use different combinations of these types of remedy. The appropriate remedy will depend on the type of case. In mergers the simplest remedy is a prohibition of the merger. Not much else may be required, as competition in the market will continue as was. However, there are many merger cases in which the authority does not wish to prohibit the merger outright, instead approving it in exchange for certain commitments by the parties aimed at preserving competition. These commitments can be structural—divesting activities or assets—or behavioural, where the merged entity promises to engage or not engage in certain behaviour. The picture is more varied for cases involving restrictive agreements and abuse of dominance. A simple prohibition may not be enough. Fines are often imposed, serving the dual purpose of punishing the perpetrators and discouraging future infringements. Some jurisdictions take punishment and deterrence a step further and impose prison sentences for hardcore cartel agreements. Many jurisdictions have endorsed the objective of compensation for the victims of the infringements, be they competitors or customers, through private damages actions before national courts (a topic discussed in Chapter 9). Where competition has been harmed by restrictive agreements or abusive conduct, remedies should aim at restoring it.

8.03 This chapter discusses the economic principles that can assist in the design of remedies in merger and conduct cases. Merger control is the area in competition law where the design of structural remedies has received most attention. Competition authorities around the world now have extensive experience with conditional merger clearances, and there is an increasing number of studies evaluating past merger remedies.[3] The market investigations regime in the United Kingdom offers useful lessons on both structural and behavioural remedies. These investigations deal with markets in which competition is not functioning effectively, but for reasons other than abuse of dominance or restrictive agreements, and therefore the remedies are often aimed at changing structural or behavioural features of the market.

---

is attributed to William Baxter, the Department of Justice Assistant Attorney General, who in 1982 broke up AT&T, a case discussed in this chapter.

[2] Department of Justice (2008), 'Competition and Monopoly: Single-firm Conduct Under Section 2 of the Sherman Act', September, Ch 9. The DOJ withdrew this report in 2009, but the chapter on remedies remains a useful contribution to the debate.

[3] For example, European Commission (2005), Deloitte (2009), Organisation for Economic Co-operation and Development (2012b and 2012c), and Kwoka (2015).

8.1.2 Structural versus behavioural remedies: Courts and competition authorities as regulators?

Competition authorities often prefer structural over behavioural remedies, especially in a **8.04** merger context.[4] Structural remedies can be horizontal or vertical. Horizontal separation involves the sale of assets that compete with each other in the same product and geographic market. Vertical separation means divesting assets in different layers of the supply chain—it is the opposite of vertical integration. Structural remedies can be used to restore competition in the market, or indeed to create more competition than there was before the intervention. Their main attraction in theory is that the authority needs to strike only once: after dissolving a position of market power (or removing a bottleneck problem in a vertical supply chain), it can leave the newly created competitive structure to its own devices without having to worry about ongoing supervision. On the other hand, structural remedies are by nature rather intrusive—the authority is forcing a company to cut off some of its limbs. This may create inefficiencies—we saw in Chapters 6 and 7 how vertical integration can be an efficient solution to co-ordination problems. Moreover, structural remedies may be complex to execute in practice. The authority needs to monitor whether a viable buyer is found within the established time period, and indeed whether the new buyer raises merger concerns itself. For example, in 2010 the European Commission allowed Unilever to buy Sara Lee's body care business on the condition that it divest the Sanex deodorant business (including all trade mark and other IP rights related to Sanex, customer contracts, production equipment, and key personnel). The acquisition of Sanex by Colgate-Palmolive Group in 2011 was then itself reviewed by the Commission, and ultimately cleared.[5]

Behavioural remedies require ongoing or periodic monitoring. This makes them less **8.05** attractive to competition authorities. A commonly held view in US antitrust law is that 'judges and juries (and antitrust enforcers) are ill-equipped to act as industry regulators deciding the terms on which a firm should be required to sell its products or services'.[6] The US Supreme Court has warned against remedies that require courts to 'assume the day-to-day controls characteristic of a regulatory agency'.[7] There is some logic in this. Sector regulators specialize in the ongoing supervision of an industry, and have specific skills and expertise to do so. Most competition authorities do not. Yet over the years this has not prevented competition authorities from applying behavioural remedies in merger and conduct cases, and taking on the supervisory burden that comes with them. Why is this? First, structural remedies may not always be proportionate. Second, appropriate sector regulations may not be in place in the market in question (or the market has recently been deregulated), which means competition law is then seen as the main tool to keep dominant companies in check. The neat separation of competition law and sector regulation as

---

[4] See, for example, Commission notice on remedies acceptable under Council Regulation (EC) No 139/2004 and under Commission Regulation (EC) No 802/2004 (2008/C 267/01); and Federal Trade Commission (2012), 'Negotiating Merger Remedies', January. The distinction between structural and behavioural remedies is not always clear-cut. For example, some authorities regard the licensing of IP as a structural remedy while others treat it as a behavioural remedy.

[5] *Unilever/Sara Lee Body Care* (Case COMP/M.5658), Decision of 17 November 2010; and *Colgate Palmolive/Sanex Business* (Case COMP/M.6221), Decision of 6 June 2011.

[6] Department of Justice (2008), 'Competition and Monopoly: Single-firm Conduct Under Section 2 of the Sherman Act', September, p. 123.

[7] *Verizon Communications Inc v Law Offices of Curtis V. Trinko, LLP* 540 US 398 (2004).

envisaged in US antitrust law is not always feasible in practice. Competition authorities often end up doing supervisory work akin to what regulators do. Third, many competition authorities seem confident these days to impose behavioural remedies, having gained experience over the years and learned useful lessons from the regulation of networks and utilities. Some competition authorities also have formal sector regulator responsibilities. The Australian Competition and Consumer Commission and New Zealand Commerce Commission have traditionally combined the functions of competition authority and sector regulator. The ACM in the Netherlands was formed in 2013 by merging the competition authority with the telecommunications regulator (with energy and transport regulation already having resided within the former). Most of the sector regulators in the United Kingdom have been given powers to apply competition law to their sector, as has the telecommunications regulator in Mexico that was formed in 2013. The field of economic regulation has developed extensive insight and sophisticated tools that can be of direct use in the design of competition law remedies, both behavioural (access and price regulation) and structural (vertical separation). Perhaps the main lesson from regulation is that effective monitoring of behaviour with regard to pricing and access is by no means impossible—the tools and practical experience exist—but the supervisory structure can be costly to implement and maintain.

8.06 Finally, we note that competition law (especially at EU level) is sometimes used as a stick to force through market changes and thereby support other regulatory policies, such as liberalization, structural separation, and cross-border integration. This chapter contains several examples of merger and conduct cases in the financial services, energy, and telecommunications industries where the remedies imposed sought to contribute to these wider policy objectives, sometimes perhaps even going beyond addressing the identified competition concerns.

8.1.3 The remainder of this chapter

8.07 Sections 8.2 and 8.3 deal with structural remedies in merger and conduct cases, respectively. The latter section also describes regulatory insights on vertical separation. Section 8.4 discusses behavioural remedies in merger and conduct cases and sets out the regulatory principles of access and price regulation. Section 8.5 covers the concept of fair, reasonable, and non-discriminatory (FRAND), which is used in a number of different contexts in access and licensing cases, and is of increasing relevance to competition law. In section 8.6 we explore the lessons from behavioural economics for designing remedies. The *Microsoft* and *Google* cases are useful illustrations. Section 8.7 deals with the principles of setting fines, with reference to the theory of incentives (including the incentives of rational criminals) and behavioural economics. The section also covers the use of economics (or possible lack of it) in the European Commission's Fining Guidelines, including in assessing companies' ability to pay fines.[8] Finally, section 8.8 covers another area where competition law can learn from regulation and public policy in general, namely that of cost–benefit analysis (CBA). In recent years, competition policy has seen an increasing emphasis on the measurement of costs and benefits, not only of specific interventions and remedies, but also of having a competition regime in the first place.

---

[8] European Commission (2006), 'Guidelines on the Method of Setting Fines Pursuant to Article 23(2)(a) of Regulation No 1/2003' [2006] OJ C210/02.

8.2 Structural Remedies in Mergers

8.2.1 Divestment as the most direct means to restore competition

Divestment remedies are common in merger cases. Short of prohibiting a merger outright, **8.08** divestments are the most direct means of restoring or maintaining competition. They are relatively straightforward where existing business units are sold off in their entirety, or the assets can be run with a high degree of independence. Going back to some of the examples of mergers we saw in Chapters 2 and 7, individual cinemas, holiday parks, and supermarkets are not difficult to separate from the rest of the chain they were part of. By the same token, they can be easily integrated into a competing chain which acquires them (sometimes not much more than a change in livery is required). The same often holds for the divestment of products and brands. Many spirit brands have changed hands following conditional merger clearances in the beverages industry, including sixteen different brands when Pernod Ricard acquired Allied Domeqc in 2005 (among which were Sauza tequila, Courvoisier cognac, and Kuemmerling bitter), and Whyte & Mackay Scotch whisky in 2014 when Diageo acquired United Spirits.[9] Several pharmaceutical mergers have been approved following divestment of products or treatments in markets where the parties had overlapping activities. In 2015, Novartis agreed to divest two of its cancer treatments when it acquired GSK's oncology business, and Mylan divested four products in five countries when it acquired part of Abbott Laboratories.[10]

In other industries, separating assets or products is less straightforward. Two merging hos- **8.09** pitals may find it difficult to divest activities that take place under the same roof. In 2013 the CC prohibited the merger between two hospitals in Bournemouth in the United Kingdom, considering divestment remedies to be infeasible:

> We found SLCs in 55 different clinical areas. Each of these would need to be addressed by any remedy. The services affected by the SLCs are not easily divisible from the rest of the merged parties' operations and it would be impossible to separate all of these services from the rest in order, for example, to divest them while allowing the remaining services to be merged.
>
> We therefore did not find that there were remedies other than prohibition that would be effective.[11]

Bank branches, like supermarkets and cinemas, can be sold off relatively easily as a **8.10** matter of divesting property. However, this may not solve the competition concerns in question if customers keep their current account with the original bank and use other branches or channels (internet, cash machines) to access their account. Italy and Switzerland had experiences with structural remedies for bank mergers before the financial crisis that began in 2007–08.[12] In Italy these included branch divestments, but also

---

[9] *Pernod Ricard/Allied Domecq* (Case COMP/M.3779), Decision of 24 June 2005; and Competition and Markets Authority (2014), 'CMA accepts Scotch whisky business sale', press release, 31 October.

[10] *Novartis/GlaxoSmithKline Oncology Business* (Case COMP/M.7275), Decision of 28 January 2015; and *Mylan/Abbott EPD-DM* (Case COMP/M.7379), Decision of 28 January 2015. We advised the acquiring party in the latter case.

[11] Competition Commission (2013), 'The Royal Bournemouth and Christchurch Hospitals NHS Foundation Trust/Poole Hospital NHS Foundation Trust', 17 October, at [9.206].

[12] See Organisation for Economic Co-operation and Development (2012b, pp. 131–2 and 293; and 2012c, pp. 94–5).

share divestments and behavioural remedies to deal with the high degree of inter-locking directorates (directors sitting on each other's boards) in Italy's banking sector. The 1998 merger between Union Bank of Switzerland and Swiss Bank Corporation created the largest Swiss bank at the time, UBS. The Swiss Competition Commission imposed structural remedies in the form of divestments of a number of subsidiaries and of bank branches in certain Swiss regions. In an evaluation of the remedies seven years later, the authority found that the attempt to attract new competitors in regional markets had failed, mainly because many of the divested branches were in economically unattractive regions, and because shifting customers of the branches to the new buyer worked only to a limited extent. The financial crisis created a wave of bank bail-outs and restructurings, and the European Commission imposed extensive branch divestment remedies on banks across Europe as a condition for approving these rescue measures. In the United Kingdom the Lloyds Banking Group and the Royal Bank of Scotland (RBS) announced plans in 2009 to divest hundreds of bank branches in order to win Commission state aid approval.[13] The process of completing the Lloyds divestments took more than five years. The RBS divestments have not been completed yet.

8.2.2 How much divestment, and to whom?

8.11 Basic questions when determining the appropriate divestments are: how many assets must be sold off, and to whom? As regards the first question, the answer is the more the original market structure can be emulated the better. But even if the divested assets represent a smaller market share than that of the smaller of the two merging parties before the transaction, the remedy can be effective if the assets are particularly attractive and are scooped up by a rival with ambitions to grow in the market. This to some extent answers the second question: who should be allowed to buy the assets? The market is generally best placed to decide on this (the keenest buyer with plans to use the assets most productively will usually step forward in a sales process), though authorities will want to avoid the assets being purchased by a competitor which already has a large market share.

8.12 The *Fortis/ABN AMRO* merger case in 2007 is one where the structural remedy went a step further than seeking to restore competition to pre-merger levels.[14] A consortium of the Royal Bank of Scotland, Banco Santander Central Hispano, and Fortis acquired ABN AMRO for €72 billion (the largest ever bank merger in Europe). This raised competition concerns in the Netherlands where ABN AMRO was one of the traditional top three banks, and Fortis (from Belgium) one of its more rapidly growing competitors. The main problem was in the provision of banking and factoring services to commercial customers (factoring is a form of financing where the bank takes over its client's outstanding invoices to third parties). The European Commission required the divestment of a significant commercial banking division that existed within ABN AMRO, together with a number of business centres and a factoring division. Altogether this divestment package was nearly twice the size of Fortis's activities in commercial banking before the merger, and it removed the overlap

---

[13] *State aid No. N 428/2009—United Kingdom Restructuring of Lloyds Banking Group*, C(2009)9087 final, Decision of 18 November 2009; and *State aid No N 422/2009 and N 621/2009—United Kingdom Restructuring of Royal Bank of Scotland following its recapitalisation by the State and its participation in the Asset Protection Scheme*, C(2009)10112 final, Decision 14 December 2009.

[14] *Fortis/ABN AMRO Assets* (Case COMP/M.4844), Decision of 3 October 2007. We advised the merging parties during this inquiry.

in factoring. The Commission was satisfied that this remedy would solve the competition concerns and that the divested assets were commercially viable if sold to the right purchaser. In addition, however, the Commission determined that the purchaser had to be a bank that was able to serve international corporate customers and that had a presence in the major world and European financial centres. This requirement effectively meant that the assets could not be acquired by one of the smaller Dutch banks, some of which had demonstrated ambitions to grow in the commercial banking market but lacked such international presence. The Commission probably saw the remedy negotiations as an opportunity to promote cross-border integration of European banking markets, a policy objective it had long sought to achieve through various means. In the event, both the deal and the execution of the remedies were delayed, and changed somewhat in nature, when the two banks had to be rescued from collapse in 2008.

The *Ryanair/Aer Lingus* case (2013) is an example where arguably far-reaching structural **8.13** remedies were offered but ultimately rejected by the European Commission. Ryanair tried several times to acquire the other major Irish airline, Aer Lingus. Following a prohibition by the Commission in 2007 and an aborted attempt in 2009, in 2013 Ryanair offered significant structural remedies:[15] divestment of Aer Lingus's operations on forty-three of the forty-six short-haul routes where the two airlines overlapped, and of take-off and landing slots to International Airlines Group (IAG, formed in 2011 after the merger between British Airways and Iberia) such that the latter could operate three major routes between London and Irish airports. Flybe, a British regional airline, was identified as an upfront buyer of the operations on the forty-three routes (and would receive access to the required aircraft, as well as support with publicity and brand awareness). Both Flybe and IAG committed to operating the newly acquired routes for a minimum of three years. The Commission welcomed the 'fix-it-first' aspects of the proposed remedies, where upfront buyers are identified and then enter into a legally binding agreement (conditional on the Commission accepting the remedy in question).[16] However, it questioned whether the forty-three routes would be a viable business (for example, they would no longer benefit from the connecting passengers on Aer Lingus's long-haul routes). The Commission also did not consider Flybe to be capable of competing effectively with Ryanair, as it was seen to have limited financial resources (despite Ryanair offering it €100 million in cash as part of the remedy) and little experience in the Irish market. The Commission found that IAG would not place a strong competitive constraint on Ryanair, and (like Flybe) would have little incentive to stay on the new routes after the three years. It doubted that the divestment remedies could be implemented in a timely manner, and ultimately prohibited the merger again.

As it happened, Ryanair was subsequently required by the UK competition authorities to **8.14** sell its minority stake in Aer Lingus which it had built up as part of the acquisition strategy (we discussed this in Chapter 7), and in 2015 it was IAG who acquired Aer Lingus—a deal approved by the Commission subject to a number of remedies, including the release

---

[15] *Ryanair/Aer Lingus* (Case COMP/M.4439), Decision of 27 June 2007; *Ryanair/Aer Lingus II* (Case COMP/M.5434), Withdrawn on 23 January 2009; and *Ryanair/Aer Lingus III* (Case COMP/M.6663), Decision of 27 February 2013. We advised Ryanair on the most recent case.
[16] Fix-it-first remedies are defined in the Commission's Remedies Notice. Commission notice on remedies acceptable under Council Regulation (EC) No 139/2004 and under Commission Regulation (EC) No 802/2004 (2008/C 267/01), at [56–7].

of five daily slot pairs at London Gatwick Airport to facilitate entry on routes to Dublin and Belfast.[17]

8.2.3 Completed mergers: Cleaning up the mess afterwards

8.15 In many jurisdictions there have been policy debates about merger notification thresholds, and indeed whether merger notification should be mandatory or voluntary (the United Kingdom is one of the few voluntary notification regimes). Mandatory notification with relatively low thresholds can be burdensome to both businesses and the competition authority. A voluntary regime relies on self-assessment by merging parties, and in practice most relevant mergers will be notified if the parties wish to have legal certainty and there is a credible threat that the competition authority will investigate the merger even after completion. The CMA (like the OFT before it) has indeed reviewed several completed mergers, as have competition authorities elsewhere. Yet unwinding a completed transaction can be costly and difficult where the two businesses have already been integrated, overlapping staff have been made redundant, and commercially sensitive information has been exchanged.

8.16 The *Twin America* case is an extreme example where a merger was unwound six years after it took place.[18] In March 2009, Coach USA and City Sights formed Twin America, a joint venture (JV) that combined their 'hop-on, hop-off' bus tour services in New York City. These services use open-top double-decker buses, and take visitors past the city's leading tourist attractions and neighbourhoods. Coach USA, using the Gray Line brand, had been the long-standing market leader in New York. City Sights entered in 2005, resulting in vigorous head-to-head competition between the two operators, with tourists benefitting from fare discounts, improved service, and novel ticket packages (e.g. tickets combined with boat tours). However, in 2009 the two companies combined their operations under Twin America, basically creating a monopoly, although continuing to operate both the Gray Line and City Sights brands. The formation of Twin America fell outside the merger notification criteria of the Hart-Scott-Rodino Act, but the DOJ and the New York State Attorney General challenged it in July 2009. The matter was put on hold for a few years because of jurisdictional questions—immediately after the challenge the parties applied to the Surface Transport Board, the federal regulator, for approval of the JV, and only when this application was rejected in 2012 could the DOJ and Attorney General pursue the case.

8.17 Sightseeing in New York through hop-on, hop-off bus tours was considered a separate relevant market. Each year, approximately 2 million visitors use these services, spending more than $100 million. As stated by the prosecutors, it was clear that a hypothetical monopolist would find it profitable to impose a SSNIP because the actual monopolist—Twin America—did in fact raise its prices significantly: the JV's stated aim was to improve profitability through raising fares by 10 per cent, and the price of Gray Line's most popular service, the All Loops Tour, increased from $49 to $54. The market was characterized by significant entry barriers, in particular the requirement to obtain authorization from the New York City Department of Transportation for each bus stop location. Gray Line and City Sights each held large portfolios of bus stop authorizations near all of the city's top

---

[17] Competition Commission (2013), 'Ryanair Holdings plc and Aer Lingus Group plc', 28 August; and *IAG/Aer Lingus* (Case COMP/M.7541), Decision of 14 July 2015.

[18] *United States and State of New York v Twin America LLC et al.*, Civil Action No. 12-cv-8989 (ALC) (GWG).

attractions. Recent entrants faced persistent difficulties in obtaining authorization for new bus stops from the department (this is an example of the absolute entry barriers we described in Chapter 3). The remedy agreed in March 2015 required Twin America to relinquish to the department the complete set of City Sights bus stop authorizations (around fifty in total). This was expected to create opportunities for new entrants to obtain bus stops at key locations. Twin America could keep the existing Gray Line bus stops, but would not be allowed to apply for new bus stop authorizations for five years.

In addition to this divestment remedy, Twin America was required to 'disgorge' $7.5 million in extra profits it had made through its unlawful formation (the DOJ and New York State shared the proceeds evenly). In US law, disgorgement is meant to prevent unjust enrichment and deter future infringements. In determining this amount, the prosecutors took into account the fact that Twin America had already agreed to pay $19 million to settle a private class action lawsuit that was filed after the DOJ and the Attorney General brought their case. The class on whose behalf the action was brought includes all persons who purchased a hop-on, hop-off ticket between February 2009 and June 2014 (they could claim back up to $20 per ticket).[19] In broad terms, if Twin America carried 2 million passengers per year, and each paid $5 extra due to the illegal merger, the total payment of $26.5 million to the prosecutors and the customer class would correspond to just over two-and-a-half years of the extra profits that the JV made. In all, remedying this completed merger took six years, and involved a combination of divestments, a prohibition on future expansion, repayment of extra profits made, and payment of damages to customers via a class action.

8.18

8.3 Structural Remedies in Conduct Cases

8.3.1 The classics: *Standard Oil* and *AT&T*

In conduct cases the use of structural remedies has been rare. The two most famous corporate break-ups in the United States—Standard Oil (1911) and AT&T (1982)—took place in very different times and circumstances, but they usefully illustrate some of the economic principles that are of relevance when designing a structural remedy.

8.19

Following a lawsuit by the DOJ, the Supreme Court ordered in 1911 that Standard Oil Company of New Jersey be dissolved and split into thirty-four companies.[20] For decades, Standard Oil—co-founded and majority-owned by John D Rockefeller—had dominated the refinement and shipment of oil in the United States, with a market share of 80–90 per cent (Scherer and Ross, 1990, pp. 450–1). It had achieved this position through a combination of superior efficiency (nothing wrong with that of course), the acquisition of more than 120 rival companies (merger control did not exist at the time), and a variety of notorious business practices. The latter included obtaining preferential treatment from railroad companies, unfair practices against competing pipelines, local price cutting at points where competition was to be suppressed, industrial espionage, and the operation of bogus independent companies. It was these practices that the DOJ condemned, and for which the

8.20

---

[19] *In Re NYC Bus Tour Antitrust Litigation*, No. 13-CV-0711 (ALC)(GWG)(S.D.N.Y. 21 October 2014). Those having been on a hop-on, hop-off tour through New York could apply for compensation on <tourbus-settlement.com>.

[20] *Standard Oil Co of New Jersey v United States* 221 US 1 (1911).

Supreme Court accepted dissolution of the company as the remedy. Reference was also made to the 'enormous and unreasonable profits' earned by Standard Oil because of its monopoly power.

8.21 Interestingly, Standard Oil argued in its defence that the companies it controlled in different parts of the United States operated quite independently and competitively (it also seemed to argue that its control of the industry was 'the result of lawful competitive methods, guided by economic genius of the highest order'). While this argument was not accepted, it did perhaps give the authorities a clue that making those companies truly independent by splitting Standard Oil was a feasible option. Indeed, rather than a single company, Standard Oil was a 'combination' or 'trust', controlling a host of other companies through shareholding arrangements—Standard Oil and its contemporaneous brethren gave rise to the term 'antitrust' when the Sherman Antitrust Act was passed in 1890. It was this 'combination' that the Supreme Court ordered to be dissolved so as to 'neutralize' its monopoly power. The court considered it insufficient for Standard Oil merely to cease the above-mentioned practices, since the market was already effectively monopolized. The position of the DOJ had been that the existence of Standard Oil, 'with the vast accumulation of property which it owns or controls, because of the infinite potency for harm and the dangerous example which its continued existence affords, is an open and enduring menace to all freedom of trade, and is a byword and reproach to modern economic methods'. The Supreme Court agreed in the end. While there have been heated debates ever since the ruling about whether the structural remedy was appropriate, the break-up did, with some delay, result in greater competition among the newly created oil companies—these included the likes of (predecessors of) ExxonMobil, Chevron, and ConocoPhillips. As for John D Rockefeller, he was said to have done rather well out of the break-up, as the minority shares he had kept in the resultant companies all increased significantly in value.

8.22 The break-up of AT&T was agreed in a settlement with the DOJ in 1982 and became effective from 1 January 1984.[21] AT&T operated the 'Bell System', which had a telephone monopoly in the United States from the early twentieth century, and consisted of entities delivering long-distance and local calls, equipment manufacturing, and R&D. In the 1960s and 1970s, new communications technologies began to compete with AT&T at the 'edges' of the Bell System. Rival telephony equipment and wireless intercity call services sought to establish a market presence, but were heavily reliant on AT&T for interconnection and compatibility with the rest of the system. AT&T responded to these competitive threats through a range of hostile actions, including refusals to interconnect and accept 'foreign' equipment, or to do so only at a high price and with delays. AT&T also heavily lobbied the sector regulator, the FCC, to help protect its monopoly status and thereby preserve the integrity of the telephone system. The DOJ filed a lawsuit against AT&T in 1974 and, after eight years of legal battles, a settlement was reached. The Bell System was to be broken up into a long-distance telephony arm—the new AT&T, which also kept the equipment-manufacturing and R&D entities—and seven separate incumbent local exchange carriers (known as the regional Bell operating companies, or 'Baby Bells'). This was therefore a combination of vertical and horizontal separation. It may seem paradoxical that such a radical intervention was made at a time when antitrust law in the United States tended more

---

[21] *United States v AT&T Co* 552 F Supp 131 (DDC 1982).

towards the laissez-faire (see Chapter 1). However, the DOJ's position was that a structural break-up would be the most effective way of introducing competition once and for all, bringing an end to the persistent disputes and need for oversight of AT&T's behaviour. The court that reviewed the case also questioned whether the FCC was realistically capable of regulating a company the size of AT&T (Scherer and Ross, 1990, pp 462–4).

What happened next? Competition certainly developed in the long-distance call market **8.23** (Sprint and MCI were major challengers). Long-distance call rates fell sharply (local call rates increased, because they had previously been subsidized by the long-distance calls). The equipment and R&D entities were not as successful as the new AT&T had hoped, again due to external rivals. As competition developed further in telephony markets over the years, consolidation took place among the Baby Bells. In 2005 AT&T was acquired by SBC Communications (keeping the name AT&T), reuniting it with three of the former Baby Bells. However, this partial reintegration was not seen as problematic given that competitive dynamics in the market had changed significantly since 1982. One thing that did not work so well after the break-up was that extensive legal and regulatory disputes continued. These have related in particular to the behaviour of the Baby Bells, which inherited local monopolies and have frequently been accused of imposing excessive access charges. In Chapter 4 we discussed the *Trinko* case (2004), which involved a refusal to supply by Verizon Communications, one of Baby Bells (formerly known as Bell Atlantic), and where AT&T was one of the affected competitors.[22] The need for extensive oversight by the courts and the FCC has therefore remained ever since the break-up.

8.3.2 More recent examples of structural remedies in conduct cases

Relatively few structural remedies have been imposed under competition law since the **8.24** *AT&T* case, although there are some examples. At one stage during the DOJ's investigation into Microsoft, in 2000, a district court ordered the company to be broken up, separating its operating system from the production of other software[23]—commentators spoke of the 'Baby Bills' (after Microsoft founder Bill Gates, then the richest man in the world). However, this was overturned on appeal, and the DOJ eventually agreed to a settlement through which Microsoft would share its application programming interfaces with third parties.[24] A break-up was off the table. In 2014 it was Google's turn to be threatened with structural separation. The European Commission opened an investigation into Google's practices in the online search market in 2010. The parties came close to a settlement (see section 8.6 below) but failed. In November 2014 the European Parliament adopted a resolution calling for the unbundling of search engines from other commercial services (though the resolution is non-binding).[25]

Energy is another sector where competition law tools have been used to enforce further lib- **8.25** eralization. In 2013 the European Commission closed an abuse of dominance investigation into CEZ, the Czech electricity incumbent, after the company offered to divest significant

---

[22] *Verizon Communications Inc. v Law Offices of Curtis V Trinko, LLP* 540 US 398 (2004).
[23] *United States v Microsoft Corp.*, 97 F.Supp. 2d59 (D.D.C. 2000).
[24] *United States v Microsoft Corp.*, Nos 98-1232 and 98-1233 (D.D.C.), Revised Proposed Final Judgment, 6 November 2001.
[25] European Parliament (2014), 'MEPs zero in on internet search companies and clouds', press release, 27 November.

generation capacity. CEZ had a market share of more than 60 per cent in electricity generation and was vertically integrated. The Commission had been concerned about a number of
practices that hindered new entry, such as pre-emptive booking of transmission capacity. It
considered that: 'Transfer of some of CEZ's generation capacity to a competitor represents a
clear-cut solution to the identified competition concerns. Transfer of generation capacity is
necessary in this case as no other type of remedy can address the effects of CEZ's conduct.'[26]

8.26 Given the variety of remedy mechanisms discussed in this chapter, this last statement by
the Commission ('no other type of remedy can address') may be somewhat pessimistic. Yet
the divestment remedy brought a long inquiry to an end, and contributed to a lower level
of concentration in electricity generation in the Czech Republic, which had been a long-
standing regulatory objective. Abuse of dominance actions by the European Commission
also resulted in structural remedies in the German and Italian domestic gas and electricity
markets.[27]

8.27 In the United Kingdom there have been some structural remedies under the market investigations regime. In Chapter 6 we discussed how in 1989 the authorities ordered vertical
separation between brewery companies and pubs.[28] A more recent example is the forced
divestment of airports by BAA, the company that used to own the main airports in London
and Scotland. In 2009 the CC required BAA to sell both Gatwick and Stansted airports (to
different purchasers), leaving it with Heathrow and Southampton airports in the south-east
of England, and to sell either Edinburgh or Glasgow airport, leaving it with two airports in
Scotland instead of three.[29] In its market investigation into private healthcare in 2014, the
CMA ordered the divestment of one of the two major London private hospitals operated
by HCA, a US-based private healthcare group.[30] This divestment was aimed at introducing
greater rivalry in this area, and thus better outcomes on price, quality, and range of services.
The London private hospital market was seen as concentrated and difficult to enter, and
HCA was the largest operator, with eight hospitals and a market share of more than 45 per
cent by number of admissions and 55 per cent by revenue. To support the remedy, the CMA
determined that the relevant insurers were required to roll over their existing contract terms
with the divested hospital for at least eighteen months following the divestment.

8.3.3 Economic insights from network regulation: Vertical separation

8.28 Vertical separation has been introduced in a number of network industries in Europe and
elsewhere since the early 1990s—among the first were the gas, electricity, and rail industries
in the United Kingdom.[31] The main aim is to facilitate entry in the potentially competitive layers of the supply chain (i.e. where there is no natural monopoly), and to restrict the
incumbents' incentives to discriminate against non-integrated competitors in the provision

---

[26] *CEZ* (Case AT/39727), Decision of 10 April 2013, at [79].

[27] *German Electricity Wholesale Market* and *German Electricity Balancing Market* (Cases COMP/39.388
and COMP/39.389), Decision of 26 November 2008; *RWE Gas Foreclosure* (Case COMP/39.402), Decision
of 18 March 2009; and *ENI* (Case COMP/39.315), Decision of 29 September 2010.

[28] Monopolies and Mergers Commission (1989), 'The Supply of Beer', March.

[29] Competition Commission (2009), 'BAA Airports Market Investigation', March. BAA in fact ended up
selling more airports and is now called Heathrow Airport Holdings Limited.

[30] Competition and Markets Authority (2014), 'Private Healthcare Market Investigation', final report,
2 April.

[31] For an international overview, see Organisation for Economic Co-operation and Development (2012a).

of network access. In other network industries where the incumbents have remained verti-cally integrated, regulators often impose accounting separation, a much milder form of separation aimed at monitoring the pricing and financial performance of the network facil-ity. In the last decade, vertical separation seems to have come back into fashion in Europe as a tool to address persistent discrimination problems where lighter forms of access regulation have failed. Due in part to pressure from their national regulators, the telecoms incumbents in the United Kingdom (BT), Italy (Telecom Italia), and Sweden (TeliaSonera) each intro-duced a type of 'functional' vertical separation. This is not full vertical separation since ownership remains the same, but the network business is set up as an independent unit that offers the same terms and conditions for access to all service providers downstream, including the incumbent's own retail business—a concept referred to as 'equivalence'. In the energy sector, the European Commission and national regulators have been promoting structural 'unbundling' of the large energy companies, in particular splitting the transmis-sion networks for electricity and gas, which are natural monopolies, from the more compet-itive activities (generation/production and distribution). We saw earlier how competition law investigations have been instrumental in further driving structural separation in several EU Member States. Debates about vertical separation have also been raging in the financial services sector, particularly as regards the vertical separation or integration of securities exchanges and clearing and settlement systems, and of payment system infrastructure and payment system providers.[32]

Over the years, a large body of economic literature has explored the relative merits of sepa-rated and integrated structures in network industries.[33] Experience has shown that it remains tempting for vertically integrated companies to engage in the vertical leveraging of market power and foreclosure of entrants downstream. Hence, the overarching question faced by regulators has been whether the efficiency benefits of integration (lower transaction costs, the elimination of double marginalization, better co-ordination) outweigh these vertical foreclosure effects. In industries that have not been separated, foreclosure has typically been dealt with through access regulation—by mandating the incumbent to provide third parties with access to its bottleneck facilities on non-discriminatory terms. However, discrimination and margin squeeze disputes have been common in this model (we saw examples in Chapter 4), and it has frequently proved difficult for regulators to monitor cases of discrimination, particularly in relation to non-price terms. For this reason vertical separation between the upstream bottleneck and downstream competitive businesses has again come to be seen as a suitable remedy, just as it was at the time of the AT&T break-up in the United States. **8.29**

The main downside of vertical separation is simply that it eliminates the benefits of vertical integration. In theory, an integrated company with market power upstream and down-stream will sell to more consumers at a lower price than its separated equivalent—this is the double-marginalization problem of separation that we discussed in Chapter 6. Vertical separation may also reduce incentives to invest or to innovate upstream, because the sepa-rated network business would no longer derive any profits from such efforts in the down-stream activities. A further argument against separation is that it hinders the co-ordination of investment and production decisions, given that the upstream company no longer has **8.30**

---

[32] See Niels et al. (2003); and Financial Conduct Authority Payment Systems Regulator (2015), 'A new regulatory framework for payment systems in the UK', policy statement, 27 March.
[33] For an overview, see Armstrong et al. (1994) and Decker (2014).

direct contact with end-user demand. Moreover, the process of separation itself comes at a cost. Separation entails a one-off direct cost, as well as the ongoing costs of maintaining the separated structure. These include the reorganization of the existing integrated company and, where ownership is still held in common, the prohibition of certain flows of information between the separated businesses.

8.31 The experience of the rail sector in Great Britain demonstrates the complexity of the co-ordination issues that can arise as a result of vertical separation. The split between the network operator and the train operators (which also exists in several other EU Member States) has proved to be an effective way of ensuring non-discrimination, but it has also led to a lack of both investment co-ordination and of focus on user requirements (and plenty of scope to blame the other entity when things go wrong).[34] The energy sector also has features that make vertical separation less attractive. Integrated companies may have greater incentives to construct interconnectors between national energy markets, and may be more able to co-ordinate the operation and scheduling of the various layers in the supply chain (balancing supply and demand at all times is an overriding imperative in energy markets). There are indications that vertically integrated energy companies tend to spend more on R&D investment—they can apply new innovations to a variety of activities, and thus have a better chance of internalizing the benefits of this investment (Markard et al., 2004). However, there are also advantages to vertical separation in the energy sector, and the introduction of competition in certain layers of the supply chain has been successful in many countries.

8.32 Given the potential upsides and downsides of vertical separation, the policy decision of whether to impose such a remedy is inherently complex. A proper CBA is needed. The outcome will depend on the specific features of the sector and the country in question. Sectors such as rail and energy tend to place greater emphasis on investment as a regulatory objective in its own right, whereas in telecoms regulation the promotion of entry and competition is considered of central importance. Another question is where in the supply chain to separate. The main criterion is to split the naturally monopolistic from the potentially competitive activities. Technological change may render a given form of separation obsolete. For example, as the telecoms industry migrates from traditional copper networks to fibre networks, local-loop unbundling, a structural remedy heavily promoted in the early 2000s, has lost some of its relevance. In the 'next-generation' networks the local exchanges are no longer the critical interconnection points in the network.

8.4 Behavioural Remedies: Price and Access

8.4.1 Behavioural remedies in competition cases

8.33 Behavioural remedies are frequently applied in both conduct and merger cases, despite competition authorities' usual preference for structural remedies. In mergers these remedies are often aimed at mitigating the effects of potential bottlenecks. Two recent examples are the acquisitions in the Netherlands and Belgium by Liberty Global, a cable operator.[35]

---

[34] For an overview, see Department for Transport and Office of Rail Regulation (2010).

[35] *Liberty Global/Corelio/W&W/De Vijver Media* (Case COMP/M.7194), Decision of 24 February 2015; and *Liberty Global/Ziggo* (Case COMP/M.7000), Decision of 10 October 2014. We advised the acquirer on both cases.

In 2014 the company merged the two major cable networks in the Netherlands. One of the behavioural remedies imposed by the European Commission was a commitment to provide sufficient internet interconnection capacity to providers of innovative over-the-top (OTT) services, such as Netflix and Amazon Instant Video, which increasingly compete with TV platforms, for a period of eight years. The Commission also required Liberty Global to remove certain restrictions from its carriage agreements with TV broadcasters, thus allowing these broadcasters to offer their content through OTT services.[36] In 2015 Liberty Global was permitted to purchase two major TV channels in Belgium, Vier and Vijf, on condition that it license these channels to other TV distributors on FRAND terms for seven years.

8.34 In conduct cases the behavioural remedy often goes hand in hand with the prohibition of the anti-competitive practice itself. A company that is found to have abused its dominant position is effectively told to stop and not do it again. A fine may help to reinforce the message and also to deter others from engaging in the same type of conduct. The judgment itself, if published and explained clearly, can become a useful part of the case law. Sometimes not much else may be required from the court or competition authority. In 2014 the English High Court ruled that Luton Airport had abused its dominant position by granting National Express exclusive access to the airport bus station for bus services to and from London for a period of seven years (the bus station being seen as an essential facility for operators of these services).[37] This finding of abuse was sufficient for the airport to agree to an access deal with the excluded operator, Arriva, without the court prescribing any of the terms for such access (Granatstein and Niels, 2015). However, in other cases the court or authority will not only want to put an end to the anti-competitive practice but also to ensure that the dominant company behaves differently in future—for example, supplying a product on FRAND terms. In 2011 the European Commission agreed a commitment with Standard & Poor's in relation to the pricing of US International Securities Identification Numbers.[38] These securities identifiers are essential for interbank communication, clearing and settlement, and for reporting to authorities. Standard & Poor's had been designated by the American Bankers Association as the monopoly numbering agency. The European Commission opened an investigation into what it considered to be unfairly high prices, and Standard & Poor's agreed to set a cost-reflective price ($15,000 per year, adjusted for inflation) for five years, and to submit a confidential report to the Commission every year on the implementation of the commitment.

8.35 Such behavioural remedies (in the United States they are often referred to as affirmative-obligation remedies) not only require ongoing monitoring, but also careful design to create the right incentives and market outcomes. This is where competition law can learn from the economic principles of price and access regulation, a theme we turn to now. Price regulation arises where there are concerns about excessive prices resulting from market power. Access regulation may also be designed to remedy high prices, but is usually concerned with remedying exclusionary practices by vertically integrated companies.

---

[36] There was also a divestment remedy further upstream, as the deal combined the two main premium film channels in the Netherlands, and one of these had to be sold off.
[37] *Arriva The Shires Ltd v London Luton Airport Operations Ltd* [2014] EWHC 64 (Ch). [2014] UKCLR 313. We acted as experts for the claimant in this matter.
[38] *Standard & Poor's* (Case COMP/39.592), Decision of 15 November 2011.

8.4.2 Economic insights from network regulation: Price regulation

8.36 The field of network and utility regulation has developed extensive theoretical and practical knowledge of price regulation.[39] Here we summarize some of the basic principles that are relevant when considering a pricing remedy in competition law. The two main types of price regulation are rate-of-return regulation and price-cap regulation.

8.37 Under rate-of-return regulation (also referred to as cost-plus regulation), prices are set at a level that reflects the cost of service, and the supplier is allowed a fixed return on its asset base. This asset base is equal to the historical investment in fixed assets, minus what has been deducted for depreciation. For an agreed base period, often twelve months, the supplier calculates its operating costs, depreciation, capital employed, and cost of capital. The regulator audits these calculations and determines the fair return—that is, revenues minus operating costs and depreciation, generating a profit that covers the cost of capital. The certainty of earning a particular return provides incentives for suppliers to invest sufficiently in the service and thus guarantee security of supply. A drawback of simple rate-of-return regulation is that it provides little incentive for efficiency. If a company's costs of service increase, it can simply raise its price and continue making the same rate of return. Companies may also have the incentive to over-invest in their asset base (referred to as 'gold-plating').

8.38 Price-cap regulation involves setting either price or revenue caps for a fixed time period (often three to five years), thereby providing an incentive for the company to reduce costs during this period. The cap itself is set with reference to a reasonable profit level similar to that in rate-of-return regulation, but because the cap doesn't change over the period, the company retains the benefits of any cost reductions for the remainder of the period. The regulator reviews the cap at the end of each period. If the company has been making high returns, the regulator will reduce the allowed prices or revenues for the next period. If returns are low (and if this is attributable to external cost or demand factors, rather than to inefficiency), prices are permitted to rise. A common form of price cap is the formula RPI – X. RPI is the retail price index, a measure of consumer price inflation. The X captures efficiency targets derived from reasonable capital and labour productivity gains for the regulated industry in question. Under this form of regulation, prices can increase with inflation but are required to decrease by X per cent in real terms per year. This mechanism incentivizes suppliers to improve their efficiency during the price-cap period as they get to keep any efficiency gains greater than X per cent. Incentives to over-invest (or gold-plate) do not arise as this would reduce the profitability of the company. This feature of the price cap may also mean, however, that suppliers have incentives to reduce investments or quality of service below optimal levels in order to save costs.

8.39 A variant of the price cap is the revenue cap. Under the former, a company's revenues will change in proportion to volumes (every unit is sold at the same price). It will therefore be incentivized to increase volumes in order to raise revenues through the course of a price control period. The downside is that the company is exposed to the risk of reduced profits due to an unanticipated decline in volumes. This risk will be exacerbated when there are high fixed costs, since these costs will be incurred irrespective of the volumes sold. In contrast,

---

[39] A classic, and very accessible, work on the economics of regulation is Kahn (1988) (first published in two separate volumes in 1970 and 1971). A leading textbook that economists often refer to is Laffont and Tirole (1993). More recent textbooks are Viscusi et al. (2005), Crew and Parker (2006), and Decker (2014).

under a revenue cap, the revenue that a company is permitted to generate remains constant irrespective of the volume of output. The company has no particular incentive to increase volumes (since price per unit would have to come down if the revenue cap is reached), but nor is it exposed to uncontrollable downward shocks in volume.

The regulatory burden is high under any of the above mechanisms. Detailed expertise **8.40** and analysis are required to assess the companies' costs and asset base, compare these with efficient benchmarks, and determine the cost of capital or reasonable return. Experience with rate-of-return regulation in the United States suggests that extensive supervision is required to avoid the gold-plating of assets. In turn, price-cap regulation often requires additional quality regulation to ensure that investments are not reduced beyond the point where quality is affected. An additional complexity arises where the market is not a natural monopoly but rather one where competition exists, or is being promoted, at the same time as prices of the dominant supplier are regulated. In a natural monopoly, reasonable profits are determined with reference to what capital providers actually invested in the asset base. In potentially competitive markets, the assets of the dominant supplier may have to be valued based on what an entrant would have to invest to replace them. This way, prices are still regulated but not at such low levels as to discourage new entry. Sector-specific regulators have been created to address these institutional and practical challenges of price regulation. Competition authorities and courts have not. The additional cost of expertise and analysis that is required by the authority or court when implementing a price remedy should be considered in the CBA of such a remedy.

8.4.3 Economic insights from network regulation: Access regulation

Access regulation has been of central importance in network industries. The first step is to **8.41** decide whether to impose an access obligation. The economic principles behind this are not very different from the assessment of essential facilities under Article 102 (see Chapter 4). In the field of regulation, the focus has mostly been on access to bottleneck and natural monopoly facilities such as rail infrastructure, electricity transmission networks, and last-mile telephone lines. With an access obligation usually comes the need to regulate the access price as well (otherwise access can be notionally offered but made prohibitively expensive). Many of the general principles of price regulation discussed above apply to access regulation as well—capping prices at competitive levels should aim to ensure that the network can earn a reasonable return and has the right incentives to invest and provide high quality. But there are additional policy objectives that are specific to access pricing: to promote efficient levels of entry in downstream markets that are reliant on the network, and to prevent vertically integrated network operators from leveraging their market power.

A general principle to achieve these objectives is that access terms should be non- **8.42** discriminatory between integrated and independent competitors. But the price level and structure also matter. Making competition work effectively in the downstream market means stimulating entry, but only by companies that are efficient (note the similarity with the as-efficient competitor test for abuse of dominance cases). Aligning efficient entry and profitable entry is generally achieved by ensuring that access prices are cost-reflective. Some of the main access pricing mechanisms are discussed below. We note here that competition law sometimes, but not always, prescribes cost-reflective access pricing—this is often a matter of judgement (and discretion), not just economics. In Chapter 4 we saw the example of *Attheraces*, where a cost-plus approach to access pricing was rejected because the input (horseracing data) had significant 'economic value' to the purchaser's downstream operations (a broadcast service) that was greater than the supplier's cost of producing the input.[40]

8.43   A first set of access-pricing mechanisms uses marginal costs as the basis. As we noted in Chapter 1, optimal pricing theory states that prices should equal marginal or incremental cost if efficient resource allocation is to be achieved. Incremental cost pricing also often means that prices are neither excessive nor predatory. The question is what to take as the relevant increment—we addressed this in Chapter 4 when discussing cost benchmarks for abuse of dominance cases. Short-run marginal cost is one option. If train operators face the actual marginal cost that their services impose on the rail network, they will be incentivized to utilize network capacity efficiently. A train service will be operated wherever the benefit of that service to the operator (in revenues) exceeds the cost that the service imposes on the network. This holds true up to the point where network capacity is fully utilized and marginal costs become much larger—that is, at that point marginal costs include the costs of network expansion required to supply the next unit. If there is effective competition in the downstream market (train services), retail prices will reflect the network access charges, thereby providing efficient incentives for usage by end-consumers. The downside is that short-run marginal costs do not include fixed costs. In most network industries fixed costs are substantial, and therefore the network operator would not recover its total costs from the access charge. This could negatively affect investment incentives and ultimately lead to sub-optimal network capacity.

8.44   A variant used frequently in regulation, and recognized in competition law as well, is long-run incremental cost (LRIC) or LRAIC pricing, which we explained in section 4. An example of a competition case in which this variant was used is *Albion Water*, concerning the access price for non-potable water to supply a paper factory in the United Kingdom.[41] LRIC pricing allows for recovery of the fixed costs of providing additional network capacity. As the relevant increment becomes larger or is considered over a longer time period, more costs become incremental. Although it deviates from short-run efficient price signals (if there is excess capacity, pricing at short-run marginal costs gives the right signals for usage of the capacity), LRIC pricing can be more efficient over time since it takes into account both short-run marginal costs and the contribution to capital costs of incremental use of the network, thus preserving incentives to invest in efficient network provision. It also allows incremental investments to be directed to those parts of the network where there is an efficient need for them.

8.45   Fully allocated cost pricing is a top-down approach whereby total costs are identified and, for a given volume projection, the access charge is set such that total revenue is sufficient to cover total costs. The European Commission inquiry into excessive charges for access to Belgacom's subscriber data is one (albeit somewhat old) example where fully allocated pricing was used in an abuse of dominance remedy.[42] This pricing mechanism is fundamentally different from marginal cost pricing. Total costs will include an appropriate return on capital and allowances for depreciation, so that this mechanism can provide for appropriate

---

[40] *Attheraces v British Horseracing Board* [2007] EWCA Civ 38, 2 February 2007.
[41] *Albion Water Limited and ors v Water Services Regulation Authority and ors* [2008] CAT 31, Judgment on Unfair Pricing, 7 November 2008.
[42] European Commission (1998), 'XXVIIth Report on Competition Policy (1997)', p. 26.

investment incentives. However, since charging is based on average rather than marginal cost, it does not provide efficient usage incentives. One particular problem arises where the network capacity is under-utilized and hence fixed costs are spread over fewer users. This increases the average costs and thereby the access price, thus perversely reducing the number of users even further.

The efficient component pricing rule is the last access pricing mechanism we discuss here. **8.46** It is also known as the Baumol–Willig rule (Baumol, 1983; Willig, 1979). Two competition cases where the rule was discussed at length (one in negative and the other in positive terms) in the context of an alleged abuse of dominance are *Albion Water* and *Telecom New Zealand*.[43] The efficient component pricing rule is applied to situations in which there is a vertically integrated network provider. Its main objective is ensuring efficient entry downstream. The access price is set such that only companies that are as efficient as the incumbent enter. It takes as a starting point the downstream (retail) price charged by the incumbent. Say this is €1.00 per unit. The access price is then equal to that retail price minus the incumbent's downstream marginal cost per unit. If this downstream marginal cost is €0.20, the access price is €0.80. At this access price, only entrants that have downstream marginal costs of €0.20 or lower get sufficient 'headroom' to make a profit (assuming that they cannot raise the retail price above the €1.00 charged by the integrated company). This mechanism is therefore also known as 'retail-minus'. In general it is relatively straightforward to implement as only downstream costs need to be analysed in detail. It is less strict on the network operator than marginal cost pricing since the retail price is taken as given—that is, there is no scrutiny of whether the €1.00 retail price reflects competitive or monopoly levels. This does not provide for any means to control end-consumer prices if those are set inefficiently high to start with. For example, if the true incremental cost of network access is €0.70, with the downstream marginal cost being €0.20, the competitive retail price would be €0.90 not €1.00. This is sometimes seen as a drawback of the efficient component pricing rule.

8.4.4 Behavioural remedies with side effects: Online hotel bookings

Competition authorities increasingly seek to resolve investigations into anti-competitive **8.47** conduct by agreeing a settlement or commitments with the parties, rather than taking the matter to a final decision. We have seen a number of examples in this chapter. This has clear advantages from the perspective of procedural efficiency, and may save significant enforcement costs. The downside is that the merits of the case may not be fully tested or made public. The parties (and sometimes the authorities) may be so keen to end the investigation that they agree to remedies even if they do not agree with the assessment of the problem. A worse situation is where a settlement agreement between the authority and the investigated parties does not sufficiently account for negative side-effects on third parties, such as competitors or customers. An example of such a situation is the online hotel booking case in the United Kingdom, which the CAT ruled on in 2014.[44]

---

[43] *Albion Water Limited and ors v Water Services Regulation Authority and ors* [2006] CAT 36, Judgment, 18 December 2006 (this was an earlier judgment in the same case cited above in the discussion of LRIC pricing); and *Commerce Commission v Telecom Corporation of New Zealand Limited and Telecom New Zealand Limited* CIV 2004-404-1333, Judgment of 9 October 2009, High Court of New Zealand.

[44] *Skyscanner Limited v Competition and Markets Authority*, [2014] CAT 16, 26 September 2014. We advised Skyscanner on this matter.

8.48 In 2010 the OFT had opened an investigation into the online sale of room-only hotel book-ings by online travel agents (OTAs). It was targeted at the two major OTAs (Expedia and Booking.com) and a large hotel chain (InterContinental Hotels Group) but the practices of concern seemed to be widespread in the market. Distribution agreements established that OTAs would offer hotel accommodation at the prices set by the hotels themselves, and would not lower these prices through discounts. The OFT considered this to be a restriction by object akin to resale price maintenance. The restrictions on discounting limited 'intra-brand' price competition for the same hotel rooms among OTAs, and between OTAs and the hotels' direct online sales channels. They also created barriers to entry for new OTAs wishing to grow by offering discounts. In January 2014 (shortly before being merged into the CMA), the OFT closed the investigation through a commitment decision. The parties agreed to remove the restrictions on discounting the headline hotel room rates. However, importantly, OTAs would offer discounts only to customers who had actively signed up to a 'closed group', and could not publicize information about the level or extent of discounts outside the closed group.

8.49 Skyscanner, a meta-search company, appealed against this commitment decision, mainly on the basis that such discounting to closed groups would reduce overall price transpar-ency in the market and threaten the business model of meta-search and price-comparison websites. The CAT agreed, and annulled the decision. It held that the OFT should have considered the potentially detrimental side-effects of the commitments. The OFT itself had acknowledged the consumer and efficiency benefits of price transparency in online mar-kets, and the growing importance of meta-search and price-comparison websites in online hotel bookings. The CAT noted that because the OFT had approached the matter as an object infringement it had not gathered sufficient information to properly assess the effects of the commitments. It found the concerns about the negative side-effects on price trans-parency and the search business to be plausible, even if no empirical evidence of such effects was available at that stage (given that the commitments had not yet been put in place). This case is a useful reminder that the costs and benefits of any remedies must be analysed care-fully and in the round, including the effects on third parties.

8.5 Behavioural Remedies: FRAND

8.5.1 FRAND remedies in competition law

8.50 FRAND is a generic formulation for the terms that can be offered under a pricing or access remedy. It is increasingly used in a variety of contexts, both in regulation and competition law. Earlier we saw the example of the *Liberty Global/De Vijver* merger in 2015 where one of the remedies was to license TV channels to rival distributors on FRAND terms. Other FRAND remedies in competition cases include BSkyB's obligation to supply access to its technical platform services in the UK pay-TV market, and Microsoft's obligation to make interface information available in order to allow rival servers to achieve full interoperability with its servers and PCs running on Windows.[45]

---

[45] Ofcom (2005), 'Provision of technical platform services: A consultation on proposed guidance as to how Ofcom may interpret the meaning of "Fair, Reasonable and Non-discriminatory" and other regulatory conditions when assessing charges and terms offered by regulated providers of technical platform services', November; and *Microsoft* (Case COMP/C-3/37.792), Decision of 24 March 2004.

The 'non-discriminatory' condition is usually interpreted in the same manner as the general **8.51** criteria for anti-competitive price discrimination under the abuse of dominance rules (see Chapter 4): the access terms should not distort competition between downstream buyers, whether vertically integrated or independent. It does not necessarily mean that all buyers get exactly the same price; there may be justifications for setting differential terms, and if buyers do not compete with each other in downstream markets there is limited risk of a competitive distortion.

The 'fair' and 'reasonable' conditions are more difficult to interpret. Some commentators **8.52** have given separate meanings to what is 'fair' and what is 'reasonable' (in the United States the concept used to be called RAND, without the 'fair', but this is mostly a matter of semantics and US commentators now also commonly refer to FRAND). However, the terms 'fair' and 'reasonable' are in essence the same, as they both seek to capture the principle that access terms must strike the right balance between facilitating efficient competition and product development in the downstream market, and providing the upstream provider with sufficient incentives to invest in the facility or input. The price and access regulation principles discussed previously in this chapter are of direct relevance here. Like in other contexts, what is fair and reasonable is usually a matter of degree and judgement, reflecting particular trade-offs that must be made—for example, between short- and long-term efficiency, and between cost- and value-based access prices.

8.5.2 FRAND remedies: IP licensing and abuse of dominance

One context in which the concept of FRAND has gained particular prominence in the last **8.53** ten years is in the licensing of IP. While FRAND terms for access to physical networks or inputs are commonly set with reference to costs, this is less straightforward for IP licences. Many products in the high-tech and telecoms industries—mobile handsets, memory chips, and game consoles, for example—are based on common technology standards, which are often set by standard-setting organizations (SSOs). Standards usually incorporate a large number of patented technologies. These patents are called standard-essential patents (SEPs) and are valuable—all users of the standard have to pay royalties to the patent holder. Patents that are excluded from the standard tend to be less valuable. Before making a particular patent part of the standard, SSOs often require the holder to commit to license it on FRAND terms. SSOs began to incorporate FRAND principles in the 1970s and 1980s, when industries were becoming increasingly aware of the potential commercial value of technology standards and had to devise practical solutions to agreeing a standard and avoiding problems of hold-up. Hold-up in this context occurs when the manufacturers in the SSO must select a particular technology for the standard, but are concerned that they will subsequently be charged exploitative royalty rates for that technology and will be unable to switch because it has become part of the standard. FRAND is designed to give IP holders a reasonable return so as to preserve their incentives to innovate, but at the same time prevent them from unreasonably benefiting from the additional value that accrues to them from being included in the standard. The use of the FRAND principle has facilitated the development and acceptance of new standards. However, SSOs that require licensing on FRAND terms, such as the European Telecommunications Standards Institute (ETSI) and the Joint Electronic Device Engineering Council (JEDEC) in the United States, have never really come up with a precise definition of the concept. For a long time this lack of definition was perhaps not a major problem because licensing disputes were relatively rare.

Yet in the last ten years the FRAND rules have led to numerous legal challenges—most notably in what has been dubbed the 'smartphone wars' since 2009, with the likes of Apple, Google, HTC, Microsoft, Nokia, and Samsung suing each other in jurisdictions across the world. These FRAND disputes under IP law increasingly end up in front of competition authorities as well.

8.54 How the competition rules apply to FRAND in IP licensing is still an undeveloped area. One question is whether not complying with FRAND obligations amounts to an abuse of dominance. Another is how FRAND should be determined. As regards the first question, there is a spectrum between laissez-faire and more interventionist approaches, just as there is in other areas of competition law. An example of the former is the *Rambus* case in the United States.[46] In 2008 a court overturned a finding by the FTC that Rambus, a technology licensing company, had breached section 2 of the Sherman Act. The FTC considered that Rambus had unfairly 'ambushed' an SSO—the JEDEC, which worked with industry participants to develop standards for random access memory chips—by not declaring its intention to acquire and subsequently enforce patent rights covering technology that was essential to implement two particular standards. The FTC also concluded that as part of this 'ambush' Rambus had charged prices above the (F)RAND levels that the SSO would have sought. Assessing this behaviour under competition law, and taking FRAND as the benchmark, was a previously untested approach. The court disagreed with the FTC and stated that:

> the Commission failed to sustain its allegation of monopolization. Its factual conclusion was that Rambus's alleged deception enabled it *either* to acquire a monopoly through the standardization of its patented technologies rather than possible alternatives, *or* to avoid limits on its patent licensing fees that the SSO would have imposed as part of its normal process of standardizing patented technologies. But the latter—deceit merely enabling a monopolist to charge higher prices than it otherwise could have charged—would not in itself constitute monopolization.[47]

8.55 The European Commission also opened an abuse of dominance investigation into Rambus, and reached a settlement in 2009 whereby Rambus would place a worldwide cap on its royalty rates for products under the JEDEC standards (and zero rates for a technology used in a particular standard that had been adopted when Rambus was a JEDEC member).[48] Another early investigation under EU competition law was into Qualcomm, following complaints by various mobile phone and chipset manufacturers (including Ericsson, Nokia, Texas Instruments, Broadcom, NEC, and Panasonic).[49] The alleged abuse concerned the terms under which Qualcomm licensed its SEPs under the WCDMA standard, which forms part of the 3G standard for European mobile phone technology (also referred to as UMTS). The investigation was closed in 2009 after the complaints were withdrawn, and hence did not shed much light on how FRAND would be treated under Article 102.

8.56 Two subsequent European Commission investigations, into Motorola and Samsung, reached a conclusion in 2014 and set out the circumstances in which SEP holders can abuse

---

[46] *Rambus Inc v FTC* 522 F 3d 456 (US Ct of Apps (District of Colombia Circuit), 2008).
[47] Ibid., at [5].
[48] *Rambus* (Case COMP/38.636), Decision of 9 December 2009.
[49] European Commission (2009), 'Antitrust: Commission closes formal proceedings against Qualcomm', press release, MEMO/09/516, 24 November.

a dominant position by filing injunctions against users of the SEP—that is, these cases did not clarify how FRAND should be interpreted, but they do circumscribe the conduct that owners of SEPs can engage in.[50] The Commission stated that where the holder of a SEP has committed to license it on FRAND terms, seeking injunctions to exclude competitors from the downstream market is anti-competitive if those competitors are 'willing' to take a licence on FRAND terms. In the case of Motorola (whose patents have been owned by Google since 2011), the Commission found that an injunction against Apple in a German court led to competitive harm: a temporary ban on Apple's sales of iPhones and iPads in the German market, and Apple having to enter into an onerous settlement agreement whereby it had to give up its claims against the validity of the Motorola patents. Apple was considered to have been a 'willing' licensee since it had agreed to a court setting the FRAND rate in the event of a dispute. In a parallel case, Samsung had sought injunctions against Apple in a number of jurisdictions. In exchange for closure of the investigation, Samsung committed not to seek such injunctions against 'willing' licensees for a period of five years. Following these decisions there is still much debate about what constitutes a 'willing' licensee, in addition to the ongoing debate about the meaning of FRAND.

8.5.3 FRAND: Economic criteria

Economics can shed some light on how to think about determining FRAND, even if the meaning of FRAND is not yet settled. The nature of IP rights means that static cost-based pricing rules do not provide useful guidance for setting price ceilings (in contrast with essential physical facilities where both capital and operating costs can be more easily identified and related to usage of the facility). The typically low marginal cost of distributing IP means that setting prices based on marginal costs—which is normally considered the efficient price level—would not generate sufficient incentives for innovation. It is therefore necessary to look for alternatives. One is to carry out a profitability analysis of the investments and returns over the lifetime of the patent. This is a more comprehensive analysis than the static cost-based pricing rules and uses the financial tools discussed in Chapter 3. With the right data, the profitability of innovative activities can be estimated, making appropriate adjustments for intangible assets, unsuccessful as well as successful innovation efforts, and risk. The price would be set such that the innovator can earn returns that cover its cost of capital. This approach still leaves open the policy question of whether it is sufficient to allow patent owners a fair return on their investments in innovation (which is often the approach for owners of essential physical facilities), or whether patent owners should be entitled to a share of the profits ('economic value') that downstream companies make by using the patented technologies. **8.57**

Another set of economic approaches tries to capture the notion that the FRAND terms should reflect the added value of the patent itself, but not the value derived from the patent's inclusion in the standard. One of these is the Swanson–Baumol approach, whereby the price that the IP holder would be willing to charge *prior* to the acceptance of the IP into the standard is taken as the fair price, as it reflects the value of the IP independently of the value of the standard (Swanson and Baumol, 2005). Another is the Shapley value approach, **8.58**

---

[50] *Motorola—Enforcement of GPRS standard essential patents* (Case AT.39985), Decision of 29 April 2014; and *Samsung—Enforcement of UMTS standard essential patents* (Case AT.39939), Decision of 29 April 2014. See also European Commission (2014).

resulting in a FRAND price that awards each IP holder the value that represents its relative contribution to the standard.[51] We discuss these two approaches below.

8.59 To alleviate concerns about exploitation of ex post market power by an IP holder that has been accepted into a standard, the Swanson–Baumol approach is based on prospective licensees negotiating licence terms *before* their acceptance into the standard, when there is still active competition between technologies. Licence terms set at that point do not reflect the value of incorporation into the standard. This is broadly the model that two SSOs—the Institute of Electrical and Electronics Engineers and the VITA Standards Organization—have been exploring: in their applications to the SSO, IP holders reveal the maximum royalty rate that would apply for the lifetime of the standard, were they to be accepted (Treacy and Kostenko, 2007). The Swanson–Baumol approach is auction-based, so the resulting licensing rates reflect the value that each patent brings to the standard over and above the value that the next-best solution could provide. While this approach is appealing in relation to the future pricing of technology that is yet to be incorporated into a standard, its usefulness as a benchmark for making ex post assessments is more limited. One would have to verify the extent to which, at the time that the particular patent was included in the standard, alternative technological solutions were available that could have been substituted for the patent in question.

8.60 The Shapley value approach to FRAND is based on a theoretical form of patent selection, and can be defined as follows (Layne-Farrar et al., 2007, p. 24):

> Suppose that there are n patent-owners, one for each patent involved . . . Suppose the patent-owners arrive at the SSO in random order each with her patent in her pocket, with all possible arrival sequences equally likely. Now suppose that in each sequence, each patent-owner receives the amount by which her patent increases the value of the best standard that can be built from the patents that are already at the SSO when she arrives . . . The Shapley value gives the average of such contributions over all possible arrival sequences—each patent thus receives the average (over arrival sequences) of its marginal contribution.

8.61 To illustrate, consider a standard with two complementary technologies: one to enable the characters in a computer game to move left, and one to enable them to move right. The end-product (the game) needs both in order to be of any use. While for most users these technologies will be of equal value, the payouts to the patent holders may not be the same under the Shapley value approach. If just one company develops the technology to move left, while two companies work out alternative technologies to move right, the payoffs would be two-thirds to the former, and one-sixth to each of the latter—this is shown in Table 8.1, which has all six arrival sequences and shows for each which technology (R1, R2, or L) renders the product valuable upon arrival, that is, once there is a left and right technology. Note that in this analysis both inventors of moving right receive a payoff, even if only one of them is ultimately included in the standard.

8.62 Despite their different approaches, the Swanson–Baumol and Shapley value methodologies share similarities in their outcomes. An IP holder that faces no competition from alternative technologies vying to be included in the standard will always earn greater returns than an IP holder for a technology for which there is competition. In practice, this could lead to

[51] This option is described as the 'Shapley solution' in Layne-Farrar et al. (2007). The underlying thinking is derived from Shapley (1953).

Table 8.1 Illustration of FRAND pay-offs based on the Shapley value approach

Arrival sequence of the technologies	Which technology adds the value?	Final pay-off to each technology after six sequences
R1, R2, L	L	R1: 1/6th
R1, L, R2	L	R2: 1/6th
R2, R1, L	L	L: 4/6ths
R2, L, R1	L	
L, R1, R2	R1	
L, R2, R1	R2	

the paradoxical outcome of a monopoly provider of a peripheral technology earning greater returns than a provider of a more fundamental element of the standard for which alternatives exist. However, economically, this outcome might still be considered efficient—scarce goods are priced more highly; this is what you get in well-functioning markets, even if it may not seem 'fair'.

In any event, it has proved difficult to translate these two theoretical approaches into practical tests. In addition, some courts have questioned the appropriateness of the theoretical result that a patent that adds significant value to a standard (like the moving right technology in the computer game example above) should get a low royalty just because it had a competitor before inclusion into the standard. In *Innovatio* (2013), an IP case in the United States involving wireless internet technology, the court accepted that the FRAND rate should reflect the value of the technology and not the hold-up value from inclusion in the standard. However, it rejected the argument that when two alternative patents compete for incorporation into the standard the FRAND rate could be driven down to zero, as 'it is implausible that in the real world, patent holders would accept effectively nothing to license their technology'.[52]

8.63

8.5.4 FRAND: A bargain?

A framework for determining FRAND (and reasonable royalties more broadly) used in IP law in the United States is that of the hypothetical negotiation between a willing licensor and a willing licensee. The reference for this is the *Georgia-Pacific* case of 1970 (concerning patents for particular types of plywood):

8.64

> The amount that a licensor (such as the patentee) and a licensee (such as the infringer) would have agreed upon (at the time the infringement began) if both had been reasonably and voluntarily trying to reach an agreement; that is, the amount which a prudent licensee—who desired, as a business proposition, to obtain a license to manufacture and sell a particular article embodying the patented innovation—would have been willing to pay as a royalty and yet be able to make a reasonable profit and which amount would have been acceptable by a prudent patentee who was willing to grant a license.[53]

---

[52] *In re Innovatio IP Ventures, LLC, Patent Litigation,* No 11-cv-09308 (N.D. Ill. 3 October 2013), Memorandum Opinion, Findings, Conclusions, and Order, at [37].

[53] *Georgia-Pacific Corp. v United States Plywood Corp.,* 318 F. Supp. 1116, 166 U.S.P.Q. (BNA) 235 (S.D.N.Y. 1970).

8.65 This negotiation framework is very broad—there are many possible outcomes—and gives great weight to what 'reasonable', 'prudent', and 'willing' buyers and sellers agree with each other in the market. The framework does have some grounding in economics, namely in the famous bargaining problem as formalized by John Nash (1950b). In its simplest general form the bargaining problem involves two parties negotiating the distribution of a fixed sum (or pie) between them. This can be a seller and a buyer (or licensor and licensee, as here). The main parameters of the bargaining are the buyer's maximum willingness to pay and the minimum price the seller is willing to accept. If the former is larger than the latter, there is scope to reach an agreement (there is a pie to be shared). Another key parameter is the 'disagreement point', which reflects the value to each player if no agreement is reached. For example, if neither party gets any value when no deal is struck, the disagreement point would be (0,0). If one of the parties has a 'walk-away' option, it would get a positive value at the disagreement point (you can see how having an alternative improves the party's bargaining position). Any resulting distribution can be an equilibrium outcome. From an economic perspective what matters most for welfare is that a deal is struck at all—any additional transaction where the buyer's willingness to pay exceeds the seller's minimum desired price enhances economic welfare (as we saw in Chapter 1).

8.66 Evidently the bargaining problem doesn't say much about distributive justice. At one extreme, the buyer may be powerful or cunning enough to appropriate the entire surplus—that is, the price ends up at the minimum level the supplier was willing to accept. At the other extreme the seller extracts the entire surplus from the buyer (in the FRAND context, this would mean that the patent holder obtains the entire downstream profit from the licensee). One type of outcome is the Nash bargaining solution, which maximizes the joint surplus made by the two parties. In the case where the two parties are symmetric (e.g. they have the same payoff at the disagreement point) the solution is to share the pie equally. This is intuitive, but also somewhat simplistic. In the *Oracle v Google* case of 2011, concerning patents related to the Java software platform, a US court rejected the 50/50 Nash bargaining solution as a basis for setting reasonable royalty rates:

> It is no wonder that a patent plaintiff would love the Nash bargaining solution because it awards fully half of the surplus to the patent owner, which in most cases will amount to half of the infringer's profit, which will be many times the amount of real-world royalty rates. There is no anchor for this fifty-percent assumption in the record of actual transactions.[54]

8.67 Quoting some formulae from an economics paper on the Nash bargaining solution, the court added that: 'No jury could follow this Greek or testimony trying to explain it. The Nash bargaining solution would invite a miscarriage of justice by clothing a fifty-percent assumption in an impenetrable facade of mathematics.'[55]

8.68 In *Microsoft v Motorola* (2013) another US court sought to adjust the *Georgia-Pacific* criteria to the specific context of FRAND for SEPs.[56] Motorola, the licensor, had offered a rate of 2.25 per cent of the end price of each Microsoft product using its SEPs (in particular the Xbox), amounting to around $4 billion in cash. The court ruled that

---

[54] *Oracle America, Inc. v Google Inc*, 798 F. Supp. 2d 1111 (N.D. Cal. 2011).

[55] Ibid.

[56] *Microsoft Corp. v Motorola, Inc.*, No. 10-cv-1823 (W.D. Wash.), Findings of Fact and Conclusions of Law, 25 April 2013.

Motorola's offer was not in line with FRAND, and determined a much lower range of FRAND rates (expressed as per-unit prices rather than as a percentage of Microsoft's product price). The court did this with reference to various comparable licensing rates in the market that had been set in a FRAND commitment context. Such benchmarking against other rates in the market is a common approach in FRAND disputes. The court referred to the hypothetical negotiation framework, but added a number of specific factors to be considered when assessing FRAND for SEPs. First, the SEP holder has committed to licensing on FRAND terms, so cannot walk away from the negotiation. Second, bargaining parties would take into account the fact that the licensee implementing the standard must deal with more than one SEP holder, and must avoid excessive 'royalty stacking' (i.e. where the SEP holders in aggregate charge such high royalties that the licensee cannot make any profit downstream). While this case has narrowed the *Georgia-Pacific* negotiation framework somewhat, it still leaves plenty of room for many different bargaining outcomes. A relatively wide range of royalty rates could be considered FRAND under the hypothetical bargaining and market benchmarking approaches.

8.6 Behavioural Remedies: Insights from Behavioural Economics

8.6.1 Nudges and liberal paternalism

8.69 In Chapter 3 we discussed behavioural economics and showed how the presence of consumer biases and bounded rationality on the demand side can have a negative impact on market outcomes. In this section we explore how behavioural economics can help in the design of remedies targeted at the demand side. These are different from the remedies discussed so far, which have focused mostly on the supply side—remedies targeted at market structure and at the behaviour of companies. Within behavioural economics there are different schools of thought about remedies (and policy interventions more broadly). One of these is 'liberal paternalism', a phrase coined by Richard Thaler and Cass Sunstein (2003). Liberal paternalist interventions try to influence consumers' choices in a way that will make them better off, and without restricting their options. These interventions have become known as 'nudges' (Thaler and Sunstein, 2008). Liberal paternalism recognizes that it is not completely understood why people behave the way they do. In addition, it acknowledges that a heavy-handed approach by policy-makers—for example, banning certain products, or subsidizing others—is not always desirable or cost-effective, and may have unintended consequences. Therefore, liberal paternalism involves designing remedies that, to some extent, work *with* consumers' biases and limited decision-making abilities, rather than seeking to correct them. This does not necessarily mean more intervention, but rather 'smarter' intervention. Given the influence of framing and bounded rationality in consumer decisions, nudging seeks to alter the choice architecture within which people make decisions. This can be of use in markets where competition is perceived to be ineffective due to a lack of customer searching and switching.

8.70 One such remedy is to simplify information disclosure to salient points—this is aimed at overcoming framing, information overload, and inertia, and hence at improving decision-making. Timing also matters, as information is most relevant at the point when a decision is made. To give an example, Cass Sunstein, retained by the US government, produced a memorandum for all executive departments and agencies entitled 'Disclosure and simplification as a regulatory tool'.[57] This stated that departments and agencies should provide 'clear, salient information at or near the time that relevant decisions are made'. This is often at the point of selection or purchase, in which 'agencies highlight the most relevant information in order to increase the likelihood that people will see it, understand it, and act in accordance with what they have learned'. In a competition context, the UK Financial Conduct Authority (FCA), the financial regulator, proposed such information-based remedies in its market study into general insurance add-ons.[58] An experiment was carried out on insurance add-ons to be purchased with a number of primary products: a home boiler, a tablet computer, a laptop, a luxury holiday for two, and a 12-day car hire in Spain. It turned out that 65 per cent of consumers bought the first insurance offer they saw without further search if the add-on was first introduced at the point of sale, whereas only 16 per cent purchased the first insurance product they saw if the add-on was introduced up front (i.e. at the start of the process of purchasing the primary product). In addition, the framing of add-on prices resulted in consumers seemingly not understanding the 'real' price of add-ons. Where monthly prices were displayed rather than the annual price, 30 per cent of consumers changed their mind about purchase once they saw the annual cost.

8.71   Another type of liberal paternalist remedy focuses on activating consumers to make a choice—the 'forced choice', which aims to prevent inertia or simply going with the default option. This could be achieved by requiring consumers to confirm pro-actively (e.g. by telephone or online) whether they wish to renew their service contract or insurance policy with their current provider, rather than the contract being renewed automatically. This may overcome the poor choices made as a result of consumer inertia. A related remedy is to use default opt-ins or opt-outs. Where a particular outcome is clearly superior from the consumers' (as opposed to the sellers') point of view, the policy might be to set that outcome as the default, without restricting consumers' ability to choose an alternative. For example, it may be that people are defaulted into an employee pension plan, but can then opt out. This can help overcome inertia and loss aversion (the fear of regret of opting into the wrong policy), and ultimately achieves an arguably better policy outcome with more people having a pension plan.

8.72   An example of such a remedy in a competition context is Ofcom's prohibition in 2011 of automatically renewable contracts (also known as rollover contracts) in retail telephony and broadband markets.[59] The UK telecoms regulator recognized the benefits of such contracts (e.g. convenience), but found that these benefits were outweighed by the negative effects on consumer switching and hence effective competition. An econometric analysis had shown that customers who were on such contracts tended to switch less frequently than those who were not. Ofcom considered a remedy aimed at providing more information to consumers about the automatic renewals. However, it found that the consumer harm resulted from the opt-out nature of these contracts, not from a lack of information as such. The remedy therefore focused on making the renewal process an opt-in rather than

---

[57] Available at: <https://www.whitehouse.gov/sites/default/files/omb/assets/inforeg/disclosure_principles.pdf>

[58] See Financial Conduct Authority (2015), 'General insurance add-ons market study—proposed remedies: banning opt-out selling across financial services and supporting informed decision-making for add-on buyers', consultation paper, March; and London Economics and YouGov (2014).

[59] Ofcom (2011), 'Automatically Renewable Contracts: Decision on a General Condition to prohibit ARCs', 13 September.

an opt-out process—that is, customers would actively have to renew their contract upon expiry. A more heavy-handed remedy that Ofcom also considered was to abolish minimum contract periods altogether and allow customers to switch at any point in time (as some other EU countries have done via legislation). However, the regulator considered this remedy to be disproportionate, as it would deprive customers of the discounts and other benefits they may receive when signing up to a contract for a particular period. This example does not mean that automatic renewals are always problematic. In its 2014 investigation into the UK motor insurance market, the CMA did not find automatic renewals of annual policies to be a major barrier to switching, as switching rates in this market were relatively high.[60] This shows the importance of careful empirical testing of the competition problems and potential remedies on a case-by-case basis.

Liberal paternalist interventions tend to come at a lower cost than more intrusive interventions, such as subsidies or education programmes. Implementing them does not require a complete understanding of consumer preferences or decision-making processes. If the intervention does not work effectively, there are often few unintended negative consequences. Liberal paternalist interventions can also be aimed at ensuring that affected consumers (e.g. naive consumers) are better off without making others (e.g. sophisticated consumers) worse off, as both types of consumer still have all choices available to them. Yet there is a fine line between liberal paternalism and simple paternalism. The CC investigation into personal current accounts in Northern Ireland perhaps came close to it. One of the competition concerns identified was that, in general, consumers do not actively search for alternative personal current accounts. However, the CC also found that 'customers are generally not particularly interested in personal current accounts', and that 80 per cent of those surveyed who had not switched bank gave as a reason that they had been with their current provider for a long time.[61] If consumers do not particularly care about a product, should competition authorities? This is a policy question that merits consideration before intervening in a market.

8.6.2 More intrusive interventions to restore consumer sovereignty

Sometimes more intrusive remedies are preferred which do restrict consumer choice sets (e.g. banning certain products), but are still aimed at increasing the power that consumers have over those choices that are available to them. These remedies are still consistent with the aim of reinforcing 'consumer sovereignty' (i.e. whereby consumer preferences determine which goods and services are produced), but go beyond just nudging consumers towards the desired behaviour. By restricting the choice set, these interventions may make some consumers better off but also make others worse off. They therefore require a great deal of caution—policymakers ultimately have to assign weights to the welfare impacts on the different groups of producers and consumers.

A far-reaching remedy proposed by the CC in the payment protection insurance (PPI) market investigation (which we also discussed in Chapter 3) was a prohibition on selling PPI at

8.73

8.74

8.75

---

[60] Competition and Markets Authority (2014), 'Private Motor Insurance Market Investigation', final report, 24 September. We advised one of the insurers in this investigation.

[61] Competition Commission (2006), 'Market Investigation into Personal Current Account Banking Services in Northern Ireland—Provisional Findings', 12 October, at [8] and Appendix 4.3. We advised one of the banks in this investigation.

the credit point of sale.[62] PPI was sold as an add-on insurance to consumers who take out credit (the primary product), and provided cover against events that may prevent them from keeping up with their repayments. The remedy prohibiting PPI at point of sale would give consumers time to shop around and encourage them to consider more carefully the price and quality features of PPI before purchasing it. It would also give stand-alone providers of PPI the opportunity to offer their products more effectively, without having the disadvantage of not being available at the point of sale. This was expected to increase competition in the PPI market. The CC concluded that other remedies, such as the provision of more information, would not be sufficient to address the competition issues. On appeal, the CAT found that the CC had failed to take into account the loss of convenience to consumers that would follow from the imposition of the point-of-sale prohibition.[63] The case was remitted to the CC for reconsideration, which then conducted further research—in particular, in the form of a number of conjoint analyses among consumers—to assess the costs and benefits of the prohibition.[64]

8.76 This consumer research raised some interesting distributional issues. The survey evidence suggested that 60 per cent of personal loan PPI customers preferred the convenience of purchasing PPI at the point of sale. Hence for this majority the prohibition remedy would remove the current preferred choice. However, the CC determined that the other 40 per cent of consumers who preferred to purchase away from the point of sale valued this option more than those who preferred to buy at the point of sale (notwithstanding the fact that those who wished to buy away from the point of sale could already do so). It therefore placed greater weight on the 40 per cent group, and confirmed its previous conclusion that, on balance, consumers as a whole would benefit from a point-of-sale prohibition. This example illustrates that it is far from straightforward to design remedies that will benefit everyone, and that a CBA of remedies often requires authorities to value the relative preferences of different groups of consumers. In this particular case, the prohibition remedy was estimated to result in an inconvenience to 60 per cent of customers and a potential benefit to the remaining 40 per cent.

8.6.3 The *Microsoft* remedies

8.77 The European Commission *Microsoft* cases are useful examples of how behavioural economics can add to the assessment of remedies in abuse of dominance investigations. Consumer biases played a role in the Media Player case, which focused on Microsoft's practice of bundling (by default and free of charge) Windows Media Player with its Windows operating system.[65] Microsoft was dominant in the operating system market, but competitors were vying to gain market share in the emerging media player market. By bundling Media Player as the default application through which all media would play when a consumer bought a PC, Microsoft was considered to have leveraged its dominance in the operating system market into the market for media players.

---

[62] Competition Commission (2009), 'Market Investigation into Payment Protection Insurance', 29 January. We advised one of the PPI providers during this investigation.

[63] *Barclays Bank PLC v Competition Commission*, [2009] CAT 27, 16 October 2009.

[64] Competition Commission (2010), 'Payment Protection Insurance Market Investigation: Remittal of the Point-of-sale Prohibition Remedy by the Competition Appeal Tribunal', 14 October.

[65] *Microsoft* (Case COMP/C-3/37.792), Decision of 24 March 2004.

Traditional approaches would suggest that this default does not matter hugely if consumers **8.78** are rational. After all, with a few clicks they could download an alternative media player free of charge. However, when viewed from the perspective of behavioural economics, it follows that many consumers may not switch away from the preloaded Microsoft software that comes as the default with the PC. The European Commission found that the pre-installation of Media Player on Windows created the potential for leveraging since, on the demand side, 'users who find WMP pre-installed on their client PCs are in general less likely to use alternative media players as they already have an application which delivers media streaming and playback functionality'.[66] Equally, the Commission found that: 'A supply-side aspect to consider is that, while downloading is in itself a technically inexpensive way of distributing media players, vendors must expend resources to overcome end-users' inertia and persuade them to ignore the pre-installation of WMP.'[67]

Hence the finding of abuse took account of the behavioural biases that consumers face. The **8.79** remedies to this competition problem also had behavioural economics aspects. Yet one remedy that the Commission put forward turned out to be ineffective, and could perhaps have been improved if it had been based more on insights from behavioural economics. This was the remedy that Microsoft should make available versions of Windows with and without Media Player installed. This came with a strict warning that Microsoft must refrain from using any technological, commercial or contractual means which would have the equivalent effect of tying Media Player to Windows. The unbundled version of Media Player had to be of the same quality as the bundled version. As it happened, few copies of the version without Media Player were sold (Ahlborn and Evans, 2009). This is perhaps not surprising since both versions were offered at the same price. When presented with the two options, consumers would be most likely to choose the version with Media Player already installed. The bundled version remained an attractive default option. A more effective remedy might have been to include a CD containing a random selection of media players for consumers to choose from. By forcing consumers to make a conscious choice in this way, and by not including a default option, consumers might have been better placed to select a media player most suited to their needs.

In a subsequent case in 2009 the Commission investigated the bundling of the Microsoft **8.80** Internet Explorer web browser with Windows (akin to the US investigation into Microsoft a decade earlier, when the Netscape browser was the victim of such bundling).[68] The remedy in this case was more in line with behavioural economics insights. Users of Windows-based PCs with Internet Explorer as their default web browser, and who received Windows Update (which updates their operating system), would be taken to what was referred to as the choice or ballot screen. This screen would give users an opportunity to choose whether to install a competing web browser and, if so, which one. It would display, at random, the main browsers that users could click on, including Internet Explorer. The Commission reasoned as follows:

> Displaying five web browsers in a prominent manner, and seven more when the user scrolls sideways, strikes an appropriate balance between the need to have a workable choice screen

---

[66] Ibid, at [845].

[67] Ibid, at [870].

[68] *Microsoft (Tying)* (Case COMP/39.530), Decision of 16 December 2009; and *United States v Microsoft Corp.*, 97 F.Supp. 2d59 (D.D.C. 2000).

that users are likely to make use of and making the choice screen as accessible as possible to web browser vendors. If the choice screen presented too many web browsers, users could be overwhelmed and as a consequence would be more likely not to exercise a choice at all, but rather to dismiss the entire choice screen.[69]

8.81   The design of the choice screen was carefully considered as part of this remedy. It had to avoid any framing biases in favour of Internet Explorer or another browser—the screen was made to look different from the Explorer environment, and the initial proposal to list the various browsers alphabetically was changed to listing them randomly. The process also had to be as simple as possible for users—only one or a few clicks were required, and the new icon would be automatically pinned to the task bar, replacing the Internet Explorer icon.

8.82   This remedy in effect eliminated the default option of having Internet Explorer, instead forcing users to make an active choice of their preferred browser. The forced-choice approach seemed more effective in cutting the tie between Windows and Internet Explorer than the unbundling remedy in the Media Player case. It should be noted that in 2013 the European Commission imposed a €561 million fine on Microsoft for not implementing the browser remedy correctly (reportedly there had been a technical error in some versions of Windows which meant that customers did not see the choice screen and thus were deprived of the choice of browser).[70] This illustrates the need for ongoing supervision when behavioural remedies are applied.

8.6.4 The *Google* remedies

8.83   As internet usage grew worldwide in the early 1990s, so did the prominence of search engines: Excite, Infoseek, AltaVista, Yahoo!, Lycos, and others. Google entered the fray only in 1998, but it did so with a new and highly innovative search technology. Existing search engines mainly ranked results by how many times the search terms appeared on a page, but had begun to struggle with helping users navigate through huge amounts of web content, a lot of it spam. Google's method revolved around links between pages as a primary metric for page relevance, and significantly improved search functionality. By 2000, Google was the largest search engine in the world, and still is today. It made it into the top five global companies by market capitalization, and 'to google' has become a widely used verb. This is a case study of successful innovation in a competitive market resulting in significant benefits to consumers and huge financial rewards and high market shares for the innovator.

8.84   With high market shares have come competition concerns, especially as Google has moved into other online activities on the back of its powerful position as a search engine—including online shopping, advertising, news, travel services, and mapping. Among a range of competition law actions against Google (and actions under other areas of law, including copyright, patents, and privacy), the European Commission opened an investigation in 2010 into abuse of dominance by Google in the online search market.[71] This followed complaints by a number of competitors in search, including Foundem, ejustice.fr, and Microsoft, who were

---

[69] *Microsoft (Tying)* (Case COMP/39.530), Decision of 16 December 2009, at [81].
[70] *Microsoft (Tying)* (Case COMP/39.530), Decision of 6 March 2013.
[71] European Commission (2010), 'Antitrust: Commission probes allegations of antitrust violations by Google', press release, 30 November; and European Commission (2015), 'Antitrust: Commission sends statement of objections to Google on comparison shopping service; opens separate formal investigation on Android', press release, 15 April 2015.

subsequently joined by several others. One of the Commission's concerns was that Google's general search services, which in Europe had a market share above 90 per cent, systematically favoured the company's own specialized or vertical search services, now called Google Shopping. In search results for particular products and services Google was said to display its own services more prominently, at the expense of other specialized search providers. In line with the findings of behavioural economics, salience in search results can have a decisive influence over consumers' choices, even if alternative options can be found lower down the list. Consumers persistently tend to select the more prominently listed options, and do not tend to make much effort looking further. In competition law terms, the Commission considered that Google used its dominant position in the market for general search to the detriment of competitors, innovation, and consumers in the market for comparison shopping (specialized or vertical search).

At one stage of the investigation, in 2014, the Commission came close to agreeing a remedy **8.85** whereby Google would present search results such that competing offerings would appear as prominently as Google's own.[72] In behavioural economics terms this remedy would seem to go a long way towards mitigating concerns about biases from the way search results are framed. It would be made clear on the screen which are the Google Shopping results and which are the alternatives the user could click on. Both sets would be presented in the same manner; if the Google results had photos or a picture then the alternatives would as well. In presenting the remedies, the Commission gave illustrations of a search for gas grills and one for cafés in Paris. The first of these is shown in Figure 8.1. The picture at the top shows the search results without the remedy. The most prominent listings are for five vendors of gas grills who have paid Google for the advertising. The picture at the bottom shows what would happen with the remedy. The first search results shown are now three options from Google Shopping (by vendors who paid Google directly), and right next to it, and equally salient, three options from rival vertical search providers (Supaprice, Kelkoo, and Shopzilla). The results page for cafés in Paris after the remedy (not shown here) similarly had a prominent listing of three alternative search providers that could be used to find such cafés (pagesjaunes.fr, viamichelin.fr and Yelp).

The Commission at that stage of the investigation rejected calls for a more heavy-handed **8.86** remedy preventing Google from displaying its own specialized search results:

> The objective of the Commission is not to interfere in Google's search algorithm. It is to ensure that Google's rivals can compete fairly with Google's own services. Google should not be prevented from trying to provide users with what they're looking for. What Google should do is also give rivals a prominent space on Google's search results, in a visual format which will attract users.[73]

One of the sticking points in discussing the remedy displaying alternatives was how to **8.87** determine which three competitors would appear in the prominent alternative slots. The suggestion was to auction these slots, which was meant to strike a fair balance by giving competitors access to a valuable position in the search results, but not without payment. In the end, the remedy was not accepted, and the investigation is ongoing at the time of writing.

---

[72] European Commission (2014), 'Statement on the Google Investigation', press conference, 5 February.
[73] European Commission (2014), 'Statement on the Google investigation', press conference, 5 February.

Figure 8.1 Before and after: Proposed (but rejected) remedies for Google

Source: European Commission (2014), 'Statement on the Google investigation', press conference, 5 February.

8.7 Setting Fines

8.7.1 Headlines and main principles

Hefty fines imposed by competition authorities now regularly grab the headlines. This has **8.88** raised awareness of competition law among business communities and even the general public. In the ten years from 2005 to 2014 the European Commission imposed cartel fines totaling €18 billion (in the decade of the 1990s total cartel fines were only €615 million).[74] The Commission fined Microsoft €899 million in 2008 and €561 million in 2013, in both instances for failing to comply with abuse of dominance remedies (the first of these fines was reduced to €860 million by the General Court in 2012).[75] Intel was fined €1.1 billion in 2009 for abuse of dominance, a decision upheld by the General Court in 2014.[76] The Bundeskartellamt in Germany imposed a record total of more than €1 billion in fines in 2014, large parts of which were imposed on the members of the sausages and sugar cartels.[77] The French competition authority has also been active on this front—on a single day in 2014 it imposed its highest-ever fines of €950 million on cartels in personal care and cleaning products (involving L'Oréal, Procter & Gamble, Sara Lee, Reckitt Benckiser, and Unilever among other companies).[78]

These high fines raise a number of questions: how do competition authorities determine the **8.89** level of a fine? Is there any economic basis for the fine? Can companies afford these fines? We address these questions in this section. Many competition authorities have published guidelines on how they set fines, such as the European Commission's 2006 Fining Guidelines.[79] Fines function as a punishment, but more importantly they are also aimed at deterring infringements. Indeed, the main objective stated in the Fining Guidelines is to ensure that the fine has the necessary deterrent effect. We start here by exploring the economic principles of fines and their effect on deterrence.

Why do you park your car neatly between the white lines of a parking bay and put enough **8.90** money in the parking meter? Economists have two answers to this. The first is: it's because you know that otherwise you'll get a fine. You respond to financial incentives. The second answer is more akin to the principles of behavioural economics: you may have an intrinsic motivation to be law-abiding, so you would pay the car park charge even if the chances of a fine were low. Economists have joined scholars of law and psychology in studying the mindset of those tempted to break the law. The traditional economic framework in essence sees

---

[74] See the European Commission document 'Cartel Statistics', which is regularly updated, at: <http://ec.europa.eu/competition/cartels/statistics/statistics.pdf>.

[75] *Microsoft* (Case COMP/C-3/37.792), Decision of 27 February 2008; Case T-167/08 *Microsoft Corp. v Commission*, Judgment of 27 June 2012; and *Microsoft (Tying)* (Case COMP/39.530), Decision of 6 March 2013.

[76] *Intel* (Case COMP/C-3/37.990), Decision of 13 May 2009; and Case T-286/09 *Intel Corp v Commission*, Judgment of 12 June 2014.

[77] See under 'Kartellverbot' on <www.bundeskartellamt.de>.

[78] Autorité de la concurrence (2014), 'Home and personal care products sold in supermarkets—The Autorité de la concurrence fines concerted practices between manufacturers a total of 345,2 € millions and €605,9 € millions on each market concerned', press release, 18 December. Note that not all competition authorities have jumped on the high-fines bandwagon. The ACM in the Netherlands prefers to resolve matters by holding a dialogue with the companies under investigation first, and persuading or nudging them to change their ways. See, for example, Vane (2015).

[79] European Commission (2006), 'Guidelines on the Method of Setting Fines Pursuant to Article 23(2)(a) of Regulation No 1/2003' [2006] OJ C210/02.

would-be offenders making a rational trade-off between the rewards of the illegal activity and the risk of being caught.[80] Behavioural economics has introduced some further subtleties to this framework.

8.91 Two conditions must hold in this framework in order to achieve deterrence: the likelihood of being caught must be sufficiently high (in some places the chance of getting a parking ticket is rather higher than in others); and the fine must be sufficiently high. Economic theory identifies two possible reference points to determine the level of fine: the harm to society caused by the crime, and the illicit gains made by the perpetrator. On the first basis, if the cost to society of a particular crime is €1,000, and the offender is caught with 100 per cent certainty, the fine should be set at €1,000. The harm to society can then be repaired (provided that the authorities redistribute the collected fines to those who have suffered—this does not always happen). In reality, very few crimes are punished with 100 per cent certainty. If the probability of detection and enforcement is only, say, 20 per cent, a fine of €1,000 is too low—only €200 is recovered on average for every crime costing €1,000. Instead, a more appropriate fine would be €5,000—one in five criminals is caught, and a total of €5,000 is collected in fines, covering the cost to society of the five crimes. This very simple framework can be expanded with additional features—for example, the cost of enforcement. Having a police force (or a competition authority) and a court comes at a cost, and this cost must be weighed against the benefits of fighting crime. As a result, the socially optimal degree of law enforcement is usually not to catch 100 per cent of criminals but some smaller proportion. It can be optimal to let some criminals get away with it. In this framework there is to some extent a trade-off between the probability of detection on the one hand, and the level of fine on the other. In theory, the same result can be achieved either through very active enforcement (leading to a high proportion of criminals being caught) and low fines, or through more limited enforcement and higher fines. The disadvantage of the former approach is that enforcement costs are high. The disadvantage of the latter is that the fines may be disproportionate for those few criminals who do get caught (in the above example, a justice system may frown upon a criminal having to pay a fine of €5,000 for a crime that cost society only €1,000).

8.7.2 Fines and deterrence

8.92 A number of additional economic principles must be considered when applying the above framework for setting fines aimed at deterrence. One problem with setting fines with reference to the cost of the crime to society is that this may not have a deterrent effect if the fine is lower than the benefit obtained by the criminal. If you are in a real hurry to get to a client meeting on time, and the fine for speeding is €30, you may well consider that a risk worth taking. However, if the fine is €300, your rational calculation may lead you to behave differently. Whether you decide to break the law to get to your meeting on time will depend on many factors—such as how much the client is worth to you, or your hourly charge-out rate—but the point is that the fine effectively becomes like a price.

8.93 A much-discussed example of where deterrence does not work if the fine becomes a price is that of a number of private day-care centres in Haifa, Israel.[81] In order to address the problem of late pick-ups by parents, the centres began to charge parents a penalty of 10 shekels per child every time they arrived more than ten minutes late for pick-up

---

[80] Leading works include Becker (1968), Landes (1983), and Polinsky and Shavell (2000).
[81] Levitt and Dubner (2005), Ch 1. The original study was Gneezy and Rustichini (2000).

(adding to their monthly bill of 1,400 shekels). The result was the opposite of what was intended: instead of having a deterrent effect, the new fining system resulted in an increase in the number of late pick-ups. Why? The reason was that parents were more than willing to pay the fine in exchange for the extra time their child was in day care. The fine effectively became like any other price in the consumers' rational calculation (to put the 10 shekel fine into context, a babysitter cost around 15–20 shekels per hour). Another way of explaining the outcome—and here behavioural biases are at work—is that the parents felt less guilty about arriving late and taking advantage of the teachers' goodwill because they were now paying for it.

These examples show that deterrence can best be achieved through fines that negate the illicit benefits obtained by offenders. If the cost to society of you speeding is €15, and the chance of being caught is 50 per cent, proponents of fines based on the harm to society would say that a fine of €30 results in the socially optimal level of crime. The fact that at this level of fine there are some well-off motorists who can afford to 'pay off' the authorities for the right to speed is simply part of the optimum in this framework. However, you can also see that deterrence is not achieved, as the propensity to break the law will be income-related. Some commentators therefore do not regard this as the optimal situation in the context of competition law, and would rather set fines with reference to illicit gains so as to achieve greater deterrence (e.g. Wils, 2006). The calculation is similar to the one above. If the extra profit from entering a cartel is €1,000 and the cartel will be punished with 100 per cent certainty, a fine of €1,000 achieves effective deterrence. If the probability of punishment is only 20 per cent, a fine of €1,000 is insufficient as the would-be cartelist will take the 80 per cent chance of receiving a positive pay-off from the crime—instead, the deterrent fine is €5,000. Behavioural economics identifies two additional reasons why fines may have to be set even higher than that. One is the 'availability bias'—people tend to forget past fines after a while and hence may not be sufficiently deterred; regularly grabbing the headlines with high fines is one way competition authorities can avoid this cognitive bias. The other reason is optimism bias; criminals tend to underestimate the probability of something bad happening to them (i.e. getting caught), and hence an uplift in the fine may be required to make deterrence effective. **8.94**

A final economic principle we discuss here relates to predictability—to achieve deterrence, should authorities make the level of fines predictable for would-be offenders? According to the CFI's ruling in the plasterboard cartel case in 2008 the answer is no: **8.95**

> Moreover, it is important to ensure that fines are not easily foreseeable by economic operators. If the Commission were required to indicate in its decision the figures relating to the method of calculating the amount of fines, the deterrent effect of those fines would be undermined. If the amount of the fine were the result of a calculation which followed a simple arithmetical formula, undertakings would be able to predict the possible penalty and to compare it with the profit that they would derive from the infringement of the competition rules.[82]

Is the court's reasoning economically sound? Isn't the 'simple arithmetical formula' precisely the one we saw earlier capturing the rational calculation made by the would-be criminal, and doesn't this calculation allow authorities to determine the fine with optimal deterrence? There is no clear-cut answer. Leaving would-be infringers in the dark about the eventual **8.96**

---

[82] Case T-53/03 *BPB v Commission*, Judgment of 8 July 2008, at [336].

penalty, as the CFI proposed, can have a deterrent effect if companies wish to avoid the risk of arbitrarily high fines. However, some companies, or individuals within those companies, may well be willing to take that risk, in which case deterrence is not achieved. In most policy contexts some predictability of penalties is usually considered desirable to achieve effective and fair law enforcement.[83] In competition law there is an additional advantage of having predictable fines: companies that are already in a cartel can make a rational calculation of the benefit of applying for leniency in exchange for blowing the whistle (and hence avoid the fine), which can have the effect of more cartels being reported voluntarily.

8.7.3 The European Commission fining guidelines: Where is the economics?

8.97   The Fining Guidelines set out the steps that the Commission follows in its calculations. They explain how the basic amount of a fine is arrived at, and how adjustments are made for factors such as whether the company has engaged in anti-competitive behaviour before (fine adjusted upwards if this is the case) or whether it was co-operative during the investigation (fine adjusted downwards, or even cancelled in the case of leniency). The Fining Guidelines are to some extent based on the economic principles discussed earlier. The basic amount is set with reference to the value of the company's sales in the relevant market and the duration of the infringement, two factors that are seen as 'an appropriate proxy to reflect the economic importance of the infringement'.[84] The term 'economic importance' can be interpreted as the importance either to the economy as a whole or to the perpetrators. Both are positively correlated with the value of sales in the relevant market in question—larger companies do more harm, and gain more by doing so, than smaller companies. But the Guidelines stop short of actually considering the harm to the economy or the illicit gains. Nor are the various steps in the Fining Guidelines very mechanistic; there is a high degree of judgement and discretion involved at each step.

8.98   To illustrate how the Guidelines work in practice, consider the example of the chloroprene rubber cartel decision of 2007 against Bayer, DuPont/Dow, ENI, and a number of other companies.[85] The starting point for the basic amount of the fine is the value of sales in the relevant market or markets. The cartel covered chloroprene rubber sales worldwide, but for the fine the relevant turnover was limited to the EEA (no detailed market definition was required here; in other cases economists play a role in delineating the relevant market and calculating the relevant sales that form the basis for the fine). For example, ENI's relevant turnover in the last full year of the infringement was €26 million. To this the Commission then applied a 'gravity factor'. This can be up to 30 per cent of the sales. There has been some debate about whether the Commission must analyse the actual effects of the cartel to determine the gravity factor,[86] but this does not normally seem to be a requirement. In the chloroprene rubber case the Commission noted that the infringement concerned a worldwide hardcore cartel, its members having a 100 per cent market share. It set the gravity

---

[83] For example, a review of regulatory penalties for the UK government recommended that regulators should be transparent in the methodology for determining or calculating administrative financial penalties. See Macrory (2006).

[84] European Commission (2006), 'Guidelines on the Method of Setting Fines Pursuant to Article 23(2)(a) of Regulation No 1/2003' [2003] OJ C210/02, at [6].

[85] *Chloroprene Rubber* (Case COMP 38.629), Decision of 5 December 2007.

[86] See, for example, the ECJ ruling on the copper tubes cartel: Case C-272/09 P, *KME v Commission*, Judgment of 8 December 2011.

factor at 21 per cent, resulting in an amount of €5.46 million (21 per cent of €26 million), and multiplied this by the duration of the cartel of nine years, so nine times €5.46 million equals €49.1 million. The Commission next added an 'entrance fee' of 20 per cent. The stated aim of this fee is to deter companies from entering into price-fixing agreements (it seems somewhat odd, if not to say arbitrary, to include such an additional deterrence factor at this stage of the calculation). This gave the basic amount for ENI of €59 million (€49.1 million plus 20 per cent).

The next step in the Fining Guidelines is to adjust the basic amount for aggravating and mitigating circumstances. In the chloroprene rubber case there was none of the latter (the Commission rejected arguments that ENI subsidiaries did not fully implement the agreements, ceased to take part in the agreements at an earlier stage, or participated only passively). The aggravating circumstance for ENI and Bayer was recidivism. Both companies had been fined for cartel behaviour before. It did not matter to the Commission that this was for different subsidiaries and different cartel products (polypropylene and citric acid, respectively), nor that many years had passed since the last cartel. ENI's fine was increased by 60 per cent to €94.4 million (Bayer's punishment for recidivism was a 50 per cent uplift of the fine). Next, for good measure, the Commission imposed a further specific increase of 40 per cent for (again) deterrence, arguing that this was appropriate for ENI, whose overall turnover was much larger than that for chloroprene rubber alone (the other members got either no or a smaller uplift for this). The result was a total of €132.16 million (€94.4 million plus 40 per cent). The final steps were to consider this amount in light of the maximum fine of 10 per cent of total turnover (not exceeded in the case of ENI), any leniency reduction (not applicable for ENI; Bayer got a 100 per cent reduction for being the first to blow the whistle, Tosoh got 50 per cent, and DuPont/Dow 25 per cent), and a possible inability to pay the fine (not applicable for any of the cartel members in this case). Hence the Commission fined ENI €132.16 million. In 2015 the ECJ confirmed an earlier ruling by the General Court which cut the recidivism uplift for ENI from 60 per cent to 50 per cent and the specific deterrence uplift from 40 per cent to 20 per cent, thus reducing ENI's fine to €106.2 million.[87]

8.99

You can see from this example that fines have some economic grounding, in that the basic amount relates to the relevant turnover made by the infringer (and economists can play a role defining the relevant market and calculating the relevant turnover). Most of the steps set out in the Fining Guidelines have some logic to them. Yet the actual setting of the fine is not a very scientific process, and it is not always clear how specific numbers are picked at each stage, either by the Commission or, subsequently, by the courts.

8.100

8.7.4 Inability to pay fines

An infringer's ability or inability to pay can be relevant in determining the fine. In countries such as Finland and Switzerland, speeding tickets are set with reference not only to the speed recorded but also to the income of the offender (headline-grabbing fines of several hundreds of thousands of euros have been imposed under these rules—some people are hard to deter). In competition law, the inability to pay has become a topical issue given the

8.101

---

[87] Joined Cases C-93/13 P and C-123/13 P, *Commission and others v Versalis and others*, Judgment of 5 March 2015.

high fines imposed by some authorities. EU case law has actually established that the financial situation of infringers should *not* in principle influence the level of the fine. In its 2002 judgment on the district heating pipes cartel, the CFI stated as follows:

> As regards the applicant's ability to pay the fine, it is sufficient to observe that, according to a consistent line of decisions, the Commission is not required, when determining the amount of the fine, to take into account the poor financial situation of an undertaking concerned, since recognition of such an obligation would be tantamount to giving an unjustified competitive advantage to undertakings least well adapted to the market conditions.[88]

8.102   Yet it has also been recognized that there are specific situations in which the inability to pay a fine is a relevant factor to consider. Causing companies to go bankrupt by imposing fines they cannot afford may harm competition. The Fining Guidelines state as follows:

> In exceptional cases, the Commission may, upon request, take account of the undertaking's ability to pay in a specific social and economic context. It will not base any reduction granted for this reason in the fine on the mere finding of an adverse or loss-making financial situation. A reduction could be granted solely on the basis of objective evidence that imposition of the fine as provided for in these Guidelines would irretrievably jeopardise the economic viability of the undertaking concerned and cause its assets to lose all their value.[89]

8.103   These are stringent conditions. The company must go beyond showing that it is loss-making. It must demonstrate a strong possibility of financial failure as a direct result of the fine. There is currently relatively little guidance or case law on how these conditions should be interpreted.[90] How can financial economics be used to meet the Commission's requirement of 'objective evidence'?

8.104   The most direct route to demonstrating an inability to pay is to show that the fine will leave the company insolvent (solvency refers to a company having enough assets to cover its liabilities). In general, the most serious problems in paying will emerge if the fine is greater than the market value of shareholders' equity. Since a company's liabilities must equal its assets, not only would shareholder equity be wiped out, but the company would not have enough assets to pay all its debts, leading to balance sheet insolvency. For companies listed on a stock exchange, the insolvency condition could be reflected in the fine being greater than market capitalization, which in general reflects the NPV of the future payments to shareholders. Solvency constraints may mean that companies with highly leveraged capital structures (i.e. a lot of debt relative to equity) may have less capacity to pay fines than companies with lower leverage.

8.105   The Fining Guidelines emphasize issues of solvency. However, liquidity is also relevant as it may threaten the survival of a company in difficulty (liquidity refers to the extent to which a company has the cash, or assets that can be quickly converted into cash, to meet its short-term obligations). There are a number of ways in which liquidity crunches can threaten survival. Companies often require a certain amount of working capital in order to operate

---

[88]   Case T-23/99 *LR af 1998 A/S v Commission*, Judgment of 20 March 2002.

[89]   European Commission (2006), 'Guidelines on the Method of Setting Fines Pursuant to Article 23(2)(a) of Regulation No 1/2003' [2006] OJ C210/02, at [35].

[90]   There is some high-level guidance in European Commission (2010), 'Inability to pay under paragraph 35 of the Fining Guidelines and payment conditions pre- and post-decision finding an infringement and imposing fines; Information note by Mr Joaquín Almunia, Vice-President of the Commission, and by Mr Janusz Lewandowski, Member of the Commission', 12 June.

effectively, and liquidity will be required to cover these needs. Similarly, many sectors have cyclical demand, and companies need to maintain a buffer of available cash or credit lines in order to be able to meet costs during downturns. In a solvent company, all of these points are essentially about timing. In theory, if a company is solvent but has insufficient liquidity to meet both a fine and its other obligations, financial markets should be willing to provide funding to the company so that it can meet its expenditure needs. However, in practice, companies may face capital rationing, which means that they cannot finance existing or new assets. It is this capital rationing that can make even solvent companies unable to raise funds (something you can expect to happen more frequently in a financial crisis). There are therefore a number of reasons why, even if sufficient funds can be raised by a company to pay a fine, the result may be a liquidity crunch which imperils its survival.

Demonstrating liquidity constraints is more complex than assessing solvency. Determining **8.106** the maximum fine that the company would be able to pay in the short run (defined here as the period over which the company cannot access financial markets) involves comparing, on one hand, the amount of cash and credit lines it has with, on the other hand, the combined total of expected short-term losses, requirements for short-term debt repayment and taxes, and working capital requirements. This would then represent the maximum fine that could be paid without the company having to access the financial markets.

The Commission has taken into account, and sometimes accepted, arguments regarding **8.107** inability to pay in a number of cases in recent years. Its published decisions provide little detail on the analysis performed (possibly for confidentiality reasons). In the bathroom fittings cartel decision of 2010—involving seventeen different companies, including the likes of Hansgrohe, Ideal Standard, and Villeroy & Boch—the Commission assessed the ability to pay as follows.

> In assessing the undertakings' financial situation, the Commission examined the companies' recent and current financial statements as well as their projections for subsequent years. The Commission considered a number of financial ratios measuring the companies' solidity, profitability, solvency and liquidity as well as its equity and cash flow situation. In addition, the Commission took into account relations with outside financial partners such as banks and relations with shareholders. The analysis also took into account restructuring plans.
>
> The Commission assessed the specific social and economic context for each undertaking whose financial situation was found to be sufficiently critical. In this context, the impact of the global economic and financial crisis on the bathroom fitting sector was taken into account. The Commission also concluded for the five undertakings concerned that the fine would cause their assets to lose significant value.
>
> As a result of the Commission's analysis, the fines of three companies were reduced by 50% and those of another two by 25% given their difficult financial situation.[91]

There will continue to be much debate about the level of fines under competition law and **8.108** the capacity of companies to pay them. Existing economic and financial criteria can be applied to produce the required 'objective evidence' of a company's inability to pay. More case law and explanation of the Commission's assessments would also be useful in providing clarity.

---

[91] *Bathroom fittings and fixtures* (Case COMP/39.092), Decision of 23 June 2010, at [18–20] of summary of decision.

8.8 Measuring the Costs and Benefits of Remedies, and of Competition Law

8.8.1 Why measure costs and benefits?

8.109 We have mentioned a number of times that any remedy that is being considered requires a careful CBA. Economics has a role to play in this kind of analysis. In the last ten years, competition authorities around the world have been placing great emphasis on measuring the effects of competition law enforcement, including remedies. Carrying out a CBA is generally good policy practice, and is increasingly required from policy-makers and regulatory authorities around the world. For example, the European Commission has issued Impact Assessment Guidelines to ensure that Commission initiatives and EU legislation are prepared on the basis of transparent, comprehensive, and balanced evidence.[92] In competition law, CBA can be applied to specific interventions and remedies, or to the competition regime itself. A thorough ex ante CBA enables better policy decisions (e.g. more effective remedy design). Ex post CBA allows for the evaluation of past remedies and lessons to be learned for future actions.

8.110 There is an additional reason why measuring costs and benefits is important for competition policy. We have seen a spectacular proliferation of competition law globally. Awareness of competition policy has probably never been so widespread among businesses and the public at large. Proponents of competition policy would consider this growing awareness to be a positive development. It makes life easier for competition authorities, and probably means that more businesses refrain from engaging in illegal anti-competitive behaviour in the first place (the deterrence effect). However, this proliferation, in combination with high fines and an increasingly proactive stance taken by competition authorities, is bound to lead to someone asking at some point: what is it all good for? Competition policy needs a robust answer when it is held to account in this way. In recent years competition authorities have, quite successfully, played the 'consumer welfare' card in justifying their actions. It is a popular message to the public that competition law is there to protect consumers against anti-competitive practices by companies. However, this consumer welfare justification has some downsides as well, and should be used with care. For one, it can create false expectations and hence place competition authorities under pressure to intervene whenever a company is seen to be 'ripping off' its customers. Competition policy requires more than the consumer welfare argument to sustain political legitimacy. This is where the measurement of the effects of competition law enforcement comes in.

8.8.2 A remedy in dispute: CBA in the grocery inquiry

8.111 An example of where competition law expressly requires a form of CBA of remedies by the authority is the market investigation regime in the United Kingdom. In its 2008 investigation into grocery retailing, the CC found the market to be too concentrated and hindered by unnecessary barriers to entry.[93] As part of a package of remedies it recommended that a

---

[92] European Commission (2009), 'Impact Assessment Guidelines', SEC(2009) 92, 15 January. See also European Commission (2014), 'Guide to Cost-benefit Analysis of Investment Projects', December.
[93] Competition Commission (2008), 'The Supply of Groceries in the UK—Market Investigation', 30 April. We advised one of the retailers in this investigation.

'competition test' be applied to retail planning applications to local government authorities for large grocery stores. The CC thus envisaged a change to local authority regulations that had previously been more or less indifferent as to who developed a particular piece of land. The competition test implied that planning permission would be granted if, in addition to satisfying the normal planning restrictions, the retailer was a new entrant in the local area; or the total number of fascias (i.e. grocery retailer brands) in the area was four or more; or there were three or fewer fascias but the retailer would have less than 60 per cent of sales within the local area. Under this test, it would be difficult for a retailer with more than a 60 per cent local market share to expand an existing store or to build a new one, as it would not obtain planning permission.

However, on appeal the CAT found that there was insufficient evidence that the costs of applying the competition test would be justified: **8.112**

> [T]here is a significant gap in the Commission's analysis in relation to the 'costs' of the competition test. The Report does not fully and properly assess and take account of the risk that the application of the test might have adverse effects for consumers as a result of their being denied the benefit of developments which would enhance their welfare, including by leaving demand 'unmet'.[94]

The CAT also criticized the CC's assessment of the likely benefits of such a test: **8.113**

> [T]he Commission seems simply to have based its proportionality assessment on an assumption that the whole of the estimated customer detriment would be remedied by the test, in combination with the other remedies... There is in the Report no recognition or weighing of the non-acknowledged possibility that the existing AEC [adverse effects on competition] might not be satisfactorily remedied or mitigated for many years.[95]

The CAT's ruling implies that advancing a remedy such as the competition test and establishing its effectiveness and proportionality requires a comprehensive CBA. Following the appeal, the CC duly undertook further analysis on the likely effects of the competition test. In a subsequent decision in 2009, it concluded that the test would deliver positive value to consumers on the basis that any reduction in consumer welfare in the short run would be offset by the longer-term benefit of increased competition.[96] However, the CC also introduced a *de minimis* provision such that the test would be passed in cases where store extensions were small (less than 300 square metres), provided that the store had not been extended in the previous five years. The CC concluded that this new provision would not have a material impact on the effectiveness of the remedy, but would be a more proportionate response to the competition problems it had identified. This case illustrates the importance of undertaking the CBA as an integral part of the competition analysis, not as an afterthought. **8.114**

8.8.3 What to measure: Identifying the counterfactual

CBA can be undertaken at distinct levels, depending on the policy question at hand. An important initial step is to identify the objective of the CBA and to be clear about the counterfactual against which costs and benefits must be measured. CBAs can be applied to **8.115**

---

[94] [2009] CAT 6, Case 1104/6/8/08 *Tesco PLC v Competition Commission*, 4 March 2009, at [111].
[95] Ibid., at [162].
[96] Competition Commission (2009), 'Groceries Market Investigation: Remittal of the Competition Test by the Competition Appeal Tribunal: Decision', 2 October.

remedies in individual competition cases, or to the competition regime more broadly. One distinction is between the costs and benefits of *competition legislation* and those of the *competition authority*. Both are relevant but distinct policy questions. To take the example of the Netherlands, a CBA could be undertaken for the Competition Law 1998. The relevant counterfactual for this analysis would be a situation in which the Competition Law was not enacted and the NMa (or its successor, the ACM) had not been created. This would basically be the situation pre-1998 when the Economic Competition Law 1956 was in place, enforced by the Ministry of Economic Affairs—a regime that was generally considered inactive (the Netherlands used to be regarded as a 'cartel paradise'). In this counterfactual some reliance might be placed on interventions by the European Commission under the EU competition rules, which would come into play in the counterfactual without the 1998 law (in other words, the CBA of a national competition authority should consider only those cases that the European Commission would not cover, or cover less well). A separate CBA can be conducted for the competition authority itself. The counterfactual is one with a competition law in place but without a competition authority enforcing it.[97] Thus, the costs and benefits of, say, the ACM would be assessed against a situation in which the Competition Law 1998 was not enforced by the authority but rather through private litigation. A relevant question to ask in such an analysis would be: which types of anti-competitive conduct can effectively be addressed through private actions? Many business-to-business disputes involving restrictive agreements or abuse of dominance probably can. The costs and benefits of these should then not be ascribed to the competition authority.

8.116 A further distinction—of most relevance for this chapter—can be made between the costs and benefits of the *competition authority* and the costs and benefits of specific *decisions and remedies*. For the former, the absence of the authority is the counterfactual. For the latter, the authority is assumed to be in place, and the incremental analysis refers to the costs and benefits that are attributable to the enforcement action or remedy in question. The analysis can be applied either to individual decisions or to a cumulative set of decisions (e.g. all merger decisions, or all abuse of dominance decisions).

8.8.4 How to measure: Categories of costs and benefits

8.117 The next question that arises is what costs and benefits should be included in the analysis, and how they should be weighed. At a superficial level you could do a very simple calculation: the substantial fines imposed by competition authorities in recent years are orders of magnitude higher than their annual budgets. Take the European Commission's figures for 2013: it imposed fines of €1.7 billion on banks for fixing Euro and Yen interest rate derivatives, and €561 million on Microsoft.[98] These fines alone far outweigh DG Competition's operating expenditure for 2013, which was just short of €400 million.[99] In one sense, therefore, it might be claimed that through its cartel and Microsoft actions

---

[97] The reverse situation—a competition authority without a competition law—seems less plausible. Yet this was the situation in Jersey for some time. The Jersey Competition Regulatory Authority (JCRA) was set up in 2001, but the Competition (Jersey) Law did not come into force until 2005 (in the intervening period the JCRA did have certain regulatory responsibilities in the telecoms sector).

[98] European Commission (2013), 'Antitrust: Commission fines banks €1.71 billion for participating in cartels in the interest rate derivatives industry', press release, 4 December 2013; and *Microsoft* (*Tying*) (Case COMP/39.530), Decision of 6 March 2013.

[99] Figure from 'DG Competition Annual Activity Report 2013', Annex 3, available at <ec.europa.eu/atwork/synthesis/aar/index_en.htm>.

alone DG Competition already provided substantially greater benefits to EU taxpayers than it has cost them.[100] However, this comparison is not quite right: an important guiding principle for CBA is that it should be performed from a total economic welfare perspective. This means that costs and benefits to all the various participants in the economy—consumers, producers, government, taxpayers—should be included in the calculations. Money transfers between different participants—such as a fine paid by a company to the competition authority (or state treasurer)—are not a net benefit to the economy. As noted in Chapter 1, economists generally have little to say about distributive effects from transfers. However, if considered appropriate from a policy perspective, different weights can be given to different groups—for example, consumer welfare may be given greater weight than producer welfare, or poor consumers may be given greater weight than rich consumers.

Table 8.2 provides an overview of the main categories of costs and benefits in CBA. These **8.118** same categories are of relevance to any policy question—that is, whether the CBA refers to competition legislation, the competition authority, or specific enforcement actions and remedies. The main difference will lie in the counterfactual against which the categories of

Table 8.2 Main categories of costs and benefits to be assessed in the CBA

Costs	Benefits
Direct (administrative) costs of the authority	
Direct costs of companies	
– Competition law compliance costs	
– Costs of specific competition proceedings	
Economic costs to the market in question (negative market impacts)	**Economic benefits to the market in question (positive market impacts)**
– Allocative inefficiency	– Allocative efficiency
– Productive inefficiency	– Productive efficiency
– Distortion of incentives (reduced dynamic competition/innovation)	– Enhanced dynamic competition/innovation
	– Increased product/service quality
– Reduced product/service quality	– Enhanced market functioning
– Restriction on market functioning	
Indirect regulatory costs	**Indirect regulatory benefits**
– Legal uncertainty	– Legal certainty
– Likelihood of regulatory capture	– Deterrent effects
	– Improved quality of competition regime
Social costs (if relevant)	**Social benefits (if relevant)**
– Distributive costs	– Distributive benefits
– Reduced security/quality of supply	– Enhanced security/quality of supply
– Negative effect on vulnerable customers	– Positive effect on vulnerable customers

Source: Based on Oxera (2004).

---

[100] Assuming that the proceeds from the fines do indeed ultimately flow to taxpayers. We don't know how realistic this assumption is.

costs and benefits are measured. For example, to assess the costs and benefits of the competition authority, the category of 'direct costs of the authority' needs to cover its entire budget. To assess a specific remedy imposed by that authority, the category covers only the costs incurred by the authority in relation to that decision (note that the table does not include income from fines as a direct benefit of the authority, for the reason set out above). The economic benefits of competition and (where this is the appropriate counterfactual) competition law enforcement can be measured in terms of productive and allocative efficiency, enhanced dynamic competition, enhanced market functioning, and wider effects on other sectors in the economy. As to the category of economic costs (negative market impacts), we note that while the objective of competition policy is to improve market functioning, actions by competition authorities can have (unintended) adverse consequences for the market as well. One indirect benefit that competition law may generate is making interventions consistent and providing clear guidance, such that regulatory certainty among businesses is enhanced.

8.8.5 When to stop measuring: Precision and priorities

8.119　The economics literature has developed a range of quantitative techniques that can be applied in CBA.[101] Quantitative analysis should be undertaken where feasible in order to obtain robust results, but this analysis should establish rough orders of magnitude of the various costs and benefits rather than seek (often spurious) precision in the calculation.[102] The optimal degree of quantification of the costs and benefits will depend on the circumstances. Not all costs and benefits can be readily quantified, either because of a lack of data or because the effects depend on various indirect economic interactions which are difficult to measure. Nevertheless, in practice, the assessment of rough orders of magnitude may be sufficient to gain insight into the costs and benefits of the policy decision or remedy in question.

8.120　In a CBA, you can often conclude that the consumer welfare benefits of intervening in price-fixing cartel cases—focusing on the total cartel overcharge paid by consumers—will be so great that they exceed the direct costs incurred by the competition authority by various orders of magnitude. Baker (2003) shows that rough estimates of the direct benefits of cartel actions in the United States far outweigh the estimates of the total costs of US antitrust enforcement (see Chapter 9 for a discussion of the overcharge levels that have been observed in past cartels). The additional indirect benefits of the interventions—in particular the enhancement of dynamic competition and the deterrent effects on other cartels—can be described in qualitative terms, because they work in the same direction and thus would reinforce the conclusion. One tentative policy conclusion that follows is that there is merit in giving priority to cartel enforcement in larger markets, as there the welfare benefits will be greatest. However, a qualification to this conclusion is that intervention against cartels in smaller markets can still fulfil an important signalling function. A handful of such actions in smaller markets may achieve a deterrent effect. Another reasonable conclusion is that if the objective of measuring costs and benefits is to show that competition policy benefits the economy as a whole, the case can be made based just on rough approximations of the benefits of the actions against cartels.

---

[101] See Sugden and Williams (1978) and Boardman et al. (2010).
[102] Manski (2013) provides a sound health warning on the limitations of CBA in an uncertain world.

The above approach to assessing the benefits of cartel actions cannot be readily applied to **8.121** mergers, agreements other than cartels, or unilateral conduct. As noted throughout this book, remedial actions against these other practices are not as unambiguously beneficial as actions against cartels. The practices produce some efficiency benefits as well as anti-competitive effects, so intervention by the authorities can lead to negative market impacts. The extent to which a competition authority is able to strike the right balance between these two effects will depend on the quality of the underlying analysis in its investigations, and will also inherently involve a degree of judgement. The extent to which market forces can be trusted depends on the views of policy-makers and competition authorities, and on whether they consider it more desirable to avoid false positives or false negatives (false positives result in over-enforcement; false negatives in under-enforcement).

A specific action against a merger or business practice can therefore not automatically be **8.122** presumed beneficial to social welfare. Indeed, CBA of a merger or abuse of dominance case runs the risk of becoming circular if it starts from the premise that the intervention is beneficial. An example of such circularity can be found in an analysis by the OFT of the effects of intervention against predatory pricing (Office of Fair Trading, 2005). In this CBA, the welfare loss of predation (and hence welfare benefit of intervention) was taken as the NPV of the low prices to consumers during the predation period (treated as a consumer welfare gain) and the high prices during the subsequent 'recoupment' period (treated as a consumer welfare loss). In calculating this, the OFT effectively assumed that, first, recoupment was indeed going to be feasible, and second, predation was about to become successful at the point of OFT intervention (i.e. the predator would switch from low to high prices at that point). However, these are precisely the factors that make preda-tory pricing cases so complex.

Should a formal CBA be required for every competition law remedy? This policy question **8.123** would perhaps merit a CBA of its own. Too formal a requirement on competition authori-ties could make competition law enforcement more like certain other policy areas where the possible effects of specific interventions are sometimes argued over for a considerable length of time. The general lesson for competition law is that CBA can be a useful policy tool that helps competition authorities develop their thinking about a competition problem and how to solve it, even if not all costs and benefits are quantified with precision in every case.

9

QUANTIFICATION OF DAMAGES

9.1 Damages Claims, Economics, and the Law

9.1.1 What is special about the economics in damages claims?

9.01   You have seen in this book how economics helps to understand the effects of business practices, and how this in turn can be used in determining whether competition law has been infringed. The use of economics does not need to stop there, however. In Chapter 8 we showed the economic principles on which competition authorities may base remedies. In this chapter we deal with the economics of quantifying damages. After a competition authority has found an infringement and imposed a remedy (often a fine), parties that have been harmed by the infringement may file a claim for damages against the infringer. Such 'follow-on' damages actions are increasingly common in many jurisdictions. In principle, the same economic analysis of effects that is used to assess the existence of an infringement can be used to determine damages. The economic principles discussed in Chapters 4 to 6 are therefore of direct relevance to damages claims as well. After all, the competition investigation assesses harm to competition and consumers, and this harm is in essence what represents the damage caused by the infringement.

9.02   Yet there are some differences. First, a significant proportion of damages claims relate to cartels. These are usually prohibited per se, such that competition authorities have little need for analysing economic effects. This means that much of the economic analysis of the actual harm caused by cartels is undertaken only in the context of follow-on damages claims. Second, it is commonly accepted that effects-based analyses in exclusionary conduct cases focus on harm to the competitive process, not individual competitors. In contrast, damages claims are filed by individual competitors or customers who believe that they have suffered harm. Nobody files a claim on behalf of the competitive process (several jurisdictions allow certain forms of class action, but that is still because the members of the class have been harmed individually). You can see that there is some potential risk here of re-opening the debate on 'harm to competition versus harm to competitors'. In original actions—where a competitor brings the case directly before a court (also called stand-alone actions)—the infringement and harm must both be established, and the court must consider whether evidence of harm to the competitor also constitutes evidence of harm to competition. The distinction is clearer in follow-on damages cases—the competition authority has already found an infringement (presumably on the basis of harm to competition more widely), and now the competitor must show that it has actually suffered from that infringement. Third, damages claims normally go further in quantifying harm than the analysis undertaken at the infringement stage. This is because a court must ultimately determine an exact monetary amount for the damages award (if any), whereas a competition authority can limit itself to establishing that such harmful effects are significant without quantifying them precisely.

9.1.2 Policy principles behind damages claims

Damages actions brought before courts by harmed parties are a form of private enforce- **9.03** ment of competition law. This complements public enforcement by competition authorities. In the United States, the majority of antitrust cases are private actions. Elsewhere, most cases tend to be taken on by competition authorities, but the importance of private actions has grown. As mentioned above, there is a distinction between original private actions—where infringement and damages must both be established by the court—and follow-on damages actions that are brought before a court after an infringement decision by a competition authority.

There are various reasons why policy-makers find private actions attractive. One is that **9.04** they save taxpayers' money. Competition authorities have limited budgets, and must prioritize their enforcement actions. As economists would say, there is scope for an efficient division of labour: business-to-business disputes about contracts and exclusionary conduct seem to lend themselves to being effectively dealt with through private actions (businesses will be willing to pay for litigation if the stakes are sufficiently high). In the United States, treble damages are awarded to parties harmed by antitrust infringements, providing an extra incentive to bring private actions. Competition authorities can then deal with the rest—in particular, cases involving end-consumers, and cartel cases, where private parties are less likely to initiate a lawsuit as they lack the investigative powers of competition authorities.

Another reason to encourage private damages actions is that they contribute to the deter- **9.05** rence of anti-competitive practices. Nowadays, hefty fines, and possible prison sentences for individuals, already constitute a strong deterrent. The prospect of having to pay damages on top of the fines may further dampen the enthusiasm to form cartels. A curious economic argument in this regard is that follow-on damages actions may actually be redundant from a deterrence perspective—the same deterrent effect can be achieved by raising the fine itself up to the level at which the damage would ultimately be determined. That might save a lot of litigation costs. However, it pre-supposes (not always realistically) that public enforcement is sufficient to catch all competition law infringements, and that competition authorities have as much information at the infringement and fining stages as would become available in a private damages action.

A further policy principle behind damages actions, and one that is embedded in EU law, **9.06** is that of the right to full compensation. As stated in the 2014 Directive on antitrust damages actions:

1. Member States shall ensure that any natural or legal person who has suffered harm caused by an infringement of competition law is able to claim and to obtain full compensation for that harm.
2. Full compensation shall place a person who has suffered harm in the position in which that person would have been had the infringement of competition law not been committed. It shall therefore cover the right to compensation for actual loss and for loss of profit, plus the payment of interest.

3. Full compensation under this Directive shall not lead to overcompensation, whether by means of punitive, multiple or other types of damages.[1]

9.07 We discuss in this chapter how the compensation principle can be made to work in practice. If followed to the letter it would imply a certain degree of precision in the determination of the harm—there should be neither under-compensation nor over-compensation. It would also mean that compensation should reach the victims of an infringement regardless of where they operate in the supply chain. If the cartel's direct customers have passed on the cartel overcharge to their own respective customers, the latter should get the appropriate compensation. We show how economics can help with these legal principles.

9.1.3 Searching for the right answer, within practical and legal bounds

9.08 Any damages assessment needs to strike a balance between two objectives: first, finding the most accurate answer—the desire to determine the real damage value as closely as possible, which is how an economist would naturally seek to approach quantification problems; and second, using approaches that are clear and easy to apply and that fit within the existing legal frameworks. Calculating the exact damage arising from an infringement requires complete information about what would have happened in a parallel world where the infringement did not take place—the 'but for' or counterfactual situation. Determining the counterfactual is inherently difficult as such complete information cannot exist. Courts generally understand this. As one judgment by the English High Court put it:

> It is common ground between the parties, and obviously right, that expert economic evidence is necessary in this case, in order to be able to establish the relevant economic factual background, and then to wander off into the realms of economic fantasy which is necessary in order to arrive at answers to questions of causation and loss, so far as liability is established...
>
> [this requires] expertise in defining relevant parameters and operations of and within the health care industry, and then the application of the fruits of that exercise, and of factual material, in economic modelling to work out what would have happened had Reckitt Benckiser not done that which it may ultimately be found they should not have done.[2]

9.09 Hence, to assess the counterfactual you need to enter into the 'realms of economic fantasy' and carry out economic modelling (don't think immediately of complicated equations; modelling can be fairly straightforward sometimes). All models are necessarily simplifications of the real world. They rely on assumptions, and can vary in the degree to which they take into account all factors that may influence the counterfactual. This variation is often driven by constraints on data, time or budgets. The fact that models simplify reality does not invalidate their use as evidence in court. As one US court stated: 'The antitrust cases are legion which reiterate the proposition that, if the fact of damages is proven, the actual computation of damages may suffer from minor imperfections.'[3]

---

[1] Directive 2014/104/EU of the European Parliament and of the Council of the European Union of 26 November 2014 on certain rules governing actions for damages under national law for infringements of the competition law provisions of the Member States and of the European Union, OJ L 349/1, 5 December 2014, at [3].

[2] *Secretary of State for Health and others/Pinewood v Reckitt Benckiser*, approved judgment, 4 December 2012, 2012 EWHC 3913 (Ch). We advised one of the parties in this case.

[3] *South-East Coal Co v Consolidation Coal Co* 434 F 2d 767, 794 (6th Cir. 1970).

Another US court similarly held that: 'The vagaries of the marketplace usually deny us sure knowledge of what plaintiff's situation would have been in the absence of the defendant's antitrust violation.'[4] **9.10**

The EU Directive on antitrust damages actions states that the difficulty of quantifying harm with precision should not make it impossible to make claims: **9.11**

> Member States shall ensure that neither the burden nor the standard of proof required for the quantification of harm renders the exercise of the right to damages practically impossible or excessively difficult. Member States shall ensure that the national courts are empowered, in accordance with national procedures, to estimate the amount of harm if it is established that a claimant suffered harm but it is practically impossible or excessively difficult precisely to quantify the harm suffered on the basis of the evidence available.[5]

Several EU Member States have rules on the degree of freedom for judges when determining damages in cases where precise quantification is difficult. Such rules often reflect the principles of equity, justice, and procedural efficiency. For example, in a follow-on damages claim regarding a car insurance cartel the Italian Supreme Court confirmed that when the exact harm is difficult to prove, the Italian courts can rely on Article 1226 of the Italian Civil Code and award an equitable amount of damages (*ex aequo et bono*).[6] The Supreme Court considered the insurance case as 'a textbook example' of where the Italian courts should make use of such a power, due to the fact that it was difficult for the claimant to prove the precise value of the loss it had suffered (essentially the cartel overcharge). **9.12**

9.1.4 The remainder of this chapter

The aim of this chapter is to take you through the economic principles and methods that are of relevance to quantifying damages. Section 9.2 sets out a conceptual framework for estimating the harm from hardcore cartels. Section 9.3 does this in relation to exclusionary practices. Section 9.4 presents a classification of methods and models that can be used for quantifying damages, and contains a general discussion on what you should look for in a model. The classification is taken from a report for the European Commission by Oxera et al. (2009), which formed the basis for the Commission's 2013 'Practical guide on quantifying harm for damages'.[7] The later sections explore each of the main approaches. Section 9.5 deals with cross-sectional comparisons; section 9.6 with time-series comparisons; section 9.7 with difference-in-differences comparisons; section 9.8 with financial-analysis-based approaches; and section 9.9 with market-structure-based approaches. Section 9.10 addresses the economics of pass-on in the context of the passing-on defence in damages actions. Section 9.11 concludes with an explanation of the principles behind interest and discounting, usually the final (but relatively unexplored) step in damages calculations. **9.13**

---

[4] *J Truett Payne Co v Chrysler Motors Corp* 451 US 557, 565; 101 S Ct 1923; 68 L Ed 2d 442 (1981).

[5] Directive 2014/104/EU of the European Parliament and of the Council of the European Union of 26 November 2014 on certain rules governing actions for damages under national law for infringements of the competition law provisions of the Member States and of the European Union, OJ L 349/1, 5 December 2014, at [17].

[6] *Fondiaria SAI SpA v Nigriello* (Italian Supreme Court, 17 February 2007).

[7] European Commission (2013), 'Practical Guide on Quantifying Harm for Damages Based on Breaches of Article 101 or 102 of the Treaty on the Functioning of the European Union', Staff working document, 11 June.

9.2 Harm from Hardcore Cartels: Conceptual Framework

9.2.1 The main effects illustrated

9.14 Hardcore cartels tend to result in higher prices. This holds not only for price-fixing cartels but also for other types. We discussed this in Chapter 5. Some hardcore cartels target quantities rather than prices because they find it easier to agree on and monitor output quotas. The OPEC petroleum cartel is a notorious example. Restrictions in output normally go hand in hand with increases in price (a simple economic principle: we saw in Chapters 1 and 2 that most demand curves slope downward). Likewise, customer-allocation and bid-rigging cartels give each member a degree of monopoly power over its allocated customers or bids, which creates scope for restricting output and increasing price.

9.15 Figure 9.1—which you will recognize from the charts in Chapter 2—shows the overcharge paid on all the units actually sold (rectangle A), and the corresponding reduction in volume (triangle B). Triangle C represents consumer surplus in this market (the difference between what consumers are willing to pay for each unit bought, and what they actually pay). While this chart is similar to the ones in Chapter 2, note that the counterfactual price here is not necessarily the same as in perfect competition. Markets are rarely perfectly competitive. Equally, the cartel price is not necessarily the same as the monopoly price. Not all cartels manage to set price at the profit-maximizing monopoly level.

9.2.2 The cartel overcharge harm

9.16 The overcharge, A, is the quantity of actual unit sales by the cartel multiplied by the difference between the actual cartel price and the counterfactual price (i.e. the price that would have been charged in the absence of the cartel). It is convenient to express the overcharge as a percentage of the actual price of the cartel. If the cartel price is €125, and the counterfactual price is €100, the overcharge would be 20 per cent (€25 is 20 per cent of €125). The overcharge is sometimes expressed as a percentage of the counterfactual price (in this case 25 per cent). This is equally valid in theory, but it is important to be clear

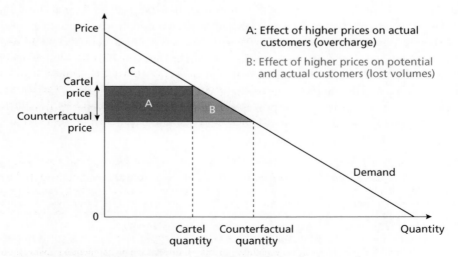

Figure 9.1 Stylized illustration of the effects of a hardcore cartel

about which percentage calculation is used. Expressing the overcharge as a percentage of the actual price makes it easy (and intuitive) to calculate the total amount of overcharge by applying the percentage to the amount that the buyer actually paid for its purchases (often known as the value of commerce). For example, if the cartel sold 1 million units at a price of €125 each and at an overcharge percentage of 20 per cent, the total overcharge would be €25 million. If one specific claimant filed a successful damages action, and it could demonstrate that its total purchases from the cartel amounted to, say, €15 million over the relevant period, the amount it was overcharged would be 20 per cent of €15 million, so €3 million.

9.2.3 Volume effects

The lost-volume effect (represented by triangle B in Figure 9.1) is known in economic theory as a deadweight welfare loss; it represents an inefficiency to the economy as a whole, as we explained in Chapters 1 and 2. This deadweight loss is greatest if the counterfactual price is equal to the price under perfect competition, but also arises if some other form of competitive interaction would have taken place in the counterfactual, such as oligopoly. From an economic perspective, the deadweight loss is inefficient as the cartel does not serve those customers who would be willing to pay the price offered under more competitive conditions.   **9.17**

In practice, cartel damages actions are mostly brought by parties that were actual (direct or indirect) customers of the cartel during the infringement period. These actions normally focus on the overcharge harm. Damages from reduced volumes are more difficult to prove. How can you identify those potential customers who did not purchase at all during the infringement period but would have done so at the non-cartelized price? Take the private schools price-fixing case in the United Kingdom.[8] Parents who could no longer afford to send their children to private schools at the inflated school fees may have been harmed as well as those who paid the higher fees and did send their children to those schools—but can they prove it? Harm from volume loss may also arise further downstream if direct purchasers of the cartel pass on the overcharge by raising prices to their own customers (we discuss this further in sections 9.3 and 9.10).   **9.18**

9.2.4 Dynamic cartel effects

In addition to the price and quantity effects illustrated in Figure 9.1, cartels can have longer-term effects on the structure and functioning of the market. The reduction in rivalry between firms can result in lower levels of innovation and a slowing of the rate at which improvements in efficiency are achieved, or at which inefficient firms exit the market. Higher cartel prices may also have a distortive effect in downstream markets—for example, if certain purchasers can no longer afford high input prices and downstream concentration consequently increases.   **9.19**

To an economist, all these longer-term effects are relevant for the damages estimation, since they may affect the counterfactual price. For example, the counterfactual price might have been even lower (and hence the overcharge even higher) if the market would have seen cost-reducing innovations in the absence of the cartel. However, such factors can be taken into   **9.20**

---

[8] Office of Fair Trading (2006), 'Independent schools agree settlement: competition investigation resolved', press release, 19 May.

account only in circumstances where estimating these effects is really feasible, and where it is legally possible to include them, since it may be difficult to demonstrate a causal link between the infringement and the alleged longer-term harm.

9.2.5 Umbrella pricing and other 'remote' cartel effects

9.21 A cartel at a particular stage of the supply chain can cause ripples along the whole chain, such that various parties may potentially be harmed. Yet legal principles such as causality, remoteness and foreseeability tend to put a limit on who can claim for damages in practice. Direct competitors and direct customers of the infringing party are relatively 'close' to the effects of the infringement. Suppliers to the infringing parties may also have suffered harm, since cartels usually result in lower levels of output. This means that fewer inputs are required, thus reducing the volumes sold by suppliers. Companies in connected markets can equally be affected—if a brick cartel has raised costs to the construction industry such that there is less construction activity overall, other suppliers to the industry are harmed as well. Or take the example of a hot dog stand outside the brick factory. The brick cartel leads to an output restriction, hence lower production in the factory, fewer workers buying hot dogs during lunch breaks, and the hot dog stand suffering harm. Economically, these are all forms of harm that would fall within the compensation principle. However, courts tend to draw the 'remoteness line' closer to where the infringement has taken place.[9]

9.22 One area where courts have accepted that damages may arise beyond the cartelized products themselves is in relation to the 'umbrella effect'. This occurs where products or geographic areas outside the cartel agreement compete so closely with the cartelized products that it is likely that their prices have been raised as well, benefitting from the pricing 'umbrella' provided by the cartel. In a 2014 judgment concerning the lifts and escalators cartel, the ECJ determined that such umbrella claims are valid in principle:

> Where a cartel manages to maintain artificially high prices for particular goods and certain conditions are met, relating, in particular, to the nature of the goods or to the size of the market covered by that cartel, it cannot be ruled out that a competing undertaking, outside the cartel in question, might choose to set the price of its offer at an amount higher than it would have chosen under normal conditions of competition, that is, in the absence of that cartel . . .
>
> It follows that . . . a loss being suffered by the customer of an undertaking not party to a cartel, but benefiting from the economic conditions of umbrella pricing, because of an offer price higher than it would have been but for the existence of that cartel is one of the possible effects of the cartel, that the members thereof cannot disregard.[10]

9.23 To analyse the umbrella effect you first need to assess whether the other products or geographic areas in question do indeed compete closely with the cartel. The techniques used for market definition and determining the closeness of competition discussed in Chapters 2 and 7 are of relevance here. If they are close substitutes, you can analyse the overcharge for these other products or areas directly, using the methods discussed later. Where limited data is available, you can sometimes assume that the overcharge for the other products

---

[9] In 2015 the Austrian Supreme Court rejected a claim for €23 million by a lift installer against the members of a lifts and escalators cartel. The installer claimed that the cartel had led to fewer new lift installations and maintenance contracts. The court considered the claim to be insufficiently substantiated, and any harm to the installer from the output reduction to be too remote. Austrian Supreme Court, Case 4Ob95/15x Judgment of 16 June 2015.

[10] Case C-557/12, *Kone AG and Others*, Judgment of 5 June 2014, at [29–30].

is a proportion of the cartel overcharge. This proportion will depend on the degree of competition between the two groups; the higher this degree, the closer the umbrella overcharge will be to the cartel overcharge. Note that the effect can also work the other way around: the cartel may pull up the price of the competing products (the umbrella effect), but competing products may also drag down the cartel price. The stronger the suppliers or products outside the cartel are relative to those inside, the more likely is this latter effect of reducing prices.

9.2.6 Presumptions on the existence of cartel overcharges

If a competition authority decision contains evidence that a hardcore cartel was operational for many years without breaking down, you might expect the cartel members to have charged higher prices than they would have in the absence of the cartel. There have been significant enforcement efforts against cartels by competition authorities worldwide in the last two decades, and substantial fines and other penalties have been imposed (see Chapters 5 and 8). Where hardcore cartels have nonetheless been active—meeting and exchanging information regularly, and using sophisticated methods to circumvent detection—it is not unreasonable to infer that the mere fact that the cartel members took such risks over a long time period indicates that they considered it worthwhile.   **9.24**

As discussed in Chapter 8, the decision as to whether a company or individual engages   **9.25**
in cartel activity can be thought of as a rational profit calculation. In a simple model, the company would be expected to commit the infringement if the expected additional profit from being part of the cartel (i.e. above the profit earned when competing) is higher than the sum of (i) the expected fine if the cartel is detected (which itself depends on the expected probability of being detected), and (ii) the expected damages payout of a subsequent successful private action. According to this logic, and on the assumption that cartel participants act rationally, they would not be taking on the risk of being prosecuted if they did not expect to achieve significant extra profits from the cartel. This basic logic is sometimes (implicitly or explicitly) followed by courts. In a vitamins cartel case, the Dortmund Regional Court applied the presumption that a cartel price is generally higher than a market price:

> The damage of a price cartel consists of the difference between the cartel price and the hypothetical competitive price in the absence of the cartel. According to the experience of life (*Lebenserfahrung*), it can be assumed that a competitive price is lower than a cartel price. The defendant did not show that it would have been different in this case and why. The difference between the competitive price and the cartel price represents a financial damage in the sense of lost wealth.[11]

The court found support for this proposition in the fact that prices increased or remained   **9.26**
stable during the cartel, but declined after the cartel ceased to operate. Similarly, in a cement cartel case, the Higher Regional Court in Düsseldorf stated that: 'The longer and more sustainable a cartel was operational, and the wider the area it was designed to cover, the higher the requirements that have to be imposed on a court if it wants to deny that the cartel agreement produced any economic benefits.'[12]

---

[11] LG Dortmund AZ 13 0 55/02 Kart *Vitaminkartell III* [2004] (Dortmund Regional Court, 1 April 2004).

[12] Oberlandesgericht Düsseldorf, *Berliner Transportbeton I*, KRB 2/05.

9.27   The court emphasized that market mechanisms were unlikely to function properly due to the imposition of cartel quotas. It thus concluded that prices set by the cartel were likely to have been higher than in a competitive market. In a damages action against a sugar cartel in Spain, the Valladolid Provincial Court relied on the competition authority's finding that the agreement on prices had caused serious harm, and therefore rejected outright the defendant's expert report which had calculated the damage as zero.[13]

9.28   The EU Directive on antitrust damages actions captures the above logic by establishing a rebuttable presumption of harm from hardcore cartels, aimed at shifting the burden of proof towards the defendants to some extent:

> To remedy the information asymmetry and some of the difficulties associated with quantifying harm in competition law cases, and to ensure the effectiveness of claims for damages, it is appropriate to presume that cartel infringements result in harm, in particular via an effect on prices. Depending on the facts of the case, cartels result in a rise in prices, or prevent a lowering of prices which would otherwise have occurred but for the cartel. This presumption should not cover the concrete amount of harm. Infringers should be allowed to rebut the presumption. It is appropriate to limit this rebuttable presumption to cartels, given their secret nature, which increases the information asymmetry and makes it more difficult for claimants to obtain the evidence necessary to prove the harm.[14]

9.2.7   Empirical insights into the magnitude of cartel overcharges

9.29   Economists have carried out many empirical studies on overcharges in past cartels. Lawyers involved in damages actions have shown great interest in the results of these studies, in order to get a feel for what sort of orders of magnitude are typically involved in such cases. We note from the outset that some care is required when interpreting this empirical data. Not all studies on cartel overcharges would qualify as sufficiently robust. There may also be a publication bias: empirical studies tend to focus on cartels that are most likely to have had an effect, and some cartels with no effect will not have been captured in these studies (although, as shown below, a small but significant proportion of the cartels studied resulted in no overcharges).

9.30   A study by Connor and Lande (2008) used a comprehensive dataset on cartel overcharges, and has been the most widely cited study on this topic.[15] It contained 674 observations of average overcharges from 200 social science studies of cartels from the eighteenth century onwards—for example, it covered a British coal cartel that started in the 1770s and a Canadian petroleum lamp oil cartel in the 1870s. The study found that the median cartel overcharge for all types of cartel was 20 per cent. An earlier study by Connor and Lande (2005) suggested that in around 7 per cent of cartel cases there was no overcharge. Oxera et al. (2009) examined the dataset underlying the 2008 Connor and Lande study, as well as an additional 350 observations provided by these authors, and tested the sensitivity of the results by limiting the sample to cartels that started after 1960 and to overcharge

---

[13]   Audiencia Provincial de Valladolid, Sentencia num. 261/2009, Judgment of 9 October 2009.

[14]   Directive 2014/104/EU of the European Parliament and of the Council of the European Union of 26 November 2014 on certain rules governing actions for damages under national law for infringements of the competition law provisions of the Member States and of the European Union, OJ L 349/1, 5 December 2014, [recital 47]. The presumption itself is at [17].

[15]   Professor Connor has updated the study a number of times since. The main findings are not very different.

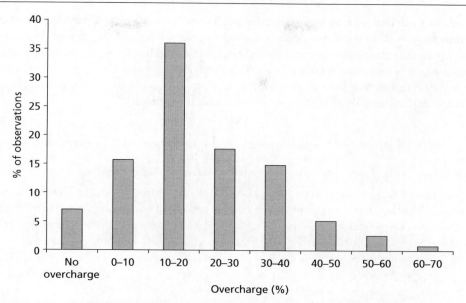

Figure 9.2 Distribution of cartel overcharges in empirical studies of past cartels
Source: Oxera et al. (2009), based on Connor and Lande (2008).

estimates obtained from peer-reviewed academic articles and chapters in published books (this reduced the sample size from over 1,000 to 114).

Figure 9.2 illustrates the distribution of cartel overcharges across this dataset. The range **9.31** with the greatest number of observations is 10–20 per cent. The median overcharge is 18 per cent—not far from the 20 per cent found by Connor and Lande. The average overcharge is around 20 per cent, compared with 23 per cent in Connor and Lande. However, since the variation in observed overcharges is large, it is informative to consider the distribution of overcharges as well as the median or average overcharge. In 93 per cent of the cases the overcharge is above zero (as in Connor and Lande, 2005). This supports the theory that in most cases the cartel overcharge may be expected to be positive, but also shows that there is a small but significant proportion of cartels where no overcharge has been found.

The important policy question is what you do with the results of this empirical literature. Is **9.32** it merely interesting background information? Do you use it to inform your calculation of the possible order of magnitude of the damage at an early stage in the case? Or do you go as far as using a presumption that the overcharge in the case you are considering is somewhere between 10 per cent and 20 per cent, as that is the most frequently observed range of past cartel overcharges? A prominent example of the latter approach is the Hungarian Competition Act, which establishes a rebuttable presumption that hardcore cartels result in a 10 per cent overcharge.[16] We see little economic merit in such presumptions (other than possibly the presumption that for hardcore cartels the overcharge is likely to be greater than zero, without specifying a number, as discussed above and reflected in the EU Directive on antitrust damages actions). The amount of the overcharge in any particular damages case ultimately

---

[16] Hungarian Competition Act (Act LVII of 1996, as amended from time to time), [88/C].

needs to be determined on the specific facts. This was also the view of the Commercial Court in Brussels in the damages action brought by the European Commission (as a purchaser) against the members of the lifts and escalators cartel. In a 2014 judgment the court accepted the notion that cartels are generally likely to increase prices, but quoted the Oxera et al. (2009) study that for a small but significant proportion of cartels no overcharge has been found and hence that a case-by-case assessment is required.[17]

9.3 Harm from Exclusionary Conduct: Conceptual Framework

9.3.1 Lost profit: Legal principles determining the relevant economic questions

9.33 Exclusionary conduct prevents existing rivals from competing effectively or forces them to exit altogether. Potential competitors may be prevented from entering the market or restricted to small-scale entry. Buyers, be they end-consumers or intermediate producers or distributors, may be harmed by exclusionary conduct if the reduction in competition leads to higher prices, less choice, or lower quality. A number of legal principles are important when considering the chances of success for certain types of claim for exclusionary damages. To economists there is a broad set of damages that may arise from a competition infringement, and each type is in principle quantifiable; to lawyers the set is narrower. Existing rivals are, in legal terms, relatively close to the exclusionary conduct, meaning that it is easier for them to substantiate a damages claim than it is for potential entrants.

9.34 From an economic perspective, harm to competitors from an exclusionary infringement may arise in two ways. First, it may be in the form of increased costs, where costs include both cash cost items, such as input goods, and other more general items, such as the cost of financing the business. Second, it may be in the form of reduced revenue, where the infringing conduct affects the price or sales volume. The effect of both increased costs and reduced revenue is a reduction in profit. From a legal perspective, it may be important (we understand from lawyers) to make explicit whether this effect falls under actual loss (*damnum emergens*) or lost profit (*lucrum cessans*). To an economist there is not much difference. The framework presented here can be used for both categories. In legal terms the evidentiary requirements may be different. Actual loss is generally easier to prove—for example, a small airline that was foreclosed from access to distribution channels by a dominant rival and had to find alternative, more expensive, distribution channels instead, should in principle be able to demonstrate the harm based on the actual additional expenditure incurred (it can show the actual invoices). It is more difficult to prove the quantum of the alleged lost profit—e.g. loss of market share or a fall in sales growth—and a causal link between the unlawful conduct and that lost profit. This is because of difficulties in establishing whether such losses were due to the anti-competitive practice or to other factors, such as incompetence, bad luck, or external economic factors. Most legal systems seem to take a relatively conservative approach when assessing claims for lost profit—or related concepts, such as loss of chance and loss of opportunity—in exclusionary damages cases. Often the damages awarded are limited to actual losses or a narrow interpretation of lost profits. We show some examples below.

---

[17] Nederlandstalige Rechtbank van Koophandel, Brussel, Vonnis in de zaak van Europese Unie tegen Otis en anderen, A.R. A/08/06816, 24 November 2014, pp. 23 and 27.

9.3.2 Lost profit: Cases where courts have been cautious

The Paris Court of Appeal ruled on an exclusionary damages case in 1998 after it had found **9.35** that Labinal, a supplier to the aerospace industry, had infringed Article 101 and Article 102 by trying to eliminate its only competitor, Mors, from a tender to supply tyre pressure measuring equipment to British Aerospace.[18] The court awarded Mors FF34.2 million (around €5.2 million) for the losses caused by Labinal. The calculation was based on the report of a court-appointed expert, with the court confining itself to assessing whether the expert's conclusions were reasonable and supported by the factual evidence. The expert considered that Mors had incurred harm in the form of: (i) additional administrative and commercial costs; (ii) loss of opportunity to participate in other tenders; and (iii) the inability to recover one-off costs. However, the expert did not consider that Mors should be awarded damages for loss of opportunity to enter adjacent markets since it had failed to prove that it would have entered these other markets had Labinal's anti-competitive conduct not taken place.

An exclusionary damages case before the Court of Appeal of Milan followed a finding **9.36** by the Italian competition authority that the members of the National Association of Employment Consultants had collectively boycotted the claimant's software packages.[19] The court compared the average number of contracts with the claimant that were terminated by the association's members in the two years of the collective boycott (1997–98) with the average number of contracts terminated in the years before the boycott. On that basis, the court awarded €148,200 in damages. The next question was whether the claimant was entitled to compensation for the slower growth of its business due to the boycott (a form of lost profit). While the claimant had shown that before the boycott its business was growing by more than 10 per cent per year and that this increase had suddenly ceased at the time of the boycott, the court considered that it could not be sure that this growth would have continued in the counterfactual. The past evidence could not be used to support a presumption that the growth rate would have been the same.

Various English courts, and at one stage the ECJ, ruled on the famous *Crehan* damages **9.37** case.[20] The claimant was a pub landlord who, in 1991, entered into an exclusive contract with Inntrepreneur to lease two pubs on the condition that he stocked only its beers. After two unsuccessful years, Inntrepreneur terminated his tenancy and sought to recover money owed to it. Mr Crehan counterclaimed that the beer tie agreement infringed Article 101 and sought to recover three heads of damages: (i) losses that he suffered during the period of the lease between 1991 and 1993; (ii) future profits he would have made in the period between 1993 and 2003 in the absence of the beer tie; and (iii) the value in 2003 of the untied leases had he wished to sell these on. Both the High Court and the Court of Appeal accepted that if liability were established, the claimant would have been entitled to recover in full the losses suffered during the period of the two-year lease. However, the Court of Appeal took a more restrictive approach than the High Court in relation to the recoverability of future profits that the claimant would have made between 1993 and 2003. The High Court (albeit hypothetically as it had dismissed the case on other grounds) calculated the total lost profit

---

[18] *Mors SA v Labinal SA*, Cour d'Appel de Paris, 1ère chambre, section A, arrêt no 334, 30 September 1998.

[19] *INAZ Paghe srl v Associazione Nazionale dei Consulenti del Lavoro* (Corte d'Appello di Milano, 10 December 2004).

[20] *Crehan v Inntrepreneur Pub Company (CPC) & Anor* [2003] EWHC 1510 (Ch); [2004] EWCA Civ 637; [2006] UKHL 38; Case C-453/99 *Courage Ltd v Bernard Crehan* [2001] ECR I–6297.

as £1,311,500. This included all three heads of damages listed above. In contrast, the Court of Appeal held that the claimant would have been entitled to only £131,336 in damages. It considered the lost profit between 1993 and 2003 to be too speculative. The case was subsequently appealed to the House of Lords, which overturned the Court of Appeal's finding that the beer tie agreement infringed Article 101. As such, the issue of the quantum of damage did not need to be addressed in this last ruling. Mr Crehan's thirteen years of battles in court ultimately left him empty-handed, but his case was instrumental in embedding in EU law the legal principle of compensation.

9.3.3 The concept of lost profit: An economic framework

9.38 The basic economic framework to determine harm from exclusionary practices—encompassing both actual loss and lost profit in the legal sense—is illustrated in Figure 9.3. The damages are calculated as the difference between the actual and the counterfactual profit of the company. To take a simple example, if the victim of the infringement—say, a small competitor airline that was harmed by a dominant airline's exclusionary conduct—had actual revenues of €10 million and actual costs of €8 million, its actual profit is €2 million. If its revenues would have been €15 million in the absence of the infringement and its counterfactual costs €12 million, then its counterfactual profit is €3 million. The small airline's lost profit is therefore €1 million.

9.39 The framework can be rearranged as illustrated in Figure 9.4, which shows a simpler expression for the fall in profit. The lost revenue in Figure 9.4 is calculated as the difference

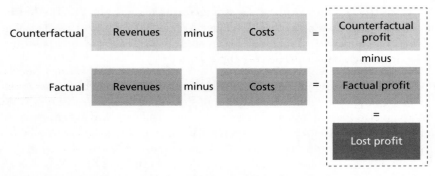

Figure 9.3 Economic framework for calculating harm from exclusionary conduct
Source: Oxera et al. (2009).

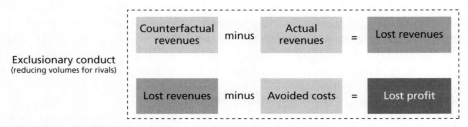

Figure 9.4 Rearranged economic framework for calculating harm from exclusionary conduct (equivalent to Fig. 9.3)
Source: Oxera et al. (2009).

between the counterfactual and actual revenues. The costs avoided due to the infringement are then deducted from the lost revenue to obtain the reduction in profit. For example, if volume falls, certain costs that vary with volume (e.g. fuel or input materials) will decrease as well. A company that experiences a reduction in sales due to exclusionary conduct by a rival will in this sense have an offsetting benefit from a cost reduction, and this cost saving should be deducted from the lost revenue to obtain the lost profit, as illustrated in Figure 9.4. This rearranged expression has the advantage over Figure 9.3 of requiring less detailed knowledge of the company's cost structure. It is not necessary to calculate all the costs that the company would have incurred in the relevant period. Instead, the focus is on the costs that the company did not incur because of the infringement—that is, the avoided costs. Following the above example, lost revenues for the small airline equal €5 million (€15 million of revenue in the counterfactual minus €10 million of actual revenue). Its avoided costs amount to €4 million (€12 million of costs in the counterfactual minus €8 million of actual costs), reflecting the fact that in the absence of the exclusionary conduct the airline would have achieved higher revenues but also incurred additional costs. Lost revenues of €5 million minus avoided costs of €4 million gives a lost profit of €1 million.

9.40 The effect on profits is often approximated by reference to variables such as lost volumes, lost customers, or lost market share. These quantifications are (or should be) consistent with the conceptual framework in the figures above. For example, damages claims based on an estimation of lost sales volume can be translated into a negative effect on profits by applying some average counterfactual profit margin to each unit of sales lost. If the airline demonstrates that it sold 50,000 fewer tickets because of the abuse by its dominant rival, and its average profit margin per ticket was €20 (and would have been €20 in the counterfactual), its lost profit can be estimated at €1 million.

9.3.4 The effect of infringements that increase input prices

9.41 Figure 9.3 can also be rearranged to capture the effect on profit from infringements that increase input prices. See Figure 9.5. This applies to exclusionary conduct that has the effect of raising prices to buyers, and to exclusionary conduct that has the effect of raising rivals' costs in downstream markets—a common theory of harm in abuse of dominance cases. Figure 9.5 can also be used to analyse the effect on the profits of customers of a cartel. In the top section of Figure 9.5, the fall in profit is calculated as the increase in costs minus the

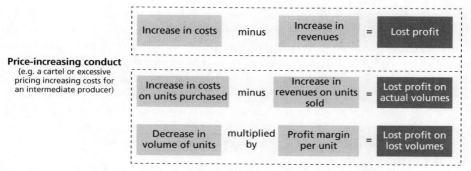

Figure 9.5 Rearranged economic framework for calculating harm from price-increasing conduct (equivalent to Figure 9.3)

Source: Oxera et al. (2009).

421

increase in revenues. In the case of a cartel or anti-competitive increase in an input price, the increase in costs to the downstream purchaser (the box to the left) will often be equal to the overcharge. The increase in revenues (the middle box) will include the pass-on of this overcharge to the purchaser's own customers. Pass-on is achieved through raising price, and the resulting higher revenues may have to be offset against the higher costs caused by the infringement. The lower part of Figure 9.5 is equivalent but splits the profit effect from a higher price into three components: the increase in costs on units actually purchased (the overcharge effect); the increase in revenues on units actually sold downstream (which covers the pass-on effect); and the effect of lost volumes of sales downstream due to the price increase upstream. Within this framework, the total lost profit equals the sum of the lost profit from actual volumes and the lost profit from lost volumes.

9.3.5 The counterfactual in exclusion cases: Competitive or barely legal conduct?

9.42 Where damages are claimed for exclusionary conduct, the counterfactual is not always straightforward to determine, as the dominant company may have behaved in a number of different ways in this hypothetical situation. In predatory pricing cases, which of a range of possible non-predatory prices would the dominant company have charged in the counterfactual? In margin squeeze cases, what would have been the dominant company's non-abusive margin between the wholesale price and the retail price, and would it have achieved this margin in the counterfactual by lowering the former or raising the latter?

9.43 This question is not always relevant to the legal assessment. Take the *2 Travel v Cardiff City Transport* damages action before the CAT.[21] Following the entry by 2 Travel with a low-cost bus service on a number of routes in Cardiff, the incumbent operator, Cardiff Bus, launched its 'white services' on the same routes to compete with 2 Travel. The OFT considered this to be predatory. In the follow-on damages claim, the counterfactual question was how much profit 2 Travel would have made had Cardiff Bus not launched the white services at all. The question was not whether Cardiff Bus might have responded in some other, legitimate, way to 2 Travel's entry, for example, by increasing service frequency or lowering fares on existing services but still recovering costs.

9.44 However, in other cases this counterfactual question can make a material difference. In a predatory pricing case, should it be assumed that the dominant company would have charged a price that covered its average total cost in full, leaving plenty of space for competitors? Or might it still have priced sharply, just staying on the right side of the law, covering average avoidable costs? This matters for the damages estimate. The higher the counterfactual price, the more profit margin there would have been available for the claimant. From an economic perspective, it depends on what is most realistic: when an incumbent faces new entry, it is not unreasonable to assume that it reacts to this entry somehow, even in a counterfactual situation where such a reaction remains within the bounds of the law. The price it charged before the entry is therefore not necessarily an accurate representation of the counterfactual price; its costs, or prices charged in other markets with existing competitors, may provide a better indication. Economics provides tools to estimate such costs and prices in order to determine the counterfactual, as further discussed in this chapter.

---

[21] *2 Travel Group Plc (in Liquidation) v Cardiff City Transport Services Limited*, [2012] CAT 19, 5 July 2012. We acted as experts for the defendant in this case.

The CAT faced this question in *Albion Water*, a follow-on damages claim against Dŵr **9.45** Cymru (Welsh Water) involving an excessive wholesale access charge and resulting margin squeeze.[22] For both conceptual and practical reasons, the CAT dismissed the notion that the counterfactual price should be set at the level of access charge that would just be on the right side of the law (in this case, the highest legitimate access charge). Instead it chose a value based on an average of a range of lawful charges:

> It will be very rare that an infringement decision, whether adopted by a domestic competition authority or by the European Commission, or indeed on appeal as in Case 1046 [where earlier the CAT had confirmed the abuse], will determine the precise borderline between lawful and unlawful conduct. If Dŵr Cymru is right that the claimant in a follow-on damages claim will have to show precisely where that line should be drawn, that will often involve the court in re-doing much of the work done in the earlier infringement decision. Further, it is a task that is almost impossible to accomplish, as is demonstrated in this case. If $16.5p/m^3$ is not abusive (a point we do not decide), what about $16.6p/m^3$ or $16.7p/m^3$, or $16.8p/m^3$? We do not see how a claimant could prove that one rather than the other is the tipping point between lawful and unlawful conduct.[23]

> There is a range of lawful access prices that Dŵr Cymru could have offered and we should take the figure in the middle of that range. The counterfactual must be based on an assumption that Dŵr Cymru would have offered a reasonable access price, rather than an access price which is the highest it could lawfully have charged.[24]

In margin squeeze cases there is a further conceptual question: in the counterfactual, is **9.46** the wholesale price lower, or the retail price higher? After all, this type of abuse involves squeezing the competitor's margin from both sides. On which side the squeeze is released can have a significant impact on the estimated damages. If the incumbent had charged a higher retail price in the counterfactual, there would have been more scope for the entrant to gain market share and grow overall demand downstream by undercutting this retail price. In contrast, if the incumbent had cut wholesale prices but kept the retail price at the same low level in the counterfactual, the entrant would have found it more difficult to grow its profits. Again, from an economic perspective it depends on what is most realistic. In telecoms markets, where several margin squeeze cases have arisen (see Chapter 4), retail markets tend to be more competitive than wholesale markets. Incumbents, acting lawfully, may be more inclined to lower wholesale prices than to raise retail prices so as to avoid losing retail market share.

9.4 A Classification of Methods and Models for Quantifying Damages

9.4.1 The classification

Having set out the conceptual frameworks for determining harm from cartels and exclusion- **9.47** ary conduct, we now turn to the practical approaches to quantifying such harm. Economics has developed a wide array of methods and models for this purpose. Figure 9.6 presents a

---

[22] *Albion Water Limited v Dŵr Cymru Cyfyngedig*, [2013] CAT 6, 28 March. We advised the defendants on this matter.
[23] Ibid., at [69].
[24] Ibid., at [71].

classification into three broad approaches: comparator-based, financial-analysis-based, and market-structure-based. This is taken from the report for the European Commission by Oxera et al. (2009). It encapsulates previous classifications, most notably that of US case law which has explicitly identified three 'common approaches to measuring antitrust damages': the before-and-after approach, the yardstick or benchmark approach, and regression analysis.[25] The classification here draws clearer distinctions between what is used as the basis for the counterfactual in each method, and the precise estimation technique. Before-and-after and yardstick are in reality two different types of comparator-based approach; the former involves making comparisons over time, the latter across product or geographic markets. Similarly, the regression analysis category does not in itself clarify the basis for the counterfactual. Regression analysis is a technique, and can be used in both the before-and-after and the yardstick approach. Figure 9.6 identifies the basis for the counterfactual that underlies each of the three approaches. It then summarizes the estimation techniques that can be used within each approach. All three approaches can be used for any type of competition law damages case. They are not mutually exclusive and in fact often complement each other, as discussed below.

9.48   Comparator-based approaches use data from sources that are external to the infringement to estimate the counterfactual. This can be done in three ways: by cross-sectional comparisons (comparing different geographic or product markets); time-series comparisons (analysing prices before, during, and/or after an infringement); and combining the above two in 'difference-in-differences' models (e.g. analysing the change in price for a cartelized market over time, and comparing that against the change in price in a non-cartelized market over the same time frame). Various techniques can be used to analyse this comparator

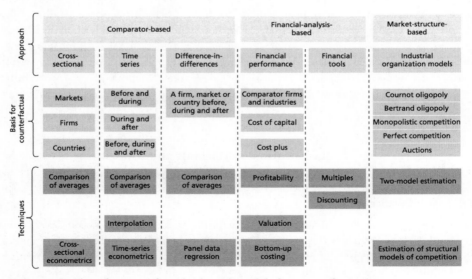

Figure 9.6 Classification of methods and models for quantifying damages
Source: Oxera et al. (2009).

---

[25] *Conwood Co LP v US Tobacco Co* 290 F 3d 768, 793 (6th Cir. 2002).

data, ranging from the simple, such as comparing averages, to the more sophisticated, such as panel data regression.

Financial-analysis-based approaches—the Commission's Practical guide calls them 'cost-based and finance-based methods'—have been developed in finance theory and practice. They use financial information on defendants, claimants or comparator companies to estimate the counterfactual. There are two types of approach that use this information. First are those that examine financial performance. These include assessing the profitability of defendants or claimants and comparing this against a benchmark, and bottom-up costing to estimate a counterfactual price. The second type is a group of more general financial tools, such as discounting and valuation, which can be used also as part of the other approaches (e.g. a time-series comparison of profit margins during and after the cartel).   **9.49**

Market-structure-based approaches are derived from IO theory and use a combination of theoretical models and empirical estimation (rather than comparisons across markets or over time) to arrive at the counterfactual. This involves identifying models of competition that best fit the market in question, and using these models to assess what prices or volumes would have been in the absence of the anti-competitive conduct. The Practical guide calls these 'simulation models'. We think this term is too general. While it captures the idea that you use a model to simulate a counterfactual, simulation is a technique that can be used in many other contexts as well.   **9.50**

9.4.2 Some notes on the use of models generally

No model can fully describe and predict the complete range of market interactions, but nor is it intended to do so. Models can be thought of as maps that simplify the real world to make it understandable and predictable. The simplifications made will depend on the intended use of the map. A geological map and a road atlas will make very different simplifications, even if describing the same piece of land, because they are used for different purposes.   **9.51**

A model will only be as good as the quality of the input data used to populate it. Thus it is important to ensure that the sourcing of data is free from potential biases and that the data used is consistent over time and over units (companies, business units, or individuals). A sophisticated model based on unreliable or biased data is less useful than a simpler model based on better data. A critical question for you, or a court, to ask when presented with a model is therefore whether the data used is of sufficient quality, and whether a simpler model could be used. There are many statistical tests to assess the reliability of the model and its results.[26] When presented with an empirical study, you are entitled to require it to show the basic diagnostic tests. One important aspect of reliability is statistical significance: does the estimated value (say, of the overcharge) reflect the true value? A 90 per cent or 95 per cent confidence interval is often used as a threshold for this purpose—the range of uncertainty around the estimated value is such that there is only a 10 per cent or 5 per cent probability that the true value does not lie within this range. The t-test and p-value are most commonly used for this purpose. If the p-value is 0.05 or smaller, the true value lies within the 95 per cent confidence interval around the estimated value, and the estimate can be considered statistically significant.   **9.52**

---

[26] These are explained in econometrics textbooks, such as Wooldridge (2013).

9.4.3 What can economic models say about causation?

9.53 Quantifying the harm and establishing a causal link between the harm and the infringement are essential parts of any damages action. What, if anything, can economic models used for quantifying damages say about causation? Econometric analysis seeks to identify statistically significant relationships between a dependent variable and various explanatory variables (see also Chapter 2). The econometric analysis itself does not prove causality. A model may be constructed with two completely unrelated variables that happen to have a high correlation (i.e. they move similarly over time, like inflation and accumulated rainfall). Such an analysis may identify a relationship that is statistically significant but economically meaningless.

9.54 Nevertheless, econometrics can help address the issue of causation because it can take into account many possible explanatory factors (subject to data availability). This is important for damages actions since the difficulties in proving causation frequently arise when a model purports to show a relationship between two variables but ignores other explanatory variables. A model may show that a competitor's sales have fallen during the period of an exclusionary abuse, but fail to address other possible explanations such as a general drop in sales in the market, the entry of a new competitor, or managerial incompetence. A good econometric model would seek to 'control' for those other explanations—that is, incorporate them into the model as additional explanatory variables. That way, the various effects can be isolated from one another, and the model may well show that, while the other factors explain some of the sales loss, the remainder of the loss is related to the infringement.

9.55 In US antitrust damages cases, where the use of econometrics is more common than in Europe, the issue of causation is often dealt with in this way. The US courts sometimes expect to see a regression analysis in order to have robust estimates and to isolate the effects of the infringement from other effects:

> The goal of a prudent economist in performing the 'before and after' analysis is to determine the hypothetical or 'counter-factual' prices that would have prevailed during the conspiracy period, but for the conspiracy. In applying the 'before and after' model of damages, it is fundamentally necessary to explain the pattern of forces outside the violation period using factors that might have changed (i.e., supply, demand, and differences in competition) to predict the prices during the conspiratorial period. In this context, as in most economic problems, failure to keep 'other things equal' is one of the known pitfalls in the path of the serious economist...A prudent economist must account for these differences and would perform a minimum regression analysis if utilizing the 'before and after' model.[27]

9.56 In a number of cases, economic evidence has been rejected on the grounds that it did not sufficiently account for other possible explanations for the harm. In *Stelwagon v Tarmac Roofing*, the expert's opinion was not accepted since it 'failed to sufficiently link any decline in Stelwagon's MAPs [modified asphalt products] sales to price discrimination. The sales may have been lost for reasons apart from price discrimination—reasons that [the expert]'s analysis apparently did not take into account.'[28] In other cases courts did accept the econometric evidence. In *Conwood v US Tobacco*, a case of alleged monopolization, the court accepted that the expert had tested for 'all plausible explanations' for the claimant's low

---

[27] *Re Aluminum Phosphide Antitrust Litigation*, 893 F Supp 1497 (D. Kan. 1995).
[28] *Stelwagon Mfg Co v Tarmac Roofing* 63 F 3d 1267 (3d Cir. 1995).

market share in his regression analysis, thus allowing the court to isolate the effect of the infringement itself.[29]

9.4.4 Choosing a single damages value

Methods and models cannot be ranked *a priori*. The choice of model is driven mainly by data availability. It is not uncommon for an economic expert to use more than one model if there are different sources of available information. It is also common to see the experts on the claimant and defendant sides using different models. Ultimately a court needs to decide on the specific amount of damages (if any) to be awarded. The main question is normally whether specific models have been applied reasonably and robustly to the case at hand, not whether one approach is inherently superior to another. It may be that several models are robust but give non-identical results, simply because they rely on different assumptions and have used different data. A court may have to decide which assumptions or data sources it prefers.   **9.57**

An alternative approach when presented with multiple robust estimates is to 'pool' them. This involves combining the results of two or more models into a single value. The economics literature has shown pooling to work well.[30] The combination of individual forecasts of the same event has often been found to outperform the individual forecasts. One approach is simply taking the mean of the available estimates. This is often done for macroeconomic forecasts. Hence, if three robust models estimate the harm to be €10.1 million, €11.2 million, and €12.0 million, respectively, the pooled model result using a simple average would be €11.1 million. This combined value can then be used as the best estimate of the actual harm.   **9.58**

An advantage of pooling is that when the models rely on different data, combining their results means that the final value reflects more of the underlying data (and hence more of the available information) than a single model alone. While it is theoretically possible to conceive of a 'unified' model that incorporates all the data sources of the individual models, it is often difficult to implement this in practice. Instead, pooling of different model results creates a form of 'unified' estimate, since it draws on all the approaches undertaken. In addition, pooling the results can help reduce biases in the individual models, as positive and negative biases may offset one another. If the biases are all in the same direction, combining results would not eliminate them, but nor would it exacerbate them. Thus, combining results can generally be expected to reduce biases, since at least some of the biases are likely to be in different directions. Pooling does need to be applied with care. It is most frequently used in cases where a single expert is using multiple approaches, or where multiple experts—such as a group of court-appointed experts—are attempting to estimate the same value for the same purpose. Pooling the results from different experts on opposing sides can also work, but only if their approaches start from similar premises and datasets.   **9.59**

The Court of Session in Edinburgh accepted the pooling approach in a commercial dispute between two paper manufacturers that led one to claim for lost profits.[31] Inveresk had sold one of its brands to Tullis, but in the five-month transition period its staff hindered   **9.60**

---

[29] *Conwood Co v US Tobacco Co* 290 F 3d 768 (6th Cir. 2002).
[30] See, for example, Hendry and Clements (2004) and Timmerman (2006).
[31] *Tullis Russell Papermakers Limited v Inveresk Limited*, 2010 CSOH 148, 10 November 2010. We acted for the claimant in this case.

operations and thereby damaged the brand. Tullis sued for lost profits as disaffected customers switched to other suppliers. The claimant's expert used various methods to estimate the lost sales from the existing customer portfolio: a before-and-after comparison of sales using simple interpolation; several before-and-after comparisons using econometric analysis; and a difference-in-differences analysis, using a comparison with sales to an unaffected group of customers before and after the infringement. The judgment, which, perhaps as yet unusually in Europe, contains a lengthy discussion of the econometric analysis, agreed with the expert that pooling of the three main model results was appropriate to come to a final damages value: 'It is accepted economic practice to use more than one benchmark, in order to reflect more of the underlying data and to reduce the effect of biases in individual approaches.'[32]

9.61   In the end the court awarded £4,250,000 in damages in line with the pooling of the estimates made by the claimant's expert.

9.5 Comparator-based Approaches: Cross-sectional

9.5.1 Choice of comparator

9.62   Cross-section comparisons can be made between companies, product markets, geographic areas, or a combination. In *Conwood v US Tobacco*, a monopolization case in moist snuff (dipping tobacco) resulting in one of the highest antitrust damages ever awarded ($1.05 billion), the plaintiff's expert used comparator market shares from US states where no exclusionary practices had taken place, and from the market for loose-leaf tobacco, in which the defendant was not active.[33] The regression analysis showed that the plaintiff had a higher sales growth in these comparator markets. The ideal cross-sectional comparison includes data from the relevant market and from unaffected markets that are otherwise similar. If a regional infringement had the effect of increasing prices nationally, comparing data from two regional markets within the country would give a biased estimate of the damage since the comparator groups would be 'contaminated' by the infringement. In a case relating to a German paper wholesaling cartel, both the higher regional court and the German Federal Court of Justice felt unable to use cross-sectional comparisons between cartelized and other regional markets for paper wholesaling to estimate the overcharge because there was some evidence of cartels existing in other regional markets, which were therefore possibly affected by overcharges as well.[34]

9.63   The strength of a cross-sectional comparison lies in how like-for-like the comparison is and how many of the differentiating factors have been controlled for in the modelling. In a US case concerning a refusal to deal with a prospective purchaser of the Chicago Bulls basketball franchise by the Chicago stadium owner, the experts and court calculated the counterfactual fair market value of the Chicago Bulls franchise using recent sales prices of comparable National Basketball Association franchises.[35] A total of ten such transactions were considered by the court to be sufficiently comparable. Factors that were considered in

---

[32]   Ibid., at [183].
[33]   *Conwood Co v US Tobacco Co* 290 F 3d 768 (6th Cir. 2002).
[34]   *German Paper Wholesale Cartel* (German Federal Court of Justice, 19 June 2007).
[35]   *Fishman v Estate of Wirtz* 594 F. Supp. 853 (ND Ill. 1984); and 807 F 2d 520 (7th Cir. 1986).

the comparison between franchises included the size and population growth of the home city; the city's interest in basketball (e.g. its history of supporting teams, stadium attendance, and advertising support—all factors that the court said are difficult to quantify objectively and ultimately gave little weight); and whether the deal concerned an 'expansion' franchise (i.e. a new team, which is normally less valuable than an existing team). Likewise, in the *Conduit* case in Spain involving exclusionary practices by the telephony incumbent in relation to directory enquiries, the court accepted the UK market as a comparator for the claimant's lost market share in Spain, given the similarities between the two markets.[36] The market for directory inquiries had recently been liberalized and Conduit was one of the new entrants in both countries, but with greater success in the United Kingdom. The damage estimate itself was not accepted by the court.

9.5.2 Comparison of averages

Several estimation techniques can be employed to derive the counterfactual price using **9.64** cross-sectional comparators, ranging from the simple to the more sophisticated. A relatively simple comparison of averages uses the average price in an unaffected comparator group as an estimate for the counterfactual price. See Figure 9.7. The price in the cartelized market is €12, while the average price in comparator markets is €10. This indicates that the overcharge is €2 (or 16.7 per cent of the cartel price). The measure used to denote the 'average price' is usually the simple average or arithmetic mean (as the €10 here), but could also be the median or the modal price. The arithmetic mean is calculated by dividing the sum of all observations by the number of observations (€10 is the simple average of €10, €10.25, €9.50, €9.50, and €10.75). The median price is identified such that half of the companies in the comparator group charge a price below this median

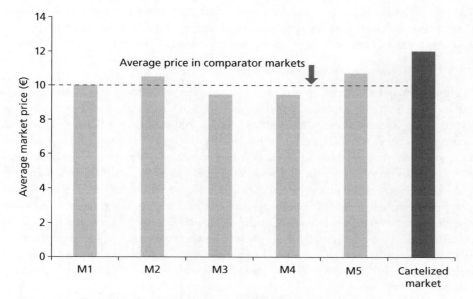

Figure 9.7 Example of a cross-sectional comparison of averages

---

[36] *Conduit Europe SA v Telefónica de España SAU* (Madrid Commercial Court, Judgment of 11 November 2005).

price and half charge above it (here the €10 in comparator market 1). The modal price is one that is observed most frequently in the comparator group (here €9.50 in markets 3 and 4). The choice among the three measures would depend on the nature of the market and the pricing pattern. If there are ten comparator markets, nine with a price of €10 and one with a price of €25, the modal or median price—both €10—might give a more accurate representation of the average price than the arithmetic mean of €11.50 which is influenced by the outlier (you may of course also conclude that this outlier is not such a good comparator market after all).

9.65 Whichever metric is used, the counterfactual price can then be compared with the actual price charged in the infringement market to calculate the overcharge. If there is sufficient data, a statistical test can be undertaken to check whether the counterfactual price is significantly different (in the statistical sense) from the actual price charged. We mentioned the *t*-test and the *p*-value earlier. Testing for statistical significance—and making the results of the tests transparent—is good practice in economics and statistics. It helps in understanding the precision of an estimate. A test for statistical significance accounts for the number and the variation of observations in the comparator group. The more observations you have, and the lower the variation, the more likely you are to obtain significant results.

9.66 What about Figure 9.7, where the actual price was €12 and the simple average of the comparator markets was €10? The variation in prices in the comparator group is relatively small—between €9.50 and €10.75—and quite different from the cartel price of €12, but you have only five comparators. The *p*-value for this comparison is 0.026, which is below the threshold of 0.05, and means that the actual difference lies within the 95 per cent confidence interval around the estimated difference. In practice, where both the comparator and cartel market observations are more varied, and some comparator prices even exceed the cartel market price, you would normally need a greater number of data points to obtain estimates that are statistically significant at standard thresholds.

9.5.3 Cross-section regression analysis

9.67 Regression analysis is a more sophisticated statistical method that can explain the variation in data using multiple factors (we explained the basics in Chapter 2). It addresses the main shortcomings of simple comparisons of averages by controlling for differences in market or company characteristics. Consider a situation in which you have prices for a number of companies (n), some of which are in the infringement market and some of which are outside it. A cross-section regression analysis will then be based on an equation such as $Pi = \alpha + \beta Xi + \delta Di + ei$. On the left-hand side of the equation is the variable to be explained, in this case price. Thus the variable Pi represents the price of company i (this i ranges from 1 to n as there are n companies in total). On the right-hand side are all the variables that can explain price. Xi includes characteristics of each company or its market, such as input costs, quality, or size—these are factors other than the infringement that may influence price, and hence should be controlled for. Di is the 'dummy' variable which is equal to one if company i belongs to the infringement market, and zero if the company belongs to a comparator market. This dummy variable is ultimately of main interest to the analysis as it gives you the estimate of the overcharge. The first term α is the intercept, and the last term ei is the error term (we explained these in Chapter 2; they are important for statistical purposes but not directly for inferring the overcharge).

The model can be estimated when sufficient data points are available for all the P and X variables. The D values are taken directly from what is known about the scope of the infringement market. The regression analysis seeks to identify the statistical relationship between these variables. The parameter of main interest in this regression is δ, which represents the average change in price attributable to the fact that a company belongs to the infringement market. In essence, this regression approach is similar to a simple comparison of average prices, but it isolates the part of the price difference that is related to the infringement rather than the other factors captured in the equation. Regression analysis, where it is feasible, generally leads to more robust results than simple price comparisons.

9.68

9.6 Comparator-based Approaches: Time Series

9.6.1 Choice of comparator period

Comparisons over time are probably the most commonly used approach to quantify damages. The approach is intuitive. In the *LePage's* monopolization case in the United States—which we also discussed in Chapter 4—the court found that the 'impact of 3M's discounts was apparent from the chart introduced by LePage's showing that LePage's earnings as a percentage of sales plummeted to below zero—to negative 10 per cent—during 3M's rebate program'.[37] In the three years before 3M introduced its bundled rebates, LePage's had a healthy operating income and significant growth in sales. After the introduction of the rebates, LePage's lost sales to key customers and saw its operating income turn into losses. The court was satisfied that there was substantial evidence that the anti-competitive effects of 3M's rebate programs caused LePage's losses. Another relatively simple comparison over time was made in a damages action before the Regional Civil Court of Graz following an earlier ruling by the Austrian Cartel Court against five driving schools.[38] The Cartel Court found that for a period of two months the schools had conspired to charge identical prices for the most popular driving courses, infringing the Austrian Cartel Act. The claim was brought by the Bundesarbeitskammer (the Federal Chamber of Workers) on behalf of customers of the driving schools. The Bundesarbeitskammer argued that the loss suffered by customers could be quantified as the 22 per cent difference between the price charged by the driving schools for the two months of the cartel's duration and the lower average price in the market after the cartel had ended. The court accepted this calculation.

9.69

Although the time-series comparison is often described generically as the 'before-and-after' approach, it is more accurate to make an explicit distinction between three variants: before and during; during and after; and before, during, and after. Ideally, time-series comparisons should be made using information from both the pre- and the post-infringement period so that more data is used. This allows 'anchoring' the predicted prices for the infringement period and increases the likelihood of robust findings. 'Before' and 'after' data each have advantages and disadvantages. Post-infringement data is more likely to be available because it is more recent. One potential problem with using post-infringement data, however, is that it may take some time for the cartel or anti-competitive behaviour to unwind fully or for the market to return to competitive pricing, so some of the earlier 'after' data may be contaminated. You may need

9.70

---

[37] *LePage's Inc. v 3M Co.*, 324 F 3d (3d Cir. 2003).
[38] *Bundesarbeitskammer v Powerdrive Fahrschule Andritz GmbH*, Landesgericht für Zivilrechtssachen Graz (Regional Civil Court of Graz), 17 August 2007.

data over a longer period and to test for different end points of the infringement. One of the advantages of pre-infringement data is that the market equilibrium that it represents is not normally contaminated by the existence of the infringement. However, it may sometimes be difficult to ascertain when the infringement actually began. A further disadvantage is that the pre-infringement period may be so long ago that good data is difficult to obtain.

9.71 Time-series analysis has the advantage over cross-sections that the comparison involves the same companies and markets within and outside the infringement period. You still have to control for other factors that could result in differences in the market over time. Time-series regression analysis allows for this, and the same approach as described above can be used. Instead of looking at variations across *n* different companies, you analyse variations across *n* different time periods. The statistical techniques may be different, because data over time often displays characteristics not seen in cross-sectional data. There may be a seasonal trend or serial dependence (autocorrelation) in time-series data, which means that a high value now (at time = *t*) is associated with a high value tomorrow (*t* + 1). This is a potential statistical problem as the different observations over time may not be independent. More advanced time-series econometrics can control for trends and serial dependence.

9.6.2 Simple time-series techniques: Averages and interpolation

9.72 Comparisons of averages over time are similar to those described under cross-sectional comparisons. The average price in the market concerned during the infringement period is compared with the period before or after. As previously, a statistical test (e.g. a *t*-test) can be conducted to determine whether the difference is statistically significant.

9.73 Interpolation involves joining the price points before and after the relevant period to indicate what the prices would have been in the intervening period (we called this 'anchoring' earlier). In its simplest form the connecting line will be straight, as in the example in Figure 9.8.

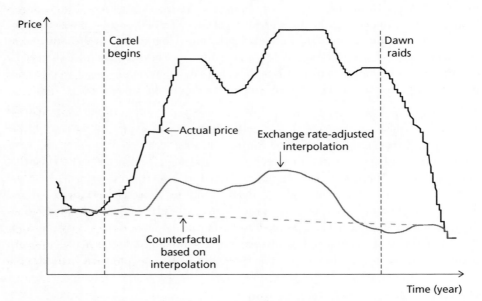

Figure 9.8 Interpolation to determine the counterfactual (prices before, during, and after the cartel)

This is loosely based on a cartel damages case we have worked on. The top line shows the development of actual prices paid by the claimant. The starting point of the cartel is the date when, according to the European Commission's infringement decision, the first meeting between cartel members was held. The starting price for the interpolation is based on an average actual price in the months before this start date. The end price is an average actual price in the months after the Commission's dawn raids took place and the cartel broke down. You can see that the actual price plummets at about that time. The dashed line between these points shows the counterfactual price according to the interpolation exercise. More sophisticated versions of interpolation can incorporate seasonal patterns if that is a feature of the market. Figure 9.8 incorporates a different adjustment, namely one for exchange rate movements, since in this case the cartel fixed prices in one European currency and the claim related to prices in another currency which had devalued during the cartel period. This results in a new counterfactual line, as shown in the figure. It can be seen that the price increase due to the exchange rate movement explains a small part of the spike in prices during the cartel period, but there is still a significant overcharge effect.

9.6.3 More sophisticated time-series techniques: ARIMA, dummy regression, and forecasting

Time-series models can be univariate ('pure') or multivariate. A univariate time-series model does not attempt to formulate a behavioural relationship between the variable under consideration (e.g. price) and other potential explanatory variables (e.g. costs). Instead, the historical pattern of the relevant variable itself is used as a predictor of its own future values. A multivariate time-series model, on the other hand, includes other explanatory variables and assesses the relationship between them to predict the relevant variable. **9.74**

ARIMA (autoregressive integrated moving average) is a widely used pure time-series technique. Rather than simple interpolation it uses the pattern of past values of the variable under investigation to forecast its future values. Figure 9.9 illustrates this technique with an example based on an exclusionary conduct case we have worked on. Historical sales volumes of the claimant (a competitor to the infringing party) are modelled using ARIMA. The results of this are then used to forecast volumes during the period of the infringement— October 2009 to October 2013 in this example. The forecasts act as estimates of the counterfactual volumes, which can then be compared with actual volumes to estimate the harm resulting from the infringement (the lost volumes must be multiplied by the relevant profit margin per unit to determine the lost profit). If the comparison is between a period during the infringement and a period after, the process can be reversed such that the model backcasts (as opposed to forecasts) to the start of the infringement. In this example, the ARIMA modelling was on past data, but the figure also shows what happened after the infringement, which served as a cross-check of the results. **9.75**

Time-series regression analysis uses the same basic equation as cross-section regression analysis: $Pt = \alpha + \beta Xt + \delta Dt + et$. Again this model specification seeks to explain prices P through a range of explanatory factors X, and a dummy variable D representing the infringement period. But can you spot the difference with the cross-section equation we saw earlier? The subscript to the variables is now t, representing different time periods, rather than i, representing different firms or markets (there are n time periods, so t ranges from 1 to n). Time-series regression controls for changes in the other explanatory variables X over time (such as changes in input costs). The dummy variable takes the value of one during **9.76**

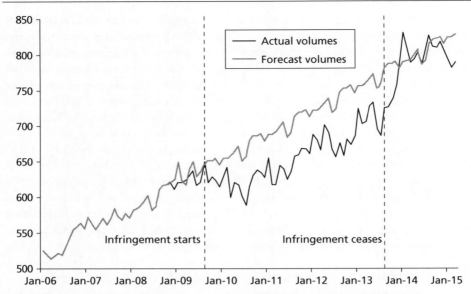

Figure 9.9 Example of forecasting using an ARIMA model (sales volumes of a competitor before, during, and after an exclusionary abuse)

Source: Oxera et al. (2009).

the infringement period and zero in outside periods. In static time-series regression the price P in period t is assumed to be explained by the other factors X in that same period t. In dynamic time-series regression the price in period t can also be explained by the price (and hence other factors) in previous periods ($t-1$, $t-2$, etc.). Dynamic modelling is appropriate if there is sufficient data and there are reasons to believe that inter-temporal effects play an important role in the market in question (e.g. if prices are negotiated with the previous year's price as a starting point).

9.77   There is sometimes heated debate among economists about the best way of doing time-series econometrics. The dummy-variable approach as described above is commonly used. The main alternative option is the forecasting approach, whereby you estimate the relationship between price and other factors for the period before or after the cartel only, but not during the cartel. Once estimated, you use the parameters to forecast or backcast what would have happened during the cartel.[39] Proponents of the forecasting approach would argue that it is difficult to infer any meaningful estimates from the cartel period itself since the relationship between price and other factors may be distorted by the cartel. Only outside the cartel period do you observe how price is determined in the 'normal' course of business. For example, the cartel may have influenced costs as well as prices, so that costs during the cartel are not a good independent variable to explain price. Say the cartel lasted from 2006 to 2012 and you have data on prices, costs and other market characteristics from 2006 to 2014. Under the forecasting approach you estimate a model using the data for 2013 and 2014, establishing the relationship between price, costs and the other factors. With this

---

[39] Note that simple interpolation and ARIMA discussed above are also forms of forecasting (or backcasting), as they determine the counterfactual based on data from outside the infringement period, not during it.

model you then predict what price would have been in the 2006–12 period. A drawback of the forecasting approach is that the 2013–14 period may not represent the earlier cartel years very well if the market has changed significantly over time. Another disadvantage is that the after period may be too short to allow for a robust regression (monthly data for the two years may be adequate, but with quarterly or annual data two years would not be a sufficiently long period). Instead, the dummy-variable approach uses the data for the whole period. You can see that both approaches have advantages and disadvantages. Good practice would be to try both and assess which one fits the data best.

9.6.4 Time-series analysis to calculate the value of commerce

Determining how much the claimant has purchased from the cartel in the relevant period is the first step in quantifying damages. This value of commerce is normally a matter of fact: a claimant should be able to prove its purchases with invoices or purchase records on a database. Yet in practice this not always so straightforward. In our experience even the most sophisticated multinational companies do not always have a good record of their purchases of particular products, especially if the cartel was operating many years ago. For legal or tax purposes companies have to retain commercial data for a particular minimum period—this varies across jurisdictions, and is usually between five and ten years—but beyond that the records tend to become patchy. This is where economics can help on value of commerce. Gaps in data may be 'plugged' using simple interpolation, or even sophisticated time-series regression analysis. Sometimes there are sensible rules of thumb that can be applied. For example, in a damages claim against a car glass cartel, if a car manufacturer has incomplete records of the amount of car glass it has purchased but good records of the number of vehicles it has produced, a simple rule of thumb is that the manufacturer will have purchased at least one windscreen per car produced. **9.78**

A US court accepted this approach in the LCD (liquid crystal display) cartel damages case.[40] **9.79** One of the claimants, mobile phone handset manufacturer Nokia, did not have full records of its LCD purchases. Its economic expert calculated the purchases based on the number of mobile devices that Nokia had sold over the relevant period. Approximately $11.6 million of the $52.3 million in claimed damages was based on these 'inferred invoices'. The court agreed with the manner in which the expert had identified that Nokia's purchase records were incomplete, and had subsequently derived the value of LCD purchases from data on mobile device shipments:

> [The expert's] finding that Nokia's available LCD purchase data for years 2001 to 2004 is incomplete and her corresponding estimate of these purchases based, in part, on Nokia's SEC reports, is grounded in facts... From her review of the LCD invoice data contained in Nokia's R3 database, [the expert] noted that LCD purchases were 'very low in the earlier years of the conspiracy compared with the later years: purchases were fewer than 50 million units in 2001, and grew to over 300 million units in 2007.'... Finding this level of growth 'questionable', [the expert] 'used other sources of data to check whether the Nokia invoice dataset reflected all of Nokia's LCD purchases', including Nokia's 'mobile device shipment data' contained in its SEC Reports... 'Relying on the fact that Nokia must purchase at least

---

[40] *In RE: TFT-LCD (Flat panel) antitrust litigation, Nokia Corporation and Nokia Inc v AU Optronics Corporation et al*, Case No. C 09-5609 SI, Order granting in part defendants' joint motion for partial summary judgment as to (1) claims based on inferred invoices; and (2) state law claims (ND Cal, 2012). We acted as experts for the claimants in this case.

one LCD to produce a mobile device', [the expert] compared the LCD invoice data and the shipment data. Based on this comparison, she concluded that 'the invoice dataset does not contain all records of all LCD purchases.'... [The expert] used the SEC reports to calculate the number of mobile phone handsets Nokia shipped for certain years, and then inferred the number of LCDs purchased by Nokia.

9.7 Comparator-based Approaches: Difference-in-Differences

9.80 Difference-in-differences analysis combines the cross-section and time-series approaches. It requires data both over time and across infringement and non-infringement markets, often referred to as a panel. The estimation techniques for panel data are similar to those often used for evaluating clinical trials and the effect of policy choices, in that one group has a 'treatment' applied to it (the infringement) while another that is not treated is used as a control group.[41] The difference-in-differences analysis compares what happens to each group before, during and after the treatment. By using the control group, the analysis removes the impact of any changes that affect both treatment and control groups.

9.81 Figure 9.10 illustrates the difference-in-differences approach. It uses the average price in the treatment group (i.e. the infringement market) in the period during the infringement (A), and the corresponding averages for B (infringement market after the infringement), C (non-infringement market during), and D (non-infringement market after). The difference (A – B) reflects the change in prices in the market concerned during and after the infringement, while (C – D) reflects the change in the comparator market. Not all of the difference (A – B) is due to the infringement. There are other factors with an effect on price, and these can be inferred from the change in price in the comparator market, so (C – D). The difference in the differences in the average prices, that is, (A – B) – (C – D), is therefore used to identify separately the change in prices in the relevant market that is due to the infringement. Say A = €10, B = €7, C = €8, and D = €6. In the cartel market the average price fell from €10 to €7 after the cartel. However, not all of the €3 difference can be ascribed to the

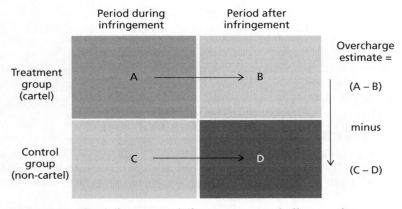

Figure 9.10 The difference-in-differences approach illustrated

---

[41] See, for example, Krum et al. (1994), and Card and Krueger (1994).

cartel, as there may be other factors resulting in lower prices, such as technological improvements or lower input costs. This can be seen from the comparator market, where average prices fell by €2 (from €8 to €6) over the same period. Only the difference between the two differences—€1—can be attributed to the cartel, so the overcharge is 10 per cent.

Conceptually, the difference-in-differences technique is an improvement on pure cross-sectional and time-series models since it exploits the variations over time as well as across firms. This increased variability helps in the estimation of the effect of the infringement, and can also account for certain factors that might affect prices in the two markets. The data requirement for a difference-in-differences panel data regression is normally greater than that for cross-sectional or time-series regression, for the simple reason that you need data both across markets and over time. **9.82**

9.8 Approaches Based on Financial Analysis

9.8.1 The role of financial analysis in determining the counterfactual

The tools for financial and profitability analysis that we discussed in Chapter 3 can also be used for damages estimations. In damages cases there is not always a clear-cut distinction between finance and non-finance methods, since a form of financial analysis is often involved at some stage. Some of the financial-analysis-based approaches can be seen as one form of application of comparator-based approaches, as counterfactual values are also often derived from comparator markets or time periods: for example, margins or profits during and after the infringement. Financial methods can also be used to construct counterfactual prices or profits by assessing information on the cost of production, cost of capital, and profit margins of the relevant market participants. This latter application of financial methods is different from the methods discussed thus far as it does not use comparators, but rather builds up the counterfactual using a combination of theory, assumptions, and empirical information. The market-structure-based approaches discussed in section 9.9 share this methodological feature. **9.83**

Financial analysis can be used in several ways. First, the deterioration in the financial performance of claimants as a result of the infringement can provide an estimate of the harm caused to them. Second, the improvement in the financial performance of the defendant as a result of the infringement can provide an estimate of the benefits derived from the infringement. From a legal perspective, this is not a direct basis for determining compensatory damages, but in certain circumstances it may be used to inform the valuation of the damage suffered by the victims of the infringement (e.g. in cartel cases). Various techniques can be used for both types of analysis of financial performance—in particular, profitability analysis and valuation. A relevant benchmark would need to be identified as well, reflecting the profitability in the counterfactual. Finally, the counterfactual price level can be estimated by assessing the infringing parties' production costs, and adding a return that reflects the degree of competition in the counterfactual. **9.84**

9.8.2 Financial performance of claimants

The damage incurred as a result of the infringement should ultimately be reflected in the financial performance of the claimant. Hence, a comparison of the claimant's actual financial performance with the financial performance that would be expected in the absence **9.85** of the infringement can be used to provide an estimate of the damage. Financial performance is usually measured in terms of either profitability or company valuation. Valuation is closely related to profitability, since valuations of assets are usually based on the expected profits that can be achieved with those assets.

9.86　One example is the (partly successful) damages action before the Versailles Court of Appeal in France, where an excluded competitor claimed damages for lost profit based on its financial performance.[42] This followed on from an earlier decision by the French Competition Council, which found that the defendants together had deliberately delayed the communication of information that was necessary for the claimant to operate in the market for media services. Since this information could not be obtained from any other source, the Competition Council concluded that the defendants' conduct contributed to raising barriers to entry, thus constituting a breach of the French equivalent of Article 101. The claimant sought damages as a result of loss of clientele (€828,103), and damages resulting from the difference between its business plan and its actual financial results (€2,027,571). The court considered that while the claimant was entitled to recover damages as a result of its loss of clientele, the quantum of those damages should be reduced due to the claimant's lack of experience in the business area in which it was starting up. The court therefore awarded only €100,000 to compensate for the lost opportunity to penetrate the market more quickly (it provided no explanation as to how it arrived at this figure). Moreover, it rejected the claim for damages resulting from the difference between the business plan and actual financial results, considering that since loss of clientele and loss of expected profits are one and the same category of harm, they can be compensated only once.

9.87　Another example is the exclusionary conduct case before the Court of Appeal of Milan, where the Italian competition authority had concluded that Telecom Italia abused its dominant position by preventing the claimant from entering the market for services for closed user groups.[43] The claimant wished to provide a service that would have linked the telephone exchanges between its customers' offices using a network infrastructure exclusively composed of switching nodes and dedicated lines leased from the defendant. The claimant was to pay Telecom Italia a fixed charge for the lease of dedicated local and trunk lines. However, it was found that Telecom Italia refused to lease the lines required to link the offices of the claimant's customers, thus abusing its dominant position. A group of court-appointed experts calculated the claimant's actual losses on the basis of documented costs that it had incurred. In relation to lost profits, the experts took into account a business plan drawn up by the claimant, but considered the projected figures relating to the acquisition of new customers to be too high. Moreover, they considered that the claimant's future expansion would have been limited by the fact that it had not made sufficient investments in publicity and other promotional activities, that it lacked sales staff, and that it had experienced significant delays between the signing of new contracts and the activation of the service. Similarly, as regards loss of opportunity, the experts doubted the claimant's argument that it would have had significant first-mover advantages, because there were no major barriers to entry into that market and it would have been difficult for the claimant to maintain customer loyalty once established.

---

[42] *SA Verimedia v SA Mediametrie, SA Secodip, GIE Audipub*, Cour d'Appel de Versailles, 12ème chambre, section 2, arrêt no 319, 24 June 2004.
[43] *Telystem SpA v SIP SpA* (now Telecom Italia SpA) (Milan Court of Appeal, December 1996).

This last case shows how courts tend to treat with caution counterfactuals based on business plan analysis, a theme we saw before in the discussion of lost profits. Business plans can suffer from optimism bias. You can get situations where several competitors are excluded by a dominant rival, with each claiming that it would have achieved a certain market share in the counterfactual, but with those lost market shares adding up to more than 100 per cent. However, with some careful scrutiny of the parameters and assumptions used, and a cross-check against actual market indicators, contemporaneous business plans can still give you a good indication of what was expected to happen in the absence of the infringement.

9.88

9.8.3 Financial performance of defendants

In some cases compensatory damages can also be inferred from the financial performance of the defendant. For example, a cartel overcharge means that a particular cash flow is transferred from the buyer (claimant) to the seller (defendant). Therefore, the financial performance of the seller would be expected to be better than in the absence of the overcharge. The value of the cash flows that are transferred to the defendant may provide an estimate of the overcharge paid by the claimant. In the case of exclusionary abuses, the financial performance of the defendant can be used as a proxy for the value of the business opportunity from which a claimant was excluded. Consider the Chicago Bulls franchise case referred to earlier.[44] The defendant prevented the claimant from acquiring an asset by refusing to enter into a contract for the provision of supplementary services. Fishman and Illinois Basketball Inc. (the unsuccessful bidders for the franchise) brought an action against the Chicago Professional Sports Corporation (the successful bidder), its shareholders, William Wirtz (the owner of the Chicago stadium), and others for refusing to contract with Illinois Basketball for the lease of the stadium and hence foreclosing competition in the market for the franchise. In this case, the actual financial performance of the defendant was considered in the damages quantification. The value of the damage to the claimant was calculated as the value of cash flows from the Chicago Bulls franchise generated by the winning bidder, effectively assuming that the claimant would have obtained this same value but for the infringement.

9.89

Another example is the Danish Supreme Court exclusion case in the ferry sector where the financial performance of the defendant was considered in the determination of the harm caused to the claimant, a competitor.[45] De Danske Statsbaner (DSB) is the state-owned train operator which owned Gedser Harbour and operated ferry transport services to Germany. As the owner of the port, DSB collected port fees from another ferry operator, GT Linien, for operating a service there. However, it did not collect fees for the use of the port by its own vessels since these were exempt from this duty under Danish law. On appeal, the Danish Supreme Court upheld an earlier Eastern High Court judgment which found that DSB had abused its dominant position in the market for ferry transport between Denmark and Germany by collecting port fees from GT Linien without charging such fees to its own vessels, and that GT Linien was entitled to recover damages. In quantifying the damages, the Supreme Court based its estimate in part on reconstructed accounts of Gedser Harbour prepared on the claimant's behalf, since the defendant was an integrated

9.90

---

[44] *Fishman v Estate of Wirtz* 594 F. Supp. 853 (ND Ill. 1984); and 807 F 2d 520 (7th Cir. 1986).
[45] *GT Linien A/S (under bankruptcy—subsequently GT Link A/S) v De Danske Statsbaner DSB and Scandlines A/Sn (formerly DSB Rederi A/S)* UFR 2005.2171H (Danish Supreme Court).

port authority and did not produce separate accounts. While the claimant argued that it should be entitled to recover DKK25 million (around €3.3 million), the court, after detailed consideration of the financial evidence, agreed with the defendant that the reconstructed accounts did not sufficiently take into account depreciations, reserves set aside for investments by the port, and interest on its invested capital. The court therefore awarded the claimant only DKK10 million (€1.3 million) in damages, but this was still based on the analysis of the financial performance of the defendant.

9.91   Financial data on the defendants can serve as a useful cross-check of damages estimates. For example, if a time-series comparator analysis produces a 25 per cent cartel overcharge, but the management accounts of the cartel members show profit margins on the product concerned of only 5–10 per cent in the same period, something may be missing from the analysis. A closer look is required. It may be that the time-series analysis has overstated the overcharge, or that the margin data does not capture all the effects of the cartel (e.g. the cartel may have resulted in higher costs as well as prices).

9.8.4 Bottom-up costing analysis to estimate the counterfactual price

9.92   This technique involves estimating the counterfactual price on the basis of bottom-up analysis of the costs and returns of the claimant or defendant. It typically involves determining unit costs of the product and adding a mark-up, expressed as a cash margin or a percentage profit margin on the costs. The resulting counterfactual price is compared with the actual price to obtain the per-unit value of the overcharge by the defendant or loss of revenue by the claimant. A 2008 exclusionary conduct case before the Düsseldorf Higher Regional Court provides an example of this approach.[46] This stand-alone damages claim was brought against a state-owned local utility company by a direct competitor, in relation to a competitive bid for the supply of gas to a particular client. Despite having offered the lowest price, the claimant lost the bid because the utility had threatened the client with an increase in its district heating price if it were to source gas or electricity from other suppliers. The court considered the defendant's conduct to be an abuse of a dominant position in the district heating market. It awarded damages corresponding to the claimant's lost profits in relation to this particular contract, amounting to around 5 per cent of supply costs. This figure was determined through a bottom-up analysis, using detailed information that the claimant had provided on its own supply costs. The court considered that the claimant had proved that at the relevant time it would actually have been able to supply the contracted amount of gas, and that under normal circumstances it would have expected to earn a 5 per cent profit margin over and above supply costs.

9.93   Another example of the bottom-up costing approach is the *Albion Water* case discussed earlier, which involved an excessive wholesale access charge and corresponding margin squeeze.[47] To determine the access fee that Dŵr Cymru would have charged in the counterfactual, the CAT took an average of three different measures of the company's costs, resulting in a figure of 14.4 p/m^3. It also determined that, in line with commercial and regulatory principles applied in the water sector, this access charge would have been increased year on year in accordance with the retail price index. The CAT then assessed whether Albion

---

[46] OLG Düsseldorf, Urteil vom 16.4.2008 VI-2 U(Kart) 8/06—*Stadtwerk* (Higher Regional Court of Düsseldorf).

[47] *Albion Water Limited v Dŵr Cymru Cyfyngedig*, [2013] CAT 6, 28 March.

Water would actually have accepted an access fee of 14.4 p/m^3 in a commercial negotiation in the counterfactual. After all, the company's initial claim was that a charge of only 7 p/m^3 would have been justified. In light of the factual evidence, the CAT considered that Albion Water's approach to negotiations was not based on 'die-in-ditch principles but on pragmatic business sense', and that it would have agreed to 14.4 p/m^3 even if this was above what it thought was justifiable.[48]

9.9 Approaches Based on Market Structure and Industrial Organization Theory

9.9.1 What are market-structure-based approaches?

IO models can be used to simulate market outcomes—particularly prices and volumes—in the counterfactual scenario. As you have seen in various places in this book, IO theory has developed a range of models of competitive interaction that predict a variety of market outcomes, from the least competitive (monopoly) to the most competitive (perfect competition). As with some of the financial-analysis-based approaches discussed above, market-structure-based approaches to quantifying damages differ from comparator analysis in that they build up the counterfactual based on a combination of theoretical models, assumptions, and empirical estimation, rather than comparisons across markets or over time. **9.94**

The choice of model is important, given that the outcomes can vary significantly depending on the assumptions adopted. For any given factual situation where a cartel or other infringement has led to an increase in price, the more intense the competition is assumed to be in the counterfactual, the higher is the estimated damage from the infringement (as the counterfactual price is lower when competition is fiercer). In *Concord Boat Corporation v Brunswick Corporation*, a US case, the expert on the plaintiff's side applied the Cournot model to determine the counterfactual.[49] Under the standard Cournot model with two identical firms in the market, the model predicts that each firm will have a 50 per cent market share. The expert used this as the counterfactual and calculated damages for all periods when the defendant possessed more than 50 per cent market share. This particular use of the Cournot model was criticized by the court on the basis that it did not take into account differences between the quality of the two suppliers' products, or external shocks, that could have led to the defendant possessing a market share of more than 50 per cent even in the counterfactual. **9.95**

9.9.2 How close is the cartel outcome to monopoly, and how competitive is the counterfactual?

In cartel cases, the actual market outcome might resemble that of a monopoly. Cartel members co-ordinate output and prices to try to maximize joint profits. The best they can achieve is the monopoly profit. Yet there are several reasons why joint profit maximization by a cartel may not succeed. As we saw in Chapters 5 and 7, cheating, monitoring problems, and external demand and supply conditions may hinder effective co-ordination. Hardcore **9.96**

---

[48] Ibid., at [77–8].
[49] *Concord Boat Corporation v Brunswick Corporation* 207 F 3d 1039 (8th Cir. 2000), 24 March 2000.

cartels may still achieve an overcharge, but the assumption that this actual cartel outcome is equivalent to a monopoly generally holds only in an upper-bound scenario.

9.97 What can be inferred from actual prices observed in periods of cartel breakdown? Are prices seen during the periodic price wars that occur in some cartels close to the counterfactual competitive outcome? The answers to these questions are not clear-cut. An important finding in economic theory is that periodic bouts of deviation and punishment, taking the form of sharp falls in prices, can be expected even in well-functioning cartels (Green and Porter, 1984). These temporary price wars give an indication of how low competitors in the market are prepared to go. However, such prices may not necessarily be sustainable in a competitive situation in the absence of the cartel.

9.98 Questions of this type were addressed in the paper wholesale cartel case before the German Federal Court of Justice in 2007.[50] This judgment did not concern the quantification of damages, but of the overcharge by the cartel in the original investigation (German competition law at the time required fines to be based on estimates of actual overcharges). Following a finding of illegal price agreements in 2004, the wholesalers involved in the cartel were fined €57.6 million by the German competition authority. The cartel spanned ten regions in Germany from 1995 to 2000, and charged higher prices to smaller customers. The Federal Court of Justice disagreed with the method used by a lower court to estimate the overcharge in this case, which consisted of comparing the cartel price with the price charged by suppliers who were attempting to undercut the cartel price. The court found that such price cuts could not serve as a reference for the competitive market price since they were still dependent on the cartel price. It concluded that the prices after the cuts were still likely to be higher than the competitive price, and therefore that this method would underestimate the overcharge. In the absence of comparable reference markets, the court was of the view that the counterfactual price for estimating the overcharge should be established by way of an overall economic analysis. The judgment suggested a bottom-up costing approach, whereby an average profit margin—informed by comparator markets—is added to costs.

9.9.3 Use of IO models to determine or cross-check the counterfactual

9.99 As discussed in Chapter 7, competition authorities use IO models in merger control to simulate post-merger outcomes. Using IO models in damages cases is like merger simulation in reverse: in damages cases the counterfactual has more competition than the factual, while for merger cases competition is reduced in the counterfactual. In practice, the degree to which the theoretical IO models are calibrated can vary (calibration in this context means assigning values to the key parameters of the model so that it fits the actual data). At one extreme, little actual data is used and the analysis relies largely on assumptions regarding the main parameters of the theoretical model to simulate market outcomes. At the other extreme, all the main parameters of the theoretical model are estimated using actual data (e.g. estimates of the demand function and profit margins). The optimal approach will depend on data availability, and this in turn determines the weight you can place on the analysis.

9.100 Even where data availability is limited, IO models can still provide the basis for a cross-check of results from other quantification methods. If there is evidence to suggest that

---

[50] *German Paper Wholesale Cartel* (German Federal Court of Justice, 19 June 2007).

the counterfactual market structure has the characteristics of perfect competition or Bertrand oligopoly with homogeneous goods, the theory suggests that the cartel over-charge can be expected to be as high as the cartel members' price–cost margin (since in competitive markets firms would set prices close to cost). If the counterfactual market structure is more like standard Cournot oligopoly, the overcharge can be approximated by reference to the cartel members' price–cost margin and the number of firms in the market. Take the example of a cartelized four-firm market. The factual situation might be approximated through a monopoly model while the counterfactual is akin to Cournot oligopoly. A comparison of price outcomes under the two IO models enables a rough approximation of the possible overcharge (referred to as two-model estimation in Figure 9.6). If the cartel price–cost margin was 20 per cent, the cartel overcharge would theoretically have been 12 per cent. If the cartel margin was 40 per cent, the overcharge would theoretically have been 24 per cent. These results are derived from a formula for the cartel overcharge where the factual is monopoly and the counterfactual an n-firm Cournot oligopoly—the formula is m times $(n-1)$ divided by $(n+1)$, where m is the cartel margin (this formula assumes linear demand and symmetric, constant marginal costs). So with four firms, n is 4, and with a margin of 20 per cent, the result is 0.2 times $(4-1=3)$ divided by $(4+1=5)$, which equals 0.12 or 12 per cent. According to this formula, the overcharge increases as the number of firms in the counterfactual increases (because more firms implies a more competitive counterfactual), and as the cartel profit margin increases (because there is more profit margin to be 'competed away' in the absence of the cartel). These results are based on a comparison with a factual characterized as a monopoly. As noted above, cartels may not be as effective at raising prices as a monopoly. If this is the case, the above formula will tend to overesti-mate the overcharge, but can still be used as an upper bound when cross-checking the results from other approaches.

9.9.4 Example of a market-structure-based approach to estimate lost profits: Bus fights in Cardiff

In 2012, the CAT awarded £33,818.79 in lost profits to 2 Travel based on a relatively straightforward market structure model (a case we also discussed in section 9.3).[51] 2 Travel had been the victim of predatory conduct by Cardiff Bus, the incumbent bus operator owned by the local government. Its original claim had been for £50 million of lost profit. In April 2004, 2 Travel began a no-frills bus service on four routes in Cardiff, with a fifth route planned to begin operating at a later date. These were in-fill ser-vices: commercial bus services operating in between the tendered morning and afternoon school services that had been awarded to 2 Travel, and for which it could use the same vehicles. In response, Cardiff Bus introduced its own no-frills bus service (the 'white ser-vices') on the same five routes. This was in addition to its existing, 'liveried', bus services, which already operated in Cardiff on routes partly overlapping those of the new entrant. 2 Travel ceased operations in December 2004 and Cardiff Bus closed down its white ser-vices shortly thereafter. 2 Travel, which also had several operations outside Cardiff, went into liquidation in May 2005. In 2008, the OFT determined that the launch of the white services was an abuse of dominance.

9.101

---

[51] *2 Travel Group Plc (in Liquidation) v Cardiff City Transport Services Limited*, [2012] CAT 19, 5 July 2012. We acted as experts for the defendant in this case.

9.102   In 2011, 2 Travel claimed £50 million in lost profit under a number of different heads of damage. The largest of these heads—various lost commercial opportunities—were dismissed as too speculative and out of line with the factual evidence. In essence, 2 Travel claimed that, had it succeeded in establishing a foothold in Cardiff, it would have grown not only in Cardiff but in other areas as well. The idea was that Cardiff Bus's actions caused it to go bankrupt before any of this commercial success could be realized. However, the factual evidence showed that even before entering the Cardiff market, 2 Travel had been a 'poorly run and administered [business] in almost constant financial difficulty'.[52] Internal communications by the company's finance director recommended going into liquidation rather than enter the Cardiff market. The CAT also found that the (limited) lost revenue resulting from the infringement would not have been enough to prevent insolvency. In the end, the only lost profit claim upheld by the CAT was that for the four routes that 2 Travel actually operated in Cardiff between April and December 2004.[53]

9.103   The OFT determined that Cardiff Bus had launched the entire white services operation for the sole purpose of driving 2 Travel out of the market. As such, the experts for both sides, and the CAT, agreed that the relevant counterfactual was one in which Cardiff Bus did not operate its white services at all. The experts and the CAT agreed that, in the counter-factual, the passengers who actually travelled on the white services would have used either 2 Travel's services or Cardiff Bus's liveried services. It was also common ground between the parties that the overall number of passengers would not have grown following entry. Since Cardiff Bus's liveried services on the same routes were operating in both the factual and the counterfactual scenarios, it was agreed that none of the actual passengers on these services would have transferred to 2 Travel. Therefore, the maximum number of additional passengers (i.e. in addition to those who already travelled on 2 Travel) that 2 Travel could possibly have attracted were the 150,727 passengers who travelled on the white services over the relevant period.

9.104   The overall approaches to determining how many of these passengers would have travelled with 2 Travel, and the revenue that would have been generated, were similar among both experts and the CAT. However, their analyses differed on some key assumptions. The expert for Cardiff Bus developed a market-structure-based model of 2 Travel's operations on the relevant bus routes that incorporated a range of facts and assumptions about the main parameters, including the number of services that 2 Travel actually ran from April to December 2004; the number and types of additional passengers that 2 Travel would have gained; and the costs that 2 Travel would have incurred. To determine counterfac-tual market shares, the expert for Cardiff Bus assumed that passengers get on the first bus that comes along. This is based on a common finding in the bus market. Passengers are more time-sensitive than price-sensitive, especially for frequent services such as those on the four routes in question (for infrequent services—running only once or twice per

---

[52] Ibid., at [223].

[53] The CAT also awarded £60,000 in exemplary damages, which is relatively rare. It emerged that Cardiff Bus had received legal advice at the time that its actions might be seen as anti-competitive, but knowingly disregarded this risk. The way the £60,000 was determined is not specified in the judgment, but it appears to be proportionate to the lost profit award.

hour—passengers are more inclined to check the timetable before turning up at the bus stop). The passenger allocation between the two operators was thus approximated by considering the relative frequencies of their services. For example, if one operator runs six buses an hour on a particular section of the route, and another operator runs two buses an hour on that same section, it is assumed that the first operator would get 75 per cent of the passengers and the second 25 per cent. In the main scenarios, it was estimated that 2 Travel would have been able to achieve an average market share of 19 per cent across all sections of the four routes, since this was the share of frequencies relative to those of the Cardiff Bus liveried services on the same routes. This is a simple market structure approach to determine the counterfactual.

Once the counterfactual passenger numbers had been calculated, they were multiplied by 2 Travel's fares to estimate its counterfactual revenue. Using an approach similar to that employed by the expert for Cardiff Bus, the CAT allocated the actual number of white service passengers to 2 Travel based on frequency. It thus estimated that, in the counterfactual, 2 Travel would have attracted an additional 41,255 passengers between April and December 2004. At an average fare of just under £0.82 per passenger per journey, the CAT estimated the lost revenues to be £33,818.79. This estimate lies within the range that was provided by the expert for Cardiff Bus, and was an order of magnitude lower than the amount claimed by 2 Travel. **9.105**

Having reached a view as to what revenue 2 Travel lost as a result of the infringement, the additional costs that the bus operator would have incurred in order to generate that revenue needed to be considered to reach a figure for its lost profits. There was some disagreement about the treatment of incremental costs in the counterfactual analysis. 2 Travel argued that it could not operate its services in full because of a driver shortage caused by Cardiff Bus's conduct. The expert for Cardiff Bus considered that if, in the counterfactual situation, 2 Travel had operated to its full registered timetable, it would have required extra drivers. These drivers would have constituted incremental costs compared with 2 Travel's costs in the actual situation. It follows logically that the additional driver costs should be deducted from the estimates of lost profit for the counterfactual scenarios in which 2 Travel operated more services than it actually did. 2 Travel and its expert had not taken such incremental costs into account. Ultimately, the issue of incremental costs was not directly addressed in the judgment, since the CAT rejected the counterfactual scenario with 2 Travel's additional services. However, the principle remains that if a claimant would have undertaken greater activity but for the infringement, and hence have achieved higher revenue, one has to deduct from this revenue the incremental costs associated with the greater activity (in line with the framework set out in section 9.3). **9.106**

9.10 Pass-on of Overcharges

9.10.1 The policy debate about the passing-on defence

There have been extensive policy debates about whether the passing-on defence should be permitted. This defence means that purchasers or competitors who have suffered harm in the form of higher costs are not entitled to damages if they have passed the higher costs on to their own customers in the form of higher prices. In the United States, pass-on has been ruled out as a defence by the federal courts, and typically only direct purchasers can claim **9.107** cartel damages (a number of US states do allow indirect purchasers to claim damages).[54] Economic incentives have played a role in this policy decision. The reasoning is that direct purchasers are best placed to file a claim, as they will generally have the best information available and may also be more likely to have the resources to make a claim (at least compared with end-consumers). Ruling out the passing-on defence gives direct purchasers better incentives to file claims.

9.108   In Europe, the general approach reflected in the 2014 Directive on antitrust damages actions (Articles 12 to 15) is that the passing-on defence should be allowed, and that direct and indirect purchasers can claim for damages. This is in line with the compensation principle: if direct purchasers have passed on an overcharge to their own customers (i.e. the indirect purchasers), the former should not be over-compensated, and nor should the latter be under-compensated. However, the EU policy to allow the passing-on defence and indirect purchaser claims does come with some further clauses. Article 12 of the Directive makes it clear that a claimant who has passed on an overcharge may still have suffered a loss of profit (this would be mainly in the form of lost sales volumes, as we saw in section 9.3). Article 14 establishes a rebuttable presumption that the overcharge has been fully passed on to the specific indirect purchaser who brings the claim—we return to this later. Article 15 seeks to ensure that claims made at different layers of the supply chain do not lead to multiple liability. This makes economic sense. Regardless of how many layers of the supply chain an overcharge is passed on to, and in what proportion, the sum of the overcharge harm claims from the various layers cannot exceed the level of the overcharge itself. In Figure 9.1 at the start of this chapter, area A is the total overcharge, so the total harm suffered across the various layers of the supply chain cannot exceed A. There should be no double-counting of harm (which in legal terms would result in a form of unjust enrichment by some parties in the chain). For example, if it is found that direct purchasers of the cartel have passed on 75 per cent of A, and their respective customers have passed on 90 per cent of their price increase to end-consumers, the direct purchasers have suffered a harm equal to 25 per cent of A, their customers a harm of 7.5 per cent of A (75 per cent of A but with 90 per cent of that passed on), and end-consumers 67.5 per cent (90 per cent of 75 per cent of A). By the same token, however, the total overcharge harm caused along the chain is still 100 per cent of area A, so if all parties in the different layers of the chain (including final consumers) found some way of making a joint claim and distributing the damages award among themselves, area A would be the right overcharge amount to claim for in that joint action.

9.10.2 Pass-on in theory: The relationship between prices and costs in economic models

9.109   In the standard economic models of competition, oligopoly and monopoly, there are defined relationships between price and marginal cost. These provide the basic theoretical understanding of how cost changes translate into price changes. In all these models, companies are assumed to maximize their profit given a certain level of marginal costs and the degree and nature of competition they face. The resulting equilibrium prices can be expressed as a function of marginal cost. For example, in perfect competition price equals marginal cost,

---

[54] *Illinois Brick Co v Illinois* 431 US 720 (1977); and *Hanover Shoe Inc v United Shoe Machinery Corp* 392 US 481 (1968).

so if the marginal cost to all suppliers increases due to a cartel overcharge on an input, the price will increase correspondingly.

Cost pass-on refers to the proportion of a cost change that is translated into a change in the final price. It is usually represented as a percentage pass-on rate: the change in price expressed as a percentage of the change in the marginal cost. If costs per unit increase by €10 and the price increases by €5, the pass-on rate is 50 per cent. This percentage pass-on rate is straightforward to interpret, and can be applied directly to the total overcharge. For example, if the overcharge is €3 million, and the percentage pass-on rate is 50 per cent, this means that €1.5 million of the overcharge has been passed on. **9.110**

9.10.3 Pass-on in competitive markets: Industry-wide versus firm-specific cost increases

A distinction must be made between firm-specific and industry-wide cost increases. In perfect competition, an overcharge that affects all competitors in a downstream market (i.e. is industry-wide) would be passed on in full. You may find this result counterintuitive, and so do some business people: 'my market is highly competitive, surely I cannot pass on any cost increase?' But it simply follows from the fact that, under perfect competition, prices equal marginal costs. All downstream firms that remain in the market therefore see no change in profit level.[55] **9.111**

In contrast, for a cost increase that affects only one, or some, of the competitors in those markets, the expected pass-on rate would be close to zero, since those competitors that do not face the increase can leave their prices unchanged. Those that do face the increase must absorb it to stay competitive or exit the market. This may also be the case if, for example, an entire industry is affected by the overcharge, but that industry competes with another industry that uses a different upstream input not subject to the overcharge. For example, if an upstream cartel operates only in Europe, and downstream companies compete with non-European producers which are unaffected by the cartel, the European downstream companies may face difficulties passing on the cartel input overcharge. A similar logic was applied by the Valladolid Provincial Court in Spain in a 2009 damages action brought by a biscuit producer against a sugar cartel.[56] Spanish sugar producers were found to have colluded to fix the prices of sugar for industrial use between February 1995 and September 1996. The court considered that biscuit producers in Spain were harmed because they compete in European markets with foreign biscuit producers which did not purchase their sugar in Spain. By implication the Spanish biscuit producers had to absorb the overcharge on sugar or else lose market share. In 2014 the Spanish Supreme Court applied the same reasoning in a parallel case against another member of the sugar cartel.[57] This claim was brought by a group of producers of biscuits, desserts and confectionary, including Nestlé, LU, and Wrigley. The Supreme Court noted that the Spanish confectionary industry exports a significant proportion of its production. The cartel overcharge on Spanish sugar **9.112**

---

[55] The cost increase could of course lead to a reduction in downstream output and the exit of a number of downstream suppliers. This may give rise to a lost profit claim separate from the overcharge claim. However, it is usually harder to prove such lost profits, especially for suppliers who are no longer in the market.

[56] Audiencia Provincial de Valladolid, Sentencia num. 261/2009, Judgment of 9 October 2009.

[57] Tribunal Supremo, STS 5819/2013, Judgment of 7 November 2014.

would therefore have affected the industry's competitiveness vis-à-vis foreign competitors and would have made pass-on difficult, with a negative effect on profit margins.

9.10.4 Pass-on in monopoly and other models of competition: An illustration

9.113 Another well-known theoretical finding is that a monopolist with linear demand and constant marginal cost passes on exactly 50 per cent of the cost increase. You may also find this result counterintuitive: why doesn't the monopolist pass on cost increases in full? The reason is not benevolence but self-interested profit maximization—if costs change, so does the profit-maximizing price (we explained this in Chapter 2). Figure 9.11 illustrates this logic. It shows the demand and marginal cost curves in the downstream market, where marginal cost includes the cartelized input. Marginal cost per unit equals 2. If the downstream market were perfectly competitive, the price would be 2 and output 8. If it were a monopoly, the price would be 6 and output 4. Now the upstream cartel causes the industry-wide marginal costs to increase from 2 to 4 (in reality a 100 per cent overcharge would be highly unlikely, but this is a stylized example). You can see that in perfect competition, the new price is 4 and output 6. So the cost increase resulting from the cartel is fully passed on—hence there is no overcharge harm to downstream manufacturers that have purchased from the cartel (as noted before, the downstream output decrease from 8 to 6 constitutes a different type of harm—a volume loss—but this is generally more difficult to claim in practice). In monopoly, marginal costs now equal marginal revenue where output is 3. The new price is 7. So the cost increase of 2 units has resulted in a 1-unit price increase, from 6 to 7—that is, a 50 per cent pass-on.

9.114 In oligopolistic markets you typically get results that are in between perfect competition and monopoly. In the standard Cournot oligopoly model (with constant marginal cost and linear demand), the pass-on rate for an industry-wide cost change can be expressed as n divided by $(n + 1)$, where n is the number of firms (ten Kate and Niels, 2005). Therefore, for two firms the pass-on rate is two-thirds, while for seven firms it would be seven-eighths. The pass-on rate increases with the number of firms, which is consistent with the 50–100 per cent range between monopoly and perfect competition, as identified above. The standard

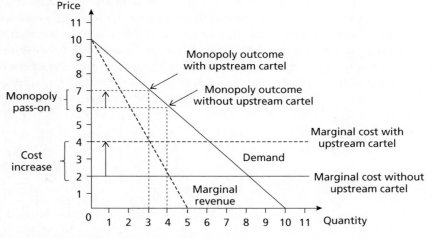

Figure 9.11 Pass-on of a cost increase

Bertrand oligopoly model with homogeneous goods has the same outcome as perfect competition, and pass-on is 100 per cent. In the Bertrand model with differentiated goods, and in monopolistic competition, firms behave like monopolists for their own product, so with linear demand and constant marginal cost the pass-on rate would be at least 50 per cent. However, it also depends of the degree of differentiation and the number of competitors. Less differentiation and more competitors gets you closer to 100 per cent pass-on.

9.10.5 Pass-on in theory: Further insights

In some cases the overcharge may have caused significant changes in the dynamics of competition in the downstream market—smaller operators may have been forced to exit, for example. In theory, this may give rise to pass-on rates greater than 100 per cent, as increased downstream concentration may result in higher downstream prices (although the term pass-on is not accurate in such a situation, as, in reality, a chain of events has taken place). Such factors would need to be assessed on a case-by-case basis. **9.115**

In the various models of competitive interaction, companies set their profit-maximizing price with reference to marginal costs. Fixed costs do not directly determine price in the same way as marginal costs, at least in the short run (in the longer run, many fixed costs tend to become variable). Therefore, a change in fixed costs due to an infringement may not be passed on in the same way. However, fixed costs can influence whether a firm can viably operate in the market in the first place—that is, the margins between price and marginal cost need to be at least sufficient to recover fixed costs. An increase in fixed costs may, in the longer term, induce exit and lead the remaining firms to increase price, in which case there may be full pass-on eventually. The effect of changes in fixed costs should also therefore be assessed on a case-by-case basis, and the duration of the infringement becomes an important factor to consider. **9.116**

Finally, buyer power of downstream customers can influence the ability of downstream suppliers to pass on the overcharge on the upstream input. If strong buyers can credibly switch to alternatives, this may limit the ability to pass on cost increases, in line with the theoretical insights presented above. However, if buyer power has already been exercised and has meant that prices equal marginal costs, the situation may be similar to that in a competitive market where pass-on is near 100 per cent. Again, in this situation, there may also be a volume effect that can give rise to a different type of damage from the overcharge. Pass-on may also depend on the type of negotiation with strong buyers. In some arrangements between suppliers and large retailers, prices may be renegotiated only if there are changes in costs of significant input items. In this case it therefore matters whether the cartelized upstream product constitutes a large and visible input into the downstream product, or whether it represents only a small fraction of total costs. We discuss this below. **9.117**

9.10.6 Small versus large cost increases

A question that arises frequently relates to the pass-on of very small cost increases, or small cost items. Car glass makes up only a small fraction of the total price of a car; methionine makes up only small fraction of the price of chicken feed (and an even smaller fraction of the price of a chicken). On the other hand, candle wax makes up a significant proportion of the costs of a candle. Does this make a difference for the pass-on rate? Assume that the overcharge on an input is 20 per cent. If the input price represents 50 per cent of the downstream product price (akin to the candle wax example), full pass-on of the overcharge **9.118** would mean a 10 per cent increase in the downstream price—that is, if the candle price is 100 cents and the candle wax costs 50 cents, and the cartel raises this by 20 per cent to 60 cents, 100 per cent pass-on means a new candle price of 110 cents, so 10 per cent higher. On the other hand, if the input price represents only 5 per cent of the downstream price, the latter increases by 1 per cent (costs were 5 cents, the cartel increases this to 6 cents, so a 1 cent increase if fully passed on). You can see how a 10 per cent price increase downstream is more significant (and noticeable) than a 1 per cent increase.

9.119   In the standard economic models it does not matter whether a particular input represents 5 per cent or 50 per cent of total marginal costs, as prices are set with respect to these total marginal costs. In practice it does matter. However, the direction of the effect is not clear-cut. If the affected input cost makes up only a small proportion of the final-product price, there may be no pass-on if the downstream producer chooses not to reset prices. This may occur where downstream prices are set, or negotiated, with respect to only major and more visible input costs, or where there are 'menu' costs associated with changing and communicating the final-product price (most restaurants don't print a new menu every time the costs of meat or vegetables change). Alternatively, small changes in the input price may well be fully passed on in some circumstances if their magnitude is sufficiently small as to avoid any significant demand reduction. In the above example, the downstream producers may get away with a 1 per cent price increase but not a 10 per cent one. This reasoning was used by the Paris Commercial Court in a 2007 vitamins cartel case (*Juva v Hoffman La Roche*).[58] The court considered vitamins to be a small part of the finished good and that a small price increase would be sufficient to offset the overcharge. It also noted that the price of the claimant's finished good had increased by more than the prices of the vitamins, and that its sales volumes had also grown.

9.120   Economic theory is divided on this point. One economic approach is to assess the relationship between price and overall costs (or overall marginal costs), and infer from this that the pass-on rate is the same for all individual cost items, be they large or small.[59] After all, when setting prices, companies may look at their total costs in the round, and hence even small items are considered in this way. Total costs are simply the sum of individual cost items. According to this logic, if the overall pass-on rate of marginal costs is found to be, say, 80 per cent, this rate can also be applied to each of the individual marginal cost items, including the small ones. The counterview is that there may well be differences between small and large cost items, both in commercial reality and in theory. In practice, companies may change prices with regard to only major or more visible input costs, while small-cost items are ignored. Can there still be pass-on in such circumstances?

9.121   Take the example of a law firm that has acquired an espresso machine for its staff area, at a price of €299. It turns out that espresso machine manufacturers had formed a cartel such that the law firm paid an overcharge of 10 per cent, so €29.90. Has the law firm passed this additional cost on through its fees to clients? Let's say this successful law firm increases its hourly rates by 10 per cent at the start of the new year. When setting the new rates, the firm's management committee did not pay much heed to the cost of the espresso machine—that is, it did not increase the fees with the espresso machine in mind. However, it did look at the

---

[58] Paris Commercial Court, *Juva v Hoffmann La Roche*, Decision of 26 January 2007.
[59] See van Dijk and Verboven (2009).

overall expenditure of the business—in particular, lawyer salaries and office costs, which include the cost of the espresso machine. The fee increase will earn the law firm a couple of million euros in extra revenue, clearly dwarfing the €29.90 it overpaid on the espresso machine. In that sense the overcharge is easily recovered. But does that mean the law firm has actually passed on the costs of the espresso machine to its clients? Or did it absorb these costs? And would its fee increase have been any different had the espresso machine been cheaper? There are different views—legal, economic, and even philosophical—on the question of whether the fee increase can be regarded as pass-on.

9.10.7 The effect of pricing practices and price friction

In any specific case you would expect there to be an analysis of the way companies in the downstream market concerned actually set prices. The theoretical relationships between costs and prices may not always hold, particularly over short time periods. Some companies price on a cost-plus basis, while others may have explicit contracts with customers through which increases in input costs are agreed to be passed on in full. Prices in some industries are changed on an annual (or other periodic) basis rather than continually in response to cost changes, or are determined at the end of a production cycle, long after input prices have been agreed. **9.122**

Cost-plus pricing occurs where a seller calculates the cost of the product and then adds a fixed mark-up. If a retailer applies a 25 per cent mark-up on all products, a product that costs €9.00 will sell for €11.25. If an upstream cartel raises the wholesale price to €10.00 (10 per cent overcharge), the retail price is increased to €12.50. The retailer has thus not only passed on the €1.00 input cost increase in full, it has raised its own price by €1.25, implying a pass-on rate of 125 per cent. Yet from both a legal and an economic perspective it is not clear that the extra €0.25 actually represents pass-on as such; it is more a resetting of price in which the change in cost was just one of the relevant factors. Another question is whether the mechanistic pricing rule—in this case, the 25 per cent mark-up—has been applied consistently during the cartel period; the retailer may have had to adjust its percentage mark-up to reflect changing market conditions. **9.123**

Another pricing practice is to use specific price points, such as €9.95 rather than €10.05, or a rounded price of €11.00 or €12.00 rather than €11.25. Sellers may also prefer simplicity and continuity in pricing. The price of the print edition of *The Times* newspaper remained at £1 for several years (it is now £1.20), while the price of a Big Mac (an international pricing benchmark monitored through *The Economist*'s Big Mac Index) in Spain was €3.50 for years.[60] Price changes in all these situations can be lumpy, and may not be directly related to changes in underlying costs. The rate of pass-on may be low as a result, at least in the short term. **9.124**

9.10.8 Empirical evidence on pass-on

Empirical studies on pass-on in competition law damages cases are rare. Fields in economic literature where pass-on has been studied empirically include tax incidence, exchange rate movements, and the transmission of intermediate goods prices. They provide some support for the theoretical insights discussed above. Various studies have confirmed very high pass-on rates where the downstream market is highly competitive—for example, in petrol **9.125**

---

[60] See http://www.economist.com/content/big-mac-index.

retailing and various agricultural products. Full pass-on is sometimes achieved only after a lag of several months, which may or may not affect the damages estimate, depending on the length of the period considered (the longer the period, the greater the pass-on). In addition, some studies have found that the pass-on rate is higher for price increases than for price decreases. In the standard IO models, such asymmetry does not exist, but for practical reasons prices may sometimes be 'sticky' downwards. This is also known as the 'rockets and feathers' phenomenon.[61] One US-based study found that the pass-on rate for an industry-wide cost shock in raw milk was 92–94 per cent in wholesale prices and 85–87 per cent in retail prices (Dhar and Cotterill, 1999). The study also tested separately for the effects of firm-specific cost shocks. It found that one supplier with significant market power had a firm-specific pass-on rate of 50–60 per cent (in line with the assumption for the monopoly level), while other suppliers with limited market power had a low pass-on rate of 13–19 per cent (in line with the theoretical result where cost changes are firm-specific).

9.126   Some studies on exchange rate pass-on provide further support for the assumption regarding high pass-on rates where downstream markets are competitive. Exchange rate pass-on is conventionally defined as the percentage change in an imported good's local-currency price for a given percentage change in the nominal exchange rate. One study on the US automobile market found that the pass-on rate for Japanese cars was 15–30 per cent when an exchange rate shock occurred, while for German cars it was above 65 per cent (Goldberg, 1995). During the period in question, Japanese car manufacturers competed mainly in the small-car segment, and were therefore constrained by domestic competitors that were not subject to the exchange rate shock. Their pass-on rate was relatively low. In contrast, German car manufacturers mainly served the luxury-car segment, where there tended to be fewer competitors. Their pass-on rate was high.

9.127   Several empirical studies have analysed how retailers pass on changes in VAT and other taxes. Overall, with some exceptions, these studies indicate high degrees of pass-on by retailers, often between two-thirds and 100 per cent. For example, Blundell (2009) estimated that 75 per cent of a 2.5 per cent VAT rise in the United Kingdom would be passed on to consumers. The Deutsche Bundesbank (2008) investigated the price effects of the VAT increase in Germany from 16 per cent to 19 per cent. Following an econometric analysis, controlling for seasonal effects, exchange rates and additional government measures, the study concluded that higher tax rates had been largely passed on to consumers.

9.128   What is the relevance of these studies for specific damages cases? As with the empirical studies on overcharges discussed earlier, the literature on pass-on provides some interesting background on what kind of pass-on rates you may encounter in practice in different types of industry. It also provides some high-level support for the theoretical insights presented here. However, the literature is not sufficiently clear-cut to derive any presumptions about actual pass-on rates. These will have to be determined on a case-by-case basis.

9.10.9 Pass-on and volume effects

9.129   Where a purchaser has passed on the overcharge in part or in full it may still have suffered a volume harm. After all, higher prices downstream often means lower sales. Legally this is a separate type of harm from the overcharge. The EU Directive on antitrust damages actions

---

[61] See, for example, Bacon (1991).

(Article 12) states that claimants are still entitled to compensation for loss of profits due to a full or partial passing-on of the overcharge. The ECJ acknowledged the possibility of such a loss-of-volume harm in the presence of complete pass-on in a 1997 judgment on port fees that were illegally levied in the French territory (this was not a competition law ruling).[62]

9.130 Claims for volume loss from pass-on of an overcharge are not yet common, in part because they are difficult to prove (though perhaps also because claimants would often prefer not to admit to a high pass-on rate when making their case). The downstream price increase would have to be significant for it to have a noticeable effect on downstream volumes. In the earlier example, if the downstream price increase was only 1 per cent it would be difficult to identify any effect on volume. Having an estimate of the own-price elasticity of demand for the downstream product would help. In that case even the effect of a 1 per cent price increase may be calculated, if not actually proven empirically. For example, if the elasticity is -2, a 1 per cent increase in the price would have resulted in a 2 per cent reduction in volume. Once the lost volumes have been estimated, the lost profit can be derived in line with the conceptual framework discussed in section 9.3.

9.10.10 Passing the buck: Remaining policy and practical questions

9.131 Court rulings on the level on pass-on are as yet rare. Best practice on how to quantify pass-on is still developing. In many cases, determining the level of pass-on will involve applying the theoretical insights on market structure, combined with an assessment of how downstream companies actually set prices. If there is sufficient data, a quantitative analysis of pass-on may be undertaken as well, considering metrics such as the correlation between claimant costs and downstream prices, or the development of the claimant's downstream profit margins over time. In any event, as with the overcharge, both claimants and defendants will have to do some homework to estimate the likely degree of pass-on; there are no presumptions that follow from economic theory.

9.132 What about the rebuttable presumption in the EU Directive on antitrust damages actions? This states (in Article 14) that wherever claimants are in the supply chain, it can be presumed that the overcharge has been passed on to them:

1. Member States shall ensure that, where in an action for damages the existence of a claim for damages or the amount of compensation to be awarded depends on whether, or to what degree, an overcharge was passed on to the claimant, taking into account the commercial practice that price increases are passed on down the supply chain, the burden of proving the existence and scope of such a passing-on shall rest with the claimant, who may reasonably require disclosure from the defendant or from third parties.
2. In the situation referred to in paragraph 1, the indirect purchaser shall be deemed to have proven that a passing-on to that indirect purchaser occurred where that indirect purchaser has shown that:
   (a) the defendant has committed an infringement of competition law;
   (b) the infringement of competition law has resulted in an overcharge for the direct purchaser of the defendant; and
   (c) the indirect purchaser has purchased the goods or services that were the object of the infringement of competition law, or has purchased goods or services derived from or containing them.

---

[62] Joined Cases C-192/95 to C-218/95 *Société Comateb and others v Directeur Général des Douanes et Droits Indirects* [1997] OJ C74/3.

9.133 This presumption reflects a policy choice to make claims by indirect purchasers easier. It does not have any economic grounding. It cannot be presumed from the outset that the overcharge has ended up with any particular layer of the chain. The presumption may also complicate matters if there are simultaneous claims by direct and indirect purchasers. Moreover, pass-on is generally difficult to prove for defendants (and hence the presumption difficult to rebut) as this requires data from direct and indirect purchasers about their pricing downstream.

9.134 A final policy point is that competition authorities should be careful what they write in their decisions. Government agencies are often under pressure to demonstrate the consumer benefits of their interventions. This is one reason why infringement decisions sometimes include statements along the lines of the effects of the anti-competitive conduct (a cartel or abuse of dominance) ultimately being felt by end-consumers. Such statements can be unhelpful to a claimant who operates at an intermediate layer of the supply chain, since they imply that all cost increases have been passed on to end-consumers. For example, in a damages action in France against the vitamins cartel, the Nanterre Commercial Court noted that the earlier European Commission decision and press release had stated that the cartel ultimately affected end-consumers, and inferred from this that direct purchasers were able to pass on the cost increase.[63] It is open to question whether the Commission's statement about end-consumers being harmed was based on any actual analysis specific to the case at hand, or whether, perhaps more likely, it was meant as a general statement about cartels ultimately being bad for end-consumers. What is clear is that the intention of competition authorities to show that their interventions benefit consumers can sometimes, inadvertently, get in the way of follow-on damages actions by providing apparent support for the passing-on defence.

9.11 Interest and Discounting

9.11.1 Relevance of interest and discounting

9.135 A competition law infringement may have started a long time ago and lasted many years. Its effects may be felt for years into the future. Quantifying damages therefore involves calculating monetary amounts for a number of years in the past, and possibly in the future. The economic principle of the time value of money means that you cannot just add up amounts of money from different years—€100 today is worth less than €100 last year, and more than €100 next year. Translating past and future monetary amounts into a present value requires discounting, as we also saw in Chapter 3. For this you apply a discount rate. Future amounts are discounted applying this rate, and past amounts are uprated. Applying interest on past damages values is a form of uprating. The time value of money has also been recognized in the EU Directive on antitrust damages actions, which regards the application of interest as being in line with the principle of compensation:

> The payment of interest is an essential component of compensation to make good the damage sustained by taking into account the effluxion of time and should be due from the time when the harm occurred until the time when compensation is paid, without prejudice to the

---

[63] *Arkopharma v Roche and Hoffmann-La Roche*, no RG2004F02643, Tribunal de Commerce de Nanterre (Nanterre Commercial Court, 11 May 2006).

qualification of such interest as compensatory or default interest under national law and to whether effluxion of time is taken into account as a separate category (interest) or as a constituent part of actual loss or loss of profit. It is incumbent on the Member States to lay down the rules to be applied for that purpose.[64]

US courts do not award interest on past damages; only post-judgment interest is awarded **9.136** (and sometimes pre-judgment interest if it can be shown that the defendant has unduly delayed the litigation process).[65] In jurisdictions across Europe and elsewhere the legal rules and practices regarding the award and calculation of interest vary significantly. The rules are also frequently at odds with economic principles. One specific issue is whether the interest is paid on a simple or a compound basis. Another is whether a statutory interest rate or some market rate is applied. There is also much debate, among economists as well as lawyers, about which rate is most appropriate if no statutory rate is prescribed: a risk-free rate, the cost of capital, or something in between? The choice of interest rate and method can have a significant effect on the damages quantification, especially in cases involving long-running cartels. In the damages action brought by National Grid, the operator of the electricity transmission network in Great Britain, against the members of a gas insulated switchgear cartel—active from 1988 to 2004—the overcharge claim amounted to £95 million without interest, and £276 million with interest.[66]

9.11.2 Principles of interest and discounting

Conceptually, the discount rate should take into account the time value of money, inflation, **9.137** and risk. Inflation means that prices tend to rise over time and hence the same nominal amount of money decreases in value. Risk means that future expected cash flows are uncertain. Applying interest on damages is a form of uprating cash flows. If an infringement has caused the victim a loss of €100 during each of the past five years, each year's loss needs to be uprated using the discount rate to determine the current value of this harm. Suppose that the discount or interest rate is 10 per cent per year. The harm from the first of the five years (i.e. the first €100) needs to be uprated five times, which is comparable to paying cumulative interest on that amount for five years. The current value of that amount is €161.05 (€100 times 1.10 to the power of 5). The harm from the second year needs to be uprated for four years (€100 times 1.10 to the power of 4, which equals €146.41), and so on. The present value of the total harm over the five years is €671.56.[67] Furthermore, if it is demonstrated, and accepted by the court, that the now ceased infringement will still cause losses to the victim in the subsequent three years (because the victim cannot immediately recover the market position it would have had in the absence of the infringement, for example), those future losses form part of the harm suffered. They need to be added to the present value of

---

[64] Directive 2014/104/EU of the European Parliament and of the Council of the European Union of 26 November 2014 on certain rules governing actions for damages under national law for infringements of the competition law provisions of the Member States and of the European Union, OJ L 349/1, 5 December 2014, [recital 12].

[65] Plaintiffs in the USA are entitled to treble damages. In Europe the payment of interest can also triple the original amount if the damage arose a long time ago.

[66] *National Grid Electricity Transmission Plc v ABB Ltd and Others*, [2012] EWHC 869 (Ch). The case settled out of court in 2014 for an undisclosed amount. We acted as experts for National Grid on this matter.

[67] For simplicity, this example assumes that the cash flows occur on 1 January of each year. Another assumption is that the interest is compounded—that is, the calculation includes interest on accumulated interest from prior periods (see below).

the harm over the first five years. Suppose the future losses are €75, €50, and €25 (as the victim is gradually regaining market share to its 'normal' levels), and the same discount rate applies. The €75 occurs in the current year, so does not require discounting. The €50 occurs in the next year, so needs to be discounted once, and is worth €45.45 in present terms (€50 divided by 1.10). The €25 in two years' time is worth €20.66 in present terms (€25 divided by 1.10 to the power of 2). The present value of the total harm over the whole eight years in this example (five past years, the current year, and the two future years) is now €812.68.

9.138   The choice of discount rate can have a significant influence on the damage value. In the above example, if the discount rate were 5 per cent instead of 10 per cent, the present value of the damage from the five past years would be €580.19 instead of €671.56. If it were 15 per cent the value would be €775.37. The higher the discount rate, the greater the present value of the past losses when uprated, but the smaller the present value of the future losses when discounted at this rate. We turn to the choice of interest or discount rate next.

9.11.3   Choice of interest or discount rate

9.139   Various jurisdictions require statutory rates of interest—generally prescribed by civil or contract/tort law provisions—to be used for uprating damages. In Germany it is five percentage points above the Bundesbank base rate; in the Netherlands it is seven percentage points above the European Central Bank base rate.[68] The date from which interest can be claimed varies across jurisdictions, and can refer to the start of the infringement (as in the EU Directive, cited above), the start of the legal action, or the date of the award. The relevant legal framework usually determines which part of the cash flows in the damages valuation should be uprated by the statutory interest rate, and for which cash flows (if any) a discount rate can be chosen according to economic criteria.

9.140   Economic and finance theories have developed a range of principles on how to determine the discount rate. For future cash flows, it may be appropriate to use the claimant's cost of capital as the discount rate. This takes into account the claimant's time value of money and business risk—that is, the fact that future factual and counterfactual scenarios, and hence estimates of losses, are uncertain. Discounting expected future losses would provide an estimate of their value as at the award date. As regards uprating past losses, there are several possible approaches. One is to use the claimant's cost of capital. The rationale is that during the period in which the damages were incurred, a claimant earning 'normal' returns would have expected to earn profits consistent with the cost of capital. Thus, damages uprated at the cost of capital would capture the expected return that the investors in the claimant company could have earned on the amounts lost, had these amounts been available for investment—i.e. it compensates investors for the use of their capital. An alternative approach is to apply the risk-free rate, which theoretically represents the guaranteed rate of return on an investment that has no risk. This is usually approximated by the rate of return on a virtually risk-free investment such as a government bond. The rationale for using the risk-free rate is that the repayment of damages is certain once awarded (subject to an inability to pay by the defendant), thus ensuring that the claimant is compensated for the time value of money without a risk premium within the interest rate. From an economic perspective, it may be appropriate to apply a risk-free rate to any damages from the point

---

[68]   Bürgerliches Gesetzbuch, Section 288 Book 2; and Burgerlijk Wetboek, Article 120 Book 6.

in time where the claimant has certainty that it will be awarded damages. This can be the court award itself, or an earlier point such as when the cartel is discovered and the claimant knows it will be able to prove harm. Without such certainty, applying a measure which captures risk (such as the cost of capital) may be more appropriate. This is still an area of debate among economists.

An example of a situation where a court preferred one discount rate over another is the **9.141** Chicago Bulls franchise case that we saw before.[69] The original claim uprated historical cash flows at the risk-free rate (in this case they were negative as the claimant had to commit additional equity to the business in the counterfactual scenario). The court agreed with most aspects of the damages valuation (including the comparators used), but not with the uprating approach. It held that historical cash flows (which in this case reflected equity contributions) needed to be uprated at the cost of equity capital to reflect the fact that the claimant would have incurred an opportunity cost of capital on the committed equity.

9.11.4 Economics and law on interest: Reconciling them ought to be more 'simple'

Interest can be applied as simple interest or compound interest. With compounding, the **9.142** calculation includes interest on accumulated interest from prior periods. For example, 10 per cent is applied to €100 in the first year, giving €110, and in the second year the 10 per cent is applied to that €110 from the first year, giving €121. From an economic perspective, compounding interest is the usual, and conceptually correct, approach to discounting. When you put your money in the bank, you expect interest to be paid on the whole balance, so on past interest too. And yet very often legal frameworks require simple interest to be applied. This means interest calculated solely as a percentage of the principal sum. So 10 per cent is applied to €100 in the first year, giving €110, and in the second year the 10 per cent is again applied to the €100, giving a total of €120. In this example the difference between the two methods is only €1. However, for longer time periods and higher interest rates the differences become substantially greater. Whether you apply simple or compound interest usually has a greater effect on the damages estimate than which particular rate you use.

In most jurisdictions simple interest is the norm. As economists we are somewhat puz- **9.143** zled by this. The Netherlands seems to be one of the few jurisdictions where the civil code prescribes compounding of interest.[70] EU case law seems to emphasize simple interest but has also referred to compound interest. In a 2001 case the General Court stated that:

> Regarding the rate of interest, it should be pointed out that, according to a principle generally accepted in the domestic law of the Member States, in an action for the recovery of a sum unduly paid based on the principle prohibiting unjust enrichment, the claimant is normally entitled to the lower of the two amounts corresponding to the enrichment and the loss. Furthermore, where the loss consists of the loss of use of a sum of money over a period of time, the amount recoverable is generally calculated by reference to the statutory or judicial rate of interest, without compounding.[71]

---

[69] *Fishman v Estate of Wirtz* 594 F. Supp. 853 (ND Ill. 1984); and 807 F 2d 520 (7th Cir. 1986).
[70] Burgerlijk Wetboek, Artikel 119a Boek 6.
[71] Case T-171/99 *Corus UK Ltd v Commission* [2002] OJ C3/23.

9.144 However, the General Court also found that, in this particular case, the actual amount to be calculated would be better reflected by applying a compound interest rate, and therefore preferred the latter. A UK House of Lords ruling, *Sempra Metals*, contains a useful discussion of these points.[72] It notes some comments made by legal representative bodies that 'the obvious reason for awarding compound interest is that it reflects economic reality', and that 'computation of the time value of the enrichment on the basis of simple interest will inevitably fall short of its true value'. On the other hand, it noted that 'The virtue of simple interest is its simplicity. That cannot be said of compound interest, which can be calculated in different ways leading to different results.' (We do not necessarily follow this last statement; indeed, compound interest is easier to compute in spreadsheets than simple interest.)

9.145 Case law in the United Kingdom also seems to increasingly recognize that the use of the statutory interest rate is not necessarily aligned with business reality. In a case outside competition law, the High Court held that:

> The Judgments Act [statutory] rate is fixed for the benefit of unpaid judgment creditors. It is not normally an appropriate rate of interest to award in the context of a dispute between two businesses…If Claymore or a company such as Claymore, had sought to borrow £750,000.00 over the period since June 2004, Claymore would have had to pay interest at more than 1% over base rate.[73]

9.146 Ultimately, there is plenty of scope for economics and law to come closer together in the area of interest and discounting in damages cases. Given the significant difference the application of interest can make to the damages estimate, this theme merits greater debate and reflection than it has received to date.

---

[72] *Sempra Metals Ltd v Revenue & Anor* [2007] UKHL 34, 18 July 2007.
[73] *Claymore v Nautilus* [2007] EWHC 805 (TCC).

10

THE USE OF ECONOMIC EVIDENCE
IN COMPETITION CASES

10.1 Smokescreens and Mud-slingers?

As we mentioned in Chapter 1, whether you are a practising lawyer, a competition official, or a judge, economics matters to you, because it matters to competition law. The very essence of competition law is based on the economic notion that competition is 'good' and monopoly is 'bad'. Competition authorities apply economic principles and tests in their decisions, and parties on both sides of a competition dispute use economic arguments and evidence to support their case. Throughout this book we have sought to give you a feel for what economics can contribute to competition law, and what its limitations are. **10.01**

We conclude by looking at the use of economic evidence, and of economists, in competition cases. Competition lawyers and economists routinely work alongside each other as complements (not substitutes). However, much still needs to be done to extend good practice in the use of economic evidence. Economists do not always have a favourable reputation, and are the butt of many a joke: the two-handed economist (on the one hand, on the other), the economist who dismisses reality because it doesn't fit the theory, ask two economists and you get three opinions, and so on.[1] To a large extent economists have themselves to blame. It is not helpful when economic experts appear to be slinging mud **10.02**

---

[1] We refer you to Judge Nicholas Green's five truisms about economists, presented at the launch of the first edition of our book (Green, 2011). He praised the rigour that mathematics has brought to economics; and the mortis.

at each other's analysis instead of providing insight. Nor is the reputation of economists enhanced when they do not explain their analysis very well, write long reports full of jargon, or worse, throw up smokescreens of unnecessarily complicated theories and equations. That competition law is a complex field is not the fault of economists—in Chapter 1 we quoted one specialized court as saying that 'competition law is not an area of law in which there is much scope for absolute concepts or sharp edges'.[2] However, economists can do a lot more to help lawyers and courts navigate through the complexities of a case. This begins with explaining economic principles and concepts clearly—something we have tried to do in this book.

10.03 In what follows, section 10.2 explores best practice in presenting economic evidence. Various competition authorities have issued guidance on this, which is a useful step in improving the contribution of economics to competition law. In section 10.3 we address the question of how courts can assess what weight and credibility to attach to the evidence of economic experts, especially in situations where two experts reach different conclusions. Useful criteria for dealing with these situations have been developed in the United States (the *Daubert* test), the United Kingdom (the 'duty to help the court'), and Australia (the 'hot tub'). Section 10.4 discusses some of the themes that have arisen in court cases with regard to economic evidence and how it can be interpreted—do economists in court always get a fair hearing? Section 10.5 concludes with some, mostly optimistic, observations about future trends in the use of economics in competition law.

10.2 Best Practice in Presenting Economic Evidence

10.04 Academic economists have a reputation for observing the world from an ivory tower. But even practising economists sometimes carry out their analyses quite separately from the legal case they are supposed to shed light on. The most effective cases are those where the business people and the economists work closely together with the lawyers on an integrated legal submission that reflects both business reality and sound economic reasoning. This can be complemented by a separate, usually more technical, economic submission containing empirical evidence.

10.05 Competition authorities and courts must take a view on how much weight to attach to this evidence. In previous chapters where we described empirical techniques, we gave some tips for critical questions that non-economists may ask when presented with quantitative results. We used the analogy of the black box, which you can look into and shake and rattle a bit to see if it holds together under scrutiny. But even for an economist it can be difficult to assess the robustness of another economist's empirical results if they are not presented clearly. This can work only if economists are able to peer-review each other's work. Despite the perception that different economists always come up with a different answer, we believe that there is actually some common understanding in our profession as to what constitutes a good piece of economics and what doesn't. Analysis based on established theory, using good data, and a robustness check of the results, are all elements of this common understanding. If it passes peer review by other economists, it is probably a good analysis. (This is

---

[2] *The Racecourse Association and the British Horseracing Board v OFT* [2005] CAT 29, 2 August 2005, at [167].

not to say that the standard of robustness should be the same as for peer-reviewed academic journals—empirical work in competition cases is usually carried out within much tighter timescales than academic work.) Economic evidence needs to be presented in such a way that it allows for a proper review by the economists at the competition authority or on the other side. Various guidance documents on best practice for economic submissions have been issued by competition authorities. These capture some common principles, articulated as follows in the UK guidance:

> Clarity and transparency: Submissions should not only present clearly the results and con-
> clusions of the economic analysis undertaken, but they should also clearly state the method-
> ology used, the assumptions made in reaching results, the justification for the methodology
> and the assumptions, and the robustness of the results to any assumptions made...

> Completeness: Submissions should contain a complete description of the analysis under-
> taken. All relevant assumptions should be discussed and the choice of techniques explained.
> Relevant econometric output, diagnostic tests and checks for robustness should be
> included...

> Replication of results: In a number of cases, the CC will want to replicate the results of the
> analysis that has been submitted. This means that parties should be prepared to respond to
> a CC request, at very short notice, for all relevant computer code and data files necessary for
> the CC's economists to reproduce the result presented in parties' submission.[3]

10.06 The European Commission's guidance contains some useful additional points on the presentation and interpretation of results.[4] It states that the results of an empirical analysis should be reported in the standard format found in academic papers. This includes reporting on statistical significance (did the result occur by chance?) and other diagnostic tests, and emphasizing those results that are statistically significant at the 5 per cent level (as discussed in Chapter 2, this is a cut-off point often used in statistics, meaning that you can be 95 per cent confident that your results did not occur by chance). The Commission also emphasizes that, by their very nature, economic models are based on simplifications of reality, but that this in itself is not a problem: 'It is therefore normally not sufficient to disprove a particular argument or model, to point out that it is based on seemingly unrealistic assumptions.'[5] Instead, the Commission expects any critique of an analysis to identify which aspects of reality should be better reflected and to indicate why this would alter the conclusions. Another point made in the Commission guidance is that:

> The credibility of an economic submission is enhanced when the limitations with regards
> to accuracy or explanatory power of the underlying data and methodology are explic-
> itly acknowledged. In this regard it is often advisable to address rather than minimize
> uncertainty.[6]

10.07 Again, clarity and transparency are key. If the analysis has certain shortcomings, it is more credible to signal these up front rather than sweep them under the carpet and hope no one notices.

---

[3] Competition Commission (2009), 'Suggested Best Practice for Submission of Technical Economic Analysis From Parties to the Competition Commission', 24 February, pp. 1–2.

[4] European Commission (2010), 'Best Practices for the Submission of Economic Evidence and Data Collection in Cases Concerning the Application of Articles 101 and 102 TFEU and in Merger Cases', January.

[5] Ibid., at [12].

[6] Ibid., at [41].

10.3 Economists in Court: When Can You Rely on Them?

10.08 Most competition authorities have economists among their staff—indeed, many now have a Chief Economist. If the best-practice guidance discussed above is followed, the submission of empirical evidence should allow for a more in-depth debate, and ultimately better decision-making. However, in competition cases before courts there is the complication that few judges have had extensive economics training. In this sense courts are generally less well equipped than competition authorities to deal with technical economic evidence. When presented with such evidence, should they limit themselves to putting some critical questions to the expert, and if these are answered satisfactorily, accept the expert's conclusions? Should they rely on the other side's expert or a court-appointed expert to provide the required peer review? Or should they just ignore the evidence? Different jurisdictions deal with these challenges in different ways. Some of the principles developed in the US, UK, and Australian courts are particularly useful, as discussed below.

10.3.1 The *Daubert* principle

10.09 US case law has developed the '*Daubert* test' on the admissibility of scientific evidence, which also applies to economic evidence in antitrust cases. Based on a 1993 Supreme Court ruling, the test has been refined through a number of subsequent judgments and is reflected in Rule 702 of the Federal Rules of Evidence.[7] It is intended to prevent testimony based on untested and unreliable theories. The main aspects of the *Daubert* test are whether: (i) the testimony is based on sufficient facts or data; (ii) the testimony is the product of reliable principles and methods; and (iii) the expert has applied the principles and methods reliably to the facts of the case. Note that admission of the evidence is just the first hurdle; it does not necessarily mean that the evidence is given much weight. The *Daubert* test has been used to great effect in many antitrust cases in the last twenty years. Indeed, quite a few economists have seen their evidence not being admitted—prominent ones include a winner of the Nobel Prize for Economics, and the author of a leading guide to using economic evidence in antitrust court cases.

10.10 Expert evidence in private damages actions (which represent a large proportion of all antitrust cases in the United States) is most likely to be admitted if it falls within one of the three 'common approaches to measuring antitrust damages': the before-and-after approach, a yardstick or benchmark approach, and regression analysis (see also Chapter 9).[8] US courts have accepted the usefulness of regression analysis. In one case it was stated that 'if performed properly multiple regression analysis is a reliable means by which economists may prove antitrust damages'.[9] US courts have also considered the question of how much of an expert the expert needs to be. In one antitrust case involving a clinic's refusal to continue to treat two patients, the plaintiffs' expert had a PhD in economics, but no expertise in competition economics. The court dismissed him:

> The district court's and the plaintiffs' difficulty in describing the relevant market was to a great measure the result of the plaintiffs' reliance on [the expert] as their sole economic

---

[7] *Daubert v Merrell Dow Pharma Inc* 509 US 579 (1993). For a more detailed discussion of the test, see Berger (2000) and Cwik and North (2003). The Federal Rules of Evidence are updated from time to time and are available on various websites, including: <http://federalevidence.com/rules-of-evidence>

[8] *Conwood Co LP v US Tobacco Co* 290 F 3d 768, 793 (6th Cir. 2002).

[9] *Petruzzi's IGA Supermarkets Inc v Darling-Delaware Co* 998 F 2d 1224, 1238 (3d Cir. 1993).

analyst/expert. Dr. [expert] is the sole qualified source cited by the plaintiffs supporting their allegation of the Clinic's market power. Yet, Dr. [expert] conceded that he was 'not an expert,' that he had no background in antitrust markets, either geographic or product, and that he had no background in 'primary care' markets. Dr. [expert] further stated that he was not a member of any associations or industrial organization groups which form the bulwark of economists specializing in antitrust law and economics. Where supposed experts have admitted that they are 'not experts,' courts have had little difficulty in excluding their testimony.[10]

The English High Court faced a similar question in an abuse of dominance case where   **10.11**
the expert was not an economist, but did have extensive business experience in the industry (local bus services). The court expressed a more nuanced view on this than its US counterpart:

> Whilst the concepts required to be investigated in a competition law case are no doubt most easily grasped, explained and opined upon by trained economists, they are concepts drawn from and related to the operation of the markets of the real world; and I regard it as unreal the thought that it is only trained economists with a list of learned articles to their name who have the expertise necessary to understand them and to help the court on their application to a particular case.[11]

Conversely, the question has arisen as to whether experts need to have had experience in the   **10.12**
industry in question. In a case involving a horizontal group boycott under section 1 of the Sherman Act, the court noted the expert's (an accountant) extensive experience in business valuation, and was satisfied that while the expert had no prior experience in the industry concerned (aluminium distribution), he had made substantial efforts to acquaint himself with the industry for the purpose of the case.[12] This seems sensible given that competition economists, like competition lawyers, can effectively work across a wide range of industries, and may not necessarily be familiar with the industry in question at the start of a case. In this particular case, the expert's evidence was rejected for another reason: it was not based on any identifiable theory or technique, but rather on the expert's own assumptions and judgement, such that the analysis could not be objectively tested or verified by others (which is another of the *Daubert* criteria).

Experts cannot rely only on their past experience. Under the *Daubert* test they are   **10.13**
expected to engage with the details of a case, and ensure that their analysis fits the facts. In *Concord Boat*, a rebate case involving boat builders and an engine manufacturer that we also discussed in Chapter 4, the appeal court rejected the plaintiff's expert because his Cournot oligopoly model 'did not incorporate all aspects of the economic reality' of the market in question, and 'ignored inconvenient evidence'.[13] The Cournot model itself was not challenged—it is after all a well-accepted model—but two experts on the other side criticized the way it had been applied in the case at hand. The court considered that there was 'simply too great an analytic gap between the data and the opinion proffered'. In another US case, concerning price discrimination in phospholipids (fat derivatives), the plaintiff's expert was rejected because his analysis was not based on authoritative industry

---

[10] *Nelson v Monroe Regional Medical Center* 925 F 2d 1555 (7th Cir. 1991).
[11] *Chester City Council v Arriva* [2007] EWHC 1373 (Ch).
[12] *Champagne Metals v Ken-Mac Metals Inc* 458 F 3d 1073, 1088 (10th Cir. 2006).
[13] *Concord Boat Corp v Brunswick Corp* 207 F 3d 1039 (8th Cir. 2000).

data or recognized financial data.[14] Instead it was based on the 'deposition testimony, estimates, feelings and beliefs' of one of the plaintiff's executives. This executive would have been the main beneficiary of the damages claim (and might therefore have been biased), and the court considered him not sufficiently qualified to provide the general opinions on which the expert had relied in calculating the damages, as he was neither an economist nor an accountant. The court also stated that the expert had not made any effort to verify the executive's estimates. That experts must do their homework is also a theme that has come up in the UK courts. In one damages action (outside competition law), where economic and business experts analysed the effect of a failed customer relationship management (CRM) system on the number of pay-TV subscribers, the court stated that:

> It is clear that [the expert] is a person who has a great deal of relevant experience in this field and could provide a valuable opinion on the effect of the CRM System on Sky's customers. However, I found that his evidence failed to live up to expectations. It seemed that he had little grasp of the detailed facts and had not properly understood some features which were necessary to make churn predictions for Sky.[15]

10.3.2 Duty to help the court

10.14 There are various ways to involve experts in court proceedings, and the rules differ across jurisdictions. Parties can each appoint their own expert, or they can appoint one expert jointly. Courts may themselves appoint an expert. We are supporters of the system of party-appointed experts used in the English courts. In our own experience, and based on what several judges have said about it, this system can be highly effective in bringing out the best in economic experts. It combines a number of powerful mechanisms that provide the right incentives for experts to do the job properly: (i) a duty on the experts to help the court; (ii) a requirement on the experts to produce a joint statement of points of agreement and disagreement; and (iii) robust cross-examination of the experts by a barrister if the case goes to trial.

10.15 Part 35 of the English Civil Procedure Rules and the accompanying Practice Direction determine that experts have a duty to help the court on matters within their expertise.[16] This duty overrides any obligation to the parties from whom experts have received instructions. Experts are expected to provide objective opinions on matters within their expertise, and not to assume the role of an advocate. They have to make it clear when a question falls outside their expertise, and when they are not able to reach a definitive opinion, for example, because they have insufficient information. In our experience, this duty to help the court in itself provides a powerful incentive to carry out the analysis with rigour—and indeed it also provides incentives for the instructing solicitors not to place undue pressure on the expert to say one thing or another. Judges tend to dismiss the evidence of an expert who does not appear to want to be helpful to the court—for example, when the expert seems unwilling to comment on a matter from another perspective when asked to do so, or appears to be hiding

---

[14] *Vernon Walden, Inc v Lipoid GmbH and Lipoid USA LLC* (Civ No 01-4826 (DRD)), (D.N.J. 2005).

[15] *BSkyB Limited and Sky Subscribers Services Limited v HP Enterprise Services UK Limited (formerly Electronic Data Systems Limited) and Electronic Data Systems LLC (formerly Electronic Data Systems Corporation)* [2010] EWHC 86 (TCC), at [288].

[16] These rules are updated from time to time and are available on the Ministry of Justice website: <http://www.justice.gov.uk/civil/procrules_fin/index.htm>.

behind narrow instructions. This can be seen in the quote below, which is from a 1995 judg-ment that was influential in the development of the duty to the court principle (the expert evidence here did not relate to economics but to architecture, as the case involved a property rights dispute over the copying of a house design):

> That some witnesses of fact, driven by a desire to achieve a particular outcome to the litiga-tion, feel it necessary to sacrifice truth in pursuit of victory is a fact of life. The court tries to discover it when it happens. But in the case of expert witnesses the court is likely to lower its guard. Of course the court will be aware that a party is likely to choose as its expert someone whose view is most sympathetic to its position. Subject to that caveat, the court is likely to assume that the expert witness is more interested in being honest and right than in ensur-ing that one side or another wins. An expert should not consider that it is his job to stand shoulder-to-shoulder through thick and thin with the side which is paying his bill.[17]

There have been several judgments in which the UK courts have explicitly stated that they found an economic expert's evidence to be credible, persuasive, and authoritative, and that they felt they could rely on the expert. Equally, courts have indicated where there were some doubts in this respect. This confirms to us that the duty to the court principle works effec-tively. The following extracts from UK court judgments illustrate the point. In an Article 101 case before the Court of Session in Edinburgh, the judge observed: **10.16**

> I noted the considered and thoughtful way in which Mr [expert] gave his evidence. I am entirely satisfied that he acted throughout as an independent expert offering his opinions to assist the court... His credentials to give expert evidence on this subject are impressive. On the material issues, I accept all of Mr [expert]'s evidence and his conclusions.[18]

In a High Court ruling on an Article 102 case, the judge made the following comment about the claimants' expert: **10.17**

> I was satisfied that Mr [expert] was giving his evidence honestly and was doing so in proper recognition of his duties to the court. I recognise, however, that he has been close to the action on the claimants' side of the record, and that there is therefore a risk that his opinion may perhaps have become unconsciously coloured by the claimants' interests.[19]

Under the Civil Procedure Rules, the experts from both sides are expected to hold dis-cussions and to produce a joint statement setting out the issues on which they agree and disagree, and the reasons for doing so. This usually also involves the experts sharing their data and calculations with each other, in line with the best-practice principles set out above. Together with the duty to the court, this requirement on experts to narrow the issues in dispute can be a powerful mechanism to help courts understand the economics of the case. Indeed it could be applied in any type of competition investigation—it would equally be helpful in administrative proceedings if the economists at the competition authority and those advising the parties discussed where they agree and where they do not, and clearly state the reasons why. The Civil Procedure Rules state that 'the purpose of discussions between experts is not for experts to settle cases but to agree and narrow issues', and that—reader take note—'neither the parties nor their legal representatives may attend experts discussions'.[20] In our experience, even if these expert discussions do not always bring the **10.18**

---

[17] *Cala Homes v Alfred McAlpine Homes East* [1995] FSR 818.
[18] *Calor Gas v Express Fuels and D Jamieson* [2008] CSOH 13, Court of Session.
[19] *Chester City Council v Arriva* [2007] EWHC 1373 (Ch).
[20] Practice Direction 35—'Experts and assessors', at [9.2] and [9.4].

parties' cases much closer together, it is already helpful if there is agreement on at least some basic principles. In one, possibly rare, case that we worked on (an arbitration involving an abuse of dominance allegation), the two experts agreed on all the economic criteria applicable to the case, and considered that the remaining areas of difference between the two sides were entirely a matter of factual evidence. As a result, there was no longer a need to cross-examine the experts at the hearing. That the mechanism of the expert meeting and joint statement can work satisfactorily is also borne out by the following quote from a damages judgment that we mentioned earlier:

> The quantum experts have managed to make very good progress in agreeing figures. This meant that the issues between them were more limited. Both [expert 1 and expert 2] were impressive witnesses and although their approaches on particular issues differed, this was the result of opinion on such matters as validation of costs. I have therefore been able to see clearly what their views are and decide which view I prefer on particular issues.[21]

10.19 Finally, in addition to the duty to the court and the requirement to meet with the other expert, an economist involved in these proceedings faces the prospect of cross-examination by a barrister representing the other side. This is the most vigorous form of rattling that the black box can get in court. The most powerful incentive for the party-appointed expert to produce a credible analysis is provided by the prospect of close scrutiny by the other expert and cross-examination by the barrister. To this can be added the desire to avoid a damning quote in the final judgment if your analysis is shown to be unreliable or unhelpful to the court.

10.3.3 Hot tubs, court experts, and economists as judges

10.20 One method through which the evidence of party-appointed experts can be tested is what is known as the expert 'hot tub' or 'conclave'. This originated in Australia, and is now starting to be introduced elsewhere. Like real hot tubs, expert hot tubs come in different shapes and sizes, but in essence they are a blend of the expert discussions and cross-examination. The experts appear together in court to exchange views and answer questions from the barristers and the judge. As explained by an Australian judge:

> In many situations calling for evidence, the 'hot tub' offers the potential for a much more satisfactory experience of expert evidence for all those involved. It enables each expert to concentrate on the real issues between them. The judge or listener can hear all the experts discussing the same issue at the same time to explain each of their points in a discussion with a professional colleague. The technique reduces the chances of the experts, lawyers, and judge, jury, or tribunal misunderstanding what the experts are saying.[22]

10.21 Jurisdictions such as Ireland, Finland, South Africa, Hong Kong, and New Zealand also mainly use party-appointed experts, as do many international arbitrations. Several of these have adopted elements of the US, UK, and Australian systems. Other jurisdictions rely largely on court-appointed experts. These assist courts in making the decision, sometimes sitting alongside the judge in the courtroom. Some specialized courts, such as the CAT, even have economists among their members (including one of the founders of our firm).

---

[21] *BSkyB Limited and Sky Subscribers Services Limited v HP Enterprise Services UK Limited (formerly Electronic Data Systems Limited) and Electronic Data Systems LLC (formerly Electronic Data Systems Corporation)* [2010] EWHC 86 (TCC), at [303].

[22] Rares (2013).

Do you get more objective and more informed outcomes if the expert is appointed by the court rather than the parties? Not necessarily. Both systems can work well, provided that they meet a number of criteria. One is that the evidence gets properly tested. Even for court experts it is a useful incentive to carry out a robust analysis when they know that they can be challenged by the parties and their experts (we know this from experience, both as court-appointed and party-appointed experts). Also, seeing the argument from both sides can be helpful both for the judge and the court-appointed expert. It is normally easier for court experts to review two well-developed economic analyses by the respective party experts, than having to do all the homework themselves. Courts in Australia have recognized that it is not inherently a bad thing that party-appointed experts do not reach the same conclusion, especially in a field like competition law. As one Australian judge stated: 'The fallacy underlying the one-expert argument lies in the unstated premise that in fields of expert knowledge there is only one answer.'[23]

10.22

Another noted that it can be useful to have contradictory evidence because the court does not normally choose between the experts, preferring all aspects of one opinion over another, but rather uses their differing views to assist in reaching its own conclusion.[24] In our view, a further key criterion is that the experts must talk to each other, exchange analyses, and seek to narrow the issues through a statement of points of agreement and disagreement. This has proven its worth in UK court cases, as noted above. It can work regardless of whether there are only party-appointed experts, or a court expert who has a dialogue with the two party experts. Such expert discussions can be held in private, without the lawyers present (as in the United Kingdom), or in a hot tub in the courtroom, or through some combination of both. In all, allowing experts to explain their evidence, subjecting them to cross-examination, and requiring the experts on all sides to narrow the issues by identifying points of agreement and disagreement, are all part of the recipe for the successful use of economic expert evidence in court cases.

10.23

10.4 Economists in Court: Do They Get a Fair Hearing?

The CAT has regularly pondered over what to make of the evidence presented by economic experts, and in a number of cases two related themes have emerged. The first is the extent to which the economic reasoning by the experts matches business reality (a theme also covered under the *Daubert* criteria). Does the theory fit the facts? The second is whether economic experts are guilty of ex post rationalization. When the economist comes up with a theory explaining business behaviour *after* the event, do you need evidence that businesses actually saw themselves behaving in that way?

10.24

10.4.1 A triumph of theory over commercial reality?

In *RCA and BHB v OFT* (2005), a large group of British racecourses sold media rights collectively to a new venture for interactive TV and internet betting on horseracing.[25] The question arose as to whether this collective selling constituted a restriction of competition

10.25

---

[23] Downes (2006), at [185].

[24] *Archer, Mortlock Murray & Woolley Pty Ltd v Hooker Homes Pty Ltd* [1971] 2 NSWLR 278, at [286E-F].

[25] *The Racecourse Association and the British Horseracing Board v Office of Fair Trading* [2005] CAT 29, 2 August 2005.

under Article 101(1). It would not be if collective selling was objectively necessary for the launch of the new venture. The parties agreed that such a new venture required a 'critical mass' of horseracing content for a successful launch (in the end, the launch never actually happened). However, the OFT found an infringement because it considered that, in a counterfactual without the agreement, the venture could have assembled a critical mass of rights by negotiating individually with each racecourse. Such separate contracts could have been made conditional on obtaining sufficient rights from other courses, so the OFT reasoned. The racecourses, in contrast, claimed that from a practical point of view collective selling was the only realistic way to achieve a sale and purchase of the rights. These rights had never been sold before, and interactive betting was a new service at the time. The CAT agreed, and dismissed the counterfactual put forward by the OFT:

> The suggestion that the acquisition of the necessary critical mass by individual negotiation with up to 37 course owners either could have been done, might have been done, or was ever contemplated as something which could or might have been done, appears to us to represent a triumph of theory over commercial reality and to ignore the evidence of the events leading up to the [agreement].[26]

10.26 Another such 'triumph of theory over commercial reality' was encountered in *Enron v EWS* (2009), a damages case following an abuse of dominance finding by the Office of Rail Regulation.[27] The question that arose was whether in the counterfactual—in the absence of the abuse—the claimant would have secured a major four-year contract to supply coal to a coal-fired power station (a 'loss of chance' claim). The economic expert for the claimant argued that the operator of the power station, as a rational economic decision-maker, would have been likely to select the claimant's bid in the counterfactual. However, neither the facts nor the executive at the power company who was responsible for the coal supply contract at the time supported this argument. The executive in question gave various business reasons why he would probably not have granted the contract to the claimant in any event. The CAT found that the executive gave his evidence 'candidly and in a straightforward manner', and was 'impressed by his overall consistency on key points'.[28] In the end it placed greater weight on this evidence from the actual decision-maker than on what the economic expert said a hypothetical rational decision-maker would have done.

10.4.2 Are economists guilty of ex post rationalization?

10.27 Nonetheless, attempts by economic experts to 'rationalize' certain business behaviour should not be dismissed outright every time the business reality is slightly different from the theory. This brings us to the second theme that has come up in cases before the CAT. *Napp*, its very first judgment in an appeal under the Competition Act 1998, concerned predatory and excessive pricing.[29] The economists acting for the defendant were accused of ex post rationalization of the company's behaviour. In other words, they came up with a justification for the behaviour *after* the event. The CAT stated that the defendant's justification

---

[26] Ibid., at [170]. We don't know whether this counterfactual was put forward by the OFT's lawyers or economists, or both.

[27] *Enron Coal Services Limited (in liquidation) v English Welsh & Scottish Railway Limited* [2009] CAT 36, 21 December. The regulator is now called the Office of Rail and Road.

[28] Ibid., at [70(a)].

[29] *Napp Pharmaceutical Holdings Limited and Subsidiaries v Director General of Fair Trading* [2002] CAT 1, 15 January.

for its behaviour did not flow from its internal documents, but from the work done by its economic advisers:

> Napp does not strike us as a naïve or badly managed company. If its pricing policy had in fact been set by Napp in the way that its economic consultants suggest, we would have expected the company's internal documents to demonstrate that.[30]

What can economists say to this in their defence? We have to go right back to the beginning. **10.28** Economics emerged in the late eighteenth century. Commerce as we know it has existed for thousands of years. So it is almost inevitable that much of what economists have done is to provide explanations of business behaviour and market mechanisms that have existed for ages. But even ex post, economics can provide critical insights into the effects of business practices. The *Napp* case involved alleged predatory pricing in sustained-release morphine products (used in the treatment of cancer-related pain) in the hospital sector, combined with excessive pricing of the same product in the pharmacy ('community') sector. The economists presented the theory that Napp's pricing policy incorporated a 'follow-on effect'. This basically meant setting low prices in the hospital sector in order to enhance subsequent sales in the community sector. The economists had described this effect in a narrow sense, in that more hospital sales would almost mechanistically lead to more community sales. There was no factual evidence that this was actually how Napp set its prices. The CAT stated that the term 'follow-on effect' was not used in the industry but rather 'coined by Napp's advisers for the purposes of this case'.[31] The managing director of Napp admitted that he had first come across the term when reading the papers for this case. However, apart from the fact that it is not uncommon for pharmaceutical companies to set low prices to hospitals in order to gain more business in the community sector (even it if isn't widely referred to as a 'follow-on effect'), is it really the case that economic theories about how companies behave must always be reflected in internal company documents? Consider the insight first provided by Adam Smith in 1776. In *Wealth of Nations* he explained that if all economic agents pursue their own self-interest this is actually a good thing, because it ensures that in the economy as a whole the right business decisions and opportunities are taken. This is the famous 'invisible hand' mechanism, through which markets work efficiently and make us all better off:

> It is not from the benevolence of the butcher, the brewer, or the baker that we expect our dinner, but from their regard to their own interest. We address ourselves, not to their humanity but to their self-love...He generally, indeed, neither intends to promote the public interest, nor knows how much he is promoting it...And by directing that industry in such a manner as its produce may be of the greatest value, he intends only his own gain, and he is in this, as in many other cases, led by an invisible hand to promote an end which was no part of his intention. Nor is it always the worse for the society that it was no part of it. By pursuing his own interest he frequently promotes that of society more effectually than when he really intends to promote it.[32]

This eighteenth-century insight still underpins the way economists think about markets **10.29** today. Applying it to *Napp*, whether or not internal business documents confirm the theory put forward by the economist is to some extent irrelevant. The fact that business executives are not aware of the economic theory according to which they behave does not mean

---

[30] Ibid., at [252].
[31] Ibid., at [235–6].
[32] Smith (1776), Book I, Ch II.

that the theory should be dismissed. Companies involved in competition proceedings are like the butcher and the baker, seeking their own self-interest (profits), and economists do have things to say about the effects of such behaviour. To use a sports analogy, just because a snooker player does not stand there with a protractor, calculator, and a list of formulae before playing every shot doesn't mean that the laws of physics don't apply to the shots played. Thus, ex post rationalization in itself is perhaps not such a terrible offence. But the other theme discussed in this section remains important: economic experts should ensure that their theories and empirical evidence contain a good dose of realism and are aligned with the facts of the case. The CAT's rejection of triumphs of theory over commercial reality is not without foundation.

10.5 The Use of Economics in Competition Law: A Promising Future?

10.5.1 Tackling new issues with the existing framework

10.30　The use of economics has spread to competition regimes across the world. It has permeated all the various areas of competition law that we have discussed in this book—abuse of dominance, restrictive agreements, mergers, and, more recently, damages. Economics has provided competition law with a better understanding of the effects of business practices, with practical concepts and criteria, and with quantitative tools that can generate empirical evidence to test theories and arguments. We have no reason to believe that this trend will change any time soon. If best practice in presenting economic evidence is adhered to more often, and courts and competition authorities become more familiar with such evidence, you can expect economics to continue to make significant contributions to competition law.

10.31　The 'mainstream' economic framework within which competition economists operate has, by and large, remained the same over recent decades. As discussed in Chapter 1, this framework was founded on the insights of the Chicago School into the efficiency benefits of many business practices that seemed restrictive, and then supplemented by modern IO theory based on game theory which has deepened economists' understanding of business practices. Econometrics, finance, and behavioural economics complete the toolkit. This basic competition economics framework is a flexible one. Throughout the book we have seen several examples of how it can be adapted to deal with new challenges, and generate new ideas and concepts (some of which have proved very useful; others having more in common with management fads or rehashing older theories).

10.32　In Chapter 2 we discussed the hypothetical monopolist test for market definition, a framework that has since been developed to deal with differentiated product markets, and evolved into methods to assess price effects of mergers directly (as covered in Chapter 7). We also saw how economics can be used in dealing with the complex interactions between competition and IP rights. Chapters 2 and 3 explored how innovation and market dynamics influence the assessment of market definition and market power. Chapter 4 showed how the effects of practices such as parallel trade, bundling, and refusal to supply can be more nuanced when IP rights are involved. Chapter 5 discussed how agreements between competitors are often used to address market failures in innovation and R&D, and how this can be assessed under the competition rules. Chapter 8 dealt with FRAND remedies in the area of IP licensing. In various chapters we came across the concept of two-sided markets, which became something of a buzzword in competition law following the credit card interchange fee cases (see Chapters 2 and 5). Two-sidedness remains in vogue today, in the context of online platforms such as price-comparison websites and search engines. We saw the examples of e-books, online hotel bookings, and Google search. Other 'new' concepts of recent times are hub-and-spoke collusion (Chapter 5), diagonal mergers (Chapter 7), and pass-on in damages cases (Chapter 9). Issues that are not so new but have nonetheless received extensive attention of late include MFN clauses (Chapter 6) and minority shareholdings (Chapter 7).

In addition to developing new theories and concepts, economists have become increas- **10.33** ingly confident at empirical analysis. The statistical tools and availability of data have improved. We have discussed the empirical estimation of concepts such as demand elasticities (Chapter 2), unilateral effects of mergers (Chapter 7), effects of competition interventions (Chapter 8), and damages (Chapter 9). Big data is a big new theme in its own right. It allows for more and better empirical measurement—sellers of online services such as e-books and music streaming can almost literally observe the demand curve in real time, as you and millions of other consumers use these products. Big data also creates its own potential competition problems. Access to data generated by tracking online consumer behaviour can become an essential input into the provision of related services. Rivals of Google complain of such a data barrier to entry, but similar issues arise in other sectors from mobile phones and gaming to cars and home appliances. Cars are becoming like computers on wheels, continuously transmitting information about your driving behaviour and whereabouts, and this data may give a competitive advantage to providers of maintenance, insurance, and other services. New online business models—such as freemium services—raise challenges as well. Is free the same as predatory? Is it an efficient or an anti-competitive form of price discrimination? Is free actually free, or is the real price we pay the valuable personal information that we provide when using the online service?

10.5.2 Other fields of application

The economic concepts and tools described in this book have relevance to legal and pol- **10.34** icy areas outside competition law. Utility regulation is one. Ever since network industries such as electricity, gas, telecoms, and rail were liberalized, policy-makers and regulators have been trying to find the optimal balance between competition and regulation. Some activities in these industries may always be natural monopolies, while in others you may get effective competition. So how should you identify and then regulate the natural monopoly activities, and at what point in the liberalization process can you withdraw regulation from the potentially competitive activities? Tools from competition economics can be of assistance in tackling these regulatory questions. Market definition and market power assessments can be used to distinguish the competitive from the less competitive areas. Several jurisdictions have built such competition tests into their regulatory frameworks in particular sectors, such as telecoms and rail. Where ex ante economic regulation of an activity is withdrawn, 'ex post regulation' through the application of competition law takes over. We saw in Chapter 4 that some of the most challenging abuse of dominance cases arise in these network industries, where the natural monopoly activities interact with competitive layers in the supply chain.

Competition economics principles are also increasingly being applied to sectors that tra- **10.35** ditionally have not relied much on market functioning but are beginning to do so. One is healthcare. Many countries have introduced market mechanisms to complement or replace public sector activities, and have tasked competition authorities or specialist regulators with overseeing this new competition.[33] In Chapters 2 and 7 we gave examples of how hospital and other healthcare mergers have been dealt with under competition law. The economics of horizontal and vertical agreements are also of relevance to this sector. The jury is perhaps still out on whether competition in healthcare services will succeed and what its limits are—doctors and patients do not quite respond to price signals and incentives in the same way as suppliers and consumers in other markets—but the tools discussed in this book can help assess this.

10.36   Competition principles also have a role to play as policy-makers and regulators try to grapple with the growth of online markets. The ever-expanding internet has raised all kinds of policy challenges—from security and privacy to issues of copyright and social inclusion— but it is at heart still a private-sector activity with a competitive supply chain of infrastructure and content providers. It has delivered huge economic welfare benefits in terms of enhancing market transparency, expanding geographic markets, and creating entirely new product markets. Competition law and economics are a means to maintain this competition, keeping markets open and preventing bottlenecks created by market or government forces. The EU's Digital Single Market initiative, announced in 2015, sees competition very much as a key means of achieving its policy goals (better access to digital goods, the right conditions for innovative services to flourish, and maximizing the growth potential of the digital economy), and was accompanied by the launch of a competition inquiry into the e-commerce sector.[34]

10.37   Trade law is a further area where competition economics principles have an obvious (but not yet commonly accepted) application. This holds true particularly for the rules on anti-dumping, as embedded in Article VI of the General Agreement on Tariffs and Trade of 1947 (last amended in 1994) and the accompanying World Trade Organization Anti-dumping Agreement of 1994. These rules allow countries to impose duties on imports that are sold below their 'normal' or 'fair' value, defined as either the price charged in the home country or a third country, or the cost of production. If you think that the description of dumping sounds just like price discrimination and predatory pricing, you are correct, but the way trade law deals with it differs dramatically from the approach under competition law. Economic studies have shown that if competition law standards were applied to dumping practices, only a tiny fraction of anti-dumping cases would result in intervention. To date, the anti-dumping rules have functioned mainly as a protectionist tool, rather than to promote efficiency and consumer welfare. Another sharp contrast with competition law is that anti-dumping policy has not had much influence from modern economic thinking, despite having generated a good deal of (mostly critical) economic literature.[35] There are indications that this might be changing. Some jurisdictions, including the European Union, now seem to be giving greater weight to the interests of domestic industries and end-consumers,

---

[33] Much has been written on competition in healthcare services. For an overview, see Organisation for Economic Co-operation and Development (2005), and Leibowitz (2010).

[34] European Commission (2015), 'A Digital Single Market for Europe: Commission sets out 16 initiatives to make it happen', press release, 6 May.

[35] For an overview of these debates, see Niels and ten Kate (1997), Blonigen and Prusa (2003), and Nelson (2006).

who are typically most affected by anti-dumping duties as they end up paying higher prices for their imports.

10.5.3 Questioning the competition paradigm

Most countries in the world now have a competition regime. Enforcement has become more active across Europe and elsewhere—witness the regularity with which competition cases make the headlines in the papers (and the relative ease with which you can now explain to friends and relatives what you do for a living). Competition law is seen as an important tool for supporting economic policies based on open markets and liberalization. A lot of the impetus towards the reliance on competitive markets has come from changes in economic policy and ideology in the late 1970s and early 1980s (Thatcherism and Reaganomics were part of this pro-market thinking, though they did not necessarily favour interventionist competition law).

10.38

Can we take for granted that the political winds will always favour free markets and competition, supported by strong competition law? The answer is no. Discontent with the promotion of competition surfaces periodically. In 2007, with political debates about the new European Treaty (or even Constitution) in full swing, there was pressure from some corners—including Paris—to downgrade the importance of competition in the central objectives of the European Union. The new TFEU, which came into force on 1 December 2009, no longer contains the text of Article 3(1)(g) of the former EC Treaty, which had obliged the European Community to establish 'a system ensuring that competition in the internal market is not distorted'. This caused something of a stir in the competition community, since many EU court decisions refer to that particular text. However, the TFEU makes several other references to the term 'competition' and, most importantly, it still contains the same core competition provisions on restrictive agreements, abuse of dominance, and state aid. The then Commissioner for Competition, Neelie Kroes (2007), was also quick to give reassurance:

10.39

> An Internal Market without competition rules would be an empty shell—nice words, but no concrete results. The Protocol on Internal Market and Competition agreed at the European Council clearly repeats that competition policy is fundamental to the Internal Market. It retains the existing competition rules which have served us so well for 50 years. It reconfirms the European Commission's duties as the independent competition enforcement authority for Europe.

Another big challenge to the general confidence in markets—and indeed in economics as a profession—came with the financial crisis of 2007–08. Financial institutions ran into difficulties as markets dried up, and the impact was felt across the economy. Years of global recession followed. Some have blamed the excessive freedom of financial markets, encouraging unhealthy risk-taking, with insufficient oversight by regulators. And some have blamed economists—for having devised the most complex mathematical formulae for derivative products that no one could really understand, and for failing to see the financial crisis coming.

10.40

Yet competition law has maintained a greater degree of political support throughout the crisis than some had feared. Indeed, it has proved to be a tool that can adapt to new circumstances. In Chapter 7 we saw how merger control can address the failing-firm defence—helpful in an environment with many business restructurings and distress sales. Chapter 8

10.41

showed what analysis can be undertaken in order to assess a company's ability to pay a fine (a defence invoked by companies in financial difficulties). All these are existing mechanisms under competition law that rely on economic principles and that have proved to be useful in the economic downturn. As regards the reputation of economics, it has perhaps helped that most of the criticism has been directed at macroeconomics, and not so much at microeconomics and IO.

10.42 Economics has an important role to play in maintaining the legitimacy of competition and competition policy, not just in times of crisis. It can help not only in improving the application of competition law, but also in communicating the message that competitive markets generally perform well for consumers and the economy as a whole. That competition is good and monopoly is bad seems on the face of it an easy message to convey to the wider public, but not when there are many visible victims of free markets—bankrupt companies and unemployed workers. In these circumstances it often falls to economists to keep reminding the public that the alternatives—such as import protection, legalized crisis cartels, or bail-outs of failed companies—may not be very wise or sustainable. As to the public legitimacy of competition policy, economics can contribute by helping competition authorities quantify the effects of their interventions, and show that (where this is the case) the benefits outweigh the costs—we discussed this in Chapter 8.

10.5.4 Consumer behaviour: Are the competition rules suited to make markets work better?

10.43 Competition policy seems increasingly focused on consumers. In part this is because political support for competition law is easier to gain when it is couched in terms of the benefits it brings to consumers. Enhanced allocative and productive efficiency as policy goals do not have quite the same public appeal. The focus on consumers is reflected in the criteria applied by competition authorities. We saw in Chapter 7 how most authorities apply a consumer welfare test in mergers rather than a total welfare test—merger efficiencies must be sufficient to offset any upwards price pressure. In the assessment of efficiencies of restrictive agreements under Article 101(3), authorities also place strong emphasis on those efficiencies being passed on to consumers. In Chapter 1 we explained how this emphasis on consumers works well most of the time, since effective competition usually brings simultaneous benefits to consumers and to overall economic welfare. However, we also warned that this is not always the case (e.g. price discrimination often increases total welfare but not always consumer welfare), and that an emphasis on consumer welfare may raise false expectations.

10.44 Yet there is another challenge to competition authorities' focus on consumers: do the current competition rules enable them to a sufficient degree to make markets work better for consumers? We dealt with behavioural economics in Chapters 3 and 8. This field has provided rich insight into how consumers behave, and how their biases and bounded rationality may give suppliers a greater and more persistent degree of market power than would follow from traditional models of competition. The expected virtuous interaction between demand and supply may be disturbed by consumer biases. We discussed how insights from behavioural economics can play a role in competition cases, including in the design of remedies. However, are the rules on abuse of dominance and restrictive agreements sufficiently suited to tackle markets where the basic demand–supply interaction is not functioning well? Often there may not be an anti-competitive agreement or abusive conduct, unless you assess practices such as add-ons and drip pricing as exploitative abuses of dominance in narrowly defined markets (we discussed this possibility in Chapter 3, but also pointed out the drawbacks). Issues arising from consumer biases are more commonly dealt with through consumer protection laws, or sector regulation such as in financial services. The FCA in the United Kingdom has enthusiastically endorsed behavioural economics, combining it with other competition economics tools to investigate financial services markets and try to make them work better for consumers. It has carried out several ground-breaking experiments to assess consumer behaviour and biases in products such as insurance add-ons, savings accounts, and structured deposits.[36]

So should competition authorities leave it to consumer protection and sector regulation to deal with problems in consumer markets? Not necessarily, if they have the right tools to tackle such problems themselves. One such tool is the market investigations regime in the United Kingdom, as established in the Enterprise Act 2002 and updated in the Enterprise and Regulatory Reform Act 2013. These are in-depth investigations of markets where competition is not functioning effectively, but for reasons other than abuse of dominance or restrictive agreements. The test for intervention under this regime is whether there are features of the market that have adverse effects on competition. These can include consumer biases hindering the effective interaction between demand and supply (e.g. a lack of switching due to inertia or informational problems). The regime gives the CMA wide-ranging powers to impose structural and behavioural measures to remedy the adverse competition effects. In this book we've seen several examples of markets where the CMA or its predecessors have dealt with issues arising from consumer biases, including in personal current accounts, home credit, PPI, and motor insurance. Another advantage of this regime is that it can serve as a deflector from political pressures to intervene directly in markets: rather than impose price caps in energy, banking, or mobile phone markets, let the CMA carry out a thorough eighteen-month market investigation, and consider remedies based on extensive economic analysis. That usually makes for better policy in the end. **10.45**

Other countries may consider introducing competition rules akin to the market investigation regime. Nevertheless, as with any extension of government power, a warning note is warranted on the risk of over-intervention. Appropriate checks and balances must be in place. Any remedies imposed by the CMA have to be proportionate to the adverse effects on competition that have been identified. Cost–benefit analysis plays an important role here, as we saw in Chapter 8. CMA decisions may be appealed to the CAT, a specialist body. Indeed, we saw a number of examples where the CAT challenged the CMA's proposed remedies or the analysis supporting them. With additional powers to intervene comes additional responsibility. Economics provides the tools that can help competition authorities use their powers in an effective and measured way. **10.46**

10.5.5 The power of ideas

Finally, a major reason for us to be optimistic about the contribution of economics to competition law is that we believe in the power of ideas. This is based on an insight **10.47**

---

[36] See Financial Conduct Authority (2013) and Hunt and Kelly (2015).

by the economist John Maynard Keynes. As he famously declared, 'In the long run we are all dead', criticizing prevailing mainstream economics for relying on markets sorting themselves out in the long run (Keynes, 1923, p. 80). However, he was more positive about the long run when it came to the spreading of ideas: good ideas will eventually gain prominence among policy-makers and the public, even if they meet strong resistance to start with. This happens in competition law too. Take the following two statements:

> I like aggressive competition—including by dominant companies—and I don't care if it may hurt competitors—as long as it ultimately benefits consumers...
>
> Dominant companies should be allowed to compete effectively.

10.48 These quotes could have been taken from an antitrust commentary in the United States in the 1970s, when the Chicago School was in full swing. The second quote echoes the famous statement by US judge Learned Hand which we have mentioned a few times before: 'The successful competitor, having been urged to compete, must not be turned upon when he wins.'[37] In fact, these two statements were made in a speech by EU Commissioner Kroes in 2005, when introducing the reform of the policy on abuse of dominance.[38] Such statements had been rare in Europe before then, and might have been dismissed as 'Chicago ideas' or simply as 'American'. What caused such a change in mindset among the European competition community? And while the European Commission subsequently pushed through a significant reform of the approach to abuse of dominance, will the EU courts hold it back through judgments such as *Intel* in 2014 (as we discussed in Chapter 4)?[39] We believe that Keynes's concept of the power of ideas is at work here. His highly influential work, *The General Theory of Employment, Interest and Money*, published in 1936, developed a new theory of how economy-wide demand and supply might not naturally tend towards equilibrium, leading to unemployment (it was the time of the Great Depression), and what governments could do about this. This represented quite a strong challenge to the prevailing orthodoxy in economics of 'classical' demand–supply theory. Keynes realized that his proposed policies (basically amounting to greater government spending in times of recession) might in the context of the period be seen as more suited to totalitarian states than to free-market economies. It was with these adverse academic and political circumstances in mind that Keynes ended his *General Theory* on a hopeful note that, if his ideas were correct, in the longer term they would be influential, even if they weren't immediately. Hence followed this passage:

> But apart from this contemporary mood, the ideas of economists and political philosophers, both when they are right and when they are wrong, are more powerful than is commonly understood. Indeed the world is ruled by little else. Practical men, who believe themselves to be quite exempt from any intellectual influences, are usually the slaves of some defunct economist. Madmen in authority, who hear voices in the air, are distilling their frenzy from some academic scribbler of a few years back. I am sure that the power of vested interests is vastly exaggerated compared with the gradual encroachment of ideas. Not, indeed, immediately, but after a certain interval; for in the field of economic and political philosophy there are not many who are influenced by new theories after they are twenty-five or thirty years of age, so that the ideas which civil servants and politicians and even agitators apply to current

---

[37] *US v Aluminum Co of America* 148 F 2d 416, 430 (2nd Cir, 1945).
[38] See Kroes (2005).
[39] Case T-286/09 *Intel Corp v Commission*, Judgment of 12 June 2014.

events are not likely to be the newest. But, soon or late, it is ideas, not vested interests, which are dangerous for good or evil.[40]

If Keynes is right, the practical men and women in authority (including competition author-   **10.49**
ities and courts) will eventually come round to what are good economic ideas. Sometimes rapidly, sometimes through 'gradual encroachment', economics will continue to play a use-ful role in competition law for decades to come.

---

[40] Keynes (1936), pp. 383–4.

BIBLIOGRAPHY

ABRANTES-METZ, R., KRATEN, M., METZ, A., and SEOW, G. (2012), 'LIBOR Manipulation', *Journal of Banking and Finance*, 36:1, 136–50.

ADAMS, W.J. and YELLEN, J.L. (1976), 'Commodity Bundling and the Burden of Monopoly', *Quarterly Journal of Economics*, 90:3, 475–98.

AGHION P., BLOOM N., BLUNDELL R., GRIFFITH R., and HOWITT, P. (2005), 'Competition and Innovation: An Inverted-U Relationship', *Quarterly Journal of Economics*, 120:2, 701–28.

AHLBORN, C. and EVANS, S. (2009), 'The Microsoft Judgment and its Implications for Competition Policy towards Dominant Firms in Europe', *Antitrust Law Journal*, 75:3, 887–932.

AKERLOF, G.A. (1970), 'The Market for "Lemons": Quality Uncertainty and the Market Mechanism', *Quarterly Journal of Economics*, 84:3, 488–500.

ALLEN, K. and ECONOMY, P. (2000), *The Complete MBA for Dummies*, IDG Books Worldwide.

ALTMAN, E. and NARAYANAN, P. (1997), 'An International Survey of Business Failure Classification Models', *Financial Markets, Institutions and Instruments*, 6:2, 1–57.

ANGRIST, J.D. and PISCHKE, J.S. (2009), *Mostly Harmless Econometrics: An Empiricist's Companion*, Princeton University Press.

ANTITRUST MODERNIZATION COMMISSION (2007), 'Report and Recommendations', April.

APESTEGUIA, J., DUFWENBERG, M., and SELTEN, R. (2006), 'Blowing the Whistle', *Economic Theory*, 31, 143–66.

AREEDA, P. and HOVENKAMP, H. (2007), *Antitrust Law*, 3rd edn, Aspen Law & Business, vol. 1.

—— and TURNER, P.F. (1975), 'Predatory Pricing and Related Practices under Section 2 of the Sherman Act', *Harvard Law Review*, 88:4, 697–733.

ARIELY, D. (2008), *Predictably Irrational*, Harper Collins.

ARMSTRONG, M., COWAN, S., and VICKERS, J. (1994), *Regulatory Reform: Economic Analysis and British Experience*, The MIT Press.

ARROW, K. (1962), 'Economic Welfare and the Allocation of Resources for Invention', in R. NELSON (ed.), *The Rate and Direction of Inventive Activity: Economic and Social Factors*, Princeton University Press, 609–26.

BACON, R.W. (1991), 'Rockets and Feathers: The Asymmetric Speed of Adjustment of UK Retail Gasoline Prices to Cost Changes', *Energy Economics*, 13:3, 211–18.

BAIN, J. (1956), *Barriers to New Competition*, Harvard University Press.

BAKER, J. (1999), 'Econometric Analysis in *FTC v Staples*', *Journal of Public Policy and Marketing*, 18:1, 11–21.

—— (2003), 'The Case for Antitrust Enforcement', *Journal of Economic Perspectives*, 17:4, 27–50.

BAKOS, Y. and BRYNJOLFSSON, E. (1999), 'Bundling Information Goods: Pricing, Profits, and Efficiency', *Management Science*, 45:12, 1613–30.

BAUMOL, W. (1982), 'Contestable Markets: An Uprising in the Theory of Industrial Structure', *American Economic Review*, 72:1, 1–15.

—— (1983), 'Some Subtle Pricing Issue in Railroad Regulation', *International Journal of Transport Economics*, 10:1–2, 341–55.

—— and BRADFORD, D.F. (1970), 'Optimal Departures from Marginal Cost Pricing', *American Economic Review*, 60:3, 265–83.

BAXTER, W.F. (1983), 'Bank Interchange of Transactional Paper: Legal and Economic Perspectives', *Journal of Law and Economics*, 26:3, 541–88.

BECKER, G. (1968), 'Crime and Punishment: An Economic Approach', *Journal of Political Economy*, 76:2, 169–217.

—— and MURPHY, K.M. (1993), 'A Simple Theory of Advertising as a Good or Bad', *Quarterly Journal of Economics*, 108:4, 941–64.

BERGER, M. (2000), 'The Supreme Court's Trilogy on the Admissibility of Expert Testimony', in Federal Judicial Center, *Reference Manual on Scientific Evidence*, 2nd edn, 9–38.

BERTRAND, J. (1883), 'Review of "Recherches sur les Principes Mathématiques de la Théorie des Richesses"', *Journal des Savants*, 48, 499–508.

BISHOP, S. and WALKER, M. (2010), *The Economics of EC Competition Law: Concepts, Application and Measurement*, 3rd edn, Sweet & Maxwell.

BLAIR, R.D. and HARRISON, J.L. (1993), *Monopsony: Antitrust Law and Economics*, Princeton University Press.

BLONIGEN, B.A. and PRUSA, T.J. (2003), 'Antidumping', in E. KWAN CHOI and J. HARRIGAN (eds), *Handbook of International Trade*, Blackwell Publishing, 251–84.

BLUNDELL, R. (2009), 'Assessing the Temporary VAT Cut Policy in the UK', *Fiscal Studies*, 30:1, 31–38.

BOARDMAN, A.E., GREENBERG, D.H., VINING, A.R., and WEIMER, D.L. (2010), *Cost–Benefit Analysis: Concepts and Practice*, 4th edn, Prentice Hall.

BOIK, A and CORTS, K.S. (2013), 'The Effects of Platform MFNs on Competition and Entry', Working Paper, October.

BORK, R.H. (1978), *The Antitrust Paradox*, The Free Press.

BOWMAN, W.S. (1957), 'Tying Arrangements and the Leverage Problem', *Yale Law Journal*, 67:1, 19–36.

BRADBURN, N.M., SUDMAN, S., and WANSING, B. (2004), *Asking Questions: The Definitive Guide to Questionnaire Design—For Market Research, Political Polls, and Social and Health Questionnaires*, revised edn, John Wiley & Sons.

BREALEY, R.A., MYERS, S.C., and ALLEN, F. (2011), *Principles of Corporate Finance*, 10th edn, McGraw Hill/Irwin.

BRENNER, S. (2009), 'An Empirical Study of the European Corporate Leniency Program', *International Journal of Industrial Organization*, 27:6, 639–45.

BUCHWALD, A. (1966), 'Samson Marries Delilah', *Washington Post*, 2 April.

BUTTON, K.J. (1993), *Transport Economics*, 2nd edn, Edward Elgar.

CAPPS, C., DRANOVE, D., GREENSTEIN, S., and SATTERTHWAITHE, M. (2001), 'The Silent Majority Fallacy of the Elzinga–Hogarty Criteria: A Critique and New Approach to Analyzing Hospital Mergers', NBER Working Paper No 8216, April.

CARD, D. and KRUEGER, A.B. (1994), 'Minimum Wages and Employment: A Case Study of the Fast-Food Industry in New Jersey and Pennsylvania', *American Economic Review*, 84:4, 772–93.

COLLINS, A. and OUSTAPASSIDIS, K. (1997), 'Below Cost Legislation and Retail Performance', Agribusiness Discussion Paper No 15, April.

COMANOR, W.S. and WILSON, T.A. (1979), 'The Effect of Advertising on Competition: A Survey', *Journal of Economic Literature*, 17:2, June, 453–76.

CONNOR, J.M. and LANDE, R.H. (2005), 'How High Do Cartels Raise Prices? Implications for Reform of the Antitrust Sentencing Guidelines', Working Paper, April.

—— and —— (2008), 'Cartel Overcharges and Optimal Cartel Fines', in W.D. COLLINS (ed.), *Issues in Competition Law and Policy*, vol. 3, ABA Section of Antitrust Law, ABA Book Publishing, 2203–18

COURNOT, A.A. (1838), *Recherches sur les Principes Mathématiques de la Théorie des Richesses*, Chez L. Hachette.

CREW, M.A. and PARKER, D. (eds) (2006), *International Handbook on Economic Regulation*, Edward Elgar Publishing.

CWIK, C. and NORTH, J. (2003), 'Scientific Evidence Review: Admissibility and Use of Expert Evidence in the Courtroom', monograph no 4, American Bar Association.

DALJORD, Ø., SØRGARD, L., and THOMASSEN, Ø. (2008), 'The SSNIP Test and Market Definition with the Aggregate Diversion Ratio: A Reply to Katz and Shapiro', *Journal of Competition Law and Economics*, 4:2, 263–70.

DAVIS, P. and GARCÉS, E. (2009), *Quantitative Techniques for Competition and Antitrust Analysis*, Princeton University Press.

DECKER, C. (2014), *Modern Economic Regulation: An Introduction to Theory and Practice*, Cambridge University Press.

DELLA VIGNA, S. and MALMENDIER, U. (2006), 'Paying Not to Go to the Gym', *American Economic Review*, 96:3, 694–719.

DELOITTE (2009), 'Review of Merger Decisions under the Enterprise Act 2002', report prepared for the Competition Commission, Office of Fair Trading and the Department for Business, Enterprise and Regulatory Reform, 18 March.

DEMSETZ, H. (1974), 'Two Systems of Belief about Monopoly', in H. GOLDSCHMID,

H.M. Mann, and J.F. Weston (eds), *Industrial Concentration: The New Learning*, Little, Brown, 164–84.

Department for Transport and Office of Rail Regulation (2010), 'Rail Value for Money: Scoping Study Report', March.

Deutsche Bundesbank (2008), 'Price and Volume Effects of VAT increase of January 2007', Monthly Report, April, 29–46.

Dhar, T.P. and Cotterill, R.W. (1999), 'Cost Pass-Through in the Case of Sequential Oligopoly: An Empirical Study of the Fluid Milk Market', University of Connecticut.

Dijk, T. van and Verboven, F. (2009), 'Cartel Damages and the Passing-On Defense', *The Journal of Industrial Economics*, 57:3, 457–91.

Dinnage, J.D. (1998), 'Joint Activities Among Gas Producers: The Competition Man Cometh', *Journal of Energy and Natural Resources Law*, 16:3, 249–85.

Doyle, C. and Inderst, R. (2007), 'Some Economics on the Treatment of Buyer Power in Antitrust', *European Competition Law Review*, 28:3, 210–19.

Downes, G. (2006), 'Problems with Expert Evidence: Are Single or Court-Appointed Experts the Answer?' *Journal of Judicial Administration*, 15:4, 185–89.

Duggan, M. and Levitt, S.D. (2002), 'Winning isn't Everything: Corruption in Sumo Wrestling', *American Economic Review*, 95:5, 1594–605.

Edwards, J., Kay, J., and Mayer, C. (1987), *The Economic Analysis of Accounting Profitability*, Clarendon Press.

Elhauge, E. (2003), 'Defining Better Monopolization Standards', *Stanford Law Review*, 56, 253–344.

Elzinga, K. and Hogarty, T. (1973), 'The Problem of Geographic Market Delineation in Antitrust Suits', *Antitrust Bulletin*, 18:1, 45–81.

—— and Mills, D.E. (1989), 'Testing for Predation: Is Recoupment Feasible?', *Antitrust Bulletin*, 34, Winter, 869–93.

Emch, E.R. (2004), '"Portfolio Effects" in Merger Analysis: Differences between EU and U.S. Practice and Recommendations for the Future', *Antitrust Bulletin*, 49:1–2, 55–100.

European Commission (2005), 'Merger Remedies Study', October.

—— (2014), 'Standard-Essential Patents', *Competition Policy Brief*, Issue 8, June, 1–5.

European Federation of Pharmaceutical Industries and Associations (2008), 'The Pharmaceutical Industry in Figures'.

Farrell, J. and Shapiro, C. (1990), 'Horizontal Mergers: An Equilibrium Analysis', *American Economic Review*, 80:1, 107–26.

—— and —— (2001), 'Scale Economies and Synergies in Horizontal Merger Analysis', *Antitrust Law Journal*, 68:3, 685–710.

—— and —— (2008), 'Improving Critical Loss Analysis', *The Antitrust Source*, 7:3, 1–19.

—— and —— (2010), 'Antitrust Evaluation of Horizontal Merger: An Economic Alternative to Market Definition', *The B.E. Journal of Theoretical Economics*, 10:1, March.

Financial Conduct Authority (2013), 'Applying Behavioural Economics at the Financial Conduct Authority', Occasional Paper No. 1, August.

Frank, R.H. (2007), *The Economic Naturalist: Why Economics Explains Almost Everything*, Virgin Books.

Gabaix, X. and Laibson, D. (2006), 'Shrouded Attributes, Consumer Myopia, and Information Suppression in Competitive Markets', *Quarterly Journal of Economics*, 121:2, 505–40.

Galbraith, J.K. (1952), *American Capitalism: The Concept of Countervailing Buyer Power*, Houghton Mifflin.

Gneezy, U. and Rustichini, A. (2000), 'A Fine is a Price', *Journal of Legal Studies*, 29:1, 1–17.

Goldberg, P. (1995), 'Product Differentiation and Oligopoly in International Markets: The Case of the U.S. Automobile Industry', *Econometrica*, 63:4, 891–951.

Granatstein, M. and Niels, G. (2015), 'Ground Rules on Airport Access: The *Arriva v Luton* Case', *Competition Law Journal*, 14:1, 59–64.

Green, N. (2010), 'From Rome to Rome: The Evolution of Competition Law into a Twenty-First Century Religion', *Competition Law Journal*, 9:1, 7–25.

—— (2011), 'It's not that Complicated Really: Truisms about Economists', *Agenda*, June.

Green, E.J. and Porter, R.H. (1984), 'Non-cooperative Collusion under Imperfect Price Information', *Econometrica*, 52:1, 87–100.

HALE, G.E. and HALE, R.D. (1966), 'A Line of Commerce: Market Definition in Anti-Merger Cases', *Iowa Law Review*, 52, 406–31.

HALL, G.R. and PHILLIPS, C.F. (1964), 'Antimerger Criteria: Power, Concentration, Foreclosure and Size', *Villanova Law Review*, 9, 211–32.

HAMAGUCHI, Y. and KAWAGOE, T. (2005), 'An Experimental Study of Leniency Programs', RIETI discussion paper.

HARRINGTON Jr., J.E. (2008), 'Detecting Cartels', in P. BUCCIROSSI (ed.), *Handbook of Antitrust Economics*, The MIT Press, 231–58.

HARRIS, B.C. and SIMONS, J.J. (1989), 'Focusing Market Definition: How Much Substitution is Necessary?', *Research in Law and Economics*, 12, 207–26.

HENDRY, D.F. and CLEMENTS, M.P. (2004), 'Pooling of Forecasts', *Econometrics Journal*, 7:1, 1–31.

HICKS, J.R. (1935), 'Annual Survey of Economic Theory: The Theory of Monopoly', *Econometrica*, 3:1, 1–20.

HINLOOPEN, J. and SOETEVENT, R. (2006), 'Trust and Recidivism: The Partial Success of Corporate Leniency Programmes in the Laboratory', Tinbergen Institute Discussion Paper.

HOSSAIN, T. and MORGAN, J. (2006), 'Plus Shipping and Handling: Revenue (Non) Equivalence in Field Experiments on eBay', *Advances in Economic Analysis and Policy*, 6:2, 1–27.

HOTELLING, H. (1929), 'Stability in Competition', *The Economic Journal*, 39:153, 41–57.

HOVENKAMP, H. (2001), 'Post-Chicago Antitrust: A Review and Critique', *Columbia Business Law Review*, 2001:2, 257–337.

HUNT, S. and KELLY, D. (2015), 'Behavioural Economics and Financial Market Regulation: Practical Policy, Rigorous Methods', *Agenda*, July.

IFF RESEARCH (2015), 'UK Businesses' Understanding of Competition Law', prepared for the Competition and Markets Authority, 26 March.

INDERST, R. and VALLETTI, T.M. (2011), 'Buyer Power and the Waterbed Effect', *Journal of Industrial Economics*, 59:1, 1–20.

IVALDI, M. (2005), 'Mergers and the New Guidelines: Lessons from Hachette-Editis', in P.A.G. VAN BERGEIJK and E. KLOOSTERHUIS (eds), *Modelling European Mergers: Theory,*

Competition Policy and Case Studies, Edward Elgar, 92–103.

—— and VERBOVEN, F. (2005), 'Quantifying the Effects from Horizontal Mergers in European Competition Policy', *International Journal of Industrial Organization*, 23:9–10, 669–91.

JACOB, B.A. and LEVITT, S.D. (2003), 'Rotten Apples: An Investigation of the Prevalence and Predictors of Teacher Cheating', *The Quarterly Journal of Economics*, 118:3, 843–77.

JENSEN, R. (2007), 'The Digital Provide: Information (Technology) Market Performance, and Welfare in the South Indian Fisheries Sector', *The Quarterly Journal of Economics*, 122:3, 879–924.

JOHNSON, C. and TURNOCK, R. (eds) (2005), *ITV Cultures: Independent Television over Fifty Years*, Open University Press.

JOHNSON, J.P. (2014), 'The Agency Model and MFN Clauses', Working Paper, January.

KAHN, A.E. (1988), *The Economics of Regulation: Principles and Institutions*, The MIT Press (first published in two separate volumes in 1970 and 1971).

KAHNEMAN, D. and TVERSKY, A. (1979), 'Prospect Theory: An Analysis of Decisions Under Risk', *Econometrica*, 47:2, 263–91.

—— (1984), 'Choices, Values and Frames', *American Psychologist*, 39:4, 341–50.

KAPLAN, R.S. and ANDERSON, S.R. (2007), *Time-Driven Activity-Based Costing: A Simpler and More Powerful Path to Higher Profits*, Harvard Business School Press.

KAPLOW, L. (2010), 'Why (Ever) Define Markets?' *Harvard Law Review*, 124:2, 437–517.

KATE, A. TEN and NIELS, G. (2003), 'Below-Cost Pricing in the Presence of Network Effects', in SWEDISH COMPETITION AUTHORITY (eds), *The Pros and Cons of Low Pricing*, Swedish Competition Authority, 97–127.

—— and —— (2005), 'To What Extent are Cost Savings Passed on to Consumers? An Oligopoly Approach', *European Journal of Law and Economics*, 20:3, 323–37.

—— and —— (2006), 'Mexico's Competition Law: North American Origins, European Practice', in P. MARSDEN (ed.), *Handbook of Research in Trans-Atlantic Antitrust*, Edward Elgar, 718–31.

—— and —— (2009), 'The Relevant Market: A Concept Still in Search of a Definition',

Journal of Competition Law and Economics, 5:2, 297–333.

—— and —— (2010), 'The Concept of Critical Loss for a Group of Differentiated Products', *Journal of Competition Law and Economics*, 6:2, 321–33.

—— and —— (2014), 'The Diversion Story: Resolving the Ambiguities Surrounding the Concept of Diversion Ratio', *Journal of Competition Law and Economics*, 10:2, 361–74.

KATZ, M.L. and SHAPIRO, C. (2003), 'Critical Loss: Let's Tell the Whole Story', *Antitrust*, Spring, 49–56.

KAVANAGH, J. (2013), 'Financing Services of General Economic Interest: The European Commission's Economic Tests', in E. SZYSZCZAK (ed.), *Financing Services of General Economic Interest: Reform and Modernization*, Springer, 149–60.

——, NIELS, G., and PILSBURY, S. (2011), 'The Market Economy Investor: An Economic Role Model for Assessing State Aid', chapter 5, in E. SZYSZCZAK (ed.), *Research Handbook on European State Aid Law*, Edward Elgar, 90–104.

KAY, J.A. (1976), 'Accountants Too, Could be Happy in a Golden Age: The Accountant's Rate of Profit and the Internal Rate of Return', *Oxford Economic Papers*, 28:3, 447–60.

KEYNES, J.M. (1923), *A Tract on Monetary Reform*, Macmillan.

—— (1936), *The General Theory of Employment, Interest and Money*, Macmillan.

KLEMPERER, P. (2005), 'Bidding Markets', Competition Commission discussion paper.

KOLASKY, W.J. (2001), 'Conglomerate Mergers and Range Effects: It's a Long Way to go from Chicago to Brussels', speech by the Deputy Assistant Attorney General, Antitrust Division, US Department of Justice, before the George Mason University Symposium, 21 November.

KOVACIC, W. (1999), 'Designing Antitrust Remedies for Dominant Firm Misconduct', *Connecticut Law Review*, 31, 1285.

—— (2007), 'The Intellectual DNA of Modern U.S. Competition Law for Dominant Firm Conduct: The Chicago/Harvard Double Helix', *Columbia Business Law Review*, 2007:1, 1–82.

—— and SHAPIRO, C. (2000), 'Antitrust Policy: A Century of Economic and Legal Thinking', *Journal of Economic Perspectives*, 14:1, 43–60.

KREPS, D.M. and WILSON, R. (1982), 'Reputation and Imperfect Information', *Journal of Economic Theory*, 27:2, 253–79.

KRISTENSEN, T., BOGETOFT, P., and MOELLER PEDERSEN, K. (2010), 'Potential Gains from Hospital Mergers in Denmark', *Health Care Management Science*, 13:4, 334–45.

KROES, N. (2005), 'Preliminary Thoughts on Policy Review of Article 82', Speech at the Fordham Corporate Law Institute, New York, 23 September.

—— (2007), 'Statement by European Commissioner for Competition Neelie Kroes on Results of 21–22 June European Council—Protocol on Internal Market and Competition', MEMO/07/250, 23 June.

—— (2009), 'Many Achievements, More To Do', speech to the International Bar Association conference on private and public enforcement of EU competition law, Brussels, 12 March.

KRUM, H., CONWAY, E.L., BROADBEAR, J.H., HOWES, L.G., and LOUIS, W.J. (1994), 'Postural Hypotension in Elderly Patients Given Carvedilol', *British Medical Journal*, 309, 775–76.

KUMBHAKAR, S.C., WANG, H., and HORNCASTLE, A. (2015), *A Practitioner's Guide to Stochastic Frontier Analysis Using Stata*, Cambridge University Press.

KWOKA, J.E. (2015), *Mergers, Merger Control, and Remedies: A Retrospective Analysis of U.S. Policy*, The MIT Press.

LAFFONT, J.J. and TIROLE, J. (1993), *A Theory of Incentives in Regulation and Procurement*, The MIT Press.

LAFONTAINE, F. and SLADE, M. (2008), 'Exclusive Contracts and Vertical Restraints: Empirical Evidence and Public Policy', in P. BUCCIROSSI (ed.), *Handbook of Antitrust Economics*, The MIT Press, 391–414.

LANDES, W.M. (1983), 'Optimal Sanctions for Antitrust Violations', *University of Chicago Law Review*, 50, 652–78.

LANE, F.C. (1968), 'Pepper Prices before da Gama', *Journal of Economic History*, 28:4, 590–97.

LAYNE-FARRAR, A., PADILLA, A.J., and SCHMALENSEE, R. (2007), 'Pricing Patents for Licensing in Standard Setting Organizations:

Making Sense of FRAND Commitments', CEMFI Working Paper No 0702, January.

LEIBENSTEIN, H. (1950), 'Bandwagon, Snob, and Veblen Effects in the Theory of Consumers' Demand', *Quarterly Journal of Economics*, 64:2, 183–207.

LEIBOWITZ, J. (2010), 'A Doctor and a Lawyer Walk into a Bar: Moving Beyond Stereotypes', Remarks by the FTC Chairman to the American Medical Association House of Delegates, available at: <http://www.ftc.gov/speeches/leibowitz.shtm>.

LERNER, A.P. (1934), 'The Concept of Monopoly and Measurement of Monopoly Power', *The Review of Economic Studies*, 1:3, 157–75.

LEVITT, S.D. and DUBNER, S.J. (2005), *Freakonomics: A Rogue Economist Explores the Hidden Side of Everything*, William Morrow Ltd.

LONDON ECONOMICS and YOUGOV (2014), 'Study into the Sales of Add-On General Insurance Products: Experimental Consumer Research', report for the Financial Conduct Authority, January.

LOZANO, S. and VILLA, G. (2010), 'DEA-Based pre-merger Planning Tool', *Journal of the Operational Research Society*, 61:10, 1485–97.

LUCEY, T.A. (2005), 'Assessing the Reliability and Validity of the Jump$tart Survey of Financial Literacy', *Journal of Family and Economic Issues*, 26:2, 283–94.

MACKIE-MASON, J. and METZLER, J. (2009), 'Links Between Markets and Aftermarkets: Kodak (1997)', in J.E. KWOKA and L.J. WHITE (eds), *The Antitrust Revolution: Economics, Competition, and Policy*, 5th edn, Oxford University Press, 558–83.

MACRORY, R.B. (2006), 'Regulatory Justice: Making Sanctions Effective', November.

MAJORAS, D.P. (2001), 'GE–Honeywell: The U.S. Decision', Remarks of Deborah Platt Majoras, Deputy Assistant Attorney General, Antitrust Division, US Department of Justice, before the Antitrust Law Section, State Bar of Georgia, 29 November.

MALMENDIER, U., MORETTI, E., and PETERS, F. (2012), 'Winning by Losing: Evidence on the Long-Run Effect of Mergers', NBER Working Paper 18024, April.

MANSKI, C.F. (2013), *Public Policy in an Uncertain World: Analysis and Decisions*, Harvard University Press.

MARKARD, J., TRUFFER, B., and IMBODEN, D.M. (2004), 'The Impacts of Liberalisation on Innovation Processes in the Electricity Sector', *Energy and Environment*, 15:2, 201–14.

MARSHALL, A. (1890), *Principles of Economics*, Macmillan.

MARSHALL, R.C. and MARX, L.M. (2012), *The Economics of Collusion: Cartels and Bidding Rings*, The MIT Press.

MAZZOCCHI, M. (2008), *Statistics for Marketing and Consumer Research*, Sage Publications.

MCCRAW, T.K. (1984), *Prophets of Regulation: Charles Francis Adams, Louis D. Brandeis, James M. Landis, Alfred E. Kahn*, Harvard University Press.

MILGROM, P. and ROBERTS, J. (1982), 'Predation, Reputation and Entry Deterrence', *Journal of Economic Theory*, 27:2, 280–312.

MITCHELL, M. L. and STAFFORD E. (2000), 'Managerial Decisions and Long Term Stock Price Performance', *Journal of Business*, 73:3, 287–329.

MOELLER, S.B., SCHLINGEMANN, F.P., and STULZ, R. (2005), 'Wealth Destruction on a Massive Scale? A Study of Acquiring-Firm Returns in the Recent Merger Wave', *Journal of Finance*, 60:2, 757–82.

MORRIS, D. (2003), 'Dominant Firm Behaviour under UK Competition Law', paper presented to the Fordham Corporate Law Institute, October.

MOTTA, M. (2004), *Competition Policy: Theory and Practice*, Cambridge University Press.

—— and POLO, M. (2003), 'Leniency Programs and Cartel Prosecution', *International Journal of Industrial Organization*, 21:3, 347–79.

NALEBUFF, B. (2003), 'Bundling, Tying, and Portfolio Effects. Part 1: Conceptual Issues', DTI Economics Paper No 1, February.

NASH, J. (1950a), 'Equilibrium Points in N-Person Games', *Proceedings of the National Academy of Sciences,* 36:1, 48–49.

NASH, J. (1950b), 'The Bargaining Problem', *Econometrica*, 18:2, 155–62.

NELSON, D. (2006), 'The Political Economy of Antidumping: A Survey', *European Journal of Political Economy*, 22:3, 554–90.

NIELS, G., BARNES, F., and VAN DIJK, R. (2003), 'Unclear and Unsettled: The Debate on Competition in Clearing and Settlement of Securities Trades', *European Competition Law Review*, 24:12, 634–39.

—— and JENKINS, H. (2005), 'Reform of Article 82: Where the Link Between Dominance and Effects Breaks Down', *European Competition Law Review*, 26:11, 605–10

—— and KATE, A. TEN (1997), 'Trusting Antitrust to Dump Antidumping; Abolishing Antidumping in Free Trade Agreements without Replacing it with Competition Law', *Journal of World Trade*, 31:6, 29–43.

—— and —— (2004), 'Antitrust in the US and the EU: Converging or Diverging Paths?', *Antitrust Bulletin*, 49:1–2, 1–27.

—— and VAN DIJK, R. (2006), 'Market Definition in the Tourism Industry', in A. PAPATHEODORU (ed.), *Corporate Rivalry and Market Power: Competition Issues in the Tourism Industry*, I.B. Tauris, 187–200.

OFFICE OF FAIR TRADING (2005), (2005), 'Positive Impact: An Initial Evaluation of the Effect of the Competition Enforcement Work Conducted by the OFT', December.

—— (2010), 'What Does Behavioural Economics Mean for Competition Policy?', OFT 1224, March.

ORGANISATION FOR ECONOMIC CO-OPERATION AND DEVELOPMENT (2005), 'Enhancing Beneficial Competition in the Health Professions', Competition Committee policy roundtable, DAF/COMP(2005)45, 16 December.

—— (2007), 'Dynamic Efficiencies in Merger Analysis', DAF/COMP(2007)41.

—— (2012a), 'Report on Experiences with Structural Separation', January.

—— (2012b), 'Remedies in Merger Cases', DAF/COMP(2011)13, 30 July.

—— (2012c), 'Impact Evaluation of Merger Decisions', DAF/COMP(2011)24, 18 September.

—— (2013a), 'The Role of Efficiency Claims in Antitrust Proceedings', DAF/COMP(2012)23, 2 May.

—— (2013b), 'Competition Issues in Television and Broadcasting', DAF/COMP/GF(2013)13, 28 October.

O'ROURKE, K.H. and WILLIAMSON, J.G. (2006), 'Did Vasco da Gama Matter for European Markets? Testing Frederick Lane's Hypotheses Fifty Years Later', CEPR discussion paper no 5418, January.

OTT, R. and ANDRUS, D. (2000), 'The Effect of Personal Property Taxes on Consumer Vehicle Purchasing Decisions: A Partitioned Price / Mental Accounting Theory Analysis', *Public Finance Review*, 28:2, 134–52.

OXERA (2003), 'Assessing Profitability in Competition Policy Analysis', OFT Economic Discussion Paper 6, July.

—— (2004), 'Costs and Benefits of Market Regulators', report prepared for the Ministry of Economic Affairs (the Netherlands), October.

—— (2005a), 'What is the Impact of a Minimum Price Rule?', report prepared for the Ministry of Economic Affairs (the Netherlands), June.

—— (2005b), 'Buying Loyalty: South African Airways and the Ongoing Saga of Rebate Cases', *Agenda*, August.

—— (2008), 'Truth or Dare: Leniency and the Fight Against Cartels', *Agenda*, January.

—— (2009), 'BSkyB's Profitability in the Context of the Ofcom Market Investigation: First Report', prepared for Ofcom, June.

—— (2010), 'BSkyB's Profitability in the Context of the Ofcom Market Investigation: Second Report', prepared for Ofcom, February.

—— (2013), 'Behavioural Economics and its Impact on Competition Policy: A Practical Assessment with Illustrative Examples from Financial Services', prepared for the Netherlands Authority for Consumers and Markets (ACM), May.

—— (2014), 'From Sports Bras to Cigarettes: Economic Analysis of Anticompetitive Agreements', *Agenda*, September.

——and a multi-jurisdictional team of lawyers led by Dr Assimakis Komninos (2009), 'Quantifying Antitrust Damages: Towards Non-Binding Guidance for Courts', report prepared for DG Competition, December.

PARETO, V. (1906), *Manual of Political Economy* (original in Italian).

PILSBURY, S. (2007), 'The Impala Decision: An Economic Critique', *European Competition Journal*, 3:1, 31–47.

POLINSKY, A.M. and SHAVELL, S. (2000), 'The Economic Theory of Public Enforcement of Law', *Journal of Economic Literature*, 38:1, 45–76.

PORTER, R.H. and ZONA, J.D. (1993), 'Detection of Bid Rigging in Procurement Auctions', *Journal of Political Economy*, 101:3, 518–38.

—— and —— (1999), 'Ohio School Milk Markets: An Analysis of Bidding', *RAND Journal of Economics*, 30:2, 263–68.

POSNER, R.A. (1976), *Antitrust Law: An Economic Perspective*, University of Chicago Press.

PUGH, E. (1995), *Building IBM: Shaping an Industry and Its Technology*, The MIT Press.

RAGHAVARAO, D., WILEY, J.B., and CHITTURI, P. (2010), *Choice-Based Conjoint Analysis: Models and Designs*, CRC Press.

RAMSEY, F.P. (1927), 'A Contribution to the Theory of Taxation', *The Economic Journal*, 37:145, 47–61.

RAO, V.R. (2014), *Applied Conjoint Analysis*, Springer.

RARES, S. (2013), 'Using the "Hot Tub": How Concurrent Expert Evidence Can Help Courts', *Agenda*, November.

RBB ECONOMICS (2011), 'Conjectural Variations and Competition Policy: Theory and Empirical Techniques', report for the OFT, October.

REY, P. and VENIT, J.S. (2015), 'An Effects-Based Approach to Article 102: A Response to Wouter Wils', *World Competition*, 38:1, 3–30.

SALOP, S. and MORESI, S. (2009), 'Updating the Merger Guidelines: Comments', available at: <https://www.ftc.gov/sites/default/files/documents/public_comments/horizontal-merger-guidelines-review-project-545095-00032/545095-00032.pdf>.

—— and SCHEFFMAN, D. (1987), 'Cost-Raising Strategies', *Journal of Industrial Economics*, 36:1, 19–34.

SCHERER, F.M. (2009), 'Retailer-Instigated Restraints on Suppliers' Sales: Toys "R" Us (2000)', in J.E. KWOKA and L.J. WHITE (eds), *The Antitrust Revolution: Economics, Competition, and Policy*, 5th edn, Oxford University Press, 441–55.

—— and ROSS, D. (1990), *Industrial Market Structure and Economic Performance*, 3rd edn, Houghton Mifflin Company.

SCHMALENSEE, R. (1982), 'Commodity Bundling by Single-Product Monopolies', *Journal of Law and Economics*, 25:1, 67–71.

SCHUMPETER, J. (1942), *Capitalism, Socialism and Democracy*, Harper and Brothers.

SELTEN, R. (1978), 'The Chain Store Paradox', *Theory and Decision*, 9:2, 127–59.

SHAPLEY, L.S. (1953), 'A Value for N-Person Games', in H.W. KUHN and A.W. TUCKER (eds), *Contributions to the Theory of Games II*, Princeton University Press, 307–17.

SHENEFIELD, J.H. (2004), 'Coherence or Confusion: The Future of the Global Antitrust Conversation', *Antitrust Bulletin*, 44:1–2, 385–434.

SHEPHERD, W. (1988), 'Competition, Contestability and Transport Mergers', *International Journal of Transport Economics*, 15:2, 113–28.

SHEPPARD, S. (ed.) (2003), *The Selected Writings and Speeches of Sir Edward Coke*, Liberty Fund.

SLADE, M. (1998), 'Beer and the Tie: Did Divestiture of Brewer-Owned Public Houses Lead to Higher Beer Prices?', *The Economic Journal*, 108:448, 565–602.

SMITH, A. (1776), *An Inquiry into the Nature and Causes of the Wealth of Nations*, Strehan and T. Cadell.

SNIDER, C. and YOULE, T. (2010), 'Does the LIBOR Reflect Banks' Borrowing Costs?', Working Paper, April.

SPAGNOLO, G. (2004), 'Divide et Impera: Optimal Leniency Programmes', Working Paper 4840, Center for European Policy Research.

SPENGLER, J.J. (1950), 'Vertical Integration and Anti-Trust Policy', *Journal of Political Economy*, 58:4, 347–52.

SPIEGLER, R. (2006), 'Competition Over Agents with Boundedly Rational Expectations', *Theoretical Economics*, 1:2, 207–31.

STEPHAN, A. (2009), 'An Empirical Assessment of the European Leniency Notice', *Journal of Competition Law and Economics*, 5:3, 537–61.

STIGLER, G.J. (1968), *The Organization of Industry*, University of Chicago Press.

SUGDEN, R. and WILLIAMS, A.H. (1978), *The Principles of Practical Cost–Benefit Analysis*, Oxford University Press.

SULLIVAN, L.E. (1995), 'Post-Chicago Economics: Economists, Lawyers, Judges, and Enforcement Officials in a Less Determinate Theoretical World', *Antitrust Law Journal*, 63:2, 669–81.

SWANSON, D. and BAUMOL, W. (2005), 'Selection of Compatibility Standards and Control of Market Power Related to Intellectual Property', *Antitrust Law Journal*, 73:1, 51–56.

THALER, R. (1980), 'Toward A Positive Theory of Consumer Choice', *Journal of Economic Behavior and Organization*, 1:1, 39–60.

—— and SUNSTEIN, C.R. (2003), 'Liberal Paternalism', *American Economic Review*, 93:2, 175–79.

—— and —— (2008), *Nudge: Improving Decisions About Health, Wealth and Happiness*, Yale University Press.

THANASSOULIS, E. (2001), *Introduction to the Theory and Application of Data Envelopment Analysis: A Foundation Text with Integrated Software*, Springer.

TIMMERMAN, A. (2006), 'Forecast Combinations', in G. ELLIOT, C.W.J. GRANGER, and A. TIMMERMAN (eds), *Handbook of Economic Forecasting*, vol. 1, Elsevier, 135–96.

TOURANGEAU, R., RIPS, L., and RASINSKI, K. (2000), *The Psychology of Survey Response*, Cambridge University Press.

TREACY, P. and KOSTENKO, M. (2007), 'Safer Standard Setting', *Competition Law Insight*, 10–11.

VANE, H. (2015), 'An Interview with Chris Fonteijn', *Global Competition Review*, 18:4, April.

VEBLEN, T.B. (1899), *The Theory of the Leisure Class: An Economic Study of Institutions*, Macmillan Publishers.

VICKERS, J. (2005), 'Abuse of Market Power', *The Economic Journal*, 115:504, 244–61.

VINER, J. (1923), *Dumping: A Problem in International Trade*, Chicago University Press (reprinted in 1991 by Augustus M. Kelley).

VISCUSI, W.K., VERNON, J.M., and J.E. HARRINGTON (2005), *Economics of Regulation and Antitrust*, 4th edn, The MIT Press.

WATERSON, M. (2009), 'Beer: The ties that bind', in B. LYONS (ed.), *Cases in European Competition Policy: The Economic Analysis*, Cambridge University Press, 245–67.

WERDEN, G. (1992), 'The History of Antitrust Market Delineation', *Marquette Law Review*, 76:1, 123–215.

—— (2000), 'Expert Report in United States v. Interstate Bakeries Corp. and Continental Baking Co.', *International Journal of the Economics of Business*, 7:2, 139–48.

—— (2006), 'Identifying Exclusionary Conduct under Section 2: The "No Economic Sense" Test', *Antitrust Law Journal*, 73:2, 413–33.

WHINSTON, M.D. (1990), 'Tying, Foreclosure and Exclusion', *American Economic Review*, 80:4, 837–59.

WHISH, R. and BAILEY, D. (2015), *Competition Law*, 8th edn, Oxford University Press.

WILLIAMSON, O.E. (1968), 'Economies as an Antitrust Defense: The Welfare Tradeoffs', *American Economic Review*, 58:1, 18–36.

WILLIG, R. (1979), 'The Theory of Network Access Pricing', in H.B. TREBING (ed.), *Issues in Public Utility Regulation*, Michigan State University Public Utility Papers, 109–52.

WILS, W. (2006), 'Optimal Antitrust Fines: Theory and Practice', *World Competition*, 29:2, 183–208, June.

—— (2014), 'The Judgment of the EU General Court in Intel and the So-Called "More Economic Approach" to Abuse of Dominance', *World Competition*, 37:4, 405–34.

WOOLDRIDGE, J.M. (2013), *Introductory Econometrics: A Modern Approach*, 5th edn, South-Western.

INDEX

References are by paragraph number; chapter numbers appear in **bold**, paragraph numbers in plain.

Printed and bound by CPI Group (UK) Ltd, Croydon, CR0 4YY